Readings
on the
Body Politic

Readings on the Body Politic

Fred R. Harris

University of New Mexico

Scott, Foresman and Company
Glenview, Illinois
London, England

Library of Congress Cataloging-in-Publication Data

Readings on the body politic.

Includes bibliographical references.
1. United States—Politics and government.
2. United States—Politics and government—
Sources. I. Harris, Fred R., 1930–
JK21.R39 1987 320.973   86-28007
ISBN 0-673-18528-1

Introduction

America's democratic system of politics and government is complex. It is not easy to understand. And it is almost impossible to use effectively for those who do not understand it well.

A basic text that cites, quotes from, paraphrases, and presents in organized and narrative form the writings and findings of those who have thought most deeply about America's politics and government is central to understanding. But it is also important and helpful when you can read from these and other primary sources yourself.

Now in my eleventh year of teaching introductory American government courses, I believe ever more strongly that understanding America's system and how it works is much enhanced when you have the chance to get its real taste and feel and smell by studying for yourself what Madison actually said in *Federalist 10*, for example, or what John Marshall actually ruled, and why, in *Marbury* v. *Madison*, and by reading contemporary views on governmental and political concepts and modern policy issues. *Readings on the Body Politic* excerpts and reprints in one convenient volume the major political science classics, early and late, landmark Supreme Court decisions, and contemporary expository essays on political science principles and political and governmental issues and practices.

The book is divided into four main parts, each with a brief introduction to the particular subject matter it covers. At the beginning of most of the thirteen chapters, there is a brief and introductory survey of the basic principles and concepts of the particular field—civil rights, interest groups, or the presidency, for example. At the beginning of most chapters, too, pieces are selected for reprinting that delineate constitutional and historical foundations.

This book excerpts and reprints political science classics—both early ones, such as selections from the *Federalist* and Edmund Burke's "Statement to the Electors of Bristol," and later ones, such as those from David Mayhew's *The Electoral Connection* or Richard Neustadt's *Presidential Power*. But the student is not left hanging like a movie viewer without the last reel, as might be true if no account were taken of more recent or opposing views. Here, later classics are often followed by pieces that offer a different point of view, a different analysis, or more recent scholarship. For example, Richard Fenno, Jr.'s *Home Style* is excerpted to follow Mayhew, and John P. Roche's "The Founding Fathers: A Reform Caucus In Action," as well as portions of Robert E. Brown's work, follow excerpts from Charles Beard's *An Economic Interpretation Of the Constitution*.

Landmark Supreme Court opinions, like that in the *Miranda* decision, for example, are reprinted or excerpted in this book, but so are more recent opinions that alter or amend the earlier holdings.

This book is also unique in that it combines both the "reader" and the "debate" approach. In addition to the reprinting of classics, Court opinions, and expository essays, there is also repeated use of the debate format. This is done to facilitate understanding and provoke thought in regard to key concepts and issues. There are debates on affirmative action, on limiting political action committees, on a one-term, six-year limit for presidents, on federal welfare and antipoverty programs, on "Star Wars," and on U.S. policy toward Nicaragua.

Unusual about this book, too, is a separate section on public policy. After a brief survey introduction to the field in the public policy part opener, two chapters excerpt and reprint recent material on economic policy, foreign policy, and national security.

Finally, the U.S. Constitution is reprinted in full at the end of the book.

I appreciate the helpful work of research assistants Jonathan Eldredge and Larry McElvain, the encouragement of my wife, Margaret S. Elliston, and the interest of my students.

Used alone or with a basic text, *Readings on the Body Politic* is designed to allow students to consult first sources and thereby better master the principles and processes of our complicated, but fascinating, political and governmental system.

Fred R. Harris

Contents

Readings
on the
Body Politic

PART I

Constitutional Framework and Rights

The American system is grounded in a written Constitution. It establishes our national government, delineates its structure and powers, and prescribes the general nature of the relationship between the national government and state governments and between governments and people.

In Chapter 1, we consider the origin and meaning of the U.S. Constitution, and, in Chapter 2, the system of federalism it created.

Chapter 3 focuses on the Bill of Rights, the first ten amendments. The Bill of Rights guarantees certain individual liberties and freedoms by limiting what governments can do.

Chapter 4 on civil rights deals with the concept of equality and the guarantees of the Fourteenth Amendment, adopted as a part of the Civil War Amendments.

Independence National Historical Park, Eastern National Parks and Monuments Association.

CHAPTER 1

The U.S. Constitution

A constitution is the fundamental and supreme law of a society. The U.S. Constitution, written in 1787, is the oldest living written constitution in the world. It not only shaped our government, but it also shaped our thinking about government. In this chapter, we will consider the philosophy behind the Constitution, the motivations of those who wrote it, James Madison's explanations of, and arguments for, some central principles of the Constitution, and, finally, recent suggestions for changing it and our system.

PHILOSOPHICAL FOUNDATIONS

Whether one emphasizes most the influence on the framers of the writings of the English philosopher John Locke, or the ideas of the Scottish Enlightenment, or the theories of French philosopher Montesquieu and others, it is clear, writes historian Gordon S. Wood, that the U.S. Constitution was drafted in the environment of a political culture that included support for the ideas of republicanism, balanced government, separation of powers, and liberty.

THE INTELLECTUAL ORIGINS OF THE AMERICAN CONSTITUTION
Gordon S. Wood

The Constitution was created at a stroke in the summer of 1787, but its intellectual origins and sources, like those of all great events, reached back deep into the past. The Constitution has been described as the climax of the Enlightenment—that great eighteenth-century attempt to apply the results of Western science and learning to human affairs. As the product of Western "enlightened" thinking, the Constitution could scarcely have sprung simply from a summer's meeting. Its sources have often seemed to be the whole of previous history. No thinker, no idea, has been too remote, too obscure, to have been involved somehow in the making of the Constitution. Thus historians and political theorists have rummaged through the past looking for the particular philosopher or book that might have especially influenced the Framers of the Constitution. Some have seized on the Englishman John Locke; others, the Frenchman Montesquieu; still others, the Scot David Hume or the Swiss Burlamaqui; and some have even made a case for the ancient Greek Polybius. . . .

. . . Although isolating the influence of any one thinker on the Founding Fathers may be impossible, describing the currents of the political culture in which they were immersed in 1787 is not. The Founders were experienced, pragmatic political leaders, but they were not such practical, down-to-earth men that they could not be bothered by questions of political philosophy and theory. On the contrary, they were men intensely interested in ideas and especially concerned with making theoretical sense of what they were doing. They were participants in a rich, dynamic political culture that helped determine the nature of the Constitution they created. Understanding the Constitution requires an understanding of that political culture.

REPUBLICANISM

The most pervasive characteristic of that political culture was republicanism, a body of ideas and values so deeply rooted that it formed the presuppositions of American thinking. This body of thought not only determined the elective political system the Founders believed in; it also determined their moral and social goals. To become republican was what the American Revolution had been about.

. . . Republicanism was the ideology of the democratic revolutions of the late eighteenth century; it was the ideology of the people against monarchs and hereditary aristocracies. Even the English who held on to their king and their House of Lords through the upheavals of this period nevertheless felt compelled to claim that, because of the power of the House of Commons, their constitution was already greatly republicanized. By the last quarter of the eighteenth century, being enlightened in the Western world, it seemed, was nearly equivalent to believing in republican values.

The deepest origins of these civic and moral values went all the way back to ancient Rome and the great era of the Roman Republic. . . .

This great body of classical literature was revived and updated by the Renaissance, especially in the writings of the Italian philosopher Machiavelli. All was blended into a tradition of what has been called "civic humanism." . . .

What precisely did this body of ideas mean? It meant most obviously the elimination of a king and the institution of an electoral system of government. But these were just incidental means to a larger end. Republicanism really meant creating a political system concerned with the *res publica*, public things, the welfare of the people. Liberal critics of eighteenth-century monarchism believed that kings had become too wrapped up in their own selfish dynastic purposes and were ignoring the good of their people. By eliminating hereditary kings and instituting governments in which the people themselves would elect their political leaders, liberal reformers hoped that governments at last would promote only the public's welfare.

This civic culture, however, had more than political significance; it had social and moral significance as well. Republics required a particular sort of egalitarian and virtuous people: independent, property-holding citizens without artificial hereditary distinctions who were willing to sacrifice many of their private, selfish interests for the good of the whole community. This dependence on a relatively equal and virtuous populace was what made republics such fragile and often short-lived polities. Monarchies were long-lasting; they could maintain order from the top down over large, diverse, and stratified populations through their use of hereditary privilege, executive power, standing armies, and religious establishments. But republics had to be held together from below, from the consent and sacrifice of the people themselves; and therefore, as Montesquieu and other theorists had warned, republics necessarily had to be small in territory and homogeneous and moral in character. . . .

Americans of 1787 were not the republican enthusiasts they had been in 1776. In a decade's time many of them had had their earlier dreams and illusions about republicanism considerably dampened. Experience with popular government, especially in the state legislatures, had cast doubt on the American people's capacity for virtue and disinterestedness. By 1787 many leaders, therefore, were ready for what James Madison called a "systematic change" of government, a change that resulted in the creation of the federal Constitution. But dissatisfied as many American leaders were with the Confederation and with the state legislatures, none of them—not even Alexander Hamilton who was the most monarchically minded among them—was prepared to give up on republican government. They knew, as Madison said, that "no other form would be reconcileable with the genius of the people of America; with the fundamental principles of the revolution; or with that honorable determination, which animates every votary of freedom, to rest all our political experiments on the capacity of mankind for self-government." Hence in the new Constitution, the Framers provided for periodically elected officers of the executive and legislative branches, and they made the federal government guarantee a republican form of government for each state (Article IV, Section 4), and forbade the United States from granting any titles of nobility (Article I, Section 9).

Still, the new federal government was sufficiently different from the Confederation and the governments of the states to arouse fears among many people that it was not "strictly republican." Did it not have a strong king-like executive and a powerful Senate with an aristocratic bearing? Unlike the Confederation, did it not operate directly on diverse peoples over half a continent despite the warnings of theorists and experience that such a large republic could not last? Fears and questions like these are what led Hamilton, Madison, and John Jay to spend so much time in *The Federalist* trying to prove that the Constitution was really "conformable to the true principles of republican government." In the process they helped to develop and shape further American ideas of republicanism.

BALANCED GOVERNMENT

In 1787, classical republicanism was the basic premise of American thinking — the central presupposition behind all other ideas. However, it alone was not responsible for the peculiar structure of the revolutionary governments, including that of the federal government created by the Constitution. There was another set of ideas encapsulated in the theory of balanced or mixed government. It came likewise out of antiquity and was closely if not inextricably entwined with the tradition of classical republicanism. The classical theory of balanced government provided much more than the foundational ideas for the structures of the several state governments. The classical theory also included the notion of an independent president, the aristocratic Senate, and the popular House of Representatives.

Since at least the time of Aristotle, theorists had categorized forms of government into three ideal types — monarchy, aristocracy, and democracy. These types were derived from the number of rulers in each: for monarchy, one person; for aristocracy, a few nobles; for democracy, all the people. Aristotle and others believed that each of these rulers when alone entrusted with political power tended to run amok and to become perverted. By itself monarchy became tyranny; aristocracy became oligarchy; and democracy became anarchy. Only by mixing each of these types together in the same constitution, only by balancing the tendencies of each of them, could order be maintained and the perfections of each type of simple government be achieved. The result would be a governmental system in equilibrium — the very kind of static model that the eighteenth-century Enlightenment admired.

For most enlightened thinkers of the eighteenth century, including those of the American colonies, there already existed at least in theory such a perfectly balanced government — the English constitution. . . .

When Americans in 1776 revolted from this perfect English constitution, most of them had no intention of repudiating the classical ideal behind it. Nor did they believe that this ideal of balanced government was incompatible with republicanism. . . . They and other English critics, speaking out of the civic humanist tradition of republicanism, thought that in the course of the eighteenth century the ideal English constitution had degenerated and become corrupted. The king was using his power to appoint men to crown offices in order to bribe and influence members of the House of Lords and House of Commons. . . .

Most of America's revolutionary state governments created in 1776–77 were meant to be miniature republican copies of the ideal English constitution. Although elected, the governors, senates, and houses of representatives of the several states were intended to resemble the king, House of Lords, and House of Commons of the English constitution; indeed, they still do. But in order to prevent their balanced governments from degenerating in the way the English constitution had, most of the states in 1776 severely limited the appointing powers of the governors or chief executives; and, more important for American con-stitutional development, all of them forbade members of both houses of the legislature and the judiciary from simultaneously holding office in the executive branch. In justifying this prohibition, some of the states in 1776 invoked a doc-trine made famous by Montesquieu of separating the executive, legislative, and judicial powers from each other. This triad of functioning powers was really not the same as the classical triad of ruling elements—governors, senates, and houses of representatives—but the goal of the two triads—the prevention of corruption—was the same.

There is no exaggerating the importance of this American exclusion of the legislators from simultaneous executive or ministerial office. This fundamen-tally divided America's constitutional tradition from that of the former mother country. By this prohibition alone, Americans prevented the development of an English or European-style parliamentary cabinet form of government. Members of America's executive branch, unlike those of most of the democracies in the world, cannot at the same time hold seats in the legislatures. The separation of the legislature from what was thought to be the perverse, corrupting influence of the executive was written into the revolutionary state constitutions of 1776–77. This division was instituted for the sake of maintaining the independence of the ruling parts and the balance that an ideal government ought to have. Since separa-tion of powers was often used to justify the maintenance of this independence and balance, there was the likelihood that separating powers and balancing parts of the government would blend in people's minds.

Separation of Powers

By the time Americans came to form the federal Constitution in 1787–88, the two sets of ideas had become thoroughly confused. Undoubtedly most of the Framers at Philadelphia thought they were creating a balanced government much in the form of the several state governments—only with a stronger chief executive and Senate than in most of the states. Although the ultimate source of this structure was the ideal English constitution, by 1787 few American political leaders felt comfortable any longer saying so in public. (John Adams was a conspicuous exception.) Referring to the chief executive as the monarchical element and the Senate as the aristocracy in a balanced government was politically impossible in the popular atmosphere of the 1780s. Thus the Framers had to find justifications for their two-house legislature and their strong, independent president in some place other than the English constitution and the classical ideal of mixed government.

What they did was blend the notion of separating the functional powers of government—executive, legislative, and judicial—with the older theory of balanced government; and they used both indiscriminately to describe the now incredibly fragmented and countervailing character of America's political system. "The constant aim," wrote Madison in *The Federalist* No. 51, which summed up the Founders' thinking on their parcelling of power, "is to divide and arrange the several offices in such a manner as that each may be a check on the other." Bicameralism, the presidential veto power, the independent judiciary, even federalism itself—the apportioning of authority between the national and state governments—all became various means of dividing, checking, and balancing a mistrusted political power.

LIBERTY

. . . Although the classical traditions of republicanism and mixed government formed the presuppositions of American thinking, they were presuppositions shared by the whole Western world. Other nations, such as eighteenth-century France, were influenced by republicanism; indeed, most countries in the world now have republican governments. Other states also have attempted balanced governments, two-house legislatures, independent executives, and separated powers. But few of them have our particular concern for personal and political liberty: for the rule of law, for private personal and property rights, for constitutional and judicial limitations on the use of governmental power. If the origins of these concerns are to be found in sources other than America's own experience, then they must be found neither in the ideas of classical antiquity nor in those of Renaissance civic humanism but in the peculiarities of the English legal tradition.

Nothing was more important for the development of American constitutionalism in 1787 and in the years following than the fact that most of the Founders had been reared as Englishmen and had thus shared in the English preoccupation with liberty and in the unique protections of the English common law. England was, as Montesquieu said in 1731, "the freest country that exists in the world," and eighteenth-century Englishmen on both sides of the Atlantic prided themselves on that reputation. The colonists began the Revolution in defense of their English liberties. Liberty was an English obsession before it was an American one.

. . . Whatever Americans did to extend liberty and protect individual rights from the encroachments of governmental power, the English had done it first: trial by jury, writs of *habeas corpus*, concern for property rights, fear of standing armies, bills of rights—all were English before they were American. Without the influence of the English constitutional and legal tradition, it is inconceivable that Americans in 1787 or later would have believed and acted as they did.

Yet ultimately, of course, the American political and legal system is not the English system, and this difference should make us aware that looking for intellectual origins and tracing intellectual influences are only part of the explanation of how we have come to be what we are. More important perhaps is what Americans have done with these inherited ideas, how they have used, expanded, and reshaped their intellectual legacies to fit the dynamics of their changing experience. ■

MOTIVATIONS OF THE FRAMERS

We can better understand our Constitution if we know something about the people who wrote it and what motivated them when they did so. Thomas Jefferson, who was himself not a delegate to the Constitutional Convention because he was at the time representing the United States as Ambassador to France, wrote afterwards that the framers were "an assembly of demigods," meaning that their motives were pure and altruistic.

A jarring dissent from that view came in 1913 with the publication of historian Charles A. Beard's famous and controversial *An Economic Interpretation of the Constitution of the United States.* Excerpted here, Beard's book, as well as his other writings, maintained that the framers were an economic elite. He wrote that out of economic motivations, they restricted the power of the majority in order to protect their own property interests, and that the most influential property owners, at the Convention and in the ratification process, were the holders of personalty, or personal property (as opposed to real estate)—that is, bankers, merchants and traders, owners of stocks and bonds, manufacturers, and shipowners.

Later scholarship demonstrated that Beard's thesis was too harsh and in some instances incorrect. Robert E. Brown, in his *Charles Beard and the Constitution: A Critical Analysis of "An Interpretation of the Constitution,"* portions of which are reprinted here, showed that there were owners of personalty on both sides of the question of adopting the Constitution. More importantly, Brown asserts that the Constitution was adopted democratically in a democratic society by middle-class property owners, mostly farmers. In another work, Brown notes that in America at the time, "practically everyone was interested in the protection of property."[1]

---

1. Robert E. Brown, *We the People: The Economic Origins of the Constitution* (Chicago: University of Chicago Press, 1958), p. vii.

The main thing to remember about the framers, though, according to the classic article, "The Founding Fathers: A Reform Caucus in Action," written by John P. Roche for the *American Political Science Review* in 1961, is that they were an elite of distinguished and practical democratic politicians who tried to fashion the kind of "new and far better national government" that a majority of Americans would approve and accept.

AN ECONOMIC INTERPRETATION OF THE CONSTITUTION
Charles A. Beard

Suppose it could be shown from the classification of the men who supported and opposed the Constitution that there was no line of property division at all; that is, that men owning substantially the same amounts of the same kinds of property were equally divided on the matter of adoption or rejection—it would then become apparent that the Constitution had no ascertainable relation to economic groups or classes, but was the product of some abstract causes remote from the chief business of life—gaining a livelihood.

Suppose, on the other hand, that substantially all of the merchants, money lenders, security holders, manufacturers, shippers, capitalists, and financiers and their professional associates are to be found on one side in support of the Constitution and that substantially all or the major portion of the opposition came from the non-slaveholding farmers and the debtors—would it not be pretty conclusively demonstrated that our fundamental law was not the product of an abstraction known as "the whole people," but of a group of economic interests which must have expected beneficial results from its adoption? Obviously all the facts here desired cannot be discovered, but the data presented in the following chapters bear out the latter hypothesis, and thus a reasonable presumption in favor of the theory is created.

Of course, it may be shown (and perhaps can be shown) that the farmers and debtors who opposed the Constitution were, in fact, benefited by the general improvement which resulted from its adoption. It may likewise be shown, to take an extreme case, that the English nation derived immense advantages from the Norman Conquest and the orderly administrative processes which were introduced, as it undoubtedly did; nevertheless, it does not follow that the vague thing known as "the advancement of general welfare" or some abstraction known as "justice" was the immediate, guiding purpose of the leaders in either of these great historic changes. The point is, that the direct, impelling motive in both cases was the economic advantages which the beneficiaries expected would accrue to themselves first, from their action. Further than this, economic interpretation cannot go. It may be that some larger world process is working through each series of historical events: but ultimate causes lie beyond our horizon. . . .

ECONOMIC INTERESTS

A survey of the economic interests of the members of the Convention presents certain conclusions:

A majority of the members were lawyers by profession.

Most of the members came from towns, on or near the coast, that is, from the regions in which personalty was largely concentrated.

Not one member represented in his immediate personal economic interests the small farming or mechanic classes.

The overwhelming majority of members, at least five-sixths, were immediately, directly, and personally interested in the outcome of their labors at Philadelphia, and were to a greater or less extent economic beneficiaries from the adoption of the Constitution.

1. Public security interests were extensively represented in the Convention. Of the fifty-five members who attended no less than forty appear on the Records of the Treasury Department for sums varying from a few dollars up to more than one hundred thousand dollars. . . .

   It is interesting to note that, with the exception of New York, and possibly Delaware, each state had one or more prominent representatives in the Convention who held more than a negligible amount of securities, and who could therefore speak with feeling and authority on the question of providing in the new Constitution for the full discharge of the public debt. . . .
2. Personalty invested in lands for speculation was represented by at least fourteen members. . . .
3. Personalty in the form of money loaned at interest was represented by at least twenty-four members. . . .
4. Personalty in mercantile, manufacturing, and shipping lines was represented by at least eleven members. . . .
5. Personalty in slaves was represented by at least fifteen members. . . .

It cannot be said, therefore, that the members of the Convention were "disinterested." On the contrary, we are forced to accept the profoundly significant conclusion that they knew through their personal experiences in economic affairs the precise results which the new government that they were setting up was designed to attain. As a group of doctrinaires, like the Frankfort assembly of 1848, they would have failed miserably; but as practical men they were able to build the new government upon the only foundations which could be stable: fundamental economic interests. . . .

RATIFICATION

New York   There can be no question about the predominance of personalty in the contest over the ratification in New York. That state, says Libby, "presents the problem in its simplest form. The entire mass of interior counties . . . were solidly anti-federal, comprising the agricultural portion of the state, the last settled and the most thinly populated. There were however in this region two Federal cities (not represented in the convention [as such], Albany in Albany county and Hudson in Columbia county. . . . The Federal area centred about New York city and county: to the southwest lay Richmond county (Staten Island); to the southeast Kings county, and the northeast Westchester county; while still further extending this area, at the northeast lay the divided county of Dutchess, with a vote in the convention of 4 to 2 in favor of the Constitution, and at the southeast were the divided counties of Queens and Suffolk. . . . These radiating strips of territory with New York city as a centre form a unit, in general favorable to the new Constitution; and it is significant of this unity that Dutchess, Queens, and Suffolk, counties broke away from the anti-Federal phalanx and joined the Federalists, securing thereby the adoption of the Constitution."

Unfortunately the exact distribution of personalty in New York and particularly in the wavering districts which went over to the Federalist party cannot be ascertained, for the system of taxation in vogue in New York at the period of the adoption of the Constitution did not require a state record of property. The data which proved so fruitful in Massachusetts are not forthcoming, therefore, in the case of New York; but it seems hardly necessary to demonstrate the fact that New York City was the centre of personalty for the state and stood next to Philadelphia as the great centre of operations in public stock.

This somewhat obvious conclusion is reinforced by the evidence relative to the vote on the legal tender bill which the paper money party pushed through in 1786. Libby's analysis of this vote shows that "No vote was cast against the bill by members of counties north of the county of New York. In the city and county of New York and in Long Island and Staten Island, the combined vote was 9 to 5 against the measure. Comparing this vote with the vote on the ratification in 1788, it will be seen that of the Federal counties 3 voted against paper money and 1 for it; of the divided counties 1 (Suffolk) voted against paper money and 2 (Queens and Dutchess) voted for it. Of the anti-Federal counties none had members voting against paper money. The merchants as a body were opposed to the issue of paper money and the Chamber of Commerce adopted a memorial against the issue."

Public security interests were identified with the sound money party. There were thirty members of the New York constitutional convention who voted in favor of the ratification of the Constitution and of these no less than sixteen were holders of public securities. . . .

South Carolina   South Carolina presents the economic elements in the ratification with the utmost simplicity. There we find two rather sharply marked districts in antagonism over the Constitution. "The rival sections," says Libby, "were the coast or lower district and the upper, or more properly, the middle and upper country. The coast region was the first settled and contained a larger portion of the wealth of the state; its mercantile and commercial interests were important; its church was the Episcopal, supported by the state." This region, it is scarcely necessary to remark, was overwhelmingly in favor of the Constitution. The upper area, against the Constitution, "was a frontier section, the last to receive settlement; its lands were fertile and its mixed population were largely small farmers. . . . There was no established church, each community supported its own church and there was a great variety in the district."

A contemporary writer, R. G. Harper, calls attention to the fact that the lower country, Charleston, Beaufort, and Georgetown, which had 28,694 white inhabitants, and about seven-twelfths of the representation in the state convention, paid £28,081:5:10 taxes in 1794, while the upper country, with 120,902 inhabitants, and five-twelfths of the representation in the convention, paid only £8390:13:3 taxes. The lower districts in favor of the Constitution therefore possessed the wealth of the state and a disproportionate share in the convention—on the basis of the popular distribution of representation.

These divisions of economic interest are indicated by the abstracts of the tax returns for the state in 1794 which show that of £127,337 worth of stock in trade, faculties, etc. listed for taxation in the state, £109,800 worth was in Charleston, city and county—the stronghold of Federalism. Of the valuation of lots in towns and villages to the amount of £656,272 in the state, £549,909 was located in that city and county.

The records of the South Carolina loan office preserved in the Treasury Department at Washington show that the public securities of that state were more largely in the hands of inhabitants than was the case in North Carolina. They also show a heavy concentration in the Charleston district.

At least fourteen of the thirty-one members of the state-ratifying convention from the parishes of St. Philip and Saint Michael, Charleston (all of whom favored ratification) held over $75,000 worth of public securities. . . .

CONCLUSIONS

At the close of this long and arid survey—partaking of the nature of catalogue—it seems worth while to bring together the important conclusions for political science which the data presented appear to warrant.

The movement for the Constitution of the United States was originated and carried through principally by four groups of personalty interests which had been adversely affected under the Articles of Confederation: money, public securities, manufactures, and trade and shipping.

The first firm steps toward the formation of the Constitution were taken by a small and active group of men immediately interested through their personal possessions in the outcome of their labors.

No popular vote was taken directly or indirectly on the proposition to call the Convention which drafted the Constitution.

A large propertyless mass was, under the prevailing suffrage qualifications, excluded at the outset from participation (through representatives) in the work of framing the Constitution.

The members of the Philadelphia Convention which drafted the Constitution were, with a few exceptions, immediately, directly, and personally interested in, and derived economic advantages from, the establishment of the new system.

The Constitution was essentially an economic document based upon the concept that the fundamental private rights of property are anterior to government and morally beyond the reach of popular majorities.

The major portion of the members of the Convention are on record as recognizing the claim of property to a special and defensive position in the Constitution.

In the ratification of the Constitution, about three-fourths of the adult males failed to vote on the question, having abstained from the elections at which delegates to the state conventions were chosen, either on account of their indifference or their disfranchisement by property qualifications.

The Constitution was ratified by a vote of probably not more than one-sixth of the adult males.

It is questionable whether a majority of the voters participating in the elections for the state conventions in New York, Massachusetts, New Hampshire, Virginia, and South Carolina, actually approved the ratification of the Constitution.

The leaders who supported the Constitution in the ratifying conventions represented the same economic groups as the members of the Philadelphia Convention; and in a large number of instances they were also directly and personally interested in the outcome of their efforts.

In the ratification, it became manifest that the line of cleavage for and against the Constitution was between substantial personalty interests on the one hand and the small farming and debtor interests on the other.

The Constitution was not created by "the whole people" as the jurists have said; neither was it created by "the states" as Southern nullifiers long contended; but it was the work of a consolidated group whose interests knew no state boundaries and were truly national in their scope.   ■

A RESPONSE TO BEARD

Robert E. Brown

At the end of Chapter XI [of *An Economic Interpretation of the Constitution of the United States*], Beard summarized his findings in fourteen paragraphs under the heading of "Conclusions." Actually, these fourteen conclusions merely add up to the two halves of the Beard thesis. One half, that the Constitution originated with and was carried through by personalty interests—money, public securities, manufactures, and commerce—is to be found in paragraphs two, three, six, seven, eight, twelve, thirteen, and fourteen. The other half—that the Constitution was put over undemocratically in an undemocratic society—is expressed in paragraphs four, five, nine, ten, eleven, and fourteen. The lumping of these conclusions under two general headings makes it easier for the reader to see the broad outlines of the Beard thesis.

Before we examine these two major divisions of the thesis, however, some comment is relevant on the implications contained in the first paragraph. In it Beard characterized his book as a long and arid survey, something in the nature of a catalogue. Whether this characterization was designed to give his book the appearance of a coldly objective study based on the facts we do not know. If so, nothing could be further from reality. As reviewers pointed out in 1913, and as subsequent developments have demonstrated, the book is anything but an arid catalogue of facts. Its pages are replete with interpretation, sometimes stated, sometimes implied. Our task has been to examine Beard's evidence to see whether it justifies the interpretation which Beard gave it. We have tried to discover whether he used the historical method properly in arriving at his thesis.

If historical method means the gathering of data from primary sources, the critical evaluation of the evidence thus gathered, and the drawing of conclusions consistent with this evidence, then we must conclude that Beard has done great violation to such method in this book. He admitted that the evidence had not been collected which, given the proper use of historical method, should have precluded the writing of the book. Yet he nevertheless proceeded on the assumption that a valid interpretation could be built on secondary writings whose authors had likewise failed to collect the evidence. If we accept Beard's own maximum, "no evidence, no history," and his own admission that the data had never been collected, the answer to whether he used historical method properly is self-evident.

Neither was Beard critical of the evidence which he did use. He was accused in 1913, and one might still suspect him, of using only that evidence which appeared to support his thesis. The amount of realty in the country compared with the personality, the vote in New York, and the omission of the part of *The Federalist* No. 10 which did not fit his thesis are only a few examples of the uncritical use of evidence to be found in the book. Sometimes he accepted secondary accounts at face value without checking them with the sources; at other times he allowed unfounded rumors and traditions to color his work.

Finally, the conclusions which he drew were not justified even by the kind of evidence which he used. If we accepted his evidence strictly at face value, it would still not add up to the fact that the Constitution was put over undemocratically in an undemocratic society by personalty. The citing of property qualifications does not prove that a mass of men were disfranchised. And if we accept his figures on property holdings, either we do not know what most of the delegates had in realty and personalty, or we know that realty outnumbered personalty three to one (eighteen to six). Simply showing that a man held public securities is not sufficient to prove that he acted only in terms of his public securities. If we ignore Beard's own generalizations and accept only his evidence, we would have to conclude that most of the country, and that even the men who were directly concerned with the Constitution, and especially Washington, were large holders of realty.

Perhaps we can never be completely objective in history, but certainly we can be more objective than Beard was in this book. Naturally the historian must always be aware of the biases, the subjectivity, the pitfalls that confront him, but this does not mean that he should not make an effort to overcome these obstacles. Whether Beard had his thesis before he had his evidence, as some have said, is a question that each reader must answer for himself. Certain it is that the evidence does not justify the thesis.

So instead of the Beard interpretation that the Constitution was put over undemocratically in an undemocratic society by personal property, the following fourteen paragraphs are offered as a possible interpretation of the Constitution and as suggestions for future research on that document.

1. The movement for the Constitution was originated and carried through by men who had long been important in both economic and political affairs in their respective states. Some of them owned personalty, more of them owned realty, and if their property was adversely affected by conditions under the Articles of Confederation, so also was the property of the bulk of the people in the country, middle-class farmers as well as town artisans.

2. The movement for the Constitution, like most important movements, was undoubtedly started by a small group of men. They were probably interested personally in the outcome of their labors, but the benefits which they expected were not confined to personal property or, for that matter, strictly to things economic. And if their own interests would be enhanced by a new government, similar interests of other men, whether agricultural or commercial, would also be enhanced.

3. Naturally there was no popular vote on the calling of the convention which drafted the Constitution. Election of delegates by state legislatures was the constitutional method under the Articles of

Confederation, and had been the method long established in this
country. Delegates to the Albany Congress, the Stamp Act Congress, the First Continental Congress, the Second Continental Congress, and subsequent congresses under the Articles were all
elected by state legislatures, not by the people. Even the Articles of
Confederation had been sanctioned by state legislatures, not by
popular vote. This is not to say that the Constitutional Convention
should not have been elected directly by the people, but only that
such a procedure would have been unusual at the time. Some of
the opponents of the Constitution later stressed, without avail, the
fact that the Convention had not been directly elected. But at the
time the Convention met, the people in general seemed to be about
as much concerned over the fact that they had not elected the
delegates as the people of this country are now concerned over the
fact that they do not elect our delegates to the United Nations.

4. Present evidence seems to indicate that there were no "propertyless
masses" who were excluded from the suffrage at the time. Most
men were middle-class farmers who owned realty and were
qualified voters, and, as the men in the Convention said, mechanics
had always voted in the cities. Until credible evidence proves otherwise, we can assume that state legislatures were fairly representative at the time. We cannot condone the fact that a few men were
probably disfranchised by prevailing property qualifications, but it
makes a great deal of difference to an interpretation of the Constitution whether the disfranchised comprised ninety-five per cent of
the adult men or only five per cent. Figures which give percentages of voters in terms of the entire population are misleading,
since less than twenty per cent of the people were adult men. And
finally, the voting qualifications favored realty, not personalty.

5. If the members of the Convention were directly interested in the
outcome of their work and expected to derive benefits from the
establishment of the new system, so also did most of the people of
the country. We have many statements to the effect that the people
in general expected substantial benefits from the labors of the Convention.

6. The Constitution was not just an economic document, although
economic factors were undoubtedly important. Since most of the
people were middle-class and had private property, practically
everybody was interested in the protection of property. A constitution which did not protect property would have been rejected
without any question, for the American people had fought the
Revolution for the preservation of life, liberty, and property. Many
people believed that the Constitution did not go far enough to protect property, and they wrote these views into the amendments to
the Constitution. But property was not the only concern of those
who wrote and ratified the Constitution, and we would be doing a
grave injustice to the political sagacity of the Founding Fathers if
we assumed that property or personal gain was their only motive.

7. Naturally the delegates recognized that protection of property was important under government, but they also recognized that personal rights were equally important. In fact, persons and property were usually bracketed together as the chief objects of government protection.

8. If three-fourths of the adult males failed to vote on the election of delegates to ratifying conventions, this fact signified indifference, not disfranchisement. We must not confuse those who could *not* vote with those who *could* vote but failed to exercise their right. Many men at the time bewailed the fact that only a small portion of the voters ever exercised their prerogative. But this in itself should stand as evidence that the conflict over the Constitution was not very bitter, for if these people had felt strongly one way or the other, more of them would have voted.

   Even if we deny the evidence which I have presented and insist that American society was undemocratic in 1787, we must still accept the fact that the men who wrote the Constitution believed that they were writing it for a democratic society. They did not hide behind an iron curtain of secrecy and devise the kind of conservative government that they wanted without regard to the views and interests of "the people." More than anything else, they were aware that "the people" would have to ratify what they proposed, and that therefore any government which would be acceptable to the people must of necessity incorporate much of what was customary at the time. The men at Philadelphia were practical politicians not political theorists. They recognized the multitude of different ideas and interests that had to be reconciled and compromised before a constitution would be acceptable. They were far too practical, and represented far too many clashing interests themselves, to fashion a government weighted in favor of personalty or to believe that the people would adopt such a government.

9. If the Constitution was ratified by a vote of only one-sixth of the adult men, that again demonstrates indifference and not disfranchisement. Of the one-fourth of the adult males who voted, nearly two-thirds favored the Constitution. Present evidence does not permit us to say what the popular vote was except as it was measured by the votes of the ratifying conventions.

10. Until we know what the popular vote was, we cannot say that it is questionable whether a majority of the voters in several states favored the Constitution. Too many delegates were sent uninstructed. Neither can we count the towns which did not send delegates on the side of those opposed to the Constitution. Both items would signify indifference rather than sharp conflict over ratification.

11. The ratifying conventions were elected for the specific purpose of adopting or rejecting the Constitution. The people in general had anywhere from several weeks to several months to decide the ques-

tion. If they did not like the new government, or if they did not know whether they liked it, they could have voted *no* and there would have been no Constitution. Naturally the leaders in the ratifying conventions represented the same interests as the members of the Constitutional Convention—mainly realty and some personalty. But they also represented their constituents in these same interests, especially realty.

12. If the conflict over ratification had been between substantial personalty interests on the one hand and small farmers and debtors on the other, there would not have been a constitution. The small farmers comprised such an overwhelming percentage of the voters that they could have rejected the new government without any trouble. Farmers and debtors are not synonymous terms and should not be confused as such. A town-by-town or county-by-county record of the vote would show clearly how the farmers voted.

13. The Constitution was created about as much by the whole people as any government could be which embraced a large area and depended on representation rather than on direct participation. It was also created in part by the states, for as the *Records* show, there was strong state sentiment at the time which had to be appeased by compromise. And it was created by compromising a whole host of interests throughout the country, without which compromises it could never have been adopted.

14. If the intellectual historians are correct, we cannot explain the Constitution without considering the psychological factors also. Men were motivated by what they believe as well as by what they have. Sometimes their actions can be explained on the basis of what they hope to have or hope that their children will have. Madison understood this fact when he said that the universal hope of acquiring property tended to dispose people to look favorably upon property. It is even possible that some men support a given economic system when they themselves have nothing to gain by it. So we would want to know what the people in 1787 thought of their class status. Did workers and small farmers believe that they were lower-class, or did they, as many workers do now, consider themselves middle-class? Were the common people trying to eliminate the Washingtons, Adamses, Hamiltons, and Pinckneys, or were they trying to join them?

As did Beard's fourteen conclusions, these fourteen suggestions really add up to two major propositions: the Constitution was adopted in a society which was fundamentally democratic, not undemocratic; and it was adopted by a people who were primarily middle-class property owners, especially farmers who owned realty, not just by the owners of personalty. At present these points seem to be justified by the evidence, but if better evidence in the future disproves or modifies them, we must accept that evidence and change our interpretation accordingly.

After this critical analysis, we should at least not begin future research on this period of American history with the illusion that the Beard thesis of the Constitution is valid. If historians insist on accepting the Beard thesis in spite of this analysis, however, they must do so with the full knowledge that their acceptance is founded on "an act of faith," not an analysis of historical method, and that they were indulging in a "noble dream," not history. ∎

THE FRAMERS WERE SUPERB DEMOCRATIC POLITICIANS
John P. Roche

Over the last century and a half, the work of the Constitutional Convention and the motives of the Founding Fathers have been analyzed under a number of different ideological auspices. To one generation of historians, the hand of God was moving in the assembly; under a later dispensation, the dialectic (at various levels of philosophical sophistication) replaced the Deity: "the relationships of production" moved into the niche previously reserved for Love of Country. . . .

. . . It is not my purpose here to argue that the "Fathers" were, in fact, radical revolutionaries; that proposition has been brilliantly demonstrated by Robert R. Palmer in his *Age of the Democratic Revolution.* My concern is with the further position that not only were they revolutionaries, but also they were democrats. Indeed, in my view, there is one fundamental truth about the Founding Fathers that *every* generation of Zeitgeisters has done its best to obscure: they were first and foremost superb democratic politicians. I suspect that in a contemporary setting, James Madison would be Speaker of the House of Representatives and Hamilton would be the *eminence grise* dominating (*pace* Theodore Sorenson or Sherman Adams) the Executive Office of the President. They were, with their colleagues, *political men*—not metaphysicians, disembodied conservatives or Agents of History—and as recent research into the nature of American politics in the 1780s confirms, they were committed (perhaps willy-nilly) to working within the democratic framework, within a universe of public approval. Charles Beard *and* the filiopietists to the contrary notwithstanding, the Philadelphia Convention was not a College of Cardinals or a council of Platonic guardians working within a manipulative, predemocratic framework; it was a *nationalist* reform caucus which had to operate with great delicacy and skill in a political cosmos full of enemies to achieve the one definitive goal— popular approbation. . . .

When the Constitutionalists went forth to subvert the Confederation, they utilized the mechanisms of political legitimacy. And the roadblocks which con-

fronted them were formidable. At the same time, they were endowed with certain potent political assets. The history of the United States from 1786 to 1790
was largely one of a masterful employment of political expertise by the Constitutionalists as against bumbling, erratic behavior by the opponents of reform.
Effectively, the Constitutionalists had to induce the states, by democratic techniques of coercion, to emasculate themselves. To be specific, if New York had
refused to join the new Union, the project was doomed; yet before New York
was safely in, the reluctant state legislature had *sua sponte* to take the following
steps: (1) agree to send delegates to the Philadelphia Convention; (2) provide
maintenance for these delegates (these were distinct stages: New Hampshire was
early in naming delegates, but did not provide for their maintenance until July);
(3) set up the special *ad hoc* convention to decide on ratification; and (4) concede to the decision of the *ad hoc* convention that New York should participate.
New York admittedly was a tricky state, with a strong interest in a *status quo*
which permitted her to exploit New Jersey and Connecticut, but the same legal
hurdles existed in every state. And at the risk of becoming boring, it must be
reiterated that the *only* weapon in the Constitutionalist arsenal was an effective
mobilization of public opinion.

The group which undertook this struggle was an interesting amalgam of a
few dedicated nationalists with the self-interested spokesmen of various parochial
bailiwicks. The Georgians, for example, wanted a strong central authority to provide military protection for their huge, underpopulated state against the Creek
Confederacy; Jerseymen and Connecticuters wanted to escape from economic
bondage to New York; the Virginians hoped to establish a system which would
give that great state its rightful place in the councils of the republic. The dominant figures in the politics of these states therefore cooperated in the call for
the Convention. In other states, the thrust towards national reform was taken
up by opposition groups who added the "national interest" to their weapons system;
in Pennsylvania, for instance, the group fighting to revise the Constitution of
1776 came out four-square behind the Constitutionalists, and in New York,
Hamilton and the Schuyler *ambiance* took the same tack against George Clinton. There was, of course, a large element of personality in the affair: there is
reason to suspect that Patrick Henry's opposition to the Convention and the Constitution was founded on his conviction that Jefferson was behind both, and a
close study of local politics elsewhere would surely reveal that others supported
the Constitution for the simple (and politically quite sufficient) reason that the
"wrong" people were against it.

To say this is not to suggest that the Constitution rested on a foundation of
impure or base motives. It is rather to argue that in politics there are no im-
maculate conceptions, and that in the drive for a stronger general government,
motives of all sorts played a part. Few men in the history of mankind have
espoused a view of the "common good" or "public interest" that militated against
their private status; even Plato with all his reverence for disembodied reason
managed to put philosophers on top of the pile. Thus it is not surprising that
a number of diversified private interests joined to push the nationalist public interest; what would have been surprising was the absence of such a pragmatic
united front. And the fact remains that, however motivated, these men did

demonstrate a willingness to compromise their parochial interests in behalf of an ideal which took shape before their eyes and under their ministrations. . . .

. . . In fact, the great achievement of the Constitutionalists was their ultimate success in convincing the elected representatives of a majority of the white male population that change was imperative. A small group of political leaders with a Continental vision and essentially a consciousness of the United States' *international* impotence, provided the matrix of the movement. To their standard other leaders rallied with their own parallel ambitions. Their great assets were (1) the presence in their caucus of the one authentic American "father figure," George Washington, whose prestige was enormous, (2) the energy and talent of their leadership (in which one must include the towering intellectuals of the time, John Adams and Thomas Jefferson, despite their absence abroad), and their communications "network," which was far superior to anything on the opposition side; (3) the preemptive skill which made "their" issue The Issue and kept the locally oriented opposition permanently on the defensive; and (4) the subjective consideration that these men were spokesmen of a new and compelling credo: *American* nationalism, that ill-defined but nonetheless potent sense of collective purpose that emerged from the American Revolution. . . .

Drawing on their vast collective political experience, utilizing every weapon in the politician's arsenal, looking constantly over their shoulders at their constituents, the delegates put together a Constitution. It was a makeshift affair; some sticky issues (for example, the qualification of voters) they ducked entirely; others they mastered with that ancient instrument of political sagacity, studied ambiguity (for example, citizenship), and some they just overlooked. In this last category, I suspect, fell the matter of the power of the federal courts to determine the constitutionality of acts of Congress. When the judicial article was formulated (Article III of the Constitution), deliberations were still in the stage where the legislature was endowed with broad power under the Randolph formulation, authority which by its own terms was scarcely amenable to judicial review. In essence, courts could hardly determine when " . . . the separate States are incompetent or . . . the harmony of the United States may be interrupted"; the National Legislature, as critics pointed out, was free to define its own jurisdiction. Later the definition of legislative authority was changed into the form we know, a series of stipulated powers, *but the delegates never seriously reexamined the jurisdiction of the judiciary under this new limited formulation.* All arguments on the intention of the Framers in this matter are thus deductive and *a posteriori*, though some obviously make more sense than others.

The Framers were busy and distinguished men, anxious to get back to their families, their positions, and their constituents, not members of the French Academy devoting a lifetime to a dictionary. They were trying to do an important job, and do it in such a fashion that their handiwork would be acceptable to very diverse constituencies. No one was rhapsodic about the final document, but it was a beginning, a move in the right direction, and one they had reason to believe the people would endorse. In addition, since they had modified the impossible amendment provisions of the Articles . . . to one demanding approval by only three-quarters of the states, they seemed confident that gaps in the fabric which experience would reveal could be rewoven without undue difficulty.

So with a neat phrase introduced by Benjamin Franklin (but devised by Gouverneur Morris) which made their decision sound unanimous, and an inspired benediction by the Old Doctor urging doubters to doubt their own infallibility, the Constitution was accepted and signed. Curiously, Edmund Randolph, who had played so vital a role throughout, refused to sign, as did his fellow Virginian George Mason and Elbridge Gerry of Massachusetts. Randolph's behavior was eccentric, to say the least—his excuses for refusing his signature have a factitious ring even at this late date; the best explanation seems to be that he was afraid that the Constitution would prove to be a liability in Virginia politics, where Patrick Henry was burning up the countryside with impassioned denunciations. Presumably, Randolph wanted to check the temper of the populace before he risked his reputation, and perhaps his job, in a fight with both Henry and Richard Henry Lee. Events lend some justification to this speculation: after much temporizing and use of the conditional subjunctive tense, Randolph endorsed ratification in Virginia and ended up getting the best of both worlds.

Madison, despite his reservations about the Constitution, was the campaign manager in ratification. His first task was to get the Congress in New York to light its own funeral pyre by approving the "amendments" to the Articles and sending them on to the state legislatures. Above all, momentum had to be maintained. The anti-Constitutionalists, now thoroughly alarmed and no novices in politics, realized that their best tactic was attrition rather than direct opposition. Thus they settled on a position expressing qualified approval but calling for a second Convention to remedy various defects (the one with the most demagogic appeal was the lack of a Bill of Rights). Madison knew that to accede to this demand would be equivalent to losing the battle, nor would he agree to conditional approval (despite wavering even by Hamilton). This was an all-or-nothing proposition: national salvation or national impotence with no intermediate positions possible. Unable to get congressional approval, he settled for second best: a unanimous resolution of Congress transmitting the Constitution to the states for whatever action they saw fit to take. The opponents then moved from New York and the Congress, where they had attempted to attach amendments and conditions, to the states for the final battle.

At first the campaign for ratification went beautifully: within eight months after the delegates set their names to the document, eight states had ratified. Only in Massachusetts had the result been close (187–168). Theoretically, a ratification by one more state convention would set the new government in motion, but in fact until Virginia and New York acceded to the new Union, the latter was a fiction. New Hampshire was the next to ratify; Rhode Island was involved in its characteristic political convulsions (the Legislature there sent the Constitution out to the towns for decision by popular vote and it got lost among a series of local issues); North Carolina's convention did not meet until July and then postponed a final decision. This is hardly the place for an extensive analysis of the conventions of New York and Virginia. Suffice it to say that the Constitutionalists clearly outmaneuvered their opponents, forced them into impossible political positions, and won both states narrowly. The Virginia Convention could serve as a classic study in effective floor management: Patrick Henry had to be contained, and a reading of the debates discloses a standard, two-stage technique.

Henry would give a four- or five-hour speech denouncing some section of the Constitution on every conceivable ground (the federal district, he averred at one point, would become a haven for convicts escaping from state authority!); when Henry subsided, "Mr. Lee of Westmoreland" would rise and literally poleaxe him with sardonic invective (when Henry complained about the militia power, "Lighthorse Harry" really punched below the belt: observing that while the former Governor had been sitting in Richmond during the Revolution, *he* had been out in the trenches with the troops and thus felt better qualified to discuss military affairs). Then the gentlemanly Constitutionalists (Madison, Pendleton and Marshall) would pick up the matters at issue and examine them in the light of reason.

Indeed, modern Americans who tend to think of James Madison as a rather dessicated character should spend some time with this transcript. Probably Madison put on his most spectacular demonstration of nimble rhetoric in what might be called "The Battle of the Absent Authorities." Patrick Henry in the course of one of his harangues alleged that Jefferson was known to be opposed to Virginia's approving the Constitution. This was clever: Henry hated Jefferson, but was prepared to use any weapon that came to hand. Madison's riposte was superb: First, he said that with all due respect to the great reputation of Jefferson, he was not in the country and therefore could not formulate an adequate judgment; second, no one should utilize the reputation of an outsider—the Virginia Convention was there to think for itself; third, if there were to be recourse to outsiders, the opinions of George Washington should certainly be taken into consideration; and finally, he knew from privileged personal communications from Jefferson that in fact the latter *strongly favored* the Constitution. To devise an assault route into this rhetorical fortress was literally impossible.

The fight was over; all that remained now was to establish the new frame of government in the spirit of its framers. And who were better qualified for this task than the Framers themselves? Thus victory for the Constitution meant simultaneous victory for the Constitutionalists; the anti-Constitutionalists either capitulated or vanished into limbo—soon Patrick Henry would be offered a seat on the Supreme Court and Luther Martin would be known as the Federalist "bulldog." And irony of ironies, Alexander Hamilton and James Madison would shortly accumulate a reputation as the formulators of what is often alleged to be our political theory, the concept of "federalism." Also, on the other side of the ledger, the arguments would soon appear over what the Framers "really meant"; while these disputes have assumed the proportions of a big scholarly business in the last century, they began almost before the ink on the Constitution was dry. One of the best early ones featured Hamilton versus Madison on the scope of presidential power, and other Framers characteristically assumed positions in this and other disputes on the basis of their political convictions.

Probably our greatest difficulty is that we know so much more about what the Framers *should have meant* than they themselves did. We are intimately acquainted with the problems that their Constitution should have been designed to master; in short, we have read the mystery story backwards. If we are to get the right "feel" for their time and their circumstances, we must in Maitland's phrase, " . . . think ourselves back into a twilight." Obviously, no one can pretend completely to escape from the solipsistic web of his own environment, but if the effort is made, it is possible to appreciate the past roughly on its own terms. The first step in this process is to abandon the academic premise that because we can ask a question, there must be an answer. . . .

There was a good deal of definitional pluralism with respect to the problems the delegates did discuss, but when we move to the question of extrapolated intentions, we enter the realm of spiritualism. When men in our time, for instance, launch into elaborate talmudic exegesis to demonstrate that federal aid to parochial schools is (or is not) in accord with the intentions of the men who established the Republic and endorsed the Bill of Rights, they are engaging in historical Extra-Sensory Perception. (If one were to join this E. S. P. contingent for a minute, he might suggest that the hard-boiled politicians who wrote the Constitution and Bill or Rights would chuckle scornfully at such an invocation of authority: obviously a politician would chart his course on the intentions of the living, not of the dead, and count the number of Catholics in his constituency.)

The Constitution, then, was not an apotheosis of "constitutionalism," a triumph of architectonic genius; it was a patch-work sewn together under the pressure of both time and events by a group of extremely talented democratic politicians. They refused to attempt the establishment of a strong, centralized sovereignty on the principle of legislative supremacy for the excellent reason that the people would not accept it. They risked their political fortunes by opposing the established doctrines of state sovereignty because they were convinced that the existing system was leading to national impotence and probably foreign domination. For two years, they worked to get a convention established. For over three months, in what must have seemed to the faithful participants an endless process of give-and-take, they reasoned, cajoled, threatened, and bargained amongst themselves. The result was a Constitution which the people, in fact, by democratic processes, did accept, and a new and far better national government was established.

Beginning with the inspired propaganda of Hamilton, Madison and Jay, the ideological build-up got under way. *The Federalist* had little impact on the ratification of the Constitution, except perhaps in New York, but this volume had enormous influence on the image of the Constitution in the minds of future generations, particularly on historians and political scientists who have an innate fondness for theoretical symmetry. Yet, while the shades of Locke and Montesquieu *may* have been hovering in the background, . . . the careful observer of the day-to-day work of the Convention finds no over-arching principles. The "separation of powers" to him seems to be a by-product of suspicion, and "federalism" he views as . . . the farthest point the delegates felt they could go in the destruction of state power without themselves inviting repudiation.

To conclude, the Constitution was neither a victory for abstract theory nor a great practical success. Well over half a million men had to die on the battlefields of the Civil War before certain constitutional principles could be defined—a baleful consideration which is somehow overlooked in our customary tributes to the farsighted genius of the Framers and to the supposed American talent for "constitutionalism." The Constitution was, however, a vivid demonstration of effective democratic political action, and of the forging of a national elite which literally persuaded its countrymen to hoist themselves by their own boot straps. . . .   ■

SEPARATION OF POWERS AND CHECKS AND BALANCES

Under the name of "Publius," Alexander Hamilton, John Jay, and James Madison wrote a number of proratification essays between October 1787 and August 1788. These essays were published separately in various New York newspapers and also appeared together in a bound volume, *The Federalist.* Hamilton's idea, the essays were intended to explain and argue for the Constitution and to respond to numerous newspaper articles critical of it.

The Federalist is virtually on an equal footing with the Declaration of Independence and the Constitution itself as a major American historical document. John P. Roche has called it "inspired propaganda," but today it is looked upon by the courts, as well as historians and others, as a prime source for determining what the framers meant when they wrote a particular provision into the Constitution.

The selections which are excerpted here—from *Federalist 47, 48* and *51*—were all written by James Madison. They deal with the idea of the separation of powers—legislative, executive, and judicial. There had been criticism of the proposed Constitution on the basis that it did not totally and rigidly separate these powers, that they would overlap somewhat in the new national government. Madison makes clear that this overlapping—where each branch could check and balance the powers of the others—was both intentional and desirable.

The U. S. system is one of fragmented power—first, between the federal, or national, government and the state governments and, then, within each of these levels, by the separation of powers. Citizens who are satisfied with the *status quo* are better served by this fragmentation than those who desire rapid change. A system that divides power in so many ways makes it easier to prevent change than to bring it about. As James Madison makes clear in the following selections, this effect was recognized and intended in order to achieve what was thought to be a more important objective: to prevent the concentration of power in the hands "of one, a few or many."

FEDERALIST 47

I proceed to examine the particular structure of this government, and the distribution of this mass of power among its constituent parts.

One of the principal objections inculcated by the more respectable adversaries to the constitution, is its supposed violation of the political maxim, that the legislative, executive and judiciary departments ought to be separate and distinct. In the structure of the federal government, no regard, it is said, seems to have been paid to this essential precaution in favor of liberty. . . .

. . . The accumulation of all powers legislative, executive and judiciary in the same hands, whether of one, a few or many, and whether hereditary, self appointed, or elective, may justly be pronounced the very definition of tyranny. Were the federal constitution therefore really chargeable with this accumulation of power or with a mixture of powers having a dangerous tendency to such an accumulation, no further arguments would be necessary to inspire a universal reprobation of the system. I persuade myself however, that it will be made apparent to every one, that the charge cannot be supported, and that the maxim on which it relies, has been totally misconceived and misapplied. . . .

The oracle who is always consulted and cited on this subject, is the celebrated Montesquieu. If he be not the author of this invaluable precept in the science of politics, he has the merit at least of displaying, and recommending it most effectually to the attention of mankind. . . .

The British constitution was to Montesquieu, what Homer has been to the didactic writers on epic poetry. / . .

On the slightest view of the British constitution we must perceive, that the legislative, executive and judiciary departments are by no means totally separate and distinct from each other. The executive magistrate forms an integral part of the legislative authority. He alone has the prerogative of making treaties with foreign sovereigns, which when made have, under certain limitations, the force of legislative acts. All the members of the judiciary department are appointed by him; can be removed by him on the address of the two Houses of Parliament, and form, when he pleases to consult them, one of his constitutional councils. One branch of the legislative department forms also, a great constitutional council to the executive chief; as on another hand, it is the sole depositary of judicial power in cases of impeachment, and is invested with the supreme appellate jurisdiction, in all other cases. The judges again are so far connected with the legislative department, as often to attend and participate in its deliberations, though not admitted to a legislative vote.

From these facts by which Montesquieu was guided it may clearly be inferred, that in saying "there can be no liberty where the legislative and executive powers are united in the same person, or body of magistrates," or "if the power of judging be not separated from the legislative and executive powers," he did not mean that these departments ought to have no *partial agency* in, or no *controul* over the acts of each other. His meaning . . . can amount to no more than this, that where the *whole* power of one department is exercised by the same hands which possess the *whole* power of another department, the fundamental principles of a free constitution, are subverted. . . .

The reasons on which Montesquieu grounds his maxim are a further demonstration of his meaning. "When the legislative and executive powers are united in the same person or body" says he, "there can be no liberty, because apprehensions may arise lest *the same* monarch or senate should *enact* tyrannical laws, to *execute* them in a tyrannical manner." Again "Were the power of judging joined with the legislative, the life and liberty of the subject would be exposed to arbitrary controul, for *the judge* would then be *the legislator.* Were it joined to the executive power, *the judge* might behave with all the violence of *an oppressor."* . . .

If we look into the constitutions of the several states we find that notwithstanding the emphatical, and in some instances, the unqualified terms in which this axiom has been laid down, there is not a single instance in which the several departments of power have been kept absolutely separate and distinct. New-Hampshire, whose constitution was the last formed, seems to have been fully aware of the impossibility and inexpediency of avoiding any mixture whatever of these departments; and has qualified the doctrine by declaring "that the legislative, executive and judiciary powers ought to be kept as separate from, and independent of each other *as the nature of a free government will admit; or as is consistent with that chain of connection, that binds the whole fabric of the constitution in one indissoluble bond of unity and amity."* Her constitution accordingly mixes these departments in several respects. The senate which is a branch of the legislative department is also a judicial tribunal for the trial of empeachments. The president who is the head of the executive department, is the presiding member also of the senate; and besides an equal vote in all cases, has a casting vote in case of a tie. The executive head is himself eventually elective every year by the legislative department; and his council is every year chosen by and from the members of the same department. Several of the officers of state are also appointed by the legislature. And the members of the judiciary department are appointed by the executive department. . . .

What I have wished to evince is, that the charge brought against the proposed constitution, of violating a sacred maxim of free government, is warranted neither by the real meaning annexed to that maxim by its author; nor by the sense in which it has hitherto been understood in America. . . .   ■

FEDERALIST 48

I shall undertake in the next place, to shew that unless these departments be so far connected and blended, as to give to each a constitutional controul over the others, the degree of separation which the maxim requires as essential to a free government, can never in practice, be duly maintained.

It is agreed on all sides, that the powers properly belonging to one of the departments, ought not to be directly and compleatly administered by either of the other departments. It is equally evident, that neither of them ought to possess directly or indirectly, an overruling influence over the others in the administration of their respective powers. It will not be denied, that power is of an encroaching nature, and that it ought to be effectually restrained from passing the limits assigned to it. After discriminating therefore in theory, the several classes of power, as they may in their nature be legislative, executive, or judiciary; the next and most difficult task, is to provide some practical security for each against the invasion of the others. What this security ought to be, is the great problem to be solved.

Will it be sufficient to mark with precision the boundaries of these departments in the Constitution of the government, and to trust to these parchment barriers against the encroaching spirit of power? This is the security which appears to have been principally relied on by the compilers of most of the American Constitutions. But experience assures us, that the efficacy of the provision has been greatly over-rated; and that some more adequate defence is indispensibly necessary for the more feeble, against the more powerful members of the government. The legislative department is every where extending the sphere of its activity, and drawing all power into its impetuous vortex. . . .

In a government, where numerous and extensive prerogatives are placed in the hands of a hereditary monarch, the executive department is very justly regarded as the source of danger, and watched with all the jealousy which a zeal for liberty ought to inspire. In a democracy, where a multitude of people exercise in person the legislative functions, and are continually exposed by their incapacity for regular deliberation and concerted measures, to the ambitious intrigues of their executive magistrates, tyranny may well be apprehended on some favorable emergency, to start up in the same quarter. But in a representative republic, where the executive magistracy is carefully limited both in the extent and the duration of its power; and where the legislative power is exercised by an assembly, which is inspired by a supposed influence over the people with an intrepid confidence in its own strength; which is sufficiently numerous to feel all the passions which actuate a multitude; yet not so numerous as to be incapable of pursuing the objects of its passions, by means which reason prescribes; it is against the enterprising ambition of this department, that the people ought to indulge all their jealousy and exhaust all their precautions.

The legislative department derives a superiority in our governments from other circumstances. Its constitutional powers being at once more extensive and less susceptible of precise limits, it can with the greater facility, mask under complicated and indirect measures, the encroachments which it makes on the co-ordinate departments. It is not unfrequently a question of real-nicety in legislative bodies, whether the operation of a particular measure, will, or will not extend beyond the legislative sphere. On the other side, the executive power being restrained within a narrower compass, and being more simple in its nature; and the judiciary being described by land marks, still less uncertain, projects of usurpation by either of these departments, would immediately betray and defeat themselves. Nor is this all: As the legislative department alone has access to the pockets of the people, and has in some Constitutions full discretion, and in all, a prevailing influence over the pecuniary rewards of those who fill the other departments, a dependence is thus created in the latter, which gives still greater facility to encroachments of the former. . . .   ■

FEDERALIST 51

To what expedient then shall we finally resort for maintaining in practice the necessary partition of power among the several departments, as laid down in the constitution? The only answer that can be given is, that as all these exterior provisions are found to be inadequate, the defect must be supplied, by so contriving the interior structure of the government, as that its several constituent parts may, by their mutual relations, be the means of keeping each other in their proper places. . . .

In order to lay a due foundation for that separate and distinct exercise of the different powers of government, which to a certain extent, is admitted on all hands to be essential to the preservation of liberty, it is evident that each department should have a will of its own; and consequently should be so constituted, that the members of each should have as little agency as possible in the appointment of the members of the others. . .

It is equally evident that the members of each department should be as little dependent as possible on those of the others, for the emoluments annexed to their offices. Were the executive magistrate, or the judges, not independent of the legislature in this particular, their independence in every other would be merely nominal.

But the great security against a gradual concentration of the several powers in the same department, consists in giving to those who administer each department, the necessary constitutional means, and personal motives, to resist encroachments of the others. The provision for defence must in this, as in all other cases, be made commensurate to the danger of attack. Ambition must be made to counteract ambition. The interest of the man must be connected with the constitutional rights of the place. It may be a reflection on human nature, that such devices should be necessary to controul the abuses of government. But what is government itself but the greatest of all reflections on human nature? If men were angels, no government would be necessary. If angels were to govern men, neither external nor internal controuls on government would be necessary. In framing a government which is to be administered by men over men, the great difficulty lies in this: You must first enable the government to controul the governed; and in the next place, oblige it to controul itself. A dependence on the people is no doubt the primary controul on the government; but experience has taught mankind the necessity of auxiliary precautions.

This policy of supplying by opposite and rival interests, the defect of better motives, might be traced through the whole system of human affairs, private as well as public. We see it particularly displayed in all the subordinate distributions of power; where the constant aim is to divide and arrange the several offices in such a manner as that each may be a check on the other; that the private interest of every individual, may be a centinel over the public rights. These inventions of prudence cannot be less requisite in the distribution of the supreme powers of the state.

But it is not possible to give to each department an equal power of self defence. In republican government the legislative authority, necessarily, predominates. The remedy for this inconveniency is, to divide the legislature into different branches; and to render them by different modes of election, and different principles of action, as little connected with each other, as the nature of their common functions, and their common dependence on the society, will admit. It may even be necessary to guard against dangerous encroachments by still further precautions. As the weight of the legislative authority requires that it should be thus divided, the weakness of the executive may require, on the other hand, that it should be fortified. An absolute negative, on the legislature, appears at first view to be the natural defence with which the executive magistrate should be armed. But perhaps it would be neither altogether safe, nor alone sufficient. On ordinary occasions, it might not be exerted with the requisite firmness; and on extraordinary occasions, it might be perfidiously abused. May not this defect of an absolute negative be supplied, by some qualified connection between this weaker department, and the weaker branch of the stronger department, by which the latter may be led to support the constitutional rights of the former, without being too much detached from the rights of its own department? . . . ■

SHOULD THE CONSTITUTION BE CHANGED?

In all the 200 years since it was written, the U. S. Constitution has only been amended twenty-six times. Ten of these changes came with the adoption of the Bill of Rights immediately after the establishment of the new government. One reason for such few amendments is the fact that the Constitution was written in brief and general language that has proved capable of interpretation and reinterpretation, without alteration of the actual words, as times and circumstances have changed.

Another reason for such few amendments, as Dom Bonafede puts it in the next selection, is the "emotional attachment" most Americans have for our Constitution and system. The basic features of our governmental structure have never been altered. Indeed, most current ideas for amending the Constitution deal only with changing substantive policies made by the President, the Congress, or the courts—to require that the federal budget be balanced or to reverse the Supreme Court's decision on abortion, for example.

Some studies *are* being made, however, of possible structural changes. Two distinguished former national officials, Lloyd N. Cutler and C. Douglas Dillon, have set up a Committee on the Constitutional System to look into the possibility of moving the United States toward a more parliamentary system. Dom Bonafede has written a report on this project, its ideas, and its chances of success.

SHOULD AMERICA CHANGE TO A PARLIAMENTARY SYSTEM?
Dom Bonafede

In 1980, while serving as counsel to President Carter, Washington attorney Lloyd N. Cutler published an article in *Foreign Affairs* magazine in which he maintained that the constitutional separation of powers between the legislative and executive branches makes it almost impossible for the President to "form a government," resulting in endemic stalemate in U.S. political leadership.

He suggested that the nation should consider amending the Constitution to incorporate elements of the parliamentary system to heal the breach caused by "divided government" and ensure that "the elected majority is able to carry out an over-all program and is held accountable for its success or failure."

In 1982, C. Douglas Dillon, Treasury Secretary in the Kennedy Administration, elaborated on that thesis in an address at Tufts University, declaring that the constitutional system, which served the country well in its first 150 years, is considerably less adaptable to political changes, international events and technological advances in today's world. Contemporary governmental problems, he said, "do not lie with the quality or character of our elected representatives. . . . Rather they lie with a system which promotes divisiveness and makes it difficult, if not impossible, to develop truly national policies."

Dillon proposed that the answer may be some form of parliamentary democracy, wherein "responsibility for policy and its execution lies clearly with the head of government and his party, which stands or falls on its over-all record."

Although not new—before the turn of the century, Woodrow Wilson, then

From *National Journal*, June 29, 1985, pp. 1521.1524. Copyright © 1985 by National Journal Inc. All Rights Reserved. Reprinted by permission.

a professor, urged movement toward a parliamentary system—the arguments put forth by Cutler and Dillon stimulated deep-seated interest in constitutional reform among prominent scholars, statesmen, officeholders, politicians, former government officials and journalists.

Numerous organizations, universities, think tanks, special committees and individual academics have been studying various facets of governmental reform, including changes in organizational structures, political and electoral procedures and leadership concepts.

James L. Sundquist, a senior fellow at the Brookings Institution, recently completed a book tentatively titled *Efficient Government and Constitutional Reform*, in which he analyzes governmental problems and offers possible remedies. . . .

About three years ago, Cutler and Dillon established the Committee on the Constitutional System, a nonpartisan, nonprofit corporation in Washington, devoted to the study and analysis of the Constitution and its impact on the nation's political and governmental systems. . . .

Cutler contends that to attain greater government responsiveness, there must be more party cohesion and less separation between the executive and legislative branches. The courts would still serve as a decisive check on their power, he says.

"The changes we are discussing . . . don't come close to a true parliamentary system," Cutler said. "But they are aimed at party responsibility and giving the elected majority a chance to promote their programs and be accountable."

Cutler argues that governmental reforms are essential because of the political and socioeconomic changes that have taken place since World War II. The government today, he observed, is required to make constant, innumerable choices and face new challenges that predictably lead to cross-party coalitions and consensus politics. The increasing interdependence—what happens in India, for example, can have an impact, economically and politically, in the United States—necessitates prompt responses from Washington.

Because of congressional reforms that have fostered a diffusion of authority, the President can no longer negotiate and strike agreements with just a small number of leaders, Cutler said. Also, the decline of political parties and the concurrent erosion in party discipline have virtually removed the parties as decisive factors in the selection and underwriting of candidates. Finally, highly organized and well-financed single-issue organizations have been thrust in the center of the political arena because of their ability to "reward or punish legislators, both in cash and at the ballot box," he said.

In defense of their argument against divided government, the reformers note that for more than half of the time since World War II, the White House has been under the control of one party and one or both houses of Congress have been in the hands of the other party. They further contend that on only three occasions in recent history have the White House and Congress worked in complete harmony—during the early periods of the Roosevelt and Johnson Administrations and, in 1981–1982, when President Reagan's comprehensive economic program was adopted.

Dillon said that divisiveness at the top levels of government has made it difficult, if not impossible, to develop national policies and has discouraged accountability. "The President blames the Congress, the Congress blames the President and the public remains confused and disgusted with government in Washington," he told the Tufts audience. The government, he added, cannot speak with "one clear voice" in foreign affairs or "act promptly and energetically in the face of a crisis."

More specifically, the Dillon-Cutler committee contends that this division of power has crippled efforts to deal with huge federal deficits and come to terms on a national budget.

Cutler recalls that although Carter negotiated and signed the second Strategic Arms Limitation Treaty, the pact was never approved by two-thirds of the Senate. Such a situation would not have occurred, he said, had the President been able to count on the total or near-total support of his party—if, in short, he had been able to "form a government." . . .

Sundquist, who is working in concert with the Cutler-Dillon committee, reported in a study written for the committee that because of divided government, "the welfare state came late to the United States, social security measures lagged several decades behind their adoption by the industrial democracies of Europe and this country still has no national system of health care and relatively little [public housing]. Civil rights legislation was likewise stalled for years, if not for decades, until the logjam was broken by the televised images of southern law enforcement officers using police dogs and fire hoses on peaceful demonstrators."

In Sundquist's view, "Constitutional reform has been a debate between liberals and conservatives, the former seeing the separation of powers as a barrier to, and the latter as a protection against, government activism." However, he said, the traditional positions are being reversed. "Currently, the country is witnessing an unprecedented political configuration—a determined, activist conservative President encountering resistance from a liberal Congress seeking to defend the status quo. It is the conservatives' turn to experience the frustration of the separate powers."

ALTERNATIVES

The specific reforms being studied by the Committee on the Constitutional System cover a broad range of subjects. Many could be achieved by legislation or revisions in party rules. Proposed constitutional amendments would involve only structural matters—how the machinery of government is assembled and works, rather than the jurisdictional authority of political institutions. There would be no proposals, for instance, affecting the fundamental executive powers of the President or the legislative responsibilities of Congress. Nor would the Bill of Rights be touched.

Reformers acknowledge that major changes in the Constitution generally come as the result of a national crisis, but they contend that the country should repair gaps in the system now so that it will be prepared for future emergencies. The most significant changes being considered would entail the adaptation of certain strains of the parliamentary concept that would narrow the line of authority between the executive and legislative branches with the intent of enhancing party cohesion. . . .

As a means of providing greater incentives for Presidents and Members of

Congress of the same party to cooperate in "forming a government," the committee is considering proposing constitutional amendments that would allow the President to include incumbent Members of Congress in his Cabinet without requiring them to give up their congressional seats. Another would make it possible for governments to "fall" by authorizing the President or Congress or both to call for new elections "when a stalemate becomes intolerable," according to the committee workbook. The provision could also be used to remove a weak, ineffectual "but nonimpeachable President" from office.

Still other constitutional changes would authorize a presidential line-item veto of appropriations bills, subject to override by majority votes of both houses, and provide for four-year terms for Members of the House to run concurrently with presidential terms and be synchronized with eight-year terms for Senators.

Among proposed federal statutes under review is a provision that provides for presidential elections to be held two–four weeks before congressional elections, enabling voters to know which party has been entrusted with the White House before they vote for Members of Congress. Another federal statute under consideration, which is aimed at reducing ticket splitting, would require every state to include a line or lever allowing a voter to cast a single ballot for all the candidates of one party.

Changes in party rules would entitle winning nominees for House and Senate seats, plus holdover Senators, to attend presidential nominating conventions as voting delegates. Others would provide government financing of congressional as well as presidential elections and make funds for broadcast advertising available to congressional candidates on the condition that they do not spend any other money on campaign broadcasts. The latter is intended to relieve the candidates from dependence on funds from single-issue groups and to build party loyalty among those elected with the help of party-allocated funds.

A major legislative change would stipulate that a party caucus in each house could, by a 60 per cent vote, bind all of its members to vote the party line on up to a specified number of bills—say, 50. The committee said: "Such a rule would be enforced by automatic loss of any chairmanship or other party office held by a member who votes against the caucus position more than the stated number of times per session. This would greatly enhance party legislative loyalty while leaving reasonable scope for party members to make occasional departures on principal from the party caucus position."

OPPOSITION

Proposals to revise the Constitution, although rarely successful, have a long history. Thomas Jefferson was convinced that each generation should modify the document to meet contemporary needs. Suggestions were made in the late 19th century by Ohio Sen. George Pendleton to allow Cabinet officials on the floor of Congress to engage in debate, an idea since suggested by other reformers. The proposal by the Cutler-Dillon committee for the creation of a joint Cabinet composed of members of the executive and legislative branches has also been offered before.

Yet the Constitution has remained remarkably durable; in almost 200 years— since 1791, when the Bill of Rights was ratified—it has been amended only 16 times—all the more extraordinary since it was written in general and sometimes vague language open to wide interpretation. The intent of the framers is often obscured by their accommodation to conflicting regions and interests. The Constitution created a strong national government but provided only the framework of our political system. Political parties, nominating conventions, primaries and presidential Cabinets are unmentioned.

Sundquist notes that of the last 16 amendments, only 2 significantly deal with the structural character of political institutions—the 17th Amendment, which provided for the popular election of Senators, and the 22nd Amendment, which limited Presidents to two terms of four years each. None address the separation of executive and legislative powers.

Acting as a deterrent to constitutional reforms, he said, are the "enormous barriers" erected by the authors—approval by two-thirds of both houses of Congress, followed by ratification by three-fourths of the states.

"To succeed, then, a proposed amendment either must have no adverse effect on anybody . . . or must distribute its adverse effects so nearly neutral that no substantial interest is offended."

Not unexpectedly, there is formidable opposition to amending the Constitution, especially provisions relating to the separation of powers. Arthur M. Schlesinger Jr., in a 1982 *Wall Street Journal* article, cautioned against the "romantic myths" of the parliamentary system. He maintained that the system "assures the almost unassailable dominance of the executive over the legislature." For example, he wrote, the British prime minister can make appointments, conclude treaties, declare war and withhold information without worrying about parliamentary confirmation or approval. And Schlesinger noted, "While constitutional reformers muse about the virtues of a fusion of powers, British reformers yearn for separation." . . .

These arguments are familiar to the reformers. Cutler said that his committee is not proposing a true parliamentary system but only the parts of it that could be blended into our system. "We would still have an elected President, we would still have two houses in Congress," he said. Several countries in the post World War II era have adopted constitutions merging the virtues of the two systems, including Canada, France, Italy, Ireland, Japan and West Germany, he said. . . .

However, in promoting its proposed reforms, the committee may find it less difficult to cope with the arguments of reform opponents than with the emotional attachment of most Americans to the Constitution. To them, it not only confers legitimacy on the government but also symbolizes what the country is all about. Consequently, it is not something to be easily tampered with.

On a more substantive level, there is the widely held conviction that a divided government is the driving force of the American political system, that its untidy procedures and time-consuming devices encourage bipartisan consultation leading to acceptable compromises and the fine-tuning of public policy.

The reformers' task is also complicated by the reality that Reagan has demonstrated that the presidency is manageable, thereby persuading many people to feel better about the institution. . . .

On their side is the universal recognition that while tripartite government may be one of the best political systems ever conceived, it is nonetheless imperfect and hence open to public discussion and potential improvement. ∎

CHAPTER 2

Federalism

W hat James Madison termed a "compound republic"—later called "the federal system" or, simply, "federalism"—represented a middle-ground solution worked out by the constitutional framers.

The United States does not have a *unitary* government. That is a system in which authority is centralized in the national government, which derives its power directly from the people and to which state and local governments owe their existence and power. Nor does the United States have a *confederation*, a system in which the national government owes its existence and power to the state governments. Instead, we have a government based on a written constitution in which power is divided between (and shared by) the national government and the states—*federalism*.

In this chapter, we will examine how Madison and Alexander Hamilton explained, and argued for, the state-national relationship the Constitution established. We will also look at two Supreme Court Decisions (one early, one recent), that have emphasized the power of the national government in that relationship. And, finally, we will consider how federalism has evolved in recent times into what some call "intergovernmental relations."

FEDERALISM AND THE CONSTITUTION

When the thirteen American colonies rebelled against Great Britain, declaring their independence formally in 1776, a major target of their rebellion was the centralized authority that had been exercised over them and their governments by the British Parliament and king. The first national govern-

no pres or Judicary cart

ment for the newly independent states was established under the Articles of Confederation (written in 1777, but not ratified by all the new states as required until 1781). It is no surprise that the Articles provided that sovereignty, or governmental authority, would principally be retained by the states. There was no national chief executive nor any national courts. Congress had to rely largely on the states for execution and enforcement of the national laws.

James Madison of Virginia and Alexander Hamilton of New York were among those early Americans who came to feel during the perilous days of the Revolutionary War and its aftermath that a more powerful national government was needed if the new nation was to survive. They and others helped bring about the Constitutional Convention, which met in Philadelphia in 1787.

There were many confederationists—such as Patrick Henry of Virginia— who took no part in the writing of the Constitution and later opposed its ratification by the states because they vigorously objected to strengthening the national government at the expense of the states.

Hamilton and Madison undertook to answer this criticism and opposition. Hamilton wrote *Federalist 16* and *17*, both excerpted here. In *16,* he argued that the new national government must be able to execute and enforce its own laws, not just by actions against state governments, but by dealing direcly with the people. In *17,* he said that the state governments would be an effective counterweight against the power of the national government— and would not be dominated by it—first, because the power of the national government would be diffused as a result of the separation of powers within it, and, second, because citizens would have greater attachment to and give greater support to the governments closer to them, the state governments.

James Madison wrote *Federalist 39* in which he first defined "republic" and showed that the new national government fit the definition. A republic, he said, is "a government which derives all its powers directly or indirectly from the great body of the people, and is administered by persons holding their offices during pleasure for a limited period, or during good behavior." Next, Madison addressed the question of whether the proposed Constitution would give too much power to the national government at the expense of the states. In this excerpt, Madison's terms of the day are a little confusing. He wrote that the new government was not meant totally to be a "national," which today we would call a unitary, government, nor was it meant totally to be a "federal," which today we would call a confederation, government. The new government, he declared, would be a composite of the two—what came to be called federalism.

Hamilton

FEDERALIST 16

It has been seen that delinquencies in the members [states] of the Union are its natural and necessary offspring; and that whenever they happen, the only constitutional remedy is force, and the immediate effect of the use of it, civil war.

It remains to enquire how far so odious an engine of government, in its application to us, would even be capable of answering its end. If there should not be a large army, constantly at the disposal of the national government, it would either not be able to employ force at all, or when this could be done, it would amount to a war between different parts of the confederacy . . . .

It seems to require no pains to prove that the States ought not to prefer a national constitution, which could only be kept in motion by the instrumentality of a large army, continually on foot to execute the ordinary requisitions or decrees of the government. And yet this is the plain alternative involved by those who wish to deny it the power of extending its operations to individuals. Such a scheme, if practicable at all, would instantly degenerate into a military despotism; but it will be found in every light impracticable. The resources of the Union would not be equal to the maintenance of an army considerable enough to confine the larger States within the limits of their duty; nor would the means ever be furnished of forming such an army in the first instance. . . .

The result of these observations to an intelligent mind must be clearly this, that if it be possible at any rate to construct a Federal Government capable of regulating the common concerns and preserving the general tranquility, it must be founded, as to the objects committed to its care, upon the reverse of the principle contended for by the opponents of the proposed constitution. It must carry its agency to the persons of the citizens. It must stand in need of no intermediate legislations; but must itself be empowered to employ the arm of the ordinary magistrate to execute its own resolutions. The majesty of the national authority must be manifested through the medium of the Courts of Justice. The government of the Union, like that of each State, must be able to address itself immediately to the hopes and fears of individuals; and to attract to its support, those passions, which have the strongest influence upon the human heart. It must in short, possess all the means and have a right to resort to all the methods of executing the powers, with which it is entrusted, that are possessed and exercised by the governments of the particular States.

To this reasoning it may perhaps be objected, that if any State should be disaffected to the authority of the Union, it could at any time obstruct the execution of its laws, and bring the matter to the same issue of force, with the necessity of which the opposite scheme is reproached.

The plausibility of this objection will vanish the moment we advert to the essential difference between a mere NON COMPLIANCE and a DIRECT and ACTIVE RESISTANCE. If the interposition of the State-Legislature be necessary to give effect to a measure of the Union, they have only NOT TO ACT or TO ACT

EVASIVELY, and the measure is defeated. This neglect of duty may be disguised under affected but unsubstantial provisions, so as not to appear, and of course not to excite any alarm in the people for the safety of the constitution. The State leaders may even make a merit of their surreptitious invasions of it, on the ground of some temporary convenience, exemption, or advantage.

But if the execution of the laws of the national government, should not require the intervention of the State Legislatures; if they were to pass into immediate operation upon the citizens themselves, the particular governments could not interrupt their progress without an open and violent exertion of an unconstitutional power. No omissions, nor evasions would answer the end. They would be obliged to act, and in such a manner, as would leave no doubt that they had encroached on the national rights. An experiment of this nature would always be hazardous—in the face of a constitution in any degree competent to its own defence, and of a people enlightened enough to distinguish between a legal exercise and an illegal usurpation of authority. The success of it would require not merely a factious majority in the Legislature, but the concurrence of the courts of justice, and of the body of the people. . . .   ■

FEDERALIST 17

An objection of a nature different from that which has been stated and answered, in my last address, may perhaps be likewise urged against the principle of legislation for the individual citizens of America. It may be said, that it would tend to render the government of the Union too powerful, and to enable it to absorb in itself those residuary authorities, which it might be judged proper to leave with the States for local purposes. Allowing the utmost latitude to the love of power, which any reasonable man can require, I confess I am at a loss to discover what temptation the persons entrusted with the administration of the general government could ever feel to divest the States of the authorities of that description. The regulation of the mere domestic police of a State appears to me to hold out slender allurements to ambition. Commerce, finance, negociation and war seem to comprehend all the objects, which have charms for minds governed by that passion; and all the powers necessary to these objects ought in the first instance to be lodged in the national depository. The administration of private justice between the citizens of the same State, the supervision of agriculture and of other concerns of a similar nature, all those things in short which are proper to be provided for by local legislation, can never be desirable cares of a general jurisdiction. It is therefore improbable that there should exist a disposition in the Federal councils to usurp the powers with which they are connected; because the attempt to exercise those powers would be as troublesome as it would be nugatory; and the possession of them, for that reason, would contribute nothing to the dignity, to the importance, or to the splendour of the national government.

But let it be admitted for argument sake, that mere wantonness and lust of domination would be sufficient to beget that disposition, still it may be safely affirmed, that the sense of the constituent body of the national representatives, or in other words of the people of the several States would controul the indulgence of so extravagant an appetite. It will always be far more easy for the State governments to encroach upon the national authorities, than for the national government to encroach upon the State authorities. The proof of this proposition turns upon the greater degree of influence, which the State governments, if they administer their affairs with uprightness and prudence, will generally possess over the people; a circumstance which at the same time teaches us, that there is an inherent and intrinsic weakness in all Federal Constitutions; and that too much pains cannot be taken in their organization, to give them all the force which is compatible with the principles of liberty.

The superiority of influence in favour of the particular governments would result partly from the diffusive construction of the national government; but chiefly from the nature of the objects to which the attention of the State administrations would be directed.

It is a known fact in human nature that its affections are commonly weak in proportion to the distance of diffusiveness of the object. Upon the same principle that a man is more attached to his family than to his neighbourhood, to his neighbourhood than to the community at large, the people of each State would be apt to feel a stronger byass towards their local governments than towards the government of the Union; unless the force of that principle should be destroyed by a much better administration of the latter.

This strong propensity of the human heart would find powerful auxiliaries in the objects of State regulation.

The variety of more minute interests, which will necessarily fall under the superintendence of the local administrations, and which will form so many rivulets of influence running through every part of the society, cannot be particularised without involving a detail too tedious and uninteresting to compensate for the instruction it might afford.

There is one transcendent advantage belonging to the province of the State governments which alone suffices to place the matter in a clear and satisfactory light. I mean the ordinary administration of criminal and civil justice. This of all others is the most powerful, most universal and most attractive source of popular obedience and attachment. It is that, which—being the immediate and visible guardian of life and property—having its benefits and its terrors in constant activity before the public eye—regulating all those personal interests and familiar concerns to which the sensibility of individuals is more immediately awake—contributes more than any other circumstance to impressing upon the minds of the people affection, esteem and reverence towards the government. This great cement of society which will diffuse itself almost wholly through the channels of the particular governments, independent of all other causes of influence, would ensure them so decided an empire over their respective citizens, as to render them at all times a complete counterpoise and not unfrequently dangerous rivals to the power of the Union. . . .   ■

Madison

FEDERALIST 39

The last paper having concluded the observations which were meant to introduce a candid survey of the plan of government reported by the Convention, we now proceed to the execution of that part of our undertaking. The first question that offers itself is, whether the general form and aspect of the government be strictly republican? It is evident that no other form would be reconcileable with the genius of the people of America; with the fundamental principles of the revolution; or with that honorable determination, which animates every votary of freedom, to rest all our political experiments on the capacity of mankind for self-government. If the plan of the convention therefore be found to depart from the republican character, its advocates must abandon it as no longer defensible.

What then are the distinctive characters of the republican form? Were an answer to this question to be sought, not by recurring to principles, but in the application of the term by political writers, to the constitutions of different States, no satisfactory one would ever be found. Holland, in which no particle of the supreme authority is derived from the people, has passed almost universally under the denomination of a republic. The same title has been bestowed on Venice, where absolute power over the great body of the people, is exercised in the most absolute manner, by a small body of hereditary nobles. Poland, which is a mixture of aristocracy and of monarchy in their worst forms, has been dignified with the same appellation. The government of England, which has one republican branch only, combined with a hereditary aristocracy and monarchy, has with equal impropriety been frequently placed on the list of republics. These examples, which are nearly as dissimilar to each other as to a genuine republic, shew the extreme inaccuracy with which the term has been used in political disquisitions.

If we resort for a criterion, to the different principles on which different forms of government are established, we may define a republic to be, or at least may bestow that name on, a government which derives all its powers directly or indirectly from the great body of the people; and is administered by persons holding their offices during pleasure, for a limited period, or during good behaviour. It is *essential* to such a government, that it be derived from the great body of the society, not from an inconsiderable proportion, or a favored class of it; otherwise a handful of tyrannical nobles, exercising their oppressions by a delegation of their powers, might aspire to the rank of republicans, and claim for their government the honorable title of republic. It is *sufficient* for such a government, that the persons administering it be appointed, either directly or indirectly, by the people; and that they hold their appointments by either of the tenures just specified; otherwise every government in the United States, as well as every other popular government that has been or can be well organized or well executed, would be degraded from the republican character. According to the Constitution of every State in the Union, some or other of the officers of government are appointed indirectly only by the people. According to most of them the chief magistrate himself is so appointed. And according to one, this mode of appointment is extended to one of the coordinate branches of the legislature. According to all the Constitutions also, the tenure of the highest offices is extended to a definite period, and in many instances, both within the legislative and executive departments, to a period of years. According to the provisions of most of the constitutions, again, as well as according to the most respectable and received opinions on the subject, the members of the judiciary department are to retain their offices by the firm tenure of good behaviour.

On comparing the Constitution planned by the Convention, with the standard here fixed, we perceive at once that it is in the most rigid sense conformable to it. The House of Representatives, like that of one branch at least of all the State Legislatures, is elected immediately by the great body of the people. The Senate, like the present Congress, and the Senate of Maryland, derives its appointment indirectly from the people. The President is indirectly derived from the choice of the people, according to the example in most of the States. Even the judges, with all other officers of the Union, will, as in the several States, be the choice, though a remote choice, of the people themselves. The duration of the appointments is equally conformable to the republican standard, and to the model of the State Constitutions. The House of Representatives is periodically elective as in all the States: and for the period of two years as in the State of South-Carolina. The Senate is elective for the period of six years; which is but one year more than the period of the Senate of Maryland; and but two more than that of the Senates of New-York and Virginia. The President is to continue on office for the period of four years; as in New-York and Delaware, the chief magistrate is elected for three years, and in South-Carolina for two years. In the other States the election is annual. In several of the States however, no constitutional provision is made for the impeachment of the Chief Magistrate. And in Delaware and Virginia, he is not impeachable till out of office. The President of the United States is impeachable at any time during his continuance in office. The tenure by which the Judges are to hold their places, is, as it unquestionably ought to be, that of good behaviour. The tenure of the ministerial offices generally will be a subject of legal regulation, conformably to the reason of the case, and the example of the State Constitutions.

Could any further proof be required of the republican complextion of this system, the most decisive one might be found in its absolute prohibition of titles of nobility, both under the Federal and the State Governments; and in its express guarantee of the republican form to each of the latter.

But it was not sufficient, say the adversaries of the proposed Constitution, for the Convention to adhere to the republican form. They ought, with equal

national + unitary
federal confederation

care, to have preserved the *federal* form, which regards the union as a *confederacy* of sovereign States; instead of which, they have framed a *national* government, which regards the union as a *consolidation* of the States. And it is asked by what authority this bold and radical innovation was undertaken. The handle which has been made of this objection requires, that it should be examined with some precision.

Without enquiring into the accuracy of the distinction on which the objection is founded, it will be necessary to a just estimate of its force, first to ascertain the real character of the government in question; secondly, to enquire how far the Convention were authorised to propose such a government; and thirdly, how far the duty they owed to their country, could supply any defect of regular authority.

real character of Govn

First. In order to ascertain the real character of the government it may be considered in relation to the foundation on which it is to be established; to the sources from which its ordinary powers are to be drawn; to the operation of those powers; to the extent of them; and to the authority by which future changes in the government are to be introduced.

On examining the first relation, it appears on one hand that the Constitution is to be founded on the assent and ratification of the people of America, given by deputies elected for the special purpose; but on the other, that this assent and ratification is to be given by the people, not as individuals composing one entire nation; but as composing the distinct and independent States to which they respectively belong. It is to be the assent and ratification of the several States, derived from the supreme authority in each State, the authority of the people themselves. The act therefore establishing the Constitution, will not be a *national* but a *federal* act.

That it will be a federal and not a national act, as these terms are understood by the objectors, the act of the people as forming so many independent States, not as forming one aggregate nation, is obvious from this single consideration that it is to result neither from the decision of a *majority* of the people of the Union, nor from that of a *majority* of the States. It must result from the *unanimous* assent of the several States that are parties to it, differing no other wise from their ordinary assent than in its being expressed, not by the legislative authority, but by that of the people themselves. Were the people regarded in this transaction as forming one nation, the will of the majority of the whole people of the United States, would bind the minority; in the same manner as the majority in each State must bind the minority; and the will of the majority must be determined either by a comparison of the individual votes; or by considering the will of a majority of the States, as evidence of the will of a majority of the people of the United States. Neither of these rules has been adopted. Each State in ratifying the Constitution, is considered as a sovereign body independent of all others, and only to be bound by its own voluntary act. In this relation then the new Constitution will, if established, be a *federal* and not a *national* Constitution.

The next relation is to the sources from which the ordinary powers of government are to be derived. The house of representatives will derive its powers from the people of America, and the people will be represented in the same proportion\ and on the same principle, as they are in the Legislature of a particular State. So far the Government is *national* not *federal*. The Senate on the other hand will derive its powers from the States, as political and co-equal societies; and these will be represented on the principle of equality in the Senate, as they now are in the existing Congress. So far the government is *federal*, not *national*. The executive power will be derived from a very compound source. The immediate election of the President is to be made by the States in their political characters. The votes allotted to them, are in a compound ratio, which considers them partly as distinct and co-equal societies; partly as unequal members of the same society. The eventual election, again is to be made by that branch of the Legislature which consists of the national representatives; but in this particular act, they are to be thrown into the form of individual delegations from so many distinct and co-equal bodies politic. From this aspect of the Government, it appears to be of a mixed character presenting at least as many *federal* as *national* features.

The difference between a federal and national Government as it relates to the *operation of the Government* is supposed to consist in this, that in the former, the powers operate on the political bodies composing the confederacy, in their political capacities: In the latter, on the individual citizens, composing the nation, in their individual capacities. On trying the Constitution by this criterion, it falls under the *national*, not the *federal* character; though perhaps not so compleatly, as has been understood. In several cases and particularly in the trial of controversies to which States may be parties, they must be viewed and proceeded against in their collective and political capacities only. So far the national countenance of the Government on this side seems to be disfigured by a few federal features. But this blemish is perhaps unavoidable in any plan; and the operation of the Government on the people in their individual capacities, in its ordinary and most essential proceedings, may on the whole designate it in this relation a *national* Government.

But if the Government be national with regard to the *operation* of its powers, it changes its aspect again when we contemplate it in relation to the *extent* of its powers. The idea of a national Government involves in it, not only an authority over the individual citizens; but an indefinite supremacy over all persons and things, so far as they are objects of lawful Government. Among a people consolidated into one nation, this supremacy is compleatly vested in the national legislature. Among communities united for particular purposes, it is vested partly in the general, and partly in the municipal Legislatures. In the former case, all local authorities are subordinate to the supreme; and may be controuled, directed or abolished by it at pleasure. In the latter the local or municipal authorities form distinct and independent portions of the supremacy, no more subject within their respective spheres to the general authority, than the general authority is subject to them, within its own sphere. In this relation then the proposed Government cannot be deemed a *national* one; since its jurisdiction extends to certain enumerated objects only, and leaves to the several States a residuary and inviolable sovereignty over all other objects. It is true that in controversies relating to the boundary between the two jurisdictions, the tribunal which is ultimately to decide, is to be established under the general Government. But this does not change the principle of the case. The decision is to be impartially made, according to the rules of the Constitution; and all the usual and most effectual precautions are taken to secure this impartiality. Some such tribunal is clearly essential to prevent an appeal to the sword, and a dissolution of the compact; and that it ought to be established under the general, rather than under the local Governments; or to speak more properly, that it could be safely established under the first alone, is a position not likely to be combated.

If we try the Constitution by its last relation, to the authority by which amendments are to be made, we find it neither wholly *national*, nor wholly *federal*. Were it wholly national, the supreme and ultimate authority would reside in the *majority* of the people of the Union; and this authority would be competent at all times, like that of a majority of every national society, to alter or abolish its established Government. Were it wholly federal on the other hand, the concurrence of each State in the Union would be essential to every alteration that would be binding on all. The mode provided by the plan of the Convention is not founded on either of these principles. In requiring more than a majority, and particularly, in computing the proportion by *States*, not by *citizens*, it departs from the *national*, and advances towards the *federal* character: In rendering the concurrence of less than the whole number of States sufficient, it loses again the *federal*, and partakes of the *national* character.

The proposed Constitution therefore is in strictness neither a national nor a federal constitution; but a composition of both. In its foundation, it is federal, not national; in the sources from which the ordinary powers of the Government are drawn, it is partly federal, and partly national: in the operation of these powers, it is national, not federal: In the extent of them again, it is federal, not national: And finally, in the authoritative mode of introducing amendments, it is neither wholly federal, nor wholly national. ■

THE SUPREME COURT AND NATIONAL POWER

The second paragraph of Article VI of the U. S. Constitution is called the Supremacy Clause. It declares that the Constitution itself, acts of Congress made "in pursuance of" the Constitution, and treaties made "under the authority of the United States" are "the supreme law of the land," and it requires state judges to respect this national, or federal, supremacy, no matter what their own states' laws or constitutions provide to the contrary.

Who determines whether an act of Congress is in pursuance of the Constitution—that is, is consistent with it? The Constitution is silent on this question. But the U. S. Supreme Court supplied the answer in the landmark 1803 case of *Marbury* v. *Madison,*[1] holding that the Court itself, under the supreme judicial power vested in it by the Constitution, has the power to

---

1. 1 Cranch 137 (1819).

interpret the Constitution and thus to declare acts of Congress "constitutional" or "unconstitutional."

In 1819, in another landmark case, McCulloch v. Maryland, excerpted here, the Supreme Court exercised this power of "judicial review," as it is called, to uphold the power of Congress to create a national bank and to declare a Maryland state tax on the bank unconstitutional. The opinion written by Chief Justice John Marshall admitted that the power of Congress to create a national bank was nowhere "enumerated," or expressly stated, in the Constitution. But the Court declared that Congress and the federal government are not just limited to "enumerated" powers. The national government also has "implied" powers—under the "necessary and proper clause." This provision, contained in Article I, Section 8 of the Constitution, follows a list of enumerated powers and states that Congress also has the power "To make all laws which shall be necessary and proper for carrying into execution the foregoing powers, and all other powers vested by this Constitution in the government of the United States, or in any department or officer thereof."

The "implied powers" allowed Congress and the national government by the Supreme Court tipped the state-federal balance of power in favor of the federal government. The balance was further tipped in the same direction by Supreme Court decisions interpreting the Commerce Clause. This provision, one of the enumerated powers in Article I, Section 8, gives Congress and the national government the power "To regulate commerce with foreign nations, and among the states, and with the Indian tribes." Very early,[2] the Supreme Court held that the power to regulate commerce among the states—the "interstate commerce" power—meant that when Congress established licensing for coastal shippers, states could not do so because such state action, even though intrastate, or within-state, affected interstate commerce and conflicted with the superior powers of the federal government in this field.

Much later, during the administration of President Franklin D. Roosevelt, the Supreme Court first held unconstitutional and, later (with some change in Court members), constitutional a whole slough of new federal laws regulating business and industry and setting standards for their conduct and activity that "touches on" or "affects" interstate commerce.[3]

Among such regulatory laws passed by Congress were those that set fair labor standards—for example, prescribing minimum wages and maximum hours for workers. But can these federal standards be imposed on state and local governments? The answer was generally thought to be yes until the 1976 decision by the U. S. Supreme Court in the case of National League of Cities v. Usery.[4] By a five-to-four vote in that case, the Court ruled that a legislative attempt of Congress to extend wage and hour laws to state and local govern-

---

2. *Gibbons* v. *Ogden*, 9 Wheaton 1 (1824).

3. See *Steward Machine Co.* v. *Davis*, 301 U.S. 548 (1937); and *National Labor Relations Board* v. *Jones & Laughlin Steel Corp.*, 301 U.S. 1 (1937).

4. 426 U.S. 833 (1976).

ment employees was unconstitutional because it impaired the ability of the state and local governments to function in the federal system.

But the Court reversed itself in 1985. The 1976 opinion had been written by conservative Justice William Rehnquist. Justice Harry Blackmun's concurring opinion then had supplied the fifth vote and a Court majority, but he had written that he was not "untroubled" by the decision. By 1985, Justice Blackmun had become so troubled that when a similar case presented itself, *Garcia* v. *San Antonio Metropolitan Transit Authority*, excerpted here, he switched to the other side and, as a matter of fact, wrote the majority opinion (five-to-four, again)—holding, after all, that state and local governments must abide by federal wage and hour laws. Justice Rehnquist, one of four dissenters this time, predicted that with new appointments to its membership, the Court would some day revert to the *National League of Cities* rule. In the state-federal relationship, the federal government is dominant—and the Supreme Court has, by its decisions, helped to foster that dominance—as the early decision in *McCulloch* v. *Maryland* and the recent decision in *Garcia* v. *San Antonio Metropolitan Transit Authority* show. It is doubtful that even a reversal of the *Garcia* decision would do much to change that.

MCCULLOCH V. MARYLAND*

Mr. Chief Justice Marshall delivered the opinion of the Court.

In the case now to be determined, the defendant, a sovereign State, denies the obligation of a law enacted by the legislature of the Union, and the plaintiff, on his part, contests the validity of an act which has been passed by the legislature of that State. The constitution of our country, in its most interesting and vital parts, is to be considered; the conflicting powers of the government of the Union and of its members, as marked in that constitution, are to be discussed; and an opinion given, which may essentially influence the great operations of the government. . . .

The first question made in the cause is, has Congress power to incorporate a bank?

In discussing this question, the counsel for the State of Maryland have deemed it of some importance, in the construction of the constitution, to consider that instrument not as emanating from the people, but as the act of sovereign and independent States. The powers of the general government, it has been said, are

_____

* 4 Wheaton 316 (1819).

delegated by the States, who alone are truly sovereign; and must be exercised in subordination to the States, who alone possess supreme dominion.

It would be difficult to sustain this proposition. The Convention which framed the constitution was indeed elected by the State legislatures. But the instrument, when it came from their hands, was a mere proposal, without obligation, or pretensions to it. It was reported to the then existing Congress of the United States, with a request that it might "be submitted to a Convention of Delegates, chosen in each State by the people thereof, under the recommendation of its Legislature, for their assent and ratification." This mode of proceeding was adopted; and by the Convention, by Congress, and by the State Legislatures, the instrument was submitted to the people. They acted upon it in the only manner in which they can act safely, effectively, and wisely, on such a subject, by assembling in Convention. It is true, they assembled in their several States—and where else should they have assembled? No political dreamer was ever wild enough to think of breaking down the lines which separate the States, and of compounding the American people into one common mass. Of consequence, when they act, they act in their States. But the measures they adopt do not, on that account, cease to be the measures of the people themselves, or become the measures of the State governments.

From these Conventions the constitution derives its whole authority. The government proceeds directly from the people; is "ordained and established" in the name of the people; and is declared to be ordained, "in order to form a more perfect union, establish justice, ensure domestic tranquillity, and secure the blessings of liberty to themselves and to their posterity." The assent of the States, in their sovereign capacity, is implied in calling a Convention, and thus submitting that instrument to the people. But the people were at perfect liberty to accept or reject it; and their act was final. It required not the affirmance, and could not be negatived, by the State governments. The constitution, when thus adopted, was of complete obligation, and bound the State sovereignties. . . .

If any one proposition could command the universal assent of mankind, we might expect it would be this—that the government of the Union, though limited in its powers, is supreme within its sphere of action. This would seem to result necessarily from its nature. It is the government of all; its powers are delegated by all; it represents all, and acts for all. Though any one State may be willing to control its operations, no State is willing to allow others to control them. The nation, on those subjects on which it can act, must necessarily bind its component parts. But this question is not left to mere reason: the people have, in express terms, decided it, by saying, "this constitution, and the laws of the United States, which shall be made in pursuance thereof," "shall be the supreme law of the land," and by requiring that the members of the State legislatures, and the officers of the executive and judicial departments of the States, shall take the oath of fidelity to it.

The government of the United States, then, though limited in its powers, is supreme; and its laws, when made in pursuance of the constitution, form the supreme law of the land, "any thing in the constitution or laws of any State to the contrary notwithstanding."

Among the enumerated powers, we do not find that of establishing a bank or creating a corporation. But there is no phrase in the instrument which, like the articles of confederation, excludes incidental or implied powers; and which requires that every thing granted shall be expressly and minutely described. Even the 10th amendment, which was framed for the purpose of quieting the excessive jealousies which had been excited, omits the word "expressly," and declares only that the powers "not delegated to the United States, nor prohibited to the States, are reserved to the States or to the people;" thus leaving the question, whether the particular power which may become the subject of contest has been delegated to the one government, or prohibited to the other, to depend on a fair construction of the whole instrument. The men who drew and adopted this amendment had experienced the embarrassments resulting from the insertion of this word in the articles of confederation, and probably omitted it to avoid those embarrassments. A constitution, to contain an accurate detail of all the subdivisions of which its great powers will admit, and of all the means by which they may be carried into execution, would partake of the prolixity of a legal code, and could scarcely be embraced by the human mind. It would probably never be understood by the public. Its nature, therefore, requires, that only its great outlines should be marked, its important objects designated, and the minor ingredients which compose those objects be deduced from the nature of the objects themselves. That this idea was entertained by the framers of the American constitution, is not only to be inferred from the nature of the instrument, but from the language. Why else were some of the limitations, found in the ninth section of the 1st article, introduced? It is also, in some degree, warranted by their having omitted to use any restrictive term which might prevent its receiving a fair and just interpretation. In considering this question, then, we must never forget, that it is *a constitution* we are expounding.

Although, among the enumerated powers of government, we do not find the word "bank" or "incorporation," we find the great powers to lay and collect taxes; to borrow money; to regulate commerce; to declare and conduct a war; and to raise and support armies and navies. The sword and the purse, all the external relations, and no inconsiderable portion of the industry of the nation, are entrusted to its government. It can never be pretended that these vast powers draw after them others of inferior importance, merely because they are inferior. Such an idea can never be advanced. But it may with great reason be contended, that a government, entrusted with such ample powers, on the due execution of which the happiness and prosperity of the nation so vitally depends, must also be entrusted with ample means for their execution. The power being given, it is the interest of the nation to facilitate its execution. It can never be their interest, and cannot be presumed to have been their intention, to clog and embarrass its execution by withholding the most appropriate means. Throughout this vast republic, from the St. Croix to the Gulph of Mexico, from the Atlantic to the Pacific, revenue is to be collected and expended, armies are to be marched and supported. The exigencies of the nation may require that the treasure raised in the north should be transported to the south, *that* raised in the east conveyed to the west, or that this order should be reversed. Is that construction of the constitution to be preferred which would render these operations difficult, hazardous, and expensive? Can we adopt that construction, (unless the words imperiously

require it,) which would impute to the framers of that instrument, when granting these powers for the public good, the intention of impeding their exercise
by withholding a choice of means? If, indeed, such be the mandate of the constitution, we have only to obey; but that instrument does not profess to enumerate
the means by which the powers it confers may be executed; nor does it prohibit
the creation of a corporation, if the existence of such a being be essential to
the beneficial exercise of those powers. It is, then, the subject of fair inquiry,
how far such means may be employed. . . .

But the constitution of the United States has not left the right of Congress
to employ the necessary means, for the execution of the powers conferred on
the government, to general reasoning. To its enumeration of powers is added
that of making "all laws which shall be necessary and proper, for carrying into
execution the foregoing powers, and all other powers vested by this constitution,
in the government of the United States, or in any department thereof." . . .

We admit, as all must admit, that the powers of the government are limited,
and that its limits are not to be transcended. But we think the sound construction
of the constitution must allow to the national legislature that discretion, with
respect to the means by which the powers it confers are to be carried into execution, which will enable that body to perform the high duties assigned to it, in
the manner most beneficial to the people. Let the end be legitimate, let it be
within the scope of the constitution, and all means which are appropriate, which
are plainly adapted to that end, which are not prohibited, but consist with the
letter and spirit of the constitution, are constitutional. . . .

It being the opinion of the Court, that the act incorporating the bank is constitutional; and that the power of establishing a branch in the State of Maryland
might be properly exercised by the bank itself, we proceed to inquire—

Whether the State of Maryland may, without violating the constitution, tax
that branch?

That the power of taxation is one of vital importance; that it is retained by
the States; that it is not abridged by the grant of a similar power to the government of the Union; that it is to be concurrently exercised by the two governments: are truths which have never been denied. But, such is the paramount
character of the constitution, that its capacity to withdraw any subject from the
action of even this power, is admitted. The States are expressly forbidden to lay
any duties on imports or exports, except what may be absolutely necessary for
executing their inspection laws. If the obligation of this prohibition must be
conceded—if it may restrain a State from the exercise of its taxing power on
imports and exports; the same paramount character would seem to restrain, as
it certainly may restrain, a State from such other exercise of this power, as is
in its nature incompatible with, and repugnant to, the constitutional laws of the
Union. A law, absolutely repugnant to another, as entirely repeals that other as
if express terms of repeal were used.

On this ground the counsel for the bank place its claim to be exempted from
the power of a State to tax its operations. There is no express provision for the
case, but the claim has been sustained on a principle which so entirely pervades
the constitution, is so intermixed with the materials which compose it, so inter-
woven with its web, so blended with its texture, as to be incapable of being
separated from it, without rending it into shreds.

This great principle is, that the constitution and the laws made in pursuance thereof are supreme; that they control the constitution and laws of the respective States, and cannot be controlled by them. From this, which may be almost termed an axiom, other propositions are deduced as corollaries, on the truth or error of which, and on their application to this case, the cause has been supposed to depend. These are, 1st. that a power to create implies a power to preserve. 2nd. That a power to destroy, if wielded by a different hand, is hostile to, and incompatible with these powers to create and to preserve. 3d. That where this repugnancy exists, that authority which is supreme must control, not yield to that over which it is supreme. . . .

If we apply the principle for which the State of Maryland contends, to the constitution generally, we shall find it capable of changing totally the character of that instrument. We shall find it capable of arresting all the measures of the government, and of prostrating it at the foot of the States. The American people have declared their constitution, and the laws made in pursuance thereof, to be supreme; but this principle would transfer the supremacy, in fact, to the States. . . .

The Court has bestowed on this subject its most deliberate consideration. The result is a conviction that the States have no power, by taxation or otherwise, to retard, impede, burden, or in any manner control, the operations of the constitutional laws enacted by Congress to carry into execution the powers vested in the general government. This is, we think, the unavoidable consequence of that supremacy which the constitution has declared.

We are unanimously of opinion, that the law passed by the legislature of Maryland, imposing a tax on the Bank of the United States, is unconstitutional and void. . . . ■

GARCIA V. SAN ANTONIO METROPOLITAN TRANSIT AUTHORITY*

Justice BLACKMUN delivered the opinion of the Court.

We revisit in these cases an issue raised in *National League of Cities v. Usery*.[1] In that litigation, this Court, by a sharply divided vote, ruled that the Commerce Clause does not empower Congress to enforce the minimum-wage and overtime provisions of the Fair Labor Standards Act (FLSA) against the States "in areas of traditional governmental functions." . . . Although *National League of Cities* supplied some examples of "traditional governmental functions," it did not offer

---

* 105 S. Ct. 1005 (1985).
1. 426 U.S. 833 (1976).

a general explanation of how a "traditional" function is to be distinguished from a "nontraditional" one. Since then, federal and state courts have struggled with the task, thus imposed, of identifying a traditional function for purposes of state immunity under the Commerce Clause.

In the present cases, a Federal District Court concluded that municipal owner- ship and operation of a mass-transit system is a traditional governmental func- tion and thus, under *National League of Cities*, is exempt from the obligations imposed by the FLSA. Faced with the identical question, three Federal Courts of Appeals and one state appellate court have reached the opposite conclusion.

Our examination of this "function" standard applied in these and other cases over the last eight years now persuades us that the attempt to draw the bound- aries of state regulatory immunity in terms of "traditional governmental func- tion" is not only unworkable but is inconsistent with established principles of federalism and, indeed, with those very federalism principles on which *National League of Cities* purported to rest. That case, accordingly, is overruled. . . .

The present controversy concerns the extent to which SAMTA [San Antonio Metropolitan Transit Authority] may be subjected to the minimum-wage and over- time requirements of the FLSA. When the FLSA was enacted in 1938, its wage and overtime provisions did not apply to local mass-transit employees or, in- deed, to employees of state and local governments. . . . In 1961, Congress ex- tended minimum-wage coverage to employees of any private mass-transit carrier whose annual gross revenue was not less than $1 million. . . . Five years later, Congress extended FLSA coverage to state and local-government employees for the first time by withdrawing the minimum-wage and overtime exemptions from public hospitals, schools, and mass-transit carriers whose rates and services were subject to state regulation. . . . At the same time, Congress eliminated the over- time exemption for all mass-transit employees other than drivers, operators, and conductors. . . . The application of the FLSA to public schools and hospitals was ruled to be within Congress' power under the Commerce Clause. . . .[2]

The FLSA obligations of public mass-transit systems like SATS were ex- panded in 1974 when Congress provided for the progressive repeal of the sur- viving overtime exemption for mass-transit employees. . . . Congress simultaneously brought the States and their subdivisions further within the am- bit of the FLSA by extending FLSA coverage to virtually all state and local- government employees. . . . SATS [San Antonio Transit System] complied with the FLSA's overtime requirements until 1976, when this Court, in *National League of Cities*, overruled *Maryland v. Wirtz,* and held that the FLSA could not be applied constitutionally to the "traditional governmental functions" of state and local governments. Four months after *National League of Cities* was handed down, SATS informed its employees that the decision relieved SATS of its overtime obligations under the FLSA.

Matters rested there until September 17, 1979, when the Wage and Hour Ad- ministration of the Department of Labor issued an opinion that SAMTA's opera- tions "are not constitutionally immune from the application of the Fair Labor

---

2. *Maryland* v. *Wirtz,* 392 U.S. 183 (1968).

Standards Act under *National League of Cities*. . . . On November 21 of that year, SAMTA filed this action against the Secretary of Labor in the United States District Court for the Western District of Texas. It sought a declaratory judgment that, contrary to the Wage and Hour Administration's determination, *National League of Cities* precluded the application of the FLSA's overtime requirements to SAMTA's operations. The Secretary counterclaimed . . .for enforcement of the overtime and record-keeping requirements of the FLSA. On the same day that SAMTA filed its action, appellant Garcia and several other SAMTA employees brought suit against SAMTA in the same District Court for overtime pay under the FLSA. . . .

The District Court voiced a common concern: "Despite the abundance of adjectives, identifying which particular state functions are immune remains difficult." Just how troublesome the task has been is revealed by the results reached in other federal cases. Thus, courts have held that regulating ambulance services, . . . licensing automobile drivers, . . . operating a municipal airport, . . . performing solid waste disposal, . . . and operating a highway authority . . . are functions *protected* under *National League of Cities*. At the same time, courts have held that issuance of industrial development bonds, . . . regulation of intrastate natural gas sales, . . . regulation of traffic on public roads, . . . regulation of air transportation, . . . operation of a telephone system, . . . leasing and sale of natural gas, . . . operation of a mental health facility, . . . and provision of in-house domestic services for the aged and handicapped, . . . are *not* entitled to immunity. We find it difficult, if not impossible, to identify an organizing principle that places each of the cases in the first group on one side of a line and each of the cases in the second group on the other side. The constitutional distinction between licensing drivers and regulating traffic, for example, or between operating a highway authority and operating a mental health facility, is elusive at best.

Thus far, this Court itself has made little headway in defining the scope of the governmental functions deemed protected under *National League of Cities*. In that case the court set forth examples of protected and unprotected functions, . . . but provided no explanation of how those examples were identified. . . .

We therefore now reject, as unsound in principle and unworkable in practice, a rule of state immunity from federal regulation that turns on a judicial appraisal of whether a particular governmental function is "integral" or "traditional." Any such rule leads to inconsistent results at the same time that it disserves principles of democratic self-governance, and it breeds inconsistency precisely because it is divorced from those principles. If there are to be limits on the Federal Government's power to interfere with state functions—as undoubtedly there are—we must look elsewhere to find them. We accordingly return to the underlying issue that confronted this Court in *National League of Cities*—the manner in which the Constitution insulated States from the reach of Congress' power under the Commerce Clause.

The central theme of *National League of Cities* was that the States occupy a special position in our constitutional system and that the scope of Congress' authority under the Commerce Clause must reflect that position. . . .

The States unquestionably do "retai[n] a significant measure of sovereign authority." . . . They do so, however, only to the extent that the Constitution has not divested them of their original powers and transferred those powers to the Federal Government. In the words of James Madison to the Members of the First Congress: "Interference with the power of the States was no constitutional criterion of the power of Congress. If the power was not given, Congress could not exercise it; if given, they might exercise it, although it should interfere with the laws, or even the Constitution of the States." . . .

When we look for the States' "residuary and inviolable sovereignty," The Federalist No. 39, . . . in the shape of the constitutional scheme rather than in predetermined notions of sovereign power, a different measure of state sovereignty emerges. Apart from the limitation on federal authority inherent in the delegated nature of Congress' Article I powers, the principal means chosen by the Framers to ensure the role of the States in the federal system lies in the structure of the Federal Government itself. It is no novelty to observe that the composition of the Federal Government was designed in large part to protect the States from overreaching by Congress. The Framers thus gave the States a role in the selection both of the Executive and the Legislative Branches of the Federal Government. The States were vested with indirect influence over the House of Representatives and the Presidency by their control of electoral qualifications and their role in presidential elections. U.S. Const., Art. I, § 2, and Art. II, § 1. They were given more direct influence in the Senate, where each State received equal representation and each Senator was to be selected by the legislature of his State. Art. I, § 3. The significance attached to the States' equal representation in the Senate is underscored by the prohibition of any constitutional amendment divesting a State of equal representation without the State's consent. Art. V.

The extent to which the structure of the Federal Government itself was relied on to insulate the interests of the States is evident in the views of the Framers. James Madison explained that the Federal Government "will partake sufficiently of the spirit [of the States], to be disinclined to invade the rights of the individual States, or the prerogatives of their government." The Federalist No. 46 . . . .

The effectiveness of the federal political process in preserving the States' interests is apparent even today in the course of federal legislation. On the one hand, the States have been able to direct a substantial proportion of federal revenues into their own treasuries in the form of general and program-specific grants in aid. The federal role in assisting state and local governments is a longstanding one; Congress provided federal land grants to finance state governments from the beginning of the Republic, and direct cash grants were awarded as early as 1887 under the Hatch Act. In the past quarter-century alone, federal grants to States and localities have grown from $7 billion to $96 billion. As a result, federal grants now account for about one-fifth of state and local government expenditures. The States have obtained federal funding for such services as police and fire protection, education, public health and hospitals, parks and recreation, and sanitation. Moreover, at the same time that the States have exercised their influence to obtain federal support, they have been able to exempt themselves from a wide variety of obligations imposed by Congress under the

Commerce Clause. For example, the Federal Power Act, the National Labor Relations Act, the Labor-Management Reporting and Disclosure Act, the Occupational Safety and Health Act, the Employee Retirement Insurance Security Act, and the Sherman Act all contain express or implied exemptions for States and their subdivisions. The fact that some federal statues such as the FLSA extend general obligations to the States cannot obscure the extent to which the political position of the States in the federal system has served to minimize the burdens that the States bear under the Commerce Clause.

We realize that changes in the structure of the Federal Government have taken place since 1789, not the least of which has been the substitution of popular election of Senators by the adoption of the Seventeenth Amendment in 1913, and that these changes may work to alter the influence of the States in the federal political process. Nonetheless, against this background, we are convinced that the fundamental limitation that the constitutional scheme imposes on the Commerce Clause to protect the "States as States" is one of process rather than one of result. . . .

Insofar as the present cases are concerned, then, we need go no further than to state that we perceive nothing in the overtime and minimum-wage requirements of the FLSA, as applied to SAMTA, that is destructive of state sovereignty or violative of any constitutional provision. SAMTA faces nothing more than the same minimum-wage and overtime obligations that hundreds of thousands of other employers, public as well as private, have to meet. . . .

Though the separate concurrence providing the fifth vote in *National League of Cities* was "not untroubled by certain possible implications" of the decision, . . . the Court in that case attempted to articulate affirmative limits on the Commerce Clause power in terms of core governmental functions and fundamental attributes of state sovereignty. But the model of democratic decision-making the Court there identified underestimated, in our view, the solicitude of the national political process for the continued vitality of the States. Attempts by other courts since then to draw guidance from this model have proved it both impracticable and doctrinally barren. In sum, in *National League of Cities* the Court tried to repair what did not need repair.

We do not lightly overrule recent precedent. We have not hesitated, however, when it has become apparent that a prior decision has departed from a proper understanding of congressional power under the Commerce Clause. . . . Due respect for the reach of congressional power within the federal system mandates that we do so now. . . .

Justice POWELL, with whom The Chief Justice, Justice REHNQUIST, and Justice O'CONNOR join, dissenting. ∎

FROM "DUAL FEDERALISM" TO "INTERGOVERNMENTAL RELATIONS"

The federal-state relationship created by the Constitution was a kind of "dual federalism" that was comparable to a layer cake—each level of government having distinct spheres of responsibility and power. The word "dual" also indicates that the relationship between the levels of government was primarily federal-state, not federal-state-local. Originally, the federal government had little dealings directly with cities, counties, and other local governments. Local governments are considered creatures of the states, and the state governments represented them in the federalism arrangement.

But, as we have seen, national power has increased far beyond what the framers might have imagined. Partly this was because of decisions by the U. S. Supreme Court. The Great Depression of the 1930s was another major cause of increased national power. President Franklin D. Roosevelt and a compliant Congress inaugurated a wide range of new federal programs, agencies, regulations, and grant-in-aid programs.

These grant-in-aid programs—later enormously expanded, especially during the 1970's Great Society years of President Lyndon Johnson—produced a kind of "cooperative federalism" under which federal "categorical" aid funds were provided for a particular purpose and with regulatory strings attached. The funds went not only to state governments, but also, in many cases, directly to local governments, too. Frequently, state and local governments, and special agencies they set up, shared with the federal government in the responsibility for funding, as well as administration and policymaking. The power of the federal government was increased because most of the money came from the federal level.

Instead of the layer cake of dual federalism, the intertwined relationships of local, state, and federal (and, incidentally, Indian tribal) governments gave way to a kind of "marble cake," as Morton Grodzins called it, of intergovernmental relations. Little if any policy areas were off limits to the national government or were the exclusive province of the states. There were Republican-led efforts for reform.

In the essay excerpted here, Harvard Professor Arnold M. Howitt gives an excellent overview of intergovernmental relations. He traces its development from earliest times through President Ronald Reagan's "New Federalism."

INTERGOVERNMENTAL RELATIONS: AN OVERVIEW
Arnold M. Howitt

Today the federal system is far more complex than the founders of our republic could have foreseen. It involves a complicated *division of legal authority* between the states and the national government on one hand, and the states and local governments on the other; tangled *fiscal relationships* between the national government and the states, between the national government and localities, and between the states and localities; extensive *administrative and regulatory ties* among these government entities; and dynamic *political interdependencies* among elected and appointed officials at all levels of government. Taken together, these aspects of American federalism can be thought of as *intergovernmental relations.* . . .

Few areas of domestic policy and government exist in which the federal government plays no part. In Fiscal Year (FY) 1984 the federal government will spend more than $95 billion on aid to states and localities. This money supports myriad programs and projects that directly or indirectly benefit American citizens. It provides financial assistance, medical care, housing, social services, job training, and food to needy individuals. It supports many basic services that all citizens use such as schools, libraries, public health care, fire protection, and public transportation. It helps states and localities build major physical facilities: highways, bridges, tunnels, transit systems, dams, water treatment plants, sewer systems, and parks. It helps older U.S. cities rebuild deteriorating business and residential districts, and it helps newer cities develop the basic infrastructure that permits growth. Beyond fiscal assistance, moreover, the federal government plays a major regulatory role—for example, by promoting a clean and healthy environment or seeking to eliminate discrimination in education, housing, and employment. . . .

FROM THE EARLY DAYS TO THE TWENTIETH CENTURY

In the first days of the new nation and during most of the nineteenth century, the level of interaction between the federal government and the states was quite low compared with what it was to become. Historians have termed this a period of "dual federalism," in which the two levels of government had largely separate sets of functions. By the latter part of the nineteenth century and the early decades of the twentieth century, however, a new pattern of "cooperative federalism" began to emerge in which the national government and the states shared responsibility for a growing number of functions, jointly financing them and managing them with some degree of federal supervision. . . .

The grant-in-aid system grew more significantly, but still slowly, during the first three decades of the twentieth century. Changing political attitudes, activist presidents such as Theodore Roosevelt and Woodrow Wilson, and—not least— the establishment of a federal income tax to generate more revenue, made possible an expansion of the federal domestic policy agenda. Congress enacted a number of new grant programs, most importantly a highway construction grant that distributed funds according to a three-factor legislative formula, matched state expenditures on a 50-50 basis, and imposed planning and administrative requirements on the states. There were also new grants for forestry, the agricultural extension service, vocational education and rehabilitation, and maternal and infant care. . . .

THE NEW DEAL'S LEGACY

President Franklin D. Roosevelt's New Deal was a major turning point in intergovernmental relations. Under the pressure of a national economic crisis, the federal government vastly expanded the scope of its domestic programs, including aid to state and local governments. . . . There was an increasing philosophical acceptance of government activism, in general, and federal activism, in particular. Between 1933 and 1938 Congress created 16 grant-in-aid programs, as well as a number of temporary emergency grants. . . .

For the intergovernmental system, the Social Security Act of 1935 was by far the most important legislation of this period, laying the foundation for a national social welfare system that remains largely intact today. The Social Security Act established categorical programs for aid to the aged, blind, and dependent children; unemployment insurance; child welfare programs; and programs for maternal and child health and crippled children's services.

The New Deal programs involved departures from previous practice in several important respects. One was the growing link between the national government and local governments. Between 1932 and 1936 the amount of federal aid received by local authorities increased from $10 million to $229 million. Previously, to the extent that it reached the localities, federal aid was channeled through the states. Now money began to flow directly to local governments or to quasi-independent local agencies, for example in the public housing program enacted in 1937. The New Deal programs also enlarged the federal government's supervisory role. . . .

World War II interrupted the growth of the intergovernmental grant system, despite the creation of several temporary aid programs oriented toward the war effort. . . .

THE POSTWAR PERIOD

For almost 20 years after the conclusion of World War II, American government wrestled with the legacy of the New Deal's domestic policy innovations. The Democrats lacked the political strength to enhance dramatically the initiatives taken during the Depression but pressed for selective expansion. The Republicans, once in power, made no attempt to dismantle New Deal programs wholesale; they even supported increased financial aid and some new program ideas. During the Truman, Eisenhower, and Kennedy administrations, therefore, the intergovernmental grant system grew gradually but steadily—both in the number of individual programs and in the amount of financial resources provided. . . .

During the postwar period, the trend toward direct aid to municipal governments or autonomous local agencies continued . . . . But the largest fiscal commitment of this era was made in 1956 to the interstate highway program, whose funds went to state governments.

Overall, by the end of 1962, the federal government supported a total of 160 grant-in-aid programs at an annual cost of $7.9 billion.

KENNEDY-JOHNSON YEARS

During the four-year period from 1963 to 1966—the last year of President John F. Kennedy's administration and the first three of the new Johnson administration—the intergovernmental grant system underwent an explosive spurt of growth in the number of programs and the level of federal financial aid. . . . These included legislative landmarks—such as Medicaid, the Elementary and Secondary Education Act, and the Model Cities program—as well as many smaller initiatives tailored to the interests of relatively narrow constituencies. In just four years, 219 new grant programs were created, with 109 being enacted in 1965 alone. . . .

The relationship with local government, in particular, was altered significantly. As the country politically recognized an "urban crisis," many of the new grant programs were set up to provide aid directly to municipal governments or local agencies rather than through the states as intermediaries.

This growth of the intergovernmental system was highly controversial, reflecting deep-rooted differences in political philosophy. The Great Society programs were a triumph for those who believed that the federal government should establish national goals and standards for social welfare and civil rights. They believed that neither state-by-state variations in political belief nor fiscal capacity should prevent any citizen from having a full opportunity to develop his potential and to enjoy the benefits of the nation's prosperity. Others believed with equal fervor in a decentralized federal system in which local preferences and priorities, reflected by political institutions closer to the people than members of Congress and bureaucrats in Washington, should determine the extent and character of government activity. For these individuals, the increasing number of programs and directives emanating from the nation's capital were an affront—and even a danger to the continued viability of the federal system. . . .

As a consequence of rapid growth, though, the intergovernmental system was becoming far more difficult to manage—both from the federal perspective and the state and local side. The proliferation of grant programs meant that federal agencies were responsible for administering a larger number of separate programs, working with a larger number of governmental units, and overseeing the expenditure of increasing amounts of federal money. These programs, moreover, were more complex than many of their predecessors. Given the political climate of the day, Congress tended to prescribe in greater detail both the goals and adminstrative means of the programs, and it delegated to federal executive agencies a great deal of authority for further specifying program purposes and operating procedures through administrative regulations. A high percentage of the new programs, moreover, involved *project* grants to which state and local governments had no automatic entitlement; they had to apply to the federal agency responsible for administering the grant, competing with other states and localities for grant support. This gave federal administrators a substantial amount of discretion in—and responsibility for—choosing recipients.

From the other side, state and local officials of nearly all political persuasions found the weaknesses of the intergovernmental system increasingly troublesome. As grant programs proliferated throughout the 1960s, a single jurisdiction might be eligible for literally dozens—perhaps hundreds—of programs. There was little standardization, however, in the way that the federal government administered these grants. Each program tended to have its own application procedures, budget cycle, fiscal arrangements, restrictions on expenditures, planning requirements, program regulations, and accounting procedures. . . .

Chief executives—whether elected or appointed—found it particularly difficult to deal with the intergovernmental system. Grants frequently went directly to the agencies that ran federal programs, giving their bureaucratic leaders a relatively independent source of funds—and power. . . .

To some extent the Johnson administration came to recognize these difficulties and took some tentative steps to ameliorate them. Several grant programs . . . either consolidated preexisting categorical programs into broader purpose grants or gave the recipient government substantially more discretion in how federal funds could be used. . . . Even taken as a whole, however, these measures did little to make the intergovernmental system easier to manage.

Notwithstanding these problems, the Great Society programs developed a strong constituency—in part because they gave recognition to social and political problems that governors, mayors, and other state and municipal officials felt pressure to act on; and in part because of the growing financial stake that these officials had in intergovernmental aid. . . .

THE NIXON-FORD 'NEW FEDERALISM'

With the election of President Richard Nixon in 1968 and the return of the Republican party to power in the federal executive branch, many thought that Great Society programs would be pruned severely and that the intergovernmental system as a whole would be subject to significant retrenchment. These expectations proved too simple. The president did seek substantial change in the structure of the grant system and hoped to rein in its fiscal growth. But determined Democratic congressional majorities strongly resisted many of Nixon's proposals and, in fact, enacted a number of new grant programs.

President Nixon made reform of the intergovernmental grant system one of the principal elements of his domestic policy. He emphasized grant consolidation, reduction of federal regulation, and, consequently, more freedom for state and local governments to set priorities for their programs. To effect this policy, Nixon proposed both *general* revenue sharing (in which states and localities would receive funds with virtually no restrictions on how they might be used) and *special* revenue sharing (in which existing categorical programs would be consolidated into a broad purpose grant in a particular policy area—for example, education—with relatively few federal restrictions on its use). . . . In 1972, . . . Congress was persuaded to adopt general revenue sharing when a coalition of state and local leaders, spearheaded by Democratic big city mayors, organized a massive lobbying campaign to support it. The six special revenue sharing proposals languished in committee, but ultimately Congress adopted several *block* grant compromises that consolidated some grants while providing for more federal regulation than the special revenue sharing proposals had intended. . . .

On the administrative front, the Nixon administration experimented with methods to strengthen chief executives' managerial role in the grant system and, more generally, sought to reduce the amount of federal regulation. Congress, however, did not fully share the latter goal. Largely as a result of congressional initiatives, a number of *cross-cutting* regulations were drafted in areas such as antidiscrimination, environmental protection, and employment practices. (This layer of regulations applied across the board to all or most grant programs, not just to ones that specifically included such provisions in their authorizing statutes.) While not a new practice, such regulations became a far more common device in the 1970s and consequently were seen as increasingly burdensome by state and local officials. Even the new block grants, which began life with a relatively simple regulatory framework, accumulated restrictions as early operating experience made executive branch monitors and congressional overseers dissatisfied with certain aspects of their performance.

Contrary to most observers' expectations when President Nixon was elected, the federal government's fiscal commitment to the intergovernmental system continued to grow at a rapid pace during the Nixon-Ford administrations. . . . Overall, the amount of intergovernmental aid provided by the federal government climbed from $20.3 billion in FY 1969 to $68.4 billion in FY 1977—an increase of nearly 109 percent in real dollars.

THE CARTER YEARS

The intergovernmental trends of President Jimmy Carter's administration are not clear-cut. In important respects he was an activist in intergovernmental affairs in the tradition of Lyndon Johnson. He worked at strengthening White House liaison with the nation's governors and mayors, secured enactment of major new programs . . . modified existing ones . . . promoted a strong federal regulatory role . . . and sought to generate consensus both within his administration and among other intergovernmental political actors for meaningful administrative reforms of the system. Although the exact expansion of categorical grant programs attributable to the Carter years is not available, the number of federal programs increased from 448 in 1975 to 498 in 1978 and to 539 in 1981.

Yet because he was cautious economically and faced tight fiscal conditions, President Carter's administration first slowed the rate of growth of federal aid to states and localities and then stabilized it. . . . The modern highwater mark of federal aid to states and localities—in real dollars—was reached in FY 1978. In light of President Ronald Reagan's subsequent policies, the Carter administration can be seen as a transition point between an era of steady expansion (that began in the postwar period and accelerated greatly during the Johnson, Nixon, and Ford years) and an era of retrenchment.

REAGAN'S NEW FEDERALISM

President Reagan entered the White House with firm views and strong campaign commitments about intergovernmental relations. . . . First, he intended to reduce the amount of money that the federal government would provide to states and localities, making them rely to an increasing degree on their own revenue sources. Second, in the areas in which the federal government continued to play a role in financing state and local programs, he intended to diminish the detail in which it prescribed program purposes, design, and management through statute and administrative regulations. Third, he planned to reduce federal monitoring of and intervention in state and local program execution. . . .

The reaction to President Reagan's proposals was heated, both in Washington and around the country. In the nation's capital his plans were challenged by those who believed firmly that the federal government should be responsible for establishing national policy goals and minimum standards of service to America's people and for providing whatever funding and regulatory prodding were necessary to see that states and localities achieved them. Many members of Congress and the spokesmen for a number of major lobbying groups especially were concerned that projected budget cuts would seriously harm poor people if the states were unwilling or unable to replace federal funds for income maintenance and specialized aid programs. They worried, too, whether many states and localities would be as zealous as the federal government in protecting civil rights, preventing housing and job discrimination, and protecting the environment. In addition, many members of Congress had grave reservations about whether it would be possible to hold state and local officials appropriately accountable for their use of federal funds; they believed the level of government that raised revenue had an obligation to taxpayers to oversee its expenditure.

In state capitals and the nation's cities and towns, reaction to the president's proposals was mixed. Many public officials welcomed aspects of the president's initiatives. Most approved of his intention to reduce federal regulation and control but were extremely wary of his budget retrenchment plans. They feared that more autonomy would come only at the cost of overburdening their own budgets and forcing them to cut back services significantly or raise taxes. Some other political actors were even less enthusiastic. Many interest group leaders—particularly those who represented the poor, racial minorities, or other groups that had had a difficult time achieving influence in state and local affairs—were bitterly opposed to President Reagan's initiatives. They saw hard-won political gains, secured with the help of federal money or regulations, being swept away by "reforms" in Washington. . . .

By 1983 the momentum behind comprehensive reform of the intergovernmontal system seemed to have run out, at least temporarily. The administration proposed a new plan built around the consolidation of 34 categorical programs into four "mega-block" grants that took account of some of the reasons for opposition to the previous year's proposals. But it did not put anywhere near so much political energy into its efforts to move them through Congress, and the opposition remained steadfast. . . .

Despite disappointments in effecting structural reform in the intergovernmental system, however, Reagan had important effects on administrative and fiscal relations with state and local governments during his first three years as president. Through both legislation and regulatory action, the Reagan administration reduced the amount of federal control over state and local affairs. . . . Reagan's first budget (for FY 1982) saw a decline in the aggregate amount of federal aid from $94.8 billion to $88.8 billion, a cutback of 122.2 percent in real dollar terms; and his subsequent budgets kept the fiscal pressure on state and local governments, proposing virtually no growth in real resources for intergovernmental aid. Whether that trend of increasing aid has been broken over the long haul cannot be foreseen, but the president's program represented the greatest shift in direction for the intergovernmental system in nearly a generation. . . . ■

The Bill of Rights

The Declaration of Independence of 1776 declared it self-evident that "all men are created equal, that they are endowed by their Creator with certain unalienable rights, that among these are Life, Liberty, and the pursuit of Happiness." Governments are instituted to protect these rights, the Declaration further stated. The "unalienable" rights of citizens that governments are bound to respect were not further spelled out. Nor was the Declaration, standing alone, self-executing. It was a political document, meant to explain and argue for—in the strongest and noblest terms—the war against England, which was already underway.

The written constitutions of the newly independent American states did each contain a detailed Bill of Rights to set limits on these governments. But Alexander Hamilton was among those who felt that no such Bill of Rights was needed in the U. S. Constitution. He argued that since the new national government was a limited government, possessing only such powers as had been given to it, there was no need to state in a negative way what rights of the people the government could not transgress. "Why, for instance," he asked in *Federalist 84,* "should it be said that the liberty of the press shall not be restrained, when no power is given by which restrictions may be imposed?"

Opponents of ratification of the Constitution disagreed. They maintained that the lack of a Bill of Rights was a fatal flaw in the document. Even Thomas Jefferson felt a national Bill of Rights was needed, though he thought it could be added later, once the Constitution had been ratified and the new government established. This, in fact, was what was done.

When the first Congress met after ratification, James Madison, now a U. S. Representative from Virginia, offered a series of amendments to the Constitution. Once agreed to by two-thirds vote in both houses of Congress and ratified by the states, these first ten amendments to the Constitution became the Bill of Rights.

In this chapter, we will first examine the philosophy behind the "democratic freedoms"—particularly the freedom of expression. We will see how state governments also came to be restricted by the federal Bill of Rights. Then, we will give particular attention to the modern interpretations of certain freedoms and rights: freedom of expression, freedom of assembly, the right of privacy, and the right against self-incrimination.

THE DEMOCRATIC FREEDOMS

The First Amendment to the Constitution states: "Congress shall make no law respecting an establishment of religion, or prohibiting the free exercise thereof; or abridging the freedom of speech, or of the press, or the right of the people peaceably to assemble, and to petition the government for a redress of grievances."

Thus, the First Amendment first deals with religion—in two ways. In the "establishment clause," it mandates what was later called a "wall of separation" between church and state. It is under this provision that the Supreme Court has held that the use of public funds for general aid to parochial schools[1] and required or prescribed prayer or other religious practice in the public schools[2] are unconstitutional. The "free exercise clause" prohibits government interference with freedom of religion. Interpreting this clause, the Supreme Court has held that children in public schools may not be required to salute the flag if, as with members of the Jehovah's Witnesses, that would violate their religious convictions.[3]

The remainder of the First Amendment deals with what have been called the "Democratic Freedoms"—freedoms of speech and press (together referred to as the freedom of expression) and freedoms of petition and assembly. These are called the Democratic Freedoms because it is difficult to imagine how a democracy, a government based upon consent of the governed, could exist without them.

The signers of the Declaration of Independence justified the democratic freedoms and their protections, even though a majority might from time to time oppose their exercise if the ideas expressed were unpopular, on the ground that they were God-given, or natural, rights. Nearly a century later, English philosopher John Stuart Mill, in his 1859 essay, *On Liberty*, excerpted here, justified continued respect for free expression on the basis of "utility;" that is, to do so was useful for the majority. Accepted opinion may be in

---

1. *Lemon v. Kurtzman; Committee for Public Education v. Nyquist; Levitt v. Committee for Public Education*, 413 U. S. 472 (1973).

2. *Abington School District v. Schempp* and *Murray v. Curlett*, 374 U. S. 203 (1963).

3. *West Virginia Board of Education v. Barnette*, 319 U. S. 624 (1943), which reversed an earlier decision in *Minersville School District v. Gobitis*, 310 U. S. 586 (1940).

error and censored opinion true, he wrote, and only through allowing the free expression of both can the majority know what is true and in its own best interests.

ON LIBERTY
John Stuart Mill

The time, it is to be hoped, is gone by when any defence would be necessary of the "liberty of the press" as one of the securities against corrupt or tyrannical government. No argument, we may suppose, can now be needed, against permitting a legislature or an executive, not identified in interest with the people, to prescribe opinions to them, and determine what doctrines or what arguments they shall be allowed to hear. This aspect of the question, besides, has been so often and so triumphantly enforced by preceding writers, that it needs not be specially insisted on in this place. Though the law of England, on the subject of the press, is as servile to this day as it was in the time of the Tudors, there is little danger of its being actually put in force against political discussion, except during some temporary panic, when fear of insurrection drives ministers and judges from their propriety; and, speaking generally, it is not, in constitutional countries, to be apprehended, that the government, whether completely responsible to the people or not, will often attempt to control the expression of opinion, except when in doing so it makes itself the organ of the general intolerance of the public. Let us suppose, therefore, that the government is entirely at one with the people, and never thinks of exerting any power of coercion unless in agreement with what it conceives to be their voice. But I deny the right of the people to exercise such coercion, either by themselves or by their government. The power itself is illegitimate. The best government has no more title to it than the worst. It is a noxious, or more noxious, when exerted in accordance with public opinion, than when in opposition to it. If all mankind minus one, were of one opinion, and only one person were of the contrary opinion, mankind would be no more justified in silencing that one person, than he, if he had the power, would be justified in silencing mankind. Were an opinion a personal possession of no value except to the owner; if to be obstructed in the enjoyment of it were simply a private injury, it would make some difference whether the injury was inflicted only on a few persons or on many. But the peculiar evil of silencing the expression of an opinion is, that it is robbing the human race, posterity as well as the existing generation; those whose dissent from the opinion, still more than those who hold it. If the opinion is right, they are deprived of the opportunity of exchanging error for truth: if wrong, they lose, what is almost as great a benefit, the clearer perception and livelier impression of truth, produced by its collision with error.

It is necessary to consider separately these two hypotheses, each of which has a distinct branch of the argument corresponding to it. We can never be sure that the opinion we are endeavoring to stifle is a false opinion; and if we were sure, stifling it would be an evil still.

First: the opinion which it is attempted to suppress by authority may possibly be true. Those who desire to suppress it, of course deny its truth; but they are not infallible. They have no authority to decide the question for all mankind, and exclude every other person from the means of judging. To refuse a hearing to an opinion, because they are sure that it is false, is to assume that *their* certainty is the same thing as *absolute* certainty. All silencing of discussion is an assumption of infallibility. Its condemnation may be allowed to rest on this common argument, not the worse for being common.

Unfortunately for the good sense of mankind, the fact of their fallibility is far from carrying the weight in their practical judgment, which is always allowed to it in theory; for while every one well knows himself to be fallible, few think it necessary to take any precautions against their own fallibility, or admit the supposition that any opinion, of which they feel very certain, may be one of the examples of the error to which they acknowledge themselves to be liable. Absolute princes, or others who are accustomed to unlimited deference, usually feel this complete confidence in their own opinions on nearly all subjects. People more happily situated, who sometimes hear their opinions disputed, and are not wholly unused to be set right when they are wrong, place the same unbounded reliance only on such of their opinions as are shared by all who surround them, or to whom they habitually defer: for in proportion to a man's want of confidence in his own solitary judgment, does he usually repose, with implicit trust, on the infallibility of "the world" in general. And the world, to each individual, means the part of it with which he comes in contact; his party, his sect, his church, his class of society: the man may be called, by comparison, almost liberal and large-minded to whom it means anything so comprehensive as his own country or his own age. Nor is his faith in this collective authority at all shaken by his being aware that other ages, countries, sects, churches, classes, and parties have thought, and even now think, the exact reverse. He devolves upon his own world the responsibility of being in the right against the dissentient worlds of other people; and it never troubles him that mere accident has decided which of these numerous worlds is the object of his reliance, and that the same causes which make him a Churchman in London, would have made him a Buddhist or a Confucian in Peking. Yet it is as evident in itself, as any amount of argument can make it, that ages are no more infallible than individuals; every age having held many opinions which subsequent ages have deemed not only false but absurd; and it is as certain that many opinons, now general, will be rejected by future ages, as it is that many, once general, are rejected by the present.

The objection likely to be made to this argument, would probably take some such form as the following. There is no greater assumption of infallibility in forbidding the propagation of error, that in any other thing which is done by public authority on its own judgment and responsibility. Judgment is given to men that they may use it. Because it may be used erroneously, are men to be told that they ought not to use it at all? To prohibit what they think pernicious, is not claiming exemption from error, but fulfilling the duty incumbent on them, although fallible, of acting on their conscientious conviction. If we were never to act on our opinions, because those opinions may be wrong, we should leave all our interests uncared for, and all our duties unperformed. An objection which applies to all conduct, can be no valid objection to any conduct in particular. It is the duty of governments, and of individuals, to form the truest opinions they can; to form them carefully, and never impose them upon others unless they are quite sure of being right. but when they are sure (such reasoners may say), it is not conscientiousness but cowardice to shrink from acting on their opinions, and allow doctrines which they honestly think dangerous to the welfare of mankind, either in this life or in another, to be scattered abroad without restraint, because other people, in less enlightened times, have persecuted opinions now believed to be true. Let us take care, it may be said, not to make the same mistake: but governments and nations have made mistakes in other things, which are not denied to be fit subjects for the exercise of authority: they have laid on bad taxes, made unjust wars. Ought we therefore to lay on no taxes, and, under whatever provocation, make no wars? Men, and governments, must act to the best of their ability. There is no such thing as absolute certainty, but there is assurance sufficient for the purposes of human life. We may, and must, assume our opinion to be true for the guidance of our own conduct: and it is assuming no more when we forbid bad men to pervert society by the propagation of opinions which we regard as false and pernicious.

I answer, that it is assuming very much more. There is the greatest difference between presuming an opinion to be true, because, with every opportunity for contesting it, it had not been refuted, and assuming its truth for the purpose of not permitting its refutation. Complete liberty of contradicting and disproving our opinion, is the very condition which justifies us in assuming its truth for purposes of action; and on no other terms can a being with human faculties have any rational assurance of being right.

When we consider either the history of opinion, or the ordinary conduct of human life, to what is it to be ascribed that the one and the other are no worse than they are? Not certainly to the inherent force of the human understanding; for, on any matter not self-evident, there are ninety-nine persons totally incapable of judging of it, for one who is capable; and the capacity of the hundredth person is only comparative; for the majority of the eminent men of every past generation held many opinions now known to be erroneous, and did or approved numerous things which no one will now justify. Why is it, then, that there is on the whole a preponderance among mankind of rational opinions and rational conduct? If there really is this preponderance—which there must be, unless human affairs are, and have always been, in an almost desperate state—it is owing to a quality of the human mind, the source of everything respectable in man either as an intellectual or as a moral being, namely, that his errors are corrigible. He is capable of rectifying his mistakes, by discussion and experience. Not by experience alone. There must be discussion, to show how experience is to be interpreted. Wrong opinions and practices gradually yield to fact and argument: but facts and arguments, to produce any effect on the mind, must be brought before it. Very few facts are able to tell their own story, without comments to bring out their meaning. The whole strength and value, then, of human judgment, depending on the one property, that it can be set right when it is wrong, reliance can be placed on it only when the means of setting it right are kept constantly at hand. In the case of any person whose judgment is really deserving of confidence, how has it become so? Because he has kept his mind open to criticism of his opinions and conduct. Because it has been his practice to listen to all that could be said against him; to profit by as much of it as was just, and expound to himself, and upon occasion to others, the fallacy of what was fallacious. Because he has felt, that the only way in which a human being can make some approach to knowing the whole of a subject, is by hearing what can be said about it by persons of every variety of opinion, and studying all modes in which it can be looked at by every character of mind. No wise man ever acquired his wisdom in any mode but this; nor is it in the nature of human intellect to become wise in any other manner. The steady habit of correcting and completing his own opinion by collating it with those of others, so far from causing doubt and hesitation in carrying it into practice, is the only stable foundation for a just reliance on it: for, being cognizant of all that can, at least obviously, be said against him, and having taken up his position against all gainsayers—knowing that he has sought for objections and difficulties, instead of avoiding them, and has shut out no light which can be thrown upon the subject from any quarter—he has a right to think his judgment better than that of any person, or any multitude, who have not gone through a similar process.

It is not too much to require that what the wisest of mankind, those who are best entitled to trust their own judgment, find necessary to warrant their relying on it, should be submitted to by that miscellaneous collection of a few wise and many foolish individuals, called the public. The most intolerant of churches, the Roman Catholic Church, even at the canonization of a saint, admits, and listens patiently to, a "devil's advocate." The holiest of men, it appears, cannot be admitted to posthumous honors, until all that the devil could say against him is known and weighed. If even the Newtonian philosophy were not permitted to be questioned, mankind could not feel as complete assurance of its truth as they now do. The beliefs which we have most warrant for, have no safeguard to rest on, but a standing invitation to the whole world to prove them unfounded. . . .

We have now recognized the necessity to the mental well-being of mankind (on which all their other well-being depends) of freedom of opinion, and freedom of the expression of opinion, on four distinct grounds; which we will now briefly recapitulate.

First, if any opinion is compelled to silence, that opinion may, for aught we can certainly know, be true. To deny this is to assume our own infallibility.

Secondly, though the silenced opinion be an error, it may, and very commonly does, contain a portion of truth; and since the general or prevailing opinion on any subject is rarely or never the whole truth, it is only by the collision of adverse opinons that the remainder of the truth has any chance of being supplied.

Thirdly, even if the received opinion be not only true, but the whole truth; unless it is suffered to be, and actually is, vigorously and earnestly contested, it will, by most of those who receive it, be held in the manner of a prejudice, with little comprehension of feeling of its rational grounds. And not only this, but fourthly the meaning of the doctrine itself will be in danger of being lost, or enfeebled, and deprived of its vital effect on the character and conduct: the dogma becoming a mere formal profession, inefficacious for good, but cumbering the ground, and preventing the growth of any real and heartfelt conviction from reason or personal experience.

Before quitting the subject of freedom of opinion, it is fit to take some notice of those who say, that the free expression of all opinions should be permitted, on condition that the manner be temperate, and do not pass the bounds of fair discussion. Much might be said on the impossibility of fixing where these supposed bounds are to be placed; for if the test be offence to those whose opinion is attacked, I think experience testifies that this offence is given whenever the attack is telling and powerful, and that every opponent who pushes them hard, and whom they find it difficult to answer, appears to them, if he shows any strong feeling on the subject, an intemperate opponent. But this, though an important consideration in a practical point of view, merges in a more fundamental objection. Undoubtedly the manner of asserting an opinion, even though it be a true one, may be very objectionable, and may justly incur severe censure. But the principal offences of the kind are such as it is mostly impossible, unless by accidental self-betrayal, to bring home to conviction. The gravest of them is, to argue sophistically, to suppress facts or arguments, to misstate the elements of the case, or misrepresent the opposite opinion. But all this, even to the most aggravated degree, is so continually done in perfect good faith, by persons who are not considered, and in many other respects may not deserve to be considered, ignorant or incompetent, that it is rarely possible on adequate grounds conscientiously to stamp the misrepresentation as morally culpable; and still less could law presume to interfere with this kind of controversial misconduct. With regard to what is commonly meant by intemperate discussion, namely, invective, sarcasm, personality, and the like, the denunciation of these weapons would deserve more sympathy if it were ever proposed to interdict them equally to both sides; but it is only desired to restrain the employment of them against the prevailing opinion: against the unprevailing they may not only be used without general disapproval, but will be likely to obtain for him who uses them the praise of honest zeal and righteous indignation. Yet whatever mischief arises from their use, is greatest when they are employed against the comparatively defenceless; and whatever unfair advantage can be derived by any opinion from this mode of asserting it, accrues almost exclusively to received opinions. The worst offence of this kind which can be committed by a polemic, is to stigmatize those who hold the contrary opinion as bad and immoral men. To calumny of this sort, those who hold any unpopular opinion are peculiarly exposed, because they are in general few and uninfluential, and nobody but themselves feels much interest in seeing justice done them; but this weapon is, from the nature of the case, denied to those who attack a prevailing opinion: they can neither use it with safety to themselves, nor, if they could would it do anything but recoil on their own cause. In general, opinions contrary to those commonly received can only obtain a hearing by studied moderation of language and the most cautious avoidance of unnecessary offence, from which they hardly ever deviate even in a slight degree without losing ground: while unmeasured vituperation employed on the side of the prevailing opinion, really does deter people from professing contrary opinions, and from listening to those who profess them. For the interest, therefore, of truth and justice, it is far more important to restrain this employment of vituperative language than the other; and, for example, if it were necessary to choose, there would be much more need to discourage offensive attacks on infidelity, than on religion. It is, however, obvious that law and authority have no business with restraining either, while opinion ought, in every instance, to determine its verdict by the circumstances of the individual case; condemning every none, on whichever side of the argument he places himself, in whose mode of advocacy either want of candor, or malignity, bigotry, or intolerance of feeling manifest themselves; but not inferring these vices from the side which a person takes, though it be the contrary side of the question to our own: and giving merited honor to every one, whatever opinion he may hold, who has calmness to see and honesty to state what his opponents and their opinions really are, exaggerating nothing to their discredit, keeping nothing back which tells, or can be supposed to tell, in their favor. This is the real morality of public discussion; and if often violated, I am happy to think that there are many controversialists who to a great extent observe it, and a still greater number who conscientiously strive towards it.   ■

THE STATES AND THE BILL OF RIGHTS

The Bill of Rights, added to the U. S. Constitution after its ratification, was intended as restrictions on what the *federal* government could do. In 1833, the U. S. Supreme Court ruled that the Bill of Rights did not operate as a restraint on *state* governments (though each state was bound, of course, by the restraints specifically stated in its own constitutional bill of rights).

Then, after the Civil War, the Thirteenth, Fourteenth and Fifteenth Amendments were added to the national Constitution. Among other things, the Fourteenth Amendment contained a provision (similar to a Fifth Amendment restriction on the federal government) that no *state* could "deprive any person of life, liberty, or property, without due process of law." In 1925, in the case of *Gitlow* v. *New York*,[4] the Supreme Court announced the *doctrine of incorporation*, holding that the word "liberty" in the Fourteenth Amend-

---

4. 268 U. S. 652 (1925).

ment includes in its meaning the freedoms of speech and press set forth in the Bill of Rights. In other words, these provisions of the Bill of Rights, originally intended as restrictions on the federal government, are also restrictions on the state governments.

Similar Supreme Court opinions followed in regard to other rights and freedoms. By the 1970s, on a case-by-case basis—as in the *Gideon* v. *Wainwright* case, excerpted here—the Supreme Court had held that the Fourteenth Amendment in effect incorporated virtually all of the important provisions of the Bill of Rights and thus made them restraints on states—not just on the federal government. (Never specifically included in this doctrine of incorporation as restraints on the states are: the right to a grand jury criminal indictment, the right to trial by jury in civil cases, the right to bear arms, protection against excessive bail and fines, and protection against involuntary quartering of troops in private homes.)

In *Gideon* v. *Wainwright,* the Supreme Court reversed an earlier decision and, for the first time, held that the right to a lawyer in a criminal case, guaranteed in the federal courts under the Sixth Amendment, is one of the fundamental rights incorporated in the Fourteenth Amendment's word "liberty." Thus, under the federal Constitution, those accused of a crime in a state court have a right to counsel, a right to be represented by a lawyer.

GIDEON V. WAINWRIGHT*

M R. JUSTICE BLACK delivered the opinion of the Court.

Petitioner was charged in a Florida state court with having broken and entered a poolroom with intent to commit a misdemeanor. This offense is a felony under Florida law. Appearing in court without funds and without a lawyer, petitioner asked the court to appoint counsel for him, whereupon the following colloquy took place:

> The COURT: Mr. Gideon, I am sorry, but I cannot appoint Counsel to represent you in this case. Under the laws of the State of Florida, the only time the Court can appoint Counsel to represent a Defendant is when that person is charged with a capital offense. I am sorry, but I will have to deny your request to appoint Counsel to defend you in this case.
>
> The DEFENDANT: The United States Supreme Court says I am entitled to be represented by Counsel.

---

* 372 U. S. 335 (1962).

Put to trial before a jury, Gideon conducted his defense about as well as could be expected from a layman. He made an opening statement to the jury, cross-examined the State's witnesses, presented witnesses in his own defense, declined to testify himself, and made a short argument "emphasizing his innocence to the charge contained in the Information filed in this case." The jury returned a verdict of guilty, and petitioner was sentenced to serve five years in the state prison. Later, petitioner filed in the Florida Supreme Court this habeas corpus petition attacking his conviction and sentence on the ground that the trial court's refusal to appoint counsel for him denied him rights "guaranteed by the Constitution and the Bill of Rights by the United States Government." Treating the petition for habeas corpus as properly before it, the State Supreme Court, "upon consideration thereof" but without an opinion, denied all relief. Since 1942, when *Betts* v. *Brady*, 316 U. S. 455, was decided by a divided Court, the problem of a defendant's federal constitutional right to counsel in a state court has been a continuing source of controversy and litigation in both state and federal courts. To give this problem another review here, we granted certiorari. . . . Since Gideon was proceeding in *in forma pauperis*, we appointed counsel to represent him and requested both sides to discuss in their briefs and oral arguments the following: "Should this Court's holding *Betts* v. *Brady*, 316 U. S. 455, be reconsidered?"

The facts upon which Betts claimed that he had been unconstitutionally denied the right to have counsel appointed to assist him are strikingly like the facts upon which Gideon here bases his federal constitutional claim. . . .

Like Gideon, Betts sought release by habeas corpus, alleging that he had been denied the right to assistance of counsel in violation of the Fourteenth Amendment. Betts was denied any relief, and on review this Court affirmed. It was held that a refusal to appoint counsel for an indigent defendant charged with a felony did not necessarily violate the Due Process Clause of the Fourteenth Amendment, which for reasons given the Court deemed to be the only applicable federal constitutional provision. . . .

The Sixth Amendment provides, "In all criminal prosecutions, the accused shall enjoy the right . . . to have the Assistance of Counsel for his defence." We have construed this to mean that in federal courts counsel must be provided for defendants unable to employ counsel unless the right is competently and intelligently waived. Betts argued that this right is extended to indigent defendants in state courts by the Fourteenth Amendment. In response the Court stated that, while the Sixth Amendment laid down "no rule for the conduct of the States, the question recurs whether the constraint laid by the Amendment upon the national courts expresses a rule so fundamental and essential to a fair trial, and so, to due process of law, that it is made obligatory upon the States by the Fourteenth Amendment." . . . In order to decide whether the Sixth Amendment's guarantee of counsel is of this fundamental nature, the Courts in *Betts* set out and considered "[r]elevant data on the subject . . . afforded by constitutional and statutory provisions subsisting in the colonies and the States prior to the inclusion of the Bill of Rights in the national Constitution, and in the constitutional, legislative, and judicial history of the States to the present date." . . . On the basis of this historical data the court concluded that "appointment of counsel is not a fundamental right, essential to a fair trial." . . . It was for this reason the *Betts* Court refused to accept the contention that the Sixth Amendment's guarantee of counsel for indigent federal defendants was extended to or, in the words of that court, "made obligatory upon the States by the Fourteenth Amendment." Plainly, had the Court concluded that appointment of counsel for an indigent criminal defendant was "a fundamental right, essential to a fair trial," it would have held that the Fourteenth Amendment requires an appointment of counsel in a state court, just as the Sixth Amendment requires in a federal court.

We think the Court in *Betts* had ample precedent for acknowledging that those guarantees of the Bill of Rights which are fundamental safeguards of liberty immune from federal abridgment are equally protected against state invasion by the Due Process Clause of the Fourteenth Amendment. This same principle was recognized, explained, and applied in *Powell* v. *Alabama*, 287 U. S. 45 (1932), a case upholding the right of counsel, where the Court held that despite sweeping language to the contrary in *Hurtado* v. *California*, 110 U. S. 516 (1884), the Fourteenth Amendment "embraced" those " 'fundamental principles of liberty and justice which lie at the base of all our civil and political institutions,' " even though they had been "specifically dealt with in another part of the federal Constitution." . . . In many cases other than *Powell* and *Betts*, this Court has looked to the fundamental nature of original Bill of Rights guarantees to decide whether the Fourteenth Amendment makes them obligatory on the States. Explicitly recognized to be of this "fundamental nature" and therefore made immune from state invasion by the Fourteenth, or some part of it, are the First Amendment's freedoms of speech, press, religion, assembly, association, and petition for redress of grievances. For the same reason, though not always in precisely the same terminology, the Court has made obligatory on the States the Fifth Amendment's command that private property shall not be taken for public use without just compensation, the Fourth Amendment's prohibition of unreasonable searches and seizures, and the Eighth's ban on cruel and unusual punishment. . . .

We accept *Betts* v. *Brady's* assumption, based as it was on our prior cases, that a provision of the Bill of Rights which is "fundamental and essential to a fair trial" is made obligatory upon the States by the Fourteenth Amendment. We think the Court in *Betts* was wrong, however, in concluding that the Sixth Amendment's guarantee of counsel is not one of these fundamental rights. Ten years before *Betts* v. *Brady*, this Court, after full consideration of all the historical data examined in *Betts,* had unequivocally declared that "the right to the aid of counsel is of this fundamental character." . . . The fact is that in deciding as it did — that "appointment of counsel is not a fundamental right, essential to a fair trial"— the Court in *Betts* v. *Brady* made an abrupt break with its own well-considered precedents. In returning to these old precedents, sounder we believe than the new, we but restore constitutional principles established to achieve a fair system of justice. Not only these precedents but also reason and reflection require us to recognize that in our adversary system of criminal justice, any person haled into court, who is too poor to hire a lawyer, cannot be assured a fair trial unless counsel is provided for him. This seems to us to be an obvious truth. Governments, both state and federal, quite properly spend vast sums of money to establish machinery to try defendants accused of crime. Lawyers to prosecute are everywhere deemed essential to protect the public's itnerest in an orderly society. Similarly, there are few defendants charged with crime, few indeed, who fail to hire the best lawyers they can get to prepare and present their defenses. That government hires lawyers to prosecute and defendants who have the money hire lawyers to defend are the strongest indications of the widespread belief that lawyers in criminal courts are necessities, not luxuries. The right of one charged with crime to counsel may not be deemed fundamental and essential to fair trials in some countries, but it is in ours. From the very beginning, our state and national constitutions and laws have laid great emphasis on procedural and substantive safeguards designed to assure fair trials before impartial tribunals in which every defendant stands equal before the law. This noble ideal cannot be realized if the poor man charged with crime has to face his accusers without a lawyer to assist him. . . .The Court in *Betts* v. *Brady* departed from the sound wisdom upon which the Court's holding in *Powell* v. *Alabama* rested. Florida supported by two other States, has asked that *Betts* v. *Brady* be left intact. Twenty-two States, as friends of the Court, argue that *Betts* was "an anachronism when handed down" and that it should now be overruled. We agree.

The judgment is reversed and the cause is remanded to the Supreme Court of Florida for further action not inconsistent with this opinion. ■

FREEDOM OF EXPRESSION

The freedoms stated in the Bill of Rights are expressed in absolute terms. For example, the Amendment declares that Congress (and, now, by interpretation, state and local governments) can make *no* law abridging freedom of speech. In practice, though, and as interpreted by the courts, the freedoms are not absolute, but conditional. The courts use a "balancing test" to determine if an attempted abridgement of these rights by government is constitutional—balancing the rights of the individual against the interests of society generally in protecting public health, safety and morals and in preserving order.

In his essay reprinted here, "The Constitution and Free Expression," Professor A. E. Dick Howard trace the origins, development and interpretation of the free-expression provisions of the Bill of Rights.

The Supreme Court has declared that the Democratic Freedoms of the First Amendment carry with them a "freedom of association and dissent"— the right to belong to whatever organization a person wants to and to disagree with government policy—even though this freedom is not expressly stated in the amendment. But the Court has not always followed a clear and straight course on this subject.

It has always been recognized that the Democratic Freedoms—speech, press, petition and assembly, and association and dissent—do not protect incitement to riot. But can mere advocacy of violence (speech) or the mere act of belonging to an organization that advocates violence (association and dissent) or merely assembling peaceably for such advocacy (assembly) be made a crime? Today, according to the Supreme Court, the answer in each case is no.

That was not always the law. Despite the fact that the Bill of Rights was intended to protect the unpopular, as well as popular, the Congress has from time to time enacted laws against unpopular ideas and organizations. For example, the Smith Act, adopted in 1940, on the eve of World War II, made it a federal crime to teach, advocate, or encourage the violent overthrow of the government or to knowingly belong to an organization that did. After the war, ten members of the Communist party were convicted under the act. The Supreme Court, in the 1951 case of *Dennis* v. *United States*,[5] upheld the convictions, even though it had not been shown that violence was imminent as a result of the advocacy or the activities of the organization.

But, by 1957, with some change in Court membership and a slackening of the Communist scare in the country, the Court held, in the case of *Yates* v. *United States*,[6] that a person could *not* be convicted of a crime for mere membership in the Communist party. This and later cases virtually nullified the Smith Act. The Court uses a kind of "advocacy-plus" rule today. Is violence likely to occur as a result of the advocacy?

In the case reprinted here, *Brandenburg* v. *Ohio,* the final nail was driven into the coffin of the *Dennis* case when the Court struck down an Ohio law under which a man was convicted for membership and activity in the Ku Klux Klan.

THE CONSTITUTION AND FREE EXPRESSION
A. E. Dick Howard

When Virginia's convention, meeting at Williamsburg in May, 1776, instructed its delegates at Philadelphia to introduce the resolution for independence, they also formed a committee to write the first American state constitution. Largely the work of George Mason, that constitution's declaration of rights declared that "any citizens may freely speak, write, and publish his sentiments on all subjects, being responsible for the abuse of that right . . . ."

---

5. 341 U. S. 494 (1951).
6. 354 U. S. 298 (1957).

A little more than a decade later, the Convention which had assembled at Philadelphia to revise the Articles of Confederation instead produced a new Constitution. When that document went to the country for approval or rejection, the lack of a bill of rights, as much as any other issue, became the stumbling block to ratification. Many of the ratifying states followed the example of the Massachusetts convention and drew up lists of specific amendments. On Virginia's list, for example, was an amendment which declared:

> That the people have a right to freedom of speech, and of writing, and of publishing their sentiments; that the freedom of the press is one of the great bulwarks of liberty, and ought not to be violated.

At the first session of the Congress in 1789, James Madison moved to add a bill of rights to the new Constitution. Tutored in the precepts of the Scottish Enlightenment, Madison offered a free speech amendment which clearly seems to have been intended to give protection far beyond that given by the common law as expounded by Blackstone. His draft stated that "no State shall violate the equal rights of conscience, or the freedom of the press." After debate, however, Congress agreed upon the language now found in the First Amendment:

> Congress shall make no law respecting an establishment of religion, or prohibiting the free exercise thereof; or abridging the freedom of speech, or of the press; or the right of the people peaceably to assemble, and to petition the Government for a redress of grievances.

Such language—a few words couched in general terms—was hardly self-defining. It is clear that the First Amendment was aimed explicitly at the federal government, not at the states; it was only in the twentieth century, using the Fourteenth Amendment as a vehicle, that the Supreme Court would hold the states to the prohibitions of the First Amendment. The breadth of the protection for expression conferred by the amendment was less than clear.

Zechariah Chafee, Jr. has argued that the framers of the First Amendment intended not only to prevent censorship, but also to wipe out the common law of sedition and make it impossible to punish criticism of the government where speech was not brigaded with direct incitement of lawbreaking. Leonard Levy, however, doubts the framers intended to go so far. In his view, a broad, libertarian theory of freedom of speech and press—a view of the kind articulated by Madison—did not begin to take hold in the United States until Thomas Jefferson and his party fought against the Sedition Act of 1798, an act which led to the prosecution and jailing of a number of newspaper editors for views hostile to policies of the ruling Federalist party.

In the nearly 200 years since the First Amendment's adoption, it is remarkable that virtually all of the judicial gloss on the amendment has come in the past sixty or so years. The Supreme Court's first significant occasion to decide just what protection the Constitution gives to expression came in cases arising out of prosecutions under antisubversion statutes enacted around the time of the First World War.

The early cases produced Justice Oliver Wendell Holmes's thesis that speech could be curtailed only if it created a "clear and present danger" of a substantive evil within the power of Congress to prohibit. Holmes argued in a 1919 case (*Abrams v. United States*) that "the best test of truth is the power of the thought to get itself accepted in the competition of the market . . . ." By and large, the Court in the subversion cases was deferential to legislative power. Hence, in a series of cases the Court upheld convictions under the Espionage Act for expression, some of which (such as publishing leaflets denouncing production of war materiel which could be used against the Bolsheviks in Russia) struck Holmes and Justice Louis Brandeis, dissenting, as not presenting the requisite "clear and present danger." In the cold war years following World War II, the Court upheld (in *Dennis v. United States*, 1951) Smith Act convictions of persons charged with conspiring to advocate and teach the overthrow of the United States government.

The subversion cases involved the Court's interpretation of statues directed at the *content* of expression. Much of the Court's First Amendment jurisprudence, by contrast, turns on the regulation of the time, place, and manner of speech — how, where, to whom, or in what way something is being said. Frequently, these cases have arisen because an unpopular group has taken to the streets to express unpopular views. Thus, when a Jehovah's Witness played anti-Catholic records on the streets of New Haven, Connecticut, and was charged with breach of the peace, the Court found no "clear and present danger" to the public peace and order and hence reversed his conviction (*Cantwell v. Connecticut,* 1940). Nevertheless, in another Jehovah's Witness case (*Cox v. New Hampshire,* 1941), the justices made it clear that a locality, in regulating its streets, may require permits for parades or otherwise regulate the time, place, and manner of speech so long as it does so in a nondiscriminatory fashion.

The "public forum" cases became more complex when civil rights activists in the early 1960s were arrested for marching or demonstrating in southern cities and towns. A majority of the justices found various grounds for overturning those convictions, some of which involved protests in traditional places such as streets and public parks, others of which were mounted in less obvious "forums" such as the reading room of a public library. The Court's patience reached its limit, however, in a 1966 decision (*Adderley v. Florida*) in which, five to four, the justices held that there was no First Amendment protection for a demonstration on the grounds of a local jail.

In both the subversion cases and the "public forum" decisions, there was no questions that expression of some kind was going on; indeed, the expression concerned such issues as war and civil rights — surely the kind of subjects of debate which should trigger First Amendment scrutiny. The typical question in these cases is whether the expression suffiiciently threatens a substantial state interest, such as public order or the public's use of the streets.

Analytically more elusive, however, are those cases in which the Court has been asked to decide whether a particular kind of expression even presumptively falls within the First Amendment. Put another way, what is meant by "speech" or "the freedom of speech" in the First Amendment?

Frequently the Court has taken a kind of "defining in-defining out" approach to speech cases. In *Chaplinsky v. New Hampshire* (1942), Justice Frank Murphy commented that punishment for certain classes of speech has "never been thought to raise any Constitutional problem." As examples, Murphy cited "the lewd and obscene, the profane, the libelous, and the insulting of 'fighting' words . . . ." Murphy reasoned that such utterances "are of such slight social value that any benefit that may be derived from them is clearly outweighed by the social interest in order and morality."

This "Murphy's law" has an appealing simplicity about it. In practice, however, as forty years' litigation has revealed, the effort to create neat categories of protected and unprotected speech has proven maddeningly difficult, if not impossible. For example, in *Cohen v. California* (1971), an opponent of the Vietnam War was arrested for wearing, in a courthouse corridor, a jacket attacking the draft with a less-than-polite, four-letter word. The state argued that it had the power to punish for the use of "offensive" speech, but Justice John Marshall Harlan could not concede the state the power to "cleanse public debate;" as he put it, "One man's vulgarity is another's lyric."

State efforts to ban traffic in pornography present another judicial quagmire. In *Roth v. California* (1957), Justice William Brennan stated that "implicit in the history of the First Amendment is the rejection of obscenity as utterly without redeeming social importance"— pornography is hence unprotected by the Constitution. Yet in case after case, the justices have struggled with first one approach, then another, trying to draw a manageable line between that which is protected and that which is not. For a time, beginning in 1967, the Court simply avoided the issue by deciding a number of obscenity cases per curiam, without full opinions. Only in 1973 did a majority of five justices finally agree on one approach to obscenity cases; Chief Justice Warren E. Burger stated that, among other things, to be declared obscene the material in question must lack "serious literary, artistic, political, or scientific value." But the last word in obscenity cases has by no means been written. Obscenity is to be judged by "contemporary community standards," and the Court has held that the relevant standards need not be those of the Nation or even a state; they may reflect the tastes and opinions of local communities. Hence the actual application of the Supreme Court's guidelines continues to require case-by-case adjudication, with local prosecutors and local juries playing a major role.

Libel cases have presented similar problems of definition. Whatever the First Amendment may have done to throttle the power of government to punish seditious libel, it was long assumed that conventional libel actions—one person's claiming that another had defamed the former's reputation—fell outside the ambit of constitutional adjudication. But in 1964, in *New York Times v. Sullivan,* the Court held that, in the interest of "robust and wide-open" debate on public issues, when a "public official" brings a libel action against critics of his official conduct, he must prove "actual malice"— that is, that a statement was made with knowledge that it was false or with reckless disregard of whether it was false. The *New*

York Times rule was subsequently extended to "public figures," and in a series of sequel cases the Court has attempted definition of just who is a "public figure."

First Amendment decisions such as those arising out of obscenity prosecutions or libel actions thus present the question of whether a verbal communication, which might be speech in a layman's eyes, is nonetheless not considered "speech" in terms of the First Amendment. In contrast, other cases present the question whether nonverbal activity—symbolic expression—may be protected "speech" under the First Amendment. For example, in 1969 (*Tinker v. Des Moines School District*), the Court found First Amendment protection for high school students' wearing of black armbands in school as a form of protest against the Vietnam War.

Attempts to regulate how money may be spent in political campaigns also raise First Amendment issues. In *Buckley v. Valeo* (1976), the Court struck down several provisions of the Federal Election Campaign Act of 1971, as amended. An appellate court had upheld the act's provisions by viewing them as restricting "conduct" rather than "speech." But the Supreme Court stressed the link between the amount of money spent on a campaign and the ability to communicate political issues. In the Court's words: "This is because virtually every means of communicating ideas in today's mass society requires the expenditure of money." The Court's *Buckley* opinion gives new meaning to the old notion that "money talks."

Those who read the Supreme Court's First Amendment opinions may find themselves overwhelmed, ironically enough, by words—by tests, by standards, by slogans. An opinion by the latter Justice Harlan or Justice Felix Frankfurter teaches that in First Amendment cases there are no "absolutes," that claims of protection for expression must be "balanced" against governmental interests involved. An opinion by Justice Hugo L. Black retorts that the framers of the First Amendment did all the "balancing" that was required, that the words "no law" in the amendment literally mean "no law." Justice Holmes tutors us on "clear and present danger," but later opinions grope for ways to apply that phrase—or even to decide whether it is helpful at all as a guide.

It is simply not possible to reduce the First Amendment's meaning to a single bromide. One reason is that the ambit of constitutionally protected expression has spread far beyond the area that most concerned many of those who voted to adopt the amendment. The amendment's protection for speech reaches above all to expression related to the political process, to dissemination of ideas about self-government by a free people. . . .

The First Amendment protects a whole matrix of rights. Protection for free expression has come to include the right to speak as well as the right to remain silent in the face of government demands for information (such as a state law requiring teachers to list every organization to which they belong) which may "chill" one's freedom to associate with others of like views. Another example of a protected First Amendment right arises when individuals associate to promote their causes in court; litigation by such groups as the National Association for the Advancement of Colored People (NAACP) has been held to be a protected form of expression. . . .

It is an accident of history that the First Amendment is in fact the first of the amendments making up the Bill of Rights (two amendments that appeared ahead of it on the list submitted to the several states in 1789 were not adopted). But the "firstness" of the First Amendment has great symbolic force all the same. Perhaps James Madison's contemporaries saw less in the First Amendment than that great son of the Enlightenment hoped would take root there. But later generations have found in the First Amendment a potent force for creating the conditions of a genuinely open and free society. ■

BRANDENBURG V. OHIO*

P ER CURIAM.

The appellant, a leader of a Ku Klux Klan group, was convicted under the Ohio Criminal syndicalism statute for "advocat[ing] . . . the duty, necessity, or propriety of crime, sabotage, violence, or unlawful methods of terrorism as a means of accomplishing industrial or political reform" and for "voluntarily assembl[ing] with any society, group, or assemblage of persons formed to teach or advocate the doctrines of criminal syndicalism." . . . He was fined $1,000 and sentenced to one to 10 years' imprisonment. The appellant challenged the constitutionality of the criminal syndicalism statute under the First and Fourteenth Amendments to the United States Constitution, but the intermediate appellate court of Ohio affirmed his conviction without opinion. The Supreme Court of Ohio dismissed his appeal, *sua sponte,* "for the reason that no substantial constitutional question exists herein." It did not file an opinion or explain its conclusions. Appeal was taken to this Court, and we noted probable jurisdiction. . . . We reverse.

The record shows that a man, identified at trial as the appellant, telephoned an announcer-reporter on the staff of a Cincinnati television station and invited him to come to a Ku Klux Klan "rally" to be held at a farm in Hamilton County. With the cooperation of the organizers, the reporter and a cameraman attended the meeting and filmed the events. Portions of the films were later broadcast on the local station and on a national network.

The prosecution's case rested on the films and on testimony identifying the appellant as the person who communicated with the reporter and who spoke at the rally. The State also introduced into evidence several articles appearing

---

* 395 U. S. 444 (1968).

in the film, including a pistol, a rifle, a shotgun, ammunition, a Bible, and a red hood worn by the speaker in the films.

One film showed 12 hooded figures, some of whom carried firearms. They were gathered around a large wooden cross, which they burned. No one was present other than the participants and the newsmen who made the film. Most of the words uttered during the scene were incomprehensible when the film was projected, but scattered phrases could be understood that were derogatory of Negroes and, in one instance, of Jews. Another scene on the same film showed the appellant, in Klan regalia, making a speech. The speech, in full, was as follows:

We are marching on Congress July the Fourth, four hundred thousand strong. From there we are dividing into two groups, one group to march on St. Augustine, Florida, the other group to march into Mississippi. Thank you.

The second film showed six hooded figures one of whom, later identified as the appellant, repeated a speech very similar to that recorded on the first film. The reference to the possibility of "revengeance" was omittted, and one sentence was added: "Personally, I believe the nigger should be returned to Africa, the Jew returned to Israel." Though some of the figures in the films carried weapons, the speaker did not.

The Ohio Criminal Syndicalism Statute was enacted in 1919. From 1917 to 1920, identical or quite similar laws were adopted by 20 States and two territories. E. Dowell, A History of Criminal Syndicalism Legislation in the United States 21 (1939). In 1927, this Court sustained the constitutionality of California's Criminal Syndicalism Act . . . *Whitney* v. *California*, 274 U. S. 357 (1927). The Court upheld the statute on the ground that, without more, "advocating" violent means to effect political and economic change involves such danger to the security of the State that the State may outlaw it. . . . But *Whitney* has been thoroughly discredited by later decisions. See *Dennis* v. *United States*, 341 U. S. 494, at 507 (1951). These later decisions have fashioned the principle that the constitutional guarantees of free speech and free press do not permit a State to forbid or proscribe advocacy of the use of force or of law violation except where such advocacy is directed to inciting or producing imminent lawless action and is likely to incite or produce such action. As we said in *Noto* v. *United States*, 367 U. S. 290, 297–298 (1961), "the mere abstract teaching . . . of the moral propriety or even moral necessity for a resort to force and violence, is not the same as preparing a group for violent action and steeling it to such ac-tion." . . . A statute which fails to draw this distinction impermissibly intrudes upon the freedoms guaranteed by the First and Fourteenth Amendments. It sweeps within its condemnation speech which our Constitution has immunized from governmental control. . . .

Measured by this test, Ohio's Criminal Syndicalism Act cannot be sustained. The Act punishes persons who "advocate or teach the duty, necessity, or pro-priety" or violence "as a means of accomplishing industrial or political reform;" or who publish or circulate or display any book or paper containing such ad-vocacy; or who "justify" the commission of violent acts "with intent to exemplify, spread or advocate the propriety of the doctrines of criminal syndicalism;" or who "voluntarily assemble" with a group formed "to teach or advocate the doctrines of criminal syndicalism." Neither the indictment nor the trial judge's instructions to the jury in any way refined the statute's bald definition of the crime in terms of mere advocacy not distinguished from incitement to imminent lawless action.

Accordingly, we are here confronted with a statute which, by its own words and as applied, purports to punish mere advocacy and to forbid, on pain of criminal punishment, assembly with others merely to advocate the described type of acton. Such a statute falls within the condemnation of the First and Fourteenth Amendments. The contrary teaching of *Whitney* v. *California* cannot be supported, and that decision is therefore overruled.   ∎

FREEDOM OF ASSEMBLY

Peaceful picketing, demonstrations, and marches are protected by the First Amendment—both under the freedom of assembly and because the courts have held such activities to be "symbolic speech."

Most Americans would agree with this as an abstract principle. But what if the demonstrating group is a small but hate-filled, antiSemitic group like the American Nazi party and the place where they want to march is Skokie, a heavily Jewish suburb of Chicago where many survivors of the Nazi holocaust and their relatives live? Are Nazis protected by the constitution?

Just such a question was presented to the courts in 1978, when the Village of Skokie attempted to block a Nazi march. The Supreme Court upheld the rights of the Nazis (although the group finally voluntarily moved the site of the march to a Chicago park).[7]

The Skokie controversy caused great and anguished disagreement among people and organizations who otherwise supported the First Amendment. The American Civil Liberties Union lost many members, many of them Jewish, when it defended the Nazi right to march. A number of other groups, such as the American Jewish Congress and the Anti-Defamation League, vigorously took the opposite side. Columnist George F. Will expressed the views of the opposition, when he asserted in a *Washington Post* article, entitled, "Nazis: Outside the Constitution," that the First Amendment should not be used to protect "those who, if they win, will destroy the Constitution and then throw people down wells."[8]

In his book excerpted here, *Defending My Enemy*, Aryeh Neier, then head of the ACLU and himself a Jew, argues that truth will prevail where it is allowed openly to compete with falsehood and that, under our system, Nazis must be free to speak so that Jews may be free to speak.

---

7. *Collin* v. *Smith*, 439 U. S. 916 (1978); and *National Socialist Party* v. *Village of Skokie*, 432 U. S. 43 (1977).
8. *Washington Post* (February 2, 1978), p. A19.

THE CONSTITUTION PROTECTS THE NAZIS
Aryeh Neier

"My only hope," said a letter I received from a man in Boston, "is that if we are both forced into a march some day to some crematorium, *you* will be at the head of the parade, at which time you will in your rapture have an opportunity to sing hosannas in praise of freedom of speech for your tormentors."

I have received many similar letters. They were provoked by the efforts of the American Civil Liberties Union, which I served as executive director, to secure free speech for a group of American Nazis who said they wanted to march in Skokie, Illinois. The most succinct letter was from the man who proposed a motto for the ACLU: "The First Amendment *über Alles*." . . .

I supported free speech for Nazis when they wanted to march in Skokie in order to defeat Nazis. Defending my enemy is the only way to protect a free society against the enemies of freedom. . . .

I am a Jew, born in Berlin. We escaped to England. . . .

When the war ended, my parents discovered what had happened to their families. Almost everyone was dead. Only fragmentary information was available on how they had been murdered. My father's mother had been shot and killed early in the war, soon after the Germans overran the village in Poland where she lived. Two of my mother's brothers had survived in Bergen-Belsen until the end, only to be killed on the eve of the camp's liberation. Others died along the way. . . .

I recite my own background to suggest why I am unwilling to put anything, even love of free speech, ahead of detestation of the Nazis. Many residents of Skokie, Illinois, have far better grounds for detesting the Nazis. They themselves experienced the death camps. I know those horrors only through the words of others. They watched the Nazis kill members of their families. I was too young ever to know the members of my family who died in the camps and I was hundreds of miles away in England when they died. I could not bring myself to advocate freedom of speech in Skokie if I did not believe thast the changes are best for preventing a repetition of the Holocaust in a society where every incursion on freedom is resisted. Freedom has its risks. Suppression of freedom, I believe, is a sure prescription for disaster. . . .

John Milton's view that truth will prevail in a free and open encounter with falsehood is my view, too. I want to keep encounters between ideas free and open, expecting to give truth the edge. . . .

John Milton's view that truth will prevail in a free and open encounter with falsehood is my view, too. I want to keep encounters between ideas free and open, expecting to give truth the edge. . . .

Albert Camus said, "Freedom is the concern of the oppressed, and her natural protectors have always come from among the oppressed." It is a matter of self-interest. The oppressed are the victims of power. If they are to end their oppression, they must either win freedom or take power themselves. Many of those who have suffered oppression prefer to take power themselves. One-fifth of all the Jews in the world have sought refuge in their own homeland, Israel. It is a place where Jews hope their oppression will end because there, they make the rules. They have the power. Some Jews have sought refuge in other countries, in scattered communities where most of their neighbors are also Jews. Because Jews loom large in the population of a town such as Skokie, it is also a place where they hope their oppression will end because they can make the rules and exercise the power there. Skokie, in that sense, is a microcosmic reflection of Israel. It is a place where the Jews believe they should be able to defend themselves against invasion. . . .

Jews cannot hide from the Nazis in Skokie. For their own safety's sake, they must give the devil—the Nazis—benefit of law. It is dangerous to let the Nazis have their say. But it is more dangerous by far to destroy the laws that deny anyone the power to silence Jews if Jews should need to cry out to each other and to the world for succor. Jews have been persecuted too many times in history for anyone to assert that their sufferings are at an end. When the time comes for Jews to speak, to publish, and to march in behalf of their own safety, Illinois and the United States must not be allowed to interfere. The Nazis, I respond to those who ask how I, a Jew, can defend freedom for Nazis, must be free to speak because Jews must be free to speak and because I must be free to speak. . . .

* * *

Sixteen months in which the Nazis had captured the attention of the nation ended on July 9, 1978. On that warm and humid Sunday, Frank Collin and about twenty-five uniformed followers held a rally in Marquette Park. A federal court's decision two weeks earlier granting the Nazis the right to demonstrate in that Chicago park had given them the excuse they sought for canceling the Skokie march at the last moment. Their exclusion from Marquette Park where they could exploit the racial tensions of the neighborhood had inspired their effort to march in Skokie.

The Nazi rally lasted less than an hour. A crowd of about two thousand people made so much noise that the speeches by Collin and his St. Louis Nazi comrade, Michael Allen, were all but drowned out. Some of the crowd shouted support for the Nazis and "Death to the Jews." Others reviled Collin and shouted "Death to the Nazis." The size of the crowd was swelled by the presence of several hundred plain-clothes police officers who broke up sporadic fights and arrested seventy-two persons, most of them charged with disorderly conduct, only a few with assault. Thanks to the police vigilance, no serious violence took place. The police also kept one group of anti-Nazis out of Marquette Park entirely. A number of anti-Nazis complained to the Illinois ACLU and secured its aid in bringing a lawsuit challenging interference with their First Amendment rights.

Hoping to create more Skokies, the Nazis announced plans for demonstrations in several other Chicago suburbs. That petered out, however, when only three Nazis showed up for one demonstration and the press virtually ignored it. The Nazis were on their way back to obscurity.

Remarkably, during those sixteen months, the Nazis gained no adherents. Although Skokie's attempt to deny the Nazis the freedom to speak had backfired, bestowing on them the opportunity to speak almost daily to the entire nation through the press, when it was all over no one had been persuaded to join them. They had disseminated their message and it had been rejected.

Why did the Nazi message fall on such deaf ears? Revolutionaries and advocates of destruction attract followers readily when the society they wish to overturn loses legitimacy. Understanding this process, revolutionaries try to provoke the government into using repressive measures. They rejoice, as the American Nazis did, when their rights are denied to them; they count on repression to win them sympathizers.

In confronting the Nazis, however, American democracy did not lose, but preserved its legitimacy. When the Chicago Park District and the village of Skokie denied the Nazis the right to speak, the courts intervened to protect that right. When the Nazis assembled in St. Louis, at the federal building in Chicago, and in Marquette Park, police power was employed to protect their rights. It cost $10,000 to clean up Marquette Park after the twenty-five Nazis demonstrated and $90,000 in overtime pay for the police. If the Nazis had gone ahead with their plan to march in Skokie, thousands of police would have been on hand to protect them at many times the cost of the Marquette Park rally.

The judges who devoted so much attention to the Nazis, the police departments that paid so much overtime, and the American Civil Liberties Union, which lost a half-million dollars in membership income as a consequence of its defense, used their time and money well. They defeated the Nazis by preserving the legitimacy of American democracy. ■

RIGHT OF PRIVACY

The Fourth Amendment states that people have a right "to be secure in their persons, houses, papers, and effects, against unreasonable searches and seizures . . . ." The courts have held that before conducting a search, the authorities must first obtain a search warrant unless there is "probably cause" to believe that a crime has been committed.

Evidence obtained by the authorities in violation of the Fourth Amendment, as interpreted by the courts, may be excluded in the trial of a person charged with a crime—under what is called the "exclusionary rule."

The U. S. Supreme Court under Chief Justice Warren Burger—the "Burger Court" (1969–present)—has interpreted the Bill of Rights slightly more in favor of the authorities and slightly less in favor of persons accused of crimes than was true of the Court when it was headed by Chief Justice Earl Warren—the "Warren Court" (1953–1969). The Burger Court's interpretation of the "exclusionary rule" is an example.

In 1985, the case of New Jersey v. T. L. O., excerpted here, was decided by the Burger court, with Justice Byron White writing the majority opinion. In it, the Court held that the Fourth Amendment does protect a public school student against an "unreasonable" search by school authorities, but, in the particular case involved, the Court said that the search was reasonable. In doing so, the Supreme Court announced a new standard: in cases involving searches of students by school authorities, the authorities do not have to have "probable cause" to believe a crime has been committed; it is sufficient that they are "reasonable" under all the circumstances in believing that a search will turn up evidence of violation of school rules.

NEW JERSEY V. T.L.O.*

Justice WHITE delivered the opinion of the Court . . .

On March 7, 1980, a teacher at Piscataway High School in Middlesex County, N.J., discovered two girls smoking in a lavatory. One of the two girls was the respondent T.L.O., who at that time was a 14-year-old high school freshman. Because smoking in the lavatory was a violation of a school rule, the teacher took the two girls to the Principal's office, where they met with Assistant Vice Principal Theodore Choplick. In response to questioning by Mr. Choplick, T.L.O.'s companion admitted that she had violated the rule. T.L.O., however, denied that she had been smoking in the lavatory and claimed that she did not smoke at all.

Mr. Choplick asked T.L.O. to come into his private office and demanded to see her purse. Opening the purse, he found a pack of cigarettes, which he removed from the purse and held before T.L.O. as he accused her of having lied to him. As he reached into the purse for the cigarettes, Mr. Choplick also noticed a package of cigarette rolling papers. In his experience, possession of rolling papers by high school students was closely associated with the use of marihuana. Suspecting that a closer examination fo the purse might yield further evidence of drug use, Mr. Choplick proceeded to search the purse thoroughly. The search revealed a small amount of marihuana, a pipe, a number of empty plastic bags, a substantial quantity of money in one-dollar bills, an index card tht appeared to be a list of students who owed T.L.O. money, and two letters that implicated T.L.O. in marihuana dealing.

Mr. Choplick notified T.L.O.'s mother and the police, and turned the evidence of drug dealing over to the police. At the request of the police, T.L.O.'s mother

---

* 105 S. Ct. 733 (1985).

took her daughter to police headquarters, where T.L.O. confessed that she had been selling marihuana at the high school. On the basis of the confession and the evidence seized by Mr. Choplick, the State brought delinquency charges against T.L.O. in the Juvenile and Domestic Relations Court of Middlesex County. Contending that Mr. Choplick's search of her purse violated the Fourth Amendment, T.L.O. moved to suppress the evidence found in her purse as well her confession, which, she argued, was tainted by the allegedly unlawful search. The Juvenile Court denied the motion to suppress. . . .

On appeal from the final judgment of the Juvenile Court, a divided Appellate Division affirmed the trial court's finding that there had been no Fourth Amendment violation . . . T.L.O. appealed the Fourth Amendment ruling, and the Supreme Court of New Jersey reversed the judgment of the Appellate Division and ordered the suppression of the evidence found in T.L.O.'s purse. . . .

With respect to the question of the legality of the search before it, the court agreed with the Juvenile Court that a warrantless search by a school official "has reasonable grounds to believe that a student possesses evidence of illegal activity or activity that would interfere with school discipline and order." . . . However, the court, with two justices dissenting, sharply disagreed with the Juvenile Court's conclusion that the search of the purse was reasonable. According to the majority, the contents of T.L.O.'s purse had no bearing on the possession of cigarettes (as opposed to smoking them in the lavatory) did not violate school rules, and a mere desire for evidence that would impeach T.L.O.'s claim that she did not smoke cigarettes could not justify the search. Moreover, even if a reasonable suspicion that T.L.O. had cigarettes in her purse would justify a search, Mr. Choplick had no such suspicion, as no one had furnished him with any specific information that there were cigarettes in the purse. Finally, leaving aside the question whether Mr. Choplick was justified in opening the purse, the court held that the evidence of drug use that he saw inside did not justify the extensive "rummaging" through T.L.O.'s papers and effects that followed. . . . Having heard argument on the legality of the search of T.L.O.'s purse, we are satisfied that the search did not violate the Fourth Amendment.

In determining whether the search at issue in this case violated the Fourth Amendment, we are faced initially with the question whether that Amendment's prohibition on unreasonable searches and seizures applies to searches conducted by public school officials. We hold that it does.

It is now beyond dispute that "the Federal Constitution, by virtue of the Fourteenth Amendment, prohibits unreasonable searches and seizures by state officers." . . . Equally indisputable is the proposition that the Fourteenth Amendment protects the rights of students against encroachment by public school officials:

"The Fourteenth Amendment, as now applied to the States, protects the citizen against the State itself and all of its creatures—Boards of Education not excepted. These have, of course, delicate, and highly discretionary functions, but none that they may not perform within the limits of the Bill of Rights. That they are educating the young for citizenship is reason for scrupulous protection of Constitutional freedoms of the individual, if we are not to strangle the free mind at its source and teach youth to discount important principles of our government as mere platitudes." . . .

These two propositions—that the Fourth Amendment applies to the States through the Fourteenth Amendment, and that the actions of public school officials are subject to the limits placed on state action by the Fourteenth Amendment— might appear sufficient to answer the suggestion that the Fourth Amendment does not proscribe unreasonable searches by school officials. On reargument, however, the State of New Jersey has argued that the history of the Fourth Amendment indicates that the Amendment was intended to regulate only searches and seizures carried out by law enforcement officers; accordingly, although public school officials are concededly state agents for purposes of the Fourteenth Amendment, the Fourth Amendment creates no rights enforceable against them. . . .

Teachers and school administrators, it is said, act *in loco parentis* in their dealings with students: their authority is that of the parent, not the State, and is therefore not subject to the limits of the Fourth Amendment.

Such reasoning is in tension with contemporary reality and the teachings of this Court. . . . Today's public school officials do not merely exercise authority voluntarily conferred on them by individual parents; rather, they act in furtherance of publicly mandated educational and disciplinary policies. . . . In carrying out searches and other disciplinary functions pursuant to such policies, school officials act as representatives of the State, not merely as surrogates for the parents, and they cannot claim the parents' immunity from the strictures of the Fourth Amendment.

To hold that the Fourth Amendment applies to searches conducted by school authorities is only to begin the inquiry into the standards governing such searches. Although the underlying command of the Fourth Amendment is always that searches and seizures be reasonable, what is reasonable depends on the context within which a search takes place. The determination of the standard of reasonableness governing any specific class of searches requires "balancing the need to search against the invasion which the search entails." . . . On one side of the balance are arrayed the individual's legitimate expectations of privacy and personal security; on the other, the government's need for effective methods to deal with breaches of public order.

A search of a child's person or of a closed purse or other bag carried on her person, no less than a similar search carried out on an adult, is undoubtedly a severe violation of subjective expectations of privacy. . . .

How, then, should we strike the balance between the schoolchild's legitimate expectations of privacy and the school's equally legitimate need to maintain an environment in which learning can take place? It is evident that the school setting requires some easing of the restrictions to which searches by public authorities are ordinarily subject. The warrant requirement, in particular, is unsuited to the school environment: requiring a teacher to obtain a warrant before searching a child suspected of an infraction of school rules (or of the criminal law) would unduly interfere with the maintenance of the swift and informal disciplinary procedures needed in the schools. Just as we have in other cases dispensed with the warrant requirement when "the burden of obtaining a warrant is likely to frustrate the governmental purpose behind the search," . . . we hold today that school officials need not obtain a warrant before searching a student who is under their authority.

We join the majority of courts that have examined this issue in concluding that the accommodation of the privacy interests of schoolchildren with the substantial need of teachers and administrators for freedom to maintain order in the schools does not require strict adherence to the requirement that searches be based on probable cause to believe that the subject of the search has violated or is violating the law. Rather, the legality of a search of a student should depend simply on the reasonableness, under all the circumstances, of the search. Determining the reasonableness of any search involved a twofold inquiry: first, one must consider "whether the . . . action was justified at its inception," . . . ; second, one must determine whether the search as actually conducted "was reasonably related in scope to the circumstances which justified the interference in the first place," . . . Under ordinary circumstances, a search of a student by a teacher or other school official will be "justified at its inception" when there are reasonable grounds for suspecting that the search will turn up evidence that the student has violated or is violating either the law or the rules of the school. Such a search will be permissible in its scope when the measures adopted are reasonably related to the objectives of the search and not excessively intrusive in light of the age and sex of the student and the nature of the infraction. . . .

There remains the question of the legality of the search in this case. We recognize that the "reasonable grounds" standard applied by the New Jersey Supreme Court in its consideration of this question is not substantially different from the standard that we have adopted today. Nonetheless, we believe that the New Jersey court's application of that standard to strike down the search of T.L.O's purse reflects a somewhat crabbed notion of reasonableness. Our review of the facts surrounding the search leads us to conclude that the search was in no sense unreasonable for Fourth Amendment purposes. . . .

Because the search resulting in the discovery of the evidence of marihuana dealing by T.L.O. was reasonable, the New Jersey Supreme Court's decision to exclude that evidence from T.L.O's juvenile delinquency proceedings on Fourth Amendment grounds was erroneous. Accordingly, the judgment of the Supreme Court of New Jersey is

Reversed. . . .

Justice BRENNAN, with whom Justice MARSHALL joins, concurring in part and dissenting in part.

I fully agree with Part II of the court's opinion. Teachers, like all other government officials, must conform their conduct to the Fourth Amendment's protections of personal privacy and personal security. . . . It would be incongruous and futile to charge teachers with the task of embuing their students with an understanding of our system of constitutional democracy, while at the same time immunizing those same teachers from the need to respect constitutional protections. . . .

I emphatically disagree with the Court's decision to cast aside the constitutional probable-cause standard when assessing the constitutional validity of a schoolhouse search. The Court's decision jettisons the probable-cause standard— the only standard that finds support in the text of the Fourth Amendment—on the basis of its Rohrschach-like "balancing test." Use of such a "balancing test" to determine the standard for evaluating the validity of a full-scale search represents a sizable innovation in Fourth Amendment analysis. This innovation finds support neither in precedent nor policy and portends a dangerous weakening of the purpose of the Fourth Amendment to protect the privacy and security of our citizens. Moreover, even if this Court's historic understanding of the Fourth Amendment were mistaken and a balancing test of some kind were appropriate, any such test that gave adequate weight to the privacy and security interests protected by the Fourth Amendment would not reach the preordained result the Court's conclusionary analysis reaches today. Therefore, because I believe that the balancing test used by the Court today is flawed both in its inception and in its execution, I respectfully dissent. . . .

Justice STEVENS, with whom Justice MARSHALL joins, and with whom Justice BRENNAN joins as to Part I, concurring in part and dissenting in part. . . .

The majority holds that "a search of a student by a teacher or other school official will be 'justified at its inception' when there are reasonable grounds for suspecting that the search will turn up evidence *that the student has violated or is violating* either the law or *the rules of the school.*" . . . This standard will permit teachers and school administrators to search students when they suspect that the search will reveal evidence of even the most trivial school regulation or precatory guideline for student behavior. . . .

The schoolroom is the first opportunity most citizens have to experience the power of government. Through it passes every citizen and public official, from schoolteachers to policemen and prison guards. The values they learn there, they take with them in life. One of our most cherished ideals is the one contained in the Fourth Amendment: that the Government may not intrude on the personal privacy of its citizens without a warrant or compelling circumstance. The Court's decision today is a curious moral for the Nation's youth. Although the search of T.L.O.'s purse does not trouble today's majority, I submit that we are not dealing with "matters relatively trivial to the welfare of the Nation. There are village tyrants as well as village Hampdens, but none who acts under color of law is beyond the reach of the Constitution." . . . ■

RIGHT AGAINST SELF-INCRIMINATION

The Fifth Amendment includes certain rights of a person accused of a crime— including, for example, the right against "double jeopardy" and the right to a grand jury indictment in serious cases. It also includes the prohibition against a person being "compelled in any criminal case to be a witness against himself." This provision is what is meant when the common phrase, "taking the Fifth," is used.

The right against self-incrimination is a very old concept that came to the United States from England and was intended to prevent coerced, or forced, confessions.

By a five-to-four vote in 1965, in the case of *Miranda* v. *Arizona,* excerpted here, the Warren Court handed down a "landmark" and controversial decision concerning the right against self-incrimination. The majority opinion was written by Chief Justice Earl Warren himself. The Court declared that unless an accused person in custody is advised of his or her rights prior to making a statement, the statement cannot be used against the accused. The Court said that such prior advice was necessary if the Fifth Amendment right was to be really meaningful. The *Miranda* advice—now as familiar to viewers of television police shows as to the police themselves—must include the right to remain silent, the fact that anything said by the accused can and will be used against him or her, and the right to a lawyer.

In 1984 and 1985, the Supreme Court—with some changed membership and (since 1969) a new chief Justice, Warren Burger, now called the Burger Court—handed down opinions that while still affirming the main principles of the *Miranda* case, nevertheless chipped away at its requirements a little. The two cases are excerpted here. In the majority opinion in *New York* v. *Quarles,* 1984, written by Justice William Rehnquist, the Court decreed a "public safety" exception to the *Miranda* rule. In the 1985 case of *Oregon* v. *Elstad,* in which Justice Sandra Day O'Connor wrote the majority opinion, the Court said that the fact that an accused person gave incriminating answers to the police without first having been advised of his or her rights did not prevent the use of a later confession if prior to the later confession, the accused *was* given the *Miranda* advice.

MIRANDA V. ARIZONA*

M̲ʀ. C̲ʜɪᴇꜰ J̲ᴜsᴛɪᴄᴇ W̲ᴀʀʀᴇɴ delivered the opinion of the Court.

The cases before us raise questions which go to the roots of our concepts of American criminal jurisprudence: the restraints society must observe consistent with the Federal Constitution in prosecuting individuals for crime. More specifically, we deal with the admissibility of statements obtained from an individual who is subjected to custodial police interrogation and the necessity for procedures which assure that the individual is accorded his privilege under the

---

* 384 U. S. 436 (1965).

Fifth Amendment to the Constitution not to be compelled to incriminate himself. . . .

Our holding will be spelled out with some specificity in the pages which follow but briefly stated it is this: the prosecution may not use statements, whether exculpatory or inculpatory, stemming from custodial interrogation of the defendant unless it demonstrates the use of procedural safeguards effective to secure the privilege against self-incrimination. By custodial interrogation, we mean questioning initiated by law enforcement officers after a person has been taken into custody or otherwise deprived of his freedom of action in any significant way. As for the procedural safeguards to be employed, unless other fully effective means are devised to inform accused persons of their right of silence and to assure a continuous opportunity to exercise it, the following measures are required. Prior to any questioning, the person must be warned that he has a right to remain silent, that any statement he does make may be used as evidence against him and that he has a right to the presence of an attorney, either retained or appointed. The defendant may waive effectuation of these rights, provided the waiver is made voluntarily, knowingly and intelligently. If, however, he indicates in any manner and at any stage of the process that he wishes to consult with an attorney before speaking there can be no questioning. Likewise, if the individual is alone and indicates in any manner that he does not wish to be interrogated, the police may not question him. The mere fact that he may have answered some questions or volunteered some statements on his own does not deprive him of the right to refrain from answering any further inquiries until he has consulted with an attorney and thereafter consents to be questioned. . . .

The Commission on Civil Rights in 1961 found much evidence to indicate that "some policemen still resort to physical force to obtain confessions," . . . The use of physical brutality and violence is not, unfortunately, relegated to the past or to any part of the country. Only recently in Kings County, New York, the police brutally beat, kicked and placed lighted cigarette butts on the back of a potential witness under interrogation for the purpose of securing a statement incriminating a third party.

The examples given above are undoubtedly the exception now, but they are sufficiently widespread to be the object of concern. Unless a proper limitation upon custodial interrogation is achieved—such as these decisions will advance—there can be no assurance that practices of this nature will be eradicated in the foreseeable future. . . .

Again we stress that the modern practice of in-custody interrogation is psychologically rather than physically oriented. As we have stated before, "Since *Chambers* v. *Florida,* 309 U. S. 227, this Court has recognized that coercion can be mental as well as physical, and that the blood of the accused is not the only hallmark of an unconstitutional inquisition." . . . Interrogation still takes place in privacy. Privacy results in secrecy and this in turn results in a gap in our knowledge as to what in fact goes on in the interrogation rooms. A valuable source of information about present police practices, however, may be found in various police manuals and texts which document procedures employed with success in the past, and which recommend various other effective tactics. . . .

The officers are told by the manuals that the "principal psychological factor contributing to a successful interrogation is *privacy*—being alone with the person under interrogation." . . .

The interrogators sometimes are instructed to induce a confession out of trickery. The technique here is quite effective in crimes which require identification or which run in series. In the identification situation, the interrogator may take a break in his questioning to place the subject among a group of men in a line-up. "The witness or complainant (previously coached, if necessary) studies the line-up and confidently points out the subject as the guilty party. Then the questioning resumes "as though there were now no doubt about the guilt of the subject." . . .

The manuals also contain instructions for police on how to handle the individual who refused to discuss the matter entirely, or who asks for an attorney or relatives. The examiner is to concede him the right to remain silent. "This usually has a very undermining effect. First of all, he is disappointed in his expectation of an unfavorable reaction on the part of the interrogator. Secondly, a concession of this right to remain silent impresses the subject with the apparent fairness of his interrogator." After this psychological conditioning, however, the officer is told to point out the incriminating significance of the suspect's refusal to talk:

> Joe, you have a right to remain silent. That's your privilege and I'm the last person in the world who'll try to take it away from you. If that's the way you want to leave this, O. K. But let me ask you this. Suppose you were in my shoes and I were in yours and you called me in to ask me about this and I told you, "I don't want to answer any of your questions." You'd think I had something to hide, and you'd probably be right in thinking that. That's exactly what I'll have to think about you, and so will everybody else. So let's sit here and talk this whole thing over.

Few will persist in their initial refusal to talk, it is said, if this monologue is employed correctly.

In the event that the subject wishes to speak to a relative or an attorney, the following advice is tendered:

> [T]he interrogator should respond by suggesting that the subject first tell the truth to the interrogator himself rather than get anyone else involved in the matter. If the request is for an attorney, the interrogator may suggest that the subject save himself or his family the expense of any such professional service, particularly if he is innocent of the offense under investigation. The interrogator may also add, "Joe, I'm only looking for the truth, and if you're telling the truth, that's it. You can handle this by yourself."

From these representative samples of interrogation techniques, the setting prescribed by the manuals and observed in practice becomes clear. In essence, it is this: To be alone with the subject is essential to prevent distraction and to deprive him of any outside support. The aura of confidence in his guilt undermines his will to resist. He merely confirms the preconceived story the police seek to have him describe. Patience and persistence, at times relentless questioning, are employed. To obtain a confession, the interrogator must "patiently maneuver himself or his quarry into a position from which the desired objective may be attained." When normal procedures fail to produce the needed result, the police may resort to deceptive strategems such as giving false legal advice. It is important to keep the subject off balance, for example, by trading on his insecurity about himself or his surroundings. The police then persuade, trick, or cajole him out of exercising his constitutional rights.

Even without employing brutality, the "third degree" or the specific strategems described above, the very fact of custodial interrogation exacts a heavy toll on individual liberty and trades on the weakness of individuals. . . .

In these cases, we might not find the defendants' statements to have been involuntary in traditional terms. Our concern for adequate safeguards to protect precious Fifth Amendment rights is, of course, not lessened in the slightest. In each of the cases, the defendant was thrust into an unfamiliar atmosphere and run through menacing police interrogation procedures. The potentiality for compulsion is forcefully apparent, for example, in *Miranda*, where the indigent Mexican defendant was a seriously disturbed individual with pronounced sexual fantasies, and in *Stewart*, in which the defendant was an indigent Los Angeles Negro who had dropped out of school in the sixth grade. To be sure, the records do not evince overt physical coercion or patent psychological ploys. The fact remains that in none of these cases did the officers undertake to afford appropriate safeguards at the outset of the interrogation to insure that the statements were truly the product of free choice.

It is obvious that such an interrogation environment is created for no purpose other than to subjugate the individual to the will of his examiner. This atmosphere carries its own badge of intimidation. To be sure, this is not physical intimidation, but it is equally destructive of human dignity. The current practice of incommunicado interrogation is at odds with one of our Nation's most cherished principles—that the individual may not be compelled to incriminate himself. Unless adequate protective devices are employed to dispel the compulsion inherent in custodial surroundings, no statement obtained from the defendant can truly be the product of his free choice. . . .

Today, . . . there can be no doubt that the Fifth Amendment privilege is available outside of criminal court proceedings and serves to protect persons in all settings in which their freedom of action is curtailed in any significant way from being compelled to incriminate themselves. We have concluded that without proper safeguards the process of in-custody interrogation of persons suspected or accused of crime contains inherently compelling pressures which work to undermine the individual's will to resist and to compel him to speak where he would not otherwise do so freely. In order to combat these pressures and to permit a full opportunity to exercise the privilege against self-incrimination, the accused must be adequately and effectively apprised of his rights and the exercise of those rights must be fully honored.

It is impossible for us to foresee the potential alternatives for protecting the privilege which might be devised by Congress or the States in the exercise of their creative rule-making capacities. Therefore we cannot say that the Constitution necessarily requires adherence to any particular solution for the inherent compulsions of the interrogation process as it is presently conducted. . . . However, unless we are shown other procedures which are at least as effective in apprising accused persons of their right of silence and in assuring a continuous opportunity to exercise it, the following safeguards must be observed.

At the outset, if a person in custody is to be subjected to interrogation, he must first be informed in clear and unequivocal terms that he has the right to remain silent. For those unaware of the privilege, the warning is needed simply to make them aware of it—the threshold requirement for an intelligent decision as to its exercise. More important, such a warning is an absolute prerequisite in overcoming the inherent pressures of the interrogation atmosphere. It is not just the subnormal or woefully ignorant who succumb to an interrogator's imprecations, whether implied or expressly stated, that the interrogation will continue until a confession is obtained or that silence in the face of accusation is itself damning and will bode ill when presented to a jury. Further, the warning will show the individual that his interrogators are prepared to recognize his privilege should he choose to exercise it.

The Fifth Amendment privilege is so fundamental to our system of constitutional rule and the expedient of giving an adequate warning as to the availability of the privilege so simple, we will not pause to inquire in individual cases whether the defendant was aware of his rights without a warning being given. Assessments of the knowledge the defendant possessed, based on information as to his age, education, intelligence, or prior contact with authorities, can never be more than speculation; a warning is a clearcut fact. More important, whatever the background of the person interrogated, a warning at the time of the interrogation is indispensable to overcome its pressures and to insure that the individual knows he is free to exercise the privilege at that point in time.

The warning of the right to remain silent must be accompanied by the explanation that anything said can and will be used against the individual in court. This warning is needed in order to make him aware not only of the privilege, but also of the consequences of forgoing it. It is only through an awareness of these consequences that there can be any assurance of real understanding and intelligent exercise of the privilege. Moreover, this warning may serve to make the individual more acutely aware that he is faced with a phase of the adversary system—that he is not in the presence of persons acting solely in his interest.

The circumstances surrounding in-custody interrogation can operate very quickly to overbear the will of one merely made aware of his privilege by his interrogators. Therefore, the right to have counsel present at the interrogation is indispensable to the protection of the Fifth Amendment privilege under the system we delineate today. . . .

Accordingly we hold that an individual held for interrogation must be clearly informed that he has the right to consult with a lawyer and to have the lawyer with him during interrogation under the system for protecting the privilege we delineate today. As with the warnings of the right to remain silent and that anything stated can be used in evidence against him, this warning is an absolute prerequisite to interrogation. No amount of circumstantial evidence that the person may have been aware of this right will suffice to stand in its stead. Only through such a warning is there ascertainable assurance that the accused was aware of this right. . . .

In order fully to apprise a person interrogated of the extent of his rights under this system then, it is necessary to warn him not only that he has the right to consult with an attorney, but also that if he is indigent a lawyer will be appointed to represent him. Without this additional warning, the admonition of the right to consult with counsel would often be understood as meaning only that he can consult with a lawyer if he has one or has the funds to obtain one. . . .

Once warning have been given, the subsequent procedure is clear. If the individual indicates in any manner, at any time prior to or during questioning, that he wishes to remain silent, the interrogation must cease. At this point he has shown that he intends to exercise his Fifth Amendment privilege; any statement taken after the person invokes his privilege cannot be other than the product of compulsion, subtle or otherwise. Without the right to cut off questioning, the setting of in-custody interrogation operates on the individual to overcome free choice in producing a statement after the privilege has been once invoked. If the individual states that he wants an attorney, the interrogation must cease until an attorney is present. At that time, the individual must have an opportunity to confer with the attorney and to have him present during any subsequent questioning. If the individual cannot obtain an attorney and he indicates that he wants one before speaking to police, they must respect his decision to remain silent. . . .

Moreover, any evidence that the accused was threatened, tricked, or cajoled into a waiver will, of course, show that the defendant did not voluntarily waive his privilege. The requirement of warnings and waiver of rights is a fundamental with respect to the Fifth Amendment privilege and not simply a preliminary ritual to existing methods of interrogation.

The warnings required and the waiver necessary in accordance with our opinion today are, in the absence of a fully effective equivalent, prerequisites to the admissibility of any statement made by a defendant. . . .

The principles announced today deal with the protection which must be given to the privilege against self-incrimination when the individual is first subjected to police interrogation while in custody at the station or otherwise deprived of his freedom of action in any significant way. It is at this point that our adversary system of criminal proceedings commences, distinguishing itself at the outset from the inquisitorial system recognized in some countries. Under the system of warnings we delineate today or under any other system which may be devised and found effective, the safeguards to be erectd about the privilege must come into play at this point. . . .

To summarize, we hold that when an individual is taken into custody or otherwise deprived of his freedom by the authorities in any significant way and is subjected to questioning, the privilege against self-incrimination is jeopardized. Procedural safeguards must be employed to protect the privilege, and unless other fully effective means are adopted to notify the person of his right of silence and to assure that the exercise of the right will be scrupulously honored, the following measures are required. He must be warned prior to any questioning that he has the right to remain silent, that anything he says can be used against him in a court of law, that he has the right to the presence of an attorney, and that if he cannot afford an attorney one will be appointed for him prior to any questioning if he so desires. Opportunity to exercise these rights must be afforded to him throughout the interrogation. After such warnings have been given, and such opportunity afforded him the individual may knowingly and intelligently waive these rights and agree to answer questions or make a statement. But unless and until such warnings and waiver are demonstrated by the prosecution at trial, no evidence obtained as a result of interrogation can be used against him.　■

NEW YORK V. QUARLES*

On September 11, 1980, at approximately 12:30 a.m., Officer Frank Kraft and Officer Sal Scarring were on road patrol in Queens, New York, when a young woman approached their car. She told them that she had just been raped by a black male, approximately six feet tall, who was wearing a black jacket with the name "Big Ben" printed in yellow letters on the back. She told the officers that the man had just entered an A & P supermarket located nearby and that the man was carrying a gun.

The officers drove the woman to the supermarket, and Officer Kraft entered the store while Officer Scarring radioed for assistance. Officer Kraft quickly spotted respondent, who matched the description given by the woman, approaching a check-out counter. Apparently upon seeing the officer, respondent turned and ran toward the rear of the store, and Officer Kraft pursued him with a drawn gun. When respondent turned the corner at the end of an aisle. Officer Kraft lost sight of him for several seconds, and upon regaining sight of respondent, ordered him to stop and put his hands over his head.

Although more than three other officers had arrived on the scene by that time, Officer Kraft was the first to reach respondent. He frisked him and discovered that he was wearing a shoulder holster which was then empty. After handcuffing him, Officer Kraft asked him where the gun was. Respondent nodded in the direction of some empty cartons and responded, "the gun is over there." Officer Kraft thereafter retrieved a loaded .38 caliber revolver form one of the cartons, formally placed respondent under arrest, and read him his *Miranda* rights from a printed card. Respondent indicated that he would be willing to answer

* U. S. Reports, Slip Opinion (June 12, 1984).

questions without an attorney present. Officer Kraft then asked respondent if he owned the gun and where he had purchased it. Respondent answered that he did own it and that he had purchased it in Miami, Florida.

In the subsequent prosecution of respondent for criminal possession of a weapon, the judge excluded the statement, "the gun is over there," and the gun because the officer had not given respondent the warnings required by our decision in *Miranda* v. *Arizona*, 384 U. S. 436 (1966), before asking him where the gun was located. The judge excluded the other statements about respondent's ownership of the gun and the place of purchase, as evidence tainted by the prior *Miranda* violation. The Appellate Division of the Supreme Court of New York affirmed without opinion. . . .

The Court of Appeals granted leave to appeal and affirmed by a 4–3 vote. . . . It concluded that respondent was in "custody" within the meaning of *Miranda* during all questioning and rejected the state's argument that the exigencies of the situation justified Officer Kraft's failure to read respondent his *Miranda* rights until after he had located the gun. The court declined to recognize an exigency exception to the usual requirements of *Miranda* because it found no indication from Officer Kraft's testimony at the suppression hearing that his subjective motivation in asking the question was to protect his own safety or the safety of the public. . . . For the reasons which follow, we believe that this case presents a situation where concern for public safety must be paramount to adherence to the literal language of the prophylactic rules enunciated in *Miranda* . . .

We hold that on these facts there is a "public safety" exception to the requirement that *Miranda* warnings be given before a suspect's answers may be admitted into evidence, and that the availability of that exception does not depend upon the motivation of the individual officers involved. In a kaleidoscopic situation such as the one confronting these officers, where spontaneity rather than adherence to a police manual is necessarily the order of the day, the application of the exception which we recognize today should not be made to depend on *post hoc* findings at a suppression hearing concerning the subjective motivaton of the arresting officer. Undoubtedly most police officers, if placed in Officer Kraft's position, would act out of a host of different, instinctive, and largely unverifiable motives—their own safety, the safety of others, and perhaps as well the desire to obtain incriminating evidence from the suspect.

Whatever the motivation of individual officers in such a situation, we do not believe that the doctrinal underpinnings of *Miranda* require that it be applied in all its rigor to a situation in which police officers ask questions reasonably prompted by a concern for the public safety. The *Miranda* decision was based in large part on this Court's view that the warnings which it required police to give to suspects in custody would reduce the likelihood that the suspects would fall victim to constitutionally impermissible practices of police interrogation in the presumptively coercive environment of the station house. . . .

The police in this case, in the very act of apprehending a suspect, were confronted with the immediate necessity of ascertaining the whereabouts of a gun which they had every reason to believe the suspect had just removed from his empty holster and discarded in the supermarket. So long as the gun was concealed somewhere in the supermarket, with its actual whereabouts unknown, it obviously posed more than one danger to the public safety: an accomplice might make use of it, a customer or employee might later come upon it.

In such a situation, if the police are required to recite the familar *Miranda* warnings before asking the whereabouts of the gun, suspects in Quarles' position might well be deterred from responding. Procedural safeguards which deter a suspect from responding were deemed acceptable in *Miranda* in order to protect the Fifth Amendment privilege; when the primary social cost of those added protections is the possibility of fewer convictions, the *Miranda* majority was willing to bear that cost. Here, had *Miranda* warnings deterred Quarles from responding to Officer Kraft's question about the whereabouts of the gun, the cost would have been something more than merely the failure to obtain evidence useful in convicting Quarles. Officer Kraft needed an answer to his question not simply to make his case against Quarles but to insure that further danger to the public did not result from the concealment of the gun in a public area.

We conclude that the need for answers to questions in a situation posing a threat to the public safety outweighs the need for the prophylactic rule protectng the Fifth Amendment's privilege against self-incrimination. We decline to place officers such as Officer Kraft in the untenable position of having to consider, often in a matter of seconds, whether it best serves society for them to ask the necessary questions without the *Miranda* warnings and render whatever probative evidence they uncover inadmissible, or for them to give the warnings in order to preserve the admissibility of evidence they might uncover but possibly damage or destroy their ability to obtain that evidence and neutralize the volatile situation confronting them. . . .

In recognizing a narrow exception to the *Miranda* rule in this case, we acknowledge that to some degree we lessen the desirable clarity of that rule. . . . The exception will not be difficult for police officers to apply because in each case it will be circumscribed by the exigency which justifies it. We think police officers can and will distinguish almost instinctively between questions necessary to secure their own safety or the safety of the public and questions designed solely to elicit testimonial evidence from a suspect.

The facts of this case clearly demonstrate that distinction and an officer's ability to recognize it. Officer Kraft asked only the question necessary to locate the missing gun before advising respondent of his rights. It was only after securing the loaded revolver and giving the warnings that he continued with investigatory questions about the ownership and place of purchase of the gun. The exception which we recognize today, far from complicating the thought processes and the on-the-scene judgments of police officers, will simply free them to follow their legitimate instincts when confronting situations presenting a danger to the public safety.

We hold that the Court of Appeals in this case erred in excluding the statement, "the gun is over there," and the gun because of the officer's failure to read respondent his *Miranda* rights before attempting to locate the weapon. Accordingly we hold that it also erred in excluding the subsequent statements as illegal fruits of a *Miranda* violation. We therefore reverse and remand for further proceedings not inconsistent with this opinion. . . . ■

OREGON V. ELSTAD*

Justice O'CONNOR delivered the opinion of the Court.

This case requires us to decide whether an initial failure of law enforcement officers to administer the warnings required by *Miranda v. Arizona*, 384 U.S. 436, 86 S.Ct. 1602, 16 L.Ed.2d 694 (1966), without more, "taints" subsequent admissions made after a suspect has been fully advised of and has waived his *Miranda* rights. Respondent, Michael James Elstad, was convicted of burglary by an Oregon trial court. The Oregon Court of Appeals reversed, holding that respondent's signed confession, although voluntary, was rendered inadmissible by a prior remark made in response to questioning without benefit of *Miranda* warnings. We granted certiorari, . . . and we now reverse. . . .

In December, 1981, the home of Mr. and Mrs. Gilbert Gross, in the town of Salem, Polk County, Ore., was burglarized. Missing were art objects and furnishings valued at $150,000. A witness to the burglary contacted the Polk County Sheriff's office, implicating respondent Michael Elstad, an 18-year-old neighbor and friend of the Grosses' teenage son. Thereupon, Officers Burke and McAllister went to the home of respondent Elstad, with a warrant for his arrest. Elstad's mother answered the door. She led the officers to her son's room where he lay on his bed, clad in shorts and listening to his stereo. The officers asked him to get dressed and to accompany them into the living room. Officer McAllister asked respondent's mother to step into the kitchen, where he explained that they had a warrant for her son's arrest for the burglary of a neighbor's residence. Officer Burke remained with Elstad in the living room. He later testified:

> I sat down with Mr. Elstad and I asked him if he was aware of why Detective McAllister and myself were there to talk with him. He stated no, he had no idea why we were there. I then asked him if he knew a person by the name of Gross, and he said yes, he did, and also added that he heard that there was a robbery at the Gross house. And at that point I told Mr. Elstad that I felt he was involved in that, and he looked at me and stated, 'Yes, I was there.'

The officers then escorted Elstad to the back of the patrol car. As they were about to leave for the Polk County Sheriff's office, Elstad's father arrived home and came to the rear of the patrol car. The officers advised him that his son was a suspect in the burglary. Officer Burke testified that Mr. Elstad became quite agitated, opened the rear door of the car and admonished his son: "I told you that you were going to get into trouble. You wouldn't listen to me. You never learn."

Elstad was transported to the Sheriff's headquarters and approximately one hour later, Officers Burke and McAllister joined him in McAllister's office. McAllister then advised respondent for the first time of his *Miranda* rights, reading from a standard card. Respondent indicated he understood his rights, and, hav-

---

ing these rights in mind, wished to speak with the officers. Elstad gave a full statement, explaining that he had known that the Gross family was out of town and had been paid to lead several acquaintances to the Gross resident and show them how to gain entry through a defective sliding glass door. The statement was typed, reviewed by respondent, read back to him for correction, initialed and signed by Elstad and both officers. As an afterthought, Elstad added and initialed the sentence, "After leaving the house Robby & I went back to [the] van & Robby handed me a small bag of grass." . . . Respondent concedes that the officers made no threats or promises either at his residence or at the Sheriff's office.

Respondent was charged with first-degree burglary. He was represented at trial by retained counsel. Elstad waived his right to a jury and his case was tried by a Circuit Court Judge. Respondent moved at once to suppress his oral statement and signed confession. He contended that the statement he made in response to questioning at his house "let the cat out of the bag," . . . and tainted the subsequent confession as "fruit of the poisonous tree." . . . The judge ruled that the statement, "I was there," had to be excluded because the defendant had not been advised of his *Miranda* rights. The written confession taken after Elstad's arrival at the Sheriff's office, however, was admitted in evidence. The court found:

> "[H]is written statement was given freely, voluntarily and knowingly by the defendant after he had waived his right to remain silent and have counsel present which waiver was evidenced by the card which the defendant had signed. [It] was not tainted in any way by the previous brief statement between the defendant and the Sheriff's Deputies that had arrested him."

Elstad was found guilty of burglary in the first degree. He received a 5-year sentence and was ordered to pay $18,000 in restitution.

Following his conviction, respondent appealed to the Oregon Court of Appeals. . . . The Court of Appeals reversed respondent's conviction, identifying the crucial constitutional inquiry as "whether there was a sufficient break in the stream of events between [the] inadmissible statement and the written confession to insulate the latter statement from the effect of what went before." . . .

When police ask questions of a suspect in custody without administering the required warnings, *Miranda* dictates that the answers received be presumed compelled and that they be excluded from evidence at trial in the State's case in chief. The Court has carefully adhered to this principle, permitting a narrow exception only where pressing public safety concerns demanded. See *New York v. Quarles* . . . . The Court today in no way retreats from the bright line rule of *Miranda*. We do not imply that good faith excuses a failure to adminster *Miranda* warnings; nor do we condone inherently coercive police tactics or methods offensive to due process that render the initial admission involuntary and undermine the suspect's will to invoke his rights once they are read to him. A handful of courts has, however, applied our precedents relating to confessions obtained under coercive circumstances to situations involving wholly voluntary admissions, requiring a passage of time or break in events before a second, fully warned statement can be deemed voluntary. Far from establishing a rigid rule, we direct courts to avoid one; there is no warrant for presuming coercive effect where the suspect's initial inculpatory statement, though technically in violation of *Miranda*, was voluntary. The relevant inquiry is whether, in fact, the second statement was also voluntarily made. As in any such inquiry, the finder of fact must examine the surrounding circumstances and the entire course of police conduct with respect to the suspect in evaluating the voluntariness of his statements. The fact that a suspect chooses to speak after being informed of his rights is, of course, highly probative. We find that the dictates of *Miranda* and the goals of the Fifth Amendment proscription against use of compelled testimony are fully satisfied in the circumstances of this case by barring use of the unwarned statement in the case in chief. No further purpose is served by imputing "taint" to subsequent statements obtained pursuant to a voluntary and knowing waiver. We hold today that a suspect who has once responded to unwarned yet uncoercive questioning is not thereby disabled from waiving his rights and confessing after he has been given the requisite *Miranda* warnings.

The judgment of the Court of Appeals of Oregon is reversed, and the case is remanded for further proceedings not inconsistent with this opinion.

It is so ordered.

Justice BRENNAN, with whom Justice MARSHALL joins, dissenting. ■

CHAPTER 4

Civil Rights

Equality, human rights, and political participation were concepts embodied in the Declaration of Independence of 1776. It took another three quarters of a century and a terrible civil war, though, before these ideals were plainly written into the U. S. Constitution (and longer, still, for their implementation).

The Thirteenth, Fourteenth and Fifteenth Amendments—called the Civil War Amendments—were proposed by the post-War Congress and ratified in 1865, 1868, and 1870. The Thirteenth Amendment, at long last, outlawed slavery. The Fifteenth Amendment guaranteed that the right to vote could not be denied by either the federal government or the state governments "on account of race, color, or previous condition of servitude." Sadly, Southern whites were soon permitted, through terrorism and legal barriers, to disenfranchise the newly freed blacks (and rigidly segregate them, too). Not until passage, nearly a century later, of the Voting Rights Act of 1965 was the voting guarantee really implemented for black people—and for many U.S. Hispanics, as well.

The Fourteenth Amendment dealt, first, with citizenship, reversing the Supreme Court holding in the prewar *Dred Scott* case that black people were never intended to be citizens. The Amendment states that "All persons born or naturalized in the United States and subject to the jurisdiction thereof, are citizens of the United States and the State wherein they reside." The Amendment declares that no state can abridge the "privileges and immunities" of a U.S. citizen—cannot, it has been held, for example, restrict free travel within the country. Like the Fifth Amendment, intended originally to restrict only the federal government, the Fourteenth Amendment also provides that states, too, cannot "deprive any person of life, liberty, or property, without the due process of law."

Finally, the Fourteenth Amendment declares that no state can "deny to

importance

any person within its jurisdiction the equal protection of the laws." This Equal Protection Clause was eventually to become the constitutional basis of the black civil rights movement and the advances toward legal and political equality finally won by black people—in the courts and in the Congress—in the 1950s and 1960s.

The Equal Protection Clause was to become the rallying point for other groups, too. More than that, it was to become the basis for more general claims to "equality," including, for example, the right to representative districts of substantially equal population.

In this chapter, we will focus on the concept of equality in general, desegregation and civil rights, affirmative action, women and equal pay, and, finally, reapportionment.

EQUALITY

First, we consider the legal applications of the concept of equality for a wide range of American groups, from blacks to women to the disabled, with excerpts from a recent book, *Equality Under the Constitution: Reclaiming the Fourteenth Amendment* by Judith A. Baer. Then, we will turn to an article, excerpted here, by political scientists Sidney Verba and Gary R. Orren, which deals with what American leaders think about the concept of equality—economic equality, political equality, and group equality—and how what leaders think can limit what government does.

EQUALITY UNDER THE CONSTITUTION
Judith A. Baer

"The nation was born with the word on its tongue." Thus one historian wrote of the idea of equality in America. "The first of those 'self-evident truths' of the Declaration was that 'all men are created equal.' Back of that was the heritage of natural rights doctrine, and back of that the great body of Christian dogma and the teaching that all men are equal in the sight of God." But equality has never been a given in American life. Those egalitarian doctrines have coexisted with inegalitarian ideas and practices; coexisted not only in the same country but in the same mind. Thomas Jefferson, for instance, wrote not only the Declaration of Independence, but also of his "suspicion" that "the blacks . . . are inferior to the whites in the endowments both of body and mind." Law has often

---

1. C. Vann Woodward, *The Burden of Southern History* (Baton Rouge: Louisiana State Unviersity Press, 1960), p. 75.

reflected such beliefs, the most notorious example being the institution of slavery. Battle after battle—literal and figurative—has been fought for equality under law, and equality has not always won.

The longest and bitterest fight has been the movement for racial equality. Its first stage, the drive to abolish slavery, culminated in a civil war and three amendments to the Constitution. One of these amendments, the Fourteenth, contains the one explicit constitutional guarantee of equality: that "no state shall . . . deny to any person within its jurisdiction the equal protection of the laws." Since the amendment was ratified in 1868, this clause has become a powerful guarantee of racial equality and a bulwark for ethnic and religious minorities. It has been an effective, though limited, tool in the revival of a long-moribund movement for women's right, and to a lesser extent has served aliens and the poor. . . .

We have long been conscious of racial and sexual inequalities, but now attention focuses on groups distinguishable by such traits as age, disability, and sexual orientation. The old, the young, the handicapped, and homosexuals have become more and more active in their own interests. All have made some gains and suffered some losses, both legislative and judicial. . . .

None of these groups enjoys full equality under law. Somehow handicapped people, homosexuals, and old or even middle-aged people are not protected against employment discrimination as blacks and women are . . .

One general argument for equality is that it is unjust to impose discriminations on all members of a class on the basis of generalizations about them, without regard to individual differences within the class. This argument insists both that those who differ—that is, the members and nonmembers of a class—must be treated alike, and, curiously enough, the very opposite: that those who are alike—that is, all the members of a class—should, in some instances, be treated differently. By this reasoning, for example, even if men, on the average, have greater muscular strength than women, laws that prohibit all women from doing heavy work are unjust because many women are in fact stronger than many men. A second general argument is that certian human characteristics are virtually never legitimate bases for legal distinctions, under any circumstances. Such an argument is frequently made about race and increasingly about sex as well.

One limited argument for equality is that there are certain fundamental human rights of which no one may justly be deprived, even a class of people generally subject to discrimination. For example, the principle that allows us to deny drivers' licenses to the severely disabled would not justify us in depriving them of the right to vote. The fourth and final argument for equality is, to use Marshall's terminology, the assertion that a difference, real as it may be, is not relevant to the particular discrimination at issue. Thus one argument advanced for sexual equality is that differences in reproductive functions have no relationship to ability to work, to earn a just wage, or to assume the responsibilities of citizenship. . . .

The equal-protection clause has been interpreted to make certain kinds of discrimination inherently suspect, and thus tenable only on demonstration of a compelling justification for them. Race, ethnic background, and religion have been ruled suspect classifications, and some judges would treat alienage and sex this way as well.

. . . The Constitution has been read to establish a "floor" or guaranteed minimum level of equality, consisting of certain basic rights that must be granted to all. Thus juveniles may not be deprived of certain procedural rights, nor may they lose all freedom of expression. Indigent people must have the right to counsel, a trial transcript, and a divorce. Homosexuals have not forfeited their First Amendment freedoms.

But other decisions . . . leave some doubt as to how solid the floor is. The rights just mentioned are ranked, explicitly or implicitly, as fundmental, but the right to an education and the right to file for bankruptcy are not. And as we have seen, trial by jury is not among the rights granted to juveniles, and the principle that prohibits school suspensions without a hearing does not extend to corporal punishment. . . .

To sum up, there are basically three kinds of differential treatment that run afoul of the Fourteenth Amendment. First, a law that lacks a close enough relationship to a good enough governmental purpose is invalid. How close is close enough varies. A law that makes arbitrary or capricious distinctions will virtually always fall, whatever the basis for the distinctions; laws that make gender-based discriminations, however, will stand if they "serve important governmental objectives" and are substantially related to achievement of these objectives. Second, a distinction that violates a fundamental right will fall, unless a compelling justification for it can be shown. Finally, certain kinds of classifications, such as those based on race, are inherently suspect and tenable only if they meet the same strict standard.

What, or whom, do these categories leave out? They exclude whatever is defined out of them: interests, such as welfare benefits or an education, which are not ranked as fundamental rights; distinctions, such as those between widows and widowers in regard to property taxes, which courts regard as relevant to a legitimate end; classifications, such as economic status or disability, not regarded as inherently suspect. . . . ■

EQUALITY AND LEADERSHIP OPINION
Sidney Verba and Gary R. Orren

To understand what Americans think about equality we surveyed a substantial sample of leaders from varied segments of American society. We chose leaders rather than average citizens, because they set the terms of public debate and play a significant role in determining public policy. The leaders we surveyed included top executives and labor leaders, as well as leaders of the major farm organizations. We also surveyed leaders of civil rights and feminist organizations in order to sample groups that challenge the system. And we included intellectuals, leaders of both political parties, leaders from the media, and a sample of future leaders—

students from prestigious colleges. The leaders' views, in fact, encompass the full range of American opinion that is not beyond the fringe. . . .

Those in the leadership study who hold conservative ideologies about equality are likely to enjoy established and privileged positions, which they want to protect. Those who would supplant the existing distribution with a more equal one generally come from those segments of society most likely to benefit. But the clash over equality entails much more. It is also a clash over ideas, over the nature of a just society. And much as cynics may doubt it, the idea of what is just does not merely reflect what is self-serving. . . .

Three areas of struggle for equal treatment and equal position illustrate the different barriers that both channel that struggle and keep it alive: the conflicts over economic equality, over political equality, and among groups—especially racial and gender groups. In the political domain, Americans cannot decide who has power; in the economic domain they cannot decide who should have wealth. The groups face a reckoning of a different sort: they must decide whether they want to be equal as members of a group or as individuals.

ECONOMIC EQUALITY

Nearly all issues of equality have an economic component. If income were equal across individuals, it would also be equal between blacks and whites, men and women. Furthermore, the main threat to political equality, the inequality of individual resources, would be eliminated. Income equality might be the key to equality in general, but it is unlikely to be achieved. Americans of every political stripe accept the premises of the capitalist system. They agree that rewards should be based on success in the competitive market; the distribution of wealth should be based on skill and effort. This belief system judges the competitive market to be highly egalitarian, and capitalism's compatibility with equality partly explains its attraction in America. The market is deemed egalitarian because it judges everyone in the same way—by how well they compete—with no reference to characteristics such as race or gender. Champions of the market as an indispensable adjunct to democracy argue rightly that it rejects the structured hierarchies of closed systems like feudalism. In practice, however, the market system, even in its own terms, is less than egalitarian. Opportunities are far from equal. Those who win at first are at a distinct advantage in further play. But the underlying premise that rewards can be widely disparate yet fair is generally accepted.

The findings of our leadership study are that some groups want more income equality, but almost none wants complete equality. Equality of results has few proponents among American leaders. Nor does any group want the government to put a ceiling on income. The most telling indication of this consensus against radical equalization occurs in attitudes toward income distribution. For example, even the group with the most egalitarian view of income considers a ratio of more than eight to one between the incomes of a top executive and an unskilled worker to be legitimate. Public opinion surveys similarly reveal little support for radical redistribution. These views are consistent with the income distribution that actually prevails. The United States is a far remove from the level of equality that has been achieved in many other industrialized democracies. Furthermore, income distribution in the United States has been remarkably stable for a long time. The consensus against redistribution hampers any radical movement toward greater equality.

Even though most leaders and citizens accept and even favor fairly wide income disparities, the United States might be pushed toward greater equality if a small and articulate vanguard of leaders held more radically redistributionist views. But there is no such group. Even among feminist, black, union, and Democratic party leaders—the leaders most critical of the current distribution in the United States—radical views are few. Such views are strikingly absent even among the members of these groups who consider themselves to be "far left" or "very liberal." . . .

The broad consensus against radical redistribution also affects actual earnings through its effect on public policy. It is not that there is no controversy over public policies relating to equality, but the consensus sets the boundaries of that controversy. The controversy exists despite Americans' ideological acceptance of the market system, because the market is imperfectly egalitarian, even in its own terms. All may begin at the same place with equal opportunity, but those who succeed in the first round will parlay that success into second-round advantages for themselves or their children. This is where politics enters the picture. Those who are successful in the market can then use their new wealth to protect their gains. Success is converted into privilege through laws that favor the accumulation of wealth, such as tax programs that are generous in their treatment of capital gains or inheritances.

The market, moreover, has never been fully open and free. Despite Americans' individualistic ideology, competition has often been limited through discrimination. Blacks and women are the most obvious examples, but other groups have suffered as well. The group that is denied an equal start in the race labors under a severe handicap.

The market's failure to live up to its own ideals fuels policy controversy. The agreement among leaders on the market norm of equality of opportunity carries with it a good deal of disagreement over the extent to which the United States lives up to that norm and, in turn, the extent to which the government should interfere with the workings of the market. The policy controversy, however, remains within bounds set by the broad value consensus. The American public largely accepts a government-supported floor under income, but only so long as the floor consists of a government guarantee of a job so one can earn that minimum. American leaders, even the most egalitarian ones, similarly opt for measures to increase equality that are consistent with the norm of opportunity. . . .

In sum, a turn toward a more radical economic egalitarianism in the United States is unlikely, because it would go against widely held values.

POLITICAL EQUALITY

The obstacles to political equality are different from, but no less significant than, those constraining economic equality. One obstacle is the mutual reinforcement of economic and political inequality; money is converted into political influence. . . . Economic equality is hard to achieve, both because few want it and because those who want it least have the most say. This in turn affects the political system, as economic inequality becomes political inequality, which makes the antiredistributionists more politically potent—thereby closing the circle.

In politics the norm is more egalitarian. Traditionally, Americans object more to differing levels of political influence than to differing levels of affluence. Violations of a one-person, one-vote rule or gross variations across individuals in campaign contributions are offensive. Americans have tried to limit these inequities by law. If they cannot and do not want to equalize income as a means of equalizing political influence, perhaps the solution is to insulate politics from economic inequalities—to keep politics, in Walzer's terminology, in its proper "sphere of justice." This is, in a sense, the logic behind laws eliminating the poll tax or limiting each citizen, rich or poor, to one vote. As the Supreme Court put it in declaring the poll tax unconstitutional, a state "violates the Equal Protection Clause of the Fourteenth Amendment whenever it makes the affluence of the voter or the payment of any fee an electoral standard. Voter qualification has no relation to wealth nor to paying or not paying this or any other tax."

Equalization of political influence by severing its connection to economic resources may be a more promising approach than attempting to establish political equality on a base of economic equality. This insulation might in turn bring about greater economic equality. If the polity were equal—if no bias were built into the system in favor of the affluent—more extensive governmental intervention aimed at economic equality might then follow. . . .

Such insulation, however, is probably impossible. Given the wide disparity of economic resources, they cannot easily be prevented from leaking into the political realm. A transfer of economic resources into politics can take place directly or indirectly. Direct transfer is hard to control; indirect is even harder. Consider the direct use of economic resources in politics:

Income/wealth → Political influence

This takes place when an individual spends money on election campaigns or in other ways directly employs economic resources to influence political outcomes. Controlling such use of money is daunting. In the first place, appropriate legislation is hard to pass, and once passed, it is often ineffective. The Campaign Finance Act, for instance, was slow in coming and mixed in result. In the second place, controls on the use of money in politics may run up against the First Amendment. Witness the Supreme Court's decision allowing individuals to spend freely on their own to support candidates. . . .

Although direct controls over spending may be hard to achieve, they are much easier than controlling the indirect effect of unequal resources. The wealthy are more likely to be highly educated, to be informed about political matters, to feel that they can influence politics, and to be acquainted with people in politics or in the media. They have, in short, more resources and stronger motivation than do the less affluent. The effect is indirect:

Income/wealth → Education /skills/motivation → Political influence

The assets found among politically influential citizens, including money, education, political involvement, information, a sense of competence, and connections, are linked: wealth buys education, which fosters motivation that leads to acquiring information, and so on. Public policies could help to equalize matters by bestowing some of these assets upon the less affluent. Such policies might include free public higher education, campaigns to increase citizen motivation and awareness, open public hearings, ombudspersons, and poverty lawyers. These policies might help motivate some people who would otherwise be inactive and might instill political activism in those at lower levels of motivation and resources. It is unlikely, though, that they would fully redress the imbalance. . . .

All this saps the practical effect of the norm of equality in politics. In the economic sphere equality is seen as opportunity, and the result is stratification in wealth and income. Equality in the political sphere, in turn, cannot defend itself from the effects of economic inequality. As long as wide disparities in economic position are legitimate and individuals are free to participate in politics, the translation of economic advantage into political advantage will be hard to limit.

A further obstacle to insulating politics from economic inequality is the unevenness of perceptions. In the absence of a metric for determining who has most political influence, the exact degree of inequality in the political system remains unclear. In the few cases where inequality is noticeable and measurable, there may be attempts to eliminate it. As Robert Dahl has pointed out, Americans would be outraged if asked to accept a three-tier system of voting as in pre-World War I Prussia, where the value of the vote varied sharply across social strata. Similarly, gross disparities in campaign contributions, because they are observable, are subject to egalitarian attention. After these inequities had become especially blatant around the time of Watergate, attempts were made to reduce them. However, political activity and influence assume a myriad of forms, some more visible than others. Differences in political influence are easily obscured and, therefore, likely to be overlooked.

This means that political equality is elusive even if all agree that it is desirable. Each group would find the others' definition of an equitable distribution to be quite unfair. For instance, labor and business might agree that America should move closer to the goal of equal political influence but they would march off in opposite directions. Furthermore, we find that the inconsistent perceptions across groups are not fully symmetrical. They tend to be biased against the disadvantaged. The more established groups, especially business, rely on less overt forms of political activity which they may not even consider to be political. Though more politically active, they tend to be less visible in their activity than the disadvantaged groups. They are thus more likely than other groups to underestimate their own influence. Less advantaged groups, lacking routine inside channels, engage in more conspicuous activity. Thus, whatever influence they have is fully acknowledged and perhaps overestimated. Business, for example, considers consumer groups to be more influential than business. . . .

GROUP EQUALITY

Neither the economic nor the political route to equality is promising. But there is another route. The drive for equality in America has been more intense when more narrowly directed toward specific groups. Here there is a passion for equality unlike the ambivalence associated with the drive for economic equality. The strength of campaigns for equality by particular groups and the weakness of more general movements for income equality are not unrelated. Equality in America has by definition always involved equality among individuals in the opportunities open to them. Furthermore, class conflict based on economic position has never been as pronounced as conflict based on other social characteristics, such as race or ethnicity. This suggests that Americans think in terms of both individuals and groups. Indeed, the two modes of thought about equality are not contradictory. The serious group-based conflicts in the United States, whether on grounds of race, ethnicity, religion, region, or more recently gender, have crosscut economic differences. In this way, they have diminished the importance of class as an organizing principle of social conflict. Thus, economic equality is relegated more to individual than to class competition. . . .

If the drive for equality continues, it may come from an alliance of disadvantaged minorities rather than from a broad majority of the less affluent. An alliance of equality-oriented minorities, each with its own agenda, seems more workable than an equality-oriented coalition including the less affluent 51 percent of the population. The less affluent coalition would be so diverse in other ways, and indeed in income, that it would lack sufficient cohesiveness and motivation to be effective.

But the prospects for an alliance of disadvantaged groups, each with its own grievance somehow related to equality, are mixed. The three challenging groups in our leadership study—blacks, feminists, and labor—each representing different equality constituencies, could together form a general equality coalition; indeed they already function as such on many issues. The concerns that bind them together tend to be economic. The three groups are close in their support of New Deal policies. They cluster together in favor of a more egalitarian distribution of income across occupations. When economic controversies arise, such as those over the Reagan administration's proposed tax changes or cuts in social welfare programs, these groups can be expected to line up together.

As an equality coalition, however, these groups have weaknesses. For one thing, each has its own set of priorities. Economic issues hold them together, but on core issues, the alliance disintegrates. Blacks rate racial equality just below jobs in importance, much higher than do the other groups. Labor puts racial equality quite far down on its list, below crime reduction, national defense, and other issues. Feminists rank racial equality higher than does labor but closer to the middle than to the top of the list. As for gender equality, blacks and union leaders rank it near the bottom of their priorities. In sum, an equality coalition might be held together by economic concerns, but because the equality issues that animate blacks and feminists differ, they are not effective political adhesives. . . .

One organization that is in a strategic position to assemble an equality coalition is the Democratic party. The several egalitarian interest groups are all overwhelmingly committed to the Democratic party. Moreover, the major parties are hardly identical on the issue of equality. Even if they offer no coherent ideologies opposed to one another, differences on equality appear at all party levels—among organizational leaders, elected officials, partisan identifiers, and voters. The differences are confirmed in opinion surveys, official platforms, and congressional voting. And they cut across the equality domains of race, gender, and economic well-being.

In this sense, equality appears on the public agenda as a thoroughly partisan issue. There are substantial differences between the two parties. . . .

The Democratic position is complicated by the fact that the positions of the groups allied to it are quite inconsistent one with another across the other equality issues. In particular, labor divides from blacks and feminists on race issues, while both blacks and labor divide from feminists on gender issues. This makes it difficult for Democratic leaders to take positions that satisfy their disparate allies. Furthermore, on these two concerns, the majority of Democratic supporters are in fact closer to the Republican leaders than to the Democrats.

In all three equality domains, then, the positions of Democratic leaders are quite distinct from those of Republican leaders. In this sense the parties do offer alternatives to the public. But the range of these alternatives is restricted, particularly in the economic realm. Furthermore, an equality coalition in the Democratic party would be a most uneasy one, with the allied groups pursuing divergent equality agendas.

CONCLUSION

At first blush, the American ideology toward equality appears straightforward. It does not take an Alexis de Tocqueville or a Gunnar Myrdal to ascertain that the nation is fundamentally concerned with equality. Americans approve of equality and actively seek it through the powers of the state and the actions of individuals. It is the *form* of equality that arouses debate. For a nation so taken with equality, there is a striking degree of contention over the goal. Americans can agree on equality only by disagreeing on what it means. . .

The future wil doubtless bring more conflict but little more equality. There is no relentless march to the perfectly egalitarian society, for there can be no such society. As Samuel Huntington has observed, to have faith in all forms of equality is incoherent. Yet Americans do not have an ideology that assigns clear priority to one value over any other. At every historical juncture where equality was an issue, its proponents failed to do all that they had set out to do. By the same token, the swell of conservatism embodied in the Reagan administration will find its limits too. Swings in the equality of social conditions are restrained not just by institutional obstacles but by fundamental conflicts of values that are a traditional element of American politics. Faith in the individualistic work ethic and belief in the legitimacy of unequal wealth retard progression to the egalitarian left. As for contemporary conservatism, the indelible tenet of political equality firmly restrains the right. A swing to the right does not eliminate America's commitment to the disadvantaged. In seeking equal opportunity over equal result, Americans forego a ceiling, not a floor. Americans may amend the uneven distribution of affluence and influence, but they will not abolish it. Intense conflict within narrow confines will remain the hallmark of the American politics of equality. ∎

DESEGREGATION AND CIVIL RIGHTS

The first major breakthrough for American black people in their long struggle for equality came with the 1954 U.S. Supreme Court decision in the landmark case of *Brown* v. *Board of Education of Topeka*.[2]

Prior to the *Brown* decision, the Supreme Court had followed the doctrine, as announced in the 1896 case of *Plessy* v. *Ferguson,*[3] that the Equal
Protection Clause of the Fourteenth Amendment did not prohibit states from
segregating black people in so-called "separate but equal" schools and other
public facilities.

In the *Brown* case, in a unanimous opinion written by Chief Justice Earl
Warren, the Supreme Court reversed the holding in the *Plessy* case and, using social science findings for saying so, declared that so-called "separate
but equal" facilities are "inherently unequal" and damaging for black people —
and, therefore, violate the Equal Protection Clause.

After this holding, the Supreme Court, in a later appeal involving the
same case, ordered the states to desegregate the schools "with all deliberate
speed." These rulings were bitterly opposed by segregationist officials and
other white people in the South. President Dwight Eisenhower ordered the
use of federal troops to enforce desegration in Little Rock, Arkansas. Later
Supreme Court decisions upheld lower court orders for busing as one means
of ending purposeful school segregation. "Busing to achieve racial balance"
in the schools sparked white opposition in the North, as well as in the South.

Little by little, the political and legal barriers to equality for black people in America began to come down. Other groups — first, American Indians,
Hispanics, and women, and, then, disabled people, older people, homosexuals, and others — followed the example of the black civil rights movement.

The *Brown* case (actually several cases were involved) had been brought
by the NAACP Legal Defense and Education Fund. The lawyer for the black
plaintiffs was Thurgood Marshall, later himself appointed by President Lyndon Johnson as a member of the Supreme Court.

Here, after the excerpt from the *Brown* opinion, we have included, in
part, some public remarks by Los Angeles Mayor Tom Bradley on the occasion of the thirtieth anniversary of the decision. Mayor Bradley says *Brown*
was a great milestone, not just in regard to desegration of public schools,
but for civil rights advances generally. On the other hand, former U.S.
Representative Barbara Jordan of Texas, now a professor, in an article reprinted
from the American Bar Association's *Human Rights* magazine, expresses her
concern that some resegregation has resulted from the policies of the Reagan
Administration.

---

2. 347 U.S. 483 (1954).
3. 163 U.S. 537 (1896).

BROWN V. BOARD OF EDUCATION OF TOPEKA*

MR. CHIEF JUSTICE WARREN delivered the opinion of the Court.

These cases come to us from the States of Kansas, South Carolina, Virginia, and Delaware. They are premised on different facts and different local conditions, but a common legal question justifies their consideration together in this consolidated opinion.

In each of the cases, minors of the Negro race, through their legal representatives, seek the aid of the courts in obtaining admission to the public schools of their community on a nonsegregated basis. In each instance, they had been denied admission to schools attended by white children under laws requiring or permitting segregation according to race. This segregation was alleged to deprive the plaintiffs of the equal protection of the laws under the Fourteenth Amendment. In each of the cases, . . . a three-judge federal district court denied relief to the plaintiffs on the so-called "separate by equal" doctrine announced by this Court in *Plessy* v. *Ferguson*, 163 U.S. 537. Under that doctrine, equality of treatment is accorded when the races are provided substantially equal facilities, even though these facilities be separate. . . .

The plaintiffs contend that segregated public schools are not "equal" and cannot be made "equal," and that hence they are deprived of the equal protection of the laws. Because of the obvious importance of the question presented, the Court took jurisdiction. Argument was heard in the 1952 Term, and reargument was heard this Term on certain questions propounded by the Court.

Reargument was largely devoted to the circumstances surrounding the adoption of the Fourteenth Amendment in 1868. It covered exhaustively consideration of the Amendment in Congress, ratification by the states, then existing practices in racial segregation, and the views of proponents and opponents of the Amendment. This discussion and our own investigation convince us that, although these sources cast some light, it is not enough to resolve the problem with which we are faced. At best, they are inconclusive. The most avid proponents of the post-War Amendments undoubtedly intended them to remove all legal distinctions among "all persons born or naturalized in the United States." Their opponents, just as certainly, were antagonistic to both the letter and the spirit of the Amendments and wished them to have the most limited effect. What others in Congress and the state legislatures had in mind cannot be determined with any degree of certainty.

An additional reason for the inconclusive nature of the Amendment's history, with respect to segregated schools, is the status of public education at that time. In the South, the movement toward free common schools, supported by general

---

* 347 U.S. 483 (1954).

taxation, had not yet taken hold. Education of white children was largely in the hands of private groups. Education of Negroes was almost nonexistent, and practically all of the race were illiterate. In fact, any education of Negroes was forbidden by law in some states. Today, in contrast, many Negroes have achieved outstanding success in the arts and sciences as well as in the business and professional world. It is true that public school education at the time of the Amendment had advanced further in the North, but the effect of the Amendment on Northern States was generally ignored in the congressional debates. Even in the North, the conditions of public education did not approximate those existing today. The curriculum was usually rudimentary; ungraded schools were common in rural areas; the school term was but three months a year in many states; and compulsory school attendance was virtually unknown. As a consequence, it is not surprising that there should be so little in the history of the Fourteenth Amendment relating to its intended effect on public education.

In the first cases in this Court construing the Fourteenth Amendment, decided shortly after its adoption, the Court interpreted it as proscribing all state-imposed discriminations against the Negro race. The doctrine of "separate but equal" did not make its appearance in this Court until 1896 in the case of *Plessy* v. *Ferguson*, *supra,* involving not education but transportation. American courts have since labored with the doctrine for over half a century. In this Court, there have been six cases involving the "separate but equal" doctrine in the field of public education. In *Cumming* v. *County Board of Education,* 175 U.S. 528, and *Gong Lum* v. *Rice,* 275 U.S. 78, the validity of the doctrine itself was not challenged. In more recent cases, all on the graduate school level, inequality was found in that specific benefits enjoyed by white students were denied to Negro students of the same educational qualifications. *Missouri ex rel. Gaines* v. *Canada,* 305 U.S. 337; *Sipuel* v. *Oklahoma,* 332 U.S. 631; *Sweatt* v. *Painter,* 339 U.S. 629; *McLaurin* v. *Oklahoma State Regents,* 339 U.S. 637. In none of these cases was it necessary to re-examine the doctrine to grant relief to the Negro plaintiff. And in *Sweatt* v. *Painter, supra,* the Court expressly reserved decision on the question whether *Plessy* v. *Ferguson* should be held inapplicable to public education.

In the instant cases, that question is directly presented. Here, unlike *Sweatt* v. *Painter,* there are findings below that the Negro and white schools involved have been equalized, or are being equalized, with respect to buildings, curricula, qualifications and salaries of teachers, and other "tangible" factors. Our decision, therefore, cannot turn on merely a comparison of these tangible factors in the Negro and white schools involved in each of the cases. We must look instead to the effect of segregation itself on public education.

In approaching this problem, we cannot turn the clock back to 1868 when the Amendment was adopted, or even to 1896 when *Plessy* v. *Ferguson* was written. We must consider public education in the light of its full development and its present place in American life throughout the Nation. Only in this way can it be determined if segregation in public schools deprives these plaintiffs of the equal protection of the laws.

Today, education is perhaps the most important function of state and local governments. Compulsory school attendance laws and the great expenditures for education both demonstrate our recognition of the importance of education to our democratic society. It is required in the performance of our most basic public responsibilities, even service in the armed forces. It is the very foundation of good citizenship. Today it is a principal instrument in awakening the child to cultural values, in preparing him for later professional training, and in helping him to adjust normally to his environment. In these days, it is doubtful that any child may reasonably be expected to succeed in life if he is denied the opportunity of an edcuation. Such an opportunity, where the state has undertaken to provide it, is a right which must be made available to all on equal terms.

We come then to the question presented: Does segregation of children in public schools solely on the basis of race, even though the physical facilities and other "tangible" factors may be equal, deprive the children of the minority group of equal educational opportunities? We believe that it does.

In *Sweatt* v. *Painter, supra,* in finding that a segregated law school for Negroes could not provide them equal educational opportunities, this Court relied in large part on "those qualities which are incapable of objective measurement but which make for greatness in a law school." In *McLaurin* v. *Oklahoma State Regents, supra,* the Court, in requiring that a Negro admitted to a white graduate school be treated like all other students, again resorted to intangible considerations: ". . . his ability to study, to engage in discussions and exchange views with other students, and, in general, to learn his profession." Such considerations apply with added force to children in grade and high schools. To separate them from others of similar age and qualifications solely because of their race generates a feeling of inferiority as to their status in the community that may affect their hearts and minds in a way unlikely ever to be undone. The effect of this separation of their educational opportunities was well stated by a finding in the Kansas case by a court which nevertheless felt compelled to rule against the Negro plaintiffs:

> Segregation of white and colored children in public schools has a detrimental effect upon the colored children. The impact is greater when it has the sanction of the law; for the policy of separating the races is usually interpreted as denoting the inferiority of the negro group. A sense of inferiority affects the motivation of a child to learn. Segregation with the sanction of law, therefore, has a tendency to [retard] the educational and mental development of negro children and to deprive them of some of the benefits they would receive in a racial[ly] integrated school system.

Whatever may have been the extent of psychological knowledge at the time of *Plessy* v. *Ferguson*, this finding is amply supported by modern authority. Any language in *Plessy* v. *Ferguson* contrary to this finding is rejected.

We conclude that in the field of public education the doctrine of "separate but equal" has no place. Separate educational facilities are inherently unequal. Therefore, we hold that the plaintiffs and others similarly situated for whom the actions have been brought are, by reason of the segregation complained of, deprived of the equal protecion of the laws guaranteed by the Fourteenth Amendment. This disposition makes unnecessary any discussion whether such segregation also violates the Due Process Clause of the Fourteenth Amendment. . . .   ■

BROWN WAS A MAJOR BREAKTHROUGH
Tom Bradley

Brown represented that first major breakthrough, changing the constitutional interpretation that made possible the legal decisions that followed. Things that today we take for granted could not have been possible before that decision.

In 1953 I bought an automobile in Lansing, Michigan, and drove back across the country. Topeka, Kansas, ironically, was my first stop, because nobody would rent me a motel room on the way. So I drove night and day until I got there and I was able to sleep in the home of some of the kind residents of that city.

Today we take for granted the right to eat in a restaurant, to stay in a beautiful hotel. But it wasn't possible before the Brown decision. All of us here tonight can thank those who were involved in the Brown case for bringing about the major breakthrough for so many other civil rights decisions that were to follow.

I can scarcely call the full roll of all those who were involved in achieving the impact of this great decision. It signaled to the community of black Americans, and all who were trapped in the vicious cycle of inequality, of bigotry, of poverty and deprivation, the long-deferred committment to racial equality in the United States. The Brown decision marked a milestone on the road to realizing that dream.

The occasion we celebrate here tonight from the perspective of thirty years' struggle to achieve full justice for all of our citizens was not the beginning of the end, to paraphrase Winston Churchill, it was the end of the beginning.

We have traveled quite a distance together as Americans in these thirty years, and achieved more in this period of time than in any comparable period in the history of this nation. I don't mean to suggest that we have achieved all that we set out to achieve nor all that we hoped to achieve. But, my friends, we've come a long way in these thirty years.

I often tell young people that you cannot measure history by what has happened in the past year. You have to look back over a longer period of time. You cannot look with me over the course of the last thirty years and say that we have not made tremendous strides in this nation.

The passage of the Voting Rights Act in 1964, for example, found us with only five hundred blacks holding public office in the entire country, with little hope of achieving any more. With the passage of the Act, new hope was given to blacks all over this nation, progress began, and today we have over 2,500 people holding public office in this nation who happen to be black. There are so many mayors that we can't begin to count them. One of these days we are going to have a governor. . . .   ■

IS RESEGREGATION OCCURRING?
Barbara Jordan

It is clear that in 1985 relations between black people and white people are not faring well. We have seen almost a resegregation in the two societies.

This should come as no surprise. We were warned about this many years ago in the Kerner Commission Report, which stated that this country was in danger of dividing into two nations—one black, one white.

And here, 20 years later, it seems that black people are building fences around themselves and their concerns, while white people are building separate fences. I often wonder whether the two races will ever mix and whether we will ever believe that society and, indeed, the Constitution of the United States is truly color blind.

We are facing another danger today—one that threatens to undo the victories won in the civil rights revolution. We are having to address issues we once thought were already settled:

• Segregation in our public schools might have been attacked in *Brown* v. *Board of Education,* but the same problem continues 31 years later. We have a new phenomenon in education today. It's called segregation by classification.

Unless we fight this new form of segregation, we will have lost all that we gained from *Brown*. This is an issue that we cannot afford to lose. The schools remain the bulwark for getting out of the vise of welfare and poverty and the cyclical degradation we feel.

• There is the issue of voting rights. Many felt that with the passage of the 1965 Voting Rights Act there would no longer be a necessity for anyone to take any definitive or positive action to ensure that black people and all people would have a right to vote. The law should have taken care of it.

It should have, but there have been people in different jurisdictions who have maneuvered to try to circumvent the basis of voting rights. There have been those who will indulge in schemes like the at-large system to dilute the power of the ballot.

It was like pulling eyeteeth to get the current Justice Department and this Administration to support amendments to the Voting Rights Act in 1982 and to support its re-enactment. We must see to it that the Act continues to be honored and that people who want to vote are able to vote.

- In 1964, Title VII of the Civil Rights Act was passed, which declared that discrimination in employment on the basis of race, color, or sex is prohibited. Shortly after that, affirmative action programs were approved, which guaranteed that minorities would have a chance at the jobs that previously had been denied.

Today we have an administration in Washington saying that affirmative action isn't working and needs to be modified, yet it has not come up with a viable alternative. We are now fighting to hold on to the gains we thought had finally been won.

Affirmative action programs are not loved by this administration, but to say that we must re-do a program like this is more than any people should have to bear, especially people who are interested in justice and fairness.

- Consider the Civil Rights Commission, established in 1957 under Dwight Eisenhower. It was once an independent, bipartisan, fact-finding commission. Today it has lost that independence.

The Reagan administration would like the commission to adopt its conservative philosophies. To that end, Clarence Pendleton was appointed by the president as chairman of the commission. Pendleton has made statements about the leadership of the black community and has managed to alienate practically every thinking black person in this country.

So, considering the state of race relations today, is it safe to assume that we are moving again into two nations—one black, one white? I would like to think not. I would like to think that we are going through a period of retrenchment, that it is only temporary, and that with proper funding, proper resources, we will be able to stand up against resegregation, attempts to weaken our affirmative action programs, and attempts to eliminate other victories earned in the civil rights revolution.

I want to know that at some point in my life, we all will stand and as one gigantic chorus say: This is the land of opportunity; there is freedom and justice for everybody; and we are truly one nation under God, indivisible, with liberty and justice for all. ■

AFFIRMATIVE ACTION

Congress passed the Civil Rights Act of 1964 to mandate the desegregation of public accommodations and to require "affirmative action" to assist women, black people, and other minorities to catch up with those who had not been so discriminated against in the past. As a result of federal requirements, great strides were made by disadvantaged groups.

With changes in the membership of the Supreme Court and with the inauguration of President Ronald Reagan, affirmative action began to come the 1978 case of *Regents of the University of California* v. ...urt ruled (in two separate majority opinions, with Justice Lewis ...ng first with four liberals and then with four conservatives) that, ...ofessional schools can use affirmative action principles and consider ...r sex as one of a number of criteria for admission, they may not set ...tas. In 1984, the Court invalidated a consent decree under which white ...refighters were laid off when the otherwise applicable seniority system would have called for the layoff of black employees with less seniority.[5] That same year, the Court also ruled that the fact that a higher education institution takes advantage of one program involving federal funds does not mean that the school must be in institution-wide compliance with federal affirmative action requirements.[6]

Justice Department officials and the Civil Rights Commission appointed by President Reagan dragged their feet on, or opposed outright, new and extensive civil rights legislation, as well as vigorous enforcement of affirmative action principles.[7]

One argument about affirmative action was whether the concept required equality of opportunity or equality of results. Clarence M. Pendleton, Jr., the controversial black Chairman of the U.S. Civil Rights Commission, appointed by President Reagan, says in the article excerpted here that opportunity is enough. On the other hand, the article written by Dorglas Huron, a lawyer who served on President Carter's staff and, earlier, in th' Justice Department's Civil Rights Division, calls for equality of results.

EQUALITY OF OPPORTUNITY IS ENOUGH
Clarence M. Pendleton, Jr.

It has been more than 20 years since the Civil Rights Act of 1964 was passed, and the debate over what Congress intended still rages.

During the last 21 years, the question has remained: Was the intent of Congress to provide equality of opportunity or equality of results?

For 84 days, the longest debate in its history, the Senate tried to resolve the issue in 1964. We still have not answered the question.

---

4. 98 S. Ct. 2733 (1978).

5. *Firefighters Local Union* v. *Stotts*, U.S. Reports Slip Opinion (June 12, 1984).

6. *Grove City College* v. *Bell*, 104 S. Ct. 1211 (1984).

7. See Robert F. Drinan, "Affirmative Action Under Attack," Vol. 12, no. 2, *Human Rights* (Fall 1984), pp. 14–17.

Many leading civil rights organizations at that time, led by Senator Hubert Humphrey, argued the equality of opportunity side. Humphrey assured his colleagues time and again that group preferences were not to be tolerated.

There is nothing in Title VII of the bill, he insisted, "that will give any power to the (Equal Employment Opportunity) Commission or to any court to require hiring, firing or promotion of employees in order to meet a racial 'quota' or to achieve a certain racial balance. That bugaboo has been brought up a dozen times; but it is nonexistent."

The opposition believed that, despite the intent of the bill, the effect would be to insure equality of results, as interpreted by the enforcing agencies of government.

The act was passed to subtantiate the rights of blacks. However, the bill's language insisted that race, color, religion, and national origin were to limit no one's rights.

The act followed the language and spirit of the 13th, 14th, and 15th amendments to the Constitution. It spoke of "citizens, individuals, and persons," not blacks, not Hispanics, native Americans, Asians, or any other group that might be subject to discrimination.

It seemed as though Justice John Marshall Harlan's famous dissent in *Plessy v. Ferguson* would be the law at last: "In view of the Constitution, in the eye of the law, there is in this country no superior, dominant ruling class of citizens. There is no caste here. Our Constitution is color-blind, and neither knows nor tolerates classes among its citizens.

"In respect of civil rights, all citizens are equal before the law. The humblest is the peer of the most powerful. The law regards man as man, and takes no account of his surroundings or of his color when his civil rights as guaranteed by the supreme law of the Land are involved."

Americans thought the eloquent words spoken by Dr. Martin Luther King Jr. from the steps of the Lincoln Memorial were cast in stone. All people, he said, were "to be judged by the content of their character not by the color of their skin."

One would be sadly and grossly mistaken to believe that a color-blind, society has been obtained. The implementation and enforcement of this law, as columnist George Will once described, succeeded in dividing "the majestic national river into little racial and ethnic creeks."

The United States, Will wrote, became "less a nation than an angry menagerie of factions scrambling for preference."

The massive societal consensus that demanded passage of the Civil Rights Act of 1964 began to break down in the 1970s. New legislation and an executive order required increased attention to race and ethnicity in hiring by any private or public employer that received federal aid or was subject to government regulation.

It was now required to count how many minorities were recruited, interviewed, trained, hired, admitted, served or enrolled.

Twenty years later, it is still necessary "to count noses" to determine if there is discrimination.

That equality of opportunity so ardently fought for and won in 1964 has given way to equality of results through such bureaucratic devices as fair share, proportional representation, special preferences, quotas, goals, timetables, and set-asides.

Today, many blacks believe that the laws were passed to ensure only their civil rights, and that blacks are due a special preference from the government to make up for the despicable institution of slavery. They sincerely believe that the government has not yet made up for past atrocities.

This is where I part company with some of my people. I believe that blacks were only due the granting of equal status, equal protection. I also believe that many of the laws and court decisions that occurred since 1964 were necessary to reassert the constitutional guarantees expressed by the 13th, 14th, and 15th amendments.

Insistence on group preference is a role reversal. Those who marched, struggled and died for equality now want separation.

In enforcing the Civil Rights Act, the government perpetuated and worsened the situation with a myriad of artificial allotments, considered incentives to assist and propel minorities into America's mainstream.

Those artificial allotments included goals, timetables, quotas and other numerical devices imposed by government to suit its notion of how society should be organized—a society where a person's standing is determined by pigment, ethnicity or gender.

Allocating social benefits on the basis of race or gender has led to bitterness and disharmony. Economist Thomas Sowell expressed a cause for concern when he stated, "There is much reason to fear the harm that (a racial preference) is doing to its supposed beneficiaries, and still more reason to fear the long-run consequences of polarizing the nation. Resentments do not accumulate indefinitely without consequences."

The U.S. Commission on Civil Rights is studying the long- and short-term consequences of these artificial allotments. Some of the issues under study are:

• *Incomes of Americans: ethnic, racial and sex differences.* The commission is examining how employment discrimination, schooling and work experience have affected income differences between men, women, racial and ethnic groups since the 1940s.

• *Affirmative action in higher education.* Techniques used by universities to increase minority and female representation among students and faculty members will be studied, along with success rates. The study will also assess the effect of affirmative action on different types of institutions and their student bodies, faculties, curricula, standards of admission, grading, progress, and graduation.

• *Voluntary and involuntary methods of achieving school desegration.* We are studying how busing, magnet schools, open enrollment, and special attendance schools have worked to achieve integration in up to 40 sites. We want to know how long integration was achieved and effects on the communities involved.

• *State and local civil rights enforcement.* The commission is evaluating how well state and local vocational rehabilitation agencies are enforcing civil rights.

• *Redistricting and minorities.* The commission has started a study of redistricting by state and local governments in order to comply with the one-person, one-vote principle for apportioning representation following 1980 census data.

We want to know whether redistricting plans dilute the voting strength of minorities in violation of the Voting Rights Act and the Constitution. We are also examining the effects of various districting plans on the opportunity of minorities to effectively participate in the political process.

• *Comparable worth.* The notion that equal pay should be given not only for equal work, but for jobs deemed comparable in the skills, knowledge and ability they require has emerged as an important civil rights issue.

The commission has published three volumes that explore the issue of equal pay for work of "comparative value," focusing on its use as a remedy for sex discrimination in employment. We have already made two recommendations to the President and Congress.

We feel that federal civil rights enforcement agencies, including the Equal Employment Opportunity Commission, should reject comparable worth and rely instead on the principle of equal pay for equal work. Moreover, we recommend that the Justice Department resist comparable worth doctrine in appropriate litigation.

The commission also feels that Congress should not adopt legislation that would establish a comparable worth doctrine in the setting of wages in the federal or private sector.

It is equality of opportunity that allows one to advance toward that laudable goal of a color-blind, race and gender neutral society. Only equality of opportunity will facilitate each individual or group to achieve to the limit of their creativity, imagination and enthusiasm.

Congress and the courts should make a commitment to pursue the moral and constitutional high ground and reject any notion that discrimination can be eliminated or minimized by racial balancing in the form of proportional representation. Nor should Congress condone equality of results in the form of preferential treatment such as quotas, goals, timetables or set-asides.

The main objective of the federal, state and local government must be to provide equal opportunity based upon individual merit. Each of us has an obligation to make sure that our children can compete based upon merit. This means they must be prepared.

A quality education must be available to all children. This nation cannot afford another generation of illiterates of any color.

Derrick Bell, dean of the University of Oregon Law School and a leading force in early court cases to end segregation, has concluded that while "there is potential strength in the argument that school desegregation is needed to improve society, the danger is that this societal personification of the benefit reduces the priority for correction of the harm suffered directly by blacks to a secondary importance when it should be the primary concern."

As W.E.B. DuBois said years ago, "The black child needs neither segregated schools nor mixed schools. What he needs is an education."

I myself survived and prospered without the so-called benefits of affirmative action and integration. The reason for my survival and success is preparation. I attended the all-black Dunbar High School in Washington, D.C. and was given a special gift.

Those black teachers demanded excellence and I left prepared to go forward. I obtained both post secondary degrees from a black college, Howard University, which gave me the tools necessary to achieve success.

We must encourage black people to support black institutions: the black church, black colleges, banks, fraternities, service organizations and countless others. We cannot depend upon philanthropy and charity to save our institutions.

We must create innovative and effective public policy that opens doors and keeps them open. We should be advocating the relaxation and repeal of various regulations that restrict entry and access to the marketplace.

Not only black Americans would benefit from such advocacy. Is it necessary for a barber or beautician to know the name of every bone in the hand to adequately cut hair? Why should a New York City taxi medallion cost $85,000 when a license in Washington, D.C. is only $200? Licensing only serves to restrict access to the market. How many people have $85,000?

Minimum wage also restricts entry into the market by black teenagers. Even the black mayors in the United States believe this to be true, yet many of us continue to work against initiation of legislation to reduce minimum wage.

Finally, affirmative action must be re-evaluated. A program which began with the best intentions and highest ideals has ended up setting white against black. It has created new protected classes, made victim status desirable and forced society to question the accomplishments of its children.

Most tragically, it has created a generation which sees no need to take risk and will never see its rewards. No quota will make any of us successful. No program of quotas will prevent the last of us from failing. Risk taking should be the engine that propels us to success.

Solving the problem of discrimination with more laws and regulations is not the answer. We have a moral responsibility to remove the barriers that deny people access to equal opportunity. We should get rid of special protections that can place more barriers to opportunity.

A passage in *The Essential Rousseau*, "Discourse on Inequality Among Men," written in 1755, sums up the situation:

"Peoples once accustomed to masters are no longer in condition to do without them. If they try to shake off the yoke, they move still farther away from freedom because they confuse it with an unbridled license that is opposed to it, and their revolutions nearly always deliver them into the hands of seducers who only make their chains heavier than before." ∎

EQUALITY OF RESULT IS REQUIRED
Douglas B. Huron

It may be fashionable to insist that affirmative action, and especially quotas for minorities, don't work. But not for the first time, the fashion is wrong. In many kinds of situations these remedies do work, providing job opportunities for qualified (or easily qualifiable) people who otherwise would not have them.

This does not mean we should turn to affirmative action to solve all the problems of America's unemployed and underemployed minorities. Affirmative action provides useful tools, not panaceas. Affirmative action cannot make an illiterate person literate, or teach good work habits, or turn someone with janitor's skills into an engineer. There is no substitute for education, training and apprenticeship.

It is clear that the White House, through the Justice Department, opposes any race-related quotas or goals for hiring or promotion of public workers. Although the Supreme Court last year, in the *Stotts* decision, upheld the seniority rights of a group of white firefighters in Memphis, it has not decided whether a racially based formula for public hiring is illegal and unconstitutional.

The Court has now agreed to review a Michigan ruling that upholds an affirmative action plan calling for layoffs of nonminority teachers who have more experience than some minority teachers, but are being laid off in order for the staff to maintain a racial balance.

The administration is arguing that the Supreme Court's ruling in *Stotts* sets the stage for striking down all preferential quotas in hiring and promoting public workers. Recently, the Justice Department has gone to court in a number of cities to overturn hiring agreements that contain racial quotas.

In many circumstances, members of minority groups have been discriminated against casually, thoughtlessly—because it has been the fashion not to hire them. Thus, many big city police and fire departments traditionally hired no blacks; many craft unions accepted no blacks as members; many big companies put no blacks in positions higher than kitchen help and janitors. When patterns of discrimination are apparent, affirmative action and quotas may be valid tools to respond. And they may also be useful for an employer who recognizes the problem and wants to change it voluntarily.

The utility of affirmative action and quotas was demonstrated in 1983 in hearings held by Reps. Don Edwards (D-Cal.) and Patricia Schroeder (D-Colo.). In those hearings I talked about public sector employment in Alabama, something I learned about as an attorney in the Justice Department's civil rights division in the Nixon-Ford administration. Another witness at the same hearings was Fred Cook, vice president for human resources at Mountain Bell in Denver.

Alabama has seen dramatic changes in the level and type of black employment in public agencies over the past decade. Most of that change is directly attributable to litigation and specifically to affirmative action and quota decrees entered by Judge Frank Johnson of Montgomery. And it is tough to imagine how blacks would have gotten those state jobs in Alabama without them.

In the late 1960s, the 70-odd Alabama state agencies employed only a handful of blacks above the menial level. At that time the Justice Department sued seven of the larger agencies which together employed over half the state government's work force. Following trial, Judge Johnson found that of the 1,000 clerical employees in these agencies, only one was black. Of over 2,000 workers in semiprofessional and supervisory positions, just 26 were black.

This paucity of black employees was no accident, since the state refused to recruit at black schools and in black media and also maintained segregated cafeteria facilities.

Even more telling, on those occasions when black applicants appeared at the top of employment registers, agencies simply passed over them in favor of low-ranked whites.

To try to remedy these entrenched discriminatory patterns, Judge Johnson enjoined the passing-over of qualified blacks and required the state to attempt to recruit black applicants. He also ordered the hiring of some 62 blacks who had been passed over and who could be identified following a laborious process of records analysis. In short, Frank Johnsin in 1970 ordered everything W. Bradford Reynolds, the current assistant attorney general for civil rights, would require of an employer guilty of discrimination.

But nothing substantive changed, despite Alabama's compliance with the specific elements of Judge Johnson's decree. Perhaps the state's attitude was still too grudging, or blacks were still too skeptical, or perhaps other factors were at work. Whatever the explanation, black employment in Alabama agencies remained low.

The one exception to this otherwise gloomy picture lay in the area of temporary employment. There Johnson had simply imposed a ratio—a quota—on temporary hires. The ratio was fixed at 25 percent—approximately the black population percentage in Alabama—and the goal was met. But there was still no improvement in permanent positions.

Then in January 1972, the Alabama NAACP filed suit against the Department of Public Safety—the state troopers. At that time everyone in Public Safety was white—the troopers, the officers and the support personnel. No blacks had ever been employed there. Throughout the '50s and '60s—from the schoolhouse door to the Selma bridge—the troopers had been the most visible instrument defending segregation.

Judge Johnson set an early trial date, then ruled from the bench, finding that Public Safety had engaged in a "blatant and continuous pattern and practice of discrimination." Having learned from his experience with the other Alabama agencies, Johnson immediately imposed a quota: he required the state to hire one black trooper for each new white hired, until blacks reached 25 percent of the trooper force. He also applied the same formula to support personnel.

The state complied, and the results have been little short of astounding. Within weeks, Alabama had hired its first black troopers. Within two years, there were a substantial number of blacks on the force, and the director of Public Safety later testified that they were competent professionals.

Today, 13 years after the entry of Judge Johnson's decree, Alabama has the most thoroughly integrated state police force in the country. Over 20 percent of the troopers and officers—and nearly 25 percent of the support personnel—are black. The day is fast approaching when Public Safety will be freed of hiring constraints. And although 13 years may seem a long time for a court order to remain in effect, the problem was years longer in the making.

When Justice contrasted the initial results on the trooper force with the lack of progress in other Alabama agencies, the department went back into court, asking that hiring ratios be applied to entry-level jobs in the other Alabama agencies. Judge Johnson gave the agencies plenty of time—over two years—to mend their ways.

When little changed, he issued a decision finding statewide discrimination, but he demurred to Justice's plea for quotas. He said that "mandatory hiring quotas must be a last resort," and he declined to order them. But he noted that the denial would be "without prejudice" to Justice's seeking the same relief one year later: "In the event substantial progress has not been made by the 70 state agencies, hiring goals will then be the only alternative."

The message—the threat—could not have been clearer, and the agencies immediately began to come around. In the eight largest departments, which together account for close to 75 percent of all state workers, black employment increased by over half between 1975 and 1983 and now stands at over 20 percent. And black workers, who used to be concentrated in menial jobs, now appear in substantial numbers in nearly all the large job categories.

No doubt problems remain in Alabama, but the only fair conclusion is that dramatic progress has been achieved in public employment for blacks over the past decade. And in view of the history of the Alabama litigation, it is clear that this would not have occurred if Judge Johnson had not first imposed a hiring quota on the state troopers—and then threatened to extend it statewide if the other agencies did not alter their discriminatory practices.

At Mountain Bell—an affiliate of AT&T before divestiture—affirmative action was also needed. In 1972, AT&T entered into a six-year consent decree with the EEOC and the Justice Department to substantially increase the number of minority and female workers, as well as the number of women in non-traditional jobs such as installers, cable repairers and frame attendants.

It was not easy at first. Fred Cook said Mountain Bell did not meet its goals for the first year of the decree, but the company then intensified its recruiting efforts and was on target for the next five. As a result, minority managers at the company have increased from under 200 to over 1,400, and there are now nearly 1,200 women in non-traditional jobs, compared to 81 in the year before the decree.

Cook defends Mountain Bell's employment practices in the '50s and '60s, saying that his company was more responsive than most to the aspirations of minorities and female workers. But, he frankly admits that the consent decree focused the company's efforts in a particularly acute and compelling way. As he put it, "It became as important as the bottom line." If it weren't for the decree, with its affirmative action goals, the progress Cook recounted would not have been made.

It is also significant that affirmative action has helped Mountain Bell in a very practical way. Fred Cook said recently that, before the consent decree, "we were reflllecting society. We were not using all the talent available." Under the decree, though, the company discovered that its minority and female work force was a "gold mine" for high-quality managers.

And in the wake of Mountain Bell's own efforts, blacks, Hispanics, and women formed organizations aimed at helping one another and at assisting the company in identifying still more talent. Cook praised the work of these groups, and he said that the net result is that Mountain Bell has done a "very good job, especially since the consent decree has ended." The company has no interest in turning back. According to Cook, "it is good business sense to take this kind of affirmative action." It is ironic that it took government action to sharpen Bell's business judgment.

Affirmative action can be a potent weapon, so it should be used only with great care. An effective affirmative action program should have a limited duration, should be aimed only at genuine problems caused by past discrimination, and should not lower standards. Otherwise the problem of selection based on race or sex may be perpetuated indefinitely.

In deciding whether affirmative action is desirable or required, the key question is, what caused a company to exclude blacks from its work force, or keep them in menial jobs? When the answer is that blacks did not have the requisite skills or training, then affirmative action is unlikely to be an effective remedy.

But when the cause is discrimination, whether it is overt or casual discrimination, affirmative action may then be required. ■

WOMEN AND EQUAL PAY

As we have seen, the Equal Protection Clause has been the basis for civil rights advances, not only for black people, but also for women and others. The Fifteenth Amendment did not give women the right to vote. That came only with the Nineteenth Amendment, ratified in 1920. For a time thereafter, the women's movement, which had agitated so long for this "woman suffrage," became somewhat dormant, at least publicly. In modern times, it began to flourish again in the wake of the black civil rights movement.

Discrimination on the basis of sex was prohibited in civil rights acts passed by Congress. Professional schools and occupations were opened to women. "Equal pay for the same work" became the law. Options and opportunities for women were greatly expanded.

In a lawsuit by state employees in Washington state, a new concept—that of "comparable worth"—has gained national attention. This concept goes further than "equal pay for the same work" and seeks "equal pay for comparable work." The problem this concept addresses is the fact that jobs that have traditionally been men's jobs pay more than jobs that have traditionally been women's jobs.

As Chairman Pendleton stated in an earlier article in this chapter, President Reagan's Civil Rights Commission has spoken out against the idea of comparable worth, arguing that the Equal Protection Clause does not require it. Though "comparable worth" has not yet been definitively held to be the law, Edith Barnett, a lawyer and civil rights advocate, in the article excerpted here, argues that it should be.

"COMPARABLE WORTH" IS A SOUND APPROACH
Edith Barnett

The fight to end sex-based wage discrimination against working women by establishing the principle of "comparable worth" or "pay equity" under federal civil rights laws continues to meet sustained and vocal opposition.

The list of amici organizations which filed briefs in the Ninth Circuit last fall on behalf of the State of Washington, seeking to reverse the plaintiffs' victory in *AFSCME v. State of Washington,* included the Eagle Forum (Phyllis Schlafly's group), the Mountain States Legal Foundation (James Watt's old group) the Pacific Legal Foundation, and the Washington Legal Foundation.

Shortly after President Reagan's reelection, the chairman of the United States Commission on Civil Rights, Clarence Pendleton, called a press conference to denounce pay equity as the "looniest idea since Looney Tunes came on screen." . . .

In March 1985, a Commission on Civil Rights report concluded that "comparable worth, as a theory of discrimination or as a remedy for discrimination, is a profoundly and irretrievably flawed idea." . . . The Commission report said that comparable worth policies of assessing the value of different jobs were "inherently subjective," and "cannot prove the existence of sex-based wage discrimination." Commission member Mary Frances Berry indicated she would issue a dissenting report. . . .

This article responds to the two main arguments used against the plaintiffs in these cases: (1) Job evaluation ("comparable worth") studies are a radical departure from traditional American wage setting practices and should therefore have no probative value in sex-based wage discrimination cases: and (2) the use of the "market" to set wages should be an absolute defense to any prima facie case of discrimination in pay.

1. Job evaluation has been long accepted by American industry and government.

Job evaluation procedures—so-called "comparable worth studies"—are attacked as if they were a radical new method for comparing different male and female jobs, such as secretary and truck driver. The argument is made that jobs which are as different as "apples and oranges" cannot be compared. This ignores the fact that job evaluation has long been accepted by government, private industry, unions, and labor arbitrators as a method for doing precisely what is at issue in sex-based wage discrimination cases — systematically comparing different jobs in order to rate their relative worth for the purpose of setting wages. . . .

It is ironic that American industry and government have uniformly supported the use and validity of job evaluation procedures until the techniques came to be used for identifying sex discrimination in pay in their workforces.

2. Job evaluation has been widely accepted as proof of wage discrimination.

During the past decade, job evaluation has been widely used by large employers, especially state governments, to attempt to isolate sex-based wage differentials. As in the *AFSCME* case, employers such as the State of Washington have contracted with well-known management consulting firms to make studies of predominantly male and female jobs, using the point method of job evaluation. The job worth scores of such traditionally female and male jobs as, respectively, nurse, secretary, librarian, and auto mechanic, highway equipment operator, and carpenter, have then been compared to the respective pay ranges of the jobs.

In every case, the female jobs have been shown to be underpaid in comparison with male jobs scoring the same or lower job worth points. The Washington State job evaluation studies, which were begun in 1974, showed that female state jobs were underpaid at least 20 percent.

Such job evaluation studies are powerful evidence of sex discrimination because they are sex neutral. Job evaluation does not evaluate *individuals*; it evaluates *jobs,* without regard to the particular characteristics of the job incumbent.

Opponents of pay equity argue that the well-known wage differential between males and females in the workforce is explained by differences in physical strength, career choices, training differences, work experience, and tenure in the work force. Such differences may explain earnings diflerentials between *individuals* based on seniority, or the decision to hire an experienced individual at a salary above the entry level rate, but they do not explain base rate differentials between *jobs* found to be of equal value by job evaluation studies, especially where the skill and other requirements of such jobs are the same.

Thus, for example, the entry level pay differential between unskilled traditionally male jobs such as laborer and unskilled traditionally female jobs such as hospital aide cannot be explained by purported differences in the training or work experience of individual male and female workers employed in such jobs. Economics professor and former Secretary of Labor Ray Marshall, who testified for the plaintiffs in the *AFSCME* case, believes that it would be very difficult to explain the assignment of different wage rates to *jobs* with the same value to the employer on grounds other than discrimination.

Long before the decision in *AFSCME v. Washington,* the courts had accepted employer use of job evaluation studies as a means for setting pay, and had found actionable discrimination where the employer determined the worth of the job, but then paid the males, according to that worth, but not the females. In the first Equal Pay Act case to be decided by the United States Supreme Court, *Corning Glass Works v. Brennan* (1974), the Court affirmed lower court findings that the defendant was violating the Equal Pay Act by paying female day inspectors less than male night inspectors. The Court relied on the company's own job evaluation plans, whch awarded the same point values to both jobs, in rejecting the company's attempt to explain away the pay differential.

In one of the first sex-based wage discrimination cases decided by the Supreme Court under Title VII of the 1964 Civil Rights Act, *Gunther v. County of Washington* (1981), the County of Washington commissioned a job evaluation study of the worth of female prison guard jobs and determined that they should be paid approximately 95 percent as much as male prison guard jobs. The county then paid the male guards the full evaluated worth of their jobs, while paying the female guards only 70 percent as much as the male guards. The Supreme Court held that the plaintiffs should be given the opportunity to prove that the failure of the county to pay them the full evaluated worth of their jobs was attributable to sex discrimination. Although the Supreme Court stated in *Gunther* that it was "not called upon in this case to decide whether respondents have stated a prima facie case of sex discrimination under Title VII," the lower courts have uniformly construed the opinion as a holding that a prima facie case was stated by the facts.

Other courts have also found actionable discrimination where the employer determines the worth of its jobs by the use of job evaluation, but then pays the males (or the white workers) according to that worth, but not the females (or the black workers).

The ritualistic invocation of the "market" cannot serve as an absolute defense to sex-based wage discrimination. Opponents commonly argue that the "market," rather than sex discrimination, is responsible for pay differentials between male- and female-dominated jobs. Proponents of ending wage discrimination are therefore suspect, as being against the "free market" and, therefore, the American way of life. . . . This argument fails to consider that: 1) wage setting in this country has not been left to the tender mercies of the so-called "free market" since the Great Depression; 2) the market for labor is heavily regulated and is so different from the market for products that neo-conservative laissez-faire theories of the product market are virtually irrelevant, and 3) the "market" argument as propounded is only a slightly disguised version of the cost justification defense which the courts have uniformly rejected in discrimination cases.

3. Is there a "free market" for labor?

The elementary laissez-faire model of the competitive labor market assumes that wages are determined purely by demand, which is derived from the demand for the product produced by labor. Under this model, it is assumed that employers pay only the minimum price needed, through a process of bargaining with individual employees or applicants, to secure and maintain what they consider to be an adequate supply of labor for their enterprises. Wages are determined by the interaction of demand and supply curves. Because discrimination in inefficient, and is therefore inconsistent with this model of a perfectly competitive labor market, it is assumed that it cannot exist.

Wage setting in this country does not operate this way, if it ever did.

Traditional wage administration programs, including job evaluation, are widely used to set wages. Federal and state protective labor legislation has for many years restricted the ability of employers to pay the lowest wages they can. For example, since 1938, the Fair Labor Standards Act has barred most employers from paying less than the minimum wage, even if their employees would accept less. Under the Act, children may not work at all in many instances even if they are willing to take what employers offer them. The National Labor Relations Act has for over 50 years protected the market limitations embodied in employer-union agreements reached through free collective bargaining.

Since 1963, the Equal Pay Act, as an amendment of the Fair Labor Standards Act, has barred employers from paying women lower wages than men for equal work, even though women would accept lower wages.

Title VII of the Civil Rights Act of 1964 further limits market forces which might permit the hiring of employees at depressed wages because of their race, color, religion, national origin or sex. The Railway Labor Act, the Age Discrimination in Employment Act and the Rehabilitation Act are other examples. Most states also have similar laws. The demand side of the labor market does not match the neo-conservative model; employers are not legally free to pay the lowest wage they can.

The supply side also does not match the neo-conservative model. This model assumes that sellers will be generally willing to supply more of any product at higher prices. In the labor market, it is not known with any degree of reliability whether people are willing to supply more or less labor at higher wages. Contrary to the usual "laws of supply and demand," some workers work more when paid higher wages while others work less, because they feel that their needs are satisfied, or wish to substitute leisure for additional money. Also, because of family and other community ties, workers are not highly mobile and cannot always move wherever necessary to obtain the highest wages.

That is not to say that supply and demand has no impact on wages, but many other forces are also at work, including protective labor legislation, collective bargaining, and traditional internal wage structures. . . .

Thus, the labor market in this country does not match the neo-conservative model of the competitive market for products. Moreover, discrimination can and does exist, as Congress recognized in enacting laws against employment discrimination.

4. The "market defense" is another version of the rejected "cost justification" defense.

The argument that sex discrimination in pay is caused by the "market" is a barely disguised version of the cost justification defense often rejected by the courts. Essentially, the argument holds that an employer should be able to pay employees the lowest wages they will take; since female employees "cost" less in the marketplace, paying females less is a defense of pay discrimination.

The lower courts have also strongly adhered to the principle that employers cannot defend against pay discrimination under the Equal Pay Act on the grounds that they pay men more because they cannot get them for less. To permit a market defense in sex-based discrimination cases under Title VII would only perpetuate the historically entrenched discrimination against women which Title VII and the Equal Pay Act were designed to eradicate. . . .

Conclusion

Job evaluation, far from being a radical new invention, is a traditional and widely accepted American method of wage setting. It has come under attack only because of its use for an unpopular purpose—isolating and identifying sex-based wage discrimination in employer work forces.

The ritualistic invocation of "the market" cannot and should not serve as a defense to any and all sex-based wage discrimination. The market for labor in this country, because of social behavior patterns, collective bargaining, protective labor legislation, and traditional internal wage structures, has little resemblance to the neo-conservative model of the market for products. Sex discrimination in pay and other employment conditions can and does exist, as Congress recognized in enacting laws against employment discrimination. "Comparable worth" analysis is a sound and legitimate technique to prove discrimination. ■

REAPPORTIONMENT

Electoral equality—"one person, one vote"—has also been held to be required by the Equal Protection Clause of the Fourteenth Amendment.

The Constitution mandates that a national census be taken every ten years—that everybody be counted in a decennial census—so that the number of members of the U. S. House of Representatives can be apportioned among the various states on the basis of their relative populations. The framers of the Constitution intended that the House of Representatives would represent the general population.

But by the 1960s, the number of people who lived in different congressional districts—established within each state by its state legislature—varied greatly. In twenty-one states, the largest congressional district had twice as much population as the smallest district. This practice of setting up representative districts with substantially unequal populations is called "malapportionment."

Not just congressional districts, but the legislative districts in the various states, established for the election of members of their own state legislatures, were equally characterized by malapportionment. This was true despite the Fourteenth Amendment's prohibition against denial of "equal protection of the laws."

Until 1962, there was no remedy through the courts for malapportionment. This was said to be a "political question," not a "justiciable issue" that the courts could decide. If state legislatures did not district properly, the courts would not order them to do so. In another one of its major, groundbreaking decisions, the Warren Court, in *Baker* v. *Carr,* held for the first time that malapportionment is, indeed, a justiciable issue—under the Equal Protection Clause.

In two important decisions that soon followed,[8] the Supreme Court ruled that districts for electing members of the U. S. House of Representatives and *both* houses of state legislatures must be substantially equal in population because, as Chief Justice Warren put it, "legislators represent people, not trees or acres."

BAKER V. CARR*

MR. JUSTICE BRENNAN delivered the opinion of the Court.

This civil action was brought under 42 U.S.C. §§1983 and 1988 to redress the alleged deprivation of federal constitutional rights. The complaint, alleging that by means of a 1901 statute of Tennessee apportioning the members of the General Assembly among the State's 95 counties, "these plaintiffs and others similarly situated, are denied the equal protection of the laws accorded them by the Fourteenth Amendment to the Constitution of the United States by virtue of the debasement of their votes," was dismissed by a three-judge court convened under 28 U.S.C. § 2281 in the Middle District of Tennessee. The court held that it lacked jurisdiction of the subject matter and also that no claim was stated upon which relief could be granted. . . . We hold that the dismissal was error, and remand the cause to the District court for trial and further proceedings consistent with this opinion. . . .

Between 1901 and 1961, Tennessee has experienced substantial growth and redistribution of her population. In 1901 the population was 2,020,616 of whom 487,380 were eligible to vote. The 1960 Federal Census reports the State's population at 3,567,089 of whom 2,092,891 are eligible to vote. The relative standings of the counties in terms of qualified voters have changed significantly. It is primarily the continued application of the 1901 Apportionment Act to this shifted and enlarged voting population which gives rise to the present controversy.

Indeed, the complaint alleges that the 1901 statute, even as of the time of its passage, "made no apportionment of Representatives and Senators in accordance with the constitutional formula . . . , but instead arbitrarily and capriciously apportioned representatives in the Senate and House without reference . . . to any logical or reasonable formula whatever." It is further alleged that "because of the population changes since 1900, and the failure of the Legislature to reapportion itself since 1901," the 1901 statute became "unconstitutional and obsolete." Appellants also argue that, because of the composition of the legislature effected by the 1901 Apportionment Act, redress in the form

---

8. *Wesberry* v. *Sanders*, 376 U.S. 1 (1964); and *Reynolds* v. *Sims*, 377 U.S. 533 (1964).
* 369 U.S. 186 (1962).

of a state constitutional amendment to change the entire mechanism for reapportioning, or any other change short of that, is difficult or impossible. The complaint concludes that "these plaintiffs and others similarly situated, are denied the equal protection of the laws accorded them by the Fourteenth Amendment to the Constitution of the United States by virtue of the debasement of their votes." They seek a declaration that the 1901 statute is unconstitutional and an injunction restraining the appellees from acting to conduct any further elections under it. They also pray that unless and until the General Assembly enacts a valid reapportionment, the District Court should either decree a reapportionment by mathematical application of the Tennessee constitutional formulae to the most recent Federal Census figures, or direct the appellees to conduct legislative elections, primary and general, at large. . . .

The District Court's dismissal order recited that it was issued in conformity with the court's *per curiam* opinion. The opinion reveals that the court rested its dismissal upon lack of subject-matter jurisdiction and lack of a justiciable cause of action without attempting to distinguish between these grounds. After noting that the plaintiffs challenged the existing legislative apportionment in Tennessee under the Due Process and Equal Protection Clauses, and summarizing the supporting allegations and the relief requested, the court stated that

> The action is presently before the Court upon the defendants' motion to dismiss predicated upon three grounds: first, that the Court lacks jurisdiction of the subject matter; second, that the complaints fail to state a claim upon which relief can be granted; and third, that indispensable party defendants are not before the Court. . . .

The court proceeded to explain its action as turning on the case's presenting a "question of the distribution of political strength for legislative purposes." For,

> From a review of [numerous Supreme Court] . . . decisions there can be no doubt that the federal rule, as enunciated and applied by the Supreme Court, is that the federal courts, whether from a lack of jurisdiction or from the inappropriateness of the subject matter for judicial consideration, will not intervene in cases of this type to compel legislative reapportionment. . . .

The court went on to express doubts as to the feasibility of the various possible remedies sought by the plaintiffs. 179 F. Supp., at 827–828. Then it made clear that its dismissal reflected a view not of doubt that violation of constitutional rights was alleged, but of a court's impotence to correct that violation:

> With the plaintiffs' argument that the legislature of Tennessee is guilty of a clear violation of the state constitution and of the rights of the plaintiffs the Court entirely agrees. It also agrees that the evil is a serious one which should be corrected without further delay. But even so the remedy in this situation clearly does not lie with the courts. It has long been recognized and is accepted doctrine that there are indeed some rights guaranteed by the Constitution for the violation of which the courts cannot give redress. . . .

In light of the District Court's treatment of the case, we hold today only (a) that the court possessed jurisdiction of the subject matter; (b) that a justiciable cause of action is stated upon which appellants would be entitled to appropriate relief; and (c) because appellees raise the issue before this Court, that the appellants have standing to challenge the Tennessee apportionment statutes. Beyond noting that we have no cause at this stage to doubt the District Court will be able to fashion relief if violations of constitutional rights are found, it is improper now to consider what remedy would be most appropriate if appellants prevail at the trial.

JURISDICTION OF THE SUBJECT MATTER

The District Court was uncertain whether our cases withholding federal judicial relief rested upon a lack of federal jurisdiction or upon the in appropriateness of the subject matter for judicial consideration—what we have designated "nonjusticiability." The distinction between the two grounds is significant. In the instance of nonjusticiability, consideration of the cause is not wholly and immediately foreclosed; rather, the Court's inquiry necessarily proceeds to the point of deciding whether the duty asserted can be judicially identified and its breach judicially determined, and whether protection for the right asserted can be judicially molded. In the instance of lack of jurisdiction the cause either does not "arise under" the Federal Constitution, laws or treaties (or fall within one of the other enumerated categories of Art. III, § 2), or is not a "case or controversy" within the meaning of that section; or the cause is not one described by any jurisdictional statute. Our conclusion . . . that this cause presents no nonjusticiable "politicl question" settles the only possible doubt that it is a case or controversy. . . .

Article III, § 2, of the Federal Constitution provides that "The judicial Power shall extend to all Cases, in Law and Equity, arising under this Constitution, the Laws of the United States, and Treaties made, or which shall be made, under their Authority . . . ." It is clear that the cause of action is one which "arises under" the Federal Constitution. The complaint alleges that the 1901 statute effects an apportionment that deprives the appellants of the equal protection of the laws in violation of the Fourteenth Amendment. Dismissal of the complaint upon the ground of lack of jurisdiction of the subject matter would, therefore, be justified only if that claim were "so attenuated and unsubstantial as to be absolutely devoid of merit," . . . or "frivolous," . . . . That the claim is unsubstantial must be "very plain." . . . Since the District Court obviously and correctly did not deem the asserted federal constitutional claim unsubstantial and frivolous, it should not have dismissed the complaint for want of jurisdiction of the subject matter. . . .

A federal court cannot "pronounce any statute, either of a State or of the United States, void, because irreconcilable with the Constitution, except as it is called upon to adjudge the legal rights of litigants in actual controversies." . . . Have the appellants alleged such a personal stake in the outcome of the controversy as to assure that concrete adverseness which sharpens the presentation of issues upon which the court so largely depends for illumination of difficult constitutional questions? This is the gist of the question of standing. It is, of course, a question of federal law.

The complaint was filed by residents of Davidson, Hamilton, Knox, Montgomery, and Shelby Counties. Each is a person allegedly qualified to vote for members of the General Assembly representing his county. These appellants sued "on their own behalf and on behalf of all qualified voters of their respective counties, and further, on behalf of all voters of the State of Tennessee who are similarly situated . . . ." The appellees are the Tennessee Secretary of State, Attorney General, Coordinator of Elections, and members of the State Board of Elections; the members of the State Board are sued in their own right and also as representatives of the County Election Commissioners whom they appoint . . .

These appellants seek relief in order to protect or vindicate an interest of their own, and of those similarly situated. Their constitutional claim is, in substance, that the 1901 statute constitutes arbitrary and capricious state action, offensive to the Fourteenth Amendment in its irrational disregard of the standard of apportionment prescribed by the State's Constitution or of any standard, effecting a gross disproportion of representation to voting population. The injury which appellants assert is that this classification disfavors the voters in the counties in which they reside, placing them in a position of constitutionally unjustifiable inequality *vis-à-vis* voters in irrationally favored counties. A citizen's right to a vote free of arbitrary impairment by state action has been judicially recognized as a right secured by the Constitution, when such impairment resulted from dilution by a false tally, . . . or by a refusal to count votes from arbitrarily selected precincts, . . . or by a stuffing of the ballot box . . . .

It would not be necessary to decide whether appellants' allegations of impairment of their votes by the 1901 apportionment will, ultimately, entitle them to any relief, in order to hold that they have standing to seek it. If such impairment does produce a legally cognizable injury, they are among those who have sustained it. They are asserting "a plain, direct and adequate interest in maintaining the effectiveness of their votes," . . . not merely a claim of "the right, possessed by every citizen, to require that the Government be administered according to law . . . ." They are entitled to a hearing and to the District Court's decision on their claims. "The very essence of civil liberty certainly consists in the right of every individual to claim the protection of the laws, whenever he receives an injury." *Marbury* v. *Madison*, 1 Cranch 137, 163.

JUSTICIABILITY

. . . The court stated: "From a review of these decisions there can be no doubt that the federal rule . . . is that the federal courts . . . will not intervene in cases of this type to compel legislative reapportionment." . . . We understand the District Court to have read the cited cases as compelling the conclusion that since the appellants sought to have a legislative apportionment held unconstitutional, their suit presented a "political question" and was therefore nonjusticiable. We hold that this challenge to an apportionment presents no nonjusticiable "political question." The cited cases do not hold the contrary.

Of course the mere fact that the suit seeks protection of a political right does not mean it presents a political question. Such an objection "is little more than a play upon words." . . . Rather, it is argued that apportionment cases, whatever the actual wording of the complaint, can involve no federal constitutional right except one resting on the guaranty of a republican form of government, and that complaints based on that clause have been held to present political questions which are nonjusticiable.

We hold that the claim pleaded here neither rests upon nor implicates the Guaranty Clause and that its justiciability is therefore not foreclosed by our decisions of cases involving that clause. The District Court misinterpreted *Colegrove* v. *Green* and other decisions of this Court on which it relied. Appellants' claim that they are being denied equal protection is justiciable, and if "discrimination is sufficiently shown, the right to relief under the equal protection clause is not diminished by the fact that the discrimination relates to political rights." . . .

The question here is the consistency of state action with the Federal Constitution. We have no question decided, or to be decided, by a political branch of government coequal with this Court. Nor do we risk embarrassment of our government abroad, or grave disturbance at home if we take issue with Tennessee as to the constitutionality of her action here challenged. Nor need the appellants, in order to succeed in this action, ask the Court to enter upon policy determinations for which judicially manageable standards are lacking. Judicial standards under the Equal Protection Clause are well developed and familiar, and it has been open to courts since the enactment of the Fourteenth Amendment to determine, if on the particular facts they must, that a discrimination reflects *no* policy, but simply arbitrary and capricious action.

This case does, in one sense, involve the allocation of political power within a State, and the appellants might conceivably have added a claim under the Guaranty Clause. Of course, as we have seen, any reliance on that clause would be futile. But because any reliance on the Guaranty Clause could not have succeeded it does not follow that appellants may not be heard on the equal protection claim which in fact they tender. True, it must be clear that the Fourteenth Amendment claim is not so enmeshed with those political question elements which render Guaranty Clause claims nonjusticiable as actually to present a political question itself. But we have found that not to be the case here.

When challenges to state action respecting matters of "the administration of the affairs of the State and the officers through whom they are conducted" have rested on claims of constitutional deprivation which are amenable to judicial correction, this Court has acted upon its view of the merits of the claim. For example, in *Boyd* v. *Nebraska ex rel. Thayer,* . . . we reversed the Nebraska Supreme Court's decision that Nebraska's Governor was not a citizen of the United States or of the State and therefore could not continue in office. In *Kennard* v. *Louisiana ex rel. Morgan* . . . and *Foster* v. *Kansas ex rel. Johnston,* . . . we considered whether persons had been removed from public office by procedures consistent with the Fourteenth Amendment's due process guaranty, and held on the merits that they had. And only last Term, in *Gomillion* v. *Lightfoot,* . . . we applied the Fifteenth Amendment to strike down a redrafting of municipal boundaries which effected a discriminatory impairment of voting rights, in the face of what a majority of the Court of Appeals thought to be a sweeping commitment to state legislatures of the power to draw and redraw such boundaries.

Gomillion was brought by a Negro who had been a resident of the City of Tuskegee, Alabama, until the municipal boundaries were so recast by the State Legislature as to exclude practically all Negroes. The plaintiff claimed deprivation of the right to vote in municipal elections. The District Court's dismissal for want of jurisdiction and failure to state a claim upon which relief could be granted was affirmed by the Court of Appeals. This Court unanimously reversed. This Court's answer to the argument that States enjoyed unrestricted control over municipal boundaries was:

> Legislative control of municipalities, no less than other state power, lies within the scope of relevant limitations imposed by the United States Constitution. . . . The opposite conclusion, urged upon us by respondents, would sanction the achievement by a State of any impairment of voting rights whatever so long as it was cloaked in the garb of the realignment of political subdivisions. "It is inconceivable that guaranties embedded in the Constitution of the United States may thus be manipulated out of existence." . . .

To a second argument, that *Colgrove* v. *Green* was a barrier to hearing the merits of the case, the Court responded that *Gomillion* was lifted "out of the so-called 'political' arena and into the conventional sphere of constitutional litigation" because here was discriminatory treatment of a racial minority violating the Fifteenth Amendment.

> A statute which is alleged to have worked unconstitutional deprivations of petitioners' rights is not immune to attack simply because the mechanism employed by the legislature is a redefinition of municipal boundaries. . . . While in form this is merely an act redefining metes and bounds, if the allegations are established, the inescapable human effect of this essay in geometry and geography is to despoil colored citizens, and only colored citizens, of their theretofore enjoyed voting rights. That was not *Colegrove* v. *Green.*
> When a State exercises power wholly within the domain of state interest, it is insulated from federal judicial review. But such insulation is not carried over when state power is used as an instrument for circumventing a federally protected right. . . .

We conclude that the complaint's allegations of a denial of equal protection present a justiciable constitutional cause of action upon which appellants are entitled to a trial and a decision. The right asserted is within the reach of judicial protection under the Fourteenth Amendment.

The judgment of the District Court is reversed and the cause is remanded for further proceedings consistent with this opinion.   ■

Courtesy The Boatmen's National Bank of St. Louis.

PART II

Democratic Citizenship

Democracy means "rule of the people." Political participation, then, is a key element of our system. What citizens say about, and how they act on, public issues is important. What people do, as voters and as members of interest groups and political parties, keenly affects political outcomes and public policy.

In Chapter 5, we consider public opinion and the mass media. Chapter 6 is devoted to interest groups and what they do. Finally, Chapter 7 is concerned with political parties and the elections that are central to a democracy.

Public Opinion and the

P̲ublic opinion is the collective and public expression of ideas and feelings about issues. Any government, even a dictatorship, ignores public opinion at its peril. In a democracy, public opinion is especially important.

From earliest childhood until the end of our days, each of us, in what is known as the process of "political socialization," learns certain political values and norms, such as support for our political system itself, as well as how our political system and government work. Our families, schools, and peers are the most important agents in this socialization process, which creates a kind of cultural environment in which we consider political questions and issues as they arise. Other agents of political socialization include public officials and government, political events and experiences, and the media—the means of mass communication.

The media—newspapers, magazines, radio, and television, especially— can directly affect public opinion in a number of ways. First, they have a powerful "agenda-setting" effect—that is, those issues and questions the media choose to report or comment on very often become the issues and questions the public focuses on and thinks about. Second, the media transmit information, and the opinions that you and I form on public issues and questions are frequently based on information we have gained from the media. Third, not only do the media serve as a conduit, passing on to us the opinions and view of others, they are, themselves, sometimes the source of such views and opinions.

It is important, then, in understanding public opinion, for us to study the media. In the first selection in this chapter, sociologist Peter Dreier points to the links between the most influential American newspaper companies and the corporate power structure in the country. He writes that the four news firms with the closest ties to the U.S. power structure—the *New York*

,vashington Post, the Wall Street Journal, and the Los Angeles
—are also the most influential, not only with the general public, but
vith public officials and other media people, too. These four newspapers,
Dreier says, share what he calls a "corporate liberal" outlook—that is, they
emphasize the stability of the political system and, thus, concede the need,
for example, for some government regulation of business, for civil rights, and
for social welfare legislation.

The media tend to perpetuate the status quo, the way things are. The
next two selections—one, from a leftist perspective, by Michael Parenti, the
other, from a more conservative viewpoint, by Walter Guzzardi—show how
the media tend to support the views of American business and government
officials.

What effect is *television* having on American public opinion? One important and ongoing study by George Gerbner, Larry Gross, Michael Morgan,
and Nancy Signorielli has found that the opinions of heavy viewers of television are different from those of light viewers. Their article, excerpted here,
says that heavy viewers are more apt to think of themselves as middle-class
and moderate than would otherwise be the case, and that they tend to become
more conservative on such issues as race and personal freedoms, but support greater spending for social programs.

THE PRESS AND THE POWER STRUCTURE
Peter Dreier

The mass media play two critical roles in society. First, they are profit-seeking
firms; their owners, directors, suppliers, and advertisers are interested in the
economic health of these firms. Second, they are ideological institutions. The
media set the agenda of political, social, and economic debate. They shape public
opinion on crucial issues; socialize individuals to social roles and behavior; and
can legitimate or undermine powerful institutions, individuals, and ideas. Who
controls these organizations is an important area for research.

Observers of and spokespersons for the mass media both view it as unique
among U.S. industries. They view the media as a "fourth estate," standing apart
from other institutions and segments of society, putting its public role and its
social responsibility above the unfettered pursuit of profits. Publishers, editors,
and journalists alike claim that their organizations are not beholden to any special
interests except the pursuit of truth. The prime function of the press, according
to the canons of the American Society of Newspaper Editors, is "to satisfy the
public's need to know." . . . Because of their unique function in society, the
mass media are, alone among U.S. industries, protected by the Constitution
through First Amendment guarantees of "freedom of the press." . . .

The media's special status is codified in an ideology extolling objectivity and impartiality. According to this ideology, the media should not reflect the views of any particular segment of society, but should try to provide a balance of all perspectives and points of view. . . . These norms are institutionalized in the daily practice of journalism. To guarantee that journalists' judgments are not colored by their own affiliations, newspapers encourage, and often require, that journalists avoid potentially conflicting commitments. The code of ethics of Sigma Delta Chi, the Society of Professional Journalists (whose officers are usually high-level editors of influential newspapers) states: "Journalists and their employers should conduct their personal lives in a manner which protects them from conflicts of interest, real or apparent. Their responsibilities to the public are paramount." Most journalists espouse these professional norms. . . .

While the Sigma Delta Chi statement includes employers (media executives) as well as journalists in its proscription against conflicts of interest, interviews with and letters from newspaper board directors, as well as their statements in various articles, reveal contradictory norms and practices among newspaper firms regarding executives' institutional affiliations. . . . Some believe that all such affiliations compromise the credibility of the press and thus should be prohibited or discouraged. For example, the chairman of one of the nation's largest newspaper firms (who requested anonymity) said: "I have turned down directorships of major banks, saving-fund societies, life insurance companies, fire insurance companies, graduate business schools, hospitals, art museums, orchestra, and Port Authority, to avoid conflict of interest and the mere appearance of conflict of interest, direct or indirect (as in news coverage of strikes against such institutions)." . . . Ben Bradlee, editor of the *Washington Post,* believes that newspaper company editors and executives should not join "any civic groups, clubs, or institutions." . . . Otis Chandler, publisher of the *Los Angeles Times,* has resigned from all his corporate directorships, citing the desire to avoid conflict of interest, although fellow board members at the parent Times-Mirror Company have not followed suit. Some firms prohibit affiliations only with profit-seeking corporations. Even among those who prohibit or discourage outside involvements, some apply such standards only to "inside" directors (employees of the firm) and not "outside" directors. Others view such involvements as part of a newspaper's role as an active "citizen" of the community, even suggesting that such involvements improve news coverage by allowing executives to feel the community's pulse. Still others suggest that affiliations related to the media's business operations, such as corporate directorships or business policy groups, are entirely separate from its journalistic activities and thus do not reflect potential conflicts of interest. Allen Neuharth, chairman of Gannett (the largest chain in terms of number of newspapers), explained that "I accepted the Marine Midland (bank) directorship because it has branches in all our communities in New York State . . . It's a good way for our company, through me, to be in touch with the business communities in the cities where we publish. You learn a lot of things about business developments that you might not otherwise know about." . . .

During the past decade, sociologists have developed a growing interest in the upper echelons of business and political power, but they have not focused on the press as a special segment. At the same time, interest in the mass media and its inner workings has also grown. Research, however, has centered on the day-to-day activities of the newsroom itself and the processes of identifying, gathering, writing and editing the news. This has provided a wealth of insight into the social construction of news and the pressures on news media person-nel. . . . But this research has not penetrated the upper echelons of the newspaper hierarchy, the top decision-makers or the boards of directors of newspaper-owning corporations. Much of what we know about these individuals comes from official and unofficial biographies of publishers, histories of par-ticular newspapers and journalistic accounts of the "lords of the press." . . . While these studies suggest that publishers and board members can have an influence on the general tone of a paper as well as upon specific stories, there has been little systematic research on the characteristics of these individuals and how (or if) they are connected to other sectors of the U.S. power structure.

. . . In this paper, I systematically examine the media elites' position in the web of institution affiliations that comprise the U.S. power structure. First, I examine the *extent* of the press' affiliations with other institutions. Despite their occupational code and ideology, the press is deeply involved in the power struc-ture network. Second, I describe the *distribution* of affiliations, particularly be-tween inside and outside directors, a distinction mentioned by several executives as the critical difference in terms of outside involvements. Third, I look at the different *patterns* of affiliation between newspaper firms. Some companies are more closely linked to the power structure than others. There is a small subset of influential papers whose affiliations are significantly greater than the others. This distinctive pattern corresponds to the ideological outlook of the pinnacle of the corporate elite, an outlook termed "corporate liberalism."

. . . I defined the U.S. power structure as the top positions in the institu-tional structure of the society, especially the elite institutions in four major sectors—corporations, business policy groups, non-profit civic organizations, and social clubs. Research has found that, despite divisions among the members of the power structure, overlapping memberships in these elite institutions form a network, or web, of inter-relationships that allows a high degree of cohesiveness within the capitalist class. At the pinnacle of this network is . . . the "inner group" within the capitalist class. This inner group includes those individuals connected to several major corporations who seek to protect the general welfare of large corporations as a class rather than the narrower interests of particular corporations, industries or regions. This inner group is the general voice of big business. Members of the inner group are disproportionately represented in in-stitutions that promote class cohesiveness and integration, such as civic organiza-tions, business policy groups, clubs, and high-level government posts. . . .

I defined the newspaper elite as the directors of the 25 largest newspaper companies in the United States (in terms of daily circulation) during 1978 and 1979. . . . The top 25 companies accounted for over one-half (53.5 percent) of the total daily circulation in 1979. In that year there were 1,764 papers in the United States with a combined circulation of 62.2 million. . . . The top 25 companies owned 425 daily papers with a total circulation of 33.3 million. These included most of the major metropolitan papers (including 20 of the 25 largest dailies) and many small- and medium-sized papers as well. The top 25 newspaper companies dominate the industry. This reflects the long-term trend, accelerated in the postwar period, toward concentration, conglomeration, and centralization within the newspaper industry. . . . While many of these companies are diversifying, they are still primarily engaged in newspaper publishing. . . . Of the top 25 companies, all except Newhouse (the third-largest chain) provided me with a list of its board of directors for 1978 and 1979. I checked the lists of directors against information from annual reports (for those that publish them) and public references such as Standard and Poor's *Register of Corporations*. Because the list of Newhouse's board could not be obtained directly or indirectly, . . . this research focuses on 24 of the top 25 chains.

This method netted a total of 290 individuals. . . . I examined affiliations with elite institutions. . . .

In fact, the data indicate that the nation's major newspaper firms *are* heavily linked with the nation's power structure. . . . [T]he 24 newspaper companies have 447 ties with elite organizations, including 196 with *Fortune's* 1,300 largest corporations, 97 with the 15 major business policy groups, 24 with the 12 major private universities, and 130 with the 47 elite social clubs. Banks and other financial institutions account for the largest number of corporate interlocks compared with other industries, a pattern found in other interlock studies. . . . This is not surprising, given the newspaper industry's rapid growth and expansion in the postwar period and these firms' need for capital. . . .

The power elite influences government policy not only through lobbying, campaign contributions, and policy groups and think tanks, but also by placing representatives (drawn disproportionately from the inner group) in high-level appointed positions in government. . . . [T]he newspaper industry shares in this pattern of "revolving door" links between the private sector and government. Thirty-six directors have been appointed to at least one (past or present) high-level federal government position. These posts include cabinet posts, presidential advisory commissions, advisory committees to federal agencies . . . and regional boards of the Federal Reserve Bank. Individuals with extensive and high-level experience in the federal government provide useful resources for newspaper companies, because these companies engage in activities (such as broadcasting and mergers) that are closely regulated by government. . . .

[T]he newspaper companies' ties with the U.S. power structure come primarily from outside directors brought onto their boards for a variety of reasons, and . . . a relatively small group of these outside directors account for a disproportionate share of these elite affiliations. . . . The inside directors, with some exceptions, run the day-to-day operations of the newspaper-owning firms (or simply benefit through trusts as beneficiaries). Their affiliations, also with some exceptions, are with industry-related activities—boards of the Associated Press, or newspaper executives' organizations, press clubs, awards committees, and so on—and reflect an industry-oriented outlook. . . . The exceptions to this rule are those inside directors who are part of the owning families—Katherine Graham of the *Washington Post,* Arthur Sulzberger of the New York Times, John Cowles and John Cowles, Jr., of the *Minneapolis Star and Tribune,* Marshall Field of Field Enterprises, Helen Copley of Copley Press, William Taylor of Affiliated Publications, and William R. Hearst, Jr., of Hearst Corporation, for example. Members of owning families tend to be part of both the social aristocracy of the nation . . . and the network of the U.S. power structure. Thus, they share more in common with the outside directors than with the professional executives hired to run the newspaper companies on a day-to-day basis. . . .

The outside directors provide a bridge between the newspaper companies and the capitalist class and its institutions. Some, as bank directors, may oversee their banks' investment in newspaper firms. Some, as former government officials, may provide expertise on government matters. But beyond these specific roles, these outside directors—many of them members of the inner group at the pinnacle of the capitalist class—provide a link to the broader interests of the business community with which the newspaper companies' future is tied. They provide important links to the major corporate decision-makers and the larger corporate world. Thus, while they may represent stockholders' interests . . . or banks, or other institutions in the narrow sense, they also provide a link to the central decision-making networks within the capitalist class.

[N]ot all newspaper companies are equally linked with the power structure. Four companies—Dow Jones Company (57 affiliations), the New York Times Company (47), the Washington Post Company (41), and the Times-Mirror Corporation (40)—together account for 185 (41.6 percent) of all elite affiliations. The next four companies account for 27.1 percent, the next four 17.2 percent, the next four 9.8 percent, the next four 3.5 percent, and the final four less than one percent. How can this disproportionate share at the top be explained? What distinguishes the companies with the most elite affiliations, and therefore the strongest institutional integration within the national power structure, from the other companies? . . .

What is clear . . . is that these four companies own the four most prestigious and politically-influential newspapers in the United States, the *Washington Post,* the *Wall Street Journal* (Dow Jones), the *Los Angeles Times* (Times-Mirror Corporation), and the *New York Times.* . . .

Journalistic influence and prestige probably accounts for the pattern of elite affiliations. There is a perfect correlation between the four newspaper companies with the most elite affiliations and the four most influential newspapers. The data does not explain the causal relationship. . . .

The four firms/papers with the closest ties to the U.S. power structure—the *New York Times,* the *Washington Post,* the *Wall Street Journal* and the *Los Angeles Times*—are distinguished from most other daily newspapers by their ideological outlook. These four papers reflect a "corporate liberal" perspective. This is the outlook identified with the inner group of the capitalist class. . . . While leaders of small and medium size businesses have characteristically opposed unions, social welfare, foreign aid, and government regulation in all forms, leaders of the major corporations (the inner group) have sought to forestall challenges from below and stabilize the long-term foundations of capitalism by implementing strategic reforms to co-opt dissent. Concerned with the stability of the entire system rather than the narrow interests of any one industry, corporation, or region, the leaders of the major corporations have conceded the need for some government regulation of business, as well as trade unionism, civil rights and social welfare legislation, foreign aid to promote free trade and stability, and other related policies. Corporate-sponsored think tanks and business policy groups generally adhere to this "corporate liberal" outlook.

Most U.S. newspapers are relatively narrow and parochial in outlook. Few have offices in Washington, D.C., or in foreign capitals. They emphasize local or regional news and economic development and growth. . . . Newspaper publishers traditionally have been politically conservative, reflecting a small-business outlook of government intervention in the marketplace, foreign aid and trade, defense policy, labor relations, and other policies. For the past 40 years, the overwhelming number of daily papers have supported the Republican party. In every presidential election since 1940, with the exception of 1964, most U.S. newspapers (between 57.7 percent in 1960 and 71.4 percent in 1972) endorsed the Republican candidate. This parochialism continues to this day. . . .

There is evidence, however, that as newspapers and newspaper companies grow as corporate entities (and as competiton between papers decline, leaving most dailies without any direct competition), they begin to broaden their political outlook. Today there are few independent, locally-owned dailies. Gradually, chains have purchased independent papers and large chains have purchased smaller chains. . . . As the chains grow, their high-level employees and executives make links outside the local community. They are no longer under the strong personal control of individuals such as William R. Hearst . . . or Col. Robert McCormick. . . . Moreover, as newspaper competition declines, monopoly or near-monopoly newspapers must appeal to a broader audience. These reasons are clearly responsible for the increasingly corporate liberal outlook of both the *Chicago Tribune* and the *Los Angeles Times,* once bastions of extreme conservatism. . . . Many papers, especially the *Wall Street Journal,* the *New York Times,* and the *Washington Post,* wish to appeal to the "upscale," affluent readers, the target for both advertisers and opinion-leaders. One indication of newspapers' increasingly "statesman-like role" is the steady increase in papers making no presidential endorsements at all—from only 13.4 percent in 1940 to 25.6 percent in 1976. . . .

Although daily newspapers are moving away from narrow parochialism, the four papers with the closest links to the power structure best reflect the corporate liberal viewpoint. They have taken the lead, among major daily papers, in exposing corporate wrongdoing and government corruption. They regularly investigate corporations and government actions that violate . . . "responsible capitalism." The *New York Times* published the Pentagon Papers, the *Washington Post* and the *Los Angeles Times* took the lead in the Watergate exposé, and the *Wall Street Journal* was the first major paper to investigate the foreign policy views and business ethics of Reagan advisor Richard Allen, to question the State Department's view of the ties between El Salvador's insurgents and both Cuba and the Soviet Union, and to expose many corporate scandals that corporate officers would have preferred to remain secret. These papers were among the first to reflect the disenchantment with the Vietnam War among the inner group of the business community. . . . Other papers also do such investigations and reporting, but none as consistently and with such national influence as these four papers. What this suggests is that these papers' corporate liberal outlook transcends the narrow interests of any one industry, corporation, or region. The corporate liberal press may criticize or expose *particular* corporate or government practices as harmful to the legitimacy and thus long-term stability of the entire system, or *particular* corporations or elected officials for the same reason. They take the long view. Thus, while at first it may seem paradoxical that the papers and firms with the *most* elite connections are the most likely to expose corporate and government practices, from the standpoint of their role as corporate liberal spokesmen for the inner group, it makes perfect sense.

In examining how the mass media functions, sociologists have usually explained the tendency of newspapers to reflect the outlook of the powerful in terms of the routines of newsgathering and the ability of powerful institutions and individuals to gain regular access to journalists. Or, they point to the attitude of journalists that those in positions of power and influence are more "responsible" news sources. . . . Certainly these factors help explain why newspapers in general reflect the world view of the powerful, but they cannot explain *variations* in ideology and world view, between newspapers, since the routines of news gathering are similar on most papers. That is why factors external to the newsroom, including the social, political, and corporate ties of newspaper directors, must be considered in explaining why some newspapers are different than others.

Our data confirm that the nation's leading newspaper companies are all linked to outside institutions. Of the 24 firms, 22 are linked to at least one elite institution of the *national* power structure. Moreover, these links are primarily through outside directors, who serve as the major link to the business community. The patterns of affiliations also suggest that four companies—those that publish the *New York Times,* the *Washington Post,* the *Los Angeles Times,* and the *Wall Street Journal*—represent the newspaper industry's part of the national power structure. These four papers speak not only for the directors and owners, but also for the inner group of the larger capitalist class. This is not to deny that they have a degree of autonomy and independence; they are not mere "tools" of this class. . . . But the structural links help to maintain and reinforce the ideology of corporate liberalism that these papers share with the inner group.   ■

THE MESSAGE OF THE MEDIA
Michael Parenti

. . . The press sees the established governmental leadership as essential to the maintenance of social order; and it gives more credence to public officials, corporate representatives, church leaders, and university officers than it does to protesters, taxpayers, consumers, workers, parishioners, and students.

The foremost leader in the United States is the president, "who is viewed as the ultimate protector of order." A systematic examination of twenty-five years of presidential news in the *New York Times* and *Time* magazine, as well as ten years of CBS broadcasts, reveals a "consistent pattern of favorable coverage of the President," with sympathetic stories outnumbering critical ones by two to one. More often than not, a president's viewpoint, especially if it has no liberal slant, is transmitted by the press with no opposing set of facts. Thus when President Reagan claimed credit for the 1982 extension of the Voting Rights Act and for appointing more minority members and females to administrative posts and waging a more vigorous enforcement of civil rights than previous administrations, the press faithfully reported his claims without pointing out that in fact he had threatened to veto the Voting Rights Act (and only signed it because it passed both houses by veto-proof majorities) and had actually cut back on minority and female appointments and on civil rights enforcement. And in the 1984 campaign when President Reagan asserted he would "never" attack Social Security, most of the major media gave top play to his statement without noting that in previous years he had repeatedly attacked Social Security, equating it and other entitlement programs with welfare—which he hated.

The 1984 presidential election campaign revealed the media's conservative bias to those who cared to look. According to a survey by *Editor and Publisher* magazine, 387 daily newspapers in the United States endorsed the right-wing Republican Ronald Reagan for president, while 63 supported the Democrat Walter Mondale. And this kind of conservative editorial bias carries over to news coverage, as media critic Ben Bagdikian found looking at earlier studies:

> Is it possible that newspapers might endorse Republicans, print conservative columnists, editorialize in favor of conservative issues, but still counterbalance this with pro-liberal bias in their news columns? In the mid-sixties I looked at the current published studies of political bias in the news. There were 84 systematic studies that found significant bias. There was a very high correlation between editorial policy and news bias. Of the 84 studies of bias, 74 found pro-Republican bias in the news in papers with pro-Republican editorial policies. There were seven instances of pro-Democratic bias in papers with pro-Democratic editorials. Only in three of the 84 cases was news bias the

opposite of editorial position. So where political bias in the news is found, it is overwhelmingly pro-Republican and pro-conservative. . . . There is much talk of a "liberal conspiracy" in the press; but the real question is how liberal electoral politics survives at all with the overwhelming opposition of the conservative press.[1]

A George Washington University study of television network evening news during the 1984 presidential campaign found that five out of six stories on Walter Mondale presented him in a negative manner focusing on minor mishaps and the candidate's presumed lack of appeal, rather than on the issues he was raising. . . .

Candidates learn that if they take a stand on controversial issues, the press is less likely to get their position across to the public than to concentrate on the controversy arising from the position taken. Suddenly their judgment and suitability will be called into question. So rather than the press using its coverage to fit the campaign, candidates trim their campaigns in anticipation of coverage. In the act of reporting on political life, the media actively help shape it.

The media create conservative effects by slighting the issues and focusing on candidate image. Even when attention is given to issues, it is usually to conjecture on how the candidate used them to help his image and advance his electoral chances. Once considered an adjunct to political discussion, image now seems to be the whole point of the discussion. "It is not the issues we are asked to judge: it is the nuances of the presentation."[2]

The George Washington University study conducted by the media specialist Michael Robinson found no liberal bias in campaign coverage but rather a "hollowness," and a lack of content. The campaign was treated more as a horse race than a clash of programs and policies. Who will run? Who will be nominated? Who's ahead? How will voters respond? Who will win? These preoccupations are supplemented with generous offerings of surface events and personality trivia. . . .

The media, like the major political parties themselves, treat campaigns not as an opportunity to develop democratic accountability and debate issues, but solely as a competiton for office. The focus is on the race itself with little thought raised about what the race is supposed to be about, what makes it so meaningful, and why should it be considered an exercise in democratic governance.

By focusing on "human interest" trivia, on contest rather than content, the media make it difficult for the public to give intelligent expression to political life and to mobilize around the issues. Thus the media have — intentionally or not — a conservative effect on public discourse. Given short shrift are the con-

1. Ben Bagdikian, *The Effete Conspiracy* (New York: Harper and Row, 1974), pp. 146, 148.
2. John Corry, "How TV Dilutes Political Debates," *New York Times* (October 21, 1984).

cerns of millions of people regarding nuclear arms escalation, Pentagon spending, tax reform, war in Central America, unemployment, and poverty. The democratic input, the great public debate about the state of the Union and its national policies, the heightening of political consciousness and information levels—all the things democratic electoral campaigns are supposed to foster— are crowded off the stage by image politics.

Not only during election campaigns but just about on every other occasion the news media prefer surface to substance, emphasizing the eye-catching visuals, the attention-catching "special angle" report, and the reassuring and comforting stories, while slighting the deeper, more important but politically more troublesome and more controversial themes. There is so much concentration on surface events that we often have trouble grasping the content of things, so much focus on action and personality that we fail to see the purposive goal of the action. For instance, during 1981, President Reagan dismantled major portions of forty years of domestic social legislation, initiated enormous tax cuts for rich individuals and corporations, dramatically escalated an already huge military spending program, and launched a series of cold-war confrontations against the Soviet Union—all policies of great import. However, the theme that predominated in most of the stories about those crucial actions was whether Reagan was "winning" or "losing" in his contests with Congress, the bureaucracy, labor, and foreign governments. Thus momentous political issues were reduced to catchy but trivial questions about Reagan's political "score card," his efficacy as a leader, and his personal popularity. . . .

Early studies of the media's impact on voting choices found that people seemed surprisingly immune from media manipulation. Campaign propaganda usually reinforced the public's preferences rather than altered them. People exposed themselves to media appeals in a selective way, giving more credence and attention to messages that bolstered their own views. Their opinions and information intake also were influenced by peers, social groups, and community, so the individual did not stand without a buffer against the impact of the media. The press, it was concluded, had only a "minimal effect."

As first glance, these findings are reassuring: People seem fairly self-directed in their responses to the media and do not allow themselves to be mindlessly directed. Democracy is safe. But troublesome questions remain. If through "selective exposure" and "selective attention" we utilize the media mainly to reinforce our established predispositions, where do the predispositions themselves come from? We can point to various socializing agencies: family, school, peer groups, work place—and the media themselves. Certainly some of our internalized political predispositions come from the dominant political culture that the media have had a hand in shaping—and directly from earlier exposure to the media themselves.

Our ability to discriminate is limited in part by how we have been conditioned by previous media exposures. The selectivity we exercise is not an autonomous antidote to propaganda but may feed right into it, choosing one or another variation of the same establishment offering. Opinions that depart too far from the mainstream are likely to be rejected out of hand. In such situations, our "selectivity" is designed to *avoid* information and views that contradict the dominant propaganda, a propaganda we long ago implicitly embraced as representative of "the nature of things." Thus, an implanted set of conditioned responses are now mistakenly identified as our self-generated political perceptions, and the public's selective ingestion of the media's conventional fare is wrongly treated as evidence of the "minimal effect" of news organizations.

In addition, more recent empirical evidence suggests that, contrary to the earlier "minimal effects" theory, the news media are able to direct our attention to certain issues and shape our opinions about them. One study found that "participants exposed to a steady stream of news about defense or about pollution came to believe that defense or pollution were more consequential problems." Other studies found that fluctuations in public concern for problems like civil rights, Vietnam, crime, and inflation over the last two decades reflected variations in the attention paid to them by the major media. . . .

If much of our informational and opinion intake is filtered through our previously established mental predilections, these predilections are often not part of our conscious discernment but of our unexamined perceptual conditioning — which brings us back to an earlier point: *Rather than being rational guardians against propaganda, our predispositional sets, having been shaped by prolonged exposure to earlier outputs of that same propaganda, may be active accomplices.*

Furthermore, there are many things about which we may not have a predetermined opinion. Lacking any competing information, we often unwarily embrace what we read or hear. In those instances, the media are not merely reinforcing previously held opinions, they are implanting new ones, although these implants themselves seldom fall upon *tabula rasa* brains and usually do not conflict too drastically with established biases. For example, millions of Americans who have an unfavorable view of the Sandinista government in Nicaragua came by that opinion through exposure to press reports rather than from direct contact with the Nicaraguan revolution. Here then is an original implant; people are prepared to hate and fear a foreign government on the basis of what they read in the papers or hear on television and radio. But this negative view is persuasive to them also because it is congruous with a long-standing and largely uncriticized anticommunist, cold-war propaganda that has shaped the climate of opinion for decades.

Thus the press can effectively direct our perceptions when we have no information to the contrary and when the message seems congruent with earlier notions about these events (which themselves may be in part media created). In this way the original implant is also a reinforcement of earlier perceptions. Seemingly distinct reports about diverse events have a hidden continuity and a cumulative impact that again support previous views. To see this process as one of "minimal effects" because it merely reinforces existing views and does not change them is to overlook the fact that it was never intended to change them and was indeed designed to reinforce the dominant orthodoxy.

As to whether the negative view of the Sandinistas translates into support for a U.S. government policy of aggression against Nicaragua is yet another question. For an entirely different set of reasons, such as fear of loss of American lives, fear of a larger war, opposition to the draft and to the higher taxes needed to pay for war, people may be reluctant to go along with U.S. intervention. Yet the negative image about Nicaragua propagated by government and press does leave policymakers with a lot of room to carry out aggressive measures short of direct intervention by U.S. troops. So even if the press does not elicit total public support for a particular policy, it is still not without a substantial influence in creating a *climate of opinion* that allows the government to get away with a lot, and it prevents a competing opinion about Nicaragua from occupying the high ground in the political arena. Even if those who are antagonistic toward Nicaragua constitute but a minority of the public, members of Congress and other politicians find it difficult, if not impossible, to say a positive word about the Sandinista revolution given the *publicly visible opinion* created by media and government around that issue and given the way that opinion hooks into decades of anticommunist propaganda.

If the press cannot mold our every opinion, it can frame the perceptual reality around which our opinions take shape. Here may lie the most important effect of the news media: they set the issue agenda for the rest of us, choosing what to emphasize and what to ignore or suppress, in effect, organizing much of our political world for us. *The media may not always be able to tell us what to think, but they are strikingly successful in telling us what to think about.*

Along with other social, cultural, and educational agencies, the media teach us tunnel vision, conditioning us to perceive the problems of society as isolated particulars, thereby stunting our critical vision. Larger causalities are reduced to immediately distinct events, while the linkages of wealth, power, and policy go unreported or are buried under a congestion of surface impressions and personalities. There is nothing too essential and revealing that cannot be ignored by the American press and nothing too trivial and superficial that cannot be accorded protracted play.

In sum, the media set the limits on public discourse and public understanding. They may not always mold opinion but they do not always have to. It is enough that they create opinion visibility, giving legitimacy to certain views and illegitimacy to others. The media do the same to substantive issues that they do to candidates, raising some from oblivion and conferring legitimacy upon them, while consigning others to limbo. This power to determine the issue agenda, the information flow, and the parameters of political debate so that it extends from ultra-right to no further than moderate center, is if not total, still totally awesome. . . . ■

THE PRESS, GOVERNMENT, AND BUSINESS
Walter Guzzardi

The idea of an adversarial relationship between the government and the press seems irresistible to members of both institutions. Widespread acceptance of this comfortable platitude has been encouraged by acerbic and colorful comments from the principal players, especially presidents of the United States. But the exchange of insults obscures the ties and common interests that bind the institutions together. Far from being separate and inimical entities, the press and the government are inextricably linked, woven together for the common purpose of strengthening the cause of democracy. In this union, the press has become a tremendous — and often unappreciated — force for legitimizing governmental institutions and free enterprise.

MUTUAL ANTIPATHY

Presidents love to complain about the media, and they can count on full quotation when they do. Harry Truman's characteristic crack that "When the press stops abusing me, I'll know I'm in the wrong pew" seems mild compared to the sequels. For Lyndon Johnson, meeting the press was like "looking down the open end of a gun barrel." Richard Nixon was more vulgar: Coming back from the rear of the presidential plane, where the press was sitting, he remarked to an aide, "It sure smells bad back there, doesn't it?" And once when the press entered the Cabinet room to take pictures, Nixon couldn't resist: "It's only coincidental that we were talking about pollution when the press walk[ed] in." Jimmy Carter found the press too dramatic and superficial. He probably shared Jody Powell's bitter belief that the media thought Carter to be "a devious, manipulative bastard, and by God they were determined to make sure the country knew about it." Although given high marks for handling the media well, Ronald Reagan often takes pot shots at the press, judging it deliberately unfair and allowing its exclusion from events such as the Grenada invasion. Some of Reagan's military chiefs go further, pitching into reporters who they say are perfectly willing to endanger American lives in their eagerness to be first to spill illicitly obtained military secrets. In what our military leaders must have regarded as a mortal blow, an officer at the State Department, Lt. General John Chain, removed a sinning reporter's portrait from a department wall.

A few barbs come from the press side, too. "We who hate your gaudy guts salute you" was William Allen White's famous greeting to FDR. Today, journalists lack that sense of style: Instead, they fill the air with self-righteous talk about their noble purposes, which, they insist, the president seeks to defeat. The media today seem to reciprocate presidential dislike and distrust, baying after Nixon, mocking Ford, disparaging Carter, resenting Reagan.

Although anecdotal and judgmental, such evidence imparts a kind of validity to the adversarial proposition: As in sex and psychoanalysis, the displeasure of either party (much less both parties) defines the experience. Still, a more useful perspective emerges when media and government are thought of as symbiotic. To consider one of them essential and the other derivative and obstructive overlooks the unbreakable nexus between the two. The point is simple, but it is often ignored: Government officials must have the media to get across their message, and the media must have the officials, for they are irreplaceable sources. In many areas, the economy being a conspicuous example, the government is the only supplier of data. Elsewhere, government officials stand comfortably on the demand side: Consumers want to know about them.

THE GRAND DESIGN

Both press and government are vital partners in the democratic experiment. Despite conflicts between them, the press accepts the presidency as an institution, and it does so surprisingly uncritically. That acceptance extends to many other government institutions, even those recently born, and to a host of American principles, values, and conventions as well. And, as it did in the early sixties, the press vigorously rejects radical change.

The widely held judgment that the press is liberal tends to obscure the authority that the press grants to traditional American government and its basic interests. "If the system were in peril," James MacGregor Burns has written, "the media would almost unanimously rally to its defense." Burns is undoubtedly correct. Columnist Richard Cohen confesses to a perplexing tendency to defend his nation from foreign threats who disguise themselves as interviewers:

> I get interviewed on foreign television as a critic of the Reagan administration. But then a funny thing happens. This critic . . . turns into John Wayne. The Duke can find hardly anything to criticize.

This is the propensity of print journalism, and it asserts itself in television news as well.

The media's central conservative strain shows up strikingly in the stylized picture of the nation that they present. That picture, although very far from the "mirror to the world" that news people insist they hold up, consistently supports American institutional life—economic as well as governmental. Reporting may sometimes be naive and obsessed with melodrama, and it too rarely questions underlying assumptions, but the flow of news is essentially benign. The media put their benedictions on private ownership, the heroics of individual entrepreneurs, and the concept of benevolent capitalism. Around those principles, the press organizes both its moral code and its definition of the news.

But the press seems to misunderstand its own mission. Among journalism's more outrageous claims is that it conveys "a true picture of life," or, in the words of White House correspondent Helen Thomas, that it seeks "only the truth." Sadly for those of us in search of enlightenment, the press knows no more than we do about life or about the truth—philosophers know more, taxi drivers and barbers know no less—and it has no idea what happened to the human race yesterday. Even if it did, it wouldn't tell us. Its deeper purpose is the undeclared one that Walter Lippmann pointed to fifty years ago: to report the central transactions in a democratic society—the transactions among institutions.

These institutions, almost invariably adjudged good by the press, make up the country's great entitlement. Fortunately for the earnings of the big companies in the news business, these good institutions often inadvertently harbor bad people. Straining at their traces, the press will see to it that these aberrant types are brought to justice, their malfeasances laid bare for all to regard. Since the press knows what is right—just listen to those editors—it sets about making things conform to that view. Hence the inclination toward institutional deification and the assumption that we are entitled to honest government. It is not thus everywhere. In Italy institutions are most often adjudged to be bad, and are usually ridiculed; malfeasants are not aberrant but commonplace. No doubt to its detriment, Italy doesn't think itself entitled to much better.

In a long, dense book called *Deciding What's News,* Columbia sociologist Herbert Gans argued that such a sense of entitlement is the ultimate arbiter of the news. By identifying people he calls "Knowns"—starting with the president, through presidential candidates, congressional leaders, members of the Supreme Court, and federal and state officeholders—and studying media attention given them, Gans found that they dominate the news with surprising consistency, and by wide margins over competitors for public attention. Among the Unknowns, the people getting the space were criminals, rioters, strikers, and other variously motivated protesters against conventional social order. Victims came next. Most people—like me, and possibly like you—who are seldom wrongdoers or victims, were left out: Editors find us a bore. "All the news that's fit to print" is defined by an exclusionist elite: It is what the editors of the *New York Times,* for reasons they would have a hard time explaining, don't like.

But an even higher set of decisions about what's news is made not by the *New York Times* but by government officials. They set the agenda, they are the real sources of the news, they are "the first-stage decision makers." To this process, which Lippmann called "the manufacture of consent," Gans attributes a circular quality. Knowns show the media where the stories are and how to get them. Then the "Knowns" monitor the media to test the reactions. From that monitoring—"the only nonfiction that most Americans see, hear, or read," according to Gans—the nation defines itself. The Knowns lead the editors, whom Gans calls "managers of the symbolic arena . . . protectors of order . . . moral guardians."

What happens to you and me is ignored by the "gatekeepers" (another neologism used to describe editors) who, in so many ways led by the Knowns, make assignments, allocate space to events they consider interesting, and bury where history can never find it the story that doesn't strike their fancy. Editors also manufacture what Daniel Boorstin called "media events": If the *New York Times* were to send Norman Mailer to Ouagadougou, for example, Ouagadougou would bust out all over your morning paper, although nothing may have happened there.

INSTITUTIONAL DEIFICATION: THE CASE OF THE FED

The search for institutions that define the news uncovers none more sacrosanct than the Federal Reserve Board. Hostages come and go, but nothing makes the wheels of news turn more regularly and predictably than the Fed. The figure of Paul Volcker—not many newspaper readers can still be ignorant of his height or his cigar-smoking habits, irrelevant as they are—and the perennial drama about his successor perpetuate Fed mythology. Enthroned, the great "independent" American institution is insulated from change: After Donald Regan, now White House chief of staff, was bold enough to suggest that radical change—maybe putting the Fed under control of the Treasury Department?—might be studied, he had to rush hastily for cover from the storm.

In the years since the popular press discovered what the Fed was, it has become the point of departure for stories about the economy. Other non-Fed-centered views are badly neglected. Some evidence supports Milton Friedman's ideas that the Fed is a ponderous bureaucracy whose principal aim is self-perpetuation, that it uses outdated technologies, and that it constantly shifts its goals. Seldom does the press point out that the source for the performance of the Fed is chiefly the Fed itself, which, some think, plays a shell game with its various measures of the money supply—all the Marvelous Ms—to argue its own case. Nor does the press examine much the thought that the Fed's recent acceleration may have little effect at all.

Although the idea would shock most businessmen, inherent conservatism is what drives most of the media's economic and financial reporting. In ways probably not fully understood by the practitioners themselves, warming waves of news support the principles that support the republic: a belief in capitalism (if properly restrained by the blessed institutions of government), a faith in free enterprise, a reverence for the risk-taking entrepreneur (but, matching another belief, only when he is successful), and an abiding affection for small business. True, the press complains a lot about business, and is unfailingly appalled to learn that men and markets often fail to conform to the media's ideals.

A few years ago, shock broke out all over the press when the huge salaries that corporate executives pay themselves came to public notice. The shudders have subsided somewhat with the nation's recent prosperity, but when the economy turns down again, and CEO salaries still go up, you can count on renewed indignation. The whole exhibition is charming in its innocence. In the press's moral order, executives are not supposed to be so grasping and greedy, nor should they give advantages to organized labor that might affect company performance long after new leaders have taken over. Anchormen raise eyebrows and offer disapproving looks when they recount the salaries of business bosses—but they usually neglect to admit that they, too, are members of the six- (or seven-) figure club.

In fact, top executives of big corporations have always taken good care of themselves, and they always will. In a crunch, they come first. Good times or bad, right or wrong, they get rich—and what's shocking about that, unless you have a code that says they shouldn't?

During the several oil crises, the press has also reacted with horror. "Obscene profits" were mulcting the helpless man in the street; Congress was aroused by headlines saying that "Exxon's profits rose 170 percent"; legislators sharpened their pencils. Neglected were the not especially difficult analytical points. When the prices of crude go up, oil company profits will follow, and they will also follow them down. Poor preceding years make increases in profit seem enormous by comparison: Afterwards, the high base makes the declines seem very steep, but that never attracts the same kind of attention. Many of the "obscenities" were inventory profits that benefited shareholders—often pension funds. The pension funds, of course, aided that man in the street who was supposedly being victimized. Anyway, companies are supposed to profit from market opportunities, raising prices ultimately to alleviate scarcity.

ALLIANCES

Behind the press's anger and numbskullery, though, lies tacit approval of our economic enterprises. Note what directions the press did *not* go in: No editorial suggested that a government official should be appointed to the boss's job at Chrysler to protect the American taxpayers' money. Nor, during the obscene profits era, was the air filled with proposals that the United States should follow the example of other countries and take over the oil companies. Even when the government had to bail out Lockheed some years ago, state ownership wasn't exactly a hot topic. Frivolous and shallow the press may be, but it adheres to its faith in our system of enterprise.

Small business, that child of free enterprise, is another media god. Jimmy Carter happily distributed medals on "Small Business Day" at the White House— one of his few media successes. The *New York Times* a few months ago ran a fulsome piece about Frank Swain, lawyer and ombudsman for the Small Business Administration, lauding him for promoting the interests of "this largely unrepresented segment of American business," and for fighting to get small business a bigger share of Pentagon procurement. Never mind that small business has plenty of clout in Washington: Not even President Reagan himself has been big enough to get rid of the scandal-ridden Small Business Administration.

Along with the Fed and the SBA stand a platoon of respected government agencies, which the press likes to think of as defenders of the underprivileged and helpless. One of the oldest is the Securities and Exchange Commission, that selfless protector of the legendary small investor. Tracking the torturous ways of the SEC some years ago, George Stigler, the Nobel prize-winning economist, was unable to uncover a single small investor better off for the Commission's activism, but the legend lives on. The Commission's own secret crusade, aimed at arrogating more and more power unto itself, goes unnoticed while it enlarges its authority in the courts, reaching in to bank regulation, better left to other bodies; to the prosecution of journalists who betray their employers by trading on advance knowledge of the next day's news—new territory for the SEC; and by aggressively pursuing the evils of insider trading, where this Commission intends to leave its mark on history. The only Commission foray to elicit an unpopular response in the press came predictably when the SEC started making noises about having reporters divulge their own financial holdings when they write business stories—an idea from which the Commission beat a hasty retreat, recognizing that it was about to alienate its best ally.

If businessmen are occasionally enraged by jabs from Dan Rather (who isn't?), they can turn to *Indiana Business* or *Corporate Report: Minnesota* for therapy. Reporting about business in regional periodicals, which apoplectic businessmen rarely mention, can be positively sycophantic. These journals, described recently as "the hottest, fastest-growing segment of today's media marketplace," consist largely of corporate press releases, canned stories from public relations firms, heartening reports about uplifted employee morale, and flattering lengthly profiles of local businessmen. Even the "liberal" *New York Times,* the *Washington Post,* and *Time* magazine as well, often run articles that the mothers of the protagonists must love. Meanwhile, the media for years laid off now classic stories like the smoking/cancer connection and food contamination. The biggest story of all, automobile safety, never showed up until a nonjournalist, Ralph Nader, broke it with *Unsafe at Any Speed.* Tobacco, food, and automobile companies make up the established order, so they are usually left alone.

TV network news reinforces the message: if much of TV news is stereotypical, shallow, and stupid, it's no accident. TV news, like TV fiction, features heroes, villains, clear dangers, simple plots, plenty of pictorial action, and final outcomes. The producers of TV news—the very phrase says a lot—fit the news into these patterns, which conform with current social outlooks.

In a broader sense, TV remains a testament to the American business system. The TV world is upbeat, materialistic, and consumption-prone. Whatever TV says that is nasty about corporate America is subsumed by the overriding assertion of the great desiderata: the products of a consumer society, the pleasures of the packaged good life. The big businessman may be a villain sometimes—on TV, he's got to be a villain or a hero, of course—but his power and perquisites are still envied. And the power of the advertiser, I believe, is greater in TV news than in print journalism: Advertisers can and do remove their sponsorship of TV programs that they don't like.

WHY NOT THE BEST

Musing on these considerations that balance the "adversarial" proposition and that highlight the media's influence for continuity over change, leads back to the kind of society we are. In the end, the media have to make their way in the world of commerce. That may lead to many kinds of reporting that we don't like, but it remains the best system. The media so often support the machinery of power because we, their audience, would not have them do otherwise. The press can be much improved despite the conclusion, but still the conclusion stands: We get the kind of press we deserve. ■

TELEVISION MOVES US TOWARD THE MIDDLE
George Gerbner, Larry Gross, Michael Morgan, and Nancy Signorielli

. . . Television is a centralized system of storytelling. Its drama, commercials, news, and other programs bring a relatively coherent world of common images and messages into every viewing home. People are now born into the symbolic environment of television and live with its repetitive lessons throughout life. Television cultivates from the outset the very predispositions that affect future cultural selections and uses. Transcending historic barriers of literacy and mobility, television has become the primary common source of everyday culture of an otherwise heterogeneous population.

Many of those now dependent upon television have never before been part of a shared national political culture. Television provides, perhaps for the first time since preindustrial religion, a strong cultural link, a shared daily ritual of highly compelling and informative content, between the elites and all other publics. What is the role of this common experience in the general socialization and political orientation of Americans? . . .

For message system analysis we record and analyze week-long samples of network television drama and have done so for each year since 1967. We subject these sample weeks of television drama to rigorous and detailed content analysis in order to reliably delineate selected features of the television world. We consider these the potential lessons of television and use them as the source of questions for the second prong of the inquiry. In this "cultivation analysis," we examine the responses of light and heavy viewers to these questions, phrased to refer to the real world. (Non-viewers are too few and demographically too scattered for serious research purposes.) We want to determine whether those who spend more of their time with television are more likely to answer these questions in ways that reflect the potential lessons of the television world (the "television answer") than are groups that watch less television but are otherwise comparable (in terms of important demographic characteristics) to the heavy viewers. . . .

On issue after issue we have found that the assumptions, beliefs, and values of heavy viewers differ systematically from those of light viewers in the same demographic groups. The differences tend to reflect both what things exist and how things work in the television world. . . .

TELEVISION IMAGES

When many millions of dollars of revenue ride on a single ratings point, there are few degrees of freedom to indulge egos or yield to many other pressures. Competition for the largest possible audience at the least cost means striving for the broadest and most conventional appeals, blurring sharp conflicts, blending and balancing competing perspectives, and presenting divergent or deviant images as mostly to be shunned, feared, or suppressed. Otherwise, no matter how skewed or off-center a view might really be, it should be "balanced" by more "extreme" manifestations, preferably on "both sides," to make its presentation appear "objective," "moderate," and otherwise suitable for mass marketing.

These institutional pressures and functions suggest the cultivation of relatively "moderate" or "middle-of-the-road" presentations and orientations. . . .

The world of prime time as seen by the average viewer is animated by vivid and intimate portrayals of over 300 major characters a week, mostly stock dramatic types, and their weekly rounds of dramatic activities. . . . Despite the fact that nearly half of the national income goes to the top fifth of the real population, the myth of middle class as the all-American norm dominates the world of television. Nearly 7 out of 10 television characters appear in the "middle-middle" of a five-way classification system. Most of them are professionals and managers. Blue-collar and service work occupies 67 percent of all Americans but only 10 percent of television characters. These features of the world of prime-time television should cultivate a middle-class or "average" incomd self-designation among viewers.

Men outnumber women at least three to one. Most women attend to men or home (and appliances) and are younger (but age faster) than the men they meet. Underrepresentation in the world of television suggests the cultivation of viewers' acceptance of more limited life chances, a more limited range of activities, and more rigidly stereotyped images than for the dominant and more fully represented social and dramatic types.

Young people (under 18) comprise one-third and older people (over 65) one-fifth of their true proportion in the population. Blacks on television represent three-fourths and Hispanics one-third of their share of the U.S. population, and a disproportionate number are minor rather than major characters. A single program like "Hawaii Five-O" can result in the overrepresentation of Orientals, but again mostly as minor characters. A study by Weigel and others . . . shows that while blacks appear in many programs and commercials, they seldom appear with whites, and actually interact with whites in only about two percent of total human appearance time. The prominent and stable overrepresentation of well-to-do white males in the prime of life dominates prime time. Television's general demography bears greater resemblance to the facts of consumer spending than to the U.S. Census. . . . These facts and dynamics of life suggest the cultivation of a relatively restrictive view of women's and minority rights among viewers.

The state in the world of prime time acts mostly to fend off threats to law and order in a mean and dangerous world. Enforcing the law of that world takes nearly three times as many characters as the number of all blue-collar and service worker characters. The typical viewer of an average week's prime-time programs sees realistic and often intimate (but usually not true-to-life) representations of the life and work of 30 police officers, 7 lawyers, and 3 judges, but only one engineer or scientist and very few blue-collar workers. Nearly everybody appears to be comfortably managing on an "average" income or as a member of a "middle class."

But threats abound. Crime in prime time is at least 10 times as rampant as in the real world. An average of five to six acts of overt physical violence per hour involves over half of all major characters. Yet, pain, suffering, and medical help rarely follow this mayhem. Symbolic violence demonstrates power; it shows victimization, not just aggression, hurt but not therapy; it shows who can get away with what against whom. The dominant white males in the prime of life score highest on the "safety scale": they are the most likely to be the victimizers rather than the victims. Conversely, old, young, and minority women, and young boys, are the most likely to be the victims rather than the victimizers in violent conflicts.

EFFECT ON VIEWERS

The warped demography of the television world cultivates some iniquitous concepts of the norms of social life. Except among the most traditional or biased, television viewing tends to go with stronger prejudices about women and old people . . . . Children know more about uncommon occupations frequently portrayed on television than about common jobs rarely seen on the screen. . . . Viewing boosts the confidence rating given to doctors . . . but depresses that given to scientists, especially in groups that otherwise support them most. . . .

Cultivation studies continue to confirm the findings that viewing tends to heighten perceptions of danger and risk and maintain an exaggerated sense of mistrust, vulnerability, and insecurity. We have also found that the prime-time power hierarchy of relative levels of victimization cultivates similar hierarchies of fears of real-world victimization among viewers. Those minority group viewers who see themselves more often on the losing end of violent encounters on television are more apprehensive of their own victimization than are the light viewers in the same groups. . . . Television's mean and dangerous world can thus be expected to contribute to receptivity to repressive measures and to apparently simple, tough, hard-line posturings and "solutions." At the same time, however, the overall context of conventional values and consumer gratifications, with their requirements of happy endings and material satisfaction, may suggest a sense of entitlement to goods and services, setting up a conflict of perspectives.

Thus we can expect the cultivation of preference for "middle-of-the-road" political orientations alongside different and at times contradictory assumptions. These assumptions are likely to include demographically skewed, socially rigid and mistrustful, and often excessively anxious or repressive notions, but expansive expectations for economic services and material progress even among those who traditionally do not share such views. . . .

Political party affiliation is traditionally related to social status. Therefore, it is not surprising that among heavy viewers, who tend to have lower status, we find more Democrats than among light viewers (45 percent to 35 percent), while proportionately more light than heavy viewers are Independents (41 to 34 percent) and Republicans (24 to 21 percent). We will see, however, that television alters the social significance and political meaning of these and other conventional labels.

An example of this transformation is the blurring of class lines and the self-styled "averaging" of income differences. . . . [L]ow socioeconomic status (SES) respondents are most likely to call themselves "working class"—but only when they are light viewers. Heavy-viewing respondents of the same low-status group are significantly less likely than their light-viewing counterparts to think of themselves as "working class" and more likely to say they are "middle class." The television experience seems to counter other circumstances in thinking of one's class. It is an especially powerful deterrent to working-class consciousness.

Middle SES viewers show the least sense of class distinction at different viewing levels. They are already "in" the mainstream. The high SES group, however, like the low SES group, exhibits a response pattern that is strongly associated with amount of television viewing. More high SES heavy viewers consider themselves to be "working class" than do high SES light viewers. Television viewing tends to blur class distinctions and make more affluent heavy viewers think of themselves as just working people of average income.

These processes show up clearly when we relate television viewing to labels of direct political relevance. We used a relatively general and presumably stable designation of political tendency, most likely to structure a range of political attitudes and positions: the self-designations "liberal," "moderate," and "conservative." . . . [3] The most general relationship between television viewing and political tendency is that significantly more heavy than light viewers in all subgroups call themselves moderates and significantly fewer call themselves conservatives. The number of liberals also declines slightly among heavy viewers, except where there are the fewest liberals (e.g., among Republicans). [This] illustrates the absorption of divergent tendencies and the blending of political distinctions into the "television mainstream." . . .

On the surface, mainstreaming appears to be a "centering"—even a "liberalizing"—of political and other tendencies. After all, as viewing increases, the per-

---

3. Political tendency was measured by the question, "We hear a lot of talk these days about liberals and conservatives. I'm going to show you a seven-point scale on which the *political* views that people might hold are arranged from extremely liberal—point 1—to extremely conservative—point 7. Where would you place yourself on this scale?" . . .

cent of conservatives drops significantly within every group (except Democrats), and the relationships of amount of television viewing with the percent of liberals are generally weaker. However, a closer look at the actual positions taken in response to questions about political issues such as minorities, civil and personal rights, free speech, the economy, etc., shows that the mainstream does not always mean "middle of the road."

Eight questions about attitudes toward blacks were asked in at least two of the four . . . years analyzed here, and explicitly assess respondents' desire to keep blacks and whites separate. Questions include, "Do you think that white students and black students should go to the same schools or to separate schools?" and "Do you think that there should be laws against marriages between blacks and whites?" . . . Light-viewing liberals are always least likely to endorse segregationist statements. Light-viewing moderates and conservatives are, interestingly, often very close; in more than one instance, light-viewing moderates are slightly *more* likely to support racial segregation than are light-viewing conservatives.

More importantly, associations between amount of viewing and these attitudes are sharply different for liberals, moderates, and conservatives. Liberals, who are least likely to hold segregationist views, show some dramatic (and always significant) associations between amount of viewing and the desire to keep blacks and whites separate. Among moderates and conservatives, in contrast, the relationships between viewing and these attitudes are smaller and inconsistent. (Four of the interaction terms are significant, showing the correlates of heavy viewing to be systematically different across political categories.) On busing, moderates and conservatives even show a significant negative association, indicating *less* segregationist attitudes among these heavy viewers; this is an instance of viewing bringing divergent groups closer together from both directions.

In general, these patterns vividly illustrate mainstreaming. There are, to be sure, some across-the-board relationships, but even these are markedly weaker for moderates and conservatives. Overall, these data show a convergence and homogenization of heavy viewers across political groups.

The differences between liberals and conservatives—i.e., the effects of political tendency on attitudes toward blacks—decrease among heavy viewers. Among light viewers, liberals and conservatives show an average difference of 15.4 percentage points; yet, among heavy viewers, liberals and conservatives differ by an average of only 4.6 percentage points. . . .

In . . . opposition to busing, we . . . see that heavy-viewing conservatives are more "liberal" and heavy-viewing liberals more "conservative" than their respective light-viewing counterparts. In . . . opposition to open housing laws, viewing is not associated with any differences in the attitudes expressed by conservatives, but among liberals . . . heavy viewing goes with a greater likelihood of such opposition. Finally, in response to a question about laws against marriages between blacks and whites, we find that heavy viewers in all groups are more likely to favor these laws than are light viewers in the same categories, but this is significantly more pronounced for liberals.

In sum, the responses of heavy-viewing liberals are quite comparable to those of all moderates and conservatives, and there is not much difference between moderates and conservatives. The television mainstream, in terms of attitudes toward blacks, clearly runs to the right. . . .

In the case of attitudes on homosexuality, abortion, and marijuana, there is considerable spread between light-viewing liberals and light-viewing conservatives (an average of 28 percentage points); the latter are always much more likely to be opposed. And, once again, the attitudes of heavy-viewing liberals and conservatives are far closer together (an average of 13 percentage points . . .), due primarily to the difference between light- and heavy-viewing liberals. (All interaction terms are significant.) In all instances, the self-designated moderates are much closer to the conservatives than they are to the liberals. . . .

The narrowing of the political spectrum is also revealed in some more explicitly "political" findings. Whatever its reasons and justifications, anti-communism has been used as the principal rationale for political repression since the first Red Scare of 1919–1920. Responses to several . . . questions tap television's relationship to anti-Communist sentiments and to the tendency to restrict free speech. . . . Five out of ten light-viewing moderates and six out of ten light-viewing conservatives consider communism "the worst form [of government] of all." Heavy-viewing moderates and conservatives nearly unite in condemning communism as "worst" by even larger margins (64 and 67 percent, respectively). But viewing makes the biggest difference among liberals: only one-third of light-viewing but half of heavy-viewing liberals agree that communism is "the worst form" of government. . . .

Responses on restricting free speech show similar patterns. Heavy viewers of all three political persuasions are more likely to agree to restrict, in various ways, the speech of "left" and "right" nonconformists than are their light-viewing counterparts. There is little difference between conservatives and moderates. But, again, the most striking difference is between light- and heavy-viewing liberals.

In general, with respect to anti-communism and restrictions on political speech of the left and right, those who call themselves conservatives are in the "television mainstream." Those who consider themselves moderates join the conservatives—or exceed them—as heavy viewers. Liberals perform their traditional role of defending political plurality and freedom of speech only when they are light viewers. Mainstreaming means not only a narrowing of political differences but also a significant tilt in the political balance.

But political drift to the right is not the full story. As we noted before, television has a business clientele which, while it may be politically conservative, also has a mission to perform that requires the cultivation of consumer values and gratifications pulling in a different direction.

A number of surveys have documented the tendency of respondents to support government services that benefit them while taking increasingly hard-line positions on taxes, equality, crime, and other issues that touch deeply felt anxieties and insecurities. The media interpreted (and election results seemed to confirm, at least in the early 1980s) these inherently contradictory positions as a "conservative trend". . . . Television may have contributed to that trend in two ways. First, as our Violence Profiles have demonstrated, heavy viewers have a keener sense of living in a "mean world" with greater hazards and insecurities than do comparable groups of light viewers. . . . Second, while television does not directly sway viewers to be conservative (in fact, heavy viewers tend to shun that label), its mainstream of apparent moderation shifts political attitudes toward conservative positions.

When positions on economic issues are examined, however, a different if perhaps complementary pattern emerges. Television needs to attract a wide following to perform its principal task of delivering the buying public to its sponsors. It could afford even less than most politicians to project austerity, to denigrate popular bread-and-butter issues, or to urge saving instead of spending for goods, services, and security. The essential mission of the television institution—mass mobilization for consumption—would seem to dictate an economically popular and even populist stance.

We examined patterns of responses to questions about government spending on 11 programs. . . . Seven are traditional "liberal" issues: health, environment, cities, education, foreign aid, welfare, and blacks. [O]n health, welfare, and blacks, . . . instead of heavy-viewing liberals taking positions closer to conservatives, the opposite happens: heavy-viewing conservatives, as well as moderates, converge toward the liberal position on six of the seven issues. The more they watch, the less they say the U.S. spends "too much." . . .

The remaining four issues are crime, drugs, defense, and space exploration. . . . Here again, with the exception of space, heavy viewers generally want to spend more. As these are somewhat more "conservative" issues, it is the moderates and conservatives who are in the "television mainstream," taking a position toward greater spending, and heavy-viewing liberals stand close to them. . . .

To investigate further the populist streak in the otherwise restrictive political mix of the typology of the heavy viewer, we look for questions that combine outlooks on both taxes and spending. The 1980 [study] permitted us to isolate those respondents who oppose reductions in government spending and yet feel their taxes are too high. . . .

As on the other economic issues, liberals and moderates are close together while heavy-viewing conservatives join the liberal-moderate mainstream; the tilt is in the liberal (if conflicted) direction. Heavy-viewing Republicans and Independents also express attitudes closer to the Democratic position than do their light-viewing political counterparts. But all heavy viewers are more likely to want a combination of more social spending *and* lower taxes.

SUMMARY

The cultural—and evidently political—television mainstream tends to absorb the divergent tendencies that traditionally shaped the political process and to contain its own cross-currents. Heavy television viewers tend more than comparable light viewers to call themselves "moderate" but take positions that are unmistakably conservative, except on economic issues.

Our analysis shows that although television viewing brings conservatives, moderates, and liberals closer together, it is the liberal position that is weakest among heavy viewers. Viewing blurs traditional differences, blends them into a more homogeneous mainstream, and bends the mainstream toward a "hard line" position on issues dealing with minorities and personal rights. Hard-nosed commercial populism, with its mix of restrictive conservatism and pork-chop liberalism, is the paradoxical—and potentially volatile—contribution of television to political orientations.

The "television mainstream" may be the true twentieth-century melting pot of the American people. The mix it creates is of central significance for the theory as well as the practice of popular self-government. . . .   ■

CHAPTER 6

Interest Groups

Americans can participate in politics and government in a number of ways. They can vote; that is probably the easiest way to participate, although many people nevertheless stay home on election day. They can run for office, but most do not do so, of course.

Political participation can take other forms. People can take part in campaigns and make campaign contributions. They can try to influence government officials by direct contact with them—that is, by "lobbying." They can engage in demonstrations, boycotts, and strikes and in other direct ways attempt to call attention to their cause and affect public policy. They can file lawsuits.

In all these activities, except voting and running for office, of course, people can participate either individually or as members of organizations. These "interest groups"—sometimes also called "lobbies" or "pressure groups"— are a prominent feature of the American political system.

An interest group has three characteristics. First, it is *organized*. Second, it is an organization of *shared attitudes or interests*. Third, it *works to affect public policy*. The activity of such groups is protected by the First Amendment right of Americans to petition their government.

But not everyone belongs to an interest group, and some interests are represented more strongly than others. In this chapter, we will first consider the role of interest groups in a democracy. Then, we will turn our attention to the activities of modern American interest groups—including that of lobbying and the financing of political campaigns through political action committees (PACs)—and the problems these activities pose for America's democracy.

DEMOCRACY AND INTEREST GROUPS

James Madison did not like the idea of "factions" in politics—what we call interest groups. But he thought that human nature made them inevitable. In his famed *Federalist 10,* excerpted here, he wrote that interest groups, or factions, could best be kept within check, and particularly powerful ones kept from dominance, by the kind of government the American Constitution provided, fragmenting power, and by competition among numerous groups of conflicting aims.

Recent years have seen a great proliferation of interest groups in the United States—what some call an "advocacy explosion." The influence of the "special interests," particularly that of business and industry, has grown, especially through lobbying and campaign financing. Political scientist Jeffrey M. Berry, a portion of whose book is reprinted here, discusses "Madison's Dilemma," as he calls it, in the light of modern developments—how citizens' rights to organize and seek to influence the government can be respected without allowing too much power for certain groups. He feels that reform in the way political campaigns are financed would both reduce the inordinate influence of some interest groups and help political parties rebuild their importance in the American system.

FEDERALIST 10

Among the numerous advantages promised by a well constructed Union, none deserves to be more accurately developed than its tendency to break and control the violence of faction. The friend of popular governments, never finds himself so much alarmed for their character and fate, as when he contemplates their propensity to this dangerous vice. He will not fail therefore to set a due value on any plan which, without violating the principles to which he is attached, provides a proper cure for it. The instability, injustice and confusion introduced into the public councils, have in truth been the mortal diseases under which popular governments have every where perished; as they continue to be the favorite and fruitful topics from which the adversaries to liberty derive their most specious declamations. The valuable improvements made by the American Constitutions on the popular models, both ancient and modern, cannot certainly be too much admired; but it would be an unwarrantable partiality, to contend that they have as effectually obviated the danger on this side as was wished and expected. Complaints are every where heard from our most considerate and virtuous citizens, equally the friends of public and private faith, and of public and personal liberty; that our governments are too unstable; that the public good is disregarded in the conflicts of rival parties; and that measures are too often decided, not according to the rules of justice, and the rights of the minor party; but by the superior force of an interested and over-bearing majority. However anxiously we may wish that these complaints had no foundation, the evidence of known facts will not permit us to deny that they are in some degree true. It will be found indeed, on a candid review of our situation, that some of the distresses under which we labor, have been erroneously charged on the operation of our governments; but it will be found, at the same time, that other causes will not alone account for many of our heaviest misfortunes; and particularly, for that prevailing and increasing distrust of public engagements, and alarm for private rights, which are echoed from one end of the continent to the other. These must be chiefly, if not wholly, effects of the unsteadiness and injustice, with which a factious spirit has tainted our public administrations.

By a faction I understand a number of citizens, whether amounting to a majority or minority of the whole, who are united and actuated by some common impulse of passion, or of interest, adverse to the rights of other citizens, or to the permanent and aggregate interests of the community.

There are two methods of curing the mischiefs of faction: the one, by removing its causes; the other, by controling its effects.

There are again two methods of removing the causes of faction: the one by destroying the liberty which is essential to its existence; the other, by giving to every citizen the same opinions, the same passions, and the same interests.

It could never be more truly said than of the first remedy, that it is worse than the disease. Liberty is to faction, what air is to fire, an aliment without which it instantly expires. But it could not be a less folly to abolish liberty, which is essential to political life, because it nourishes faction, than it would be to wish the annihilation of air, which is essential to animal life, because it imparts to fire its destructive agency.

The second expedient is as impracticable, as the first would be unwise. As long as the reason of man continues fallible, and he is at liberty to exercise it, different opinions will be formed. As long as the connection subsists between his reason and his self-love, his opinions and his passions will have a reciprocal influence on each other; and the former will be objects to which the latter will attach themselves. The diversity in the faculties of men from which the rights of property originate, is not less an insuperable obstacle to a uniformity of interests. The protection of these faculties is the first object of Government. From the protection of different and unequal faculties of acquiring property, the possession of different degrees and kinds of property immediately results: and from the influence of these on the sentiments and views of the respective proprietors, ensues a division of the society into different interests and parties.

The latent causes of faction are thus sown in the nature of man; and we see them every where brought into different degrees of activity, according to the different circumstances of civil society. A zeal for different opinions concerning religion, concerning Government and many other points, as well of speculation as of practice; an attachment to different leaders ambitiously contending for pre-eminence and power; or to persons of other descriptions whose fortunes have been interesting to the human passions, have in turn divided mankind into parties, inflamed them with mutual animosity, and rendered them much more disposed to vex and oppress each other, than to co-operate for their common good. So strong is this propensity of mankind to fall into mutual animosities, that where no substantial occasion presents itself, the most frivolous and fanciful distinctions have been sufficient to kindle their unfriendly passions, and excite their most violent conflicts. But the most common and durable source of factions, have been the various and unequal distribution of property. Those who hold, and those who are without property, have ever formed distinct interests in society. Those who are creditors, and those who are debtors, fall under a like discrimination. A landed interest, a manufacturing interest, a mercantile interest, a monied interest, with many lesser interests, grow up of necessity in civilized nations, and divide them into different classes, actuated by different sentiments and views. The regulation of these various and interfering iterests forms the principal task of modern Legislation, and involves the spirit of party and faction in the necessary and ordinary operations of Government.

No man is allowed to be a judge in his own cause; because his interest would certainly bias his judgment, and, not improbably, corrupt his integrity. With equal, nay with greater reason, a body of men, are unfit to be both judges and parties, at the same time; yet, what are many of the most important acts of legislation, but so many judicial determinations, not indeed concerning the rights of single persons, but concerning the rights of large bodies of citizens; and what are the different classes of legislators, but advocates and parties to the causes which they determine? Is a law proposed concerning private debts? It is a question to which the creditors are parties on one side, and the debtors on the other. Justice ought to hold the balance between them. Yet the parties are and must be themselves the judges; and the most numerous party, or, in other words, the most powerful faction must be expected to prevail. Shall domestic manufactures be encouraged, and in what degree, by restrictions on foreign manufactures? are questions which would be differently decided by the landed and the manufacturing classes; and probably by neither, with a sole regard to justice and the public good. . . .

It is in vain to say, that enlightened statesmen will be able to adjust these clashing interests, and render them all subservient to the public good. Enlightened statesmen will not always be at the helm: Nor, in many cases, can such an adjustment be made at all, without taking into view indirect and remote considerations, which will rarely prevail over the immediate interest which one party may find in disregarding the rights of another, or the good of the whole.

The inference to which we are brought, is, that the *causes* of faction cannot be removed; and that relief is only to be sought in the means of controling its *effects*.

If a faction consists of less than a majority, relief is supplied by the republican principle, which enables the majority to defeat its sinister views by regular vote:

It may clog the administration, it may convulse the society; but it will be unable to execute and mask its violence under the forms of the Constitution. When a majority is included in a faction, the form of popular government on the other hand enables it to sacrifice to its ruling passion or interest, both the public good and the rights of other citizens. To secure the public good, and private rights, against the danger of such a faction, and at the same time to preserve the spirit and the form of popular government, is then the great object to which our en-quiries are directed: Let me add that it is the great desideratum, by which alone this form of government can be rescued from the opprobrium under which it has so long labored, and be recommended to the esteem and adoption of mankind.

By what means is this object attainable? Evidently by one of two only. Either the existence of the same passion or interest in a majority at the same time, must be prevented; or the majority, having such co-existent passion or interest, must be rendered, by their number and local situation, unable to concert and carry into effect schemes of oppression. If the impulse and the opportunity be suffered to coincide, we well know that neither moral nor religious motives can be relied on as an adequate control. They are not found to be such on the injustice and violence of individuals, and lose their efficacy in proportion to the number com-bined together; that is, in proportion as their efficacy becomes needful.

From this view of the subject, it may be concluded, that a pure Democracy, by which I mean, a Society, consisting of a small number of citizens, who assem-ble and administer the Government in person, can admit of no cure for the mischiefs of faction. A common passion or interest will, in almost every case, be felt by a majority of the whole; a communication and concert results from the form of Government itself; and there is nothing to check the inducements to sacrifice the weaker party, or an obnoxious individual. Hence it is, that such Democracies have ever been spectacles of turbulence and contention; have ever been found incompatible with personal security, or the rights of property; and have in general been as short in their lives, as they have been violent in their deaths. Theoretic politicans, who have patronized this species of Government, have erroneously supposed, that by reducing mankind to a perfect equality in their political rights, they would, at the same time, be perfectly equalized and assimilated in their possessions, their opinions, and their passions.

A Republic, by which I mean a Government in which the scheme of represen-tation takes place, opens a different prospect, and promises the cure for which we are seeking. Let us examine the points in which it varies from pure Democracy, and we shall comprehend both the nature of the cure, and the efficacy which it must derive from the Union.

The two great points of difference between a Democracy and a Republic are, first, the delegation of the Government, in the latter, to a small number of citizens elected by the rest: secondly, the greater number of citizens, and greater sphere of country, over which the latter may be extended.

The effect of the first difference is, on the one hand to refine and enlarge the public views, by passing them through the medium of a chosen body of citizens, whose wisdom may best discern the true interest of their country, and whose patriotism and love of justice, will be least likely to sacrifice it to temporary or partial considerations. Under such a regulation, it may well happen that the public voice pronounced by the representatives of the people, will be more consonant to the public good, than if pronounced by the people themselves convened for the purpose. On the other hand, the effect may be inverted. Men of factious tempers, of local prejudices, or of sinister designs, may by intrigue, by corruption or by other means, first obtain the suffrages, and then betray the interests of the people. The question resulting is, whether small or extensive Republics are most favorable to the election of proper guardians of the public weal: and it is clearly decided in favor of the latter by two obvious considerations.

In the first place it is to be remarked that however small the Republic may be, the Representatives must be raised to a certain number, in order to guard against the cabals of a few; and that however large it may be, they must be limited to a certain number, in order to guard against the confusion of a multitude. Hence the number of Representatives in the two cases, not being in proportion to that of the Constituents, and being proportionally greatest in the small Republic, it follows, that if the proportion of fit characters, be not less, in the large than in the small Republic, the former will present a greater option, and consequently a greater probability of a fit choice.

In the next place, as each Representative will be chosen by a greater number of citizens in the large than in the small Republic, it will be more difficult for unworthy candidates to practise with success the vicious arts, by which elections are too often carried; and the suffrages of the people being more free, will be more likely to centre on men who possess the most attractive merit, and the most diffusive and established characters.

It must be confessed, that in this, as in most other cases, there is a mean, on both sides of which inconveniencies will be found to lie. By enlarging too much the number of electors, you render the representative too little acquainted with all their local circumstances and lesser interests; as by reducing it too much, you render him unduly attached to these, and too little fit to comprehend and pursue great and national objects. The Federal Constitution forms a happy combination in this respect; the great and aggregate interests being referred to the national, the local and particular, to the state legislatures.

The other point of difference is, the greater number of citizens and extent of territory which may be brought within the compass of Republican, than of Democratic Government; and it is this circumstance principally which renders factious combinations less to be dreaded in the former, than in the latter. The smaller the society, the fewer probably will be the distinct parties and interests composing it; the fewer the distinct parties and interests, the more frequently will a majority be found of the same party; and the smaller the number of individuals composing a majority, and the smaller the compass within which they are placed, the more easily will they concert and execute their plans of oppression. Extend the sphere, and you take in a greater variety of parties and interests; you make it less probable that a majority of the whole will have a common motive to invade the rights of other citizens; or if such a common motive exists, it will be more difficult for all who feel it to discover their own strength, and to act in unison with each other. . . .

Hence it clearly appears, that the same advantage, which a Republic has over a Democracy, in controling the effects of faction, is enjoyed by a large over a small Republic—is enjoyed by the Union over the States composing it. Does this advantage consist in the substitution of Representatives, whose enlightened views and virtuous sentiments render them superior to local prejudices, and to schemes of injustice? It will not be denied, that the Representation of the Union will be most likely to possess these requisite endowments. Does it consist in the greater security afforded by a greater variety of parties, against the event of any one party being able to outnumber and oppress the rest? In an equal degree does the encreased variety of parties, comprised within the Union, encrease this security. Does it, in fine, consist in the greater obstacles opposed to the concern and accomplishment of the secret wishes of an unjust and interested majority? Here, again, the extent of the Union gives it the most palpable advantage.

The influence of factious leaders may kindle a flame within their particular States, but will be unable to spread a general conflagration through the other States: a religious sect, may degenerate into a political faction in a part of the Confederacy; but the variety of sects dispersed over the entire face of it, must secure the national Councils against any danger from that source: a rage for paper money, for an abolition of debts, for an equal division of property, or for any other improper or wicked project, will be less apt to pervade the whole body of the Union, than a particular member of it; in the same proportion as such a malady is more likely to taint a particular county or district, than an entire State.

In the extent and proper structure of the Union, therefore, we behold a Republican remedy for the diseases most incident to Republican Government. And according to the degree of pleasure and pride, we feel in being Republicans, ought to be our zeal in cherishing the spirit, and supporting the character of Federalists. ■

INTEREST GROUPS AND MADISON'S DILEMMA
Jeffrey M. Berry

A troubling dilemma lies at the core of the American political system. In an open and free society in which people have the right to express their political views, petition their government, and organize on behalf of causes, some segments of the population are likely to pursue their own selfish interests. Dairy farmers will push Congress to adopt price subsidies even though it means consumers will have to pay more for milk at the grocery store. Auto companies and auto workers will want the government to impose import restrictions against Japanese car manufacturers, despite the great popularity these cars have won with Americans. And environmentalists will fight for increasing the number and area of parks and wilderness preserves though development of those lands might provide jobs for some who are out of work. In short, people will pursue their self-interest even though the policies they advocate may hurt others, and may not be in the best interest of the nation.

The dilemma is this: If the government does not allow people to pursue their self-interest, it takes away their political freedom. When we look at the nations of the world in which people are forbidden to organize and to freely express their political views, we find that there the dilemma has been solved by authoritarianism. Although the alternative—permitting people to advocate whatever they want—is far preferable, it carries dangers. In a system such as ours, interest groups constantly push government to enact policies that benefit small constituencies at the expense of the general public.

This dilemma is as old as the country itself, yet never more relevant than today. As lobbying has grown in recent years, anxiety has mounted over the consequences of interest group politics. Political action committees (PACs) threaten to dominate financing of congressional elections. Liberal citizen groups are blamed for slowing economic development with the regulatory policies they have fought for. Labor unions are held responsible because America fails to compete effectively in many world markets, while recent tax cuts granted to influential business lobbies seem to increase their profits at the expense of huge federal budget deficits. Beyond the sins allegedly committed by segments of the interest group community is a broader worry. Is the sheer number of interest groups and their collective power undermining American democracy?

Many agree that interest groups are an increasingly troublesome part of American politics, yet there is little consensus on what, if anything, ought to be done about it. The dilemma remains: Interest groups are no less a threat than they are an expression of freedom.

CURING THE MISCHIEFS OF FACTION

Is there no middle ground between these two alternatives? Must a government accept one or the other? Contemporary discussions of this question inevitably turn to *The Federalist*, for James Madison's analysis in essay No. 10 remains the foundation of American political theory on interest groups. With great foresight, Madison recognized the problem that the fragile new nation would face. Although at the time he was writing the country had no political parties or lobbies as we know them, Madison correctly perceived that people would organize in some way to further their common interests. Furthermore, these groupings, or "factions" as he called them, were a potential threat to popular government. . . .

Madison worried that a powerful faction could eventually come to tyrannize others in society. What, then, was the solution for "curing the mischiefs of faction"? He rejected out of hand any restrictions on the freedoms that permitted people to pursue their own selfish interests, remarking that the remedy would be "worse than the disease." Instead, he reasoned that the effects of faction must be controlled rather than eliminating factions themselves. This control could be accomplished by setting into place the structure of government proposed in the Constitution.

In Madison's mind, a *republican* form of government, as designed by the framers, would provide the necessary checks on the worst impulses of factions. A republican form of government gives responsibility for decisions to a small number of representatives who are elected by the larger citizenry. Furthermore, for a government whose authority extends over a large and dispersed population, the effects of faction would be diluted by the clash of many competing interests across the country. Thus, Madison believed that in a land as large as the United States, so many interests would arise that a representative government with its own checks and balances would not become dominated by any faction. Instead, government could deal with the views of all, producing policies that would be in the common good.

Madison's cure for the mischiefs of faction was something of a leap of faith. The structure of American government has not, by itself, prevented some interests from gaining great advantage at the expense of others. Those with large resources have always been better represented by interest groups, and the least wealthy in society have suffered because of their failure to organize. Still, even though the republican form of government envisioned by Madison has not always been strong enough to prevent abuse by factions, the beliefs underlying *Federalist* No. 10 have endured.

This view that the natural diversity of interests would prevent particular groups from dominating politics found a later incarnation in American social science of the 1950s and 1960s. *Pluralist* scholars argued that the many (that is, plural) interests in society found representation in the policy-making process through lobbying by organizations. The bargaining that went on between such groups and government led to policies produced by compromise and consensus. Interest groups were seen as more beneficial to the system than Madison's factions, with emphasis placed on the positive contributions made by groups in speaking for their constituents before government. . . .

INTEREST GROUPS AND THEIR FUNCTIONS

When an interest group attempts to influence policy makers, it can be said to be engaging in *lobbying*. (The word comes from the practice of interest group representatives standing in the lobbies of legislatures so that they could stop members on their way to a session and plead their case. In earlier times, when many legislators had no office of their own, the lobbies or anterooms adjoining their chambers were a convenient place for a quick discussion on the merits of a bill.) Although "lobbying" conjures up the image of an interest group representative trying to persuade a legislator to vote in the group's favor, we should see it in a broader context. Lobbying can be directed at any institution of government—legislative, judicial, and executive. Interest groups can even try to influence those institutions indirectly by attempting to sway public opinion, which they hope in turn will influence government. Lobbying also encompasses many tactics. Initiating a lawsuit, starting a letter-writing campaign, filing a formal comment on a proposed regulation, talking face to face with a congressman or bureaucrat; just about any legal means used to try to influence government can be called lobbying.

In their efforts to influence government, interest groups come to play diverse roles in American politics. First and foremost, interest groups act to *represent* their constituents before government. They are a primary link between citizens and their government, forming a channel of access through which members voice their opinions to those who govern them. . . .

Interest groups also afford people the opportunity to *participate* in the political process. . . . By contributing money to a lobbying organization, and possibly participating through it to do other things such as writing letters or taking part in protests, members come to feel they have a more significant role in the political process. Interest groups give them that opportunity.

Another function performed by interest groups is helping to *educate* the American public about political issues. With their advocacy efforts, publications, and publicity campaigns, interest groups can make people better aware of both policy problems and proposed solutions. . . .

A related activity is *agenda building*. Beyond simply educating people about the sides of an issue, interest groups are frequently responsible for bringing the issue to light in the first place. The world has many problems, but not all are political issues being actively considered by government. Agenda building turns problems into issues, which become part of the body of policy questions that government feels it must deal with. . . .

Finally, interest groups are involved in *program monitoring*. Lobbies closely follow programs affecting their constituents, and will often try to draw attention to shortcomings they observe through such tactics as issuing evaluative reports and contacting people in the media. They may also directly lobby agency personnel to make changes in program implementation or even go to court in an effort to exact compliance with a law. . . .

THE RISE AND FALL OF PLURALISM

The early forerunner of pluralism in political science was known as "group theory," most widely associated with David Truman's *The Governmental Process*, published in 1951.[1] Truman makes a simple assertion: Politics can be understood only by looking at the interaction of groups. He casts his lot with Madison, agreeing that "tendencies toward such groupings are 'sown in the nature of man.' "[2] He also draws on cultural anthropology and social psychology to prove his case that political man is a product of group influences. "In all societies of any degree

---

1. David B. Truman, *The Governmental Process* (New York: Knopf, 1951). . . .
2. Truman, *The Governmental Process*, p. 17.

of complexity the individual is less affected directly by the society as a whole than differentially through various of its subdivisions, or groups."[3]

The pluralist influence in political science reached its zenith a decade later when Robert Dahl published *Who Governs?*, a study of local politics in New Haven, Connecticut.[4] Dahl examined three areas of local politics to see just who influenced policy outcomes. His crucial finding was that in the three areas — political party nominations, urban redevelopment, and public education — different groups of people were active and influential. New Haven did not have a small, closed circle of important people who together decided all the important issues in town politics.

Dahl found policy making in New Haven to be a process by which loose coalitions of groups and politicians would become active on issues they cared about. Although most citizens might be apathetic about most issues, many do get interested in the issues that directly affect them. . . . Through bargaining and compromise between affected groups and political elites, democratic decisions are reached, with no one group consistently dominating.

The influence of pluralist thought, and Dahl's writings in particular, was enormous. He had gone a step further than Truman by putting his findings in such an approving light. That is, he not only seemed to be saying this is the way things are, but this is the way things should be. Policy making through group interaction is a positive virtue, not a threat to democracy. . . .

To most social scientists who stood in the ideological mainstream of their disciplines, pluralism was an attractive counterpoint to radical critiques of American society. Books like C. Wright Mills's *The Power Elite* (1956) had gained a good deal of attention with the claim that America was ruled by a small stratum of wealthy and powerful individuals.[5] This power elite of corporate executives, fabulously rich families, military leaders, and politicians were said to be the true decision makers in society, "democracy" being an effective illusion perpetrated on the masses. But if the power elite thesis was false, as most social scientists believed it was, what was the countertheory?

Pluralism thus became the refutation of this damning interpretation of American politics. *Who Governs?* acknowledged that political elites had disproportionate amounts of resources, but said that . . . group politics forced elites to be responsive to a broad range of constituencies rather than to a small group of powerful individuals. . . .

Two main lines of scholarly criticism soon came to the fore, one *methodological* and the other *normative.* The methodological criticism of pluralism was that studies like *Who Governs?* focused on far too narrow a set of questions. . . . What of the larger issues, such as relative distribution of wealth among different segments of society, which really are never directly addressed by governmental bodies? The issues Dahl analyzed did not threaten to change the basic structure of New Haven society or its economy, no matter how

---

3. Truman, *The Governmental Process,* p. 15.
4. Robert A. Dahl, *Who Governs?* (New Haven: Yale University Press, 1961).
5. C. Wright Mills, *The Power Elite* (New York: Oxford University Press, 1956). . . .

they were resolved. In this view, only issues that do not fundamentally alter the position of elites enter the political agenda and become subject to interest group politics. . . .

A second strain of criticism stressed the consequences of pluralist theory rather than the research questions that guided it. Critics like Jack Walker and Theodore Lowi attacked pluralism because it justified the status quo. In *The End of Liberalism*[6] Lowi concludes that government through interest groups is conservative because it creates resistance to change. He points out that lobbying groups arise to protect the interests of some segment of society. Once government begins to make policies by bargaining with those groups, they then act to favor them at the expense of others. This privileged access of groups even favors them against newly organizing interests from the same strata of society, such as business competitors trying to enter a tightly regulated market.

These critics were not making the more radical argument of those who, like Mills, said America was governed by a small ruling class. Rather, they were saying that there was disproportionate privilege, and that privilege was rationalized by pluralism. Not all relevant interests were adequately represented by interest groups, and pluralism falsely suggested that all those significantly affected by an impending decision were taken into the policy-making process.

The validity of pluralism was thrown open to question not only by scholars, but by real-world events as well. The civil rights movement that began in the early 1960s made it all too clear that blacks were wholly outside the normal workings of the political system. As the marches and occasional violence continued during the decade, the inadequacy of pluralist theory to explain the positions of blacks in society became increasingly evident. On top of the civil rights movement came the anti-Vietnam War movement. Spreading disillusionment with the war increased alienation toward the federal government. Questions arose in people's minds not only about the wisdom of the war, but about the way the government was run. By the end of the 1960s, neither intellectuals nor ordinary citizens were likely to believe contemporary interest group politics was the basis for democratic policy making. . . .

CONCLUSION

During the 1960s, Americans became increasingly dissatisfied with the way their democratic system was operating. For their part, American political scientists were more and more disillusioned with the dominant theory in their discipline that purported to explain how that democracy worked. Both alienation from American government and scholarly rejection of pluralism contributed to a powerful new idea: Increased participation was needed to balance a system of interest groups that skewed policy making toward organizations unrepresentative of the American people.

Although no new theory as such came along to replace pluralism, the idea

---

6. Theodore J. Lowi, *The End of Liberalism*, 2nd ed. (New York: Norton, 1979).

of expanded interest group participation by the chronically underrepresented was at least a first step toward finding a new solution to the dilemma of *Federalist* No. 10. The real-world events and the philosophical musings of scholars that contributed to the movement toward increased participation by interest groups could not be selective in their influence. The new interest group politics went far beyond citizen participation programs and public interest groups for those traditionally unrepresented in the governmental process. Rather, extraordinary growth in all types of lobbying organizations raised anew questions about curing the mischiefs of faction. . . .

The growth of interest group politics can be applauded for the broadened representation it has brought the political system. If there are to be lobbying organizations, it is best that they be as representative as possible of all segments of American society. Yet it would be naive to assume that interest groups are ever going to fairly reflect the different interests of all Americans. Upper- and middle-class interests will always be better represented by interest groups.

Government is realistically limited in what it can do to address this imbalance. It should continue to try to ensure representation for the chronically underrepresented. Financial support for advocacy groups for the poor should be expanded, not decreased as part of the overall move to cut back government funding of welfare and social services. Such cuts actually create a greater need for this kind of surrogate representation. Citizen participation programs, which have had mixed success, ought to be continued and improved upon. They make government more accountable to the people it serves and create a potential channel of influence for those who may not be adequately represented by interest groups. There is little that the federal government ought to do aside from changing current campaign finance practices, however, to curb the activities of interest groups. Worrisome as the spiraling growth of interest group politics may be, it is not desirable to have the government trying generally to inhibit the efforts of various constituencies to find more effective representation in the political system.

Because government's role will always be limited, prospects for further curbing the influence of faction must come from the political parties. They are the natural counterweight to interest groups, offering citizens the basic means of pursuing the nation's collective will. . . .

A stronger party system can be furthered by the one major reform that should be imposed on interest groups: changes in the campaign finance laws that would reduce candidates' dependence on PAC funds. Otherwise, party renewal must come from the parties and not from restrictions on interest groups. Weak parties are not an inevitable condition of American politics, and the vision and capacity of those active in national politics is surely equal to the task of making the two parties more attractive to the American public. The progress that Republicans have recently made in efforts to build their party offers some reason for hope. Their sophisticated fundraising apparatus, along with their efforts at recruiting and supporting attractive congressional challengers, have helped foster a stronger, more centralized national Republican party. The Democrats, in turn, are beginning to take similar steps to strengthen themselves.

Interest groups need to continue to play their traditional role of articulating this nation's multitude of interests. They offer a direct link to government on the everyday issues that interest a particular constituency but not the nation as a whole. The role they play is not ideal, but interest groups remain a fundamental expression of democratic government. ■

INTEREST GROUP ACTIVITY

Litigation—filing lawsuits, as the NAACP did when, in *Brown* v. *Board of Education*, it got the Supreme Court to reverse an earlier ruling and hold segregation in the public schools unconstitutional—is one tactic sometimes used by interest groups. Recently, conservative interests, such as the Mountain States Legal Fund, have gone to court to further their goals.

More prevalent are the interest group tactics of mass propaganda, grass roots pressure, lobbying, and campaign activity, particularly providing campaign funds. Interest groups establish offices in Washington (as well as in state capitals) and hire consultants and lawyers to press for their positions—with both the executive and legislative branches.

Using modern techniques, today's interest groups, as pointed out in the article by Ann Cooper, excerpted here, combine some or all of these tactics for maximum effect.

HIGH-TECH LOBBYING
Ann Cooper

. . . Washington's influence industry today relies less on the well-connected individual lobbyist and more on an infrastructure of workers who specialize in direct mail, coalition building or other activities that seldom take them to the halls of government. . . .

In their race to round up "grass-roots" support, lobbyists increasingly rely on high-tech intermediaries, who specialize in targeting messages at both the public and the decision makers. Thus, much of the dialogue between Washington and the rest of the country is in the form of prefabricated messages produced by middlemen. . . .

Today's lobbyist is more technocrat than backslapper. Campaign contributions are one form of lobbying currency, but so are opinion polls, petitions and fact sheets.

And many lobbyists have learned that a fact sheet offered by a constituent often has more value than the same facts presented by a Washington representative.

"Senator So and So doesn't want to talk to me," said a Washington-based chemical industry lobbyist, who estimates that 90 per cent of his time is spent at "the grunt level," working with congressional staff. When he does visit Members, a local plant manager or corporate official is usually included in the entourage because "Members want to hear from people in the district."

Whole businesses have been built on that belief. National Strategies and Marketing Group Inc., formed earlier this year by a trio of Democrats that includes Walter F. Mondale's former campaign manager, specializes in setting up grass-roots support for its corporate clients.

The theory is that non-Washington voices will make a more persuasive "public-interest" argument. But public interest isn't necessarily what motivates a National Strategies client. Consider the case of Rollins Environmental Services Inc., a toxic waste disposal company whose land-based incinerators might get less business if the Environmental Protection Agency (EPA) approves a rival firm's pending application to burn wastes at sea. To lobby EPA for Rollins's position, National Strategies formed something called the Alliance to Save the Ocean, which talks about the perils of sea pollution rather than the threat to Rollins's bottom line.

The seeds that led to services like National Strategies were sown by the public-interest movement. Groups that set up shop in the 1970s to lobby on issues such as the environment and consumer protection substituted scrappy public relations and clamorous grass-roots organizations for the more refined persuasions of lawyer-lobbyists.

Those groups, now a permanent part of the influence community, still rely heavily on the news media and activist memberships to bolster their messages in Washington. Their tactics are being taught to new generations of liberal activists by the Advocacy Institute, an educational center recently opened by former Common Cause president David Cohen and Michael Pertschuk, who was Federal Trade Commission chairman during the Carter Administration.

One legacy of the public-interest tactics was that business began to copy them, organizing employees, stockholders and customers to send in grass-roots messages from outside of Washington. Grass roots also became the foundation of the New Right, which honed direct-mail techniques to activate millions of conservative sympathizers. . . .

Today, cultivating grass roots is part of the strategy in most major lobbying campaigns. In 1981–82, Boston College professors John T. Tierney and Kay Lehman Schlozman conducted in-depth interviews on lobbying with representatives of 175 unions, corporations, public-interest groups and others with

Washington offices; 80 per cent reported using grassroots as one influence technique.

"Grass roots is an obsession. But it may be an illusion how important it is," said Tierney, whose study is described in *Organized Interests and American Democracy* (Harper & Row Publishers Inc., 1985). Tierney believes grass-roots campaigns may get undue attention because "we're aware of those activities in a way that we're not aware of a lobbyist taking a committee staff director out to lunch."

But others say that the multiplicity of messages has made many Members of Congress more pressure-sensitive to grass-roots campaigns. As a lobbyist told Tierney and Schlozman: "The congressman has to care that *somebody* out there in his district has enough power to get hundreds of people to sit down and write a postcard or a letter—because if the guy can get them to do *that*, he might be able to influence them in other ways. So, a Member has no choice but to pay attention. It's suicide if he doesn't."

The search for grass-roots support has turned into a full-time living for some Washington consultants. For those who can afford it, consultants will use sophisticated computer technology to search out likely pockets of supporters and prepare ready-made communications for them to mail to Capitol Hill. Sometimes supporters for a single issue are lured by targeted messages, which the consultant varies according to his or her analysis of what different groups of people want to hear.

The targeted message approach is "incredibly expensive" and "a bit manipulative, to say the least," said Anne Wexler, a lobbyist who was President Carter's assistant for public liaison. Nevertheless, Wexler says, such campaigns can identify and educate supporters who otherwise would not be aware of an issue, making them a useful tactic "when you need to demonstrate massive public support."

"Whether all of this increasingly sophisticated communication between constituents and elected officials is a net gain or loss for democracy cannot be answered with certainty," direct mail consultant Robert M. Smith told a congressional hearing in 1983. "My own belief is that virtually any additional communication between constituents and their elected officials is a net plus for democracy."

Not everyone is as sanguine about technology's expanding role in lobbying. As the emphasis on mail generation grows, "certain groups, because of their size and their easy access to huge numbers of people, are going to get a distorted, tilted capacity to influence the legislative process," said Common Cause president Fred Wertheimer. "The more the edge is given to very large resources, the more distortion we're going to face."

As an example, Wertheimer cites the banking industry's 1983 use of monthly customer statements to urge communications to Congress opposing withholding of taxes on interest and dividends. Many Members of Congress were bitter about the bankers' campaign, which they believed misled the public into thinking that withholding was a new tax. But little mail was generated in support of withholding, and in the end, only a few Members chose to ignore the millions of banker-inspired messages sent to Capitol Hill. Withholding, approved in 1982, was repealed less than a year later with minimal opposition.

GROWING PROFESSION

Solid numbers elude anyone who tries to count the lobbyists, trade association representatives, public relations specialists and others who work in Washington's influence industry. The industry's own professional organization, the American League of Lobbyists, has just 300 members, who meet for monthly lunches. Another group, Women in Government Relations, counts 600 members, but some work for Congress or federal agencies.

Perhaps the most comprehensive accounting is *Washington Representatives,* a privately published listing of "persons working to influence government policies and actions to advance their own or their client's interest." In 1977, a mere 4,000 names were listed. By 1981, that number had doubled, and the 1985 edition lists 10,000 people who fit the book's definition—including representatives for such specialized interests as the Frozen Potato Products Institute and the United States Hang Gliding Association.

While the editors note that they have developed new sources of information, the listings also have grown because of "a continuing migration of association offices in Washington, an increase in the number of advocacy groups and a gradual expansion of the public affairs-government relations profession."

Along with the growth has come a proliferation of titles. The media still describe former deputy Treasury secretary Charls E. Walker as a "tax lobbyist," but Charls E. Walker Associates Inc.'s downtown Washington headquarters bills itself as a "business-political consulting firm." Former White House chief of staff Michael K. Deaver says his new Georgetown business offers "communications and public affairs" services. Meanwhile, clients go to Wexler, Reynolds, Harrison and Schule for "issues management and government relations," says co-founder Wexler.

Regardless of the title used, each of these companies is in business for one purpose: to influence the decisions made by Congress, the White House and federal bureaucrats. "It's a one-industry town, and we all do the same thing," said John M. Damgard, president of the Futures Industry Association.

Increasingly, that work is being done under names created for a specific campaign. Sometimes the name represents a coalition of established organizations. Sometimes it masks corporate roots and hints at connections with the public-interest movement. Natural gas producers called themselves the Alliance for Energy Security when they pushed for decontrol of gas prices in 1983–84. Consumers United for Rail Equity, which wants new restrictions put on freight rail rates, does have significant consumer group support. But its $2.6 million budget came from electric utilities and coal companies.

The lobbying-for-hire business has pursued two seemingly opposite trends in recent years. Some newer firms concentrate on a single, narrow specialty, such as masterminding Mailgram campaigns or organizing constituent coalitions. At the same time, more established, specialized firms have broadened into "full-service" lobbying organizations.

Typical of the latter trend is Burson-Marsteller, an international public relations firm whose Washington office was once a minor league player in the influence game. Clients used to turn to Burson-Marsteller for press conferences or background kits for the media. Now they may hire the firm to run a mail campaign or send lobbyists directly to Capitol Hill. . . .

"We're trying to position ourselves as a comprehensive lobbying firm," said Patrick J. Griffin, who left his post as secretary to the minority in the Senate to set up the firm's new lobbying arm.

That doesn't mean clients won't hire other help, Griffin said. For example, in its work for Morgan Stanley & Co., which wants to buy Consolidated Rail Corp., the federally owned freight railroad, Burson-Marsteller is part of a three-company team. One element of the Morgan Stanley strategy was to organize a coalition outside Washington, to convince Congress that the company's purchase proposal has broad support. Using mailings and telephone calls, Wexler's firm rounded up shippers, mayors and others. Burson-Marsteller handled the formal announcement of the coalition to the press. Capitol Hill gets information about the coalition from lobbying visits by Griffin and lawyers from the Washington office of the Dallas law firm of Akin, Gump, Strauss, Hauer & Feld.

"Any issue of any consequence in this town usually has more than one member of the [lobbying] team," said Griffin. "You need to use every avenue available to you to get your message across to the decision maker." ∎

SHOULD WE LIMIT THE PACs?

Political action committees, or PACs, the campaign financing arms of interest groups, are not recent inventions, although their alarming growth is relatively recent. The American Federation of Labor-Congress of Industrial Organizations (AFL-CIO) consolidated labor union PACs into the Committee on Political Education (COPE) in 1947. By the early 1960s, a few trade and professional associations had followed labor's lead and established their own PACs—AMPAC of the American Medical Association and BIPAC, the Business-Industry Political Action Committee of the National Association of Manufacturers, for example.

Under federal law, it is illegal for unions or corporations to use their "treasury," or general, funds for political purposes. Under a 1971 act of Congress, backed by both labor and business, unions and corporations were permitted to use *voluntary* member or employee contributions for political campaigns. Thus, the PACs were made legitimate. This act also provided that union dues and corporate-treasury funds could be used for "nonpartisan" get-out-the-vote drives and for communicating with members and stockholders about political matters.[7]

Then came the Watergate scandal of the Nixon Administration, which revealed, among other things, that a good many of America's best known business corporations had, in violation of federal law, contributed corporate-treasury funds to President Nixon's reelection campaign. There was strong public-opinion backing for campaign financing reform. The citizen lobby, Common Cause, formed in 1970, was in the forefront of reform efforts.

In 1974, Congress passed a comprehensive election reform act. It provided for public financing in presidential campaigns. The Senate adopted an amendment providing for public financing of congressional campaigns, too, but the House killed this provision. Again with both labor and business support, PACs were approved in the law. Labor did not foresee that it would soon be outstripped by business in the raising and contributing of campaign funds. Common Cause foresaw the consequences of public financing for presidential campaigns and private financing for congressional campaigns, and its president says, "We knew where we were headed."[8] Where we were headed was toward a fantastic jump in the number of PACs and the amounts they spent in House and Senate races. Campaign money previously spent in presidential campaigns now was diverted to congressional candidates.

In 1974, there were approximately 600 PACs, in 1982, 3400—1497 corporate PACs, 350 labor PACs, 613 trade association PACs, and the rest independent, cooperative, and ideological PACs. In 1976, PACs contributed $23 million to congressional campaigns, in 1982, nearly four times as much—$80 million!

The average cost of winning a U. S. Senate seat skyrocketed from $600,000 in 1976 to $2.9 million in 1984. In the 1984 congressional elections, some 4,000 PACs spent $104.9 million on House and Senate races, an increase of 25 percent over 1982 (which had itself seen an increase of 51 percent over 1980).[9]

The great increase in congressional campaign costs and the rise of the PACs produced many suggestions for reform. One suggestion was for public financing of congressional campaigns. But since the PACs favored incumbents by a significant margin, this idea got nowhere in the Congress. In 1986, Senator David Boren, a Democrat from Oklahoma, offered a floor amendment to a bill being considered in the Senate to limit PAC contributions in congressional campaigns. After debate, the Senate postponed action on the proposal until the following year. In the selections excerpted here from the debate on that bill, Senator Boren and Senator Barry Goldwater, a Republican

7. The history of PACs recounted here is based upon Larry J. Sabato, *PAC Power: Inside the World of Political Action Committees* (New York: W. W. Norton, 1985), pp. 1–6; and Elizabeth Drew, *Politics and Money: The New Road to Corruption* (New York: Macmillan, 1983), pp. 6–11.

8. Elizabeth Drew, *Politics and Money,* p. 10.

9. See *Congressional Quarterly Weekly Report* (June 8, 1985), pp. 1115–1117.

from Arizona, state the case for limits on the PACs, while Senators Lowell Weicker of Connecticut and Phil Gramm of Texas, both Republicans, state the case for the opposition.

The question before the Senate was: Should we limit the PACs?

YES, LIMIT THE UNDUE INFLUENCE OF PACs
David Boren

. . . We Americans often dispatch groups to observe elections in other countries to make sure that they are honest, free and fair. It is ironic that we continue to ignore a serious problem with our own election system.

In the most recent election, 163 successful candidates for Congress received over half of their campaign contributions from special interest political action committees [PAC's] instead of from individual contributors in their home States. The mushrooming influence of PAC's is beginning to threaten the basic concept of grass-roots democracy.

In the past 10 years PAC spending has grown at an explosive rate. In 1974 there were 600 PAC's in existence. Today there are over 4,000. In 1972 PAC's contributed only about $8 million to congressional campaigns. In 1984 they contributed over $104 million. While contributions by PAC's have been growing, the percentage of campaign funding provided by small donations of less than $100 has been cut in half.

It is frightening to consider the impact on the political system and the cost of campaigns if PAC contributions continue to double every 4 years as they are now.

When additional money is pumped into the system, it ends up being spent and campaign costs soar. In just 8 years, the average cost of a winning U.S. Senate campaign has risen from a little over $600,000 to more than $2.9 million, an increase of 385 percent.

In addition, the growth in the influence of PAC's further fragments our Nation and its elected legislative bodies. It makes it increasingly difficult to reach a national consensus and hold our decisionmaking process hostage to the special interests which PAC's represent.

A PAC does not judge a Senator or Congressman on his or her overall record or personal integrity. It does not balance his entire record to see if it serves the national interest. It rates the Member solely on how he voted on bills affecting the particular financial interest group or single issue constituency.

Several of my fellow Senators have joined with me in a bipartisan effort to apply the brakes to the accelerating power of special interest groups. Those of us from both political parties represent a broad political cross-section.

We intend to use every possible parliamentary vehicle to do something to reduce the undue influence of PAC's on the political process.

Our proposal has four main provisions. First, it sets limits on the total amount of PAC funds which congressional candidates may receive. For House Members, it would be $100,000 for an election cycle, or $125,000 if the Member faced both a primary and a general election challenge. For Senate candidates, the maximum amount would range from $175,000 to $750,000 depending upon the size of the State. This formula should approximately cut in half the current amount of PAC spending.

Second, it puts contributions by PAC's and by individuals on a more equal footing. Presently PAC's can contribute $5,000 per election and individuals only $1,000. Our proposal sets the limits at $3,000 for PAC's and $1,500 for individuals.

I might say that this increase in the amount allowed to individuals goes along with a recommendation recently made by a distinguished panel looking at the need for campaign reform.

Third, it closes a loophole in the current election laws under which PAC's can serve as a conduit for individual contributions which they solicit. It is possible for PAC's to receive these individual contributions, bundle them together and send them on to candidates without falling under the $5,000 spending limit.

Fourth, it tightens the definition of what constitutes independent campaign spending. Groups which are independent of a candidate can spend to attack opponents without any spending limits. In fact, they are often staffed by former employees or consultants of a candidate's campaign committee and are not truly operating independently. Under our proposal the media would also be required to provide free response time to candidates who are attacked or opposed in advertisements by these so-called independent groups.

I might say that that is a proposal made earlier by the distinguished Presiding Officer, the Senator from Missouri [Mr. DANFORTH, and the Senator from South Carolina [Mr. HOLLINGS].

No one would pretend that this proposal will solve all of the problems in the current election process. It is, however, an important first step in the right direction.

Former Solicitor General Archibald Cox put it very directly in a recent statement when he said:

> We must decide whether we want government of, by and for the people or government of the PAC's, by the PAC's and for the PAC's.

We cannot expect Members of Congress to act in the national interest when their election campaigns are being financed more and more by special interests.   ■

YES, CAMPAIGNS COST TOO MUCH
Barry Goldwater

What disturbs me is the fact that it is becoming more and more obvious—that money can get people elected. When I think back to my first campaign in 1952, where I spent $45,000, and then think of my last one just five years ago, where I put out $1.25 million, there is a vast difference there, not just in the sums of money, but in the campaign itself and what is going on.

We now have experts in the field campaigning in almost every big city in the country. They tell the candidate how to comb his hair, what color shirt to wear, what kind of tie to wear, and what is the best suit for them to wear. They take polls in every nook and cranny of the state or city or country to determine what issues should be discussed on this street corner and the next street corner and, frankly, I do not think that is any way to elect people in this country.

. . . I remember one prominent politician, and I am not going to mention his name, who had a rather unruly head of hair but who appeared on television with hair that was rather scintillating, and later I asked him what happened, and he said, "Oh, we just sprinkled a little gold dust in it." Now that might be all right, but I do not think it is exactly the way to run a campaign.

Also, I recall after one of my campaigns a person asking me for a few of my fat cat names so he could start a fund to promote conservatism. I provided him with a relative few of these names and I understand now his annual intake is over ten million dollars. I will not swear to that, but I have heard from rather dependable sources that this is true.

You know and I know that there is not a night in the week in every month during the year that a member of Congress cannot attend one or two fund raising dinners for a colleague. Every one of us is asked to be sponsors for I do not know how many candidates, all in the interest of raising money.

Now my idea of a candidate running for office is a person who will stand four square with the principles of the Constitution and our way of life, and of party, if he agrees with party positions, but he will stand for something other than the mishmash of everything that comes out of support from hundreds of different PACs and other sources of money in this country.

A man or woman should run with a demonstration of personal regard for the Constitution, regard for the American form of government, for protecting that government from foreign sources and, I might add, from harmful domestic sources, too.

To sum it all up, I think the whole matter has gone far enough . . .

The answer is not greater spending by political parties or anyone else. The answer is less campaign spending by all sources and PACs are the place to start. ■

NO, PUBLIC DISCLOSURE OF CONTRIBUTIONS IS ENOUGH
Lowell Weicker

First of all, let me address what is continually referred to in this matter of political campaigns and their financing as the present system being the result of Watergate reform.

It might be many things, but it never came out of the Watergate Committee. I think I have a fair idea of what went on insofar as that body is concerned.

The fact is, for example, and I realize this is not in the [Boren] bill as presently written, but it is mentioned often that we should have public financing of Federal campaigns, that this is really what came out of Watergate.

I do not know if anyone ever bothers to read the report written by the committee but on that point alone let me read from the report:

> The committee recommends against the adoption of any form of public financing in which tax moneys are collected and allocated to political candidates by the Federal Government.
>
> The Select Committee opposes the various proposals which have been offered in the Congress to provide mandatory public financing of campaigns for Federal office. While recognizing the basis of support for the concept of public financing and the potential difficulty in adequately funding campaigns in the midst of strict limitations on the form and amount of contributions, the committee takes issue with the contention that public financing affords either an effective or appropriation solution. Thomas Jefferson believed "to compel a man to furnish contributions of money for the propagation of opinions which he disbelieves and abhors, is sinful and tyrannical."
>
> The committee's opposition is based like Jefferson's upon the fundamental need to protect the voluntary right of individual citizens to express themselves politically as guaranteed by the first amendment.

I think that is appropriate to this argument here.

> Furthermore, we find inherent dangers in authorizing the Federal bureaucracy to fund and excessively regulate political campaigns.
>
> The abuses experienced during the 1972 campaign and unearthed by the Select Committee were perpetrated in the absence of any effective regulation of the source, form, or amount of campaign contributions. In fact, despite the progress made by the Federal Elections Campaign Act of 1971, in requiring full public disclosure of contributions, the 1972 campaign still was funded through a system of essentially unrestricted, private financing.
>
> What now seems appropriate is not the abandonment of private financing, but rather the reform of that system in an effort to vastly expand the voluntary participation of individual citizens while avoiding the abuses of earlier campaigns.

That is what was said by the Watergate Committee and that is certainly far afield from what is represented to the public in terms of Watergate reform of the financing of Federal elections.

What is needed is full disclosure.

I commend the Washington Post in its editorial today. I think it hit the nail right on the head. What is needed is full disclosure.

On the heels of Watergate I stood on the floor of the Senate during debate concerning establishment of the Ethics Committee and put in a substitute, as some of my colleagues who were here then will recall, saying we did not need the Ethics Committee, we did not need all the separate rules and opinions of a separate committee. What we needed was full disclosure of assets and liabilities of each Senator so each constituency could pronounce judgment in each case.

What goes in Kansas or what goes in Mississippi might not sell in Connecticut, and vice versa. That is up to the voters to decide. True, they can only decide if they have all the facts before them.

I was defeated in that measure. Instead we have this mishmash of rules and every little nit-picking item has to get thrown to the Ethics Committee. It ties up five of our colleagues overseeing us. That was not meant to be our job. That is the job of the people who put us here, as long as they are in full possession of all the facts.

Now the same holds true insofar as campaign financing is concerned. I think the PAC system is abhorrent.

May I point out to you that it came to pass by virtue of all the reformers after Watergate and when they reformed they created something far worse than the system that existed then.

So I do not think that I care to see any more "reform" in the sense of new rules and regulations by either the bureaucracy or the Federal Government.

What we need is full disclosure, total disclosure, and with those facts in hand the people can decide in the State of Connecticut as to whether or not their Senator is influenced far too much by the defense industry or by the electric utilities or by environmental groups or by unions or whoever.

They can make their decision as to whether or not this Senator should be elected or should be thrown out of office. It is just as simple as that. . . .

That is the issue here. It is not as to whether or not we are going to have more laws and regulations as to this matter of personal conduct, be it in terms of election campaigns or performance on the Senate floor. What the American people are deserving of is full disclosure. Fair enough. If they are too damn lazy not to vote, and they are doing that in increasing numbers, then they deserve what they get.

But you cannot get good politicians by enacting something into law any more than you can have a balanced budget by enacting a balanced budget constitutional amendment. . . .

I do not believe broad new regulations are necessary. Redirecting campaign money does nothing to further empower the American people. And further empowering the American people is finally the only good reason for reform.

The essential power of individuals in the electoral process is of course, the vote; a vote furthermore that is cast by individuals exposed to the widest range of information. An important part of this information deals with the sources of money in a campaign. Full disclosure of this information puts the tools of campaign reform where they belong, in the hands of the voters.

It is the voters who must decide if the performance of their political leaders is tied to special interest money. If it is bribery we are talking about, let us encourage indictments. But if it is not, if it is the gray area of influence or access, then the voters can best judge their leaders, even if it means judging the politicians by the cash they keep.

I remain a supporter of any proposal that furthers voluntary participation in the political process. The key to this participation remains the same as it did in the crises of the early 1970's; information, the product of mandatory disclosure. . . .   ■

NO, THAT WOULD LIMIT POLITICAL COMPETITION
Phil Gramm

Political power is a zero sum game. PAC's did not create political power. Political power exists because the Government sets the price of commodities, because the Government grants contracts, and because the Government is a megaplayer in the economy of the United States, spending almost a trillion dollars a year.

People try to influence Government for a lot of reasons. They try to influence Government because they love their country, because they have a philosophy and values.

Some people, obviously, try to influence Government to benefit themselves or to hurt others.

If we take action to limit the contributions that PAC's can make, we will not change that process. . . . In no way will those who want to see the Government employ more people and exercise more power be less inclined to affect the decisions of Congress.

All we are going to do . . . is limit the ability of one of the competitors to compete. We are not going to eliminate any power by limiting the contributions of certain PAC's. What we are going to do is to enhance the power of those interest groups which are not limited.

I think it is very interesting to look at whose power PAC's have taken away. PAC's did not create any new power; that power which they have, they have taken away from other special interest groups. They have taken some power away from the media. It, therefore, comes as little shock to me that the media almost uniformly supports limiting PAC's. They have taken power away from the political parties and, as a result, there are those who would like to see the political parties strengthened by limiting PAC's. The PAC's have taken power away from the smoke-filled rooms and from the powerbrokers. They, too, would like to regain power by limiting PAC's.

PAC's have taken power away from those organizations which have powerful endorsements. Not surprisingly, virtually all such organizations want to limit PAC's.

How interesting it is that those who created the first PAC's, the labor unions, now would like to see contributions limited so that they might fully fund their candidate, but so that business-oriented PAC's cannot outspend them.

. . . I do not understand how, if a rich person gives $1,000 to my campaign, that is not special interest, but if 100 hardware and implement dealers in Texas give $10 apiece to their PAC and that PAC contributes to me, somehow that is supposed to be special interest.

The truth is I am proud of the PAC's and the people who support me. You walk down Main Street, America, and you see the people who support me. The percentage of money I have gotten from PAC's has always been low relative to the total money I have raised, but free enterprise oriented PAC's have always strongly supported me.

The point is that the people of my State knew that the employees of McDonald's and Burger King, that the people who worked at Sears and Roebuck and Montgomery Ward, and the local member of the National Bakers Association and the local movie house, that the people who were members of the Texas Restaurant Association, that the people who ran the local automobile dealers supported me, and I am proud of their support.

I have always thought it was interesting that there are those who want to portray that somehow, if you take a contribution from somebody you belong to them, and they often find ways of trying to make their theory fit. I remember when we voted on limiting the general rulemaking power of the Federal Trade Commission over the doctors. . . . Do you remember all those studies that were done to show that the people who voted to exempt the physicians were the biggest recipients of their largess in terms of campaign contributions? It was interesting when the initial study came out that I was left out.

It just so happened that because of a quirk where there had been a consent agreement by the American Medical Association and the Texas Medical Association with the Federal Election Commission, I received more PAC money from physicians than any Member of Congress that year. Yet I voted against exempting physicians from general rulemaking by the Federal Trade Commission. However, when the various groups who wanted to prove the theory that somebody controls you by contributing to your campaign wrote their articles and releases, they just conveniently left me out.

I did not feel any compulsion to vote for the Chrysler bailout because Chrysler dealers contributed to me. I have more Chrysler dealers supporting me now than before I voted against the Chrysler bailout.

I do not worry about being bought because I am not for sale. I have a philosophy and a set of values that I try to represent. I try to represent the interest of Texas. And I am never ashamed of those values and I am never ashamed of the interest of Texas. I always try to be on the side of those values and that interest. . . .

Limiting PAC giving . . . simply takes power away from those who have used the PAC to support their views and interest. It does not take any ability to promote views and interest away from Common Cause which spends $8 million a year lobbying here in Congress to try to influence legislation. It does not change Ralph Nader's ability to manipulate the media. It does limit the ability of private citizens through PAC's from giving a candidate the funds to respond to Nader's charges.

You either believe in freedom or you do not. And I do. The issue here is freedom: should people have the freedom to collectively contribute through PAC's to candidates for public office. I say yes. The question is, Should we put restrictive limits on one group of people and not limits on another? I say no. . . .   ■

CHAPTER 7

Political Parties and Elections

A political party is a group of people organized for the purpose of running candidates—with their names on the ballot under the party label—in order to control the policies and conduct the business of government.

American political parties are different from European parties in a number of ways. They are decentralized and fragmented—in ways that parallel both federalism and the separation of powers concept. Membership is by self-identification only. Party voters in direct primaries, rather than the party organization, control party nominations for public office. There is little party discipline—that is, the party organization has very little control over the public official elected under its label.

But political parties are still an important feature of America's political system. To understand them, it is important to be precise. A political party may be thought of as having three different guises or aspects. First, there is the *party-in-the-electorate* (or party-as-electorate)—those potential voters who identify themselves with one or another party label: "I am a Democrat" or "I am a Republican." Second, there is the *party organization*—the formal structure of the party, such as the Republican State Central Committee of New Mexico or the Democratic National Committee. Finally, there is the *party-in-government*—public officials who hold office under a party label.

In this chapter, we will consider, first, realignment: Did the 1984 elections signal a permanent shift of party identification, from the Democratic label to the Republican, sufficient to make the Republicans America's majority party-in-the-electorate. Next, we will turn our attention to today's competitors with political parties—especially political consultants of various kinds and political action committees (PACs).

Political parties focus on elections, and that will be the final focus of this chapter, as we consider modern political communications, generally, and their function in elections and, more specifically, the impact of television "spot" commercials in political campaigns.

HAS THERE BEEN A PARTY REALIGNMENT?

In 1955, political scientist V. O. Key, Jr. wrote that some American elections are "critical elections" that result in a permanent realignment of the party-in-the-electorate and signal a basic shift in public opinion.[1] The election of Franklin D. Roosevelt as President in 1932 was a critical election. Some at first thought that Ronald Reagan's election in 1980 was, too. But, by the next year, party identification had switched back to the more normal 45 percent for the Democrats and 25 percent for the Republicans. President Reagan's landslide reelection victory in 1984 and the more durable party shift that accompanied it have fueled the realignment speculation again. Party identification is important because, among other reasons, it remains the best single predictor of how people will vote in a general election. Political scientist Seymour Martin Lipset has surveyed all the evidence, and, in his essay excerpted here, says that there has still not been a *national* realignment; instead, he says, there has been a dealignment—that is, fewer Americans now feel attached to either party label. He agrees, though, with Alexander P. Lamis, who writes that, in the South, a switch from the Democratic party to the Republican party has long been underway. In the last selection on realignment, an Englishment, Philip M. Williams, finds it ironic, but important, that American political parties—in all three guises—are becoming more ideologically distinct from each other, just when greater numbers of Americans are saying that parties are of lessening importance.

NOT REALIGNMENT, BUT DEALIGNMENT
Seymour Martin Lipset

Many commentaries on the recent American elections conclude that the United States has taken a long-term move to the right. This shift seemingly began in the late sixties as a reaction to the turmoil occasioned by militant, sometimes violent protest tactics used by the civil rights and antiwar movements, and by the sharp challenge to traditional values encompassed in the changes in family and sex behavior, dress styles, the increased use of drugs, and the like. The

Republicans have been victorious in four out of the last five presidential elections, those held from 1968 on. Only one of these, that in 1968, was close, but in that contest a right-wing and racist candidate, George Wallace, received 13 percent. The one election of the five which the Democrats won, that in 1976, was the first one after Richard Nixon's resignation following the Watergate scandal.

Yet the conclusion that America has been in a conservative mood for some time is challenged by the results of the races for Congress and state offices and by the findings of the opinion polls. In 1984, in the same election in which Ronald Reagan received 59 percent of the vote, eight percent more than in 1980, his party lost two seats in the Senate and gained only 14 in the much larger House, leaving it behind the Democrats by 252 to 183. The Democrats still hold 34 of the 50 governships, down by only one. Judged by which party holds most electoral offices, the Democrats remain the majority party.

THE PUBLIC AND THE ISSUES

A similar contradiction is indicated by the opinion polls. The responses to the numerous sample surveys taken during the Reagan era suggest that Americans, while voting conservative on the presidential level, are programmatically liberal. That is, they give liberal answers to most queries requesting their opinion on assorted domestic welfare issues, on military spending and on America's role abroad. During 1982–83, large majorities (3 to 1 in different polls) favored a federal job program for the unemployed. When asked to choose between cuts in domestic programs or military spending in order to reduce the federal deficit, significant majorities in recent years persistently have favored cuts in military spending, but retention of or increases in expenditures for domestic programs in areas like health, education, support for the aged, and the like. Richard Wirthlin, the President's pollster, and the various national surveys, ABC News/*Washington Post*, Harris, Gallup, CBS News/*New York Times*, and the *Los Angeles Times*, have repeatedly reported a widespread impression that the administration's policies harm the poor and benefit the rich. Wirthlin has stressed that this perception, the so-called "fairness issue," hurt Reagan's standing more than any other. In 1984, various survey analysts suggested that Mondale's best issue was "fairness." In a post-election report, Louis Harris noted that those interviewed agreed by 56–40 percent that "under the Reagan administration the elderly, the poor, and the handicapped have been especially hard hit, while the rich and big business have been much better off. . . . The 1984 mandate includes a strain of compassion for the less privileged" (The *Harris Survey*, November 12, 1984). Similarly, the *Washington Post*/ABC News Poll found, in a survey taken shortly before Reagan's inauguration in January, that his approval rating was at an all-time high 68–28 percent, "though majorities question many of Reagan's specific policies," especially as they relate to the poor and the aged. Only 35 percent favored a substantial cut in "social programs" in order "to reduce the budget deficit," but 65 percent said that there will be such a reduction.

Questions dealing with defense and foreign policies prior to the beginning of the election campaign in the spring of 1984 produced similar results. While strongly anti-Communist, most Americans voiced opposition during 1983 and 1984 to increases in the defense budget and to American military intervention in El Salvador, Nicaragua, and Lebanon. They repeatedly expressed disagreement with Reagan's "handling of the situation" in El Salvador and Lebanon. In November 1983 and again in October 1984, the CBS News/*New York Times* poll found that the American public rejected by 58 to 23 percent in 1983 and by 44 to 30 percent in 1984 "U.S. assistance to the people trying to overthrow the pro-Soviet government of Nicaragua."

The Republicans have been well aware of these poll results for some time. In 1980, Richard Wirthlin noted "a substantial ideological gap," not only between Reagan and the electorate generally, but even as compared with "the average Republican" who was considerably to the left of the party's presidential nominee. And in September 1983, after Reagan had held office for 20 months, Senator Paul Laxalt, a close personal friend of the President and the chairperson of the Republican National Committee, noted "the strange phenomenon" that most Americans expressed approval of the President although they disliked much of what he supported. As Laxalt pointed out: "People have deep differences with his policies. But they still have trust in him and they will look beyond the issues to style and character, not his policies. And Ron will run next year on his record of honesty and consistency, of conducting office with style and no real embarrassment."

The exit polls taken on election day, as well as surveys conducted soon afterward, indicated that the majority of the electorate still disagreed with Ronald Reagan on many issues. Comparing the results of its first post-election national poll with those four years earlier, the CBS News/*New York Times* one pointed to an increase in liberal sentiments on domestic issues. "There is no suggestion in this poll that the American public has grown more conservative during the four years of the Reagan administration. If anything, there is more willingness now to spend money on domestic programs and a better assessment of the social programs of the 1960's."

The electorate also showed opposition to some of Reagan's stands on social issues. Thus, the NBC News Exit Poll reported that two-thirds favored continued legalization of abortion, that "the decision be left to the woman and her physician," while a quarter disagreed. The *Los Angeles Times* found that only 23 percent supported a "constitutional amendment to prohibit abortion." Even Reagan voters were not enthusiastic about their candidate's policy; only 32 percent of them endorsed it. The ABC News poll reported that support for abortion on demand, for the right of women to have one "no matter what the reason," actually increased by 12 percentage points between January 1981 and January 1984. As Louis Harris pointed out in a post-election evaluation: "There is no real mandate for the President over so-called social or moral issues. . . . People oppose . . . requiring school prayer by 51–43 percent, and a 60–34 percent majority favors passage of the Equal Rights Amendment [ERA]. Should the President push his views on abortion, school prayer and the ERA, he is likely to meet stiff resistance from many who supported him."

In discussing these social issues, the President endorsed the positions and efforts of the politicized wing of the evangelical fundamentalists, of whom the Reverend Jerry Falwell, the head of the Moral Majority, is the most prominent leader. But again there is little evidence in the exit polls that Reagan's re-election meant a popular endorsement of their cause. When asked by the *Los Angeles Times* Exit Poll on election day for an evaluation of Jerry Falwell, 16 percent were favorable, 46 percent unfavorable, and 36 percent had no opinion. As expected, a larger proportion of Reagan's voters (23 percent) than of Mondale's (six percent) endorsed Falwell, but more Reagan voters (33 percent) were unfavorable than favorable. Clearly, voting for Reagan did not imply endorsement of the hard-line conservative position on the social issues.

Replies to polls dealing with defense spending and foreign affairs also pointed up the majority's disagreement with the President's policies. The annual General Social Survey conducted by the National Opinion Research Center found that those saying that "too little is spent on defense" declined from 29 percent in 1982 to 17 percent in 1984 while the percentage feeling "too much" is spent increased from 30 percent to 38 percent. With respect to an activist foreign policy, Richard Lugar, the Republican Chairperson of the Senate Foreign Relations Committee, noted at the start of Reagan's second term: "In poll after poll, Americans express their concern about hostile governments which imperiled our interests in Latin America and elsewhere. But in the same polls, Americans display an equal and overwhelming opposition to any course of action which might actually frustrate governments which are harmful to us."

If the electorate voiced less than full approval for Reagan's policies, why did he secure three-fifths of the vote? There is no one answer to this question. But a large part of the explanation lies in the advantage which any incumbent president has over his rival and in the desire of Americans for continuity in leadership after having experienced a high turnover among presidents from 1961 to 1981, Kennedy, Johnson, Nixon, Ford and Carter.

The American presidency is inherently a charismatic office. It places incumbents far above other politicians. Challengers for the post are inevitably handicapped by the fact that they cannot demonstrate that they are presidential, while their opponents have usually done so by the fact of holding the office. The advantage incumbency gives can be seen in the fact that 12 incumbents have been re-elected and only four defeated in presidential contests from 1900 on. And the four defeated ones suffered from particular handicaps. William Taft lost in 1912 because his popular predecessor, Theodore Roosevelt, ran on a third-party ticket and split the Republican vote. Herbert Hoover was unable to overcome the greatest depression in history in 1932. Gerald Ford, the appointed successor of Watergate villain Richard Nixon, was never able to recover from public resentment over his pardon of the ex-President. And Jimmy Carter failed in 1980 as a result of double-digit inflation, national humiliation in Iran, and his inability to communicate a sense of leadership. In July 1979, he delivered two speeches in which he complained the biggest problem with the country was that the American people lacked confidence in their leaders.

Issues apart, Ronald Reagan clearly led in 1984 in the image contest. As Louis Harris put it: "It has been evident all year that there's virtually no contest in this presidential campaign on personality grounds." All the polls agree that he is viewed as a strong leader and an effective communicator, who comes across extremely well on television. Walter Mondale was a weak candidate, handicapped by his link to a failed administration (he was Jimmy Carter's vice-president), his need to make visible concessions to most Democratic interest groups in the bitter struggle for the party nomination with Gary Hart, Jesse Jackson and others, and strangely, his fear of and reluctance to use television, a disastrous weakness today. (Mondale actually turned down a number of invitations to appear on television interview programs.)

Ronald Reagan benefited from the fact that by 1984 his presidency was seen as a successful one. The country was recovering from economic troubles. Inflation and unemployment rates were down, and the gain in per capita real personal income was the highest in 20 years. The President was given credit for having presided over the recovery. In 1980, Ronald Reagan had frequently asked, if you think you or the country are better off economically than four years ago vote for my opponent, if you think not, vote for me. Four years later, when the polls put similar questions to national samples, majorities said the U.S. is better off today. Thus the CBS News/*New York Times* Exit Poll reported 58 percent replying the economy has improved as compared to four years ago, only 18 percent said it is worse now. And when the *Los Angeles Times* Exit Poll asked what has happened to "your personal finances" over the past four years, 41 percent said they had gotten better, 19 percent replied they had worsened, and 40 percent felt they had "stayed the same." Not surprisingly, given these results, those interviewed in the NBC Exit Poll who gave credit to Reagan for an improved economy outnumbered those who did not by 52 to 35 percent.

Reactions to the performance of the economy have become the major determinant of electoral outcomes the world over. As many statistical studies by political scientists have documented, governments tend to be re-elected when unemployment and inflation rates are low or visibly improving, and to be defeated when the opposite is true. The United States is no exception to this rule, a fact well evident before Reagan's election in 1980.

The public opinion polls conducted during Reagan's first term reveal that his approval ratings, as well as his record in trial heats against Walter Mondale, varied in tandem with the changes in the economic indicators. As recession took over in the fall of 1981, many turned against the President. The Gallup Poll reported a decline from 60 percent approving "of the way Ronald Reagan is handling his job as President" in September 1981 down to 41 percent in January 1983, the month in which the recession bottomed out. The ABC News/*Washington Post* poll's findings were similar, a steady decline from 61 percent approval in October 1981 to 54 percent disapproval in January 1983.

The growth in negative evaluations of the President, closely related to the worsening economy and an increase in unemployment from seven to 11 percent, had direct effects on political choices. In early and mid-1981, Reagan invariably led Mondale by a decisive margin in all the surveys which inquired as to how respondents would vote today if they had to choose between the two. By late 1982, the former vice-president had taken the lead. The downswing in the economy also had a strong impact on the attitudes of Americans toward the two major parties. The CBS News/*New York Times* poll reported striking shifts in the party named as best able to handle the problem respondents felt was the most important one facing the country. In 1981, the Republican party was ahead — generally by a margin of ten points. In the January 1982 poll, for the first time, the Democratic party led by 36 to 32 percent, a sharp reversal from the 46 to 31 percent advantage held by the Republicans in September 1981. By late October 1982, the Democratic plurality had widened to 41 to 34 percent. Party allegiance followed a similar pattern.

The results of the congressional and state elections held in November 1982 were striking evidence of the way the recession had hurt the Republicans. The Democrats captured 55–56 percent of the national vote in the races for the House of Representatives, the Senate, and the various governorships, an increase of four to five percent over previous contests.

From the spring of 1983 on, as the various economic indicators steadily improved, the unemployment rate dropped gradually to seven percent, inflation fell to three to five percent, and economic growth revived (almost seven percent in 1984), Americans expressed a sharp increase in optimism both for themselves and for the nation, and increased confidence in the leadership of their institutions. Not surprisingly, the national surveys reported that Ronald Reagan and his economic policies were given credit for these improvements, and that his ratings, both with respect to handling the economy and performing as President, moved up considerably to a point comparable to those he obtained when first taking office in 1981. His approval rating in the ABC News/*Washington Post* survey climbed from 41 percent in January to 49 in mid-April, to 53 in mid-June, and remained in the mid-fifties to low sixties from then on in most polls taken up to the 1984 election.

As noted earlier, the majority of the electorate was still concerned in November 1984 that Ronald Reagan was "unfair," that he was more supportive of the rich than the poor, and most voters still favored government policies to aid the underprivileged. But as William Schneider pointed out, in 1984 "prosperity tended to override the fairness issue." Citing results of the *Los Angeles Times* Exit Poll reported earlier, he concluded "Reagan won because twice as many voters believed their personal financial situation had gotten better rather than worse under Reagan. The *Times* also asked voters to describe the nation's economy. Those who believed it was beginning a long-term recovery (44 percent of those who answered) were for Reagan, 92–8 percent; those who felt it was not getting any better (21 percent) were for Mondale, 87–13 percent."

Given that opinion polls indicated that many, often a majority, of Americans expressed concern that Ronald Reagan might take the country into military adventures abroad or even into war, it is noteworthy that the "peace issue" did not hurt him electorally. Clearly in 1984, Ronald Reagan was perceived at home and abroad as favoring a much more "hawkish," militarist, anti-Soviet, and interventionist stance than Walter Mondale. And as we have seen, opinion surveys taken prior to the election year suggested that the majority of Americans were more "dovish" than the President. The celebrated "gender gap," the lesser support for Reagan among women than among men, which dogged his first term in all the polls, seems related to the fact that females are consistently more likely to support peace proposals and to oppose spending for the military than men.

Two things can be said about the relationship of foreign policy issues to the electoral outcome. First, foreign affairs generally have much less effect on vote choice than domestic ones, except in the context of a major event or policy choice that has an impact during the election season. Second, by stressing the fact that the nation was at peace, and by exhibiting a willingness to negotiate arms control with the Soviets, Ronald Reagan was able to overcome concerns about prospective intervention abroad, particularly in Central America, and the sorry state of negotiations with the Soviet Union over arms control. To these judgments must be added the evidence that a series of events in the latter half of 1983, the shooting down by the Soviets of the Korean airliner, the terrorist attack on the American marines in Lebanon, and the short triumphal war in Grenada, produced higher approval ratings for the administration generally, as well as major improvements in Reagan's standing in trial heats against prospective Democratic opponents, a gain in support for increases in military spending (although most remained opposed), and a general toughening of attitudes toward the Soviet Union. Thus, although Americans who feared the President's behavior was overly bellicose outnumbered those who favored his policies, the foreign affairs record probably helped Ronald Reagan more than his opponents. When Gallup asked in October 1984: "Looking at American relations with other countries, do you think our country's situation is better today, worse today, or about the same as it was in 1980?" 40 percent replied, better; 27 percent, worse; and 29 percent, the same.

Perhaps the strongest evidence that many who voted for Ronald Reagan consciously realized that they disagreed with him on many issues is the fact that most people preferred the outcome, a divided government in which the Democrats controlled at least one House of Congress. As the Harris Survey reports: "By 54–39 percent, a majority hold the view that the country would be worse off, not better off, 'if voters gave him [Reagan] a Republican-controlled Congress that would pass nearly everything he wants.' The voters' reasons for feeling this way were not hard to find. On a whole host of key issues, voters disagree with many of the policies President Reagan has advocated. . . . The voters want at least one house controlled by the Democrats as a check on the President and his programs."

REALIGNMENT OR DEALIGNMENT

Given the Republican victories in four out of the last five presidential contests, this last time by close to a 20 percent margin, and striking gains in the proportion of identified voters, the question has been raised, is the American party system finally realigning? Is the Republican party in the process of becoming the majority party?

The answer appears to be not realignment, but dealignment. By the latter term, political scientists mean a decline in the numbers who identify with or have strong commitments to one of the two parties, as well as a growth in the proportion of those who change party identification as they shift their candidate preference. Both processes seem to be occurring. Prior to the Reagan era, the "ratio of Democrats to Republicans increased from about 3–2 in the 1950s to about 5–3 in the 1960s and 2–1 in the 1970s." But during the eighties, the electorate has shown a willingness to move back and forth. Republicans initially gained from 21 to 28 percent, while Democrats fell from 48 to 41 percent between 1980 and 1981. But in reaction to the 82–83 recession, the distribution of party identifications shifted back to the pre-Reagan level of Democratic domination, 45 to 25 percent, according to the Gallup Poll. During 1984, Gallup and other pollsters reported a steady increase in Republican identifiers, so that by Election Day, Democrats barely outnumbered Republicans, 37 to 33 percent, averaging the results of five different polling organizations. In comparing the results of his post-election surveys in 1980 and 1984, Richard Wirthlin found that the Republicans had gained 11 percent. He and Peter Hart, Mondale's pollster, agreed in a post mortem discussion on the election that the "single most dramatic factor of 1984 was movement in party identifications."

These findings suggest that party identification no longer means much for many Americans. Those who change their electoral choice report a party identification in harmony with their candidate preference. To the 30–33 percent who have described themselves as "independents" since the early seventies (up from a fifth in the early sixties) must be added at least another 20 percent who change their identification as they shift their vote preference. These results are simply another way of documenting that the American electorate has become more volatile, that a large part of it can be easily moved from one party to another. But realignment, a large-scale shift in partisan loyalties by major segments of the electorate, such as occurred in 1896 and from 1932 on, has not occurred.

With few major exceptions, the basic factors which have correlated with party support in the United States since the 1930s continue to operate. Thus, . . . higher income and occupational status still correlate with voting Republican. Trade union members, particularly those belonging to the AFL-CIO, are much more likely to vote Democratic than other workers. Blacks are much more disposed to vote Democratic (they did not shift at all in 1984) than whites. Hispanics favor the Democrats, although less so than blacks. White Protestants continue to vote more Republican than Catholics, while Jews are heavily Democratic.

These relationships are basically the same ones that have been reported in every election since 1936, the first election analyzed using opinion polling techniques. During landslide years like 1964, 1972 or 1984, the victorious party may gain a majority among a group normally leaning to the opposite camp, such as a majority of white Protestants voting for Lyndon Johnson in 1964, or most Catholics going for Ronald Reagan in 1984, but in both cases, Catholics were significantly less Republican than white Protestants.

There were, however, some exceptions to this pattern in 1984, one of which constitutes a genuine example of realignment. Southern whites, who were committed to the Democratic party from the Civil War to World War II, have been engaged in a process of realignment since 1948. In that year, five states in the deep South supported the Dixiecrat third-party candidacy of Strom Thurmond in opposition to Harry Truman's campaigning on a platform promising civil rights for blacks. And with the exception of 1976, when southerner Jimmy Carter was the Democratic candidate, Republican candidates have had considerable success in the South, generally gaining most of the southern states. As of 1984, the large majority of whites cast Republican ballots for President, while the growing number of black voters are almost unanimously Democratic. Half of all Democratic party identifiers in the South are black. According to the *Los Angeles Times* Exit Poll, the Republicans, probably for the first time in history, lead the Democrats in party identification in the region.

The changes in the voting pattern of the South is part of a general process of nationalization of American politics. The two-party presidential vote was almost identical in all four regions, East, South, Midwest and West. Reagan received 58 or 59 percent in each. For election purposes, the country has become one.

Two preponderantly Democratic groups, the blacks and the Jews, resisted the Republican tide. The blacks, who gave Walter Mondale over 90 percent of their votes, were slightly more Democratic than in 1980. Their continued opposition to the Republicans was based on the perception that the President and his party were against black interests with respect to civil rights legislation and government income transfer and welfare policies.

The dramatic increase in Jewish support for the Democrats as compared to 1980 (up 23 percent) occasioned real surprise among political observers. Ronald Reagan's strong support for Israel in tandem with the overt expressions of anti-Semitism by black presidential candidate for the Democratic nomination Jesse Jackson, were expected to move many Jews away from the Democratic party. In fact, the Republican party's links with the evangelical fundamentalists of the Moral Majority and its endorsement of their positions on the social issues and religion in the public schools were even more alienating. The *Los Angeles Times* Exit Poll found that almost none of the Jews—five percent—were favorable to Jerry Falwell, the leader of the Moral Majority.

To the impact of the church-state issue may be added the fact that Walter Mondale was perceived as the protege of Hubert Humphrey, the man whom American Jews regard as their best political friend in recent times. In 1968, Humphrey secured 80 percent of the Jewish vote, close to twice that he received from the electorate at large.

The variations in the voting patterns of the three major religious groups have been explained in status terms. Protestants, as the original dominant and highest status group, have supported the more conservative party; Catholics and Jews, as latter day immigrants, who experienced discrimination from the WASPS (White Anglo Saxon Protestants) historically linked to the Republicans, have backed the more liberal one. But as adherents of the latter two religions have overcome their status and economic inferiority, another set of explanations seems relevant. The

Jews, out of their history as a persecuted group, developed a strong emphasis on charitable giving, to Jews in need as well as others. This Jewish ethic with its emphasis on community welfare may be contrasted to the Protestant ethic with its stress on individualism, on the dictum that "God helps those who help themselves." The former has obvious links to the principles espoused by American liberals and the Democratic party; the latter has clear relations with the values subsumed under laissez-faire competitive individualism as expressed by conservatives and the Republican party.

The Catholic tradition, recently reiterated by the statement on economic principles of the American bishops, resembles the welfare values held by most Jews and Democrats, although church leaders express themselves in terms much closer to the Republicans on church-state and social issues, particularly abortion. The electoral division in 1984 and earlier reflected these variations, Jews for Mondale, white Protestants for Reagan, and Catholics in the middle.

Gender had not been a source of partisan division until recently. In 1984, however, there was a seven percentage point difference between the way the two sexes voted. Part of this gap may be related to the fact that the Democrats have endorsed most positions of the organized feminists and that they nominated the first woman vice-presidential candidate on a majority party ticket in 1984, while the Republicans have either opposed or not supported feminist demands. But as indicated earlier the survey data suggest that gender differences in reacting to foreign policy and defense issues are more important.

The 1984 election was the first one in which the major trade union movement, the AFL-CIO, endorsed a candidate for President, Walter Mondale, long before the party conventions and campaigned actively for his nomination. Detemined to defeat Ronald Reagan, whom they viewed as an active enemy whose appointees helped resist union organization efforts, the AFL-CIO devoted considerable resources to the campaign. Some argued that this action was a mistake, that it would alienate both non-unionists and union members.

The evidence is not yet in to evaluate the effect of organized labor's efforts. The critics of the policy point to the evidence from exit polls that Reagan was supported by 48 percent of voters who belonged to a "union household," a family which had a member who was a trade unionist. But the AFL-CIO stresses that two election night telephone surveys conducted by pollsters Peter Hart and Victor Fingerhut found that 61 percent of members of the AFL-CIO voted for Mondale, as compared to 41 percent of the electorate.

For the first time since World War II, the Republican presidential vote among young voters, those under 30 years of age, was similar to that among those 50 and over. In 1984, age was not a differentiating factor between the candidates. The most common interpretation for the failure of young people, particularly new voters, to favor the more liberal candidate, is economic. It has been argued that young people are especially sensitive to the state of the labor market and that satisfaction with the economic recovery of 1983–84 outweighed the reformist orientations of some youth. Whatever the reason, the fact remains that Ronald Reagan did relatively well among young people.

The fact that most of the traditional relationships between various social factors and party vote continued in 1984 does not mean that their relative weight did not change. Comparing the bases of support of two defeated Democratic candidates who received a similar share of the vote, Adlai Stevenson in 1956 and Walter Mondale in 1984, William Schneider reports: "Mondale did significantly better than Stevenson among black voters, college graduates, women, Jews and professionals. On the other hand, Stevenson's support was much stronger among white southerners, men, blue-collar workers, union members, and Catholics." But these differences do not constitute realignment. The size of the correlations varies from election to election and reflects changes in interests, issues, and candidate appeal. Basically, however, no fundamental change has occurred, other than increased volatility.

Finally, it may be noted that there is a real sense in which the 1984 elections should be seen as reflecting a conservative mood, even if most voters still voice liberal opinions on a variety of issues. A sizeable majority voted for the status quo, both on the presidential and congressional level. Challengers for various offices were frustrated by the fact that voters who agreed with them on the issues nevertheless opted for the incumbent. Many Americans voted for the continuation of peace and prosperity, even if it meant opposing the candidate with whom they were more ideologically compatible. Opinion surveys indicated that the overwhelming majority of those who agreed with Mondale on the issues, but felt they would be better off under Reagan, supported the President's re-election. The Jews apart, many of the liberally disposed put their perception of their economic interests first.

Ronald Reagan won the 1984 election by a decisive majority. But like Dwight D. Eisenhower and Richard Nixon before him, he was unable to help carry both Houses of Congress or more than a minority of state offices with him. There is as yet no evidence of a decisive partisan realignment, the white South excepted. There is, however, considerable indication that the proportion of Americans who are firmly committed to a party is at an all-time low for modern (post World War II) times. This means that major turnovers from one election to another in response to events and candidates are more possible than ever. The Democrats clearly need not despair. If a change in the business cycle does not facilitate their return to the White House in 1988, the "normal" swing of the political pendulum may do so. Of the five presidential elections since World War I in which there was no incumbent candidate, the party in power was defeated four times. To point up this possibility, it may be noted that the first poll of the 1984–88 campaign season to present a trial heat found the Democrats ahead. Terry Dolan, the head of the National Conservative Political Action Committee, after finding that George Bush and Gary Hart are the favorite choices of their parties' supporters for 1988, asked a national sample to choose between them. Hart led Bush by 45–42 percent as of early January. There clearly is still no majority party. ■

THE RISE OF THE TWO-PARTY SOUTH
Alexander P. Lamis

Rarely, if ever, has a region of the United States undergone as dramatic a political transformation as that experienced in the South over the last two decades. When the national Democratic party forcefully took up the banner of civil rights in the early 1960s the basis for the one-party (Democratic) South was destroyed. For generations Southern politics had been dominated by race. The main purpose of the one-party system was to preserve white control and "supremacy." The argument ran that if whites divided their votes between two parties, blacks would hold the balance of power and could bargain for concessions which would put an end to their second-class status. But when blacks entered the political process with strong federal and Democratic support, this precipitated the breakup of the Solid South. Consequently, the present top-heavy, two-party system took hold throughout the eleven states of the former Confederacy.

THE COLLAPSE OF THE ONE-PARTY SOUTH

Actually, the destruction of the one-party-dominated Southern system began in the late 1940s, but it proceeded in an uneven fashion until the critical events of the mid-60s — the passage of the Civil Rights Act of 1964 and the Voting Rights Act of 1965 — both sponsored by national Democratic leaders . . . as whites saw themselves "betrayed" by Democratic advocacy of civil rights. With a Democrat in the White House leading federal integration efforts, the national Democratic party may have truly "walked into the bright sunshine of human rights," as Hubert Humphrey urged the party to do in 1948, but it also confirmed the worst fears of Southern segregationists.

President Johnson's championing of the cause of civil rights for blacks would not have had the partisan impact it did in the South without the highly publicized opposition to the Civil Rights Act by the Republican presidential nominee in 1964. Sen. Barry Goldwater of Arizona, the GOP nominee, voted against both the imposition of cloture to break the Southern filibuster — which was the critical decision and which succeeded by only four votes — and the bill itself. Despite Goldwater's protestations that he was "unalterably opposed to discrimination of any sort" and voted against the bill because parts of it "fly in the face of the Constitution," his vote was heralded in the most race-conscious Southern circles. In November, 1964, Johnson won a landslide Democratic victory nationwide, but Republican Goldwater swept the Deep South states of Mississippi (with 87.1 percent of the vote!); Alabama (69.5 percent); South Carolina (58.9 percent); Louisiana (56.8 percent); and Georgia (54.1 percent).

The significance of Goldwater's candidacy in restructuring Southern politics cannot be underestimated. Nor should one forget that Goldwater did little more than step forward to pick up what national Democratic leaders had discarded— the votes of those Southern white Democrats who placed the preservation of racial segregation above other issues. The loss of this bloc of voters marked the end of the road for a Southern Democratic-dominated system based on white racial unity.

The 1968 and 1972 Democratic presidential nominees, Hubert Humphrey and George McGovern, received the full brunt of Southern reaction to the national party's "abandonment" of the white South. In the 1968 election, Alabama's George Wallace and Richard Nixon, the Republican nominee, divided the South; Humphrey won only President Johnson's home state of Texas. McGovern in 1972 was a weak finisher outside of the South, getting 39.7 percent of the vote in the rest of the nation; but he ran especially poorly in the South, receiving only 28.9 percent. While there were national reasons for his defeat that have nothing to do with Southern politics, McGovern's pronounced weakness in the region suggests a Democratic decline consistent with Humphrey's candidacy four years earlier. . . .

A DEMOCRATIC RESURGENCE

Steady Republican growth in the South dating from the Goldwater campaign ended temporarily in the middle 1970s when the GOP suffered a short-lived decline of varying magnitude, depending on which office is considered. . . . The drop in Republican victories bottomed out in 1976 and . . . by 1978 the party was once again on the upswing.

Why did the GOP decline in these years? The most common explanation attributes the decline to the detrimental effects of the Watergate scandal and the subsequent resignation of President Nixon. There can be no doubt that Watergate was a Republican disaster nationwide, and its effects were felt in several Southern elections. But, to attribute the GOP dip solely to Watergate, or to other national causes, such as the economic decline of 1974–1975, overlooks certain underlying dynamic elements at work in Southern politics. As previously mentioned, a key regional element contributing to this Democratic upsurge was the abatement of the race issue in the early 1970s and the impetus this altered situation gave to the formation of potent black-white Democratic coalitions throughout the region.

In the altered racial atmosphere of the early 1970s, Republicans increasingly came to recognize the weak position the loss of black support left them in. It was, of course, ironic that the traditional party of segregation in the South should become the home of, and dependent on, black voters, many of whom were enfranchised by the national Democrats' passage of the Voting Rights Act. The irony was not lost on one Georgia Republican party chairman who ruefully bemoaned the diverse coalition that demolished GOP statewide challenges in his state, complaining that there was "no tie-in" between the twin pillars of the post-civil rights era Georgia Democratic Party—rural, small-town whites of South Georgia and black voters. "They're as far apart as night and day," he noted. And yet, "They're voting hand in hand, and . . . they're squeezing the lives out of us."

Blacks in the Deep South constituted a larger percentage of the population than in the Rim South and this contributed to a contradictory result. Having a larger percentage of blacks in their states made it easier in the traditionally race-conscious Deep South for white Democratic candidates in the post-civil rights era to attain statewide majorities than was the case for their Rim South counterparts. At the same time, however, the black-white coalition in the Deep South was more volatile because of the long history of racial antagonism there. This Deep South volatility was exhibited in Mississippi in 1978 when blacks abandoned the Democratic senatorial nominee for the independent candidacy of a black leader, Charles Evers, resulting in the first statewide victory by Mississippi Republicans in a century.

At the presidential level, the cooling of the racial situation removed the major issue that in the 1960s had driven sizeable segments of the white population from the Democratic party's national standard-bearers. And in 1976 many of those white traditional Democratic voters in both the Deep South and the Rim South who had followed Goldwater, switched to Wallace, and favored Nixon over McGovern, returned to the Democratic party to vote for Jimmy Carter, the epitome of the Southern Democracy of the mid-1970s.

In addition, the power of traditional Democratic party allegiance joined with the abatement of the race issue to bring these once disgruntled Democrats back. This combination was especially noticeable in the small towns and rural areas. One Arkansas politician-observer expressed the point well: "Tradition is important to rural people. They are looking for ways to stay with the Democratic party; they have to be run off." Three decades ago, V. O. Key, Jr. articulated the powerful nature of this element: "Although the great issues of national politics are potent instruments for the formation of divisions among the voters, they meet their match in the inertia of traditional partisan attachments formed generations ago."[2]

And then there was Jimmy Carter's singular regional and national role. His impressive personal achievement in securing the 1976 Democratic presidential nomination despite the great odds against him was a godsend to Southern Democratic leaders. They were now being led by one of their own, and their campaigns in 1976 were upbeat, vigorous, and confident. For the first time since the 1960 elections, Democratic politicians throughout the South united behind their party's national standard-bearer.

Carter embodied both segments of the newly formed Southern black-white Democratic coalition. His support among blacks was solid, dating from his positive treatment of blacks and their interests while he was Governor of Georgia. And his personal background was firmly rooted in the culture of the white rural South. He spoke a language that Wallace voters could relate to; many of them trusted Carter and counted him as one of them. For Carter this coalition in 1976

---

2. V. O. Key, Jr., *Southern Politics in State and Nation* (New York: Alfred A. Knopf, 1949), p. 285.

was nothing new. It was the same one he put together in the 1970 general election to win the Georgia governorship. The nature of Carter's broad Southern coalition was exemplified by the contrasting personalities who campaigned for him in 1976: George Wallace and Martin Luther King, Sr., father of the slain civil rights leader.

SOUTHERN CLASS DIVISIONS

Although one knows intuitively that Carter's "Southernness" was important to his sweep of the region, and that it was critical for Southern Democratic politicians who only shortly before had to carry the albatross of Humphrey and Carter's success should not be allowed to obscure the changed nature of Democratic party support in the South after the disruptions of the civil rights era. In the 1976 presidential election, white urban voters throughout the South divided along class lines. . . . Sharp economic-class divisions among whites took hold at the presidential level.

But, importantly, though Southern whites were dividing along class lines in 1976, a majority of them did not vote for Carter. The Republican standard-bearer, President Gerald R. Ford, a Midwestern Republican, received 53 percent of the Southern white vote to Carter's 46 percent, survey data disclosed. Therefore, Carter's victory margins in the South rested on his solid support among Southern blacks.

SOUTHERN VS. NATIONAL FACTORS: THE 1980 AND 82 ELECTIONS

Republican Ronald Reagan swept to victory nationwide in 1980 over President Carter, 50.7 percent to 41.0 percent, with John Anderson, the independent, receiving 6.6 percent. While Reagan carried ten of the eleven Southern states, the regional picture was anything but a clear rout. Six of the ten states he won fell by extremely narrow margins: Tennessee (48.7 percent to 48.4 percent); Arkansas (48.1 percent to 47.5 percent); Mississippi (49.4 percent to 48.1 percent); South Carolina (49.4 percent to 48.1 percent); Alabama (48.8 percent to 47.4 percent); and North Carolina (49.3 percent to 47.2 percent). Three states were Reagan's by large margins: Florida (55.5 percent to 38.5 percent); Texas (55.3 percent to 41.4 percent); and Virginia (53.0 percent to 40.3 percent). Louisiana occupied a middle position, going for Reagan 51.2 percent to 45.7 percent. Carter carried his home state of Georgia, 55.8 percent to 41.0 percent.

But this election witnessed an upsurge in Southern Republican fortunes for offices other than president. . . . After the 1980 balloting the Republican party held 45.4 percent of the South's combined twenty-two U.S. Senate seats and eleven governorships. U.S. House seats won by the GOP in 1980 amounted to 36.1 percent of the Southern total, and state legislative seats increased three percentage points to 16.6 percent—a figure that still lagged behind that for other offices.

The most visible gains came in the five Republican statewide successes in 1980. . . .

National factors in 1980, perhaps for the first time, were having an impact in the region in a manner similar to the other regions of the country. . . . By placing presidential elections within the Southern context in the mid-60s and early post-civil rights era, it can be appreciated readily why the Southern vote diverged from the result in the rest of the nation; the Goldwater election is the most prominent one, although Nixon in 1972 ran nearly 10 percentage points higher in the South than in the nation. But in 1980 for the first time in decades the South reacted to a presidential campaign in about the same way as the rest of the country. The national concerns of this election are well-known: discontentment with high inflation, high interest rates, and relatively high unemployment; frustration over the Iranian hostage crisis; the perception that Carter lacked leadership ability; the unfavorable reaction to Carter's "vicious" attempt to paint Reagan as an irresponsible warmonger—to mention a few of the most prominent ones. Among white voters Carter received similar support in all regions: 35 percent in the South, 33 percent in the Northeast, 34 percent in the Midwest, and 31 percent in the West.

There had been speculation when Ronald Reagan and his brand of conservatism captured the GOP nomination that the former California governor would generate the type of enthusiasm in the South that his ideological forerunner, Barry Goldwater, did sixteen years earlier. One Mississippi Delta Republican declared: "I consider that God is giving the country a second chance to elect Barry Goldwater." But 1980 was a far cry from 1964. The transformation of the region's partisan structure by 1980 created a political environment far more sophisticated and complex then that faced by the Arizona Republican in 1964. The partisan changes wrought by the civil rights revolution had taken hold throughout the South, and, despite the tide running against the Democrats, the black-white Democratic coalition still gave the Carter-Mondale ticket a respectable Southern vote.

The 1982 mid-term elections also demonstrated the continuing strength of the black-white Democratic coalition in the South as well as the increasing importance of national factors in the region's electoral behavior. Nationwide the trend in 1982 was toward the Democrats—partly as a reaction to the deep recession of 1981–1982 with its double-digit unemployment rates, and partly as a response by "those who have less" to the perception that the policies of the Republican Administration of President Reagan excessively favored the interests of the nation's well-to-do. Democrats gained 26 seats in the U.S. House overall in 1982 with a quarter coming from the South. Southern Republican representation in the House, which had reached 36.1 percent two years earlier, dropped to 29.3 percent in 1982. In the high visibility contests for governorships and U.S. Senate seats in 1982, the GOP suffered a net loss of two of the thirty-three positions, dropping from 45.4 percent in 1980 to 39.4 percent in 1982. And there were other statewide contests that did not result in partisan changes, but which cast considerable light on the nature of the partisan struggle in the region for the 1980s. Heading the list was George Wallace's recapture of the Alabama Governorship as a bona fide post-civil rights era Democrat ironically dependent on the same black voters he had once vowed to keep segregated forever.

PARTISAN CLEAVAGES IN THE 80s

The above overview of two-party development in the South has demonstrated the importance for Southern politics of the potent, if volatile, black-white Democratic alliance that formed in the post-civil rights era.

. . . The contours of the black-white Democratic coalition in Alabama — where Carter was a narrow loser in 1980 — can be glimpsed. . . . Virtually all blacks supported Carter, but only 38 percent of the whites favored the Democratic president. The Center for Political Studies (CPS) survey presents the same basic picture for the South as a whole. . . . Reagan's Southern victory coalition . . . was made up almost exclusively of whites.

GENERATIONAL AND CLASS DIVISIONS

Two other variables — economic-class and generational — cast further light on the composition of the Southern electorate. . . . economic class in 1980, as in 1976, consistently differentiated white Southern voters. Among those with family incomes of less than $15,000, the Democratic standard-bearer received 58 percent of their votes, but only 23 percent of the votes of those whites with incomes over $35,000.

These findings confirming the existence of New Deal-style cleavages at the presidential level in 1980 also appear when party identification is substituted for candidate choice as the chief partisan measure . . . . Southern white Democrats are far more numerous among "those who have less ." . . .

A fascinating finding of the survey research done in recent years has been the sharp differences in partisan behavior among different generations. For the South, divisions among age groups are quite sharp and contain important suggestions concerning future trends. For example, among white Southerners, Carter's support was proportionally highest with those over 60 years of age; Carter defeated Reagan in that age category by 49 percent to 47 percent.

The same pattern appears when examining party identification and age among white Southerners . . . . The gap between Democratic and Republican partisans narrows considerably for the generation that came of voting age in the past 20 years. Those younger citizens who entered the electorate during and after the great partisan watershed of the middle 1960s were considerably less likely to identify with the Democratic party than were members of the older generation, whose partisan leanings were influenced by the Solid South mentality that persisted until the civil rights question had been resolved. Among white Mississippians 18 to 36 years old, for example, only 30 percent in 1982 identified with the Democratic party compared to 57 percent among those white Mississippians 61 years of age or older.

While these generational findings offer hope for the GOP, it would be an error to view the trend of Republican growth among the young as predetermined. Such an interpretation would deny to political forces their pivotal role. The major changes in Southern politics over the last two decades have had political causes at their heart. The Solid Democratic South was not destroyed by some inevitable movement predestined by socioeconomic forces—such as the rise to middle-class prosperity of many white Southerners after World War II. Socioeconomic factors played a role, but the primacy of political initiatives ought never to be forgotten.

What the ultimate partisan division of the current younger generation of Southerners, and the next one, is to become will be decided in large measure by the future actions of political elites. Republican strategists can, however, remain thankful that, with the destruction of the Solid South mindset, they are now getting a fairer shot at making lasting partisan gains among the South's youth.

CLASHES OVER ISSUES

The survey information examined so far adds a measure of insight into the partisan divisions existing in the South in the early 1980s. More, however, can be learned by focusing on what public opinion polls disclose about various issue positions prevalent among the electorate.

The 1980 CPA survey asked a marvelous question for tapping the central issue that has divided the nation's parties since the New Deal: "Some people feel the government in Washington should see to it that every person has a job and a good standard of living. Others think the government should just let each person get ahead on his own. Where would you place yourself . . . ?" The sharpest differences were between Carter's black and white Southern allies. Sixty-seven percent of the Southern blacks favored a government role while only 28 percent of Carter's Southern white backers were so inclined. This result quantitatively confirms part of the underlying basis for the tensions visible in the ideologically diverse black-white Southern Democratic coalition, which is the dominant force in Southern politics today . . . . Southern whites for Carter were somewhat more inclined to favor a role for government than were Southern for Reagan, 28 percent to 21 percent. Carter's Northern white supporters stood farther to the liberal side on the question than did their Southern counterparts, 40 percent to 28 percent.

Racial attitudes are more clearly apparent in . . . answers to a question concerning the proper role of the national government in aiding blacks. The differences between white and black Southern supporters of Carter stand out sharply: 44 percent of the blacks see a role for the national government, but only 16 percent of the whites take that position. This discrepancy indicates the potential for tensions and conflict over racial issues in the South's powerful biracial Democratic coalition. Northern whites for Carter were twice as favorable to the liberal position as were their Southern counterparts. Republicans of both regions overwhelmingly favored leaving minorities to their own devices.

Sharp differences appear between Southern whites for Carter and their Northern Democratic allies over the issue of prayer in the public schools as well; 91 percent of the former are in favor of allowing prayer, while only 58 percent of the Northerners would allow it. On this issue, Carter's Southern black and white supporters were identical in their stances. On another highly charged social issue—abortion—Carter's Southern whites were the most conservative among the five voter categories; while 46 percent of Carter's Northern white supporters favored the view that a woman should always be able to get an abortion, only 26 percent of his Southern white supporters selected the pro-choice position. The GOP responses across the two sections of the country were similar again, pointing to the homogeneous nature of national Republican politics. This was demonstrated again when on a query concerning support for increasing defense spending, Reagan white voters North and South were in agreement, but Carter's Southern white voters were far more willing to increase spending on arms than were the Democrat's Northern supporters.

THE SOUTH'S PARTISAN FUTURE

These survey findings highlight the partisan cleavages existing in the electorate of the early 1980s. White Southern and Northern Reagan voters more frequently than not came down very close to each other on the issue propositions examined. Among Democrats, the white Southern and Northern wings of the party—as measured by presidential candidate support—showed sizable attitudinal differences, especially on racial and social matters.

On the one question that best captured support for national government involvement in economic matters . . . important differences appeared among the major groupings of Carter supporters. Two-thirds of the Southern blacks strongly favored a central role for the national government in seeing to it that everyone has a job and a good standard of living while only about a quarter of Carter's Southern whites took that view; Northern whites for Carter fell somewhere in between. Given these differences, what is the future of the diverse black-white Democratic coalition in the South?

In the early 1980s, this broad Democratic alliance has held together partly as a result of the canny maneuvers of white Democratic leaders, who are among its chief beneficiaries. They often walk a political tightrope that requires Olympian balancing. It is a straddling performance that ought to evoke periodic standing ovations from the gods of equivocation, if such exist.

Forces are at work in the South, however, that could make the delicate positioning of nonideological Democratic straddlers more and more difficult to maintain. It has been stressed that the black-white Democratic coalition is diverse. That is true in the main and was the coalition's most striking feature, especially in the first years of the post-civil rights era. But by the early 1980s there was a growing tendency for rank-and-file Democrats of both races to recognize their common class interests. . . . Low-income whites are far more likely to be members of the Southern Democratic coalition than are upper-income whites. Furthermore, an examination of the issue responses uncovers a substantial percentage of whites in agreement with the views of the black wing of the alliance. And the tendency is in the direction of greater issue agreement. (In national terms, the same phenomenon can be charted under the heading of the penetration of the New Deal-style alignment into Southern politics.)

The pace at which this tendency proceeds will depend on the rise to prominence of left-leaning Southern Democratic leaders who advocate policies favorable to "those who have less" of both races. Exactly when and where these leaders will surface cannot be predicted, but the net result will probably be to push more conservative Democrats over to the Republican party. How strong the Republican party will grow in the South in the next decade or so involves many imponderables — national as well as Southern. But grow it will, for its foundations are secure in the partisan configuration that emerged in the South by the second decade of the post-civil rights era.   ■

PARTIES ARE BECOMING MORE IDEOLOGICALLY DISTINCT
Philip M. Williams

There is something baffling to the European (particularly perhaps to the British) observer in the current laments about the loss of power of political parties in the United States. Qualified writers disagree somewhat about the extent of their decline and the prospects of reversing it, but with virtual unanimity they accept the fact and regret it. Yet from across the Atlantic it seems hard to understand the disappearance of a phenomenon that had no discernible existence in the first place. From Roosevelt's single-vote majority for conscription in 1939, to Truman's resort to bipartisanship to pass Marshall Aid and the Atlantic Pact through Congress, to Eisenhower's reliance upon the Democratic leaders to save him from his own Republican fellow-partisans, to Kennedy's inability to get his tax cut even discussed in Congress for eighteen months, to Nixon's inability to stop the War Powers Act and Carter's humiliating failure over SALT II and almost equally humiliating success over Panama, Presidents have repeatedly found it impossible to rely on their parties even in the foreign and defence field, where they are supposed to have most influence.

There is another surprising feature of the debate. Sixty years ago, party allegiance in the United States seemed so totally detached from political outlook that, whatever the functions that parties were supposed to perform nationally, support for any specific policy orientation could never conceivably be among them. Republicans were mostly conservatives who believed the business of the United States to be business, yet the midwestern agrarians in their ranks were the most radical politicians in the country. Franklin Roosevelt made the Democrats a progressive big-government party, relying on the support of trade unionists, northern blacks, and working-class Catholics in the big cities — yet also of a solid South dominated by an elite committed to white supremacy, suspicious of

Catholics and organised labour, and increasingly conservative in its general outlook. But in the subsequent years a very considerable reshuffle of groups and attitudes took place. In so huge and diverse a country it would be too much to expect two united and homogeneous coalitions, which even the much smaller nation-states of Europe have been unable to generate (although Britain came nearest, once Southern Ireland was detached). But the extremes have vanished, with no radical Republicans left and precious few really reactionary Democrats; the incongruent wings have shrunk, leaving the conservative Democrats a dwindling band and the liberal Republicans a pathetic and isolated rump. Their old homes find increasing difficulty in accommodating either, and in all parts of the country, at almost every election, the Democratic candidate is more liberal or at least more moderate than his Republican opponent. Yet we constantly read that the parties were more powerful in earlier days when they were almost meaningless, and are becoming less powerful as they grow more meaningful. It is a strange paradox.

The explanation is simple. When U.S. writers and British readers consider the power of the parties and the distribution of power within them, they have quite different considerations in their minds because they conceptualise parties quite differently. To Britons the essential feature of a political party is understood (not always rightly) to be the common outlook binding its members together and translating, however imperfectly, that outlook into political practice through the control of government. To Americans historically, parties have rarely had even the most rudimentary common outlook, or any recognised membership, or even a government over which they could reasonably hope to exercise real control. Britons have seen their parties (in realistic not legal terms) as units linked, more or less effectively, from the top to the bottom of a hierarchical structure subject to more or less complete central direction; even though independent power centres could often maintain their distinct existence, they rarely attained sufficient influence to challenge the established leadership. No such established leadership existed at all in the United States unless the party held the Presidency, and even then it was temporary, contingent, and contested at every turn by the numerous independent baronies that were the only permanent power centres in the system.

This was in part the consequence of federalism and the dispersal of authority to fragmented geographical units. Occasionally a state party (Ohio Republicans or Virginia Democrats) would exercise a continuous power in its own area, which the national party never tried to match on its bigger scale. Far more often the state party, like the national one, would depend for coherent leadership on having its candidate in the chief executive post, relapsing into warring factions whenever the Governor came from the other side. Local parties were more likely to be durable, being dominated in the great cities by bosses without public office, or by strong mayors; more recently where machines still survived, the mayor was usually the boss. Their perspectives and objectives were overwhelmingly local; elderly Chicago Democrats would go to Congress to retire, or promising young ones to learn their trade before returning to serious politics as city aldermen. Progressives saw the parties—with some reason—as obstacles to change, not instruments for achieving it, and that tradition still exerts a powerful influence; those who wish to promote reforming policies often seek to tear down existing organisations, rather than use them to mobilise support and clarify priorities. Where the parties were weakened by these efforts, or declined for other reasons, they have become unable to control the nomination of candidates. Instead, the direct primary, in its manifold forms, enabled the party's regular supporters or its prospective supporters or even its opponents (according to the state law) to choose its standard-bearer—who, having won on his own, was unlikely docilely to accept advice, still less discipline, from any organ of the party.

Fragmentation was not merely geographical, for the separation of powers was designed to achieve the same result at the centre. The two houses of the legislature, elected in different units and at different times, each had their internal power structures in which, for two-thirds of a century (1910 to the mid-1970s), the committee chairmen who controlled the flow of business, and usually the terms of legislation, held their posts by seniority within the majority party, whether or not they shared the views of its congressional leadership or rank-and-file members, still less of its Presidents. When the Democrats controlled Congress, as they did for all but four years from 1930 to 1980, that nominal control was primarily exercised through these baronial chairmen who, being mostly conservative southerners, were increasingly out of touch with the majority of their party.

Before the New Deal the national parties were coalitions held together above all by the need, once every four years, to keep their rivals out of the most important office of all, the Presidency. Under a parliamentary and cabinet system with a collegial executive, a multi-party system might well have arisen; with a single chief executive, the barons were obliged to make their alliances before not after the election. The territorial barons played the main but not the only role; their legislative counterparts were rarely serious rivals in this arena, but other groups could sometimes exercise great influence, notably the labor unions in the Democratic party in and after Roosevelt's day. Major parties are really coalitions not only in the United States, but in all two-party systems including the British. . . . In the United States, however, it was thought politically unprofitable and divisive to emphasise ideological differences, and the two coalition-parties preferred to appear no more distinct than Tweedledum and Tweedledee: bottles with different labels, both empty. Appearing only every four years to elect a president, they did not enunciate a party policy but proclaimed support for his—a claim in no way binding on the party's spokesmen either in the national legislature or in the states.

Americans do not, therefore, write about their political parties as units with interlocking parts, which are supposed to mesh but inevitably clash from time to time. Instead, they write separately about segments of parties, operating independently at the different levels of government; the party-in-the-electorate (who supports it, and how realiably?); the party organisation (who runs it, and how much influence do they wield?); the party-in-the-legislature (how much notice, if any, do the members take of their leaders, and in what circumstances?); and, last and decidedly least, the party-in-government (when, if ever, does it exist?). . . .

BREAKING UP THE BARONIES

Everywhere the old baronies have crumbled. It has been less widely remarked that those baronies were as much obstacles to coherent party action as they were instruments of it, for the wielders of baronial power did not necessarily share and indeed often thoroughly detested the views of the majority of their party. Shifts of population, blacks voting in the south and the growth of a new breed of political activists interested in new issues have contributed to a redistribution of electoral preferences and a great simplification of the old helplessly confused relationship between policy views and party allegiance. While that confusion prevailed, party coherence on policy was inconceivable; it still remains inhibited by many factors, both short- and long-term. But in a more congenial political climate it can now be conceived of, and some of the institutional changes of recent years could be well adapted to encourage it. These include the new if little-used powers of the Democratic party leadership in Congress, the spectacular growth of the national organisation of the Republican party, and a number of Democratic reforms that have either survived the storms of the last ten years and opened up party channels to its active supporters or have been introduced more recently to restore some influence to the office-holders and spokesmen who have a long-term stake in the party and in its successful performance on the national stage. . . .

Institutional changes in the United States have had contradictory effects, weakening party structures in some respects, yet strengthening them in others. Traditionally, American party organisations had been held together by patronage. But in the more affluent post-1945 world, ill-paid spoils-system posts were much less attractive. A more prosperous and educated society generated a new type of political activist, more committeed to particular policies or candidates and less to organisational maintenance and loyalty for their own sakes . . . . Among Democrats, the reform activists first appeared in Adlai Stevenson's campaign in 1952, and in a number of state parties, notably New York, California, and Illinois. Their conservative equivalents in the Republican party emerged a little later, to overthrow the dominant eastern establishment wing and nominate Barry Goldwater in 1964. Similar tensions, latent among the Democrats, developed over civil rights and then erupted during the Vietnam war in furious protest against the measures by which the old guard preserved its control at the 1968 convention. The consequent moves to reform party procedures began with widespread support. The established baronial powers were a target for all reformers who, however, while all aiming to democratise the party, disagreed on their priorities.

Most of them sympathised in differing degrees with four principal aims. Parties should not merely be vehicles for winning power, they should be committed to agreed policies. They should be effective in carrying out those policies. They should not be managed by established powers (whether or not holding elective office) but subject to democratic control from below, which implies a thoroughly decentralised structure open to participation at the local level. The members participating should be representative of the whole population, not confined to the social groups most accustomed to these activities, and those groups hitherto disadvantaged (by colour, age or sex) should be helped to secure their full share.

Unfortunately many of the reformers were inexperienced, and few were willing to recognise that these aims were incompatible. A party could not be an effective instrument for implementing policy without organisation and discipline; if these were demolished by "tumbleweeds" in the name of openness and decentralisation, it would have no way of ensuring that its democratically agreed policies would be applied by its spokesmen in public office. If democratic choice by the local membership was paramount, representation for minorities could not be guaranteed. If the party represented all interests in the society, with all groups having their due weight, it was unlikely to develop a distinctive outlook and ideology separating it from its rival, offering different policies and so giving the voters a real choice. Instead, two catch-all parties were likely to emerge, each straddling every issue for fear of offending a section of its clientele, restoring the old Tweedledum and Tweedledee combination rather than the committed programmatic parties sought by so many reformers.

Even in Congress, where the reform decisions were made on more limited issues by practising politicians, there was a somewhat similar confusion of objectives. By the mid-1970s a broad coalition was ready to strip the committee barons of their overweening power and security of tenure. But it was broad only because its members' aims were diverse. . . .

Senior members can now be denied chairmanships, and even the unlikely possibility of this encourages them to behave responsively rather than autocratically. Subcommittees have proliferated, giving opportunities for influence and activity to quite junior members. Committee specialisation is less effective and committee prestige less recognised, so that their decisions are much more frequently challenged and even overturned on the floor. The legislative process is more fragmented than ever, and it becomes increasingly difficult to obtain timely decisions on any controversial or divisive subject; so that junior members feel no more satisfaction in congressional life, while seniors retire in frustration much more often and earlier than their predecessors.

. . . The Speaker has regained many of the powers he had lost in 1910. He appoints the Rules Committee, for years the principal fortress of the conservatives in the House, and he has much discretion in referring bills to committee. The Democratic caucus meets monthly, instead of every two years at the start of each congress. It has exercised less influence than optimists hoped, partly because members cherish their independence and the will to reach an agreed party compromise has been weak, but also because a caucus of nearly 300 members is a quite unsuitable forum for doing so; and if it tries to impose majority decisions on the minority, they can easily frustrate it by staying away and denying a quorum. Nevertheless the Speaker and the caucus can impose ideological and loyalty conditions for membership or leadership of committees in a way that had not been possible for 70 years. Moreover, should the political climate become more congenial to centripetal forces within the party, there is now a viable alternative for hammering out party policy: the Steering and Policy Committee of 24, composed half of members elected by the Democratic congressmen (in regional groups) and half of party leaders or spokesmen for other categories (blacks, freshmen, etc.). Chaired by the Speaker and largely selected by him, representing all sectors within the Democratic ranks, it offers an instrument with more potential for acceptable party leadership than ever before.

OLD LOYALTIES IN ECLIPSE

. . . Among individual voters, particularly the young, the party label no longer attracts automatic loyalty. For highly visible offices—governor, U.S. senator, above all President—most people, whatever their nominal party identification, now insist that they evaluate the individual candidates on their personal merits (even if many nevertheless end up always choosing the same side). Whenever two or three of these offices are at stake simultaneously, large numbers of voters split their tickets and pick candidates from different parties to fill them. For less visible offices such as that of congressman, the challenger is usually less known and the advantage of the incumbent much greater. Either way, party affiliation does little to elect or defeat the member, who must organise, finance and publicise his own campaign and consequently feels little gratitude to his party for past services and has no expectation of future favours. There is not much electoral incentive for party loyalty when it brings no reward for observance and no penalty for breach.

Developments in the technique of electioneering reinforce these tendencies. The media, especially television, are indispensable to the projection of a candidate's message. Sophisticated technology and professional advice enable him to direct the message to receptive audiences and to make profitable use of his resources, which have to be substantial because every element in the process is expensive. Huge sums are spent to support or defeat an individual politician loved or hated by a well-financed single-issue group (promoting environmentalism, for instance, or opposing abortion or gun control) or by a political action committee seeking to ensure access to a congressional committee member dealing with its industry. Party discipline and the party ticket no longer cushion the politician against such pressures, and he has a strong incentive to avoid making himself a conspicuous target for a strong challenger financed by an interest-group seeking his electoral demise. . . .

The destruction of the baronies has been most evident in the most visible political arena of all, that of presidential nominating politics. Before the last decade or so, the chief examples of concentrated and irresponsible power influencing that process occurred in the Democratic party, where reformers were consequently most active. (The Republicans needed to make fewer and less sweeping changes but were still affected by some of the same pressures or indeed obliged to conform to similar rules under new legislation in particular states.) The grip of the southern segregationist Democrats had been gradually loosened. They lost their absolute veto when the requirement of a two-thirds majority for the party's presidential nomination was dropped in 1936. Their habit of repudiating any obligation to the party while enjoying the advantages of continued membership was discouraged by the requirement of loyalty to its candidates by state parties in 1956 and the denial of seniority to the Goldwater Democrats in Congress in 1965. Their hold on their own state parties was broken when Mississippi's segregationist delegation was unseated at the 1968 Convention.

Hubert Humphrey's nomination provoked the frustrated anti-Vietnam-war wing of the party into attacking all the devices by which the professional politicians, disturbed by the newly-active middle-class enthusiasts, had manipulated the rules to their detriment. . . .

IDEOLOGICAL SHIFTS

. . . The United States is becoming far more of a single nation, though a very big one; and while its various regions have conflicting interests and distinct outlooks, they no longer cherish cultures and ways of life so mutually opposed as to make them see other Americans as dangerous enemies. Instead, the New Deal began and the civil rights movement has continued a gradual shift of allegiances, which means that, while political attitudes differ greatly in different parts of the country, virtually everywhere the locally most conservative elements overwhelmingly belong to the Republican party, and the relative liberals are Democrats. Supporters of either party still disagree with one another on many issues . . . . But the growth of a loose party consensus, defined in opposition to the loose consensus on the other side, has in the last 20 years become possible for the first time.

. . . As population shifted out of the central cities and into the suburbs, it carried away an axiom of American politics. Liberals able to mobilise the big-city vote were no longer essential to carry the big marginal states for senator, governor or president, as Nixon and Reagan showed. Liberal Republicans were not, therefore, indispensable to their party after all, and its keen supporters could at least afford to express their old mistrust for those ideological misfits and indulge in their real preferences. In New York alone they were able in 1970 to replace Senator Goodell by a Conservative, James Buckley, in 1980 to defeat Senator Javits in a primary and elect the right-wing Senator D'Amato, and even in New York City to deny Mayor Lindsay the Republican nomination (he won re-election as a Liberal and subsequently switched to the Democrats). On the other side of the party divide, the conservative southern Democrats also found their opportunities restricted as they lost the protection of the other half of the double gerrymander. In the south, it was the cities that offered the best hope of Republican penetration, while the rural areas, as long as they could keep the modern world from intruding and the blacks from voting, remained solid bastions of traditionalism—grossly over-represented as their people left, but their representation nevertheless remained intact. But the Supreme Court imposed equal electoral districts, and the Voting Rights Act of 1965 belatedly but effectively enfranchised the blacks, substantially reinforcing the Democrats' more liberal wing and enabling moderate politicians to assert their views. Senators in the south became vulnerable to both Republican and even liberal challenges. . . . Thus conservative Democrats are no longer secure electorally; and their tenure of positions of committee power is threatened both by their northern colleagues reaching the top of the seniority ladder, and by the caucus penalising those who defy the party's majority wishes too outrageously. . . .

Even without the drastic new developments transforming the south, northern politicians from the minority wings of their parties increasingly found their positions untenable, since the same views that helped them win the uncommitted voter at general elections offended their own partisans. In 1968, primary defeats removed Senator Kuchel of California, the minority whip, in a state where liberal Republicans had ruled almost without serious challenge until ten years before, and also Senator Lausche of Ohio, the last thoroughly conservative Democrat from a northern state. Above all, the parties became less and less congenial to those of their members who found themselves out of sympathy with the prevailing view and who have consequently switched their allegiance in large numbers. In the south, the prominent former Democrats turned Republican include Senators Helms and Thurmond of North and South Carolina and ex-Secretary of the Treasury Connally of Texas; in the north, President Reagan and Senator Hayakawa of California, Senator Hatch of Utah, and ex-attorney General Mitchell of New York. In return, the northern Democrats recruited Senator Riegle of Michigan, ex-Senator Haskell of Colorado, ex-Mayor Lindsay of New York, Representatives Panetta of California, Foglietta of Pennsylvania and Peyser of New York. All these men headed the long lists of conservative Democrats or liberal Republicans who switched, while to count those who did so from the majority wings of either party, the fingers of one hand would need to be painfully amputated. Before the days of the New Deal such changes would have been thought unseemly as well as unnecessary, and so they were often delayed by a generation or two: Attorney General La Follette of Wisconsin is the Democratic heir of the state's great dynasty of progressive Republican congressmen; the leading Rockefeller in politics today is the Democratic governor of West Virginia; the grandfather of ex-Senator Brock of Tennessee, the architect of the 1980 Republican revival, was a conservative Democratic senator from the same state; the grandson of Speaker Garner of Texas, F. D. Roosevelt's conservative vice-president, was a Republican candidate for Congress in the state of Washington. . . .

BUILDING NATIONAL PARTIES?

The Republicans began the process of developing a coherent national organisation. Their national chairman, Bill Brock, set out to rebuild the party that Richard Nixon had so neglected and damaged—and to do so from the ground up. He made a major nation-wide effort to recruit strong candidates both at the lowest level, for the state legislatures, and also from within those nurseries of American political talent, to select able people to run for Congress and for statewide office . . . . Brock also skillfully exploited the ability of the Republican party to raise much more money than its rival; although its more numerous wealthy supporters were now restricted by campaign finance legislation, they were also supplemented by successful efforts to raise large amounts through small direct-mail contributions, a source the Democrats quite failed to tap.

Brock used these resources to excellent purpose. The Republicans have always given their National Committee more attention than their rivals; the party's staff has almost invariably been bigger, and in 1977 the disparity had already reached a peak (220 as against 40). Brock used it to provide centrally, with resulting economies of scale, the elaborate technical assistance and services that have become necessary as campaign methods have grown so immensely sophisticated and expensive in recent years. Developing a practice begun under his predecessor, he identified winnable contests and directed money to them at the time it was most useful—early in the campaigning season when it helped challengers to make themselves known, show a respectable prospect of success, and so raise more money from other sources. . . . Amendments to the campaign finance law allowed national parties to contribute directly to state parties and to House and Senate candidates; with more money and effective control of it, the Republicans made the best use of this provision. Local Republican organisations were revived, with the help of 57 professional field organisers, and began appearing in towns across the south where the party had never existed before, although its presidential candidates had been making substantial electoral inroads for two decades or more. There was no such corresponding effort on the Democratic side. What little money that party had was absorbed by the President's campaign; candidates for Congress or for governorships received very little if anything, and those for state legislatures none at all. . . .

The Democrats [in 1976] lost the White House, half of the Senate seats and a third of the governorships they were defending, and 33 seats in the House of Representatives—a record number for any party losing the Presidency since 1932. . . . The voters' wrath was directed not against a party with a clear yet unpopular policy, but against one in total disarray, for President Carter's own course was far from consistent or coherent, and he had neglected party wishes and advice even more than his predecessors had. There was no Democratic effort organistionally to match the Republicans; they had neither the money nor the impulse, since the President was determined to keep the national committee under his own control in order to avoid any policy embarrassments from his critics or any diversion of its limited resources to any election campaigns but his own. Nevertheless, the Democrats did make drastic changes of a different kind, both before and during Carter's term of office. These changes began with the factional battles of 1968 and 1972, which had led first to defeat and then to disaster. During the subsequent decade serious efforts were made to arrive at a lasting settlement acceptable to the party's rival wings, retaining the reforms that ensured wider access while modifying those that tilted the balance too far against the party's regular supporters and elected spokesmen. . . .

COMPETITIVE PRESSURES

. . . [A] party preferred by most voters from every social, geographical and ideological group in the country—as the Democrats were in 1977—is bound to alienate some professed supporters, whatever stand it takes. Quarrels and defections are inevitable, and united acceptance of a single presidential candidate is all the harder when policy decisions and symbolic affirmations are embodied in the choice. Without such severe internal strains, the Republicans, in spite of their minority status, are sustained by many and growing assets. Their regular adherents are more likely to vote. Their ranks are regularly swollen by disaffected Democrats. They have easier access to money—and that advantage will increase if they can hold the Senate and attract the funds that business political action committees have hitherto more or less reluctantly given to the Democrats to ensure legislative goodwill for their interest. They have a far better organisation at the centre and better links with the party in the country. They will benefit at all levels—the electoral college, the House, above all the Senate—if they can keep their ascendancy in the west and south-west and continue their expansion in the south; for these areas are enhancing their political influence as the old industrial north-east and midwest decline through migration. The 1982 election disappointed these hopes in the south, but not necessarily permanently. . . .

No one would expect American parties to become as disciplined and centralised as British ones, with some exaggeration, were supposed to be a few years ago. But, with the Republicans leading the way, they might begin to converge towards the looser but still recognisable form of unity that their British counterparts may be approaching from the other direction. . . .

The United States is not nearly there yet. But the sweeping generalisations inspired by the bipartisan politics of the issueless Eisenhower years were to prove inapplicable to the bitter ideological conflicts, within or between the parties, that dominated the next decade and a half. Already it seems unlikely that the conservative outlook and often fragmented politics of the later 1970s will prevail indefinitely. When the climate changes, and politicians sense and respond to a new mood in the electorate, some neglected institutional developments will reveal their latent potential. "Even as the parties have become weaker, the general realignment of the party system . . . makes both parties more homogeneous ideologically in the nation at large. This is reflected in the Congress and is a force for cohesion there in an era of individualism. Ideological kinship will also facilitate cooperation between presidents and their congressional party colleagues . . . of immense significance in the long run will be the destruction during the 1970s of old barriers to effective and responsive government. The obstacles to harmonious legislative-executive relations . . . have for the most part been overcome."[3] No doubt the old-style American parties have decayed, probably past the point of no return. No doubt there are continuing problems

---

3. James L. Sundquist, *The Decline and Resurgence of Congress* (Wash., D. C.: American Enterprise Institute, 1981), pp. 478, 483.

in the way of developing parties with a purpose, recognisable as such to European observers. But if Americans come to decide they need such parties, as has occasionally happened for short periods in the past, the political components are there waiting to be assembled and the main institutional obstructions have been removed. Neither condition has ever before been met in the history of the United States.   ■

COMPETITORS OF POLITICAL PARTY ORGANIZATIONS

Modern techniques—such as polling, mass media advertising, and direct mail solicitation of campaign contributions—have made hired political consultants increasingly essential to modern political campaigns. In their importance to candidates, these consultants have become rivals of the political party organizations. So, too, because they furnish a lot of the campaign funds for national office, have political action committees (PACs), which we discussed in the preceding chapter.

In an essay excerpted here, political scientist Larry Sabato discusses the effect on political parties of the rise of the PACs and the political consultants. He finds that as they have sought to meet this competition, party organizations—particularly of the Republican party—have been strengthened. He recommends that the Democratic party follow the Republican example.

CONSULTANTS AND PACs AS PARTY RIVALS
Larry Sabato

Not many years ago, an American president was likely to reward one of his party's organizational kingpins from the Irish-American community with the coveted post of U.S. ambassador to Dublin. However, in 1982 President Ronald Reagan chose his campaign media consultant, Peter Dailey, to be the U.S. representative in Ireland—and the choice symbolized recent changes that have occurred in American politics.

The political parties have been weakened by a multitude of circumstances, and in many respects the influence party leaders once wielded in election campaigns now is exercised by independent political consultants, just as the vital electoral roles once performed almost exclusively by parties are now available to anyone who masters the new campaign technologies such as polling, media advertising, and direct mail. The growth of political consultancy and the development of advanced campaign techniques were combined with the new election finance laws that hurt the parties, favored the prospering consultants, and encouraged the mushrooming of party-rivaling political action committees. . . .

FROM PARTY POLS TO POLITICAL CONSULTANTS

It is easy to exaggerate the changes that have occurred in the American system in recent decades, and it is especially dangerous to exaggerate the damage sustained by the political parties. Certainly the parties have declined. But that must be tempered by the knowledge that they have survived all the tumult and remain flexible enough to adapt to new political realities. As this chapter will show, the Republican party, in particular, has become a showcase of new vitality, and it has learned to use to its own benefit the campaign techniques that had threatened to make it obsolete. Slowly but surely, the Democrats are beginning to make similar adjustments.

To understand the transformation of the parties within the American electoral system, it is important first to understand how the perception that the electorate has of them has changed over the years. Martin P. Wattenberg has recently argued[4] that American voters have *not* grown more alienated from the parties (contrary to journalistic myth). Rather, voters have become more neutral in their evaluations of the parties. Why has this happened? As Wattenberg explains it:

> The reason for party decline has not been that people no longer see any important differences between the parties. . . . Rather the problem which the parties must face is that they are considered less relevant in solving the most important domestic and foreign policy issues of the day. *In the voters' minds, the parties are losing their association with the candidates and the issues which the candidates claim to stand for.* [Emphasis added.]

That association between parties and candidates is weakening partly because the parties have ceased to be very important in the process of electing their candidates. Since candidates are not beholden to the party for their elections, they are not responsive to the party's needs or platform once in office.

As the parties have moved to the sidelines, independent political consultants have rushed forward to replace them. Pollster Patrick Caddell clearly identified the alternate nonparty route that consultants have provided to willing politicians:

> Parties traditionally provided the avenue by which candidates reached voters. What we've done with media, what we've done with polling, and what we've done with direct organizational techniques is that we have provided candidates who have the resources (and that's the important thing, the resources), the ability to reach the voters and have a direct contact with the electorate without regard to party or party organization.[5]

---

4. Martin P. Wattenberg, "The Decline of Political Partisanship in the United States: Negativity or Neutrality?" *American Political Science Review* 75 (1981): 941–50.

5. This and other quotations from political consultants are taken from the author's own interviews.

The value of consultants to candidates is perhaps best described by the technologies at the consultants' command. The design and production of media advertising is among the essential skills that consultants offer political aspirants. It is difficult to find a contested race for major office in the United States today which does not feature television and radio commercials, and even campaigns for minor posts such as city councilor and state legislator often employ professional advertising. Quite simply, the paid media advertisements (together with the "free" media of press coverage) have replaced the political party as the middleman between candidate and voter. The candidate no longer depends so heavily on party workers to present his case to voters in his constituency; television can do it more directly and efficiently. The media consultant who can design effective and pleasing advertisements is thus worth his weight in gold to the modern candidate.

Equally prominent in modern campaigns is another kind of political consultant, the pollster. At every stage of the campaign the pollster, his survey data in hand and his role as *vox populi* foremost in mind, aids the candidate and staff in crucial decisions—whether to run at all, how to run, what issues to emphasize and which ones to avoid, which aspects of his opponent's platform and personality are vulnerable, and so on. In doing so, the pollster substitutes for party leaders, since it was exactly this kind of advice that the party kingpins used to dispense and their candidates used to follow. Once again, the new technology replaces the political party as the middleman between candidate and voter. Office seekers formerly depended on party workers to convey to them grassroots sentiment and the opinions of average voters in the constituency. Now random-sample surveys can perform the same chore, but with relative certainty and with a wealth of semiprecise detail that party wheel-horses could only guess at. For example, it would be difficult even for a modern-day George Washington Plunkitt to know which television shows are watched by a population sub-group targeted by the campaign. Simple crosstabulations of standard survey questions used by the political pollsters reveal this, and more, today. While the process of polling has many weaknesses and is rarely as error-free as the unwittingly arrogant disclaimer accompanying most surveys suggests—"this poll is accurate to within a margin of error of plus or minus 4 percent"— survey sampling is usually more accurate and normally more directly useful than the surmises of party leaders. Candidates know it, and that is why polling consultants like Jimmy Carter's Patrick Caddell and Ronald Reagan's Richard Wirthlin have had far more influence on the course of their client's campaigns than have party chiefs. It should be noted, too, that the pollster's dominance has recently been extended to governance as well as campaigning. Caddell, for instance, clearly had major influence on a number of President Carter's decisions (including his crucial 1979 Camp David domestic summit and subsequent "crisis of confidence" speech). Wirthlin's frequent polling studies on a wide range of subjects are reportedly closely studied by President Reagan and his key aides; Wirthlin himself is a frequent White House visitor.

Clever polling analysis and creative media can help a candidate to win, but nothing is more fundamental to a successful campaign than money. Only presidential elections are funded even partially from the public treasury at the federal level, and just a handful of states have substantial public financing of statewide campaigns. So, most candidates must themselves raise the tremendous sums necessary to seek major office in the United States. While campaign finance has always been primarily the candidate's responsibility, the political parties used to bear a reasonable share of the load, directly contributing in many states perhaps as much as a fifth of their standard-bearer's kitty. As in so many other respects, the parties were in financial decline for much of the 1970s, and observers charted the fall in the percentage of funds provided to congressional candidates by the parties. Once more, a group of political consultants has filled the vacuum, using the technology of direct mail. By carefully selecting mailing lists and finding those who are committed to a cause or a candidate, the direct mailers raise campaign cash with thousands of under-$100 contributions, and also cumulatively amass invaluable information about the contributory habits of millions of political donors. The letters they send are often complex stylized packages, highly personalized and intensely emotional and negative. The techniques of direct mail have been refined considerably over the years, and, given the right candidate and circumstances, direct mail can provide a substantial portion of a candidate's warchest—far more, certainly, than the party is likely to ante up.

Even the political party's greatest remaining strength, its precinct organization and network of volunteers, is being duplicated by independent consultants. Some consultants use a technique called "Instant Organization" (IO), which utilizes paid callers to ring up voters from centralized banks of telephones. Using various tested scripts, block captains are recruited and office volunteers solicited. Subsequent mail and telephone contracts, as well as get-togethers with the candidate and his surrogate, keep the "instant" volunteers motivated.

THE RELATIONSHIP OF CONSULTANTS TO THE POLITICAL PARTIES

The consultants and their new campaign technologies have, then, increasingly been replacing the parties as the middlemen between candidate and voter. If the relationship between the consultants and the parties is a symbiotic or mutually reinforcing one, little harm—and potentially much good—is done. Unfortunately for the political parties, few consultants are vitally interested in the health of the party system. It is fair to describe most political consultants as businessmen, not party ideologues. There are exceptions, and a few are fierce partisans, having had their political baptism as party functionaries and occasionally having had years of direct party employment. One of these, Robert Odell, is inclined to take on just about any Republican in his direct-mail firm because, "Democrats do little or nothing that I respect and Republicans do nearly everything I respect." Striking a rare pose for a private consultant, Odell declares, "The most important goal for me is to make the Republican party effective." Matt Reese holds the Democratic party in similar esteem, observing only half in jest that he is "a partisan without apology. I don't even *like* Republicans, except for Abraham

Lincoln." And few professionals have shown as long and abiding a concern for a political party as Stuart Spencer and his partner, Bill Roberts, who both began their political careers as volunteers for the Republican party in California. Their consulting shop actually developed around the GOP and was encouraged by the party. Spencer explained that he and Roberts "wanted to be an extension of the party, a management tool that the party could use," and they viewed each of their early consultant outings as "an opportunity for the Republican party."

The greatest number of consultants, though, are simply not committed in any real sense to a political party. Michael Kaye, for instance, proclaims himself to be an Independent and the parties to be "bull." Revealingly, however, he still sensed that it was a mistake to work both sides of the street, comparing it to his practice while a product advertiser:

> People in political office, most of them are paranoid anyway. And I think it would make someone uncomfortable to think that I was working for a Republican at the same time I was working for a Democrat. That is why I work only for Democrats. I don't work for just Democrats because I think they are the only good pure people on this planet. It is the same reason that in the [product] advertising business I didn't work for two clients in the same business.

Yet, for all of the danger supposedly involved in crossing party lines, consultants seem to yield frequently to the temptation. Democrat Peter Hart conducted Republican U.S. Senate nominee John Heinz's surveys in Pennsylvania in 1976 (and claimed he was told he could not take polls for Jimmy Carter as a consequence). Media consultant David Garth has been "all over the lot," as one of his detractors termed his tendency to take moderate-to-liberal Democrats and Republicans indiscriminately, and it was a surprise to no one in the profession when GOP Congressman John Anderson tapped Garth to help with his 1980 Independent presidential bid. Another Democratic-leaning liberal firm, Craver, Matthews, Smith, and Company, took on Anderson's direct-mail program. The now-defunct firm of Baus and Ross in California secured the accounts of Richard Nixon, Barry Goldwater, and Edmund G. "Pat" Brown, Sr., within a few years of one another. The survey firm of D.M.I. not only worked for both Democrats and Republicans, it actually polled both sides of the same congressional election district in 1966. Vincent Breglio, the D.M.I. vice president, took one side, and President Richard Wirthlin took the other. They ran the research independent of one another and provided consulting services to each side without crossing communications. Apparently the candidates were rather trusting souls who reportedly agreed to this outrageous arrangement (although it was quite a useful one for the firm's "win ratio"). D.M.I. converted permanently to Republicanism in 1967 when Michigan Governor George Romney asked the firm to join his presidential effort on condition that it work only for the GOP. Convinced that the move was good for business, Wirthlin and Breglio made the switch over the objections of the Democratic members of the firm, who nevertheless stayed.

A few consultants work closely with party committees as well as party candidates, helping to strengthen the organization. A third to a half of all Market Opinion Research's political polling work is done for the Republican National

Committee or state and local GOP groups, and MOR's president, Robert Teeter, wishes the proportion were even higher: "If I have a preference between working for the party or for individual candidates, it would be for the party because it's more stable—an ongoing, operating entity where our work continues after each campaign." Robert Odell is fully in agreement with his fellow Republican, and perhaps even more dedicated to and enthusiastic about the party. His direct-mail firm has contracts with 13 state party organizations, one-third of his business, and he has taken great pride in building up their fund-raising capacities.

Even though virtually all consultants identify with one of the parties (primarily for business purposes, as Michael Kaye suggested), most of them are at least passively hostile to the parties, some of them openly contemptuous. At times consultants can sound like the evangelical populists they often portray their candidates to be, railing against the evils of boss rule. "Really the only major function of the political party structure these days is to nominate the candidates for president, and my personal feeling is that we'd all be better off if this responsibility also were placed in the hands of the people," consultant Joe Napolitan has written. Media consultant Bob Goodman, in tones echoed time and again by his fellow independent professionals, lauds consultants for unshackling candidates, putting them beyond the reach of the petty party barons:

> We have enabled people to come into a party or call themselves independent Democrats or Republicans and run for office without having to pay the dues of being a party member in a feudal way. Meaning kiss the ass of certain people and maybe down the line they'll give you a shot at public office.

Parties are usually viewed as one more obstacle in the way of the client's election. "In most places the party operation does not do a great deal to help a candidate get elected the first time, and [it] is more of a hassle than it's worth," concludes GOP media consultant Douglas Bailey. Many party-consultant relationships are marked by sharp conflict, explained by Napolitan as the result of party workers' jealousy of consultants, who "have replaced organization regulars in making important campaign decisions" and who are possible usurpers of "what they [party workers] consider their rights to patronage."

A natural consequence of the consultant's antagonism toward the party is his willingness to run his candidates apart from, or even against, their party label. It was difficult to know whether GOP nominee John Heinz was a Democrat or Republican in his 1976 Pennsylvania Senate race, since media consultant David Garth fashioned his advertising campaign around an antiparty theme: "If you think Pennsylvania needs an *Independent* senator, elect John Heinz." One of Garth's spots actually featured a glowing "endorsement" of Heinz's character by Jimmy Carter (delivered in March of 1975), to further confuse the voter. Scrambling labels may seem unfortunate to those concerned about the role of party in elections, but at least the party is not under direct attack, a common tactic in party primaries. Milton Shapp, for instance, won the Democratic nomination for the Pennsylvania governorship in 1966 in a major upset, thanks to Joe Napolitan's "Man Against the Machine" theme.

When they are not running against it, most consultants simply ignore the party, in campaigns and in the way they run their business. Sanford L. Weiner, a former president of the American Association of Political Consultants, who began by representing conservative Republicans and whose clientele is now increasingly Democratic and liberal, dismissed his party contradictions by noting that "no one in California cares that any firm represents both Democrats and Republicans. . . . Strict partisanship just isn't that important anymore." Another pace-setting California firm, the Butcher-Forde direct-mail agency, is positively proud of the agency's and directors' utter lack of personal professional adherence to any party or political philosophy. One of the firm's senior associates described himself and his fellows as "pure advocates," declaring, "We're businessmen first, and politics is our business. . . . It's whoever gets to us first." Their list of recent clients is a grab bag of politicians on right and left, from liberal Democratic U.S. Senator Alan Cranston to Howard Jarvis and State Senator John Schmitz (former presidential candidate of George Wallace's American Independent Party). In addition to toying with the idea of an independent candidacy of his own and aiding George Wallace's direct-mail efforts, rightwing fund-raiser Richard Viguerie has at times been quoted as favoring the dissolution of the Republican party and enjoys working against either party's moderate or liberal candidates. Viguerie's hostility to the organized party and his designs against it are only slightly more grandiose than those of many consultants and leaders of ideological political action committees. As Viguerie's right-wing associate, Paul Weyrich of the Committee for the Survival of a Free Congress, put it, "The parties—they water down, water down, water down until they get something that everybody agrees on, which means nothing to anybody. The political parties have helped to destroy the political parties." With a little help from political consultants, he might have added.

EFFECTS OF NEW CAMPAIGN FINANCE LAWS ON POLITICAL PARTIES AND CONSULTANTS

The parties' slide and the rise of political consultants has been aided in some respects by the passage of the Federal Election Campaign Act of 1971 (FECA) and the major amendments of 1974 and 1976. . . .

It should be noted at the outset that a number of FECA provisions take reasonable account of the parties' interests. Each national party committee is permitted to make a special general election expenditure on behalf of its presidential nominee (2 cents for each person of voting age, plus a cost of living increase, amounting to $4.6 million in 1980). The Democratic and Republican senatorial campaign committees are also given the right to donate up to $17,500 to each of their Senate nominees. And the parties can make very substantial "coordinated expenditures" on behalf of both their Senate and House candidates. FECA is also broadly supportive of the two-party system in its restriction of access to public funds by third parties. A new third party or Independent presidential nominee can only receive public funds retroactively, once the election is concluded, and only if the party or candidate received more than 5% of the national popular vote. Any monies so received will be in proportion to the third party's percentage of the vote.

But in other important ways FECA has proved to be *harmful* to the major parties. It simply does not create a party-centered system of campaign finance. The stringent reporting requirements and the intricate specifications for the splitting of costs when an expenditure benefiting all of a party's candidates is made have discouraged party umbrella spending, for example, and have encouraged candidates to stay clear of the party and its other nominees. The finance law also restricts the direct contributions of a political party to each of its own candidates to just $5,000 per election—putting the political parties on exactly the same footing as nonparty political action committees.

The campaign laws also cause the national party committees to compete with their own candidates for limited fund-raising dollars to a greater degree than ever before, through a combination of contribution limits and a single small income tax credit covering both candidate and party gifts. It is little wonder that the national party committees guard so jealously their direct-mail lists and generally refuse to share them with party candidates. Moreover, FECA dealt a severe blow to local party organizational and volunteer activity because the limited campaign dollars that were permitted to be spent had to be carefully managed, controlled, and disclosed, resulting in a centralization of most campaign tasks and an elimination of grass-roots programs. The intimidation of the new rules, the threat of prosecution, and the bulky expenditure reporting requirements also have taken their toll. One Republican county chairman in 1976 was actually photographed on a ladder, painting out the name of Gerald Ford from a campaign sign, since the local party committee had discovered it had exceeded the tiny $1,000 maximum it was permitted to spend on behalf of the national ticket. In reflecting on the 1976 presidential campaign, David Broder remembered that "In many big-city neighborhoods and in most small towns, there was nothing to suggest that America was choosing a president—no local headquarters, no bumper stickers, no buttons, and almost no volunteer activity."[6]

FECA's $1,000 contribution limit on individual gifts has also been a godsend for the parties' vibrant rivals, political action committees. PACs, with a $5,000 contribution limit, can offer a greater reward for a more efficient expenditure of a candidate's time and efforts, since individual donations are usually solicited in high-overhead dinners and parties, while PACs are organized and centralized. As a consequence, the proportion of money raised by congressional candidates from PACs doubled between 1972 and 1978, to fully a quarter of congressional campaign expenditures. Because of the role of public funding in presidential campaigns (and the matching funds available for individual but not PAC gifts), political action committees have generally played a lesser role in presidential politics, however.

---

6. *Washington Post,* September 30, 1979.

Not only have the new campaign finance laws weakened parties by strengthening PACs, they have also boosted the role and influence of another group of party competitors, political consultants. Many consultants viewed FECA with concern at first, primarily because the 1974 amendments mandated overall spending limits on congressional campaigns that the professionals feared would drastically reduce the amount of money expended on their services. But after the Supreme Court struck down the spending ceiling sections of FECA in the 1976 case *Buckley* v. *Valeo*, consultants saw FECA in a new light, and for good reason. Since the disclosure requirements naturally tend to direct campaign money to easily disclosable activities such as media advertising and polling, media and polling consultants' roles in a centralized campaign structure are probably increased. Certainly the power and profits of direct mailers and other campaign fund raisers have been enhanced by FECA. The contribution limitations and matching funds for $250-and-under individual gifts fit direct mail like a glove, and contemporary candidates rely on direct mailers and professional money raisers the way their predecessors did on "fat cats" and "financial angels." "Blessed are the gatherers," President Ford's finance chairman in 1976, Robert Mosbacher, was quoted as saying. "No $1,000 contributor is of tremendous value. It's the guy who'll go out and raise $100,000." Consultants also gain from FECA's stimulus to centralized planning. Because of limits, campaigns are forced to plan better and map out their budgets earlier and more precisely—exactly the skills that generalist consultants are touted to possess. There is little doubt that FECA makes the management of cash flow and an early start in fund raising at least as critical to a candidate's success as any issue proposal he might make in the course of his campaign. Almost 60% of the GOP House winners in 1978, for instance, began their fund-raising efforts in the first quarter of 1978, while losers started much later and sought over half their money in the last months of the campaign.

Enough of FECA's shortcomings had become evident by 1979 to prod Congress into making some minor and a few moderately significant reforms in the law. The Congress passed HR_{5010} in December 1979 after bipartisan agreement was reached within the House and Senate Administration Committees. While it avoided the more controversial and serious reforms needed in the areas of PACs and public funding and only went a little way toward redressing the unhealthy tilt of the present system against political parties, HR_{5010} did achieve some useful objectives. The paperwork requirements were reduced in several respects, with fewer reports and less detail being asked for from most candidates. More important, the law permitted state and local party groups to revive grass-roots participation and make unlimited purchases of campaign materials for volunteer activities (buttons, bumper stickers, yard signs, brochures, and the like). Certain kinds of voter registration and get-out-the-vote drives on behalf of presidential tickets were also permitted without financial limit at the state and local levels, and financial reports to the Federal Election Commission (FEC) were waived if annual expenditures for volunteer programs did not exceed $5,000 or nonvolunteer projects more than $1,000. (Previously, if total spending went above $1,000—a ridiculously low threshold—a party committee was forced to fulfill all the FEC's reporting stipulations.) Volunteer political activity itself was encouraged by an increase from $500 to $1,000 in the amount of money an individual could spend in providing his home, food, or personal travel to a candidate without having to file a contributor's report. And, in yet another small step in the right direction, a volunteer was permitted to spend up to $2,000 on behalf of a party before the amount was treated as a contribution.

THE GROWTH OF POLITICAL ACTION COMMITTEES

Possibly the most far-reaching change wrought by FECA was in its legitimizing the use of corporate funds to establish and administer Political Action Committees (PACs). Labor unions already had that right, and the PAC had long been an essential political tool for organized labor. Now business and trade interests could benefit as well.

Once the floodgates were opened, the growth of corporate and trade PACs was nothing short of phenomenal.

Just between 1976 and 1978, the number of PACs rose from 1,242 to 1,938 and by 1982 PACs totaled 3,371. Their total spending increased from $30.1 million in 1976 to $127.7 million in 1980 and on to $190.4 million in 1982. New business PACs comprised by far the largest share of the growth. In 1978, for instance, when all PACs accounted for $34.1 million of the $199 million in contributions received by congressional candidates, one researcher estimated that business and business-related groups outspent labor by better than two to one. Between 1976 and 1978, corporate PAC gifts to candidates more than doubled, while labor's PAC donations showed only a 25% gain.[7] Business and trade PACs, which at first favored incumbents (and thus gave more to Democratic candidates), have gradually moved to the GOP's banner.

Of far greater concern to the political parties is another increasingly prominent form of political action committee: the ideological PAC. The National Committee for an Effective Congress (NCEC) on the left and the Committee for the Survival of a Free Congress (CSFC) on the right are typical examples. Both provide organizational assistance to ideologically compatible candidates, irrespective of party. The NCEC is much the elder of the two and was founded in 1948. It describes itself as a "bipartisan progressive" group dedicated to civil rights, civil liberties, and internationalism. Rather than giving money, the NCEC provides specific services, such as the hiring and paying of the campaign manager, polling, targeting, and organizing. In a normal election year the NCEC will assist in some way up to 60 House candidates and a dozen Senate contenders. Russell Hemenway, executive director of the NCEC, sees his organization as a substitute for the Democratic National Committee, which "provides almost no services to

---

7. Labor's figures do not, however, include separate spending for registration, get-out-the-vote, and other activities, which may amount to as much as $20 million in an election year.

candidates," and for political consultants who "are looking for campaigns that can pay hefty bills."

Many of the same goals are shared by the CSFC, which has sought to imitate somewhat the NCEC and the AFL-CIO's Committee on Political Education (COPE). "I make no secret of the fact that I admire their [COPE's] operations and have to some extent modeled our committee on the labor groups" says CSFC director Paul Weyrich. Founded in 1974 with financial support from Joseph Coors, the conservative Colorado brewer, the CSFC plays a central role in the so-called "New Right," along with Richard Viguerie's direct-mail outfit and other political committees, such as Sen. Jesse Helms' Congressional Club and the National Conservative PAC. Like the NCEC, the CSFC helps candidates assemble a skilled campaign team, usually contributing about $500 a month to pay the salary of a field organizer. The CSFC acts almost like a political party, recruiting candidates, refining candidates' political abilities, performing electoral organizational chores, devising strategy, and constructing campaign staffs. An extensive five-day "candidate school" is held by the CSFC four to six times every two years, and it is attended by prospective congressional contenders and campaign managers from the conservative wings of both parties, who pay a registration fee of $500 per person. The schools enlist incumbent congressmen and consultants as instructors and are organized around problem-solving groups that enable the CSFC directors to evaluate each political candidate's performance. At the end of the course, a simulated election is held, which sometimes serves as an informal primary of sorts since more than one candidate from the same district attends. In 1978, three Republican House contenders from the same Wisconsin constituency attended the CSFC school, and the PAC decided that one of them, Toby Roth, was clearly superior (and the most conservative). After the school's adjournment, Roth received the group's blessing, and he went on to win his party's nomination and to defeat an incumbent Democratic congressman in November.

Ideological PACs are proliferating and strengthening. In 1981–82, the six largest conservative PACs raised a combined total of $29.4 million, up by 25% from the previous election cycle. Liberal PACs did less well, raising about $9.4 million, but five of the six top groups were new-formed in reaction to the conservative PACs' 1980 election successes—and the comparable liberal total was a scant $400,000.

In explaining the explosive growth of all forms of PACs, most (but not all) roads lead to FECA. The 1974 lifting of the ban on corporate funding of PACs was crucial, and the tighter public disclosure requirements, by revealing the previously obscured extent of each corporation's involvement in politics, have produced a "keep up with the Joneses" mentality among business and trade association circles. FECA's $1,000 limitation on individual contributions and its more permissive $5,000 PAC limit encourage candidates to rely on PACs as a more generous source of funds. Also having an effect on the extent and pace of PAC expansion is a growing group of political consultants, who specialize in assisting PAC formation and activity. The professionals are finding PAC consulting to be more stable, continuous, and profitable than candidate work, and almost all consultants have advised at least one or a few PACs from time to time.

Even though PACs are clearly party rivals, both parties seem to be resigned to the age of PACs. Like Willie Sutton who robbed banks "because that's where they keep the money," the parties have begun to direct their attentions to the overflowing PAC treasuries and have hired consultants to ensure that they get their fair share of PAC money. The GOP assists its candidates in soliciting PACs, helping its nominees to secure appointments with PAC officials and directing them toward committees that are likely to donate to them. Behind the facade of cooperation , however, lies the inescapable incompatibility and competitiveness between parties and PACs. Many political action committees are slowly but surely developing into rival institutions that raise money, develop memberships, recruit candidates, organize campaigns, and influence officeholders just as the parties do (or are supposed to do). PACs already outfinance the parties, partly because they drain away potential gifts to them, permitting supporters to tell the Democratic or Republican committee that they have already given at the office. PACs also outspend the parties by a large margin. While the two parties were contributing $21.9 million to their congressional nominees in 1982, for instance, PACs mustered $83.1 million in congressional contributions.

PACs are not organized along party lines and are never likely to be. In the words of one PAC official, "We believe you have to be pretty cold-blooded concerning your giving policy. You simply have to support candidates who support you . . . regardless of party or philosophy." The ideological PACs, of course, make no pretense about their aims. Most of them view the parties with undisguised hostility, attacking them for a lack of ideological clarity and working to defeat the more moderate choices of party leaders in primaries. Paul Weyrich of CSFC proudly cites the case of Republican right-wing political novice Gordon Humphrey of New Hampshire, a former airline pilot who upset incumbent Democratic U.S. Senator Thomas McIntyre in 1978. The GOP senatorial campaign committee gave assistance to Humphrey's more moderate primary opponent, but CSFC helped to engineer a primary victory for him. Now, reports Weyrich, "Gordon is less than enthusiastic about the party," which suits CSFC just fine. It is easy to agree with Weyrich's observation that "both political parties would have an all-night celebration if we were to go out of business." The problem for the parties can be succinctly stated: Groups like CSFC are in no danger of going out of business. In fact, they are flourishing.

THE INDEPENDENT EXPENDITURE LOOPHOLE

One particular anomaly of the federal election rules gives PACs a tremendous potential advantage over parties and could play havoc with attempts to limit the influence of large donors. That anomaly, the provision for independent expenditures on behalf of a candidate, was not a part of FECA but a Supreme Court mandate (from *Buckley* v. *Valeo*). The Court held that Congress could not impose spending limitations on PACs and individuals who desire to advocate a candidate's election without consultation with his campaign. The Federal Election Commission, acting after the Court's decision, defined an independent expenditure as one made by a person or committee "expressly advocating the election or defeat" of a candidate that is "not made with the cooperation, or with the prior consent of, or in consultation with, or at the request or suggestion of, a candidate or any agent or authorized committee" of the candidate. The expenditure, in other words, must truly be independent of the candidate and his campaign; otherwise it would come under the regular contribution limitations. There is no ceiling on the amount, nor stipulation regarding frequency of, independent expenditures. While less than 0.2% of all campaign money spent in 1976 was independent in nature, the 1978 figures indicate that the two top independent spenders alone exceeded the entire total of independent expenditures for 1976 House and Senate candidates, and new records were set again in 1980 at both the presidential and congressional levels. Independent expenditures in 1982 totaled $5.3 million, representing 1.4% of all campaign spending. To this point, independent expenditures have almost always involved advertising in some form, where an individual or committee purchases time and space to endorse or attack a candidate or support or oppose a group of candidates based on an issue or set of issues. Henry C. Grover, a former Texas legislator and Ronald Reagan supporter, independently spent more money than any other individual in 1976 ($63,000) for pro-Reagan newspaper advertisements prior to the Texas and Michigan GOP primaries. And in 1980 Reagan was assisted by an independent backer in the South Carolina primary. Having already spent two-thirds of the nationwide spending limit, Reagan's campaign was unwilling to invest a significant amount of money in the Magnolia State, so U.S. Senator Jesse Helms used funds from his own PAC to launch a television promotion on behalf of the eventual Republican nominee. Liberal financier Stewart Mott spent well over $100,000 just a few weeks later to air advertisements for John Anderson's presidential effort while he was still competing in the GOP primaries.

Political action committees have been slower to investigate the independent route, but when they do, the result is often a major investment. PACs are better situated than most individuals to organize an effective independent program, since they have the administrative structure and the experienced staff that individuals lack. PACs also have direct access to the expertise of political consultants, many of whom are on retainer to them. The American Medical Association's AMPAC has been a path breaker in exploring independent action. In 1978 the committee spent over $42,000 on advertisements supporting favored congressional candidates in six popular magazines distributed throughout 16 congressional districts and the state of Georgia. AMPAC's 1982 independent spending topped $210,000. The National Conservative Political Action Committee (NCPAC) has also concentrated on independent expenditures, but of the negative variety. The group spent about $700,000 in 1979 alone primarily for television advertising to attack liberal U.S. senators up for reelection the following year. All told, in 1980 NCPAC's independent spending in the congressional contests and presidential race (where it backed Ronald Reagan) exceeded $2.3 million; in 1982 NCPAC spent almost $3.2 million independently in congressional races alone.

There are notable obstacles in the path of any group or individual attempting to undertake an independent course of action. Beyond the reporting burdens imposed by the FEC, which are particularly onerous for individuals, there is the frustrating and difficult prohibition against contact with the candidate or his agents. The AMPAC executive director, for example, felt obliged to require each member of the committee's staff and board of directors to identify any congressional candidate with whom he had had direct or indirect contact for over a full year, so as to eliminate possible violations of the FEC's standards. Additional FEC regulations restrict the flexibility of independent campaigns. Individuals are forbidden to pool their money for an independent effort, thus preventing liberal or conservative persons from combining their resources in order to afford national television time, for instance. Even if the time could be afforded, there is no guarantee advertisements would be run. Many stations refuse to consider the sale of spots or programs for independent campaigns, and the Federal Communications Commission does not require them to do so. The Internal Revenue Service added another inhibiting factor in 1980 by preliminarily ruling that contributions to "negative campaigns" are not eligible for the income tax credit on political donations. Lastly, there is the fear and the danger that an independent campaign would distort or interfere with a candidate's strategy, by perhaps raising an unpleasant issue on a controversial subject or erroneous charges. Candidates, therefore, often try to discourage independent efforts on their behalf. In Idaho, for example, the Anybody But Church Committee, a PAC affiliated with NCPAC, ran independent television commercials against Democratic U.S. Senator Frank Church in 1980. One spot showed empty Titan missile sites in the state and accused Church of opposing a strong national defense. But the advertisement backfired when Church pointed out that the Titans had been replaced by a new generation of more effective missiles under a program he backed. After this incident, Republican U.S. Senate candidates in two other states denounced similar NCPAC media campaigns against their liberal incumbent opponents, openly fearing a sympathy backlash.

Despite all of the real and potential problems involved with independent expenditures, political observers are virtually unanimous in predicting expansion in the field. There is talk among PAC officials of independent polling for a favored candidate to design a better independent media package, of independent telephone banks to identify a candidate's voters and get them to the polls on election day, and of independent persuasive direct-mail programs. One executive of AMPAC was willing to predict that within a decade, half of all the money in the growing treasuries of political action committees would be spent for independent activities—a challenge to the limitation goals of FECA, certainly, but no less a challenge to the influence of political parties.

A PARTY'S REJOINDER: GOP RENEWAL

One of the two major parties decided to fight back in the mid-1970s and began to acquire the techniques of the political consultant to further its own candidates—and, in the process, nurse itself back to health. The Republican party at the national level has organized exemplary direct-mail and media operations centered around two subsidiaries of the Republican National Committee (RNC), The National Republican Senatorial Committee (NRSC) and the National Republican

Congressional Committee (NRCC). The NRSC assists GOP U.S. Senate candidates, while the NRCC aids Republican contenders for the U.S. House of Representatives. It is difficult not to be impressed by the GOP's assemblage of organizational and technological tools. For example, each election year, the NRCC carefully selects 80 to 120 target House districts where Republicans are believed to have a chance to oust incumbent Democrats or fill open seats, and the committee's five full-time field representatives then go to work to recruit outstanding candidates, normally identifying willing participants in 40 to 50 of the districts. If the party feels it has located a particularly strong candidate in a "likely-to-win" district, and other key Republicans in the district and state agree, the NRCC will even back the candidate in a party primary.

The assistance, in both a primary and general election, can be considerable. Both the NRCC and the NRSC have collected voluminous records on House and Senate members' votes and activities. There is also a growing storehouse of postelection research, including studies of voters, nonvoters, campaign managers, and candidates conducted by national polling firms. Key congressional campaigns have instant access to the information by means of portable video display terminals located in their local headquarters and connected to the GOP computer data bank in Washington. The Republican national organizations also help their candidates to solicit PACs and political consultants. An extensive and somewhat evaluative list of consultants is kept current, as is a roster of PACs that have donated to GOP candidates in the past. The party assists candidates in securing appointments with PAC decision makers as well.

Campaign management colleges are yet another regular project of the Republican National Committee. In operation since 1974, the college consists of a week's strenuous training in campaign techniques for twelve-hour-per-day sessions. About 20 "students" are selected to participate in each college, most of them slated to manage GOP House or Senate campaigns. All costs are paid by the Republican party, and the sessions can be held for new groups as often as once a month in an election year. In addition, the special projects division of the RNC sponsors a separate school for campaign press secretaries and more than a dozen three-day "Basic instructional" workshops for all interested campaign staffers at sites scattered throughout the country. (On average, a workshop will draw about 80 participants.) The candidates themselves are not ignored, and the RNC, in cooperation with incumbent Republican congressmen, frequently brings candidates and prospective candidates to Washington long before the advent of the campaign to polish their skills and learn new ones.

The media division of the NRCC is particularly noteworthy, and its evolution is powerful evidence of campaign technology's potential usefulness to a party and its nominees. In 1971 the old broadcast services division of the RNC employed just three people and offered a very limited list of services. The new media division is so active and involved that it is difficult to summarize all of its programs. Audio and videotape "actualities" (i.e., tapes featuring the candidate) are transmitted to every radio and television station in a House member's district and are then used (normally unedited) by the unpaid media on news programs. The taping and transmission can be accomplished within a single working day, so that a congressman's activity in the morning can be highlighted on the six o'clock news. In some respects the NRCC media division has become a part-time Washington correspondent for many stations across the country.

Campaign needs, though, are the major focus of the media division. Commercials for both radio and television are produced for a phenomenally low price (at least compared to what political consultants charge). An entire advertising package, counting salaries, overhead, and all production costs, can be delivered for less than the $5,000 contribution the national party is permitted to make to each of its candidates. The media division is flexible enough to do as much or as little as a campaign needs, sometimes doing the entire advertising package from start to finish, at other times simply working with a candidate's political consultant or local agency to plan Capitol Hill filming. As of 1980, even the time-buying for many GOP candidates was done by the NRCC, saving campaigns as much as 90% of the normal 15% agency commission fee. Postproduction and editing facilities were also added in 1980, a measure that resulted in even lower media charges for GOP candidates. A major expansion of the division's scope occurred as well. While only 8 media campaigns were taken by the NRCC in 1978, almost 50 were handled in 1980, and 300 individual commercials were produced; in 1982, the number of markets jumped to 90.

The most interesting part of the media division's program is the attempt to improve the image of the Republican party with television advertisements. FECA has indirectly encouraged the party to expend funds in this way by limiting its contributions to candidates, and the GOP has made a virtue of necessity, marketing its party label in a way that it hopes will have beneficial side effects for its nominees. After Watergate's devastation, in-house media research indicated that the GOP could not talk about issues effectively until its general image and credibility improved. Out of that finding came the "America Today" series, a group of well-targeted five-minute spots that centered around a "human interest" topic (such as the needs of the disabled or the cardiopulmonary-resuscitation method) and showed what individual members of the Republican congressional delegation were doing about it. "We picked as narrators congressmen who could project what we wanted to say institutionally about the party: that Republicans care about people," reported NRCC media director Ed Blakely. A service element was built into each spot, and viewers were urged to "write REPUBLICANS, Box 1400, Washington, D.C., and we will send you a free brochure telling how you can get involved and what you can do." Each advertisement closed with pictures of all the GOP House members flashed for a third of a second each, as an announcer reminded listeners that "American Today was brought to you as a public service by the Republicans in Congress, 146 men and women working to improve the government and the quality of life of the people of this nation." Each stage of the development and production was accompanied by careful audience testing, and a cyclical schedule of broadcasting (three weeks on the air, then two weeks off, then two weeks on again, and so forth), with different spots shown in each cycle, was designed, similar to an advertising schedule for a commercial product. An extensive study by GOP consultant Robert Teeter's polling firm demonstrates that the advertisements "succeeded in producing changes in the evaluation of the GOP." Viewers thought that Republicans were more caring individuals than they had previously believed and, interestingly, the advertisements concurrently reduced viewers' favourable impressions of Democrats by 3 to 13% on rating scales for nine desirable attributes. The image polishing did not necessarily translate into more votes, but Independent voters, in particular, appeared more receptive to Republicanism afterward.

The same study found that another GOP series of commercials was much more directly useful in corralling voters. The "Issues of the '80s" spots, aired once "America Today" 's image making had run its course, gave standard Republican dogma on a host of topics, such as government spending and rising food prices. After seeing the advertisements (in the absence of countervailing advertisements, of course) a gain of 19% was registered for the GOP side. This package led to an even more strongly partisan advertising campaign first aired early in 1980, a $9.5 million series that attacked the Democratic Congress using themes from a Teeter poll conducted for the RNC. With the tag line "Vote Republican—for a Change," the 30-second, 60-second, and five-minute advertisements attacked the Democratic Congress and lampooned its leaders. One spot had an actor resembling House Speaker Tip O'Neill driving a car until it ran out of gas. Another featured an unemployed factory worker asking pointedly, "If the Democrats are so good for working people, then how come so many people aren't working?" (The inspiration for the series, incidentally, was provided by the advertising package run by the British Conservative party in 1979). The 1980 advertisements were considered so effective that, once in power in 1981, the GOP aired a $2.3 million advertising campaign designed to capitalize on President Reagan's congressional budget successes, on the theme "Republicans: Leadership that works for a change." Yet another $10 million institutional package was run prior to the 1982 midterm congressional elections, claiming "Republicans are beginning to make things better."

Many of the RNC and associated divisions' activities are paid for with profits from a remarkably successful direct-mail operation. Direct mail has brought the Republican party from near-bankruptcy (in 1975 the party raised just $300,000 of its $2.3 million budget) to a financial position unrivaled in its history. The direct-mail packages for all of the national GOP groups collected about $20 million in 1979, at a cost of only about 35 cents per dollar raised; in 1982, those groups raised $130 million in direct mail. The Republican party now has reliable lists containing the names of over 1,000,700 donors, which are maintained by a 25% annual replacement (because of donor mobility, death, etc.). All the GOP's direct-mail programs are coordinated by the Stephen Winchell and Associates firm. (Winchell, a former employee of Richard Viguerie, was selected after his old boss refused to take the account, demurring because he wanted "to destroy the Republican party by drying up all the contributions to it"—or so charged NRCC finance director Wyatt Stewart.) The GOP has been taking full advantage of a provision passed by Congress in 1978 that gave "qualified political parties" the right to mail letters under the nonprofit rate of 2.7 cents a letter, rather than the usual third-class rate of 8.4 cents. The RNC has even experimented with direct response, combining television advertisements and toll-free numbers with credit card contribution pledging. After some strained negotiation in 1978, for example, the NRCC convinced former President Ford and Ronald Reagan to appear together in a 60-second spot attacking the Democratic Congress and urging credit card contributions to the GOP by means of a toll-free number.

The NRCC plans to stay at its present level of direct-mail solicitation so as to reserve contribution potential for state party committees. In fact, much of the effort in the direct-mail division and in the other RNC subsidiaries is to transfer technology to the state level and strengthen state parties in the process. More than 20 state organizations are already tied into the RNC's "mother computer" via long-distance telephone lines. Access to the computer is made available for a very small fee (about $7 an hour, plus a one-time $300 start-up fee), and each of the subscribers gains entry to a sophisticated data processing network called "REPNET" that contains five major programs for financial mailing list maintenance, donor preservation and information, and correspondence and word processing. In another attempt to help the state parties (and to improve the GOP's congressional redistricting fortunes in the wake of the 1980 census), the RNC formed a political action committee called "GOPAC," headed by Delaware Governor Pierre DuPont, which contributed well over $1 million to state legislative candidates in 1979 and 1980 contests.

There are few Democratic equivalents of the advanced Republican technological programs. In almost every respect, the Democratic operations are pitifully inadequate by comparison with the GOP's; even where there is some visible activity, the effort is a pale shadow of its rival's work. The Democratic National Committee (DNC) and the Democratic Congressional Campaign Committee (DCCC) do schedule several dozen campaign training programs around the country, and they have recently established a Democratic National Training Academy in Des Moines, Iowa, but the workshops held so far do not compare with the more extensive Republican gatherings. The DNC's direct-mail program, under contract to Craver, Mathews, Smith, and Company, has only just begun in earnest, and it will take years to reach the GOP's level of sophistication. Thanks mainly to the difference in their direct-mail systems, the Democratic party was able to give less than one-fourth as much as its Republican counterpart to its 1980 House and Senate candidates. During 1979 and 1980, the national Republican party and its allied Senate and House campaign committees raised $122.1 million. The comparable figure for the Democratic party and committees was a paltry $23 million raised. In 1981–82, the ratio actually continued to worsen for the Democrats: the Republican groups raised seven times as much as their Democratic counterparts ($190.9 million compared to $31.4 million).

The technological and organizational gap between the two parties is certainly wider now than it has ever been, but Republicans have generally been more willing and able than Democrats to experiment with new techniques during the entire age of political consultantship. Media consultant Robert Squier, who has worked closely with some officials of the Democratic National Committee, suggested that the Democrats have not matched the GOP in campaign technology "because of a lack of money, a lack of leadership, and a lack of understanding how and why a party has to be involved in modern campaigning."

There are other factors at work as well. The pre-1980 Republican party, as the perennially disappointed underdog, had to try harder and had to be willing to experiment with new ideas, since the old ways were obviously not enough for victory. The Democratic party had been more electorally secure and consequently had less incentive to build the party or change its ways. "The Democratic party as the majority party is simply not frustrated enough," surmised William Sweeney, executive director of the Democratic Congressional Campaign Committee, before his party's 1980 disasters. Many more of the Democratic elite had been in office as well, with the personal staff perquisites that accompany incumbency, making the strengthening of party staff somewhat less important than for office-hungry Republicans. Labor's COPE operations also proved to be a ready substitute for the party's weaknesses, and, until the growth of PACs, COPE's efforts could only be directly challenged with GOP resources. Moreover, it may be that the business and middle-class base of the modern Republican party naturally produced a greater managerial emphasis among its directors, many of whom are drawn from the same sector of society. Whatever the roots of its technological edge, it has proved to be a significant advantage to the GOP in electing its candidates, in strengthening itself, and in competing effectively with rival PACs and political consultants.

The Democrats' jarring defeats in 1980 appear to have shaken the party out of its lethargy and spurred it on to modernization. There is little question that the Democratic party's potential is great if it chooses to exploit its base. RNCC's Wyatt Stewart boasted that he could apply GOP direct-mail techniques to the much broader based Democratic party and "do twice what the Republican party is doing today."

SUMMARY AND CONCLUDING COMMENTS

While the GOP has made the best of the circumstances, both political parties have been buffeted by a number of forces unleashed by new campaign finance laws and the technologies of political consultants. With a contribution limit five times greater than that of individuals and equal to the parties', a political action committee rivals the party for the affections of candidates, and if the PAC is ideological and organization oriented, it can become a sort of surrogate party. A further expansion of PAC activity and influence is almost guaranteed.

While FECA was strengthening PACs, it was weakening the parties, despite its objectives to the contrary. Political consultants were among the biggest gainers, becoming more necessary than ever for long-range planning and efficient management of larger staffs, and direct-mail fund raising from small donors became one of the most sought-after technologies. Not just FECA but also the weakened parties themselves gave political consultants their modern opening, and they used the opportunity to hawk techniques that replaced the party as the middleman between candidate and voter. A few independent consulting professionals are strongly supportive of the party system, but most are indifferent or even hostile to it, frequently running their client-candidates against or around the party label and also assisting the development of PACs' competitive facilities. Whereas most consultants are nominally loyal to one or the other party for business reasons, a growing number are proud switch-hitters, mercenaries available for hire to the first or top bidder. Others, for ideological reasons, are openly contemptuous of the parties, opposing a flexible party system in toto. However, one of the parties has begun to fight back; the Republicans are showing the way, and their shrewd and sophisticated moves suggest one solution to the dilemmas posed by the rise of political consultants and the new campaign technology.

The GOP's new directions are beneficial not just to its own electoral fortunes but to the political system as a whole. The Republican institutional advertising, media services, candidate schools, and policy briefings are having the effect of drawing candidates closer to the party. The candidates voice similar policy themes, take much the same approach on at least some fundamental issues, and have a stake in the party's present wellbeing and future development. They are beholden to the party, too; sizeable contributions and significant campaign services are not easily forgotten, and there is always the implied threat of their withdrawal in reelection campaigns, should the officeholder prove too much of a maverick. Is it any wonder, then, the House and Senate Republicans were unusually and exceedingly unified on the Reagan budget and tax votes in 1981?

Clearly, the GOP has shown one route of escape from the current candidate-centered and consultant-oriented system of American politics. The Democratic party should follow its rival's lead, and the Republicans can go further. State and local parties, for the most part, have yet to benefit fully from the revolution in campaign techniques. The technology must be transferred there if the parties are to have a vibrant base. Direct mail, party-sponsored telephone banks, and even television solicitation can be used to rebuild and revitalize the atrophied organizational foundations of the American parties. The national parties need to adopt, not just new techniques, but their own version of "New Federalism," if parties are to be the representative and broad-based agencies needed for a healthy democracy. ■

ELECTIONS

Communication is the heart and purpose of political campaigns. In recent times, campaign communications have changed, both quantitatively and qualitatively. In a recent book, *Mass Media Elections,* excerpted here, Richard Joslyn discusses those changes and then calls our attention to how the real functions of elections in our system may be somewhat more complex than we at first blush might imagine.

Finally, the role and impact of the television "spot" commercial in political campaigns is discussed in an excerpt from a recent book by Edwin Diamond and Stephen Bates.

MODERN CAMPAIGN COMMUNICATIONS AND THEIR FUNCTION
Richard Joslyn

There have been a number of recent changes in the nature of campaign communication. Although comparisons with historical times for which memories are blurred and data are sparse are always risky, it appears that the U.S. electoral process has been significantly altered by modern campaign communication.

The recent change in electoral communication has both a quantitative and a qualitative dimension. In *quantitative* terms, the number of campaign messages devised and delivered by candidates has never been greater. Certainly more money is being spent by candidates on campaign communication than ever before, and the use of spot advertising, broadcast debates, and pseudoevents to stimulate news coverage means that the electorate is probably exposed to candidate messages more frequently than ever before. It is possible that in the late nineteenth and early twentieth centuries, when party organizations were at their strongest, candidate messages were delivered to as large a proportion of the eligible electorate as they are today. It is also likely, however, that those party organizations were not uniformly strong in all areas of the country or across time. Consequently, although the prominence of candidate (actually *party* at that time) communication may have occasionally, reached the levels of contemporary campaigns, it is unlikely that the total amount of candidate-devised messages was generally as great as it is now.

In addition, the amount of campaign coverage provided by news organizations is probably greater now than ever before. Daily television news shows; press coverage of special events such as conventions and primaries; broadcast transmission of major speeches, news interviews, debates, and press conferences; and print coverage of the campaign in the daily press, weekly news magazines, and specialized opinion magazines have all combined to acquaint ever increasing audiences with at least a minimum of information about election campaigns. Again, it is possible that daily *newspaper* coverage of campaigns was more prevalent years ago when there were more daily papers in operation, but the contributions of other media to campaign coverage today more than make up for this loss.

There is also a *qualitative* aspect to contemporary changes in campaign communication. Not only is there simply more campaign-related information available to the public, but this information is qualitatively different. Generalizations here are particularly hazardous since there is little systematic data available on electoral communication prior to the television age. If thirty years is a long enough period to indicate trends in campaigning, however, then a number of qualitative changes are notable.

It may well be that today's candidate appeals are pretty much the same as they were in previous eras. Politicians have always promised peace, prosperity, and justice to the electorate; challengers have always attempted to blame incumbents for social problems and policy failures; campaigns have utilized nonsensical jingles, slogans, and image making throughout U.S. history; and, with a few notable exceptions, the natural tendency of candidates has typically been to avoid revealing specific, detailed policy preferences.

There are at least two ways in which contemporary candidate appeals are different, however. First, candidate communication is definitely much less party-oriented now than it was in the first half of the twentieth century. Party appeals are seldom visibly made by presidential candidates and are hardly ever the cornerstone of a presidential campaign. Instead, candidate appeals usually focus attention on the *candidate* rather than on the party that nominated him or her, and attempt to create favorable *candidate* rather than party impressions. A number of researchers have argued that this leads to less party-based voting, more drastic fluctuations in the partisan division of the vote, more ticket splitting across electoral levels, and more cases of divided partisan control of governing institutions. It may also leave incumbent officeholders more vulnerable to public dissatisfaction as the impressions that resulted in one's election typically turn sour and the public becomes uninterested in, skeptical of, or hostile toward officeholders.

Second, candidate messages are devised with much more awareness of and concern for public perceptions and preferences now than ever before. Candidate appeals are increasingly based on public opinion polls and delivered to targeted portions of a constituency. This may mean that the messages are more interesting, familiar, or persuasive to the public; and it may also prevent campaign rhetoric from being bold, provocative, or challenging. In the extreme case, if political leaders tell the public *only* what the public is comfortable with, political change becomes a less likely consequence of electoral politics.

Most of the qualitative change in campaign communication, however, is a result of the changing behavior of journalists. Here a number of observations seem warranted. First, I have commented many times in previous chapters about the tendency of the press to focus on "horserace" aspects of campaigns. This focus leads to an emphasis on candidate prospects and strategy, indications of electoral strength and success, and a competitive struggle among journalists to be first to predict the electoral outcome. Furthermore, there is some evidence that the current presidential delegate-selection process and products of the public opinion-polling industry have allowed journalists to become even more obsessed with the horse race than ever before. This focus clearly delimits the understanding that the public is able to acquire during an election campaign and trivializes the significance of an election into little more than a spectator sport.

Second, journalists have shown a notable tendency recently to portray candidates and dramatize the electoral contest thematically. This tendency results from audience presumptions, economic incentives, and professional training; it yields campaign accounts that are candidate-, event-, and theme-oriented; exaggerates the significance of particular campaign episodes; constrains public awareness to impressions of a few "viable" candidates; and submerges programmatic and philosophical matters in a sea of metaphors and dramatizations. Although it is unclear whether this campaign coverage differs from the coverage provided in previous years, the presence of television news has probably made a major contribution to this development.

Third, there is some evidence that contemporary journalism approaches election campaigns with a much more skeptical, cynical, and derisive orientation than was true just twenty years ago. Portrayals of candidates have become increasingly negative, and the electoral process itself has been treated as a meaningless or unseemly exercise. This tendency may be the result of an emerging adversarial relationship between journalists and politicians, and it may have contributed to the decline in political efficacy and political trust of the U.S. public. Although evidence for this effect is sketchy and adversarial journalism might also have beneficial consequences, the change in the *tone* of campaign coverage in recent years is surely a significant phenomenon.

Since we have only had about ten or fifteen years experience with the campaign communication of our new electoral process, it is unclear what the long-term consequences of these changes—both quantitative and qualitative—might be. The content of contemporary campaign communication, however, suggests a number of possibilities, mostly worrisome. Specifically, if current trends in electoral communication continue, we might reasonably expect the U.S. electorate of the future to be more cynical, less partisan, less frequently confronted with challenging political discourse, and more narrowly informed about the electoral choices available than was the case in the not-too-distant past. Any one of these consequences would have profound implications for the U.S. political process.

ELECTIONS AS COMMUNICATIONS PROCESSES

. . . Even passive citizens affect campaign communication indirectly through public opinion poll results, historical voting returns, and media-exposure patterns. Furthermore, campaign communication can be seen as a process by which the main electoral participants come to a mutually satisfactory accommodation concerning the messages that will be delivered to the public. Candidates anticipate the behavior of journalists, campaign contributors, and voters when they engage in campaign activities; journalists have developed an informal set of norms that attempt to accommodate their need for daily newsworthy stories and access to news-makers with the candidates' desire for factually accurate and favorable coverage; and the public remains the final arbiter of which messages are attended to, ignored, distorted, remembered, and persuasive.

The end result of this interaction among campaign participants is that campaign communication is unlike what any one participant would unilaterally prefer. Candidates and journalists provide more campaign discourse than the public would probably independently desire or demand, the inquiries and commentary of journalists (in debate settings, for example) force candidates to reveal more specific policy-related preferences than candidates themselves would voluntarily reveal, and audience predispositions and economic considerations force journalists to be more circumspect and nonideological in their campaign coverage than they might be otherwise. In this way the net flow of campaign messages is shaped by a number of campaign participants with differing motives, goals, and roles.

THE EFFECTS OF CAMPAIGN COMMUNICATION

Of course, there is no guarantee that the communication that is acceptable to campaign participants will be optimal in any other sense. For example, it is not at all clear that contemporary election campaigns have the educative effect that is often ascribed to them. Candidates have devised forms of campaign communication that provide them with a satisfactory way to deliver their messages without having to reveal much in the way of policy specifics or without having to be too careful about the accuracy of the claims they make. Journalists have developed methods of campaign coverage that allow them to cultivate sources, compete for a portion of their organization's news-hole, avoid attacks on the legitimacy of their coverage, and interest a sufficiently large segment of the public in their campaign accounts without informing the public about the policy preferences and philosophical positions of the candidates. The public is probably fairly well satisfied with campaign communication that can be easily ignored, may be selectively perceived, and is generally reassuring. The collective outcome of all this mutually reinforcing activity, however, may be to constrain severely the educative value of the electoral process.

We have seen, after all, that although the direct impact of campaign communcation on the voting intentions of the U.S. electorate is modest, the campaign does influence other popular perceptions and preferences. In particular, the public tends to learn horse-race information, to alter the salience of political issues and candidates for public office, to form stylistic impressions of political unknowns, and to increase slightly the accuracy of perceptions of candidate policy positions. The fact that most of this learning is shallow and superficial, or pertains mainly for the knowledge-rich, suggests that the educative effect of election campaigns is quite modest.

This raises the question of what U.S. elections actually accomplish and how the nature of campaign communication delimits the meaning of elections and the significance of electoral outcomes. Elections have always had a central position within the U.S. political system. From the early days of the Republic to the present, we have expected the electoral process to check the tyrannical designs of public officials, resolve divisive political conflict, ensure the representation of constituent interests, educate the public, and provide the public with an avenue for constraining the policy choices of public decision makers. It is quite possible, however, that what we hope elections do and what they actually do are two entirely different things. . . .

In the pages that follow we will discuss four perspectives on elections, which I will refer to as the *prospective policy choice* approach, the *retrospective policy satisfaction* approach, the *selection of a benevolent leader* approach, and the *election-as-ritual* approach. . . .

THE PROSPECTIVE-POLICY-CHOICE APPROACH

Americans are particularly fond of the notion that elections provide a mechanism by which the public can express policy preferences and constrain the future policy choices of public officials. We are often told that we can "send a message" with our vote, that this message can help shape future policy enactments by public officials, and that the aggregate message embodied in an election outcome confers a *mandate* on victorious candidates to pursue their policy preferences aggressively.

There are few political scientists who believe that elections are exclusively policymaking mechanisms. Many more political scientists, however, believe that this is a reachable goal with which the behavior of the U.S. electorate is more consistent than is often appreciated and toward which reform of the electoral process should be directed. Although numerous empirical shortcomings of this approach have been acknowledged, the normative hold of this approach on most Americans often leads to optimistic appraisals of the progress made toward the realization of this goal in the last twenty years, and to suggestions for reforming the electoral process so as to accelerate the pace of this presumed progress. . . .

In summary, this approach holds that elections may be viewed as a process by which citizens become informed about *future* public policy alternatives, by which citizens have the opportunity to choose a like-minded public official, and through which electoral outcomes shape future policy outcomes. . . .

THE RETROSPECTIVE-POLICY-SATISFACTION APPROACH

A second policy-oriented approach to elections argues that although public policies are an important consideration in election campaigns, the policies debated are as often as not past rather than future policies, and the standard of evaluation voters use is likely to be a more global assessment of satisfaction with *past* policy *performance* than agreement with *future* policy *proposals*. . . .

There is much evidence . . . for the retrospective-policy-satisfaction approach. The campaign rhetoric of candidates is largely consistent with it, the content of interelection news coverage supports it, the expectations the approach has of public opinion are reasonable and within reach, and many voters in many different elections have shown signs of policy-satisfaction-related voting. In fact, the behavior of both candidates and the populace suggests that of the two policy-oriented approaches considered here, the one that is backward-looking is the more empirically compelling one . . . .

THE SELECTION-OF-A-BENEVOLENT-LEADER APPROACH

Both of the approaches to elections we have considered so far focus on the public policy content and consequences of campaigns and elections. Yet it is clear that elections also involve *nonprogrammatic* competition between two or more *human beings* for the support and loyalty of the population. This nonprogrammatic competition involves attempts to convince the populace that the personal attributes of a candidate make him or her a "fit leader." Viewed in this way, elections become one of a number of processes by which human societies select leaders to make authoritative decisions. As is often the case in other forms of leadership selection—such as combat—this process may elevate the personal, nonprogrammatic attributes of the potential leader to a more central position than the consideration of policy decisions, conditions, or proposals. . . .

When elections are seen as an exercise in *leadership* rather than *policy* selection, our attention is directed toward the nonpolicy aspects of electoral communication and behavior. This perspective requires us to consider instead the desirable leadership attributes in cultures like our own, and to study the ways in which these attributes are presented, contrasted, and emphasized. More specifically, the approach to elections as selection of a benevolent leader reminds us of a number of features of campaign communication that we have discussed in previous chapters.

First, this benevolent-leader approach asserts that a fair amount of the campaign communication of both candidates and journalists focuses on the nonprogrammatic personal characteristics of candidates for public office. This recognizes that a candidate represents not only past and future policy decisions, but also a personality and character to which other people respond. Communication regarding these personal characteristics, both verbal and nonverbal, is thought to be prevalent both before and during an election campaign. In fact, even communication involving policy alternatives may really be concerned with the creation of impressions about a candidate's personality; hence public policies become simply one of many vehicles through which such impressions may be created.

Second, this approach assumes that citizens are willing and able to form perceptions concerning the nonprogrammatic attributes and character traits of candidates. This is partly because information regarding these characteristics is so readily available (unlike information concerning prospective policy preferences) and partly because judging the character of another human being is something we do frequently and know something about. The perceptions that citizens form in this way may not be particularly rich or accurate—we often speak of a citizen's *image* or *impression* of a candidate—but they are thought to be part of the natural process of responding to human communication and choosing between prospective leaders.

Third, this approach argues that the evaluation of the character traits or personalities of candidates is an important determinant of the citizen's candidate choice and vote. In this view, voter images or impressions of the personality or character of candidates help voters decide for whom to vote; candidates capable of creating the most positive personal impression are more likely to achieve electoral success.

Finally, the benevolent-leader approach to elections argues that the meaning of the election is not to be found in any programmatic preferences (either past or future) indicated by the citizenry, but rather in the conferral of approval on an officeholder who begins his or her tenure with a measure of support and legitimacy. The victorious candidate is more likely to embody culturally desirable leadership traits and to have been the most successful at creating a reassuring or comforting personal impression than to represent any sort of aggregate preference or mandate for specific policy choices. In fact, in this view, an electoral victory grants to the benevolent leader considerable policy latitude within which to maneuver, experiment, and bargain. In other words, this perspective does not view elections as a process by which the citizenry controls or influences public policy, except in the most inadvertent or indirect way. It is, however, a process by which human societies select an attractive, comforting focus of attention possessing, initially, a measure of legitimacy and support.

There is considerable evidence in support of this benevolent-leader approach to election campaigns. First, . . . candidate communication contains frequent references to the nonprogrammatic personal attributes of candidates. At the presidential level, both campaign rhetoric in general and political spot ads in particular contain frequent explicit attempts to create favorable, personal, nonprogrammatic impressions. If we had also considered the more implicit, nonverbal types of candidate appeals—including, for example, the use of props, settings, and camera angles to create impressions—we might well have found that *the* single most prevalent type of presidential campaign appeal is an attempt to communicate an image of a benevolent leader.

. . . . there is also clear evidence that these personal impressions of candidates show a strong relationship to electoral choices. . . . At the presidential level a number of character traits—such as strength, warmth, competence, and trustworthiness—are continuously at the center of both candidate rhetoric and citizen behavior; other personal traits, such as activity (vigor), religion, and geographical origins, appear and disappear in different contexts. Similarly, at the congressional level, Richard Fenno has pointed out that constituents may well want things other than policy agreement—for example, assurances of access and trustworthiness—from their legislators.

In sum, both the nature of campaign information and the public's reaction to that information suggest that the benevolent-leader approach is largely consistent with the available evidence. Unlike the first two approaches, however, this approach accords very little intended policymaking significance to election campaigns and electoral outcomes. In fact, if this is an accurate approach to the understanding of contemporary election campaigns, the normative consequences could be quite troubling:

> Even if . . . the electoral process casts up a paragon of benevolent leadership every time, we would still have to ask whether it is not a debasement of

language to call this democracy. It has about it a flavor of citizen abdication, of giving up on instrumental benefits of government and settling for the symbolism of a father figure or a dignified elected monarch.

In isolation, certainly, the selection of a benevolent leader is a weak sort of democracy. "Rule by the people" must concern substance as well as style, and the connections between presidential personality and policy and performance, while significant, are not sufficient to dictate in detail what government does. *Only in conjunction with other processes* of democratic control does the selection of an appropriate presidential personality take on normative importance [emphasis added].[8]

THE ELECTIONS-AS-RITUAL APPROACH

The three approaches to election campaigns discussed so far differ in many significant ways regarding the meaning of electoral communication and electoral outcomes. All three, however, share a common assumption that elections are useful for or serve the interests of the general citizenry. A fourth approach to election campaigns does not share this assumption but argues instead that elections serve the interests of political elites by preserving social stability, keeping the citizenry misinformed, and channeling political participation into a routine, nonthreatening, and impotent form. This approach, here called the *ritualistic* approach, clearly looks at electoral behavior in a fundamentally different way.

The elections-as-ritual approach holds that elites shape public opinion through the communication of myths and cultural values such as "free enterprise, honesty, industry, bravery, tolerance, perseverance, and individualism." These myths strike a responsive—but noncognitive—chord in the mass citizenry, and are capable of stimulating political controversy as individuals differ over which myth to apply to which circumstance. Communication of these myths tends to be dramatic and filled with imagery or symbols, and its imprecision permits multiple interpretations on the part of the citizenry. The myths themselves are selected from a rigid cultural consensus concerning the limits of acceptable debate and rhetoric, and they stimulate recognition and response from the deepest levels of our consciousness. Election campaigns, in this view, are a ritual in which mythical representations are transmitted to and reinforced among the populace . . . .

One way in which these myths are transmitted to the populace is through the electoral appeals made by candidates. Although many observers have criticized what they see as the emptiness of candidate rhetoric, this type of rhetoric may be seen as the essence of any political ritual. According to this view the symbolism, drama, ambiguity, and nonspecificity of candidate communication are what is typical of and meaningful about candidate appeals, since this rhetoric reveals what elections are *not* about and serves to *delimit* public understanding. . . .

---

8. Benjamin I. Page, *Choices and Echoes in Presidential Elections* (Chicago: University of Chicago Press, 1978), p. 265.

Although it is clear that much candidate communication is mythical in nature, what is much less clear is whether candidate communication and campaign news coverage are *completely* devoid of substantive information and whether the campaign truly has an insignificant educative effect on the citizenry. Candidates, after all, do reveal some fairly specific policy preferences, particularly in debate appearances; and public perceptions of the policy preferences of candidates are somewhat responsive to the clarity of campaign news coverage and candidate policy positions.

At present, the elections-as-ritual approach is useful primarily because it forces us to reconsider our commonly held assumptions about elections. Future research should illuminate the extent to which campaign communication emphasizes consensually held but empty symbols, takes place within a narrow range of programmatic disagreement, legitimizes the positions of political authorities, and defuses more violent political behavior. Until then it is difficult to assess empirically the central assertions of this approach.

CONCLUSION

. . . The empirical evidence regarding campaign communication and the public's response to that communication would seem to be more consistent with the retrospective-policy-satisfaction and selection-of-a-benevolent-leader approaches than with the other two. Candidate appeals and daily campaign news stories are filled with the type of information emphasized by these approaches, and citizen perceptions and candidate choices depend on this information flow. This means that elections may best be understood as processes by which the electorate reveals global feelings of policy satisfaction or dissatisfaction, indicates a preference for change or continuity of a general sort, and selects as a focus of attention political leaders who possess reassuring and comforting personalities.

In contrast, campaign communication and the behavior of the electorate are less consistent with the prospective-policy-choice perspective (and the dearth of evidence makes it difficult to tell how accurate the elections-as-ritual view is). Neither candidate appeals, campaign news coverage, nor citizen interest and capabilities convincingly support this approach. Consequently, it is difficult to see how electoral outcomes could possibly confer specific, future-oriented policy mandates on victorious candidates. The attractiveness of this approach, then, must be accounted for on other than empirical grounds. Perhaps because this approach to elections conforms the closest to the standard civic-education justification for elections, there is a special interest in protecting its status.

This does not mean that election campaigns and electoral outcomes have no policy significance. The fact that one set of officials rather than another is selected means that the outcome may well make a considerable difference. Throughout our nation's history there have been times in which the policy preferences of competing sets of candidates have differed significantly and the selection of one party or candidate over another had an important programmatic effect. Surely it mattered, after all, whether Taft or Bryan was selected in 1896, whether Hoover or Roosevelt won in 1932, whether Johnson or Goldwater was elected in 1964, and in 1980 whether Ronald Reagan and a host of Republican senators or Jimmy Carter and a group of Democratic senators were elected. The argument here, however, has been that because of the nature of campaign communication, these policy consequences are often *inadvertent* rather than intended by the electorate, or are at most intended only insofar as the electorate reveals a general tolerance for change.

Whether or not the retrospective-policy-satisfaction and benevolent-leader approaches to elections provide a large enough role for the citizenry and a strong enough avenue for constraining public officials to advance self-government is a provocative and complex question. Whether any other type of campaign communication and electoral process in our cultural, economic, and political environment is *possible* is also a perplexing but worthwhile query. At this point, however, it appears that the campaign communication that characterizes the contemporary electoral process does more to entertain than enlighten, to reassure than challenge, and to disorient than empower the U.S. public. Although this campaign communication may be functional for all involved, meaningful public choice—and hence self-government—would seem to be less than it might be.   ■

THE TV SPOT
Edwin Diamond and Stephen Bates

Political commentator Mark Shields tells this story:

The weekend before a Presidential election, a lowly Democratic Party hanger-on in the Second Ward of a small town in Iowa worried about the outcome. "Our voters don't know there's an election coming up," he complained to the ward committeeman. "We need a truck with a big sign and music to get people to notice." The committeeman brushed him off, but the man persisted; finally the committeeman gave in: "Here's a hundred bucks to rent a truck from your brother-in-law down at the garage, if that's what you want to do." Off rushed the man, and on Saturday afternoon, as Iowans shopped, the truck rumbled by, music blaring, placards urging a vote for the Democratic Party. On Tuesday Democrats across the nation swept into office, winning the Presidency, 15 U.S. Senate seats, 10 governorships, including Iowa's, the local Congressional district as well as control of the U.S. House of Representatives, the city manager race and three out of five ward alderman races. At Second Ward headquarters, amid all the joy, the hanger-on came up to the committeeman and with a big smile, punched him on the arm and exclaimed: "What did I tell you! It was the truck!"

Unlike this hanger-on, professional media managers rarely celebrate the effectiveness of their "trucks" in the making of political victory. Because just about every major campaign now has media specialists working for each candidate, more than half of the advertising done in any election year will be for unsuccessful candidates. Just as obviously, many things influence an election besides paid advertising, including the nature and disposition of the voters, the strength of incumbency, the character of the candidates and the unpredictable events of the campaign and of the wider society. There is, in short, a real world outside the artfully arranged realities of the media campaign.

Beyond these obvious truths, is there anything definitive that can be said about the effectiveness of paid political television advertising—which advertisements work, and why?

Social scientists tend to be cautious about the effects of television campaigns. Political scientist Kay Israel did a 1983 survey of the existing academic literature on political advertising and found little that went beyond the standard textbook conclusion offered by Bernard Berelson of the University of Chicago in the pretelevision 1940s. Berelson wrote, "Some kinds of communication on some kinds of issues, brought to the attention of some kinds of people under some kinds of conditions, have some kinds of effects." For this cautious judgment we are tempted to say to Berelson, "Thanks a little," except that Berelson's words were a welcome counterpoint to the then-existing, overwrought ideas of the powers of political persuasion and propaganda. Messages sent, it was thought in those days, were messages received, understood and acted on. By Berelson's time, however, the verdict had begun to move the other way. Social scientists, using survey-research techniques, reported that most messages didn't get through at all, and that few of those that did had an appreciable effect on attitudes.

Conversion is the obvious goal for a political advertising spot, or "polispot." But it is not the only goal. There is evidence that polispots may be better at reinforcement—keeping the committee in line. That is because people pay attention principally to messages that reflect their preexisting views; that is, the most attentive audience for a Reagan spot will be people who have already decided to vote for Reagan. As Marshall McLuhan argued two decades ago, people attend to advertisements extolling goods they already own. Supporters of Reagan's opponent, on the other hand, may ignore the message, or they may receive it, argue with it and reject it.

Polispots also seem suited for activation—prodding the already committed to go out and vote on the basis of their commitments. The academic consensus is that advertising can matter in campaigns, as one of several variables. Some of the best purely statistical work, including studies by political scientist Gary Jacobson, found that incumbency and voter partisanship explain more electoral outcomes than do broadcast expenditures. In cases where these factors are nullified—in primaries for vacant seats in Congress, for example—broadcast spending seems to make a difference in who wins.

Several of the media managers we interviewed keep up with the social science literature. Indeed, they often sound like academics themselves when talking for the record about the effectiveness of political advertising. We hear echoes of

Berelson in Stuart Spencer's answer, when asked if spots work: "Some do, some don't. Not everything you put on the air is going to move somebody. But if you have the right issue and it's handled in the right manner, and you're getting it to the right audiences . . . media can have an effect." One reason for this caution is the difficulty of isolating and identifying the impact of paid television advertising, as opposed to any other influences. Nevertheless, Charles Guggenheim notes, "No one in his right mind, in a senatorial or gubernatorial or Presidential election, can not use television—if for no other reason than self-defense, to neutralize what will undoubtedly be coming from the other side. It's like air power in a battle. Can you fight a major campaign without air power? The North Vietnamese showed you could. But I don't think you want to do away with your air force."

Much more important than paid advertising is free media exposure, according to David Garth. He cites the 1979 polls showing Kennedy leading Carter in August by 36 points. By December Kennedy was trailing by 13, not because of any commercials (there were none) but because of Roger Mudd's intervening interview with a stumbling Kennedy. Garth also argues that George Bush "went up something like 30 points in the national polls in 1980. He didn't do national spots; all he did was local spots. Bush went that far up nationally because the influence of free media far surpasses the influence of TV commercials." Is that proof enough for the primacy of free media exposure? Another media manager, John Deardourff, points to a case that seems to prove just the opposite. His client, Gov. James Thompson, had poor personal ratings in polls at the start of the 1982 governor's race in Illinois. An ad campaign for Thompson's reelection began during the summer, when news media carried relatively few stories. The paid media campaign, Deardourff claims, "shifted the focus away from Thompson's personal problems and onto the question of his record and the issues. Before-and-after polling showed a clear shift in favorability toward Thompson, both generally and in terms of his ability to deal with those issues we were showing on television. The shift happened at a time when there wasn't enough other outside coverage of the campaign. You could have no doubt about where it came from."

Media managers do extensive proprietary research, not for publication in academic journals but for guiding clients' campaigns and for sharing with prospective clients. Videotape screenings, polling data on flip charts, results from film previews and testimonial letters from past winners—the big payoff—go into these presentations. Each of the media managers we interviewed at length shared at least some of his work with us, while others provided examples of their presentation materials. Based on the evidence of these interviews and research materials, we have tried to write down some of the "unwritten rules" of political advertising.

First of all, many major campaigns now have spots previewed by samples of voters, and most managers have a moderate degree of confidence in the value of such testing. In the 1972 Nixon campaign, Peter Dailey produced and pretested several negative spots. A given spot was found to be much more effective, he later said, when it was identified as sponsored by the group called Democrats for Nixon rather than by the Committee to Re-Elect the President. Such sponsorship, Dailey said, reinforced the idea that people like John Connally, who were highly credible Democrats (at that time, at least), were throwing their support to Nixon.

In 1976, pretesting by the Ford campaign led to the shelving of several spots. Malcolm MacDougall had made a commercial arguing that agribusinessman Jimmy Carter had taken advantage of tax loopholes, paying $1,375 in federal tax on an adjusted income of more than $120,000, while candidate Jimmy Carter was railing against tax loopholes and three-martini lunches. During previews, the viewers reported that the tax spot was too complicated. They also thought that the tax laws were complex, and that most people tried to pay as little in taxes as possible. The spot was shelved. In the same campaign, Douglas Bailey made a five-minute spot showing Ford campaigning in an open car in Dallas, evoking comparison with John Kennedy and 1963 and playing on the "Feelin' Good" theme. The media man agreed it was terrific stuff, very emotional, but also risky: No one could predict how the voters would react to being reminded of the assassination. In pretesting, viewers found the spot upsetting, and it too was shelved.

Gerald Rafshoon also made similar judgments about the effectiveness of various negative spots that had been produced for Carter. He rejected such spots as the one using an off-camera voice to list all the Ford "against" positions — against Medicare, against job training, against subsidized school lunches, against food stamps, against day-care. The voice-over asks: "Who'd believe a nice man like Gerald Ford would vote against or oppose all these?" Rafshoon rejected this and others, he told us, because they were trying to show that Ford was inhumane, and "people didn't think he was inhumane; they thought he was kind of bumbling and stupid."

Pretesting measures some effects better than others. Previews, for example, are more useful for assessing positive media spots than negative ones. As Robert Squier says, "No focus group I've ever seen liked a negative spot. They think it's dirty politics." Deardourff also does extensive pretesting and says that the technique "helps eliminate the clinkers, the commercials that are relatively ineffective, or maybe even dangerous in some unanticipated way." As for the reverse — determining which spots will work best — Deardourff says, "We are not even close to being able to do that."

The second rule we found is that commercials do work in getting the candidate known. With enough dollars, the name and face of a low- or zero-recognition candidate like Lew Lehrman (the unsuccessful Republican candidate for governor of New York in 1982) can become familiar to just about every likely voter. The money simply buys enough air time so that eventually no viewer can escape seeing the candidate several times. The advertising rule of thumb is to buy enough gross ratings points (based on Nielsen ratings) to make a half-dozen hits per viewer. Roger Ailes spent $1 million a month on ads for Lehrman, to buy 400 to 500 gross rating points a week throughout the state. The ads identified Lehrman as a successful businessman, "not a politician." He lost a very close race to Mario Cuomo.

A third rule is that negative advertising is the riskiest element of the campaign. The candidate, as Deardourff told us, must be viewed by the public "in the most positive possible terms" before going on the attack. Also, any implicit messages in the negative spot must work to the campaign's advantage.

The negative themes implicit in the unused spots for Carter in 1976 would have been counterproductive, or so Rafshoon believed when he shelved them. Further, negative advertising tends, as Deardourff told us, to "harden the lines quickly—people leaning heavily toward a candidate will probably be firmed up in his favor by any attacks on him." It also tends to incite the opposition to let loose with its own attack spots, perhaps more effective ones. Besides, there is the risk, especially for incumbents battling less well-known challengers, that negative advertising will increase the opponent's name identification without significantly reducing his support. Also, negative advertising must be seen as credible. Incumbent Rep. Margaret Heckler's 1982 ads, accusing opponent Barney Frank of wanting to establish prostitution zones in every city in Massachusetts, didn't ring true. (Frank was actually opposed to restrictions on adult entertainment, a position he defended on the basis of the First Amendment.) Neither did a 1972 Nixon spot that accused McGovern of wanting to put half of the country on welfare.

Most important, the attack must be seen as fair. An extreme attack, saying that Barry Goldwater might push the button, can best be made indirectly, as in Johnson's "daisy" spot; "daisy" never mentioned Goldwater's name, though even the implied message was widely viewed as unfair. Certain personal themes are so touchy as to be considered unmentionable in negative spots (Chappaquiddick), though they can be raised implicitly ("You may not agree with President Carter, but you'll never find yourself wondering if he's telling you the truth"). Even nuances can make a major difference in whether an attack seems fair. In his work for Edward M. Kennedy in 1980, David Sawyer found that voters rejected as unfair the message that Carter, perceived as a decent man, had broken his promises, but they were receptive to the message that Carter was incapable of keeping his promises. Consequently the Kennedy campaign, Sawyer told us, "changed the argument from morality to competence." Sawyer's caution was justified for voters tend to resent unfair attacks on an incumbent President. And they also feel uncomfortable when the President goes on the attack. As Rafshoon—who successfully challenged a sitting President but failed to defend one—told us, "There's a different standard. You can play fast and loose if you're a challenger, but if you're President, they expect you to act Presidential. You can't be irresponsible."

To complicate the situation further, attacks are judged by the press as well as by the electorate. Political scientists are divided on whether press comment alone can affect voter attitudes, but most media managers believe it can; therefore they try to anticipate the press's likely response to an attack commercial. Deardourff told us that he sometimes gives reporters memos substantiating the charges made in spots—"footnotes, in effect"—in order to forestall criticism. But, as Deardourff discovered in Chicago in 1983, footnotes sometimes aren't enough, for press or public.

In January 1983, Bailey and Deardourff went to work for the Republican mayoral candidate after Harold Washington won the Democratic primary. The GOP candidate was Bernard Epton, who was Jewish and white. While Chicago had not elected a Republican as mayor since the 1920s, Democratic nominee Washington had a number of liabilities on his record, including a conviction for failure to pay his income taxes, suspension from his law practice and a string of lawsuits for nonpayment of all sorts of personal bills. Washington also was black, in a city that still has segregated neighborhoods.

Deardourff now says that "the Epton media campaign had to be against Washington on a personal basis; his character was the issue. We had just six weeks to go so we did an indictment of Washington, and wrote a tag line for the commercials." The tag line was, "Epton: Before It's Too Late." As Deardourff sees it, "The whole idea was to summarize the notion that there were a few weeks remaining before Chicago was going to have a new and entirely different kind of mayor. Our message was, 'Wake up, Chicago—look what you're getting here.' " Deardourff professes not to have seen the racial connotation in the line: Before it's too late—before a black becomes mayor.

The effort to frame the campaign around Washington's record framed the campaign instead around race. Black voters turned out in record numbers to vote for Washington on Election Day; thousands of white voters deserted the Democratic line to pull the lever for Epton. Washington won.

The fourth unwritten rule we found is that political advertising can polish a candidate's image considerably. Especially since Jimmy Carter's come-from-nowhere success in 1976, it has been widely believed that image-making is easier than image remaking, and that unknown challengers, if they're well-heeled, have an advantage over candidates with familiar—and imperfect—images. We found otherwise. A well-planned, well-executed media campaign can shift voter perceptions of a candidate, even a highly visible incumbent. One of the best examples is the remaking of former Chicago Mayor Jane Byrne, who in 1983 used a series of ads to successfully improve her badly tarnished image. Her media managers did not go on the attack against Washington, however, and he edged her out on primary day.

The intrusion of reality into campaigns sets limits on what paid media can accomplish, and all evidence of effectiveness must be read in the light of these real-world events. There is something called the Ottinger Effect (so named after Richard Ottinger, unsuccessful candidate for the New York Senate) that often influences elections; Ottinger couldn't match up to the vigorous image he tried to portray, and the dissonance between the TV image and the real thing is thought to have dissuaded voters. Similarly, Gerald Ford had been moving up in the polls against Jimmy Carter in 1976 until Ford's Eastern European stumble in the second debate. (He incorrectly stated that Poland was not within the Soviet sphere of influence.) Suddenly, the real Ford seemed at odds with the advertised Ford. The media managers were spending millions on TV spots to convey the notion that one of the major differences between the candidates was Ford's experience in international politics; he was the man who had sat at the bargaining table with Brezhnev. "Suddenly, 80 million people are exposed to a new reality," Deardourff says. "What good is your television, showing Ford riding a railroad car with a bunch of Russians, when he can't correctly position Poland?"

The fifth rule, then, is that the best advertising in the world can't paint the face of victory on a moribund campaign. The attentive, honest George McGovern of Guggenheim's spots made excellent television but couldn't overcome the candidate's self-inflicted wounds, notably his selection and subsequent rejection of Sen. Thomas Eagleton as his running mate. Rose Garden advertising couldn't overcome the intrusion of the prolonged Iranian hostage crisis in the 1980 general election. John Glenn's ads soared; his candidacy stayed earthbound.

Not all polispots, as we've indicated, aim directly at voters. Another target of spot advertising is the elites of the metacampaign, the campaign within the campaign. Media managers often preview their next commercials at special screenings for reporters or potential contributors to convey a sense of movement, strategy and organization. Political consultant Eddie Mahe argues that a spot campaign is now expected by both the insiders and the public. "You can, for example, use direct-mail appeals until hell freezes over," he says. "But broadcast media buy authenticity. I might be persuaded by the 17 direct-mail letters you send me, but if I never see your campaign on TV, I wonder if I'm the only one who got those letters." Beyond legitimizing the campaign in the eyes of its audiences, television ads also can be used to attract contributors' dollars in a more direct sense. Humphrey in 1968, McGovern in 1972 and Reagan in the 1976 primaries all used paid media to raise money.

Some spots, particularly negative spots, may be aimed partly at the strategists of the other side. Ford in his memoirs recalls that the attacks on Carter in 1976 were intended "to provoke him into a serious mistake." One such mistake, Ford's advisers agreed, would have been commercials attacking Ford. But, as Rafshoon says, the Carter camp didn't allow itself to be baited.

Perhaps the major target of the metacampaign is the press. Sometimes spots by themselves generate news stories that can affect the campaign. One Ford spot, for example, received heavy press attention and considerable negative comment. The screen showed a close-up of a blond woman, around 30, smiling slightly as she said: "If you've been waiting for this Presidential campaign to become a little clearer so that you can make a choice, it's happened. Last Wednesday, Ronald Reagan said that he would send American troops to Rhodesia. Thursday, he clarified that. He said they could be 'observers' or 'advisers.' What does he think happened in Vietnam? Or was Governor Reagan playing with words?"

Then the camera pulled back revealing a campaign poster of Ford in a dark suit. The woman continued: "The President of the United States can't play with words. When you vote Tuesday, remember: Governor Reagan couldn't start a war; President Reagan could."

Ford lost the California primary badly, and most metacampaign observers thought that his harsh attack on a native son hadn't helped. But Ford strategist Spencer told us the campaign had already written off California. Spencer knew that the press would jump on the spot, effectively providing national exposure for the price of statewide exposure. "They all watched in the East," Spencer says. "Newspaper reporters all had to write about it. That ad accomplished our purpose—it ensured us those other states."

Finally, metacampaign spots can frame the overall electoral dynamics, telling voters and elites alike: "These are the points that matter." The first polispot strategy in 1952 succeeded in this respect, when Eisenhower convinced voters that the election centered on whether it was "Time for a Change." In 1956, Stevenson tried, unsuccessfully, to make the election a referendum on Richard Nixon, given Ike's presumed failing health. In 1980, Carter tried to make "cowboy" Reagan the issue, while Reagan ran against "ineffectual" Carter. In 1984, Glenn's primary campaign against Walter Mondale pictured Glenn as the candidate of the future, in contrast to the discredited policies of the past. Mondale's response was to frame himself as the leader for the 1980s, while continuing to travel the old politics route of strong organization and institutional endorsements.

In the aftermath of Richard Nixon's victory in 1968, reporter Joe McGinniss concluded that the new Nixon was the product of the "adroit manipulation and use of television" by Ailes, Harry Treleaven and the other image makers. As McGinniss recorded Ailes, the hyper-energetic young producer, at Nixon's Election-Eve telethon: "This is the beginning of a whole new concept. This is it. This is the way they'll be elected forevermore. The next guys up will have to be performers." In 1983 an older, fleshed-out, bearded—and calmer—Ailes offered a different conclusion: "The TV public is very smart in the sense that somewhere, somehow, they make a judgment about the candidates they see. Anybody who claims he can figure out that process is full of it." In 1984 and beyond we are sure the media managers will continue their search for the key to the voter's decision process. Just as surely they will fail to find it. The creation of political advertising will remain a problematic art.   ■

Courtesy of The New York Historical Society, New York City.

Democratic Government

We have earlier considered the constitutional framework of America's governmental system and how what citizens say and do may affect politics and government. Now, in Part III, we will give our attention to the institutions of our national government—what they do, how they work, and how they may be used by citizens.

Chapter 8 deals with the principal lawmaking branch, the Congress. Chapter 9, on the presidency, and Chapter 10, on the bureaucracy, examine the functions and workings of the executive branch of the federal government.

Finally, Chapter 11 deals with the judicial branch, the courts.

The Congress

U nder the national separation-of-powers system of the United States—with separate legislative, executive, and judicial branches of government—the chief legislative, or lawmaking, power is vested in the U. S. Congress. The Congress is a *bicameral,* or two-house, national legislature—and a very powerful one.

In addition to its principal power, that of lawmaking, the Congress also has other powers. Its fiscal power includes authority over federal spending, taxation, and borrowing. Its investigating power is a broad one and is not limited to legislation under consideration. Its impeachment power—with charges to be brought by majority vote in the House, followed by trial in the Senate, two-thirds vote there being necessary for conviction—provides a means for removing national executive and judicial officials from office.

The foreign affairs powers of the Congress includes the sole authority to declare war and the requirement that no treaty can become effective until ratified by two-thirds vote in the Senate. Lastly, there is the constitutional amendment power of the Congress. It allows Congress—under the only constitutional amendment method used up to now—by a two-thirds vote in both houses to propose an amendment, which then must be ratified by three-fourths of the states before it becomes effective. (The other, unused method of amending the Constitution also involves Congress: Congress is to call a constitutional convention upon the petition of two-thirds of the states.)

In this chapter, we will first consider the constitutional foundations of the Congress and, then, how Congress has developed through the years. Still focusing on Congress as an institution, we will next give attention to the present law in regard to the "legislative veto."

Congress is not only an institution, though. It is also a collection of individual members, and these members will be the subject of the balance

269

of this chapter, as we consider two questions: What does it mean to be a "representative"? What is it like to serve in Congress?

CONSTITUTIONAL FOUNDATIONS

Attending the Constitutional Convention in Philadelphia in 1787 were "nationalists," like James Madison and Alexander Hamilton, who wanted a stronger national government that could deal directly with the people, and "confederationists," who wanted to continue a system under which the national government resulted from a kind of contract among the states, with the states retaining principal sovereignty, or governmental authority. The ultimate product of the Convention was a compromise between these two approaches: federalism, or shared sovereignty.

The central feature of the Connecticut Compromise—or Great Compromise—adopted by the Convention was the United States Congress. One house, the U. S. House of Representatives, would represent "people." All its members would be elected by the people every two years. The other house, the U. S. Senate, would represent "states." Its members—with each state having two—would be elected by state legislatures (changed to direct election by the people as a result of a 1913 constitutional amendment).

Excerpted here are *Federalist 53,* by James Madison, and *Federalist 57* and *58*—all of which discuss the House of Representatives. *Federalist 53* responds to an objection that House members should be elected for one-year terms, not two. *Federalist 57* denies, giving reasons, that the House will represent the interests of the privileged and powerful, rather than the great mass of people. *Federalist 58* seeks to answer arguments that the House will add members and become too large and that its quorum for action should be more than a majority.

Excerpted here, also, are *Federalist 62* and *63*, dealing with the Senate. They argue in favor of the stability offered by the Senate and its check on the House and on majority public passions.

FEDERALIST 53

. . . The important distinction so well understood in America between a constitution established by the people, and unalterable by the government; and a law established by the government, and alterable by the government, seems to have been little understood and less observed in any other country. Wherever the supreme power of legislation has resided, has been supposed to reside also, a full power to change the form of the government. Even in Great-Britain, where the principles of political and civil liberty have been most discussed; and where we hear most of the rights of the constitution, it is maintained that the authority of the parliament is transcendent and uncontroulable, as well with regard to the constitution, as the ordinary objects of legislative provision. They have accordingly, in several instances, actually changed, by legislative acts, some of the most fundamental articles of the government. They have in particular, on several occasions, changed the periods of election; and on the last occasion, not only introduced septennial, in place of triennial, elections; but by the same act continued themselves in place four years beyond the term for which they were elected by the people. An attention to these dangerous practices has produced a very natural alarm in the votaries of free government, of which frequency of elections is the corner stone; and has led them to seek for some security to liberty against the danger to which it is exposed. Where no constitution paramount to the government, either existed or could be obtained, no constitutional security similar to that established in the United States, was to be attempted. Some other security therefore was to be sought for; and what better security would the case admit, than that of selecting and appealing to some simple and familiar portion of time, as a standard for measuring the danger of innovations, for fixing the national sentiment, and for uniting the patriotic exertions. The most simple and familiar portion of time, applicable to the subject, was that of a year; and hence the doctrine has been inculcated by a laudable zeal to erect some barrier against the gradual innovations of an unlimited government, that the advance towards tyranny was to be calculated by the distance of departure from the fixed point of annual elections. But what necessity can there be of applying this expedient to a government, limited as the federal government will be, by the authority of a paramount constitution? Or who will pretend that the liberties of the people of America will not be more secure under biennial elections, unalterably fixed by such a Constitution, than those of any other nation would be where elections were annual, or even more frequent, but subject to alterations by the ordinary power of the government?

The second question stated is, whether biennial elections be necessary or useful. The propriety of answering this question in the affirmative will appear from several very obvious considerations.

No man can be a competent legislator who does not add to an upright intention and a sound judgment a certain degree of knowledge of the subjects on which he is to legislate. A part of this knowledge may be acquired by means of information which lie within the compass of men in private as well as public stations. Another part can only be attained, or at least thoroughly attained, by actual experience in the station which requires the use of it. The period of service ought, therefore, in all such cases, to bear some proportion to the extent of practical knowledge requisite to the due performance of the service. The period of legislative service established in most of the States for the more numerous branch is, as we have seen, one year. The question then may be put into this simple form: does the period of two years bear no greater proportion to the knowledge requisite for federal legislation than one year does to the knowledge requisite for State legislation? The very statement of the question, in this form, suggests the answer that ought to be given to it.

In a single State, the requisite knowledge relates to the existing laws, which are uniform throughout the State, and with which all the citizens are more or less conversant; and to the general affairs of the State, which lie within a small compass, are not very diversified, and occupy much of the attention and conversation of every class of people. The great theatre of the United States presents a very different scene. The laws are so far from being uniform, that they vary in every state; whilst the public affairs of the union are spread throughout a very extensive region, and are extremely diversified by the local affairs connected with them, and can with difficulty be correctly learnt in any other place, than in the central councils, to which a knowledge of them will be brought by the representatives of every part of the empire. Yet some knowledge of the affairs, and even of the laws of all the states, ought to be possessed by the members from each of the states. How can foreign trade be properly regulated by uniform laws, without some acquaintance with the commerce, the ports, the usages, and the regulations, of the different states? How can the trade between the different states be duly regulated without some knowledge of their relative situations in these and other points? How can taxes be judiciously imposed, and effectually collected, if they be not accommodated to the different laws and local circumstances relating to these objects in the different states? How can uniform regulations for the militia be duly provided without a similar knowledge of many internal circumstances by which the states are distinguished from each other? These are the principal objects of federal legislation, and suggest most forceably, the extensive information which the representatives ought to acquire. The other inferior objects will require a proportional degree of information with regard to them.

It is true that all these difficulties will by degrees be very much diminished. The most laborious task will be the proper inauguration of the government, and the primeval formation of a federal code. Improvements on the first draught will every year become both easier and fewer. Past transactions of the government will be a ready and accurate source of information to new members. The affairs of the union will become more and more objects of curiosity and conversation among the citizens at large. And the increased intercourse among those of different states will contribute not a little to diffuse a mutual knowledge of their affairs, as this again will contribute to a general assimilation of their manners and laws.

But with all these abatements the business of federal legislation must continue so far to exceed both in novelty and difficulty, the legislative business of a single state as to justify the longer period of service assigned to those who are to transact it.

A branch of knowledge which belongs to the acquirements of a federal representative, and which has not been mentioned, is that of foreign affairs. In regulating our own commerce he ought to be not only acquainted with the treaties between the United States and other nations, but also with the commercial policy and laws of other nations. He ought not to be altogether ignorant of the law of nations, for that as far as it is a proper object of municipal legislation is submitted to the federal government. And although the house of representatives is not immediately to participate in foreign negotiations and arrangements, yet from the necessary connection between the several branches of public affairs, those particular branches will frequently deserve attention in the ordinary course of legislation, and will sometimes demand particular legislative sanction and cooperation. Some portion of this knowledge may no doubt be acquired in a man's closet; but some of it also can only be derived from the public sources of information; and all of it will be acquired to best effect by a practical attention to the subject during the period of actual service in the legislature. . . .

A few of the members, as happens in all such assemblies, will possess superior talents, will by frequent re-elections, become members of long standing; will be thoroughly masters of the public business, and perhaps not unwilling to avail themselves of those advantages. The greater the proportion of new members, and the less the information of the bulk of the members, the more apt will they be to fall into the snares that may be laid for them. This remark is no less applicable to the relation which will subsist between the house of representatives and the senate. . . .

All these considerations taken together warrant us in affirming that biennial elections will be as useful to the affairs of the public, as we have seen that they will be safe to the liberties of the people. ∎

FEDERALIST 57

The aim of every political Constitution is or ought to be first to obtain for rulers, men who possess most wisdom to discern, and most virtue to pursue the common good of the society; and in the next place, to take the most effectual precautions for keeping them virtuous, whilst they continue to hold their public trust. The elective mode of obtaining rulers is the characteristic policy of republican government. The means relied on in this form of government for preventing their degeneracy are numerous and various. The most effectual one is such a limitation of the term of appointments, as will maintain a proper responsibility to the people.

Let me now ask what circumstance there is in the Constitution of the House of Representatives, that violates the principles of republican government; or favors the elevation of the few on the ruins of the many? Let me ask whether every circumstance is not, on the contrary, strictly conformable to these principles; and scrupulously impartial to the rights and pretensions of every class and description of citizens?

Who are to be the electors of the Federal Representatives? Not the rich more than the poor; not the learned more than the ignorant; not the haughty heirs of distinguished names, more than the humble sons of obscure and unpropitious fortune. The electors are to be the great body of the people of the United States. They are to be the same who exercise the right in every State of electing the correspondent branch of the Legislature of the State.

Who are to be the objects of popular choice? Every citizen whose merit may recommend him to the esteem and confidence of his country. No qualification of wealth, of birth, of religious faith, or of civil profession, is permitted to fetter the judgment or disappoint the inclination of the people.

If we consider the situation of the men on whom the free suffrages of their fellow citizens may confer the representative trust, we shall find it involving every security which can be devised or desired for their fidelity to their constituents.

In the first place, as they will have been distinguished by the preference of their fellow citizens, we are to presume, that in general, they will be somewhat distinguished also, by those qualities which entitle them to it, and which promise a sincere and scrupulous regard to the nature of their engagements.

In the second place, they will enter into the public service under circumstances which cannot fail to produce a temporary affection at least to their constituents. There is in every breast a sensibility to marks of honor, of favor, of esteem, and of confidence, which, apart from all considerations of interest, is some pledge for grateful and benevolent returns. Ingratitude is a common topic of declamation against human nature; and it must be confessed, that instances of it are but too frequent and flagrant both in public and in private life. But the universal and extreme indignation which it inspires, is itself a proof of the energy and prevalence of the contrary sentiment.

In the third place, these ties which bind the representative to his constituents are strengthened by motives of a more selfish nature. His pride and vanity attach him to a form of government which favors his pretensions, and gives him a share in its honors and distinctions. Whatever hopes or projects might be entertained by a few aspiring characters, it must generally happen that a great proportion of the men deriving their advancement from their influence with the people, would have more to hope from a preservation of the favor, than from innovations in the government subversive of the authority of the people.

All these securities however would be found very insufficient without the restraint of frequent elections. Hence, in the fourth place, the House of Representatives is so constituted as to support in the members an habitual recollection of their dependence on the people. Before the sentiments impressed on their minds by the mode of their elevation, can be effaced by the exercise of power, they will be compelled to anticipate the moment when their power is to cease, when their exercise of it is to be reviewed, and when they must descend to the level from which they were raised; there for ever to remain, unless a faithful discharge of their trust shall have established their title to a renewal of it.

I will add as a fifth circumstance in the situation of the House of Representatives, restraining them from oppressive measures, that they can make no law which will not have its full operation on themselves and their friends, as well as on the great mass of the society. This has always been deemed one of the strongest bonds by which human policy can connect the rules and the people together. It creates between them that communion of interests and sympathy of sentiments of which few governments have furnished examples; but without which every government degenerates into tyranny. If it be asked what is to restrain the House of Representatives from making legal discriminations in favor of themselves and a particular class of the society? I answer, the genius of the whole system, the nature of just and constitutional laws, and above all the vigilant and manly spirit which actuates the people of America, a spirit which nourishes freedom, and in return is nourished by it.

If this spirit shall ever be so far debased as to tolerate a law not obligatory on the Legislature as well as on the people, the people will be prepared to tolerate anything but liberty.

Such will be the relation between the House of Representatives and their constituents. Duty, gratitude, interest, ambition itself, are the chords by which they will be bound to fidelity and sympathy with the great mass of the people. It is possible that these may all be insufficient to controul the caprice and wickedness of man. But are they not all that government will admit, and that human prudence can devise? Are they not the genuine and the characteristic means by which Republican Government provides for the liberty and happiness of the people? Are they not the identical means on which every State Government in the Union, relies for the attainment of these important ends? . . .   ■

FEDERALIST 58

Within every successive term of ten years, a census of inhabitants is to be repeated. The unequivocal objects of these regulations are, first, to readjust from time to time the apportionment of representatives to the number of inhabitants; under the single exception that each state shall have one representative at least; Secondly, to augment the number of representatives at the same periods . . .

As far as experience has taken place on this subject, a gradual increase of representatives under the state constitutions, has at least kept pace with that of the constituents; and it appears that the former have been as ready to concur in such measures, as the latter have been to call for them.

There is a peculiarity in the federal constitution which ensures a watchful attention in a majority both of the people and of their representatives, to a consitutitional augmentation of the latter. The peculiarity lies in this, that one branch of the legislature is a representation of citizens; the other of the states: in the former consequently the larger states will have most weight; in the latter, the advantage will be in favour of the smaller states. From this circumstance it may with certainty be inferred, that the larger states will be strenuous advocates for increasing the number and weight of that part of the legislature in which their influence predominates. And it so happens that four only of the largest, will have a majority of the whole votes in the house of representives. Should the representatives or people therefore of the smaller states oppose at any time a reasonable addition of members, a coalition of a very few states will be sufficient to overrule the opposition; a coalition, which notwithstanding the rivalship and local prejudices which might prevent it on ordinary occasions, would not fail to take place, when not merely prompted by common interest, but justified by equity and the principles of the constitution.

It may be alledged, perhaps, that the senate would be prompted by like motives to an adverse coalition; and as their concurrence would be indispensable, the just and constitutional views of the other branch might be defeated. This is the difficulty which has probably created the most serious apprehensions in the zealous friends of a numerous representation. Fortunately it is among the difficulties which, existing only in appearance, vanish on a close and accurate inspection. The following reflections will, if I mistake not, be admitted to be conclusive and satisfactory on this point.

Notwithstanding the equal authority which will subsist between the two houses on all legislative subjects, except the originating of money bills, it cannot be doubted that the house composed of the greater number of members, when supported by the more powerful states, and speaking the known and determined sense of a majority of the people, will have no small advantage in a question depending on the comparative firmness of the two houses.

This advantage must be increased by the consciousness felt by the same side, of being supported in its demands, by right, by reason, and by the constitution; and the consciousness on the opposite side, of contending against the force of all these solemn considerations.

It is farther to be considered that in the gradation between the smallest and largest states, there are several which, though most likely in general to arrange themselves among the former, are too little removed in extent and population from the latter, to second an opposition to their just and legitimate pretensions. Hence it is by no means certain that a majority of votes, even in the senate, would be unfriendly to proper augmentations in the number of representatives.

It will not be looking too far to add, that the senators from all the new states may be gained over to the just views of the house of representatives, by an expedient too obvious to be overlooked. As these states will for a great length of time advance in population with peculiar rapidity, they will be interested in frequent reapportionments of the representatives to the number of inhabitants. The large states therefore, who will prevail in the house of representatives, will have nothing to do, but to make reapportionments and augmentations mutually conditions of each other; and the senators from all the most growing states will be bound to contend for the latter, by the interest which their states will feel in the former.

These considerations seem to afford ample security on this subject; and ought alone to satisfy all the doubts and fears which have been indulged with regard to it. Admitting however that, they should all be insufficient to subdue the unjust policy of the smaller states, or their predominant influence in the councils of the senate; a constitutional and infallible resource, still remains with the larger states, by which they will be able at all times to accomplish their just purposes. The house of representatives can not only refuse, but they alone can propose the supplies requisite for the support of government. They in a word hold the purse; that powerful instrument by which we behold in the history of the British constitution, an infant and humble representation of the people, gradually enlarging the sphere of its activity and importance, and finally reducing, as far as it seems to have wished, all the overgrown prerogatives of the other branches of the government. This power over the purse, may in fact be regarded as the most compleat and effectual weapon with which any constitution can arm the immediate representatives of the people, for obtaining a redress of every grievance, and for carrying into effect every just and salutary measure. . . .

In this review of the constitution of the house of representatives, I have passed over the circumstance of economy which in the present state of affairs might have had some effect in lessening the temporary number of representatives; and a disregard of which would probably have been as rich a theme of declamation against the constitution as has been furnished by the smallness of the number proposed. I omit also any remarks on the difficulty which might be found, under present circumstances, in engaging in the federal service, a large number of such characters as the people will probably elect. One observation however I must be permitted, to add, on this subject, as claiming in my judgment a very serious attention. It is, that in all legislative assemblies, the greater the number composing them may be, the fewer will be the men who will in fact direct their proceedings. In the first place, the more numerous any assembly may be, of whatever characers composed, the greater is known to be the ascendancy of passion over reason. In the next place, the larger the number, the greater will be the proportion of members of limited information and of weak capacities. Now it is precisely on characters of this description that the eloquence and address of the few are known to act with all their force. In the antient republics, where the whole body of the people assembled in person, a single orator, or an artful statesman, was generally seen to rule with as compleat a sway, as if a sceptre had been placed in his single hands. On the same principle the more multitudinous a representative assembly may be rendered, the more it will partake of the infirmities incident to collective meetings of the people. Ignorance will be the dupe of cunning; and passion the slave of sophistry and declamation. The people can never err more than in supposing that by multiplying their representatives, beyond a certain limit, they strengthen the barrier against the government of a few. Experience will forever admonish them that on the contrary, *after securing a sufficient number for the purposes of safety, of local information, and of diffusive sympathy with the whole society,* they will counteract their own views by every addition to their representatives. The countenance of the government may become more democratic; but the soul that animates it will be more oligarchic. The machine will be enlarged, but the fewer and often, the more secret will be the springs by which its motions are directed.

As connected with the objection against the number of representatives, may properly be here noticed, that which has been suggested against the number made competent for legislative business. It has been said that more than a majority ought to have been required for a quorum, and in particular cases, if not in all, more than a majority of a quorum for a decision. That some advantages might have resulted from such a precaution, cannot be denied. It might have been an additional shield to some particular interests, and another obstacle generally to hasty and partial measures. But these considerations are outweighed by the inconveniencies in the opposite scale. In all cases where justice or the general good might require new laws to be passed, or active measures to be pursued, the fundamental principle of free government would be reversed. It would be no longer the majority that would rule; the power would be transferred to the minority. Were the defensive privilege limited to particular cases, an interested minority might take advantage of it to screen themselves from equitable sacrifices to the general weal, or in particular emergencies to extort unreasonable indulgences. Lastly, it would facilitate and foster the baneful practice of secessions; a practice which has shewn itself even in states where a majority only is required; a practice subversive of all the principles of order and regular government; a practice which leads more directly to public convulsions, and the ruin of popular governments, than any other which has yet been displayed among us.   ∎

FEDERALIST 62

Having examined the constitution of the house of representatives, and answered such of the objections against it as seemed to merit notice, I enter next on the examination of the senate. The heads into which this member of the government may be considered, are I. the qualifications of senators. II. the appointment of them by the state legislatures. III. the equality of representation in the senate. IV. the number of senators, and the term for which they are to be elected. V. the powers vested in the senate.

I. The qualifications proposed for senators, as distinguished from those of representatives, consist in a more advanced age, and a longer period of citizenship. A senator must be thirty years of age at least; as a representative, must be twenty-five. And the former must have been a citizen nine years; as seven years are required for the latter. The propriety of these distinctions is explained by the nature of the senatorial trust; which requiring greater extent of information and stability of character, requires at the same time that the senator should have reached a period of life most likely to supply these advantages; and which participating immediately in transactions with foreign nations, ought to be exercised by none who are not thoroughly weaned from the prepossessions and habits incident to foreign birth and education. The term of nine years appears to be a prudent mediocrity between a total exclusion of adopted citizens, whose merit and talents may claim a share in the public confidence; and an indiscriminate and hasty admission of them, which might create a channel for foreign influence on the national councils.

II. It is equally unnecessary to dilate on the appointment of senators by the state legislatures. Among the various modes which might have been devised for constituting this branch of the government, that which has been proposed by the convention is probably the most congenial with the public opinion. It is recommended by the double advantage of favouring a select appointment, and of giving to the state governments such an agency in the formation of the federal government, as must secure the authority of the former; and may form a convenient link between the two systems.

III. The equality of representation in the senate is another point, which, being evidently the result of compromise between the opposite pretensions of the large and the small states, does not call for much discussion. If indeed it be right that among a people thoroughly incorporated into one nation, every district ought to have a *proportional* share in the government; and that among independent and sovereign states bound together by a simple league, the parties however unequal in size, ought to have an *equal* share in the common councils, it does not appear to be without some reason, that in a compound republic partaking both of the national and federal character, the government ought to be founded on a mixture of the principles of proportional and equal representation. But it is superfluous to try by the standards of theory, a part of the constitution which is allowed on all hands to be the result not of theory, but "of a spirit of amity, and that mutual deference and concession which the peculiarity of our political situation rendered indispensable." A common government with powers equal to its objects, is called for by the voice, and still more loudly by the political situation of America. A government founded on principles more consonant to the wishes of the larger states, is not likely to be obtained from the smaller states. The only option then for the former lies between the proposed government and a government still more objectionable. Under this alternative the advice of prudence must be, to embrace the lesser evil; and instead of indulging a fruitless anticipation of the possible mischiefs which may ensue, to contemplate rather the advantageous consequences which may qualify the sacrifice.

In this spirit it may be remarked, that the equal vote allowed to each state, is at once a constitutional recognition of the portion of sovereignty remaining in the individual states, and an instrument for preserving that residuary sovereignty. So far the equality ought to be no less acceptable to the large than to the small states; since they are not less solicitous to guard by every possible expedient against an improper consolidation of the states into one simple republic.

Another advantage accruing from this ingredient in the constitution of the senate, is the additional impediment it must prove against improper acts of legislation. No law or resolution can now be passed without the concurrence first of a majority of the people, and then of a majority of the states. It must be acknowledged that this complicated check on legislation may in some instances be injurious as well as beneficial; and that the peculiar defence which it involves in favour of the smaller states would be more rational, if any interests common to them, and distinct from those of the other states, would otherwise be exposed to peculiar danger. But as the larger states will always be able by their power over the supplies to defeat unreasonable exertions of this prerogative of the lesser states; and as the facility and excess of law-making seem to be the diseases to which our governments are most liable, it is not impossible that this part of the constitution may be more convenient in practice than it appears to many in contemplation.

IV. The number of senators and the duration of their appointment come next to be considered. In order to form an accurate judgment on both these points, it will be proper to enquire into the purposes which are to be answered by a senate; and in order to ascertain these it will be necessary to review the inconveniencies which a republic must suffer from the want of such an institution.

First. It is a misfortune incident to republican government, though in a less degree than to other governments, that those who administer it, may forget their obligations to their constituents, and prove unfaithful to their important trust. In this point of view, a senate, as a second branch of the legislative assembly, distinct from, and dividing the power with, a first, must be in all cases a salutary check on the government. It doubles the security to the people, by requiring the concurrence of two distinct bodies in schemes of usurpation or perfidy, where the ambition or corruption of one, would otherwise be sufficient. . . .

Secondly. The necessity of a senate is not less indicated by the propensity of all single and numerous assemblies, to yield to the impulse of sudden and violent passions, and to be seduced by factious leaders, into intemperate and pernicious resolutions. Examples on this subject might be cited without number; and from proceedings within the United States, as well as from the history of other nations. But a position that will not be contradicted need not be proved. All that need be remarked is that a body which is to correct this infirmity ought itself be free from it, and consequently ought to be less numerous. It ought moreover to possess great firmness, and consequently ought to hold its authority by a tenure of considerable duration.

Thirdly. Another defect to be supplied by a senate lies in a want of due acquaintance with the objects and principles of legislation. It is not possible that an assembly of men called for the most part from pursuits of a private nature, continued in appointment for a short time, and led by no permanent motive to devote the intervals of public occupation to a study of the laws, the affairs and the comprehensive interests of their country, should, if left wholly to themselves, escape a variety of important errors in the exercise of their legislative trust. It may be affirmed, on the best grounds, that no small share of the present embarrassments of America is to be charged on the blunders of our governments; and that these have proceeded from the heads rather than the hearts of most of the authors of them. What indeed are all the repealing, explaining and amending laws, which fill and disgrace our voluminous codes, but so many monuments of deficient wisdom; so many impeachments exhibited by each succeeding, against each preceding session; so many admonitions to the people of the value of those aids which may be expected from a well constituted senate? . . .

Fourthly. The mutability in the public councils, arising from a rapid succession of new members, however qualified they may be, points out in the strongest manner, the necessity of some stable institution in the government. Every new election in the states, is found to change one half of the representatives. From this change of men must proceed a change of opinions; and from a change of opinions, a change of measures. But a continual change even of good measures is inconsistent with every rule of prudence, and every prospect of success. The remark is verified in private life, and becomes more just as well as more important, in national transactions. . . .

No government any more than an individual will long be respected, without being truly respectable, nor be truly respectable without possessing a certain portion of order and stability. ■

FEDERALIST 63

A FIFTH desideratum illustrating the utility of a Senate, is the want of a due sense of national character. Without a select and stable member of the government, the esteem of foreign powers will not only be forfeited by an unenlightened and variable policy, proceeding from the causes already mentioned; but the national councils will not possess that sensibility to the opinion of the world, which is perhaps not less necessary in order to merit, than it is to obtain, its respect and confidence. . . .

Yet however requisite a sense of national character may be, it is evident that it can never be sufficiently possessed by a numerous and changeble body. It can only be found in a number so small, that a sensible degree of the praise and blame of public measures may be the portion of each individual; or in an assembly so durably invested with public trust, that the pride and consequence of its members may be sensibly incorporated with the reputation and prosperity of the community. . . .

I add as a *sixth* defect, the want in some important cases of a due responsibility in the government to the people, arising from that frequency of elections, which in other cases produces this responsibility. This remark will perhaps appear not only new but paradoxical. It must nevertheless be acknowledged, when explained, to be as undeniable as it is important.

Responsibility in order to be reasonable must be limited to objects within the power of the responsible party; and in order to be effectual, must relate to operations of that power, of which a ready and proper judgment can be formed by the constituents. The objects of government may be divided into two general classes; the one depending on measures which have singly an immediate and sensible operation; the other depending on a succession of well chosen and well connected measures, which have a gradual and perhaps unobserved operation. The importance of the latter description to the collective and permanent welfare of every country needs no explanation. And yet it is evident, that an assembly elected for so short a term as to be unable to provide more than one or two links in a chain of measures, on which the general welfare may essentially depend, ought not to be answerable for the final result, any more than a steward or tenant, engaged for one year, could be justly made to answer for places or improvements, which could not be accomplished in less than half a dozen years. Nor is it possible for the people to estimate the *share* of influence which their annual assemblies may respectively have on events resulting from the mixed transactions of several years. It is sufficiently difficult at any rate to preserve a personal responsibility in the members of a *numerous* body, for such acts of the body as have an immediate, detached and palpable operation on its constituents.

The proper remedy for this defect must be an additional body in the legislative department, which, having sufficient permanency to provide for such objects as require a continued attention, and a train of measures, may be justly and effectually answerable for the attainment of those objects.

Thus far I have considered the circumstances which point out the necessity of a well constructed senate, only as they relate to the representatives of the people. To a people as little blinded by prejudice, or corrupted by flattery, as those whom I address, I shall not scruple to add, that such an institution may be sometimes necessary, as a defence to the people against their own temporary errors and delusions. As the cool and deliberate sense of the community ought in all governments, and actually will in all free governments ultimately prevail over the views of its rulers; so there are particular moments in public affairs, when the people stimulated by some irregular passion, or some illicit advantage, or misled by the artful misrepresentations of interested men, may call for measures which they themselves will afterwards be the most ready to lament and condemn. In these critical moments, how salutary will be the interference of some temperate and respectable body of citizens, in order to check the misguided career, and to suspend the blow meditated by the people against themselves, until reason, justice and truth, can regain their authority over the public mind? What bitter anguish would not the people of Athens have often escaped, if their government had contained so provident a safeguard against the tyranny of their own passions? Popular liberty might then have escaped the indelible reproach of decreeing to the same citizens, the hemlock on one day, and statues on the next. . . .

. . . I am not unaware of the circumstances which distinguish the American from other popular governments, as well antient as modern; and which render extreme circumspection necessary in reasoning from the one case to the other. But after allowing due weight to this consideration, it may still be maintained that there are many points of similitude which render these examples not unworthy of our attention. Many of the defects as we have seen, which can only be supplied by a senatorial institution, are common to a numerous assembly frequently elected by the people, and to the people themselves. There are others peculiar to the former, which require the controul of such an institution. The people can never wilfully betray their own interests: But they may possibly be betrayed by the representatives of the people; and the danger will be evidently greater where the whole legislative trust is lodged in the hands of one body of men, than where the concurrence of separate and dissimilar bodies is required in every public act. . . .

In answer to all these arguments, suggested by reason, illustrated by examples, and enforced by our own experience, the jealous adversary of the constitution will probably content himself with repeating, that a senate appointed not immediately by the poeple, and for the term of six years, must gradually acquire a dangerous preeminence in the government, and finally transform it into a tyrannical aristocracy.

To this general answer the general reply ought to be sufficient; that liberty may be endangered by the abuses of liberty, as well as by the abuses of power; that there are numerous instances of the former as well as of the latter; and that the former rather than the latter is apparently most to be apprehended by the United States. But a more particular reply may be given.

Before such a revolution can be effected, the senate, it is to be observed, must in the first place corrupt itself; must next corrupt the state legislatures, must then corrupt the house of representatives, and must finally corrupt the people at large. It is evident that the senate must be first corrupted, before it can attempt an establishment of tyranny. Without corrupting the state legislatures, it cannot prosecute the attempt, because the periodical change of members would otherwise regenerate the whole body. Without exerting the means of corruption with equal success on the house of representatives, the opposition of that coequal branch of the government would inevitably defeat the attempt; and without corrupting the people themselves, a succession of new representatives would speedily restore all things to their pristine order. Is there any man who can seriously persuade himself, that the proposed senate can, by any possible means within the compass of human address, arrive at the object of a lawless ambition, through all these obstructions? . . .

Besides the conclusive evidence resulting from this assemblage of facts, that the federal senate will never be able to transform itself, by gradual usurpations, into an independent and aristocratic body; we are warranted in believing that if such a revolution should ever happen from causes which the foresight of man cannot guard against, the house of representatives with the people on their side will at all times be able to bring back the constitution to its primitive form and principles. Against the force of the immediate representative of the people, nothing will be able to maintain even the constitutional authority of the senate, but such a display of enlightened policy, and attachment to the public good, as will divide with that branch of the legislature, the affections and support of the entire body of the people themselves.   ■

DEVELOPMENTS THROUGH THE YEARS

Structurally, the elements of our national government, including the Congress, have remained largely unchanged ever since they were first written into the Constitution in 1787. One political scientist, Samuel C. Patterson, has written:

> If Henry Clay were alive today, and he were to serve again in the House and Senate to which he was chosen so many times in the 19th century, he would find much that was very familiar. He would certainly recognize where he was, and perhaps after some initial shock he surely would be reasonably comfortable in the modern congressional envelope.[1]

Yet, as Professor Patterson himself has catalogued, the Congress *has* changed in a number of ways. In an article, excerpted here, by then Speaker of the House Thomas P. "Tip" O'Neill, Jr., who served in that capacity through 1986, we consider some of the changes that have taken place in the first 200 years in the life of Congress. Speaker O'Neill mentions, for example, the early advent of political parties, as well as the recent weakening of their hold. He also mentions the great increase in the number and influence of congressional staff and the relative increase in presidential power in the executive-legislative relationship.

Excerpted here, too, is a report of a Select Committee on Committees of the U. S. House of Representatives. This report details congressional changes in the 1970s, indicating, among other things, that House power has

---

1. Samuel C. Patterson, "The Semi-Sovereign Congress," in Anthony King, ed., *The New American Political Systems* (Washington, D. C.: American Enterprise Institute, 1977), p. 131.

become both more centralized, with an increase in the authority of the Speaker, and more decentralized, as a result of the enhancement of subcommittee authority at the expense of committees and committee chairs.

CONGRESS: THE FIRST TWO HUNDRED YEARS
Thomas P. O'Neill, Jr.

As we approach the Bicentennial of the Constitution and the Congress it created, it is appropriate to consider how the legislative branch of our federal government has developed during its nearly 200 years of existence. It might be both interesting and useful to see how much Congress has turned out the way the Drafters of the Constitution conceived it, as well as how much of the evolution of Congress was not anticipated by them.

Take the development of political parties, for example. It is hard to imagine our government functioning without a strong two-party system. Yet the Continental Congress and the Articles of Confederation Congress existed without parties. The idea of political parties apparently never arose at the Constitutional Convention, either; a careful reading of James Madison's *Notes of Debates in the Federal Convention of 1787* does not reveal any indication that political parties were at all anticipated by the delegates.

Such a remarkable lack of prescience on the part of this talented and experienced group has had incredible consequences for the Congress and for the Nation. We normally consider the role of political parties in the House or the Senate only in terms of partisan votes on legislative issues or the means for selection of internal leadership positions. The existence of political parties, however, has changed dramatically the basic relationship between the Congress and the president in a way unanticipated in 1787.

Specifically, when the Constitutional Convention considered the method of electing the president, only one state delegation—Pennsylvania—felt that the president of the United States should be elected directly by the people. After much discussion and negotiation, the delegates decided upon indirect election of the president, using electors meeting in their separate states to cast their votes. Because of the lack of communications facilities at the time and the lack of nationally popular leaders other than George Washington, it was commonly assumed that the electoral vote generally would be indecisive. George Mason, one of the luminaries of the Revolutionary War period and a delegate to the Convention, guessed that "nineteen times in twenty" there would be no presidential majority in the electoral college.

How, then, did the delegates think that the president would be elected? The answer, found in Article II, Section 1 of the Constitution, is that the House of Representatives—each state delegation having one vote—would usually elect the president. The candidate with the majority of state delegations would become president. The second-place finisher would become vice president. If there were a tie for second, the Senate would choose the vice president. Coupled with modifications by the Twelfth Amendment to the Constitution, this is the arrangement today.

The two-party system completely wrecked this carefully wrought plan, for only twice (Thomas Jefferson in 1801 and John Quincy Adams in 1825) has the House been called upon to elect the president. This is not to say that the way things have developed is bad or wrong. On the contrary, I believe we have a much better system than anticipated. But the plan to make the president dependent upon the Congress for election in most instances was all part of the balance designed by the men who wrote the Constitution.

Delegates to the Convention seem to have anticipated that a candidate for president would have to forge an alliance with the House of Representatives in order to attain the presidency. Presidents would not assume office with what has been too often the case in recent years—a highly personal interpretation that they have been given a specific mandate by the American people to whip the Congress into shape and force it to respond to their own interpretation of what is best for the country. On the contrary, the Constitution does not give to the president alone the power to interpret and execute the popular will.

Even during my thirty-some years in Congress, the party system has changed a lot, and some of these changes have hurt the ability of Congress to act effectively. When I first entered the House in 1953, it seemed that most of the members had worked their way up through the ranks to get to the House of Representatives. They had worked for their party on the local or state level and had served in some kind of local office, like mayor or alderman or city commissioner. Perhaps they had served in the state legislature, as I did, and they knew what it meant to follow the leadership and learn the art of legislation. There were not many members in those days who set out on their own with complete disregard for the party to which they belonged. They had some understanding of government and how it works.

The party system is much different today, and I believe it works to our detriment as a Congress. Men and women are elected to the House without having previously held elective office. They can get elected because they raise the money and hire a media consultant and get on television. Some of them do not care about what party they belong to, and they feel as if they owe the party nothing when they take office. The House has always been a difficult body to lead; I do not believe, though, that even Henry Clay, despite the many problems he had with John Randolph of Roanoke who brought his hunting dogs on the floor of the House, ever had to deal with as many independent members as are found in the modern House of Representatives. The result has been a breakdown of party discipline and a refusal to follow party leadership, which leads in turn to congressional paralysis and an inability to act coherently as a legislative body.

Other fundamental changes have occurred in Congress over the past 200 years. Congressional tenures, for instance, have become much longer. Most of the men—there were only men in the Congress in those days—who served in the first years of the Republic stayed for only a term or two. The custom was that a representative would leave his farm or business or profession and go to Washington for a few years. He would stay in a boarding house, eat his meals with other members of the House and Senate, and curse the insects, Washington's heat and humidity, and the open sewer that ran near the Capitol building.

For the first fifty or so Congresses, very few men made a career of service in the House or the Senate. Until about 1880, more than half the men elected to each Congress were first-termers. Service of long duration, like that of Nathaniel Macon (1791–1828), Samuel Smith (1793–1833), and William R. King (1811–16, 1819–44, 1848–52), was most unusual. As we passed into the twentieth century, elective office became more of a career than a temporary public service.

Concurrent with the longer tenure in office, seniority began to acquire greater significance in leadership assignments in the Congress. Throughout the first century or so in the House of Representatives, the Speaker switched committee chairmen as he wished, often naming large numbers of new ones at the beginning of each Congress. His power to do this was enhanced by the relatively short careers of most congressmen of the time. By 1900, when the trend toward longer service in Congress was well-established, it had become accepted practice in both the House and the Senate that a member would move up in seniority as he outlasted other members of his party on a particular committee. When he reached the top of the ladder, he would become the committee chairman, provided that his party had a majority in his branch of the Congress. It still works this way in the Senate.

The House, however, has recently introduced an element of flexibility into the process of committee chair selection. The Democratic Caucus, whose rules control the House as long as the Democras have a majority, adopted a series of reforms in 1974. These changes require a secret ballot election for committee chairmen at the beginning of each Congress and limit a member to one subcommittee chairmanship. As a practical matter, seniority is still quite important in deciding who will chair a House committee, but it is no longer the only consideration.

There are other developments in the Congress that would surprise the men who drafted the Constitution in 1787. The Constitutional Convention, for example, was able to get by with only one staff person to help with its work. The growth of federal responsibilities and activities over the past 200 years, however, has meant that every branch of the government has increased in size since the first years of the Republic. This is as true for the Congress, which began in 1789 with only ninety-one members and a miniscule staff, as for any other branch.

For their first fifty years, the House and the Senate were able to function without having staff for particular congressional committees. By 1891, the first year for which we have good data, a total of 103 persons worked full-time for congressional committees. This assistance helped ease the committee members' workload, and as committee responsibilities have increased over the past ninety years, the number of committee staff persons has grown to just over 3000. Until almost the end of the nineteenth century, however, there was no such thing as personal staff support for a member of Congress. By 1930, the total of these congressional staffs was some 1569 persons. Fifty years later, some 14,000 individuals served the Congress as personal or committee staff members, an eightfold increase. By comparison, the national budget, for which Congress is responsible, increased by more than 172 times during this same period.

It is not unreasonable to believe that Congress has required an increase in staff assistance to enable it to cope with the growth of the national budget and the increased complexity of the federal government as a whole. The president is able to obtain information and advice from the Office of Management and Budget, the White House staff, and the thousands of analysts, statisticians, and managers elsewhere in the executive branch of the government. If the Congress is to consider legislation, appropriate hundreds of billions of dollars, perform its oversight of executive branch operations, answer millions of letters, and act as ombudsman for harassed constituents, it needs a staff much greater than the one man who served the delegates to the Constitutional Convention in 1787.

Although the role of members of Congress has expanded greatly over the past 200 years, they still have a responsibility to their constituencies. The difference, however, is the scope of these duties. Just over 100 years ago (1882) a congressman from Michigan, Roswell G. Horr, placed in the record an account of the typical constituent-service duties and activities:

> . . . I think it is safe to say that each member of this House receives fifty letters each week; many receive more . . . . Growing out of these letters will be found during each week a large number of errands, a vast amount of what is called department work. One-quarter of them, perhaps, will be from soldiers asking aid in their pension cases, and each soldier is clear in his own mind that the member can help his case out if he will only make it a special case and give it special attention.
>
> Another man writes you to look up some matter in reference to a land patent. Another says his homestead claim should be looked after and he wants you to learn and let him know why he does not receive his full title. Another has invented some machine and the department have [sic] declared his discovery to be already supplemented by some former inventor, and have [sic] refused his patent. He would like you to go through the Patent Office and look over the patent laws and see if great injustice has not been done in his case. Another has a son or brother in the Regular Army whom he would like to have discharged.
>
> Another has a recreant son whom he would like to get into the Regular Army or Navy. In conformity with these requests you are liable to be called upon, perhaps several times in one week, by these applicants in personam, and they will require you to go at once and exert your enormous powers.

Recall that the members who preceded Representative Horr, as well as those who came along many years after, performed all of these functions personally. The fifty letters a week received by Representative Horr, however, have become more than 5000 a week for the typical member of the House. All of this mail needs to be answered, even if it is only a simple acknowledgement.

Much of this incoming mail is issue-oriented, and the marriage of the computer to the high-speed printer enables a well-organized, well-financed interest group to generate literally millions of letters to Congress on a given topic. If members did not in turn rely upon their own computers and computer operators to respond to this mass-generated correspondence, they would slowly disappear beneath a sea of paper. The computer age is upon us, and for better or worse the Congress has had to adjust its way of doing business to reflect this reality.

Certain realities have not changed. Constituents need help with some agency or department of the executive branch. By the time someone writes his or her member of Congress, you can be fairly certain that a long and frustrating history has already taken place. Many citizens today feel with some justification that too much of government has become large and impersonal. When there is a problem with their Social Security benefits or their Veterans Administration benefits, the ordinary citizen often feels reduced to nothing more than a multidigit number, dealt with in an impersonal fashion. The member can step in, cut through the Gordian knot of bureaucracy, and see to it that the citizen receives his or her due. Members of Congress have been helping their constituents in this manner since the beginning of the Republic, and I cannot imagine that anyone today would suggest that this is not an appropriate role for the Congress.

Finally, I would like to consider the relationship of the Congress and the president, in its idealized state, as it actually exists, and as I believe it should exist. When most of us were going through what used to be called civics class, we were taught that there were three branches of government at the national level. The legislative branch, we were taught, makes the laws; the executive branch enforces the laws; and the judicial branch interprets the laws. In a general sense, this scheme is correct.

But the distinction between making and enforcing laws has become blurred over the years with the advent of executive branch regulation making and the congressional veto. Even the courts have gone far beyond merely "interpreting' the law and have been performing such executive functions as administering state prison systems and redrawing school district boundaries. I believe that this blurring of duties will continue for the foreseeable future, and no amount of railing for a return to the good old days will do one bit of good.

If I could accomplish one thing as Speaker of the House of Representatives, it would be to teach the American public that the Congress is a coequal branch of the federal government, with its own set of powers and responsibilities. It is not the duty of the House or the Senate to accede to the wishes of the president, just because the president occupies the Oval Office. Indeed, the Congress and the president were intentionally set at cross-purposes by the men who drafted the Constitution. Sometimes a powerful president has been able to dominate the Congress; sometimes the Congress has run over a president. The locus of power in the government swings back and forth between these two branches.

In my own lifetime, the man who was most responsible for concentrating power in the presidency was Franklin D. Roosevelt. A dynamic individual, he knew how to make the Congress bow to his will. After him other presidents, regardless of party, were able to build on Roosevelt's legacy and increase the power of the presidency.

The growth of personal and committee staffs has certainly given the Congress a better chance to meet the president on an equal basis. There are also certain congressionally initiated statutes that have recently increased the power and influence of the House and Senate, specifically the War Powers Act and the anti-impoundment provisions of the Budget Act of 1974.

The War Powers Act was passed over President Richard M. Nixon's veto in 1973 by a Congress that was reasserting its constitutional primacy in the war area. Twice since 1950 — in Korea and in Vietnam — the United States has found itself in a hot war without a specific congressional declaration of war. Some people might argue that the War Powers Act is too much of a restriction on the president, but I see it as a return to the intent of the Constitution. I see the same principle in the anti-impoundment law incorporated in the Budget Act of 1974, which was largely a reaction to President Nixon's refusal to spend certain funds that had been appropriated by Congress.

In 1972 alone, President Nixon refused to spend $2.5 billion for highway construction, $1.9 billion in defense funds, and $1.5 billion for such programs as food stamps, rural water and waste disposal, and rural electrification. The proper and constitutional way for him to object to these appropriations would have been to veto the appropriations bill. Such action would have given the Congress an opportunity to override him; impoundment — refusing to spend the money that had been appropriated — leaves the Congress high and dry with little means to protest effectively. I believe this law was greatly needed and helps restores a balance to the government. Parenthetically, I would point out that the much-discussed presidential line-item veto would undermine congressional power in the budget process and could result in the elimination of many programs, such as federal aid to libraries or museums, that are favored by a majority of the Congress but opposed by an administration. The anti-impoundment law is the sole protector of these programs today.

The biggest advantage a modern president has is the six o'clock news. Presidents can be on the news every night if they want to — and usually they want to. They can easily make themselves the focus of every major news report, because the president of the United States is unarguably the most powerful individual in the world. And it is precisely for this reason that the Congress has a duty and a responsibility to act to counterbalance this power. The Congress is composed of the collective wisdom of 435 members of the House and 100 members of the Senate, men and women who bring to the Nation's capital every conceivable combination of education and experience, 535 individuals who together represent the richness and diversity of our country. Who is to say that this group, this Congress, should bow to the wishes of any one individual, no matter who that individual may be? No, the Congress has its own role to play, and it has always been a difficult one.

One of my predecessors as Speaker, Nicholas Longworth, a Republican who served with a Republican president in a Republican Congress, spoke some sixty years ago of the public perception problem faced by the Congress. His words are humorous, but I do not feel they are exaggerated:

> I have been a member of the House of Representatives ten terms. That is twenty years. During the whole of that time we have been attacked, denounced, despised, hunted, harried, blamed, looked down upon, excoriated, and flayed.

I refuse to take it personally. I have looked into history. I find that we did not start being unpopular when I became a Congressman. We were unpopular before that time. . . .

From the beginning of the Republic it has been the duty of every free-born voter to look down upon us, and the duty of every free-born humorist to make jokes at us.

Always there is something—and, in fact, almost always there is almost everything—wrong with us. We simply can not be right.

Let me illustrate. Suppose we pass a lot of laws. Do we get praised? Certainly not. We then get denounced by everybody for being a "Meddlesome Congress" and for being a "Busybody Congress." Is it not so?

But suppose we take warning from that experience. Suppose that in our succeeding session we pass only a few laws. Are we any better off? Certainly not. Then everybody . . . denounces us for being an "Incompetent Congress" and a "Do-Nothing Congress."

We have no escape—absolutely none.

We have no chance—just absolutely no chance. The only way for a Congressman to be happy is to realize that he has no chance.

Speaker Longworth's words often seem as accurate to me today as when they were first published in the mid-1920s. I hope we can change this situation in the future. If we can use this Bicentennial to restore in the public mind the equality that was intended between the Congress and the president, then we will have accomplished something truly significant and historic. In so doing we offer the greatest possible tribute to those men who almost 200 years ago sat through a hot summer in Philadelphia and drafted the greatest Constitution the world has ever known, and we will have accomplished something that will have a lasting effect on our great nation long after we and this Bicentennial are only distant memories. ■

CONGRESSIONAL CHANGES IN THE 1970s
Select Committee on Committees, U.S. House of Representatives

SECTION I—OVERVIEW OF PRINCIPAL LEGISLATIVE DEVELOPMENTS OF THE 1970s

The 1970s have been a period of fundamental change in the House of Representatives. Not since the congressional revolution of 1910 and the accompanying progressive era has there been a comparable overhaul of House procedures and practices. These modern changes have been influenced by the steady influx of new members who differ in their attitudes and experiences from an earlier generation of Representatives. Changes have also occurred through reform in the procedures and norms of the House.

Government at all levels has been the target of public criticism during the past decade. Public confidence in governmental institutions and elected leaders has declined to unprecedented levels. The number and complexity of public policy issues seem immune to remedial action by government at both the federal and local levels. Rivalry and conflict between the branches of the federal government have increased, and seem likely to continue.

In response to these pressures, the Congress generally, and the House in particular, has made a number of significant changes in its organization and procedure. The goals of these reforms were (1) to increase the public accountability of the Congress; (2) to strengthen the legislative branch to maintain its constitutional role as a "co-equal" partner in the federal system; and (3) to make the House a more democratic institution, while, at the same time, making the congressional leadership more effective.

The issues delineated below have contributed significantly to a number of key legislative developments during the 1970s:

1. More openness.
2. The expanding workload of Congress.
3. Growth in the number of ad hoc groups.
4. Larger membership turnover.
5. Greater dispersal of power of subcommittees.
6. Some steps toward a stronger Speakership.
7. New multiple referral process.
8. Increase in staff.
9. Resurgence of the party caucus.
10. Decline of informal membership norms.

OPENNESS

During the 1970s, the Congress responded to demands for greater public accountability. One manifestation of this spirit was in opening many congressional activities which previously had been closed to the public and the press.

Although congressional committees had, on rare occasions, permitted live coverage of their proceedings, provisions were included in the 1970 Legislative Reorganization Act establishing standard committee guidelines for broadcast media coverage of their hearings. In 1974, House Rules were amended to additionally permit broadcast coverage of committee markup sessions.

Prior to 1970, no public accounting of members' votes in Committee of the Whole was possible. The Reorganization Act of that year established procedures for a "recorded teller vote" through which members votes in Committee of the Whole could be published in the Congressional Record. Subsequently, the House installed an electronic voting system with which to expedite the conduct of all of its votes and quorum calls. Some observers have claimed the installation of the electronic voting system, by reducing the time required for the House vote, has, in fact, contributed to the overall frequency with which recorded votes are demanded.

The 1970 Reorganization Act also dealt with voting in committee. Previously, no written public record of votes in committee was maintained. The Reorganization Act required that the results of each rollcall vote in committee, and each member's vote, be recorded, and made available for public inspection. Committees were also required to include in their reports on bills the results of the vote by which the committee approved the measure.

In 1973, the House adopted rules changes requiring that most committee meetings be open to the public. In prior years, approximately 30 percent of all committee meetings were held in executive, or closed, session. Some committees held upwards of 90 percent of their meetings in closed session. Now, virtually all committee meetings, hearings, and markup sessions are open to the public.

Increasingly, opposition to committee openness has been voiced: Open meetings unnecessarily slow the legislative process; open sessions are inherently formal sessions, and thus, require more time to achieve the same decisions that could have been reached more informally. Open sessions may inhibit the range of discussion in committee meetings as members are mindful of press coverage and hesitate to publicly explore controversial issues. Open sessions make it more difficult for members to change their positions once they have been publicly announced. Open sessions generally assure the presence of lobbyists and representatives of special interest organizations at committee meetings. Their presence may put undue pressure on members. Some observers also charge that open sessions inhibit the discussions and compromises which are an essential part of House-Senate conference committee meetings; increasingly, conferees meet informally to agree upon a position which will then be offered *pro forma* at an open session.

EXPANDING WORKLOAD OF CONGRESS

Between the 92nd and the 95th Congress, the number of days in session has increased, but not markedly, from 295 to 323. During the same period, there has been a decline in the number of bills enacted, from 265 to 250. The increase in the number of congressional committee and subcommittee meetings is even more significant. Between the 91st and the 95th Congresses, the number of committee meetings increased by over 30 percent, from 5,066 to 6,771. Moreover, the number of record votes has increased from 193 in the 92d Congress to 505 in the 95th Congress.

Other indexes of congressional workload have increased as well. The House Post Office has steadily increased the amount of mail processed. It is estimated to have tripled in volume from 1972 to 1979. More specifically, the volume of mail has increased over 300 percent during the past six years.

Changes in the volume of congressional workload seem to have been accompanied by an increase in its complexity, as well.

GROWTH IN NUMBER OF AD HOC GROUPS

Within recent Congresses, there has been an unprecedented growth in both the number, and organizational complexity of informal member associations which seek to influence the policymaking process. Prior to 1970, only three informal congressional groups were organized: DSG (1959), the House (Republican) Wednesday Group (1964), and the bicameral, bipartisan members of Congress for Peace Through Law (1966). As of May 1979, the number of member groups has risen more than three dozen.

In recent years, the major emphasis among new informal groups has been a bipartisan orientation which underscores economic and regional shared interests over partisan considerations. Since the 91st Congress, 19 bipartisan groups have been formally organized, only three new partisan groups have emerged.

Along with this bipartisan orientation has been an informal group orientation toward single issue concentration and regional organizations. During the 94th and 95th Congresses, informal groups organized with a concentration on Vietnam-era veterans affairs, problems affecting seaports, textiles, the steel industry, oceans policy, the Washington metropolitan area, suburban areas, the "Sunbelt," the "Frostbelt," blue-collar workers, congressional employees, and alternative energy resources, among others.

Three new bipartisan groups supplemented earlier groups organized to examine policy issues relating to the New England States, The Great Lakes Region, rural areas, and black Americans.

LARGE MEMBERSHIP TURNOVER

In recent years, the House has undergone significant membership turnover, especially considering that at the beginning of the 92d Congress, 20 percent of its membership had been elected to at least 10 terms. Howeever, at the beginning of the second session of the 94th Congress in 1976, only 14 percent of House members met the 10-term criterion (the lowest since 1955).

Over one third of House members at the beginning of the 94th Congress were beginning their first or second term, and the middle House members, in terms of seniority, were beginning their fourth term. By the start of the 96th Congress, 54 percent of House members had served three terms or less.

There are changes in the membership of the House. The average age of House members has dropped. The average age, at the beginning of the 94th Congress of a House member was less than 50 for the first time since World War II, and 87 of the members were 40 years old or under, a 50 percent increase over the 93rd Congress.

There have also been changes in the racial and sexual composition of the House. Although the number of black House members has not changed dramatically during the 70s, a larger number of black members hold committee and subcommittee leadership positions than ever before. The first black member has been elected to the Rules Committee during this decade, as were the first black whips.

Relative to the increased activity of women in politics, there has also been an increase in the number of women elected to the House. In 1974, all 12 women incumbents (10 Democrats and 2 Republicans) who sought reelection to the House were successful, and six other women won seats for the first time. The election of 18 women to the House set a record.

GREATER DISPERSAL OF POWER
TO SUBCOMMITTEES

The period of the 1970s has seen increasing restraint on the power of committee chairmen, and an increasing shift of power to subcommittee chairmen. Beginning in the 92d Congress, members could chair only one legislative subcommittee. The immediate effect was to increase the total number of members who held subcommittee chairmanships, and to place relatively junior members in positions of subcommittee leadership. In 1975, committees were required to establish a minimum number of subcommittees. With the increasingly large membership turnover of recent Congresses, coupled with the larger number of subcommittees, it is not uncommon for members in their second or third terms to rise to the chairmanship of a subcommittee.

The absolute power of committee chairmen has also been weakened by reforms in the seniority system. In 1975, three committee chairmen were deposed by the House Democratic Caucus, and more junior members chosen as chairmen to replace them.

The relative influence of subcommittees on legislation is shown by committee meeting statistics. In the 95th Congress, roughly 80 percent of all committee meetings were subcommittee meetings. Action, either markups or hearings, taken by the full committees normally was done merely to ratify previous action taken by a subcommittee. Increasingly, subcommittees have also become the focus of oversight activity in the House.

STEPS TOWARD STRONGER SPEAKERSHIP

Today, the floor leadership of the Democratic Party in the House has more potential instruments of power, according to some authorities, than has been the case in recent years. Recent actions by the House of Democratic Caucus have strengthened the floor leadership. In 1973, the Caucus established the Democratic Steering and Policy Committee. (The Speaker serves as Chairman, the majority leader as Vice Chairman, and the caucus chairman as Second Vice Chairman.) The Speaker has the authority to appoint up to eight (8) of the total 23 members. Moreover, the stated functions of the Committee are vague and as a result, the Speaker is given discretionary power in defining the stated functions.

At the beginning of the 94th Congress, the function of serving as the party "Committee on Committees" was included in the mandate of the Steering and

Policy Committee. Consequently, the Speaker is the leader of a committee that can greatly affect the members' careers.

Finally, the Speaker now has the prerogative to choose Democratic nominees to the Committee on Rules, subject to their approval by the Caucus. Additionally, the Speaker is given broad discretion in the reference of bills to committees, especially in the case of multiple referrals. The net effect has been to increase the theoretic power of the Speaker, but to limit it in practice by the continuing need to seek a majority party consensus on major issues.

THE MULTIPLE REFERRAL PROCESS

Prior to the 94th Congress, bills were required to be referred to the single committee which had the predominant legislative jurisdiction over the subject of a bill. Beginning with the 94th Congress, the Speaker was given the authority to refer bills (or parts of bills) to more than one committee. The general process is called a "multiple referral," although it refers to three different procedures: joint referrals, sequential referrals, and split referrals. A joint referral occurs when a measure is referred to two or more committees simultaneously. In a sequential referral, a bill is referred to one committee with the understanding that after the first committee acts, the bill will be referred to the second, or next, committee in the sequence. In a split referral, a portion (title or section) of a bill is referred to one committee, while other committees are referred other sections of the bill. Various permutations and combinations of these procedures are possible, and the Speaker is permitted under the rule to establish whatever conditions to the referral (for example, time limits) he may think necessary. The various referrals (joint, sequential, and split) have many advantages. They serve as avenues for flexibility, as facilitators of intercommittee cooperation and allow for the input, wisdom, and differing points of view to be considered on a measure.

During the 94th Congress, there were 1,161 bills multiply referred. Of that number, 38 were reported. During the 95th Congress, 1,855 bills were multiply referred. Of that number, 84 were reported. Given the complexity of much legislation and the overlapping jurisdiction characteristic of the congressional committee system, the Bolling Commission, as a result of its works, found it desirable that various bills, or titles thereof, be capable of referral to two or more House Committees.

Recently, opposition to the large number of multiple referrals has been voiced. Critics charge that the process is unnecessarily complex, and causes substantial delays in the legislative process.

GROWTH OF COMMITTEE STAFF

The Legislative Reorganization Act of 1970 provided for six professional and six clerical staff persons. H. Res. 988, effective in January 1975, set staff size at 18 professional staff members and 12 clerical persons except for two House committees—Appropriations and Budget. From 1973 to 1978, committee staffs increased from 878 to 1,844 with the largest increase occurring between 1974 and 1975 (326).

All House committees except Appropriations and Budget are authorized to employ up to 30 statutory staff (18 professional and 12 clerical).

The Appropriations and Budget Committees are permitted by House rules to establish their own staff levels, and their own required amount of funding.

There are two categories of committee staff in the House, statutory and investigative. Statutory employees are hired solely on the basis of their ability to perform required duties and are prohibited from performing work other than committee business during their hours of employment. Statutory committee staff may receive higher salaries than their investigative staff counterparts. Investigative personnel are hired pursuant to annual "studies and investigations" funding resolutions. Investigative staff are not covered by the legal protections and prohibitions under which statutory staff functions.

RESURGENCE OF PARTY CAUCUSES

The revival of the party caucuses has been one of the most significant developments in the Congress over the last decade. Since 1969, the following developments have occurred:

1. Debates have been held on legislative policy, and party rules and procedures at regular monthly meetings of the House Democratic Caucus.
2. The caucus has adopted party positions on certain issues and has accomplished significant changes in party rules and procedures (i.e., means of selecting committee chairmen).

Use of the Conference of policy discussions by House Republicans predates the revitalization of the Democratic Party Caucus.

Since the institution of monthly caucus meetings, House Democrats have significantly reduced the powers of their committee chairmen. Specifically, they have empowered caucuses of Democrats on each standing committee with the authority to adopt rules which:

1. Establish powers and duties of subcommittees.
2. Fix subcommittee jurisdictions and provide for referral of legislation.
3. Permit subcommittee chairmen to select staff, subject to budgetary limits and the control of Democratic Committee Caucus.
4. Set party ratios on subcommittees at least as favorable to Democrats as the full committee ratio.
5. Limit the chairman's power to assign members to vacant subcommittee seats.
6. Thoroughly revised the procedures by which subcommittee chairmen are selected.

House Republicans like their Democratic colleagues have also provided for secret ballot votes on nominees for party leadership positions on committees.

DECLINE OF INFORMAL NORMS PARTICULARLY APPRENTICESHIP

Several significant and unusual developments have occurred in the last three Congresses:

1. Junior members have been appointed to the very powerful "exclusive" committees shortly after entering the House.
2. A large number have been appointed to the exclusive committees.
3. The participation of junior members in floor debates and sponsoring floor amendments.
4. The development of new freshmen member organizations.

There have been a number of junior members assigned to the very powerful "exclusive committees" (Appropriations, Ways and Means, and Budget). Half of the Democratic members on the Rules Committee have been elected to the House since 1975. Fourteen members of the 24 Democratic members of the House Ways and Means Committee have served for three or fewer consecutive terms. On the Appropriations Committee, there are three—first-term Democratic members.

The development of new freshmen member organizations is another significant development which occurred during the 1970s. During the 94th Congress, when the "New Members' Caucus" was virtually unheard of, the group requested nominees for committee chairmanships to present themselves for interviews. It is generally agreed that the votes of the "New Members' Caucus" were instrumental in removing three incumbent chairmen from their posts in 1975.

SECTION II—RELEVANCE OF 1970s LEGISLATIVE CHANGES TO CONTEMPORARY COMMITTEE REORGANIZATION

The transformation of the House brought about by the 1970s changes will clearly affect 1979–1980 committee reorganization efforts. It is not possible to identify every direct or indirect consequence of the 1970s changes for committee reorganization. However, the task force believes there are seven particularly noteworthy developments of the 1970s that will likely affect the work of the Select Committee on Committees. These include:

1. Shift from Committee Government to Subcommittee Government

Policymaking authority in the House has significantly devolved upon subcommittees. Changes adopted by the Democratic Caucus during the 1970s (and several House rule changes) granted subcommittees new authority and independence from full committee control. No longer do full committee chairmen control the internal organizational structure of their committee. Under the Subcommittee

Bill of Rights adopted in 1973 by the Democratic Caucus, the Democratic members of each standing committee – subject to regulations established by the Caucus – determine such matters as the size, jurisdiction, and budget of their subcommittees. Heretofore, these matters were the prerogatives of the committee chairman.

The Democratic Caucus also made other changes during the 1970s that opened subcommittee chairmanships to numerous members, including junior legislators. Today, many more members have subcommittees to nurture and protect. They have a stake in subcommittee government, and are likely to oppose any proposal that significantly reduces the number of subcommittees standing committees may have. Contemporary committee reorganization, in short, must consider how any proposed changes affect committees and subcommittees.

2. More Difficult for House to Formulate Coherent Public Policies Given So Many Participants in Policymaking

Committees, subcommittees, and the Caucus play significant roles in the legislative process. Despite its assets, committee government does have serious liabilities. There are flaws that undermine the ability of Congress to fulfill its constitutional responsibilities, to make legislative policy, and oversee the implementation of that policy. The view is that internally, Congress needs central leadership because most major questions of public policy (such as economic or the energy issues) cut across individual committee jurisdictions. Since each committee and subcommittee may differ in its policy orientation, and since the support of all relevant committees will be essential to an overall program, it is difficult to enact a coherent general approach to broad policy questions.

A central party leader or central congressional steering committee with extensive control over the standing committees could provide the leadership necessary to assist the development and passage of a coherent policy across the various committees. However, committee government resists the centralization of power in a single person or unit.

Centralized leadership requires a willingness of members to cede their smaller grants of authority. However, members are likely to do this only if general agreement exists regarding the policies a stronger leadership would follow. On most current issues, no coherent party policy exists which has the general support of all party members. Hence, it is unlikely that the dispersed legislative authority in the House soon will be centralized. Too much effort has been expended in the last decade dispersing leadership authority for this tendency to be easily or quickly reversed.

3. Staffing and Space Needs

During the 1970s, the Congress generally, and the House in particular, made concerted efforts to expand its staff. The Congress in 1970 was incapable of countering the massive information and analytic resources available to the Executive Branch. The Congress, in many instances, was forced to rely upon information provided by the agencies and departments. Lacking adequate staff resources in many areas, the Congress was not always able to exercise independent judgment on Executive Branch proposals. The expansion of staff for members, for committees, and for the Congress generally, was caused by this need for independent analysis.

The growth in staff, however, has placed unforeseen strains on congressional facilities. Space in the principal House office buildings was rapidly filled, and more space in two annex office buildings was required. The growth in high technology office equipment has also contributed to space shortages, while enabling staff to handle an ever increasing volume of work. Inadequate space for staff and equipment limits the ability of the Congress to perform its duties efficiently.

In recent years, there has been concern voiced over the growth of congressional staff. Some observers, both inside and outside of Congress, believe that staff growth should be slowed, if not halted outright. In a period of fiscal restraint, it is claimed that the public will oppose continuing growth of the congressional establishment. As staff grows, the administrative duties of members increase commensurately, restricting time available to members to consider policy issues. Fiscal constraints additionally may make it impossible for the Congress to increase its office space further, thereby implicitly limiting future staff growth.

This combination of factors must be considered by the select committee in any action it takes regarding staffing and facilities of House committees.

4. Numerous Committee Scheduling Conflicts

The efficacious handling of the nation's business through the committee process cannot proceed orderly and properly if House members are not at committee meetings because of conflicting committee meeting scheduling. Conflict problems have increased in severity as the number of committee and subcommittee meetings continue to rise (from 5,066 in the 91st Congress to 6,771 in the 95th Congress).

An equitable and logical procedure for scheduling committee meetings remains an urgent priority for the House leadership and members. The ingenuity and resources of the House members must be collectively brought to bear on a resolution of conflicting meeting scheduling. Failure to address this critical matter may result in an erosion of the efficiency and productivity of the House in working its will in the legislative process.

5. Jurisdictional Overlaps

In a simpler age, it was not considered necessary to enumerate House committees' subject jurisdiction in House Rules. Since 1947, however, fairly detailed subject guidelines have been a part of House Rule X. Several previous attempts at codifying these jurisdictions, and eliminating subject overlaps and archaic language have failed. Concurrently, the complexity of policy issues facing the Congress has increased enormously. Often, new policy issues do not accommodate themselves to the committee jurisdictions enumerated in the House Rules.

As part of the Bolling reforms, House Rules were amended to permit the referral of bills (or parts of bills) to more than one committee. To a degree, this minimized jurisdictional conflicts among committees sharing partial responsibility for a major policy issue. However, the experience of four years of multiple referrals casts doubt on its legislative effectiveness. Each year, more and more bills are being referred to several committees. In the 95th Congress, more than 3,000 bills (or one out of every five House bills) was referred to more than one committee. While multiple referrals assure that divergent committee viewpoints are reflected, they also appear to delay committee and full House action on bills.

Jurisdictional fragmentation and the rise of multiple committee consideration of bills are issues which will influence the work of the select committee. Currently, no standard procedures exist for the referral of legislation to more than one committee. If the number of multiple referrals continues to rise, the establishment of such mechanisms may be considered essential. The Bolling Committee believed that multiple referrals would be required in only a few instances each year because that committee also strove to restructure existing committee jurisdictions. In failing to consolidate major policy issues in a single committee, the House was forced into greater reliance upon multiple referrals. If the House were to adopt restrictive guidelines on the use of multiple referrals, the conflicting jurisdictional claims of House committees may increase in severity. Conversely, if the House acted to reduce jurisdictional overlap among its committees, the need for bills to be referred to more than one committee might be reduced.

6. Concern About Committee Capacity to Conduct Oversight

The factor of promise and fulfillment has become a pivotal and critical element in the oversight function in recent times. Congressional leadership and House members have been enormously concerned that the plethora of legislation enacted by the Congress accomplishes what it was intended to achieve and is carefully monitored and evaluated. There is a "chasm" that continues in regard to the enactment of legislation in determining its efficacy and impact on the citizenry. The effectiveness in the last analysis in oversight responsibilities may well be determined, in large measure, by the extent of the members, their intent and commitment, particularly as it serves their constituents and their own political careers. This factor suggests that the House leadership may wish to give greater care to the assignment of members to committees based upon their interests.

7. Leadership Has Harder Time Governing the House

Vigorous congressional leadership is inhibited, not only by the decentralized power centers in the House but also by the lack of a firm base upon which to build leadership power. The political parties are shaky foundations on which to erect a viable system of legislative leadership. The party has rarely, in modern times, been a dominant force in the national legislature. The Democratic Caucus reforms of the past decade have yet to prove themselves as something more than the instruments of factional advance by the liberal bloc. Moreover, as other entities have assumed functions which historically were the responsibility of parties, formal party organizations have lost much of their influence. Weakened party loyalties have further reduced the influence of the congressional leadership.

Changed member attitudes have reinforced the decline of congressional leadership. Members frequently are elected without the aid of a strong, local party organization. Relying on their own electoral skills, new members are acutely sensitive to constituent opinion, and will normally support constituency attitudes, even if they must, therefore, oppose their party's congressional leadership. Many new members do not see House service as the high point of their political career. Consequently, they are not content to serve a lengthy apprenticeship before taking a visible part in the legislative process. Junior member activism has further contributed to the weakening of House leadership.   ■

THE LEGISLATIVE VETO

Patterned after the "laying system" of the British Parliament, used there as early as 1386, the legislative veto of the U.S. Congress has long been written into new laws to allow Congress to retain some control over powers otherwise delegated to the President or the executive branch.[2]

In 1804, for example, after dividing the new Louisiana Purchase into two territories, the Congress delegated rulemaking authority in each of them to a governor and council, with the proviso that all rules made had "to be laid before Congress; which, if disapproved of by Congress, shall henceforth be of no force." Thus, the advent of the legislative veto in the U.S. Congress.

Through the years, the legislative veto was increasingly written into new legislation. But actual use of the veto under these laws was somewhat sparing—only 125 vetoes since 1932. The legislative veto took various forms. Sometimes it was provided that the veto would only go into effect if there was affirmative action in Congress, overruling executive action. Other times, the legislative veto written into a delegation of authority provided that executive action would automatically be vetoed unless Congress acted to approve it—a negative veto. Some vetoes could be exercised by one house acting alone, or even by a committee of one house.

Then, came the 1982 Supreme Court decision in the case of *Immigration and Naturalization Service* v. *Chadha*, excerpted here. In it, the court struck down the one-house veto in words broad enough to call into question any legislative veto power of Congress not required to be exercised affirmatively by *both* houses and by means of a legislative measure that itself would be subject to a *presidential* veto. The decision was based upon the Court's interpretation of the principles of separation of powers and bicameralism.

---

2. For a discussion of the history of the legislative veto as well as argumemnt in favor of a constitutional amendment to permit it, see Dennis DeConcini and Robert Faucher, "The Legislative Veto: A Constitutional Amendment," Vol. 21, no. 1, *Harvard Journal on Legislation* (Winter 1984), pp. 29–59.

IMMIGRATION AND NATURALIZATION SERVICE v. CHADHA*

Chief Justice Burger delivered the opinion of the Court.

Chadha is an East Indian who was born in Kenya and holds a British passport. He was lawfully admitted to the United States in 1966 on a nonimmigrant student visa. His visa expired on June 30, 1972. On October 11, 1973, the District Director of the Immigration and Naturalization Service ordered Chadha to show cause why he should not be deported for having "remained in the United States for a longer time than permitted." Pursuant to § 242(b) of the Immigration and Nationality Act, a deportation hearing was held before an Immigration Judge on January 11, 1974. Chadha conceded that he was deportable for overstaying his visa and the hearing was adjourned to enable him to file an application for suspension of deportation under § 244(a)(1) of [an Act of Congress which] provided:

> As hereinafter prescribed in this section, the Attorney General may, in his discretion, suspend deportation and adjust the status to that of an alien lawfully admitted for permanent residence, in the case of an alien who applies to the Attorney General for suspension of deportation and—
> (1) is deportable under any law of the United States except the provisions specified in paragraph (2) of this subsection; has been physically present in the United States for a continuous period of not less than seven years immediately preceding the date of such application, and proves that during all of such period he was and is a person of good moral character; and is a person whose deportation would, in the opinion of the Attorney General, result in extreme hardship to the alien or to his spouse, parent, or child, who is a citizen of the United States or an alien lawfully admitted for permanent residence."

After Chadha submitted his application for suspension of deportation, the deportation hearing was resumed on February 7, 1974. On the basis of evidence adduced at the hearing, affidavits submitted with the application, and the results of a character investigation conducted by the INS, the Immigration Judge, on June 25, 1974, ordered that Chadha's deportation be suspended. The Immigration Judge found that Chadha met the requirements of § 244(a)(1): he had resided continuously in the United States for over seven years, was of good moral character, and would suffer "extreme hardship" if deported.

Pursuant to § 244(c)(1) of the Act, the Immigration Judge suspended Chadha's deportation and a report of the suspension was transmitted to Congress. Section 244(c)(1) provides:

> Upon application by any alien who is found by the Attorney General to meet the requirements of subsection (a) of this section the Attorney General may in his discretion suspend deportation of such alien. If the deportation of any alien is suspended under the provisions of this subsection, a complete and

---

*462 U. S. 919 (1982).

detailed statement of the facts and pertinent provisions of law in the case shall be reported to the Congress with the reasons for such suspension. Such reports shall be submitted on the first day of each calendar month in which Congress is in session."

Once the Attorney General's recommendation for suspension of Chadha's deportation was conveyed to Congress, Congress had the power under § 244(c)(2) of the Act to veto the Attorney General's determination that Chadha should not be deported. Section 244(c)(2) provides:

(2)In the case of an alien specified in paragraph (1) of subsection (a) of this subsection—
if during the session of the Congress at which a case is reported, or prior to the close of the session of the Congress next following the session at which a case is reported, either the Senate or the House of Representatives passes a resolution stating in substance that it does not favor the suspension of such deportation, the Attorney General shall thereupon deport such alien or authorize the alien's voluntary departure at his own expense under the order of deportation in the manner provided by law. If, within the time above specified, neither the State nor the House of Representatives shall pass such a resolution, the Attorney General shall cancel deportation proceedings.

On December 12, 1975, Representative Eilberg, Chairman of the Judiciary Subcommittee on Immigration, Citizenship, and International Law, introduced a resolution opposing "the granting of permanent residence in the United States to [six] aliens," including Chadha. The resolution was referred to the House Committee on the Judiciary. On December 16, 1975, the resolution was discharged from further consideration by the House Committee on the Judiciary and submitted to the House of Representatives for a vote. . . . The resolution was passed without debate or recorded vote. Since the House action was pursuant to § 244(c)(2), the resolution was not treated as an Art I legislative act; it was not submitted to the Senate or presented to the President for his action.

After the House veto of the Attorney General's decision to allow Chadha to remain in the United States, the Immigration Judge reopened the deportation proceedings to implement the House order deporting Chadha. Chadha moved to terminate the proceedings on the ground that § 244(c)(2) is unconstitutional. . . .

After full briefing and oral argument, the Court of Appeals held that the House was without constitutional authority to order Chadha's deportation; accordingly it directed the Attorney General "to cease and desist from taking any steps to deport this alien based upon the resolution enacted by the House of Representatives." The essence of its holding was that § 244(c)(2) violates the constitutional doctrine of separation of powers. . . .

The Constitution sought to divide the delegated powers of the new Federal Government into three defined categories, Legislative, Executive, and Judicial, to assure, as nearly as possible, that each branch of government would confine itself to its assigned responsibility. The hydraulic pressure inherent within each of the separate Branches to exceed the outer limits of its power, even to accomplish desirable objectives, must be resisted. . . .

We turn now to the question whether action of one House of Congress under § 244(c)(2) violates strictures of the Constitution. We begin, of course, with the presumption that the challenged statute is valid. Its wisdom is not the concern of the courts; if a challenged action does not violate the Constitution, it must be sustained . . . .

By the same token, the fact that a given law or procedure is efficient, convenient, and useful in facilitating functions of government, standing alone, will not save it if it is contrary to the Constitution. Convenience and efficiency are not the primary objectives — or the hallmarks — of democratic government and our inquiry is sharpened rather than blunted by the fact that congressional veto provisions are appearing with increasing frequency in statutes which delegate authority to executive and independent agencies:

> Since 1932, when the first veto provision was enacted into law, 295 congressional veto-type procedures have been inserted in 196 different statutes as follows: from 1932 to 1939, five statutes were affected; from 1940–49, nineteen statutes; between 1950–59, thirty-four statutes, and from 1960–69, forty-nine. From the year 1970 through 1975, at least one hundred sixty-three such provisions were included in eighty-nine laws.[3]

Explicit and unambiguous provisions of the Constitution prescribe and define the respective functions of the Congress and of the Executive in the legislative process. Since the precise terms of those familiar provisions are critical to the resolution of this case, we set them out verbatim. Article I provides:

> All legislative Powers herein granted shall be vested in a Congress of the United States, which shall consist of a Senate *and* House of Representatives. Art I, § 1. (Emphasis added.)
>
> Every Bill which shall have passed the House of Representatives *and* the Senate, *shall*, before it becomes a Law, be presented to the President of the United States. . . . Art I, § 7, cl 2. (Emphasis added.)
>
> *Every* Order, Resolution, or Vote to which the Concurrence of the Senate and House of Representatives may be necessary (except on a question of Adjournment) *shall be* presented to the President of the United States; and before the Same shall take Effect, *shall be* approved by him, or being disapproved by him, *shall be* repassed by two thirds of the Senate and House of Representatives, according to the Rules and Limitations prescribed in the Case of a Bill. Art I, § 7, cl 3. (Emphasis added.)

These provisions of Art I are integral parts of the constitutional design for the separation of powers. We have recently noted that "[t]he principle of separation of powers was not simply an abstract generalization in the minds of the Framers: it was woven into the document that they drafted in Philadelphia in the summer of 1787." Buckley v Valeo, 424 US, at 124 . . . . Just as we relied on the textual provision of Art II, § 2, cl 2, to vindicate the principle of separation of powers in Buckley, we see that the purposes underlying the Presentment Clauses, Art I, § 7, cls 2, 3 and the bicameral requirement of Art I, § 1, and

---

3. Abourezk, "The Congressional Veto: A Contemporary Response to Executive Encroachment on Legislative Prerogatives," 52 *Indiana Law Review* (1977), pp. 323, 324.

§ 7, cl 2, guide our resolution of the important question presented in these cases. The very structure of the articles delegating and separating powers under Arts I, II, and III exemplifies the concept of separation of powers, and we now turn to Art I.

THE PRESENTMENT CLAUSES

The records of the Constitutional Convention reveal that the requirement that all legislation be presented to the President before becoming law was uniformly accepted by the Framers. Presentment to the President and the Presidential veto were considered so imperative that the draftsmen took special pains to assure that these requirements could not be circumvented. During the final debate on Art I, § 7, cl 2, James Madison expressed concern that it might easily be evaded by the simple expedient of calling a proposed law a "resolution" or "vote" rather than a "bill." As a consequence, Art I, § 7, cl 3, was added.

The decision to provide the President with a limited and qualified power to nullify proposed legislation by veto was based on the profound conviction of the Framers that the powers conferred on Congress were the powers to be most carefully circumscribed. It is beyond doubt that lawmaking was a power to be shared by both Houses and the President. In The Federalist No. 73, Hamilton focused on the President's role in making laws:

> If even no propensity had ever discovered itself in the legislative body to invade the rights of the Executive, the rules of just reasoning and theoretic propriety would of themselves teach us that the one ought not to be left to the mercy of the other, but ought to possess a constitutional and effectual power of self-defence.

The President's role in the lawmaking process also reflects the Framers' careful efforts to check whatever propensity a particular Congress might have to enact oppressive, improvident, or ill-considered measures. The President's veto role in the legislative process was described later during public debate on ratification:

> It establishes a salutary check upon the legislative body, calculated to guard the community against the effects of faction, precipitancy, or of any impulse unfriendly to the public good, which may happen to influence a majority of that body.
> . . . The primary inducement to conferring the power in question upon the Executive is, to enable him to defend himself; the secondary one is to increase the chances in favor of the community against the passing of bad laws, through haste, inadvertence, or design. The Federalist No. 73 . . . .

BICAMERALISM

The bicameral requirement of Art I, §§ 1, 7, was of scarcely less concern to the Framers than was the Presidential veto and indeed the two concepts are interdependent. By providing that no law could take effect without the concurrence of the prescribed majority of the Members of both Houses, the Framers reemphasized their belief, already remarked upon in connection with the Presentment Clauses, that legislation should not be enacted unless it has been carefully and fully considered by the Nation's elected officials. . . .

Hamilton argued that a Congress comprised of a single House was antithetical to the very purposes of the Constitution. Were the Nation to adopt a Constitution providing for only one legislative organ, he warned:

[W]e shall finally accumulate, in a single body, all the most important prerogatives of sovereignty, and thus entail upon our posterity one of the most execrable forms of government that human infatuation ever contrived. Thus we should create in reality that very tyranny which the adversaries of the new Constitution either are, or affect to be, solicitous to avert. The Federalist No. 22 . . . .

We see therefore that the Framers were acutely conscious that the bicameral requirement and the Presentment Clauses would serve essential constitutional functions. The President's participation in the legislative process was to protect the Executive Branch from Congress and to protect the whole people from improvident laws. The division of the Congress into two distinctive bodies assures that the legislative power would be exercised only after opportunity for full study and debate in separate settings. The President's unilateral veto power, in turn, was limited by the power of two-thirds of both Houses of Congress to overrule a veto thereby precluding final arbitrary action of one person. It emerges clearly that the prescription for legislative action in Art I, §§ 1, 7, represents the Framers' decision that the legislative power of the Federal Government be exercised in accord with a single, finely wrought and exhaustively considered, procedure.

. . . We see that when the Framers intended to authorize either House of Congress to act alone and outside of its prescribed bicameral legislative role, they narrowly and precisely defined the procedure for such action. There are four provisions in the Constitution, explicit and unambiguous, by which one House may act alone with the unreviewable force of law, not subject to the President's veto:

(a) The House of Representatives alone was given the power to initiate impeachments. Art I, § 2, cl 5;

(b) The Senate alone was given the power to conduct trials following impeachment on charges initiated by the House and to convict following trial. Art I, § 3, cl 6;

(c) The Senate alone was given final unreviewable power to approve or to disapprove Presidential appointments. Art II, § 2, cl 2;

(d) The Senate alone was given unreviewable power to ratify treaties negotiated by the President. Art II, § 2, cl 2.

Clearly, when the Draftsmen sought to confer special powers on one House, independent of the other House, or of the President, they did so in explicit, unambiguous terms. These carefully defined exceptions from presentment and bicameralism underscore the difference between the legislative functions of Congress and other unilateral but important and binding one-House acts provided for in the Constitution. These exceptions are narrow, explicit, and separately justified; none of them authorize the action challenged here. On the contrary, they provide further support for the conclusion that congressional authority is not to be implied and for the conclusion that the veto provided for in § 244(c)(2) is not authorized by the constitutional design of the powers of the Legislative Branch.

Since it is clear that the action by the House under § 244(c)(2) was not within any of the express constitutional exceptions authorizing one House to act alone, and equally clear that it was an exercise of legislative power, that action was subject to the standards prescribed in Art I. The bicameral requirement, the Presentment Clauses, the President's veto, and Congress' power to override a veto were intended to erect enduring checks on each Branch and to protect the people from the improvident exercise of power by mandating certain prescribed steps. To preserve those checks, and maintain the separation of powers, the carefully defined limits on the power of each Branch must not be eroded. To accomplish what has been attempted by one House of Congress in this case requires action in conformity with the express procedures of the Constitution's prescription for legislative action: passage by a majority of both Houses and presentment to the President.

The veto authorized by § 244(c)(2) doubtless has been in many respects a convenient shortcut; the "sharing" with the Executive by Congress of its authority over aliens in this manner is, on its face, an appealing compromise. In purely practical terms, it is obviously easier for action to be taken by one House without submission to the President; but it is crystal clear from the records of the Convention, contemporaneous writings and debates, that the Framers ranked other values higher than efficiency. The records of the Convention and debates in the States preceding ratification underscore the common desire to define and limit the exercise of the newly created federal powers affecting the states and the people. There is unmistakable expression of a determination that legislation by the national Congress be a step-by-step, deliberate and deliberative process.

The choices we discern as having been made in the Constitutional Convention impose burdens on governmental processes that often seem clumsy, inefficient, even unworkable, but those hard choices were consciously made by men who had lived under a form of government that permitted arbitrary governmental acts to go unchecked. There is no support in the Constitution or decisions of this Court for the proposition that the cumbersomeness and delays often encountered in complying with explicit constitutional standards may be avoided, either by the Congress or by the President. With all the obvious flaws of delay, untidiness, and potential for abuse, we have not yet found a better way to preserve freedom than by making the exercise of power subject to the carefully crafted restraints spelled out in the Constitution.

We hold that the congressional veto provision in § 244(c)(2) is severable from the Act and that it is unconstitutional. Accordingly, the judgment of the Court of Appeals is affirmed.   ∎

WHAT IS MEANT BY "REPRESENTATION"?

The United States has a "representative democracy"—that is, a system of rule by the people through elected representatives. This concept of "representation" seems simple at first. But, on reflection, one realizes that it is in reality more complex.

What do we mean when we say that an official whom we elect "represents" us? Hanna F. Pitkin divided the concept into four distinct aspects:

formal representation, descriptive representation, symbolic representation, and substantive representation.[4]

\ Formal representation requires institutionalized, regular elections that are free and fair. Descriptive representation, far from achievement in U. S. legislatures, of course, requires that the legislative bodies be mirror images of their constituents—in race, sex, economic class, and other categories. Symbolic representation requires that the people believe in their representative— that they are psychologically satisfied.

Lastly, substantive representation requires that the representative act in the interests of constituents and be responsible to them. This latter aspect of representation, substantive representation, raises other questions as old as representative government: Should a representative follow his or her own conscience, and thus act as a "trustee," as the political scientists put it, or, regardless of the representative's own view of what is right, follow the majority opinion of constituents, thus acting as a "delegate"?

An eighteenth-century member of the British House of Commons, Edmund Burke, whose famous statement is reprinted here, took the trustee side of the issue. John F. Kennedy, when he was a member of the U. S. Senate, as well as House Speaker Jim Wright, a Democrat from Texas, both declared that, at least some of the time and on great matters of principle, representatives must lead, must act as trustees. Excerpts from their books, Kennedy's *Profiles in Courage* and Wright's *You and Your Congressman,* are excerpted here for their views on this subject of the representative's role. An article by Martin Tolchin deals with the question of how the need for compromise in Congress affects a new member's devotion to principle.

A REPRESENTATIVE SHOULD FOLLOW CONSCIENCE
Edmund Burke

Certainly, gentlemen, it ought to be the happiness and glory of a representative to live in the strictest union with his constituents. Their wishes ought to have great weight with him; their opinion high respect; their business unremitted attention. It is his duty to sacrifice his repose, his pleasures, his satisfactions, to theirs; and in all cases, to prefer their interest to his own. But his unbiased opinion, his mature judgment, his enlightened conscience, he ought

---

4. Hanna F. Pitkin, *The Concept of Representation* (Berkeley, Calif.: University of California Press, 1967), pp. 38–59.

not to sacrifice to you; to any man, or to any set of men living. These he does not derive from your pleasure; no, nor from the law and the constitution. They are a trust from Providence, for the abuse of which he is deeply answerable. Your representative owes you, not his industry only, but his judgment; and he betrays, instead of serving you, if he sacrifices it to your opinion.

If government were a matter of will upon any side, yours, without question, ought to be superior. But government and legislation are matters of reason and judgment, and not of inclination; and what sort of reason is that in which the determination precedes the discussion; in which one set of men deliberate, and another decide; and where those who form the conclusion are perhaps 300 miles distant from those who hear the arguments?

Parliament is not a *congress* of ambassadors from different and hostile interests; which interests each must maintain, as an agent and advocate, against other agents and advocates; but parliament is a *deliberative* assembly of *one* nation, with *one* interest, that of the whole; where, not local purposes, not local prejudices ought to guide, but the general good, resulting from the general reason of the whole. You chose a member indeed; but when you have chosen him, he is not member of Bristol, but he is a member of *parliament*.

If the local constituent should have an interest, or should form an hasty opinion, evidently opposite to the real good of the rest of the community, the member for that place ought to be as far, as any other, from any endeavor to give it effect.

Your faithful friend, your devoted servant, I shall be to the end of my life: a flatterer you do not wish for. On this point of instructions, however, I think it scarcely possible we ever can have any sort of difference. Perhaps I may give you too much, rather than too little trouble. ■

A REPRESENTATIVE MUST HAVE THE COURAGE TO LEAD
John F. Kennedy

The primary responsibility of a Senator, most people assume, is to represent the views of his state. Ours is a Federal system—a Union of relatively sovereign states whose needs differ greatly—and my Constitutional obligations as Senator would thus appear to require me to represent the interests of my state. Who will speak for Massachusetts if her own Senators do not? Her rights and even her identity become submerged. Her equal representation in Congress is lost. Her aspirations, however much they may from time to time be in the minority, are denied that equal opportunity to be heard to which all minority views are entitled.

Any Senator need not look very long to realize that his colleagues are representing *their* local interests. And if such interests are ever to be abandoned in favor of the national good, let the constituents—not the Senator—decide when and to what extent. For he is their agent in Washington, the protector of their rights, recognized by the Vice President in the Senate Chamber as "the Senator from Massachusetts" or "the Senator from Texas."

But when all of this is said and admitted, we have not yet told the full story. For in Washington we are "United States Senators" and members of the Senate of the United States as well as Senators from Massachusetts and Texas. Our oath of office is administered by the Vice President, not by the Governors of our respective states; and we come to Washington, to paraphrase Edmund Burke, not as hostile ambassadors or special pleaders for our state or section, in opposition to advocates and agents of other areas, but as members of the deliberative assembly of one nation with one interest. Of course, we should not ignore the needs of our area—nor could we easily as products of that area—but none could be found to look out for the national interest if local interests wholly dominated the role of each of us.

There are other obligations in addition to those of state and region . . . We believe in this country in the principle of party responsibility, and we recognize the necessity of adhering to party platforms—if the party label is to mean anything to the voters. . . .

Of course, both major parties today seek to serve the national interest. They would do so in order to obtain the broadest base of support, if for no nobler reason. But when party and officeholder differ as to how the national interest is to be served, we must place first the responsibility we owe not to our party or even to our constituents but to our individual consciences.

But it is a little easier to dismiss one's obligations to local interests and party ties than to face squarely the problem of one's responsibility to the will of his constituents. A Senator who avoids this responsibility would appear to be accountable to no one, and the basic safeguards of our democratic system would thus have vanished. He is no longer representative in the true sense, he has violated his public trust, he has betrayed the confidence demonstrated by those who voted for him to carry out their views. "Is the creature," as John Tyler asked the House of Representatives in his maiden speech, "to set himself in opposition to his Creator? Is the servant to disobey the wishes of his master?"

How can he be regarded as representing the people when he speaks, not their language, but his own? He ceases to be their representative when he does so, and represents himself alone.

In short, according to this school of thought, if I am to be properly responsive to the will of my constituents, it is my duty to place their principles, not mine, above all else. This may not always be easy, but it nevertheless is the essence of democracy, faith in the wisdom of the people and their views. To be sure, the people will make mistakes—they will get no better government than they deserve—but that is far better than the representative of the people arrogating for himself the right to say he knows better than they what is good for them. Is he not chosen, the argument closes, to vote as they would vote were they in his place?

It is difficult to accept such a narrow view of the role of United States Senator—a view that assumes the people of Massachusetts sent me to Washington to serve merely as a seismograph to record shifts in popular opinion. I reject this view not because I lack faith in the "wisdom of the people," but because this concept of democracy actually puts too little faith in the people. Those who would deny the obligation of the representative to be bound by every impulse of the electorate—regardless of the conclusions his own deliberations direct—do trust in the wisdom of the people. They have faith in their ultimate sense of justice, faith in their ability to honor courage and respect judgment, and faith that in the long run they will act unselfishly for the good of the nation. It is that kind of faith on which democracy is based, not simply the often frustrated hope that public opinion will at all times under all circumstances promptly identify itself with the public interest.

The voters selected us, in short, because they had confidence in our judgment and our ability to exercise that judgment from a position where we could determine what were their own best interests, as a part of the nation's interests. This may mean that we must on occasion lead, inform, correct and sometimes even ignore constituent opinion, if we are to exercise fully that judgment for which we were elected. But acting without selfish motive or private bias, those who follow the dictates of an intelligent conscience are not aristocrats, demagogues, eccentrics or callous politicians insensitive to the feelings of the public. They expect—and not without considerable trepidation—their constituents to be the final judges of the wisdom of their course; but they have faith that those constituents—today, tomorrow or even in another generation—will at least respect the principles that motivated their independent stand.

If their careers are temporarily or even permanently buried under an avalanche of abusive editorials, poison-pen letters, and opposition votes at the polls— as they sometimes are, for that is the risk they take—they await the future with hope and confidence, aware of the fact that the voting public frequently suffers from what ex-Congressman T. V. Smith called the lag "between our way of thought and our way of life." . . .

Moreover, I question whether any Senator, before we vote on a measure, can state with certainty exactly how the majority of his constituents feel on the issue as it is presented to the Senate. All of us in the Senate live in an iron lung— the iron lung of politics, and it is no easy task to emerge from that rarefied atmosphere in order to breathe the same fresh air our constituents breathe. It is difficult, too, to see in person an appreciable number of voters besides those professional hangers-on and vocal elements who gather about the politician on a trip home. In Washington I frequently find myself believing that forty or fifty letters, six visits from professional politicians and lobbyists, and three editorials in Massachusetts newspapers constitute public opinion on a given issue. Yet in truth I rarely know how the great majority of the voters feel, or even how much they know of the issues that seem so burning in Washington. . . .

We can compromise our political positions, but not ourselves. We can resolve the clash of interests without conceding our ideals. And even the necessity for the right kind of compromise does not eliminate the need for those idealists and reformers who keep our compromises moving ahead, who prevent all political situations from meeting the description supplied by Shaw: "smirched with compromise, rotted with opportunism, mildewed by expedience, stretched out of shape with wirepulling and putrefied with permeation." Compromise need not mean cowardice. Indeed it is frequently the compromisers and conciliators who are faced with the severest tests of political courage as they oppose the extremist views of their constituents. It was because Daniel Webster conscientiously favored compromise in 1850 that he earned a condemnation unsurpassed in the annals of political history.

His is a story worth remembering today. So, I believe, are the stories of other Senators of courage—men whose abiding loyalty to their nation triumphed over all personal and political considerations, men who showed the real meaning of courage and a real faith in democracy, men who made the Senate of the United States something more than a mere collection or robots dutifully recording the views of their constituents, or a gathering of time-servers skilled only in predicting and following the tides of public sentiment. . . .   ■

AND THEN SOMETIMES
HE'S A STATESMAN
Jim Wright

"Y ou owe this one to your country, no matter what the political consequences. I'll make it up to you somehow."

It was August, 1941. A beleaguered Sam Rayburn was pleading with a colleague for a vote to extend the terms of enlistment under the draft. He was having more than the usual amount of trouble.

Only four months later, with Pearl Harbor in ruins and the American public in a full-throated cry of righteous indignation as the Japanese overran with humiliating ease our forward defense bastions in the Pacific, Congressmen would be striving zealously to outdo one another in ardent, vocal support for measures to promote the nation's military might. But now, in August, it was a vastly different story.

The first peacetime Selective Service Act in the nation's history had been in operation for almost a year, and the right to keep trainees in service would expire if not extended. Many were ready, even anxious, for it to lapse. The draft had been unpopular. Mothers and fathers wanted their sons back home. Throughout the land, drafted youth, their schooling and careers harshly interrupted, felt themselves victims of a cruel and unnecessary discrimination. Psychologically, the very presence of military training camps seemed to bring the war that much closer. Letters poured across Congressional desks complaining of the mistreatment of draftees and condemning the draft as "militaristic," "warmongering," even "un-American."

Such was the national mood in the late summer of 1941. Isolationist sentiment still was strong in many parts of the country. The war in Europe was going badly for England, but to the uninformed the United States seemed in no danger. After all, it wasn't *our* war. If we just could manage to avoid acts of provocation, we probably could ride it out without ever having to spill American blood—so went the current of wishful thinking popular at the time.

Mr. Rayburn was firmly convinced that such an air of complacency had no basis in fact. The issue, with him, was neither partisan nor sectional; it was national. He personally buttonholed every doubtful member in the House. Some shook their heads sadly, replied that they just couldn't do it. Their people simply did not want the draft extended, they explained, and after all it was their duty to represent the wishes of their constituents. Others, although fearful that such a vote might defeat them at the polls in the forthcoming Congressional elections, said they'd think it over.[5] For days Rayburn worked incessantly, trying to fashion a majority. "You owe this one to your country," he kept saying.

The resolution to extend the Selective Service terms finally was passed in the House of Representatives on August 12, 1941, by a single vote—203 to 202.

It is dismal to contemplate what might have happened if Rayburn's efforts had failed—if, in fact, just one Congressman who voted for extension of the draft that day had decided to "play it safe" and appease the popular misconceptions of a wishful-thinking constituency. Our standing military forces critically reduced in number, the nation would have been even greatly more vulnerable than it was on that fateful December morning. If perhaps it might be safe to assume that the ultimate outcome of the war would not have been altered, at the very least it is certain that failure to pass this particular resolution unavoidably would have prolonged hostilities for many brutal months while the Japanese plunged much more deeply into Allied territory, and many thousands of additional lives would have inevitably been consumed in our efforts to stem the tide.

As this event illustrates, a Congressman must be not only a servant of his individual constituents and an advocate for the local interests of his district. Above and beyond these duties, he is primarily a trustee for the Republic.

Almost weekly when Congress is in session, on a considerably less spectacular scale, little private dramas of decision are enacted on the House and Senate floors. Occasionally the national interest will conflict with a local interest. Sometimes a member's personal convictions as to what is best for the nation will run in direct opposition to what he perceives to be the overwhelming sentiment of his district. What, in these circumstances, is his duty? To serve his district or his nation? His constituents or his conscience?

---

5. As it turned out, those who voted against extension found themselves in more political hot water when the 1943 elections came around than did those who voted in favor. But nobody, of course, could know this at the time. The electorate can be capable of a very well-developed hindsight in such matters.

This philosophical question was seriously debated during the first Congress of the United States. Representatives Page of Virginia and Gary of Massachusetts wanted to amend the Constitution, making it mandatory for members of Congress to receive instructions from their electorate and to obey such instructions. Madison opposed. The suggested amendment was finally voted down, 41–10. . . .

Walter Lippmann, neither a sensationalist nor a muckracker, rendered a gloomy verdict of the successful political figures of our time as basically "insecure and intimidated men" whose decisive consideration is "not whether the proposition is good but whether it is popular—not whether it will work well and prove itself, but whether the active-talking constituents like it immediately." Lippmann's theme, eloquently set forth in his book *The Public Philosophy,* was that public opinion is a far from reliable criterion of right and wrong in the delicate and difficult matters of foreign affairs. Reviewing the history of the past twenty-five years, he claimed public opinion has been "destructively wrong at the critical junctures." Pointing out that "strategic and diplomatic decisions call for a kind of knowledge—not to speak of an experience and a seasoned judgment—which cannot be had by glancing at newspapers," he argued that the politicians in our country are too much at the mercy of this benighted public sentiment. "In war and peace," Lippmann said, "the answer in the democracies is likely to be No."

The movement of opinion, Lippmann asserted, is almost always slower than the movement of events, and this sets up a "compulsion to make mistakes." In his judgment, the public officials on whose shoulders the great decisions rest have too often been timid souls: "Democratic officials—over and above their own human propensity to err—have been compelled to make the big mistakes that public opinion insisted upon." . . .

But I am convinced that Lippmann's blanket judgment was too harsh, his characterization too severe. While most public officials, including Congressmen, do yearn for public approbation and aspire to please those they represent, it is extreme to equate this natural desire with a lack of intellectual honesty or to conclude from it that they are "insecure and intimidated men."

As we have seen, there are two fundamental concepts of a legislator's duty. Occasionally the two will clash. Bearing in mind that he is the chosen *representative* of the people who elected him, one must ask himself what this means. Is he to represent his constituency by accurately reflecting their wishes and subordinating any divergent views of his own, giving voice primarily to their thoughts? Or is he to represent them in the sense of a free agent, by using his own best judgment in their behalf?

If happily his independent judgment confirms the sentiments of those who have chosen him to be their spokesman, there is no problem. Frequently this is the case. Indeed if it were not usually so, then the Congressman or Senator in question probably would not be a good representative for that particular constituency, and it is likely that he would not be one of any kind for long. There is nothing improper in a legislator's seeing things generally as his constituents do. This is the way it was intended to be. To say that he can be right only by disagreeing with the majority is to assume that the majority always will be wrong. To conclude that the public instincts are generally at variance with sound legislative policy would be to confess a rather shocking lack of faith in this thing we call democracy.

But what of those situations, relatively less common perhaps, when the member of Congress will be deeply and sincerely convinced that a given course of action is best for our country and when most of his constituents will firmly believe otherwise? What if his long and careful personal study of the problem, abetted by factual information not generally known to the electorate at large, convinces him that the public is mistaken for want of specific understanding? What if he realizes that the periodicals generally read in his district and from which local opinions necessarily are formed have emphasized only one side of the issue?

And, finally, what if he regards public sentiment on the matter in question to be not only mistaken but so unyieldingly so that it will mean his own defeat if he follows the dictates of his mind and conscience? It is at this point that the mettle of his intellectual honesty is tested. . . .

Few if any in the public life today can be as disdainful of public sentiment as to echo precisely the words of John C. Calhoun, who said: "I never know what South Carolina thinks of a measure. I never consult her. I act as to the best of my judgment and according to my conscience. If she approves, well and good. If she does not and wishes anyone to take my place, I am ready to vacate."

Some, however, honestly could come close to this expression. Sam Rayburn did not believe that a Congressman should be oblivious to public sentiment, but he believed it the Representative's duty to mold opinion, not to follow it. He had a rich contempt for organized efforts to influence Congress by newspaper campaigns and letter-writing forays, matched only by his contempt and pity for any Congressman whom Rayburn might privately describe as being "afraid of his district." Once he expressed to me his conviction that "any congressman worth his salt can *lead* his district." Rayburn in truth could and did. Others are less fortunate. . . .

When a freshman Congressman from Atlanta, Georgia, votes *for* the Civil Rights Bill, as Charles Longstreet Weltner did on July 2, 1964, you have an example of political courage in action. Weltner was the only member from the Deep South to cast a vote for the Civil Rights Act of 1964. He made a speech on the floor of the House pointing out that, since his name begins with a *W*, the issue would be already decided by the time he would be casting his vote, so therefore it would be easy to play it safe and vote "No." However, his conscience would not let him do this, and he voted "Aye."

His brief speech was a classic. When he took the floor, not even his home state colleagues knew the position he was about to take. It had been an agonizing choice for Charlie Weltner himself. There were passages in the bill that he didn't like. A plebiscite of his district surely would have revealed a majority of the voters strongly opposed the measure.

"What, then, is the proper course?" he asked. "Is it to vote 'no' with tradition, safety—and futility? I believe a greater cause can be served. Change, swift and certain, is upon us, and we in the South face some difficult decisions.

"We can offer resistance and defiance, with their harvest of strife and tumult. We can suffer continued demonstrations, with their wake of violence and disorder. Or, we can acknowledge this measure as the law of the land. We can accept the verdict of the Nation . . . most assuredly, moderation, tranquility, and orderly processes combine as a cause greater than conformity. . . . I shall cast my vote with that greater cause they serve. I will add my voice to those who seek reasoned and conciliatory adjustment to a new reality."

Weltner risked his entire future on that one statement. He knew very well that he was doing it. Whether one agrees with his conclusion or not, nobody can deny that it took courage. He did not seek reelection. . . .   ■

IDEALS AND THE NEED FOR COMPROMISE
Martin Tolchin

They come to Congress hoping to change the world, or at least a corner of it. They bring their ideals, their values and priorities, their vision of where the nation should be headed. But then they discover that almost everyone else has a vision, too, and to get anything at all done, they must learn the art of compromise.

"It's a paradox of sorts," Senator Howard H. Baker Jr. of Tennessee, the majority leader, said. "People come here with ideals, and this place reinforces their idealism. But Congress is an institution of compromises, and that's the antithesis of idealism."

Those most idealistically committed seldom arrive here, the old hands point out. Such people seem to find it difficult to make the compromises needed to wage successful campaigns for Congress. Instead, a quest for ideological purity leads them to spend their days in splinter groups, working out third-party platforms.

Those who do arrive here, like the hero of Frank Capra's "Mr. Smith Goes to Washington," find their ideals immediately tested by an array of imposing forces, including party leadership and interest groups. "You lose sight of what you really believe in," said Michael Johnson, an aide to the House Republican leadership. "Your beliefs are put to the test every minute of every hour of every day. You have some of the finest minds, greatest resources of information and the influences of politics and power all smothering your fragile, delicate, individual beliefs."

LONG RECALLS HIS DECISION

Representative Gillis W. Long, a Louisiana Democrat who is chairman of his party's caucus, agrees that Washington is "a very tough place" to be an idealist. He was elected to Congress in 1962, and got caught in the power conflict between President Kennedy and Howard W. Smith, chairman of the Rules Committee, who was blocking Kennedy legislation. The young Congressman cast a vote to expand the Rules Committee to negate Mr. Smith's power, and paid dearly for it.

"I got defeated as a result," he recalled. "They just waved the Southern flag and played Dixie and said, 'Vote against the man who voted against the South.' After you suffer something like that and you have another opportunity, you can't help but give political consideration to every vote you cast." Mr. Long, was reelected in 1972.

But like most of his colleagues, Mr. Long says that he has in his own mind a set of principles that he will not give up. In his case, he said, they deal for the most part with civil rights and human rights. "Everyone here has that problem, to a greater or lesser degree," he said.

Still, no one goes out looking for trouble. Senator Jim Sasser, a Tennessee Democrat, recalls waiting until the last moment before casting a tie-breaking vote against a proposal to bar funds to medical schools that taught abortion techniques. The vote came in 1982, when he was running for re-election. "You have to be able to live with yourself," he said.

But a Southern Democrat confesses that his instinct for political survival has led him into votes against abortions, although he adds, "Every time I cast a vote on abortion, I hold my nose."

Members nevertheless discover that most issues involve gradations, rather than simple right and wrong. In addition, Congressional leaders are adept at packaging legislation that has something for everyone, producing hard choices for some highly committed members.

Ideals also can be buried in Congressional work; members can get so caught up in round-the-clock negotiations on committee markups and House-Senate conferences that they sometimes forget their priorities in their desire to get it over with and get home for a decent night's sleep. "They get so bogged down worrying about minutiae that they don't have enough time or energy to step back and think about what they're doing," said an aide to the Senate Republican leadership.

Highly idealistic members who refuse to compromise often find themselves rendered ineffective. Their colleagues usually consider them more interested in taking positions than in passing legislation. "The idealists all stand over in the corner and posture, and let us compromisers get things done for them," said Representative Barber B. Conable, an upstate New York Republican who is the ranking minority member of the Ways and Means Committee.

SOLARZ LOST 'ILLUSIONS'

Members also find it difficult to delude themselves for very long. "What I've lost in the Congress is not my ideals, but my illusions," said Representative Stephen J. Solarz, a Brooklyn Democrat. The illusions, he said, included a belief in the nearly total virtue of his positions, and the irredeemable evil of his opponents. "The reality is that there are responsible and often persuasive arguments on both sides of an issue, and that no one has a monopoly on truth and wisdom," he said. "The good and the bad are frequently totally intertwined, and often the only way to get something good is to accept something bad."

As examples, he pointed to the immigration bill now hanging fire between the House and the Senate. He supported it because it legalized the status of millions of aliens, even though the bill included a guestworker program that he opposed. He similarly voted for a foreign aid bill that provided "desperately needed" funds for Israel, which he supported, but also included unrestricted aid to El Salvador, which he opposed. Similarly, the military budget provides needed money for defense, he said, but also "unjustfied weapons systems we'd be better off without."

THE USES OF COMPROMISE

Representative Bill Gradison, Ohio Republican, put it another way: "The public has the view that the shortest distance between two points is a straight line, but that's not true in government. If you see 'compromise' as a dirty word, you're in the wrong place."

But the consensus is that, without some guiding ideals, most members would find their Congressional careers meaningless.

"I've never seen a bunch of more idealistic people, on both the left and right," said Representative Don Edwards, a California Democrat, who has spent 22 years in Congress. "It's not a way to make money. It's disruptive of family life. Without ideals, this place wouldn't be any fun." ■

WHAT IS IT LIKE TO BE A REPRESENTATIVE OR SENATOR?

As noted earlier, Congress is both an institution and a collection of individuals. What is it like to be one of those individuals? What motivates them?

In an excerpt of a book by David R. Mayhew, *The Electoral Connection,* it is said that the desire for reelection is the paramount drive of members of Congress. For Richard F. Fenno, Jr., though, congressional motivations can also include the desire to be influential in Washington and the desire to help make good public policy. In the Fenno book excerpted here, *Home Style,* Fenno draws a distinction between members of Congress who follow "constituency careers" and those who follow "Washington careers."

New Yorker writer Elizabeth Drew once tagged along day after day with former U.S. Senator John Culver, Democrat from Iowa, who was later defeated for reelection. She recorded in detail everyting Culver did each day. In an excerpt from her resulting book, *Senator*, we see what one typical day in the life of a senator can be like.

CONGRESS: THE ELECTORAL INCENTIVE
David R. Mayhew

Whether they are safe or marginal, cautious or audacious, congressmen must constantly engage in activities related to reelection. There will be differences in emphasis, but all members share the root need to do things—indeed, to do things day in and day out during their terms. The next step here is to present a typology, a short list of the *kinds* of activities congressmen find it electorally useful to engage in. The case will be that there are three basic kinds of activities. It will be important to lay them out with some care . . .

One activity is *advertising,* defined here as any effort to disseminate one's name among constituents in such a fashion as to create a favorable image but in messages having little or no issue content. A successful congressman builds what amounts to a brand name, which may have a generalized electoral value for other politicians in the same family. The personal qualities to emphasize are experience, knowledge, responsiveness, concern, sincerity, independence, and the like. Just getting one's name across is difficult enough; only about half the electorate, if asked, can supply their House members' names. It helps a congressman to be known. "In the main, recognition carries a positive valence; to be perceived at all is to be perceived favorably." A vital advantage enjoyed by House incumbents is that they are much better known among voters than their November challengers. They are better known because they spend a great deal of time, energy, and money trying to make themselves better known. There are standard routines—frequent visits to the constituency, nonpolitical speeches to home audiences, the sending out of infant care booklets and letters of condolence and congratulation. Of 158 House members questioned in the mid-1960s, 121 said that they regularly sent newsletters to their constituents, 48 wrote separate news or opinion columns for newspapers; 82 regularly reported to their constituencies by radio or television; 89 regularly sent out mail questionnaires. Some routines are less standard. Congressman George E. Shipley (D., Ill.) claims to have met personally about half his constituents (i.e. some 200,000 people). For over twenty years Congressman Charles C. Diggs, Jr. (D., Mich.) has run a radio program featuring himself as a "combination disc jockey-commentator and minister." Congressman Daniel J. Flood (D., Pa.) is "famous for appearing unannounced and often uninvited at wedding anniversaries and other events." Anniversaries and other events aside, congressional advertising is done largely at public expense. Use of the franking privilege has mushroomed in recent years; in early 1973 one estimate predicted that House and Senate members would send out about 476 million pieces of mail in the year 1974, at a public cost of $38.1 million—or about 900,000 pieces per member with a subsidy of $70,000 per member. By far the heaviest mailroom traffic comes in Octobers of even-numbered years. There are some differences between House and Senate members in the ways they go about getting their names across. House members are free to blanket their constituencies with mailings for all boxholders; senators are not. But senators find it easier to appear on national television—for example, in short reaction statements on the nightly news shows. Advertising is a staple congressional activity, and there is no end to it. For each member there are always new voters to be apprised of his worthiness and old voters to be reminded of it.

A second activity may be called *credit claiming,* defined here as acting so as to generate a belief in a relevant political actor (or actors) that one is personally responsible for causing the government, or some unit thereof, to do something that the actor (or actors) considers desirable. The political logic of this, from the congressman's point of view, is that an actor who believes that a member can make pleasing things happen will no doubt wish to keep him in office so that he can make pleasing things happen in the future. The emphasis here is on individual accomplishment (rather than, say, party or governmental accomplishment) and on the congressman as doer (rather than as, say, expounder of constituency views). Credit claiming is highly important to congressmen, with the consequence that much of congressional life is a relentless search for opportunities to engage in it.

Where can credit be found? If there were only one congressman rather than 535, the answer would in principle be simple enough. Credit (or blame) would attach in Downsian fashion to the doings of the government as a whole. But there are 535. Hence it becomes necessary for each congressman to try to peel off pieces of governmental accomplishment for which he can believably generate a sense of responsibility. For the average congressman the staple way of doing this is to traffic in what may be called "particularized benefits." Particularized governmental benefits, as the term will be used here, have two properties: (1) Each benefit is given out to a specific individual, group, or geographical constituency, the recipient unit being of a scale that allows a single congressman to be recognized (by relevant political actors and other congressmen) as the claimant for the benefit (other congressmen being perceived as indifferent or hostile). (2) Each benefit is given out in apparently ad hoc fashion (unlike, say, social security checks) with a congressman apparently having a hand in the allocation. A particularized benefit can normally be regarded as a member of a class. That is, a benefit given out to an individual, group, or constituency can normally be looked upon by congressmen as one of a class of similar benefits given out to sizable numbers of individuals, groups, or constituencies. Hence the impression can arise that a congressman is getting "his share" of whatever it is the government is offering. (The classes may be vaguely defined. Some state legislatures deal in what their members call "local legislation.")

In sheer volume the bulk of particularized benefits come under the heading of "casework"—the thousands of favors congressional offices perform for supplicants in ways that normally do not require legislative action. High school students ask for essay materials, soldiers for emergency leaves, pensioners for location of missing checks, local governments for grant information, and on and on. Each office has skilled professionals who can play the bureaucracy like an organ—pushing the right pedals to produce the desired effects. But many benefits require new legislation, or at least they require important allocative decisions on matters covered by existent legislation. Here the congressman fills the traditional role of supplier of goods to the home district. It is a believable role; when a member claims credit for a benefit on the order of a dam, he may well receive it. Shiny construction projects seem especially useful . . .

The third activity congressmen engage in may be called *position taking*, defined here as the public enunciation of a judgmental statement on anything likely to be of interest to political actors. The statement may take the form of a roll call vote. The most important classes of judgmental statements are those prescribing American governmental ends (a vote cast against the war; a statement that "the war should be ended immediately") or governmental means (a statement that "the way to end the war is to take it to the United Nations"). The judgments may be implicit rather than explicit, as in: "I will support the president on this matter." But judgments may range far beyond these classes to take in implicit or explicit statements on what almost anybody should do or how he should do it: "The great Polish scientist Copernicus has been unjustly neglected"; "The way for Israel to achieve peace is to give up the Sinai." The congressman as position taker is a speaker rather than a doer. The electoral requirement is not that he make pleasing things happen but that he make pleasing judgmental statements. The position itself is the political commodity. Especially on matters where governmental responsibility is widely diffused it is not surprising that political actors should fall back on positions as tests of incumbent virtue. For voters ignorant of congressional processes the recourse is an easy one. The following comment by one of Clapp's House interviewees is highly revealing: "Recently, I went home and began to talk about the _____ act. I was pleased to have sponsored that bill, but it soon dawned on me that the point wasn't getting through at all. What was getting through was that the act might be a help to people. I changed the emphasis: I didn't mention my role particularly, but stressed my support of the legislation."

The ways in which positions can be registered are numerous and often imaginative. There are floor addresses ranging from weighty orations to mass-produced "nationality day statements." There are speeches before home groups, television appearances, letters, newsletters, press releases, ghostwritten books, *Playboy* articles, even interviews with political scientists. On occasion congressmen generate what amount to petitions; whether or not to sign the 1956 Southern Manifesto defying school desegregation rulings was an important decision for southern members. Outside the roll call process the congressman is usually able to tailor his positions to suit his audiences. A solid consensus in the constituency calls for ringing declarations; for years the later Senator James K. Vardaman (D., Miss.) campaigned on a proposal to repeal the Fifteenth Amendment. Division or uncertainty in the constituency calls for waffling; in the late 1960s a congressman had to be a poor politician indeed not to be able to come up with an inoffensive statement on Vietnam ("We must have peace with honor at the earliest possible moment consistent with the national interest"). On a controversial issue a Capitol Hill office normally prepares two form letters to send out to constituent letter writers—one for the pros and one (not directly contradictory) for the antis. . . .

Probably the best position-taking strategy for most congressmen at most times is to be conservative—to cling to their own positions of the past where possible and to reach for new ones with great caution where necessary. Yet in an earlier discussion of strategy the suggestion was made that it might be rational for members in electoral danger to resort to innovation. The form of innovation available is entrepreneurial position taking, its logic being that for a member facing defeat with his old array of positions it makes good sense to gamble on some new ones. It may be that congressional marginals fulfiill an important function here as issue pioneers—experimenters who test out new issues and thereby show other politicians which ones are usable. An example of such a pioneer is Senator Warren Magnuson (D., Wash.), who responded to a surprisingly narrow victory in 1962 by reaching for a reputation in the area of consumer affairs. Another example is Senator Ernest Hollings (D., S.C.), a servant of a shaky and racially heterogeneous southern constituency who launched "hunger" as an issue in 1969—at once pointing to a problem and giving it a useful nonracial definition. One of the most successful issue entrepreneurs of recent decades was the late Senator Joseph McCarthy (R., Wis.); it was all there—the close primary in 1946, the fear of defeat in 1952, the desperate casting about for an issue, the famous 1950 dinner at the Colony Restaurant where suggestions were tendered, the decision that "Communism" might just do the trick.

The effect of position taking on electoral behavior is about as hard to measure as the effect of credit claiming. Once again there is a variance problem; congressmen do not differ very much among themselves in the methods they use or the skills they display in attuning themselves to their diverse constituencies. All of them, after all, are professional politicians. . . .

There can be no doubt that congressmen believe positions make a difference. An important consequence of this belief is their custom of watching each other's elections to try to figure out what positions are salable. Nothing is more important in Capital Hill politicians than the shared conviction that election returns have proven a point. . . .

These, then, are the three kinds of electorally oriented activities congressmen engage in—advertising, credit claiming, and position taking. . . . ■

HOME STYLE: HOME AND WASHINGTON LINKAGE
Richard F. Fenno, Jr.

. . . When we speak of constituency careers, we speak primarily of the pursuit of the goal of reelection. When we speak of Washington careers, we speak primarily of the pursuit of the goals of influence in the House and the making of good public policy. Thus the intertwining of careers is, at bottom, an intertwining of member goals.

So long as they are in the expansionist stage of their constituency careers, House members will be especially attentive to their home base. They will pursue the goal of reelection with single-minded intensity and will allocate their resources disproportionately to that end. As noted in Chapters Two and Six, first-term members go home more frequently, place a larger proportion of their staff in the district, and more often leave their families at home than do their senior colleagues. Building a reelection constituency at home and providing continuous access to as much of that constituency as possible requires time and energy. Inevitably, these are resources that might otherwise be allocated to efforts in Washington. "The trouble is," said one member near the end of his second term,

> I haven't been a congressman yet. The first two years, I spent all of my time getting myself reelected. That last two years, I spent getting myself a district so that I could get reelected. So I won't be a congressman until next year.

By being "a congressman" he means pursuing goals above and beyond that of reelection (i.e., power in the House and good public policy).

In a House member's first years, the opportunities for gaining inside power and policy influence are limited. Time and energy and staff can be allocated to home without an acute sense of conflict. At rates that vary from congressman to congressman, however, the changes to have some institutional or legislative effect improve. As members stretch to avail themselves of the opportunity, they may begin to experience some allocative strain. It requires time and energy to develop a successful career in Washington just as it does to develop a successful careeer in the district. Because it may not be possible to allocate these resources to House and home, each to an optimal degree, members may have to make allocative and goal choices.

A four-term congressman with a person-to-person home style described the dilemma of choice:

> I'm beginning to be a little concerned about my political future. I can feel myself getting into what I guess is a natural and inevitable condition—the gradual erosion of my local orientation. I'm not as enthused about tending my constituency relations as I used to be and I'm not paying them the attention I should be. There's a natural tension between being a good representative and taking an interest in government. I'm getting into some heady things in Washington,

and I want to make an input into the government. It's making me a poorer representative than I was. I find myself avoiding the personal collisions that arise in the constituency—turning away from that one last handshake, not bothering to go to that one last meeting. I find myself forgetting people's names. And I find myself caring less about it than I used to. Right now, it's just a feeling I have. In eight years I have still to come home less than forty weekends a year. This is my thirty-sixth trip this year. What was it Arthur Rubinstein said? "If I miss one practice, I notice it. If I miss two practices, my teacher notices it. If I miss a week of practice, my audience notices it." I'm at stage one right now— or maybe stage one and stage two. But I'm beginning to feel that I could be defeated before long. And I'm not going to change. I don't want the status. I want to contribute to government.

The onset of a Washington career is altering his personal goals and his established home style. He is worried about the costs of the change; but he is willing to accept some loss of reelection support in exchange for his increased influence in Congress.

This dilemma faces every member of Congress. It is built into the twin requirements that Congress be a representative and a legislative institution. Some members believe they can achieve reelection at home together with influence or policy in Washington without sacrificing either. During Congressman O's first year as a subcommittee chairman, . . . I asked him whether his new position would make it more difficult to tend to district matters. He replied,

If you mean, am I getting Potomac fever, the answer is no. If you mean, has the change in my official duties here made me a better congressman, the answer is, yes. If you mean has is taken away from my activity in the constituency, the answer is no.

Congressman O, we recall, has been going home less; but he has been increasing the number and the activity of his district staff. Although he speaks confidently of his allocative solution, he is not unaware of potential problems. "My staff operation runs by itself. They don't need me. Maybe I should worry about that. You aren't going back and say I'm ripe for the plucking are you? I don't think I am."

A three-term member responded very positively when I paraphrased the worries of the congressman friend of his who had quoted Arthur Rubinstein:

You can do your job in Washington and in your district if you know how. My quarrel with [the people like him] of this world is that they don't learn to be good politicians before they get to Congress. They get there because some people are sitting around the table one day and ask them to do it. They're smart, but they don't learn to organize a district. Once you learn to do that, it's much easier to do your job in Washington.

This member, however, has not yet tasted the inside influence of his friend. Moreover, he does not always talk with such assurance. His district is not so well organized that he has reduced his personal attentiveness to it.

Ralph Krug [the congressman in the adjacent district] tells me I spoil my constituents. He says, "You've been elected twice; you know your district; once a month is enough to come home." But that's not my philosophy. Maybe it will be someday. . . . My lack of confidence is still a pressure which brings me home. This is my political base. Washington is not my political base. I feel I have to come home to get nourished, to see for myself what's going on. It's my security blanket—coming home.

For now, he feels no competing pulls; but he is not unaware of his friend's dilemma.

Members pose the dilemma with varying degrees of immediacy. No matter how confident members may be of their ability to pursue their Washington and their constituency careers simultaneously, however, they all recognize the potentiality of conflict and worry about coping with it. It is our guess that the conflict between the reelection goal on the one hand and the power or policy goals on the other hand becomes most acute for members as they near the peak of influence internally. For, at this stage of their Washington career, the resource requirements of the Washington job make it nearly impossible to meet established expectations of attentiveness at home. Individuals who want nothing from their Washington careers except the status of being a member of Congress will never pursue any other goal except reelection. For these people, the dilemma of which we speak is minimal. Our concern is with those individuals who find, sooner or later, that they wish to pursue a mix of goals in which reelection must be weighted along with power or policy.

One formula for managing a mix of goals that gives heavy weight to a Washington career is to make one's influence in Washington the centerpiece of home style. The member says, in effect, "I can't come home to present myself in person as much as I once did, because I'm so busy tending to the nation's business; but my seniority, my influence, my effectiveness in Washington is of great benefit to you." He asks his supportive constituents to adopt a new set of expectations, one that would put less of a premium on access. Furthermore, he asks these constituents to remain sufficiently intense in their support to discourage challengers—especially those who will promise access. All members do some of this when they explain their Washington activity—especially in connection with "explaining power." And, where possible, they quote from favorable national commentary in their campaign literature. But [few have] made Washington influence the central element of . . . home style.

One difficulty of completely adopting such a home style is that the powerful Washington legislator can actually get pretty far out of touch with his supportive constituents back home. One of the more senior members of my group, and a leader of his committee, recounted the case when his preoccupation with an internal legislative impasse affecting Israel caused him to neglect the crucial Jewish element of his primary constituency—a group "who contribute two-thirds of my money." A member of the committee staff had devised an amendment to break the deadlock.

Peter Tompkins looked at it and said to rne, "Why don't we sponsor it?" So we put it forward, and it became known as the Crowder-Tompkins Amendment. I did it because I respected the staff man who suggested it and because I wanted to get something through that was reasonable. Well, a member of the committee called people back home and said, "Crowder is selling out." All hell broke loose. I started getting calls at two and three in the morning from my friends asking me what I was doing. So I went back home and discussed the issue with them. When I walked into the room, it made me feel sad and shocked to feel their hostility. They wanted me to know that they would clobber me if they thought I was selling out. Two hours later, we walked out friends again. I dropped the Crowder-Tompkins Amendment. That's the only little flare up I've ever had with the Jewish community. But it reminded me of their sensitivity to anything that smacks of discrimination.

The congressman survived. But he would not have needed so forceful a reminder of his strongest supporters' concerns were he nearer the beginning of his constituency career. But, of course, neither would he have been a committee leader, and neither would the imperatives of a House career bulked so large in his mix of goals.

Another way to manage conflicting reelection and Washington career goals might be to use one's Washington influence to alter support patterns at home. That is, instead of acting—as is the normal case—to reenforce home support, to keep what he had "last time," the congressman might act to displace that old support with compensating new support. He might even accomplish this inadvertently, should his pursuit of power or policy attract, willy-nilly, constituents who welcomed his new mix of goals. The very Washington activity that left him out of touch with previously supportive constituents might put him in touch with newly supportive ones. A newly acquired position of influence in a particular policy area or a new reputation as an effective legislator might produce such a feedback effect. . . .

. . . [There is] a tendency for successful home styles to harden over time and to place stylistic constraints on the congressman's subsequent behavior. The pursuit of a Washington career helps us explain this constituency phenomenon. That is, to the degree that a congressman pursues power or policy goals in the House, he will have that much less time or energy to devote to the consideration of alternative home styles. His predisposition to "do what we did last time" at home will be further strengthened by his growing preoccupation with Washington matters. Indeed, the speed with which a congressman begins to develop a Washington career will affect the speed with which his home style solidifies. . . .

In all of this speculation about career linkages, we have assumed that most members of Congress develop, over time, a mix of personal goals. We particularly assume that most members will trade off some of their personal commitment to reelection in order to satisfy a personal desire for institutional or policy influence. It is our observation, based on only eighteen cases, that House members do, in fact, exhibit varying degrees of commitment to reelection. All want reelection in the abstract, but not all will pay any price to achieve it; nor will all pay the same price. . . .

One senior member contemplated retirement in the face of an adverse redistricting but, because he had the prospect of a committee chairmanship, he decided to run and hope for the best. He wanted reelection because he wanted continued influence; but he was unwilling to put his present influence in jeopardy by pursuing reelection with the same intensity that marked his earlier constituency career. As he put it,

Ten years ago, I whipped another redistricting. And I did it by neglecting my congressional duties. . . . Today I don't have the time, and I'm not going to neglect my duties. . . . If I do what is necessary to get reelected and thus become chairman of the committee, I will lose the respect and confidence of my fellow committee members because of being absent from the hearings and, occasionally, the votes.

He did not work hard at reelection, and he won by his narrowest margin ever. But he succeeded in sustaining a mix of personal goals very different from an earlier one. . . .

The congressman's home activities are more difficult and taxing than we have previously recognized. Under the best of circumstances, the tension involved in maintaining constituency contact and achieving legislative competence is considerable. Members cannot be in two places at once, and the growth of a Washington career exacerbates the problem. But, more than that, the demands in both places have grown recently. The legislative workload and the demand for legislative expertise are steadily increasing. So is the problem of maintaining meaningful contact with their several constituencies. Years ago, House members returned home for months at a time to live among their supportive constituencies, soak up the home atmosphere, absorb local problems at first hand. Today, they race home for a day, a weekend, a week at a time. Only seven of the eighteen maintain a family home in their district. The other eleven stay with relatives or friends or in barely furnished rooms when they are at home. The citizen demand for access, for communication, and for the establishment of trust is as great as ever. So members go home. But the quality of their contact has suffered. "It's like a one-night stand in a singles bar." It is harder to sustain a genuine two-way communication than it once was. House member worries about the home relationship—great under any circumstances, but greater now— contribute to the strain and frustration of the job. Some cope; but others retire. It may be those members who cannot stand the heat of the home relationship who are getting out of the House kitchen. If so, people prepared to be more attentive to home . . . are likely to replace them.

The interplay between home careers and Washington careers continues even as House members leave Congress. For, in retirement or in defeat, they still face a choice—to return home or to remain in Washington. The subject of postcongressional careers is too vast to be treated here. But students of home politics can find, in these choices, indications of the depth and durability of home attachments in the face of influential Washington careers. It is conventional wisdom in the nation's capital that senators and representatives "get Potomac fever" and that "they don't go back to Pocatello" when their legislative careers end. Having pursued the goals of power and policy in Washington with increasing success, they prefer, it is said, to continue their Washington career in some nonlegislative job rather than to go back home. In such a choice, perhaps, we might find the ultimate displacement of the constituency career with the Washington career.

An examination of the place of residence of 370 individuals who left the House between 1954 and 1974, and who were alive in 1974, sheds considerable doubt on this Washington wisdom. It appears that most House members do, indeed, "go back to Pocatello." Of the 370 former members studied, 253 (68 percent) resided in their home states in 1974; 91 lived in the Washington, D.C., area;

and 26 resided someplace else. Of those 344 who chose either Washington or home, therefore, nearly three-quarters chose home. This simple fact underscores the very great strength of the home attachments we have described in this book.

No cross section of living former members will tell us for sure how many members lingered in Washington for a while before eventually returning home. Only a careful tracing of all individual cases, therefore, will give us a full and accurate description of the Washington-home choice. Even so, among the former members most likely to be attracted to Washington—those who left Congress from 1970 to 1974—only 37 percent have chosen to remain there. A cursory glance at all those who have chosen to prolong their Washington careers, however, tells us what we might expect—that they have already had longer congressional careers than those who returned home. Our data also tells us that these members are younger than those who choose to return home. Thus, we speculate, the success of a member's previous career in Congress and the prospect that he or she still has time to capitalize on that success in the Washington community are positive inducements to stay. And these inducements seem unaffected by the manner of his or her leaving Congress—whether by electoral defeat (for renomination or reelection) or retirement. . . .

In probing for linkages between home and Washington, it is natural to ask if there are any connections between home style and Washington behavior. If we mean to ask whether members of Congress do certain things in Washington to shore up constituent support at home, the answer is obviously yes. And what they do is well known and straightforward. They allocate the tasks of their staffs in ways they think helpful in getting reelected. They choose committee assignments they think will bring identification with and benefit to their supportive constituencies. They vote in ways they think will be approved by their supportive constituents. Or, better, they avoid voting in ways they believe will be intensely disapproved by their supportive constituents. They will also vote in ways that help them structure their need to explain back home. . . .   ■

A DAY IN THE LIFE OF A SENATOR
Elizabeth Drew

WEDNESDAY, JULY 12th: The Senate went into session at eight o'clock this morning on another military bill, this one for construction of military buildings, and so on, as opposed to the "hardware" authorized in yeterday's military-procurement bill. By now, at ten-thirty, Culver has met on the Senate steps with a 4-H Club delegation from Council Bluffs, posed for pictures with them, and given them a brief tour of the Capitol, telling its history and describing the fresco under the dome in some detail; gone, along with Clark, to the Russell Office

Building to make a statement introducing the director of the Iowa Department of Transportation's Railroad Division to the Surface Transportation Subcommittee of the Senate Commerce Committee, before which the director was to testify (Culver says that he does this sort of thing about a half-dozen times a year); posed for pictures with two young women who are representing Iowa at Girls Nation, an American Legion program (they were supposed to meet Culver on the Senate steps, but were late, and finally caught up with him at the subcommittee hearing). Now he is heading for a meeting of the Judiciary Committee, in the Dirksen Building.

As Culver moves through the halls, his size makes him appear to be lumbering along, but actually he covers a lot of ground quickly. While he makes his way to the Judiciary Committee meeting, he is briefed by Josy Gittler, a petite, dark-haired woman who is the chief counsel of Culver's Juvenile Delinquency Subcommittee. (She was the first woman law professor at the University of Iowa.) Yesterday, Miss Gittler gave Culver memorandums on the bills that are to come up before the committee, for him to read last night, and now she briefs him on them: a bill to give the Attorney General the right to sue, and intervene in suits, on behalf of persons who are in state institutions and whose rights have allegedly been violated (she tells him that the vote will be very close, and that Birch Bayh, who is sponsoring the proposal, and the Justice Department are very anxious to have him there, and than she reports how various members of the committee are expected to vote), and measures concerning bankruptcy laws and off-track betting.

Room 2300, where the Judiciary Committee is meeting, is a small room; the senators sit at a long table, and aides and officials and whatever onlookers have managed to get in stand against the walls. Eastland, the chairman, is at one end of the table. The committee is made up of a number of very liberal Democrats and very conservative Republicans and includes a couple of somewhat eccentric types, and the meetings are often lively and sometimes nearly chaotic. As the deliberations proceed, Culver studies the memorandums. These are other people's bills, and he will take no major role; what he wants to do here is understand as best he can what he is voting on. When bills or amendments are offered in the committee by someone whose views he generally shares, and whom he trusts, his inclination will be to go along, but still he wants to be sure of what he's doing. Paul Laxalt, Republican of Nevada, asks that consideration of Bayh's bill be postponed, because Strom Thurmond, Republican of South Carolina, is occupied on the Senate floor with the military-construction bill and has asked for a deferral. (Any senator can block a committee meeting when the Senate is in session.) Laxalt is a pleasant man, liked by his colleagues, and he makes the request in a reasonable tone. Bayh, who has struggled to get enough senators here who back his bill, says, "My problem is, Paul, everyone around this table is busier than a one-armed paperhanger, yet they have squeezed time to be here today." William Scott, a conservative Republican from Virginia, who has the reputation of being a rather limited man, and unpredictable, remarks that Thurmond is a retired general and therefore it's important for him to be on the floor. Culver says, "How about a retired member of the Marine Corps? I'm here."

The senators put the Bayh bill aside, and go on to take up two bankruptcy-law bills and some amendments to one of them, and pass them, and then they take up a bill dealing with interstate regulation of off-track betting. It is sponsored by Senator Charles McC. Mathias, a moderate Republican from Maryland, who is a well-liked man, and who usually lines up with the liberal Democrats on the committee. But Howard Metzenbaum, Democrat of Ohio, has some problems with the bill and asks that consideration of it, too, be postponed. Culver joins him in the request. Culver would like to know more about the implications of the bill. "Let's put it over, Mac, just so we can study it more," he says quietly. Mathias agrees. So these busy people have just given themselves another meeting to attend, more work to do. Dennis DeConcini, Democrat of Arizona, brings up Senate Joint Resolution 135, designating a weekend in late April as Days of Remembrance of Victims of the Holocaust. Eastland asks if there is any objection, and the committee quickly approves the resolution. After the meeting, Culver asks Miss Gittler to take another look at the off-track betting bill, and he goes back to his office to go over the schedule for his trip to Iowa this weekend. No Senate votes are scheduled before one o'clock.

In his office, Culver scans the press clippings and the news summary from the Iowa papers that Don Brownlee prepares for him each day. Culver is pleased that the Des Moines *Register* is running a two-part series explaining why the Endangered Species Act needs to be amended, and that this morning's Washington *Post* has an editorial supporting his approach. Earlier this morning, he asked his staff to prepare a statement for him to insert in the *Congressional Record* about the retirement of a political reporter for the Davenport-area *Quad-City Times*. Next, Culver looks over the notice sent out by the Democratic Whip about what is supposed to come up this week. He has been told that it is still possible that the endangered-species bill will come up Friday, and therefore he doesn't know whether he can be in Iowa then, as he had planned. At the other end, he is scheduled to return from Iowa—via Chicago, where he is to make a speech—about three o'clock on Monday. Dick Oshlo tells him that some of the staff have met with Nelson's staff, and it now seems that Nelson may not actually move to kill Culver's proposal but may simply engage in a colloquy with him on it and then offer some "perfecting amendments." Culver is pleased by this news. He goes over the various possibilities for the schedule in Iowa with Jim Larew, his appointments secretary. Larew, who is twenty-four, worked in Culver's 1974 Senate campaign as a field organizer, and in 1977 received a summa cum laude from Harvard for an honors thesis he wrote on the history of the Democratic Party in Iowa.

Culver goes into the scheduling in great detail—dealing with it as methodically as he deals with legislation: where each event will take place, what the possibility is for television coverage for each one, how many events can be worked in. He is not satisfied with an event that has been tentatively planned for Cedar Rapids, and asks Larew to come up with a better one. He considers whether he can go to a certain city and see just one group without offending others, and decides that he can't, and will go to that city on another trip, when he will have more time to spend there. Culver had been considering going to the Rath packing plant, but he won't be able to get to Waterloo until Saturday and the plant will be closed, so that is out. He decides to go instead to an armed-services recruiting center in Waterloo and talk with the recruiters about how they are coming in meeting their quotas for the volunteer service. "Get representatives of all the services there," he says. "Saturday afternoon is Sleepy Hollow for the media; we should give them notice of this event well in advance—it's a good, substantive story. I'll make a statement on the status of the volunteer services. Let's try to encourage as much interest in the Waterloo-area media as we can, and I think it's a suitable story for the wires out of Des Moines."

The fact that many senators can't get to their states except on weekends without missing votes—and they even take chances if they are gone on Fridays or Mondays—is a problem: it is hard to gather people for political events or for tours of facilities, or even to interest much of the local press, on a weekend. It's difficult to understand how these people can go as hard as they do during the week and then virtually campaign on the weekend, but they are expected to. There is an insatiability in the demands made on them by constituents, by staff and by others who can get at them in Washington. Culver tries to make an average of one working weekend trip to Iowa a month, and he is under some criticism in the state for not doing it more often. (Clark, by contrast, spends a great deal of time in the state. Culver and Clark, while they are friends and have similar—though not identical—voting records, have different temperaments and different political strengths and styles.) Culver rarely goes back to Iowa during the week for an event—a trip would take a lot of time out of his Senate schedule. He keeps up with what is happening within the Party in the state, but he doesn't find petty intra-Party squabbles interesting, and he thinks it is more important to do his work in Washington than to take the twenty-four hours or so it requires to attend one more midweek meeting of some club or other in the state. Senators whose states are nearer to Washington can, of course, get back and forth more easily. New York's senators, for example, virtually have offices on the shuttle. Senators are expected to be both in Washington and in their states, and little consideration seems to be given to the fact that they might also want to spend some time with their families, and to be whole people. Culver does take a great interest in his family and does want to live like a normal human being at least a certain amount of the time. Each senator has limits on what he can do without losing his dignity—or sanity. Culver establishes real human connections to a greater degree than most people in public life; it is clear that he genuinely likes people (some politicians, oddly, don't), and he is interested in what is happening in his friends' lives. He also reads books. The relentless and conflicting demands are what turn many Washington politicians into driven, machinelike people—if they were not that way before they got here—and are a large part of what destroys many families. But it doesn't make news when a senator reads a book, spends time with his family, or sits around talking with friends. There are no votes in doing those things, and it takes some strength, and some innner wholeness, to resist the pressures to almost never do them.

Today, Culver will have lunch in the Democratic senators' dining room. "It's one of the few opportunities, if any, around here to be in a genuinely relaxed and social setting with other senators," he says. "It gives us a chance to talk about what's going on in committees, on the floor, to trade rumors or scuttlebutt, or to talk about sports, about what went on at a party the night before." Some members hardly ever eat there. Some do quite frequently, among them Magnuson, Stennis, Nelson, Hollings, and Long. After lunch, Culver will preside over the Senate for an hour: a chore that—in the absence of the Vice President, who usually presides only when he might have to cast a tie-breaking vote—is rotated primarily among the more junior members of the Senate. Whoever presides is guided by the Parliamentarian if any complications arise.

After Culver gets back to his office this afternooon, things begin to pile up. He gives an interview to the reporter from Iowa who wants to talk to him about the endangered-species bill and whose appointment was postponed from yesterday. The interview takes longer than was scheduled; when Culver gets interested in a subject he keeps going. Several constituents have dropped by. Pat Sarcone, Culver's secretary, has been talking with the constituents, seeing if there's anything she can do to help them. The tone of a senator's office is often set by such a person. She must understand his needs and moods, protect him, and, at the same time, see that the right people do get through to him, and, also at the same time, be pleasant to callers and visitors. Some senators' secretaries become so protective as to cause their bosses' problems with constituents and others. Miss Sarcone, who comes from a political family in Des Moines and has worked for Culver ever since he came to the Senate, understands her boss's temperament and handles the demands on him, and on herself, efficiently, perceptively, and with good humor.

When Culver finishes with the reporters, a half hour behind schedule, he drops into an outer office to greet two constituents—nuns from Clarke College, in Dubuque. "I'm afraid I'm running a little behind," he tells them. They thank him for writing in their behalf to some federal education officials, and he tells them he hopes to see them in Dubuque. A meeting with Phil Hilder, who has been a mail clerk on his staff and is leaving for law school in the fall, is postponed until tomorrow. Now Culver meets with two men—one of them used to be on his staff—who work for the Small Business Administration and are directors of a forthcoming White House conference and want to brief him on their plans. "Now, wait," Culver says to them as they explain their plan. "Why are you having regional conferences before you have state conferences?" It's late in the afternoon, and Culver is pressed, and tired, and he gets a bit cranky. The staff tries not to schedule many meetings for him after four o'clock; in order to give him time to be on the Senate floor, to get caught up on his work, to regroup, to see what needs to be done. Shortly after he begins talking to the S.B.A. men, the buzzers sound, indicating a roll-call vote. Culver buttons his collar, tightens his tie, and puts on his jacket to go over to the Senate floor.

On the way, he tells me that Mike Naylor, his legislative director, has just given him a memorandum asking him to make calls to Frank Moore, the President's assistant for congressional liaison, and to an official of the Office of Management and Budget about his proposal to provide a tax deduction for small businesses that insure themselves for product liability. Naylor has heard that a final decision is going to be made tomorrow about the Administration's position, and the rumor is that it is going to be contrary to Culver's proposal. Culver doesn't know whether the roll call will be on the military-construction bill or on an amendment to another bill: there were indications earlier that the Senate might set the military-construction bill aside temporarily to take up the other one. On the floor, Culver learns that the vote is on the Commodity Futures Trading Commission and after he votes he chats with Dale Bumpers for a while about the Soviet trials and then goes out to the cloakroom to call Frank Moore. He tells Moore of his interest in the legislation, and says that he has received signals that the Administration's position is going to be adverse to his own, and asks him to call the O.M.B. official and relay his message. He suggests that Moore tell the O.M.B. official that he and Nelson, and also Representative Abner Mikva, Democrat of Illinois, have held hearings on the subject, and to consider that they might be in a position to oppose the Administration. Now, having learned that there will not be another vote for at least a half hour, he goes to the Senate gym for a swim, as he often does to get a break from the pressure. He tells me that he gets relief from the strain by going to the gym and kidding around with his colleagues. I have heard some senators and House members talk about literally hiding from their staff members by going to the gym.

At six-thirty, Culver returns to his office, looking refreshed. He has already been to the Senate floor for several votes. A staff member gives him some briefing material for a meeting tomorrow, and Culver asks him a number of questions. Sometimes when Culver is being briefed one can see that he is being told more than he wants to hear. He catches on quickly, but the staff, after all, is steeped in information and wants to pass it along. His eyes will start to fade out, and he will say, somewhat abruptly, to move the conversation along, "O.K. Anything else?" (The other side of this is that he does not like to have to explain something to a staff member more than once.) Culver has an unusually retentive mind, and it is not just one that can spew back what he has been told, or what he has read, but one that absorbs, generates questions, makes connections between things he knows. One of his Senate colleagues says, "Culver has a towering intellect and an inquisitive mind and is intellectually enormously demanding of himself and of associates. When he gets hold of an issue, he studies it, he reads it, he thinks it, he absorbs it." Now Culver talks with Dick Oshlo and Jim Larew about tomorrow's schedule, signs his mail, returns several phone calls, and makes arrangements to have his baggage transferred to the home of some old friends, where he will be staying.

Culver tells me, "What subcommittee you're on is often the luck of the draw. You might not be on it because you have a burning interest in the issue it's concerned with, and we are all spread too thin already. Then you get a bright staff person who works for months on something in the subcommittee that he's particularly interested in, and finally you don't want to disappoint him or her, and so you say 'Go ahead,' only to regret it later because you find yourself involved in something that you don't have sufficient interest in, and spending your energy and political capital on frustrating and unsatisfying efforts."

At seven-thirty, Culver and I join two of his close friends, Alan Baron and Jim Johnson, for dinner at the Palm, a steak restaurant where a number of political people like to eat. Baron is from Iowa, has been heavily involved in national politics, and publishes a political newsletter called *The Baron Report;* Johnson, who is from Minnesota and is executive assistant to Vice President Mondale, first met Culver when Johnson worked in Iowa, among other places, on Edmund Muskie's 1972 Presidential campaign, and then he spent a lot of time helping Culver with his campaign for the Senate two years later. Both Baron and Johnson are very intelligent and have a good sense of humor, and Culver enjoys their company and dines with them from time to time at the Palm. (Often, they are joined by John Reilly, another former Iowan, who is now a Washington attorney, but Reilly cannot make it this evening.) The conversation consists of political gossip, some serious talk about what has been happening, and a great many stories and jokes. As is usually the case in such situations, Culver's humor dominates. It ranges through quick reactions, one-liners, clowning, kidding and reactions to being kidded, and stories. Many of the stories are on himself, in what he recognizes are ludicrous or absurd situations. He gets wound up in the telling of stories; he feeds in little subjokes, puts a lot of energy, even his bulk, into it, laughing so hard himself, and usually repeating the punch line two or three times — interrupting with a "Huh?" and laughing harder each time — that one is swept along by the force as well as the substance. Culver has several laughs: sometimes his mouth turns up and he laughs silently, his big body shaking; sometimes he laughs aloud, at various decibel levels; sometimes he laughs so hard that he doubles over, holding his stomach with one arm. ■

CHAPTER 9

The Presidency

T he Constitution—in Article II—establishes the office of the president of the United States and vests in it "the executive power" of our national government. The president is, then, the Chief Executive.

But the holder of this powerful office has a good many more roles and responsibilities than that. Some, such as that of Commander in Chief, are expressly stated in the Constitution. Others, such as that of leader of his or her party and symbolic leader of the country, are roles which have evolved in practice.

In this chapter, we turn first to the constitutional roles and responsibilities of the office. We then turn to a consideration of presidential power, and, after that, to a debate on the question of whether presidents should be limited to one, six-year term.

Next, we will focus on presidential personality, its importance and the possibilities of predicting it before a president takes office. And, finally, we will give attention to presidential images and the relationship between the president and the media.

THE OFFICE OF THE PRESIDENT

The Constitution of the United States gives a considerable bundle of powers to the president. Excerpted here is an article by a presidential incumbent, Ronald Reagan, giving his impression of those powers—especially the president's roles and responsibilities in regard to executive management, defense and foreign affairs, and in the legislative process. Note that President Reagan feels that the president should have, as do most state governors, a "line-item veto" power—the power to reject individual items within appropriations bills without having to accept or veto the entire bill.

PRESIDENTIAL ROLES AND RESPONSIBILITIES
Ronald Reagan

. . . The Framers looked primarily to the president to provide the critical element of "energy" in the government. The problem with the government of the Articles of Confederation had been that it was "destitute of energy." The Drafters of the Constitution redressed that problem by vesting "competent powers" in the executive to lead the Nation. As Hamilton wrote:

> Energy in the executive is a leading character in the definition of good government. It is essential to the protection of the community against foreign attacks; it is not essential to the steady administration of the laws; to the protection of property against those irregular and high-handed combinations which sometimes interrupt the ordinary course of justice; to the security of liberty against the enterprises and assaults of ambition, of faction, and of anarchy.

The president's popular mandate justified this grant of authority. The president and the vice president with whom he runs are the only officials in our government elected through a process involving all the voters. Only the president can claim to speak for all the people, because, as Hamilton wrote, his selection looks "in the first instance to an immediate act of the people of America." The office of president has "a due dependence on the people, and a due responsibility."

EXECUTIVE MANAGEMENT

Perhaps the most pervasive responsibility of the president is to administer the executive branch. The Framers were practical men who recognized, as Hamilton wrote, "that the true test of a good government is its aptitude and tendency to produce a good administration." The people look ultimately to the president to ensure the efficient performance of duty by the millions of federal employees scattered among the various departments and agencies. I doubt that any of the Framers, prescient as they were, could have imagined the size and scope of today's federal establishment. They nonetheless afforded the presidency the tools necessary "to produce a good administration."

The Framers gave the president the responsibility to "take Care that the Laws be faithfully executed" and the power to appoint officers to assist him in discharging that responsibility. The Constitution provides that the president shall nominate, and by and with the advice and consent of the Senate, shall appoint the officers of the United States. In the landmark case of *Myers v. United States*, Chief Justice William Howard Taft, a former president, wrote that it was a "reasonable implication" from the president's obligation to execute the laws that "he should select those who were to act for him under his direction in the execution of the laws."

The chief justice went on to recognize the principle that the president's appointment power carried with it the corollary power to remove those officers in whom he could no longer place his confidence: "as his selection of administrative officers is essential to the execution of the laws by him, so must be his power of removing those for whom he can not continue to be responsible." As the Framers recognized, this power to appoint and remove officers of the United States is necessary if the president is to be responsible for the faithful execution of the laws and the provision of "a good administration."

The challenge confronting the modern presidency is to "produce a good administration" when the federal establishment has grown so far beyond anything the Framers could have imagined. It is an amazing fact that there are more federal employees today than people living in America when the Framers drafted the Constitution. Perhaps President George Washington could play an active role in supervising the details of the first administration, but it is now the responsibility of his successors to create mechanisms for the control and coordination of the executive branch. One such mechanism is Executive Order 12291, which I issued during my first month in office. Executive Order 12291 for the first time provided effective and coordinated management of the regulatory process. Under the Executive Order, all regulations issued by executive departments and agencies must be reviewed by the Office of Management and Budget before being issued in order to determine whether they conform to the president's policies and to consider, to the extent possible, whether their social benefits will exceed their social costs. The administration has issued a comprehensive statement of regulatory policy, and established procedures to ensure that this policy is reflected in the actions of individual agencies.

Other initiatives include the recent establishment of the President's Council on Management Improvement, an interagency committee charged with improving management and administration throughout government; the President's Council on Integrity and Efficiency, established in 1981 to root out fraud, waste, and mismanagement; and the President's Private Sector Survey on Cost Control's comprehensive review of the functioning of the government. Given the size and scope of the federal bureaucracy, Hamilton's admonition that the executive "produce a good administration" requires careful, continuous attention to regulatory and managerial reform.

At the same time, however, it is fitting to consider whether the federal government is trying to do too much. The Framers did not charge the national government with solving all the problems that might confront the citizens of the Republic: the early Americans were too jealous of their freedom to sanction such an expansive view of central authority. It is the responsibility of the president not only to manage government efficiently, but also to offer leadership in recognizing that government spending must be limited to functions that are the proper responsibility of government and that taxing by government must be limited to providing revenue for legitimate government purposes.

DEFENSE AND FOREIGN AFFAIRS

The president has no more important responsibility under the Constitution than the conduct of foreign affairs. As John Marshall noted on the floor of the House of Representatives, "The President is the sole organ of the nation in its external relations, and its sole representative with foreign nations." In the famous *Curtis-Wright* decision of 1936, the Supreme Court agreed with Marshall's assessment: "In this vast external realm . . . the President alone has the power to speak or listen as a representative of the nation." The president's foreign policy powers derive from the general grant of executive power, the more specific grants of authority to make treaties and appoint and receive ambassadors, and his role as commander in chief of the armed forces.

The Framers recognized that of the two democratic branches, only the executive could successfully conduct foreign relations. Hamilton noted in his description of the executive that "Decision, activity, secrecy, and dispatch will generally characterize the proceedings of one man in a much more eminent degree than the proceedings of any greater number," and John Jay—himself one of our most successful early diplomats—argued that "the President will find no difficulty to provide" those qualities, though they were beyond the capability of a basically deliberative body such as Congress.

When it came to the defense of the Nation, the Framers were even more unambiguous. Hamilton, who served at General Washington's side during the American War of Independence, knew that:

> the direction of war most peculiarly demands those qualities which distinguish the exercise of power by a single hand. The direction of war implies the direction of the common strength; and the power of directing and employing the common strength forms a usual and essential part in the definition of the executive authority.

In the areas of defense and foreign affairs, the Nation must speak with one voice, and only the president is capable of providing that voice.

This is not to denigrate the role of Congress in the development of foreign policy. On the contrary, the Framers required the assent of two-thirds of the senators to a treaty, and of course only Congress possesses the power to declare war. Beyond these defined roles, the support of Congress has been indispensable to an effective foreign policy throughout our history.

The 1970s saw a rapid rise in congressional efforts to affect directly the formulation and implementation of foreign policy by the executive. A large number of prohibitions and restrictions on presidential authority were enacted in the areas of trade, human rights, arms sales, foreign aid, intelligence operations, and the deployment of United States armed forces abroad. Scholars and officials differ over the constitutionality of several of these initiatives. It is important to note, however, that efforts by Congress to participate in the development of American foreign policy must be accompanied by a recognition of the concomitant responsibility for developing bipartisan consensus. We need to restore the honorable American tradition that partisan politics stops at the water's edge. As Congress attempts to augment its foreign policy role, it must ensure that its efforts do not result in America presenting multiple and perhaps discordant voices to the world, to the detriment of its security and interests. The president—"the sole organ of the nation in its external relations"—must continually seek the means of developing a bipartisan legislative-executive consensus on America's role in the world and the means of safeguarding that role. As Congress increasingly enters the foreign policy realm, it too must recognize a greater responsibility for developing such a consensus.

LEGISLATIVE ROLE

Apart from executive functions, the Constitution accords the president a significant role in the legislative process. The president has not merely the power but the duty to "from time to time give to the Congress Information of the State of the Union, and recommend to their Consideration such Measures as he shall judge necessary and expedient . . . ." The people have grown to expect leadership from the president not only in executing the laws but also in presenting a legislative program to Congress for consideration.

Perhaps the most prominent of the president's legislative power is the qualified veto power. This power is qualified in the sense that a bill returned by the president with disapproval can nonetheless be enacted into law by a two-thirds vote of both houses. The Framers accorded the president a veto power for two reasons. First, they recognized the "propensity of the legislative department to intrude upon the rights, and to absorb the powers, of the other departments" and provided the president a veto so that he could defend the prerogatives of his office. The second purpose of the veto was as "an additional security against the enaction of improper laws."

The unique perspective the president can bring to bear on legislation was recognized by Chief Justice Taft:

> The President is a representative of the people just as the members of the Senate and of the House are, and it may be, at some times, on some subjects, that the President elected by all the people is rather more representative of them all than are the members of either body of the Legislature whose constituencies are local and not countrywide.

The intent of the Framers in providing the president a qualified veto power has been frustrated to a large extent by the development of the congressional practice of combining various items in a single appropriations bill. The Framers undoubtedly anticipated that Congress would pass separate appropriations bills for discrete programs or activities, and that the president would be able to review each program. Until about the time of the Civil War, this was the practice of Congress. Since that time, however, Congress has increasingly combined various items of appropriation in omnibus appropriations bills. This makes it difficult for the president to discharge the responsibility vested in him by the Framers, because a president cannot consider the individual items of appropriations separately, but must either veto or approve the package as a whole. The president is thus prevented from using the veto as the Framers intended, "to increase the changes in favor of the community against the passing of bad laws, through haste, inadvertence, or design."

It is for this reason that we have proposed restoring the Framers' original design through a constitutional amendment granting the president line-item veto authority. The constitutions of no fewer than forty-three states grant some such authority to the governor, and the experience at the state level suggests a line-item veto would work well at the federal level.

The powers of the presidency are limited, and the president discharges constitutional responsibilities in a system according other powers to the coordinate branches of the legislature and the judiciary. As the Supreme Court has remarked, there is a

> . . . never-ending tension between the President exercising the executive authority in a world that presents each day some new challenge with which he must deal and the Constitution under which we all live and which no one disputes embodies some sort of system of checks and balances.

The members of all three branches take an oath to uphold the Constitution, and it is a momument not only to the genius of the Framers but also to the statesmanship of those who have held office under the Constitution that the system has worked as well as it has. . . . ■

PRESIDENTIAL POWER

The office of president of the United States is a very powerful office, much more powerful today than the framers anticipated. The Constitution states the formal extent and limits of presidential power. But each occupant has shaped the office somewhat to his own style and the needs of the time as he saw them. Franklin D. Roosevelt, for example, was a very active wielder of presidential power. Dwight Eisenhower, by contrast, was seen as being much less active and aggressive in the exercise of the power of the office. Richard Nixon's failed presidency was a story of misused power. Jimmy Carter never found the levers of power. Ronald Reagan picked them up and used them with relish and effectivness.

What is presidential power? Richard E. Neustadt's classic book, *Presidential Power*, excerpted here, maintains that it is the "power to persuade." Neustadt's book had great influence on John F. Kennedy and his brief presidency.

Political scientist Thomas E. Cronin, on the other hand, is critical of Neustadt's views. In the excerpt printed here, Cronin argues that Neustadt put too great faith in the president as "great leader" and too much emphasis on presidential power and the use of it, regardless of the ends sought.

Presidential power is—and should be—limited, of course. Among other things, it is limited by Supreme Court interpretations of the Constitution, as shown by the excerpt here from the opinion in *United States* v. *Nixon*. In it, the Court denied President Nixon's "executive privilege" claim that he could withhold information—secret tapes—from a court in a Watergate scandal criminal case.

THE POWER TO PERSUADE
Richard E. Neustadt

The limits on command suggest the structure of our government. The constitutional convention of 1787 is supposed to have created a government of "separated powers." It did nothing of the sort. Rather, it created a government of separated institutions *sharing* powers. "I am part of the legislative process," Eisenhower often said in 1959 as a reminder of his veto. Congress, the dispenser of authority and funds, is no less part of the administrative process. Federalism adds another set of separated institutions. The Bill of Rights adds others. Many public purposes can only be achieved by voluntary acts of private institutions; the press, for one, in Douglass Cater's phrase, is a "fourth branch of government." And with the coming of alliances abroad, the separate institutions of a London, or a Bonn, share in the making of American public policy.

What the Constitution separates our political parties do not combine. The parties are themselves composed of separated organizations sharing public authority. The authority consists of nominating powers. Our national parties are confederations of state and local party institutions, with a headquarters that represents the White House, more or less, if the party has a President in office. These confederacies manage presidential nominations. All other public offices depend upon electorates confined within the states. All other nominations are controlled within the states. The President and congressmen who bear one party's label are divided by dependence upon different sets of voters. The differences are sharpest at the stage of nomination. The White House has too small a share in nominating congressmen, and Congress has too little weight in nominating Presidents for party to erase their constitutional separation. Party links are stronger than is frequently supposed, but nominating processes assure the separation.

The separateness of institutions and the sharing of authority prescribe the terms on which a President persuades. When one man shares authority with another, but does not gain or lose his job upon the other's whim, his willingness to act upon the urging of the other turns on whether he conceives the action right for him. The essence of a President's persuasive task is to convince such men that what the White House wants of them is what they ought to do for their sake and on their authority.

Persuasive power, thus defined, amounts to more than charm or reasoned argument. These have their uses for a President, but these are not the whole of his resources. For the men he would induce to do what he wants done on their own responsibility will need or fear some acts by him on his responsibility. If they share his authority, he has some share in theirs. Presidential "powers" may be inconclusive when a President commands, but always remain relevant as he persuades. The status and authrotiy inherent in his office reinforce his logic and his charm.

Status adds something to persuasiveness; authority adds still more. When Truman urged wage changes on his Secretary of Commerce while the latter was administering the steel mills, he and Secretary Sawyer were not just two men reasoning with one another. Had they been so, Sawyer probably would never have agreed to act. Truman's status gave him special claims to Sawyer's loyalty, or at least attention. In Walter Bagehot's charming phrase "no man can *argue* on his knees." Although there is no kneeling in this country, few men — and exceedingly few Cabinet officers — are immune to the impulse to say "yes" to the President of the United States. It grows harder to say "no" when they are seated in his oval office at the White House, or in his study on the second floor, where almost tangibly he partakes of the aura of his physical surroundings. In Sawyer's case, moreover, the President possessed formal authority to intervene in many matters of concern to the Secretary of Commerce. These matters ranged from jurisdictional disputes among the defense agencies to legislation pending before Congress and, ultimately, to the tenure of the Secretary, himself. There is nothing in the record to suggest that Truman voiced specific threats when they negotiated over wage increases. But given his *formal* powers and their relevance to Sawyer's other interests, it is safe to assume that Truman's very advocacy of wage action conveyed an implicit threat.

A President's authority and status give him great advantages in dealing with the men he would persuade. Each "power" is a vantage point for him in the degree that other men have use for his authority. From the veto to appointments, from publicity to budgeting, and so down a long list, the White House now controls the most encompassing array of vantage points in the American political system. With hardly an exception, the men who share in governing this country are aware that at some time, in some degree, the doing of *their* jobs, the furthering of *their* ambitions, may depend upon the President of the United States. Their need for presidential action, or their fear of it, is bound to be recurrent if not actually continuous. Their need or fear is his advantage.

A President's advantages are greater than mere listing of his "powers" might suggest. The men with whom he deals must deal with him until the last day of his term. Because they have continuing relationships with him, his future, while it lasts, supports his present influence. Even though there is no need or fear of him today, what he could do tomorrow may supply today's advantage. Continuing relationships may convert any "power," any aspect of his status, into vantage points in almost any case. When he induces other men to do what he wants done, a President can trade on their dependence now *and* later.

The President's advantages are checked by the advantages of others. Continuing relationships will pull in both directions. These are relationships of mutual dependence. A President depends upon the men he would persuade; he has to reckon with his need or fear of them. They too will possess status, or authority, or both, else they would be of little use to him. Their vantage points confront his own; their power tempers his.

Persuasion is a two-way street. Sawyer, it will be recalled, did not respond at once to Truman's plan for wage increases at the steel mills. On the contrary, the Secretary hesitated and delayed and only acquiesced when he was satisfied that publicly he would not bear the onus of decision. Sawyer had some points of vantage all his own from which to resist presidential pressure. If he had to reckon wih coercive implications in the President's "situations of strength," so had Truman to be mindful of the implications underlying Sawyer's place as a department head, as steel administrator, and as a Cabinet spokesman for business. Loyalty is reciprocal. Having taken on a dirty job in the steel crisis, Sawyer had strong claims to loyal support. Besides, he had authority to do some things that the White House could ill afford. Emulating Wilson, he might have resigned in a huff (the removal power also works two ways). Or emulating Ellis Arnall, he might have declined to sign necessary orders. Or, he might have let it be known publicly that he deplored what he was told to do and protested its doing. By following any of these courses Sawyer almost surely would hve strengthened the position of management, weakened the position of the White House, and embittered the union. But the whole purpose of a wage increase was to enhance White House persuasiveness in urging settlement upon union and companies alike. Although Sawyer's status and authority did not give him the power to prevent an increase outright, they gave him capability to undermine its purpose. If his authority over wage rates had been vested by a statute, not by revocable presidential order, his power of prevention might have been complete. So Harold Ickes demonstrated in the famous case of helium sales to Germany before the Second World War.

The power to persuade is the power to bargain. Status and authority yield bargaining advantages. But in a government of "separated institutions sharing powers," they yield them to all sides. With the array of vantage points at his disposal, a President may be far more persuasive than his logic or his charm could make him. But outcomes are not guaranteed by his advantages. There remain the counter pressures those whom he would influence can bring to bear on him from vantage points at their disposal. Command has limited utility; persuasion becomes give-and-take. It is well that the White House holds the vantage points it does. In such a business any President may need them all—and more.

II

This view of power as akin to bargaining is one we commonly accept in the sphere of congressional relations. Every textbook states and every legislative session demonstrates that save in times like the extraordinary Hundred Days of 1933—times virtually ruled out by definition at mid-century—a President will often be unable to obtain congressional action on his terms or even to halt action he opposes. The reverse is equally accepted: Congress often is frustrated by the President. Their formal powers are so intertwined that neither will accomplish very much, for very long, without the acquiescence of the other. By the same token, though, what one demands the other can resist. The stage is set for that great game, much like collective bargaining, in which each seeks to profit from the other's needs and fears. It is a game played catch-as-catch-can, case by case. And everybody knows the game, observers and participants alike.

The concept of real power as a give-and-take is equally familiar when applied to presidential influence outside the formal structure of the Federal government. The Little Rock affair may be extreme, but Eisenhower's dealings with the Governor—and with the citizens—becomes a case in point. Less extreme but not less pertinent is the steel seizure case with respect to union leaders, and to workers, and to company executives as well. When he deals with such people a President draws bargaining advantage from his status or authority. By virtue of their public places or their private rights they have some capability to reply in kind.

In spheres of party politics the same thing follows, necessarily, from the confederal nature of our party organizations. Even in the case of national nominations a President's advantages are checked by those of others. In 1944 it is by no means clear that Roosevelt got his first choice as his running mate. In 1948 Truman, then the President, faced serious revolts against his nomination. In 1952 his intervention from the White House helped assure the choice of Adlai Stevenson, but it is far from clear that Truman could have done as much for any other candidate acceptable to him. In 1956 when Eisenhower was President, the record leaves obscure just who backed Harold Stassen's effort to block Richard Nixon's renomination as Vice-President. But evidently everything did not go quite as Eisenhower wanted, whatever his intentions may have been. The outcomes in these instances bear all the marks of limits on command and of power checked by power that characterize congressional relations. Both in and out of politics these checks and limits seem to be quite widely understood.

Influence becomes still more a matter of give-and-take when Presidents attempt to deal with allied governments. A classic illustration is the long unhappy wrangle over Suez policy in 1956. In dealing with the British and the French before their military intervention, Eisenhower had his share of bargaining advantages but no effective power of command. His allies had their share of counter pressures, and they finally tried the most extreme of all: action despite him. His pressure then was instrumental in reversing them. But had the British government been on safe ground *at home,* Eisenhower's wishes might have made as little difference after intervention as before. Behind the decorum of diplomacy— which was not very decorous in the Suez affair—relationships among allies are not unlike relationships among state delegations at a national convention. Power is persuasion and persuasion becomes bargaining. The concept is familiar to everyone who watches foreign policy.

In only one sphere is the concept unfamiliar: the sphere of executive relations. Perhaps because of civics textbooks and teaching in our schools, Americans instinctively resist the view that power in this sphere resembles power in all others. Even Washington reporters, White House aides, and congressmen are not immune to the illusion that administrative agencies comprise a single structure, "the" Executive Branch, where presidential word is law, or ought to be. Yet . . . when a President seeks something from executive officials his persuasiveness is subject to the same sorts of limitations as in the case of congressmen, or governors, or national committeemen, or private citizens, or foreign governments. There are no generic differences, no differences in kind and only sometimes in degree. The incidents preceding the dismissal of MacArthur and the incidents surrounding seizure of the steel mills make it plain that here as elsewhere influence derives from bargaining advantages; power is a give-and-take.

Like our governmental structure as a whole, the executive establishment consists of separated institutions sharing powers. The President heads one of these; Cabinet officers, agency administrators, and military commanders head others. Below the department level, virtually independent bureau chiefs head many more. Under mid-century conditions, Federal operations spill across dividing lines on organization charts; almost every policy entangles many agencies; almost every program calls for interagency collaboration. Everything somehow involves the President. But operating agencies owe their existence least of all to one another — and only in some part to him. Each has a separate statutory base; each has its statutes to administer; each deals with a different set of subcommittees at the Capitol. Each has its own peculiar set of clients, friends, and enemies outside the formal government. Each has a different set of specialized careerists inside its own bailiwick. Our Constitution gives the President the "take-care" clause and the appointive power. Our statutes give him central budgeting and a degree of personnel control. All agency administrators are responsible to him. But they *also* are responsible to Congress, to their clients, to their staffs, and to themselves. In short, they have five masters. Only after all of those do they owe any loyalty to each other.

"The members of the Cabinet," Charles G. Dawes used to remark, "are a President's natural enemies." Dawes had been Harding's Budget Director, Coolidge's Vice-President, and Hoover's Ambassador to London; he also had been General Pershing's chief assistant for supply in the First World War. The words are highly colored, but Dawes knew whereof he spoke. The men who have to serve so many masters cannot help but be somewhat the "enemy" of any one of them. By the same token, any master wanting service is in some degree the "enemy" of such a servant. A President is likely to want loyal support but not to relish trouble on his doorstep. Yet the more his Cabinet members cleave to him, the more they may need help from him in fending off the wrath of rival masters. Help, though, is synonymous with trouble. Many a Cabinet officer, with loyalty ill-rewarded by his lights and help withheld, has come to view the White House as innately hostile to department heads. Dawe's dictum can be turned around.

A senior presidential aide remarked to me in Eisenhower's time: "If some of these Cabinet members would just take time out to stop and ask themselves 'What would I want if I were President?', they wouldn't give him all the trouble he's been having." But even if they asked themselves the question, such officials often could not act upon the answer. Their personal attachment to the President is all too often overwhelmed by duty to their other masters.

Executive officials are not equally advantaged in their dealings with a President. Nor are the same officials equally advantaged all the time. Not every officeholder can resist like a MacArthur, or like Arnall, Sawyer, Wilson, in a rough descending order of effective counter pressure. The vantage points conferred upon officials by their own authority and status vary enormously. The variance is heightened by particulars of time and circumstance. In mid-October 1950, Truman, at a press conference, remarked of the man he had considered firing in August and would fire the next April for intolerable insubordination:

> Let me tell you something that will be good for your souls. It's a pity that you . . . can't understand the ideas of two intellectually honest men when they meet. General MacArthur . . . is a member of the Government of the United States. He is loyal to that Government. He is loyal to the President. He is loyal to the President in his foreign policy. . . . There is no disagreement between General MacArthur and myself . . . .[1]

MacArthur's status in and out of government was never higher than when Truman spoke those words. The words, once spoken, added to the General's credibility thereafter when he sought to use the press in his campaign against the President. And what had happened between August and October? Near-victory had happened, together with that premature conference on *post*-war plans, the meeting at Wake Island.

If the bargaining advantages of a MacArthur fluctuate with changing circumstances, this is bound to be so with subordinates who have at their disposal fewer "powers," lesser status, to fall back on. And when officials have no "powers" in their own right, or depend upon the President for status, their counter pressure may be limited indeed. White House aides, who fit both catagories, are among the most responsive men of all, and for good reason. As a Director of the Budget once remarked to me, "Thank God I'm here and not across the street. If the President doesn't call me, I've got plenty I can do right here and plenty coming up to me, by rights, to justify my calling him. But those poor fellows over there, if the boss doesn't call them, doesn't ask them to do something, what *can* they do but sit? Authority and status so conditional are frail reliances in resisting a President's own wants. Within the White House precincts, lifted eyebrows may suffice to set an aide in motion; command, coercion, even charm aside. But even in the White House a President does not monopolize effective power. Even there persuasion is akin to bargaining. A former Roosevelt aide once wrote of Cabinet officers:

> Half of a President's suggestions, which theoretically carry the weight of orders, can be safely forgotten by a Cabinet member. And if the President asks about a suggestion a second time, he can be told that it is being investigated. If he asks a third time, a wise Cabinet officer will give him at least part of what he suggests. But only occasionally, except about the most important matters, do Presidents ever get around to asking three times.[2]

1. Presidential press conference, October 19, 1950.
2. Jonathan Daniels, *Frontier on the Potomac* (New York: Macmillan, 1946), pp. 31–32.

...s well as to the Cabinet, and certainly has been applied ... time and Eisenhower's.

...s will have more vantage points than a selective memory. Sher-...us, for example, as The Assistant to the President under Eisenhower, ...ely deserved the appellation "White House aide" in the meaning of the term before his time or as applied to other members of the Eisenhower entourage. Although Adams was by no means "chief of staff" in any sense so sweeping—or so simple—as press commentaries often took for granted, he apparently became no more dependent on the President than Eisenhower on him. "I need him," said the President when Adams turned out to have been remarkably imprudent in the Goldfine case, and delegated to him even the decision on his own departure. This instance is extreme, but the tendency it illustrates is common enough. Any aide who demonstrates to others that he has the President's consistent confidence and a consistent part in presidential business will acquire so much business on his own account that he becomes in some sense independent of his chief. Nothing in the Constitution keeps a well-placed aide from converting status into power of his own, usable in some degree even against the President—an outcome not unknown in Truman's regime or, by all accounts, in Eisenhower's.

The more an officeholder's status and his "powers" stem from sources independent of the President, the stronger will be his potential pressure *on* the President. Department heads in general have more bargaining power than do most members of the White House staff; but bureau chiefs may have still more, and specialists at upper levels of established career services may have almost unlimited reserves of the enormous power which consists of sitting still. As Frankin Roosevelt once remarked:

> The Treasury is so large and far-flung and ingrained in its practices that I find it is almost impossible to get the action and results I want—even with Henry [Morgenthau] there. But the Treasury is not to be compared with the State Department. You should go through the experience of trying to get any changes in the thinking, policy, and action of the career diplomats and then you'd know what a real problem was. But the Treasury and the State Department put together are nothing compared with the Na-a-vy. The admirals are really something to cope with—and I should know. To change anything in the Na-a-vy is like punching a feather bed. You punch it with your right and you punch it with your left until you are finally exhausted, and then you find the damn bed just as it was before you started punching.[3]

In the right circumstances, of course, a President can have his way with any of these people. . . . As between a President and his "subordinates," no less than others on whom he depends, real power is reciprocal and varies markedly with organization, subject matter, personality, and situation. The mere fact that persuasion is directed at executive officials signifies no necessary easing of his way. Any new congressman of the Administration's party, especially if narrowly elected, may turn out more amenable (though less useful) to the President than any seasoned bureau chief "downtown." *The probabilities of power do not derive from the literary theory of the Constitution.*

---

3. Marriner S. Eccles, *Beckoning Frontiers* (New York: Knopf, 1951), p. 336.

III

There is a widely held belief in the United States that were it not for folly or for knavery, a reasonable President would need no power other than the logic of his argument. No less a personage than Eisonhower has subscribed to that belief in many a campaign speech and press-conference remark. But faulty reasoning and bad intentions do not cause all quarrels with Presidents. The best of reasoning and of intent cannot compose them all. For in the fist place, what the President wants will rarely seem a trifle to the men he wants it from. And in the second place, they will be bound to judge it by the standard of their own responsibilities, not his. However logical his argument according to his lights, their judgment may not bring them to his view.

The men who share in governing this country frequently appear to act as though they were in business for themselves. So, in a real though not entire sense, they are and have to be. When Truman and MacArthur fell to quarreling, for example, the stakes were no less than the substance of American foreign policy, the risks of greater war or military stalemate, the prerogatives of Presidents and field commanders, the pride of a pro-consul and his place in history. Intertwined, inevitably, were other stakes, as well: political stakes for men and factions of both parties; power stakes for interest groups with which they were or wished to be affiiliated. And every stake was raised by the apparent discontent in the American public mood. There is no reason to suppose that in such circumstances men of large but differing responsibilities will see all things through the same glasses. On the contrary, it is to be expected that their views of what ought to be done and what they then should do will vary with the differing perspectives their particular responsibilities evoke. Since their duties are not vested in a "team" or a "collegium" but in themselves, as individuals, one must expect that they will see things *for* themselves. Moreover, when they are responsible to many masters and when an event or policy turns loyalty against loyalty—a day by day occurrence in the nature of the case—one must assume that those who have the duties to perform will choose the terms of reconciliation. This is the essence of their personal responsibility. When their own duties pull in opposite directions, who else but they can choose what they will do?

When Truman dismissed MacArthur, the latter lost three posts: the American command in the Far East, the Allied command for the occupation of Japan, and the United Nations command in Korea. He also lost his status as the senior officer on active duty in the United States armed forces. So long as he held those positions and that status, though, he had a duty to his troops, to his profession, to himself (the last is hard for any man to disentangle from the rest). As a public figure and a focus for men's hopes he had a duty to constituents at home, and in Korea and Japan. He owed a duty also to those other constituents, the UN governments contributing to his field forces. As a patriot he had a duty to his country. As an accountable official and an expert guide he stood at the call of Congress. As a military officer he had, besides, a duty to the President, his constitutional commander. Some of these duties may have manifested themselves in terms more tangible or more direct than others. But it would be nonsense to argue that the last *negated* all the rest, however much it might be claimed to override them. And it makes no more sense to think that anybody but MacArthur was effectively empowered to decide how he, himself, would reconcile the competing demands his duties made upon him.

Similar observations could be made about the rest of the executive officials . . . Price Director Arnall, it will be recalled, refused in advance to sign a major price increase for steel if Mobilization Director Wilson or the White House should concede one before management had settled with the union. When Arnall did this, he took his stand, in substance, on his oath of office. He would do what he had sworn to do in *his* best judgment, so long as he was there to do it. This posture may have been assumed for purposes of bargaining and might have been abandoned had his challenge been accepted by the President. But no one could be sure and no one, certainly, could question Arnall's right to make the judgment for himself. As head of an agency and as a politician, with a program to defend and a future to advance, *he* had to decide what he had to do on matters that, from his perspective, were exceedingly important. Neither in policy nor in personal terms, nor in terms of agency survival, were the issues of a sort to be considered secondary by an Arnall, however much they might have seemed so to a Wilson (or a Truman). Nor were the merits likely to appear the same to a price stabilizer and to men with broader duties. Reasonable men, it is so often said, *ought* to be able to agree on the requirements of given situations. But when the outlook varies with the placement of each man, and the response required in his place is for each to decide, their reasoning may lead to disagreement quite as well—and quite as reasonably. Vanity, or vice, may weaken reason, to be sure, but it is idle to assign these as the cause of Arnall's threat or MacArthur's defiance. Secretary Sawyer's hesitations, cited earlier, are in the same category. One need not denigrate such men to explain their conduct. For the responsibilities they felt, the "facts" they saw, simply were not the same as those of their superiors; yet they, not the superiors, had to decide what they would do.

Outside the Executive Branch the situation is the same, except that loyalty to the President may often matter *less.* There is no need to spell out the comparison with Governors of Arkansas, steel company executives, trade union leaders, and the like. And when one comes to congressmen who can do nothing for themselves (or their constituents) save as they are elected, term by term, in districts and through party structures *differing* from those on which a President depends, the case is very clear. An able Eisenhower aide with long congressional experience remarked to me in 1958: "The people on the Hill don't do what they might *like* to do, they do what they think they *have* to do in their own interest as *they* see it . . . This states the case precisely.

The essence of a President's persuasive task with congressmen and everybody else, *is to induce them to believe that what he wants of them is what their own appraisal of their own responsibilities requires them to do in their interest, not his.* Because men may differ in their views on public policy, because differences in outlook stem from differences in duty—duty to one's office, one's constituents, oneself—that task is bound to be more like collective bargaining than like a reasoned argument among philosopher kings. Overtly or implicitly, hard bargaining has characterized all illustrations offered up to now. This is the reason why: persuasion deals in the coin of self-interest with men who have some freedom to reject what they find counterfeit. . . .

PRESIDENTIAL POWER SHOULD BE HELD ACCOUNTABLE

Thomas E. Cronin

What of the problems and confusion raised by *Presidential Power?* . . . Perhaps the most frequent complaint about the 1960 study was that it seemed too preoccupied with the will to power, the acquisition of power, and increasing power, divorced from any discussion of the purposes to which power should be put. Such extraordinary emphasis on means without any clear discussion of ends left the impression that the art of leadership is the art of manipulation. Neustadt was faulted too for his failure to emphasize the role that a "sense of direction" plays in presidential leadership, and how a president would call upon or consider ideological values in his power exchanges.

One critic went so far as to suggest that Neustadt "baptizes" political ambition just as Dale Carnegie and kindred self-help manuals baptize greed. Does power tend to purify, and absolute power to purify absolutely? Many of his readers would have liked a more thoughtful discussion of the ends of presidential power, of the ethical boundaries. What are the higher claims on a president and how does the creative president join together the ethic of responsibility and the ethic of ultimate ends?

Neustadt's prime objective is to examine a president's capability as a seeker and wielder of influence, influence of a president upon others involved in the governing process. His analysis implies it is wise, indeed necessary, for a president to build up a vast reserve of power. No doubt Neustadt was trying to steer away from having to make value judgments about the content and consequences of presidential power. But his concentration and emphasis on the acquisition of power left him open to the charge that certain presidential activities that might look like "effective leadership" according to Neustadt were merely actions of a blatant power grab quite unrelated to substantive policy leadership.

Put another way, Neustadt's methodology does not allow political science to distinguish between the use and the abuse of Presidential power. He made little claim beyond that, although he does suggest that a president's sensitivity to the means of power had a good deal to do with "viable" public policy. To some people, this seems as if in Neustadt's terms, public purpose *is* linked directly to presidential power. In any event, he does not apologize for this focus (nor for this implicit theory of political and social change). Certainly he does not try to broaden it in his 1976 essay.

John Hart notes that the passage of the Tonkin Gulf Resolution in 1964 would show, according to Neustadt's frame of reference, President Johnson as an effective wielder of influence; that the action led to a disastrous Vietnam War policy is irrelevant. "Johnson would rate highly on Neustadt's scale insofar as this episode was concerned."[4] Examples of influence seeking and even influence wielding are Nixon's extensive policy impoundments and his efforts to centralize more administrative authority at the White House level, but they are not viewed as acceptable presidential leadership.

Neustadt, however, chose to write primarily, perhaps even exclusively, about the means of leadership. He made little claim beyond that. He does not apologize for this focus, nor does he try to broaden it in his 1976 essay. This will not quiet certain critics. They will, and with some reason, contend the analysis and discussion of power devoid of content is a shallow, even an empty, exercise. In Neustadt's defense it can be said the ends were, and perhaps still remain, implicitly embedded in the liberal vision of the 1960s.

A second criticism of Neustadt's book was that it is too worshipful of presidential power. It seems to say: Find the right president and teach him what power is all about and progress will be realized. It portrays presidents as potential saviors. If only we had the Second Coming of Franklin Roosevelt, all would be well! It comes close to suggesting we need a "Big-Daddy" figure on whom to lean to make the system work. Further, the book speaks almost exclusively about the Washington political community and makes little or no reference to the people's role or to social movements.

Two problems arise from this emphasis on FDR and on presidents as the answer to our needs. First, Neustadt fails to take into account the degree to which presidents are almost invariably stabilizers or protectors of the status quo rather than agents of redistribution or progressive change. Neustadt gives little attention to the way the prevailing American elite values, or ideology, severely limit a president's freedom. . . . One gets the impression from reading Neustadt that he thinks that a president can roam at will, providing he is shrewed enough to be able to persuade others that their interests are the same as his. In fact, however, all of our presidents have had to prove their political orthodoxy and their acceptability to a wide array of established powers, especially corporate leaders, entrenched interest-group leaders, and so on. Thus, Neustadt raises countless hopes that the presidency will be an instrument for the progressive transformation of American politics. (Neustadt apparently sees no other alternative). This complaint is a provocative one and it will doubtless be a lasting one.

The plight of the president in the special-interest state is of course one of the reasons Neustadt is on the side of the presidency as opposed to other forces in American life. President Carter, whom many people hoped would be suf-

---

4. John Hart, "Presidential Power Revisited," *Political Studies* (March 1977), p. 56.

ficiently fresh and sufficiently unburdened by campaign debts and the traditional ways of doing business in Washington, fell prey to the tenacious pressure groups. Carter expressed his plight this way:

> Almost every pressure that I feel on me as President that leads to later inflation comes from a very fine group of people—those who want to build weapons, those who want to build highways, farmers, educators, veterans, and others—all have demands upon the Federal Government that are legitimate. But when you add them all together, it creates an almost impossible financial circumstance, and the budget deficits increase because very fine people press for special attention to their problem which is very costly.[5]

The point is that a president's options are necessarily limited, if not by the accommodations he makes to get elected, then by the accommodations he makes to get reelected or to keep his party or friends in power.

Just how much and how often can we turn to the White House and hope that a benevolent and bright president will provide truly inspired leadership? Sometimes we must turn there, but a reading of history suggests that breakthroughs and leadership often come from the bottom (or at least the middle) up. Civil-rights workers, consumer organizers, women's rights activists, environmental protectionists, tax-revolt champions, and antiwar protestors are illustrative of the catalysts that more often than not bring about policy change in the United States. John W. Gardner, himself a citizen-activist, cautions that "crusading citizens' groups may not always be wise, as witness the Prohibitionists. Or they may be wise but unsuccessful in persuading their fellow citizens. For every citizens' group that changes the course of history, there are thousands . . . that never create a ripple."[6]

In Neustadt's defense it can be said that although the book is often a hymn of praise for FDR, the author really doesn't go so far as to say: defer completely to your president and trust him. He appears instead, at least most of the time, to say that without a good engineer the train just won't go.

There is, however, an undeniable elitist cast to Neustadt's formulation. There is an implicit, if not explicit, fear of the masses juxtaposed with a robust faith in the great leader. This was, of course, a prevailing and accepted view among most academics at the time Neustadt wrote. Roosevelt may have been a grand manipulator and sometimes deceptive as well, but wasn't this increasingly necessary? Leaders need a free hand. It was as if Roosevelt on occasion deceived people, including the American people, much as the physician who lies to the patient "for the patient's own good." Walter Lippmann, George Kennan, Hans Morganthau, and others had previously and often eloquently argued a similar case. What was needed was an activist helmsman to define the national interest, to subdue or avoid the passions of the electorate and the parochialisms of the special-interest groups and Congress. Look to your presidents for leadership,

5. President Jimmy Carter at the White House, June 30, 1978, *Weekly Compilation of Presidential Documents* (July 3, 1978), p. 1211.

6. Henry Etzkowitz and Peter Schwab, eds., *Is America Necessary?* (Denver: West Publishing, 1976), p. 579.

for in Lippmann's oft-quoted words, "The unhappy truth is that the prevailing public opinion has been destructively wrong at the critical junctures."

In a way, Neustadt's book was the culmination of revisionist thinking in the 1950s. The populist identification of the 1930s had been rejected. Intellectuals were reassessing the romantic aspects of the populist heritage. No one has captured this reversal in intellectual trends as well as C. Vann Woodward:

> Disenchantment of the intellectual with the masses was well under way in the forties. Mass support for evil causes in Germany and elsewhere helped to undermine the faith. The liberal's feelings of guilt and impotence were reflected in the interest that the writings of Sören Kierkegaard and Reinhold Niebuhr aroused, and the mood of self-flagellation was expressed in the vogue of the novels of Franz Kafka and George Orwell. The shock of the encounter with McCarthyism sustained and intensified the mood. Liberals and intellectuals bore the brunt of the McCarthyite assault on standards of decency. They were rightly alarmed and felt themselves betrayed. They were the victims of a perversion of the democracy to which they now guiltily realized they had too often turned a blind or indulgent eye. Stung by consciousness of their own naiveté, they responded with a healthy impulse to make up for lost time. . . .[7]

The writings of these intellectuals, surprisingly, are not discussed in the Neustadt book, but their theories and themes were in high fashion during the years Neustadt was preparing his treatise. He was doubtless unconsciously steeped in this new realism, this new orthodoxy about leaders and the led.

Neustadt was influenced by this tradition just as this tradition would be reinforced by him. The message is plain: the whole system revolves around an activist, persuasive president who knows how to avoid the pitfalls and the sand traps of the Washington obstacle course. Neustadt believes this still. Presidential power is as contingent, as uncertain, as tenuous as ever. The press, the attentive public, or a mindless Congress can too easily do enormous harm to a president's ambitions. Do not, Neustadt tells us, worry too much about an imperial presidency. Do not weaken the powers of the presidency. In Watergate and Vietnam we witnessed the *abuse* of power, not an *excess* of power. The absence or weakness of power can also corrupt.

In June 1978 Neustadt was asked why the disillusionment in our national leaders was so great. He began by saying Americans expect too much of their presidents. He added this was a bad time to be president. He suggested too that the times often make the leader or at least make us more respectful of a leader.

> It will continue to be a bad time until events that aren't very controllable conspire to create a background against which Carter's strong points come into sharp focus . . . This negative mood probably will last until there is a new conjunction of personalities and events that does what FDR in the Depression did. . . .
>
> Our perception of good leaderhsip depends enormously on the time. One can't imagine Lincoln doing well in the 1870s, say, or the 1840s. What you need is a conjunction of man and circumstances.[8]

---

7. C. Vann Woodward, "Populism and Intellectuals," in R. J. Cunningham, ed., *The Populists in Historical Perspective* (Lexington, Mass.: D. C. Health, 1968), pp. 61–62.

8. Richard E. Neustadt, "We're Fresh Out of Heroes," *U. S. News & World Report* (June 26, 1978), p. 29.

The Neustadt injunction that power-maximizing individuals are necessary if we want the presidency to function properly is now questioned in some quarters. For example, a theme in Henry Fairlie's provocative, if overstated, *The Kennedy Promise* is that Americans who were once so sure that strong leadership (of the Neustadt type) was necessarily wholesome leadership no longer hold that belief as axiomatic. Fairlie has nice words for FDR, but he saves most of his applause for Eisenhower. James David Barber's notable study of presidential character is another attempt to amend the Neustadt formula. He concludes, for example, that a strong power-maximizing president is not automatically a good president. Barber, of course, had the Johnson experience much in mind. But he broadened his account and his scope and in the end he urges us to look at much more than just an individual's power-maximizing qualities. Thus, he says, look at whether a would-be president is result-oriented, does he actively shape his environment, or is he passively made by it? But also ask: Is his effort in life and in politics a burden to be endured or an opportunity for personal enjoyment? Barber's analysis extends and clarifies certain themes, which were underdeveloped or even misleading in *Presidential Power*. Doris Kearns's book on Lyndon Johnson attempts to blend the Neustadt and Barber perspectives for a richer understanding of an undeniably complex president. New research on the Eisenhower presidency also challenges certain aspects of Neustadt's criticism of Ike.

Another body of post-Neustadt research stresses that however important the president may be, he is not the only person critically involved in the nation's policymaking processes. Neustadt of course recognized this. But he sometimes wrote as if the primary thing that mattered was how the president could control and dominate the others—the advisory circles and so on—at the upper reaches of the government. This was an unfortunate impression to leave, for plainly political science has an obligation to think and write also about the quality of the policymaking process as a whole and not to just assume that what is wholesome for a president will necessarily be good or in the best interests of a thoughtful policy-formulation process. I do not think it was Neustadt's intent to leave this impression. Rather, his near-exclusive concentration on how to help presidents help themselves caused this impression of indifference to the advisory process. Fortunately, several scholars have looked beyond the president and explored ways in which the country might be better served by alterations in how a president obtains and processes advice and information.

Some readers will be disappointed by Neustadt's explanation of Lyndon Johnson's failings in his Vietnam War leadership. There are those, for example, who will say that how a president behaves and acts in office depends not only on his character (on what is in him, i.e., his fears and insecurities, etc.) and his feel for power but also and perhaps even especially *on what others expect him to do*. To be more specific, there are many analysts who contend that our tragic participation in Vietnam was neither a mistake nor a series of miscalculated gambles. No, Vietnam was a presidential war that arose almost inevitably out of this nation's commitment to South Vietnam that went back at least to 1949. The key question was not why Johnson failed but why this commitment was made and reaffirmed and expanded by a succession of five postwar American presidents. The root causes of this presidential commitment and America's unusual grant to the post-World War II presidency to command the national security establishment and rule "the free world" are not given the attention they cry out for in these refllections on Johnson and Nixon. Then again, these are only reflections, an addendum to an earlier book, and not a major treatise on the Johnson and Nixon period. But it seems clear that much of what a president does or does not do is shaped significantly by such compelling factors as a nation's economic needs, its domestic politics, the prevailing climate of public opinion, prevailing elite values, ideology, and so on, quite apart from a president's sensitivity to his power stakes or his capacity to persuade. (Of course, Neustadt did talk somewhat about policy expectations being a major contraint on the presidency.)

Ultimately Neustadt is a realist. For those who cherish more open and more participatory forms of governmental arrangements and for those who like to view Congress as the *people's branch,* the *seat* of republican government, and the agency of *popular action,* his message is unpleasant—at times even chilling. He knows that so much depends on clever leadership in the White House. He knows, too, how to help those presidents whom we want to succeed, although ironically his analysis and prescriptions are just as available to those presidents we wish to constrain. His optimism about the presidency may be a bit too comforting. Thus he dwells in his discussions of Nixon and Johnson on *their* deficiencies as men and seldom on the possibility that the presidency itself or our political arrangements could have contributed to each man's downfall. We need more attention to the persistence of the conditions that encouraged the imperial presidency. Have that many things changed in the past ten or fifteen years? Could it not happen again?

One further reservation. Much of what Neustadt advised a president to do makes considerable sense. The only problem is that taken collectively his admonitions and prescriptions, especially all the suggestions about going into business as your own political intelligence officer, constant backward mapping, and so on, add one more set of improbable expectations to an already crushing set of expectations by which we judge our presidents. Few students who have read Neustadt believe it is possible for a president to do all the calculating, persuading, and bargaining Neustadt insists upon. Neustadt, of course, is merely suggesting the ideal set of circumstances, the ideal kind of performance. If taken too literally, however, his advice may well produce communications overload and a paralysis of information.

However valuable his book is, Neustadt has not said the last word on this subject, nor is his analysis altogether satisfying as the nation tries, or at least should be trying to find answers to the question: How can the presidency be made more effective and more accountable at the same time? . . . What about the prevailing attitudes toward the presidency today? . . . There are compelling indications that the experiment of trying to curb presidential power and relying more on Congress for national leadership has been canceled. Americans may have lost their confidence in their leaders, but they have not lost hope in the efficacy of strong purposive leadership. Thanks to Gerald Ford and Jimmy Carter, the fears of another Watergate presidency have disappeared. All the revelations about the crimes of Watergate and the dramatic resignation of a president lulled people into believing, perhaps, that "the system worked," that checks checked and balances balanced. Perhaps the very cataloging of the misuses of presidential powers, solved, or seemed to solve, the problem. The very revelations may have appeared the same as remedies. By 1980 people are asking "Whatever happened to the imperial presidency?" As the new decade dawns, observers are more likely to complain of an imperial judiciary, an imperial bureaucracy, or an imperial Congress. . . .

Defenders of a powerful presidency, such as Samuel Huntington and others, wondered how a government could conduct a coherent foreign policy if legislative ascendancy really meant the development of a Congress into a second United States government. Could the United States afford to have two foreign policies? A nation cannot retain for long a leadership role in the world unless it is both clear and decisive. In the absence of those cherished Hamiltonian virtues chaos would reign. They feared, too, that in establishing its foreign-policy decisions congressional government would operate almost entirely on the basis of domestic politics, a purview that limits its competence in the field of foreign affairs. . . .

The same verdict is heard from those who yearn for strong creative leadership in domestic or economic matters. Thus, Arthur Schlesinger, Jr., even as he condemns the imperial presidency, says that "history has shown the presidency to be the most effective instrumentality of government for justice and progress."[9]

Time and again, people caution against overreacting to Watergate. Do not be ahistorical, they say. Quoting Harold Laski, they say, "Great power makes great leadership possible."

Supporters of a strong, powerful presidency worry also about the effect of congressional assertion because they believe a president has too little power today—and has all along despite the talk of an imperial presidency—to tackle economic and energy-resource problems effectively. For example, he has very little influence over the Federal Reserve Board's policies on credit and money. He has few tools for effective, long-range economic planning. As President Carter learned, his authority over government reorganization is puny compared to expectations of him as the so-called Chief Executive. . . .

The central challenge, then, is not to reduce the president's power to lead, to govern, and to persuade but to ensure that the means to lead, to govern, and to persuade is not corrupted. Such is the neo- or modified-Neustadt conception today. . . .

The cycle theory of presidential-congressional relations has long been a fashionable one. This holds that there will be periods of presidential ascendancy followed by periods of congressional reaction and reassertiveness. Usually these have been periods of a decade or more, often a generation in length. A modest but brief congressional assertion took place in the immediate post-Watergate years. But the responsibilities of the presidency in this modern era, coupled with the complexities of foreign and economic policy, did not really permit any weakening of the presidency. . . .

---

9. Arthur M. Schlesinger, Jr., *The Imperial Presidency* (Boston: Houghton Mifflin, 1973). p. 404.

The American presidency—as an institution—is still strong. Its powers are such that the country will rally behind a president if the nation's vital interests are threatened. A post-Watergate president has a greater obligation to communicate more persuasively than in the past about when and why the national security is threatened. When persuasive presidential leadership is linked with purpose, Congress and the people are prepared to follow. ∎

UNITED STATES v. NIXON*

Mr. Chief Justice Burger delivered the opinion of the Court.

This litigation presents for review the denial of a motion, filed in the District Court on behalf of the President of the United States, in the case of United States v Mitchell . . . to quash a third-party subpoena duces tecum issued by the United States District Court for the District of Columbia pursuant to Fed Rul Crim Proc 17(c). The subpoena directed the President to produce certain tape recordings and documents relating to his conversations with aides and advisers. . . .

Having determined that the requirements of Rule 17(c) were satisfied, we turn to the claim that the subpoena should be quashed because it demands "confidential conversations between a President and his close advisors that it would be inconsistent with the public interest to produce." . . . The first contention is a broad claim that the separation of powers doctrine precludes judicial review of a President's claim of privilege. The second contention is that if he does not prevail on the claim of absolute privilege, the court should hold as a matter of constitutional law that the privilege prevails over the subpoena duces tecum.

In the performance of assigned constitutional duties each branch of the Government must initially interpret the Constitution, and the interpretation of its powers by any branch is due great respect from the others. The President's counsel, as we have noted, reads the Constitution as providing an absolute privilege of confidentiality for all Presidential communications. Many decisions of this Court, however, have unequivocally reaffirmed the holding of Marbury v Madison . . . that "[i]t is emphatically the province and duty of the judicial department to say what the law is." . . .

No holding of the Court has defined the scope of judicial power specifically relating to the enforcement of a subpoena for confidential Presidential communica-

* 418 U. S. 683 (1973).

tions for use in a criminal prosecution, but other exercises of power by the Executive Branch and the Legislative Branch have been found invalid as in conflict with the Constitution. . . . In a series of cases, the Court interpreted the explicit immunity conferred by express provisions of the Constitution on Members of the House and Senate by the Speech or Debate Clause, US Const Art I, § 6. . . . Since this Court has consistently exercised the power to construe and delineate claims arising under express powers, it must follow that the Court has authority to interpret claims with respect to powers alleged to derive from enumerated powers.

Our system of government "requires that federal courts on occasion interpret the Constitution in a manner at variance with the construction given the document by another branch." . . .

> Deciding whether a matter has in any measure been committed by the Constitution to another branch of government, or whether the action of that branch exceeds whatever authority has been committeed, is itself a delicate exercise in constitutional interpretation, and is a responsibility of this Court as ultimate interpreter of the Constitution.

Notwithstanding the deference each branch must accord the others, the "judicial Power of the United States" vested in the federal courts by Art III, § 1, of the Constitution can no more be shared with the Executive Branch than the Chief Executive, for example, can share with the Judiciary the veto power, or the Congress share with the Judiciary the power to override a Presidential veto. Any other conclusion would be contrary to the basic concept of separaton of powers and the checks and balances that flow from the scheme of a tripartite government. The Federalist, No. 47 . . . . We therefore reaffirm that it is the province and duty of this Court "to say what the law is" with respect to the claim of privilege presented in this case.

In support of his claim of absolute privilege, the President's counsel urges two grounds, one of which is common to all governments and one of which is peculiar to our system of separation of powers. The first ground is the valid need for protection of communications between high Government officials and those who advise and assist them in the performance of their manifold duties; the importance of this confidentiality is too plain to require further discussion. Human experience teaches that those who expect public dissemination of their remarks may well temper candor with a concern for appearances and for their own interests to the detriment of the decisionmaking process. Whatever the nature of the privilege of confidentiality of Presidential communications in the exercise of Art II powers, the privilege can be said to derive from the supremacy of each branch within its own assigned area of constitutional duties. Certain powers and privileges flow from the nature of enumerated powers; the protection of the confidentiality of Presidential communications has similar constitutional underpinnings.

The second ground asserted by the President's counsel in support of the claim of absolute privilege rests on the doctrine of separation of powers. Here it is argued that the independence of the Executive Branch within its own sphere . . . insulates a President from a judicial subpoena in an ongoing criminal prosecution, and thereby protects confidential Presidential communications.

However, neither the doctrine of separation of powers, nor the need for confidentiality of high-level communications, without more, can sustain an absolute, unqualified Presidential privilege of immunity from judicial process under all circumstances. The President's need for complete candor and objectivity from advisers calls for great deference from the courts. However, when the privilege depends solely on the broad, undifferentiated claim of public interest in the confidentiality of such conversations, a confrontation with other values arises. Absent a claim of need to protect military, diplomatic, or sensitive national security secrets, we find it difficult to accept the argument that even the very important interest in confidentiality of Presidential communciations is significantly diminished by production of such material for in camera inspection with all the protection that a district court will be obliged to provide.

The impediment that an absolute, unqualified privilege would place in the way of the primary constitutional duty of the Judicial Branch to do justice in criminal prosecutions would plainly conflict with the function of the courts under Art III. In designing the structure of our Government and dividing and allocating the sovereign power among three co-equal branches, the Framers of the Constitution sought to provide a comprehensive system, but the separate powers were not intended to operate with absolute independence.

> While the Constitution diffuses power the better to secure liberty, it also contemplates that practice will integrate the dispersed powers into a workable government. It enjoins upon its branches separateness but interdependence, autonomy but reciprocity. Youngstown Sheet & Tube Co. v Sawyer, 343 US, at 635 . . . .

To read the Art II powers of the President as providing an absolute privilege as against a subpoena essential to enforcement of criminal statutes on no more than a generalized claim of the public interest in confidentiality of nonmilitary and nondiplomatic discussions would upset the constitutional balance of "a workable government" and gravely impair the role of the courts under Art III.

Since we conclude that the legitimate needs of the judicial process may outweigh Presidential privilege, it is necessary to resolve those competing interets in a manner that preserves the essential functions of each branch. The right and indeed the duty to resolve that question does not free the judiciary from according high respect to the representations made on behalf of the President. . . .

The expectation of a President to the confidentiality of his conversations and correspondence, like the claim of confidentiality of judicial deliberations, for example, has all the values to which we accord deference for the privacy of all citizens and added to those values the necessity for protection of the public interest in candid, objective, and even blunt or harsh opinions in Presidential decision making. A President and those who assist him must be free to explore alternatives in the process of shaping policies and making decisions and to do so in a way many would be unwilling to express except privately. These are the considerations justifying a presumptive privilege for Presidential communications. The privilege is fundamental to the operation of government and inextricably rooted in the separation of powers under the Constitution. In Nixon v Sirica, . . . the Court of Appeals held that such Presidential communications are "presumptively privileged," . . . and this position is accepted by both parties in the present litigation. We agree with Mr. Chief Justice Marshall's observation, therefore, that "[i]n no case of this kind would a court be required to proceed against the President as against an ordinary individual." . . .

But this presumptive privilege must be considered in light of our historic commitment to the rule of law. This is nowhere more profoundly manifest than in our view that "the twofold aim [of criminal justice] is that guilt shall not escape or innocence suffer." . . . We have elected to employ an adversary system of criminal justice in which the parties contest all issues before a court of law. The need to develop all relevant facts in the adversary system is both fundamental and comprehensive. The ends of criminal justice would be defeated if judgments were to be founded on a partial or speculative presentation of the facts. The very integrity of the judicial system and public confidence in the system depend on full disclosure of all the facts, within the framework of the rules of evidence. To ensure that justice is done, it is imperative to the function of courts that compulsory process be available for the production of evidence needed either by the prosecution or by the defense.

Only recently the Court restated the ancient proposition of law, albeit in the context of a grand jury inquiry rather than a trial,

> that "the public . . . has a right to every man's evidence," except for those persons protected by a constitutional, common-law, or statutory privilege . . . .

The privileges referred to by the Court are designed to protect weighty and legitimate competing interests. Thus, the Fifth Amendment to the Constitution provides that no man "shall be compelled in any criminal case to be a witness against himself." And, generally, an attorney or a priest may not be required to disclose what has been revealed in professional confidence. These and other interests are recognized in law by privileges against forced disclosure, established in the Constitution, by statute, or at common law. Whatever their origins, these exceptions to the demand for every man's evidence are not lightly created nor expansively construed, for they are in derogation of the search for truth.

In this case the President challenges a subpoena served on him as a third party requiring the production of materials for use in a criminal prosecution; he does so on the claim that he has a privilege against disclosure of confidential communications. He does not place his claim of privilege on the ground they are military or diplomatic secrets. As to these areas of Art II duties the courts have traditionally shown the utmost deference to Presidential responsibilites. In C. & S. Air Lines v Waterman S. S. Corp. 33 US 103, 111 . . . (1948), dealing with Presidential authority involving foreign policy considerations, the Court said:

> The President, both as Commander-in-Chief and as the Nation's organ for foreign affairs, has available intelligence services whose reports are not and ought not

to be published to the world. It would be intolerable that courts, without the relevant information, should review and perhaps nullify actions of the Executive taken on information properly held secret.

In United States v Reynolds, 345 US1, . . . (1953), dealing with a claimant's demand for evidence in a damage case against the Government the Court said:

It may be possible to satisfy the court, from all the circumstances of the case, that there is a reasonable danger that compulsion of the evidence will expose military matters which, in the interest of national security, should not be divulged. When this is the case, the occasion for the privilege is appropriate, and the court should not jeopardize the security which the privilege is meant to protect by insisting upon an examination of the evidence, even by the judge alone, in chambers. . . .

No case of the Court, however, has extended this high degree of deference to a President's generalized interest in confidentiality. Nowhere in the Constitution, as we have noted earlier, is there any explicit reference to a privilege of confidentiality, yet to the extent this interest relates to the effective discharge of a President's powers, it is constitutionally based.

The right to the production of all evidence at a criminal trial similarly has constitutional dimensions. The Sixth Amendment explicitly confers upon every defendant in a criminal trial the right "to be confronted with the witnesses against him" and "to have compulsory process for obtaining witnesses in his favor." Moreover, the Fifth Amendment also guarantees that no person shall be deprived of liberty without due process of law. It is the manifest duty of the courts to vindicate those guarantees, and to accomplish that it is essential that all relevant and admissible evidence be produced.

In this case we must weigh the importance of the general privilege of confidentiality of Presidential communications in performance of his responsibilities against the inroads of such a privilege on the fair administraton of criminal justice. The interest in preserving confidentiality is weighty indeed and entitled to great respect. However, we cannot conclude that advisers will be moved to temper the candor of their remarks by the infrequent occasions of disclosure because of the possibility that such conversations will be called for in the context of a criminal prosecution.

On the other hand, the allowance of the privilege to withhold evidence that is demonstrably relevant in a criminal trial would cut deeply into the guarantee of due process of law and gravely impair the basic function of the courts. A President's acknowledged need for confidentiality in the communications of his office is general in nature, whereas the constitutional need for production of relevant evidence in a criminal proceeding is specific and central to the fair adjudication of a particular criminal case in the administration of justice. Without access to specific facts a criminal prosecution may be totally frustrated. The President's broad interest in confidentiality of communications will not be vitiated by disclosure of a limited number of conversations preliminarily shown to have some bearing on the pending criminal cases.

We conclude that when the ground for asserting privilege as to subpoenaed materials sought for use in a criminal trial is based only on the generalized interest in confidentiality, it cannot prevail over the fundamental demands of due process of law in the fair administration of justice. The generalized assertion of privilege must yield to the demonstrated, specific need for evidence in a pending criminal trial. . . .

Since the matter came before the Court during the pendency of a criminal prosecution, and on representations that time is of the essence, the mandate shall issue forthwith.

Affirmed.

Mr. Justice Rehnquist took no part in the consideration or decision of these cases. ■

SHOULD WE HAVE A ONE-TERM, SIX-YEAR PRESIDENT?

The founders provided for unlimited four-year terms for America's presidents. They rejected a proposal, made at the Constitutional Convention, to permit a president only one term.

Beginning with George Washington, however, no presidential incumbent sought a third term until Franklin D. Roosevelt did so in 1940. Not only did Roosevelt seek a third term, he also sought, and was reelected to, a fourth term in 1944, dying soon thereafter. In reaction to the Roosevelt example, Congress proposed a constitutional amendment in 1947 to limit the president to two terms. This restriction was ratified as the Twenty-Second Amendment in 1951. The amendment thus limits the power of the people to elect whomever they want as president for as long as they want.

In recent times, there has been agitation for limiting the power of the people in this regard even further. For example, certain distinguished former Cabinet officials—Griffiin B. Bell and Herbert Brownell, each of whom formerly served as Attorney General, William E. Simon, a former Secretary of the Treasury, and Cyrus R. Vance, former Secretary of State—are national cochairmen of the Committee for a Single Six-Year Presidential Term. Reprinted here is an article which these former officials coauthored for the *New York Times*. In it, they argue that a one-term, six-year president would manage better and be freer to do what he or she thought was right.

On the other side is historian Arthur Schlesinger, Jr., whose answering *New York Times* article is also reprinted here. Schlesinger says that the limited-term idea violates democratic principles, and he declares that reelection possibilities make better presidents of the occupants of that office.

The question these two sides address is: Should we amend the Constitution to limit our presidents to one, six-year term?

YES, REELECTION CAMPAIGNS IMPAIR GOOD MANAGEMENT

Griffin B. Bell, Herbert Brownell,
William E. Simon, and Cyrus R. Vance

Once again, thanks to President Reagan's observations about the 22nd Amendment, the nation is turning its attention to the Presidential term. How long can—or should—a chief executive run the country? Does reelection enhance or diminish a President's ability to govern effectively?

Mr. Reagan has advocated repeal of the 22d Amendment so that Presidents may again run for an unlimited number of four-year terms. We agree that it *is* time to repeal the 22d Amendment: However, we believe a new amendment should replace it. It is our belief—a belief shared by many Americans—that the national interest would be better served by a Constitutional amendment providing for a single six-year term.

The idea of a single term is older than the Republic. The length and number of Presidential terms was debated at the Constitutional Convention, and the decision was left to the discretion of George Washington. Once in office, he ran for a second term—but reluctantly—because he believed that service in official capacities should be limited. Sixteen Presidents since Washington, beginning with Andrew Jackson and continuing through Jimmy Carter, have endorsed a single six-year term as a preferable alternative to multiple terms. The six-year term proposal was a part of the Democratic platform in 1913 and passed the Senate that year.

The single six-year term has received renewed attention in recent years because of widespread bipartisan concern that, under the two-term system, re-election pressures lie at the heart of our inability to manage complex, long-term national problems, domestic and foreign. Opponents of the idea declare that the potential hazards facing "lame duck" Presidents under a single term outweigh the damage now caused by delays in decision-making during a re-election campaign. Historical evidence contradicts that view.

According to Kenneth P. O'Donnell, President John F. Kennedy's appointments secretary, in early 1963 Mr. Kennedy told Senator Mike Mansfield that although he knew there was no future for us in Vietnam, he could not expect to be re-elected, given the mood of the country, if he withdrew American forces before the election.

Richard M. Nixon acknowledged in his book "The Real War" that he exaggerated the potential of détente in 1972 because he wanted "political credit" in the coming election. The break-in at the Watergate Hotel and subsequent upheaval were directly attributable to the Nixon Administraton's obsession with re-election.

Gerald R. Ford did not press to a conclusion the strategic arms agreements reached at the Vladivostok summit meeting when those agreements were opposed by his challenger in the Presidential primaries, Ronald Reagan.

In 1980, the Middle East autonomy negotiations were not pushed by President Jimmy Carter as vigorously as they might have been in a non-election year.

In the 1984 election, if President Reagan did not have to face the Federal deficit as a campaign issue, he would likely have acknowledged its importance earlier and begun addressing it as early as 1982 and 1983, rather than now.

These examples indicate that important policy decisions are often deferred because of the enormous pressures a re-election campaign places on Presidents. The result is that long-term foreign and domestic policies often lack steadiness, continuity and predictability.,

Regardless of party affiliation or popularity, all Presidents have delayed some of the hardest and most important decisions until a second term. Lyndon B. Johnson summed it up when he said, after leaving office: "If a fellow knew from the beginning that he had a definite limitation and the bell is going to ring at a certain time, he might be able to tackle some of the problems he's inclined to postpone."

What of being a "lame duck" President? That factor is largely a myth. If it now appears more difficult for Presidents to get the job done at the beginning of the second term, it is because there is a strong temptation built into the two-term system to defer the hard, unpopular decisions until the second term.

Dwight D. Eisenhower, as the only President to have served two full terms under the 22d Amendment, provides a test case of the "lame duck" theory. Despite Democratic control of Congress in both terms, he won passage of more constructive legislation in his second term than in his first. The time spent on re-election activity was minimized, permitting the President to function more effectively as a political leader. In 1959, he declared he would veto major spending bills and, if overridden, would increase taxes. That decision would have been very unpopular in a first-term election period but it helped contribute to low inflation and unemployment in his second term.

Ronald Reagan now has the opportunity to dispel the "lame duck" notion that clouds perceptions of his second term. We're already talking about who will be the next President. Yet the responsibility for managing this nation is in the hands of today's, not tomorrow's, chief executive. That responsibility begins the moment a President takes office and remains until the moment his term ends.

President Eisenhower entered his second term opposing the 22d Amendment for the same reason as President Reagan. He left office a vigorous proponent of a single six-year term because of his strong belief that he was able to function more effectively once the pressures of re-election were removed. Perhaps experience will also lead Mr. Reagan to this view.

As the nation approaches 1987, the 200th anniversary of the drafting of the Constitution, it is appropriate to respond to Thomas Jefferson's plea that each generation re-examine it in light of contemporary needs. Dr. Milton Eisnhower, founder of the current national movement for the single six-year Presidential term, spoke for many Americans when he wrote that he favored a single six-year term so that a President would "have no incentive to propose and fight for measures conceived mainly to enhance his chances for re-election or merely to confound the opposition."

Rather than relegate Mr. Reagan prematurely to a "lame duck" status, we would more profitably spend our time determining how we can enable a modern President to manage government more effectively during his whole term. The single six-year term is the right place to start, and Congressional hearings are the first essential step to put the issue squarely before the American people.   ■

NO, LET'S CONTINUE TO PRACTICE DEMOCRACY
Arthur Schlesinger, Jr.

The proposal of a single six-year Presidential term has been around for a long time. High-minded men have urged it from the beginning of the Republic. The Constitutional Convention turned it down in 1787, and recurrent efforts to put it in the Constitution have regularly failed in the two centuries since. Quite right: It is a terrible idea for a number of reasons, among them that it is at war with the philosophy of democracy.

The basic argument for the one-term, six-year Presidency is that the quest for re-election is at the heart of our problems with self-government. The desire for re-election, it is claimed, drives Presidents to do things they would not otherwise do. It leads them to make easy promises and to postpone hard decisions. A single six-year term would liberate Presidents from the pressures and temptations of politics. Instead of worrying about re-election, they would be free to do only what was best for the country.

The argument is superficially attractive. But when you think about it, it is profoundly anti-democratic in its implications. It assumes Presidents know better than anyone else what is best for the country and that the people are so wrongheaded and ignorant that Presidents should be encouraged to disregard their wishes. It assumes that the less responsive a President is to popular desires and needs, the better President he will be. It assumes that the democratic process is the obstacle to wise decisions.

The theory of American democracy is quite the opposite. It is that the give-and-take of the democratic process is the best source of wise decisions. It is that the President's duty is not to ignore and override popular concerns but to acknowledge and heed them. It is that the President's accountability to the popular will is the best guarantee that he will do a good job.

The one-term limitation, as Gouverneur Morris, final draftsman of the Constitution, persuaded the convention, would "destroy the great motive to good behavior," which is the hope of re-election. A President, said Oliver Ellsworth, another Founding Father, "should be re-elected if his conduct prove worthy of it. And he will be more likely to render himself worthy of it if he be rewardable with it."

Few things have a more tonic effect on a President's sensitivity to public needs and hopes than the desire for re-election. "A President immunized from political considerations," Clark Clifford told the Senate Judiciary Committee when it was considering the proposal some years ago, "is a President who need not listen to the people, respond to majority sentiment or pay attention to views that may be diverse, intense and perhaps at variance with his own. . . . Concern for one's own political future can be a powerful stimulus to responsible and responsive performance in office."

We all saw the tempering effect of the desire for re-election on Ronald Reagan in 1984. He dropped his earlier talk about the "evil empire," announced a concealed passion for arms control, slowed down the movement toward intervention in Central America, affirmed his loyalty to Social Security and the "safety net" and in other ways moderated his hard ideological positions. A single six-year term would have given Reaganite ideology full, uninhibited sway.

The ban on re-election has other perverse consequences. Forbidding a President to run again, Gouverneur Morris said, is "as much as to say that we should give him the benefit of experience, and then deprive ourselves of the use of it." George Washington stoutly opposed the idea. "I can see no propriety," he wrote, "in precluding ourselves from the service of any man, who on some great emergency shall be deemed universally most capable of serving the public."

Jefferson, after initially favoring a single seven-year term, thought more carefully and changed his mind. Seven years, he concluded, were "too long to be irremovable"; "service for eight years with a power to remove at the end of the first four" was the way to do it. Woodrow Wilson agreed, observing that a six-year term is too long for a poor President and too short for a good one and that the decision belongs to the people. "By seeking to determine by fixed constitutional provision what the people are perfectly competent to determine by themselves," Wilson said in 1913, "we cast a doubt upon the whole theory of popular government."

A single six-year year term would release Presidents from the test of submitting their records to the voters. It would enshrine the "President-knows-best" myth, which has already got us into sufficient trouble as a nation. It would be a mighty blow against Presidential accountability. It would be a mighty reinforcement of the imperial Presidency. It would be an impeachment of the democratic process itself. The Founding Fathers were everlastingly right when they turned down this well-intentioned but ill-considered proposal 200 years ago. ∎

PRESIDENTIAL PERSONALITY

The formal constitutional powers of the presidency, as we have seen, have not been altered through the years. Yet, presidents, and the way they use the office, have often differed markedly.

In an important and controversial 1972 book, *The Presidential Character,* political scientist James David Barber focused on the importance of presidential personality for success in office. In the excerpt reprinted here, Barber offers a system by which voters may gauge in advance the personality—or, as Barber terms it, with a slightly different meaning, "character"—of a person who seeks to be president.

Another political scientist, Michael Nelson, whose essay is also excerpted here, says that James David Barber made a valuable contribution by emphasizing the importance of presidential personality, but that serious criticisms, which he lists, have been leveled at Barber's system: too simple, too subjective, and personality is not all that matters.

PRESIDENTIAL CHARACTER AND HOW TO FORESEE IT
James David Barber

When a citizen votes for a Presidential candidate he makes, in effect, a prediction. He chooses from among the contenders the one he thinks (or feels, or guesses) would be the best President. He operates in a situation of immense uncertainty. If he has a long voting history, he can recall time and time again when he guessed wrong. He listens to the commentators, the politicians, and his friends, then adds it all up in some rough way to produce his prediction and his vote. Earlier in the game, his anticipations have been taken into account, either directly in the polls and primaries or indirectly in the minds of politicians who want to nominate someone he will like. But he must choose in the midst of a cloud of confusion, a rain of phony advertising, a storm of sermons, a hail of complex issues, a fog of charisma and boredom, and a thunder of accusation and defense. In the face of this chaos, a great many citizens fall back on the past, vote their old allegiances, and let it go at that. Nevertheless, the citizen's vote says that on balance he expects Mr. X would outshine Mr. Y in the Presidency.

This book is meant to help citizens and those who advise them cut through the confusion and get at some clear criteria for choosing Presidents. To understand what actual Presidents do and what potential Presidents might do, the first need is to see the man whole—not as some abstract embodiment of civic virtue, some scorecard of issue stands, or some reflection of a faction, but as a human being like the rest of us, a person trying to cope with a difficult environment. To that task he brings his own character, his own view of the world, his own political style. None of that is new for him. If we can see the pattern he has set for his political life we can, I contend, estimate much better his pattern as he confronts the stresses and chances of the Presidency.

The Presidency is a peculiar office. The Founding Fathers left it extraordinarily loose in definition, partly because they trusted George Washington to invent a tradition as he went along. It is an institution made a piece at a time by successive men in the White House. Jefferson reached out to Congress to put together the beginnings of political parties; Jackson's dramatic force extended electoral partisanship to its mass base; Lincoln vastly expanded the administrative reach of the office, Wilson and the Roosevelts showed its rhetorical possibilities— in fact every President's mind and demeanor has left its mark on a heritage still in lively development.

But the Presidency is much more than an institution. It is a focus of feelings. In general, popular feelings about politics are low-key, shallow, casual. For example, the vast majority of Americans knows virtually nothing of what Congress is doing and cares less. The Presidency is different. The Presidency is the focus for the most intense and persistent emotions in the American polity. The President is a symbolic leader, the one figure who draws together the people's hopes and fears for the political future. On top of all his routine duties, he has to carry that off—or fail.

Our emotional attachment to Presidents shows up when one dies in office. People were not just disappointed or worried when President Kennedy was killed; people wept at the loss of a man most had never even met. Kennedy was young and charismatic—but history shows that whenever a President dies in office, heroic Lincoln or debased Harding, McKinley or Garfield, the same wave of deep emotion sweeps across the country. On the other hand, the death of an ex-President brings forth no such intense emotional reaction.

The President is the first political figure children are aware of (later they add Congress, the Court, and others, as "helpers" of the President). With some exceptions among children in deprived circumstances, the President is seen as a "benevolent leader," one who nurtures, sustains, and inspires the citizenry. Presidents regularly show up among "most admired" contemporaries and forebears, and the President is the "best known" (in the sense of sheer name recognition) person in the country. At inauguration time, even Presidents elected by close margins are supported by much larger majorities than the election returns show, for people rally round as he actually assumes office. There is a similar reaction when the people see their President threatened by crisis: if he takes action, there is a favorable spurt in the Gallup poll whether he succeeds or fails.

Obviously the President gets more attention in schoolbooks, press, and television than any other politician. He is one of very few who can make news by doing good things. *His* emotional state is a matter of continual public commentary, as is the manner in which his personal and official families conduct themselves. The media bring across the President not as some neutral administrator or corporate executive to be assessed by his production, but as a special being with mysterious dimensions.

We have no king. The sentiments English children—and adults—direct to the Queen have no place to go in our system but to the President. Whatever his talents—Coolidge-type or Roosevelt-type—the President is the only available object for such national-religious-monarchical sentiments as Americans possess.

The President helps people make sense of politics. Congress is a tangle of committees, the bureaucracy is a maze of agencies. The President is one man trying to do a job—a picture much more understandable to the mass of people who find themselves in the same boat. Furthermore, he is the top man. He ought to know what is going on and set it right. So when the economy goes sour, or war drags on, or domestic violence erupts, the President is available to take the blame. Then when things go right, it seems the President must have had a hand in it. Indeed, the flow of political life is marked off by Presidents: the "Eisenhower Era," the "Kennedy Years."

What all this means is that the President's *main* responsibilities reach far beyond administering the Executive Branch or commanding the armed forces. The White House is first and foremost a place of public leadership. That inevitably brings to bear on the President intense moral, sentimental, and quasi-religious pressures which can, if he lets them, distort his own thinking and feeling. If there is such a thing as extraordinary sanity, it is needed nowhere so much as in the White House.

Who the President is at a given time can make a profound difference in the whole thrust and direction of national politics. Since we have only one President at a time, we can never prove this by comparison, but even the most superficial speculation confirms the commonsense view that the man himself weighs heavily among other historical factors. A Wilson re-elected in 1920, a Hoover in 1932, a John F. Kennedy in 1964 would, it seems very likely, have guided the body politic along rather different paths from those their actual successors chose. Or try to imagine a Theodore Roosevelt ensconced behind today's "bully pulpit" of a Presidency, or Lyndon Johnson as President in the age of McKinley. Only someone mesmerized by the lures of historical inevitability can suppose that it would have made little or no difference to government policy had Alf Landon replaced FDR in 1936, had Dewey beaten Truman in 1948, or Adlai Stevenson reigned through the 1950s. Not only would these alternative Presidents have advocated different policies—they would have approached the office from very different psychological angles. It stretches credibility to think that Eugene McCarthy would have run the institution the way Lyndon Johnson did.

The burden of this book is that the crucial differences can be anticipated by an understanding of a potential President's character, his world view, and his style. This kind of prediction is not easy; well-informed observers often have guessed wrong as they watched a man step toward the White House. One thinks of Woodrow Wilson, the scholar who would bring reason to politics; of Herbert

Hoover, the Great Engineer who would organize chaos into progress; of Franklin D. Roosevelt, that champion of the balanced budget; of Harry Truman, whom the office would surely overwhelm; of Dwight D. Eisenhower, militant cursader; of John F. Kennedy, who would lead beyond moralisms to achievements; of Lyndon B. Johnson, the Southern conservative; and of Richard M. Nixon, conciliator. Spotting the errors is easy. Predicting with even approximate accuracy is going to require some sharp tools and close attention in their use. But the experiment is worth it because the question is critical and because it lends itself to correction by evidence.

My argument comes in layers.

First, a President's personality is an important shaper of his Presidential behavior on nontrivial matters.

Second, Presidential personality is patterned. His character, world view, and style fit together in a dynamic package understandable in psychological terms.

Third, a President's personality interacts with the power situation he faces and the national "climate of expectations" dominant at the time he serves. The tuning, the resonance—or lack of it—between these external factors and his personality sets in motion the dynamic of his Presidency.

Fourth, the best way to predict a President's character, world view, and style is to see how they were put together in the first place. That happened in his early life, culminating in his first independent political success.

But the core of the argument (which organizes the structure of the book) is that Presidential character—the basic stance a man takes toward his Presidential experience—come in four varieties. The most important thing to know about a President or candidate is where he fits among these types, defined according to (a) how active he is and (b) whether or not he gives the impression he enjoys his political life.

Let me spell out these concepts briefly before getting down to cases.

PERSONALITY SHAPES PEFORMANCE

I am not about to argue that once you know a President's personality you know everything. But as the cases will demonstrate, the degree and quality of a President's emotional involvement in an issue are powerful influences on how he defines the issue itself, how much attention he pays to it, which facts and persons he sees as relevant to its resolution, and, finally, what principles and purposes he associates with the issue. Every story of Presidential decision-making is really two stories: an outer one in which a rational man calculates and an inner one in which an emotional man feels. The two are forever connected. Any real President is one whole man and his deeds reflect his wholeness.

As for personality, it is a matter of tendencies. It is not that one President "has" some basic characteristic that another President does not "have." That old way of treating a trait as a possession, like a rock in a basket, ignores the universality of aggressiveness, compliancy, detachment, and other human drives. We all have all of them, but in different amounts and in different combinations.

THE PATTERN OF CHARACTER, WORLD VIEW, AND STYLE

The most visible part of the pattern is style. *Style is the President's habitual way of performing his three political roles: rhetoric, personal relations, and homework.* Not to be confused with "stylishness," charisma, or appearance, style is how the President goes about doing what the office requires him to do—to speak, directly or through media, to large audiences; to deal face to face with other politicians, individually and in small, relatively private groups; and to read, write, and calculate by himself in order to manage the endless flow of details that stream onto his desk. No President can escape doing at least some of each. But there are marked differences in stylistic emphasis from President to President. The *balance* among the three style elements varies; one President may put most of himself into rhetoric, another may stress close, informal dealing, while still another may devote his energies mainly to study and cogitation. Beyond the balance, we want to see each President's peculiar habits of style, his mode of coping with and adapting to these Presidential demands. For example, I think both Calvin Coolidge and John F. Kennedy were primarily rhetoricians, but they went about it in contrasting ways.

A President's *world view consists of his primary, politically relevant beliefs, particularly his conceptions of social causality, human nature, and the central moral conflicts of the time.* This is how he sees the world and his lasting opinions about what he sees. Style is his way of acting; world view is his way of seeing. Like the rest of us, a President develops over a lifetime certain conceptions of reality—how things work in politics, what people are like, what the main purposes are. These assumptions or conceptions help him make sense of his world, give some semblance of order to the chaos of existence. Perhaps most important: a man's world view affects what he pays attention to, and a great deal of politics is about paying attention. The name of the game for many politicians is not so much "Do this, do that" as it is "Look here!"

"Character" comes from the Greek word for engraving; in one sense it is what life has marked into a man's being. As used here, *character is the way the President orients himself toward life*—not for the moment, but enduringly. Character is the person's stance as he confronts experience. And at the core of character, a man confronts himself. The President's fundamental self-esteem is his prime personal resource; to defend and advance that, he will sacrifice much else he values. Down there in the privacy of his heart, does he find himself superb, or ordinary, or debased, or in some intermediate range? No President has been utterly paralyzed by self-doubt and none has been utterly free of midnight self-mockery. In between, the real Presidents move out on life from positions of relative strength on weakness. Equally important are the criteria by which they judge themselves. A President who rates himself by the standard of achievement, for instance, may be little affected by losses of affection.

Character, world view, and style are abstractions from the reality of the whole individual. In every case they form an integrated pattern: the man develops a combination which makes psychological sense for him, a dynamic arrangement of motives, beliefs, and habits in the service of his need for self-esteem.

THE POWER SITUATION AND "CLIMATE OF EXPECTATIONS"

Presidential character resonates with the political situation the President faces. It adapts him as he tries to adapt it. The support he has from the public and interest groups, the party balance in Congress, the thrust of Supreme Court opinion together set the basic power situation he must deal with. An activist President may run smack into a brick wall of resistance, then pull back and wait for a better moment. On the other hand, a President who sees himself as a quiet caretaker may not try to exploit even the most favorable power situation. So it is the relationship between President and the political configuration that makes the system tick.

Even before public opinion polls, the President's real or supposed popularity was a large factor in his performance. Besides the power mix in Washington, the President has to deal with a national climate of expectations, the predominant needs thrust up to him by the people. There are at least three recurrent themes around which these needs are focused.

People look to the President for *reassurance,* a feeling that things will be all right, that the President will take care of his people. The psychological request is for a surcease of anxiety. Obviously, modern life in American involves considerable doses of fear, tension, anxiety, worry; from time to time, the public mood calls for a rest, a time of peace, a breathing space, a "return to normalcy."

Another theme is the demand for a *sense of progress and action.* The President ought to do something to direct the nation's course—or at least be in there pitching for the people. The President is looked to as a take-charge man, a doer, a turner of the wheels, a producer of progress—even if that means some sacrifice of serenity.

A third type of climate of expectations is the public need for a sense of *legitimacy* from, and in, the Presidency. The President should be a master politician who is above politics. He should have a right to his place and a rightful way of acting in it. The respectability—even religiosity—of the office has to be protected by a man who presents himself as defender of the faith. There is more to this than dignity, more than propriety. The President is expected to personify our betterness in an inspiring way, to express in what he does and is (not just in what he says) a moral idealism which, in much of the public mind, is the very opposite of "politics."

Over time the climate of expectations shifts and changes. War, depressions, and other national events contribute to that change, but there also is a rough cycle, from an emphasis on action (which begins to look too "political") to an emphasis on reassurance and rest (which comes to seem like drift) and back to action again. One need not be astrological about it. The point is that the climate of expectations at any given time is the political air the President has to breathe. Relating to this climate is a large part of his task.

PREDICTING PRESIDENTS

The best way to predict a President's character, world view, and style is to see how he constructed them in the first place. Especially in the early stages life is experimental; consciously or not, a peson tries out various ways of defining and maintaining and raising self-esteem. He looks to his environment for clues as to who he is and how well he is doing. These lessons of life slowly sink in: certain self-images and evaluations, certain ways of looking at the world, certain styles of action get confirmed by his experience and he gradually adopts them as his own. If we can see that process of development, we can understand the product. The features to note are those bearing on Presidential performance.

Experimental development continues all the way to death; we will not blind ourselves to midlife changes, particularly in the full-scale prediction case, that of Richard Nixon. But it is often much easier to see the basic patterns in early life histories. Later on a whole host of distractions—especially the image-making all politicians learn to practice—clouds the picture.

In general, character has its *main* development in childhood, world view in adolescence, style in early adulthood. The stance toward life I call character grows out of the child's experiments in relating to parents, brothers and sisters, and peers at play and in school, as well as to his own body and the objects around it. Slowly the child defines an orientation toward experience; once established, that tends to last despite much subsequent contradiction. By adolescence, the child has been hearing and seeing how people make their worlds meaningful, and now he is moved to relate himself—his own meanings—to those around him. His focus of attention shifts toward the future; he senses that decisions about his fate are coming and he looks into the premises for those decisions. Thoughts about the way the world works and how one might work in it, about what people are like and how one might be like them or not, and about the values people share and how one might share in them too—these are typical concerns for the post-child, pre-adult mind of the adolescent.

These themes come together strongly in early adulthood, when the person moves from contemplation to responsible action and adopts a style. In most biographical accounts this period stands out in stark clarity—the time of emergence, the time the young man found himself. I call it his first independent political success. It was then he moved beyond the detailed guidance of his family; then his self-esteem was dramatically boosted; then he came forth as a person to be reckoned with by other people. The *way* he did that is profoundly important. Typically he grasps that style and hangs onto it. Much later, coming into the Presidency, something in him remembers this earlier victory and re-emphasizes the style that made it happen.

Character provides the main thrust and broad direction—but it does not *determine,* in any fixed sense, world view and style. The story of development does not end with the end of childhood. Thereafter, the culture one grows in and the ways that culture is translated by parents and peers shapes the meanings one makes of his character. The going world view gets learned and that learning helps channel character forces. Thus it will not necessarily be true that compulsive characters have reactionary beliefs, or that compliant characters believe in compromise. Similarly for style: historical accidents play a large part in furnishing special opportunities for action—and in blocking off alternatives. For example, however much anger a young man may feel, that anger will not be expressed in rhetoric unless and until his life situation provides a platform and an audience. Style thus has a stature and independence of its own. Those who would reduce all explanation to character neglect these highly significant later channelings. For beyond the root is the branch, above the foundation the superstructure, and starts do not prescribe finishes.

FOUR TYPES OF PRESIDENTIAL CHARACTER

The five concepts—character, world view, style, power situation, and climate of expectations—run through the accounts of Presidents in the chapters to follow, which cluster the Presidents since Theodore Roosevelt into four types. This is the fundamental scheme of the study. It offers a way to move past the complexities to the main contrasts and comparisons.

The first baseline defining Presidential types is *activity-passivity.* How much energy does the man invest in his Presidency? Lyndon Johnson went at his day like a human cyclone, coming to rest long after the sun went down. Calvin Coolidge often slept eleven hours a night and still needed a nap in the middle of the day. In between the Presidents array themselves on the high or low side of the activity line.

The second baseline is *positive-negative affect* toward one's activity—that is, how he feels about what he does. Relatively speaking, does he seem to experience his political life as happy or sad, enjoyable or discouraging, positive or negative in its main effect. The feeling I am after here is not grim satisfaction in a job well done, not some philosophical conclusion. The idea is this: is he someone who, on the surfaces we can see, gives forth the feeling that he has *fun* in political life? Franklin Roosevelt's Secretary of War, Henry L. Stimson wrote that the Roosevelts "not only understood the *use* of power, they knew the *enjoyment* of power, too. . . . Whether a man is burdened by power or enjoys power; whether he is trapped by responsibility or made free by it; whether he is moved by other people and outer forces or moves them—that is the essence of leadership."

The positive-negative baseline, then, is a general symptom of the fit between the man and his experience, a kind of register of *felt* satisfaction.

Why might we expect these two simple dimensions to outline the main character types? Because they stand for two central features of anyone's orientation toward life. In nearly every study of personality, some form of the active-passive contrast is critical; the general tendency to act or be acted upon is evident in such concepts as dominance-submission, extraversion-introversion, aggression-timidity, attack-defense, fight-flight, engagement-withdrawal, approach-avoidance. In everyday life we sense quickly the general energy output of the people we deal with. Similarly we catch on fairly quickly to the affect dimension—whether the person seems to be optimistic or pessimistic, hopeful or skeptical, happy or sad. The two baselines are clear and they are also independent of one another: all of us know people who are very active but seem discouraged, others who are quite passive but seem happy, and so forth. The activity baseline refers to what one does, the affect baseline to how one feels about what he does.

Both are crude clues to character. They are leads into four basic character patterns long familiar in psychological research. In summary form, these are the main configurations:

Active-positive: There is a congruence, a consistency, between much activity and the enjoyment of it, indicating relatively high self-esteem and relative success in relating to the environment. The man shows an orientation toward productiveness as a value and an ability to use his styles flexibly, adaptively, suiting the dance to the music. He sees himself as developing over time toward relatively well defined personal goals—growing toward his image of himself as he might yet be. There is an emphasis on rational mastery, on using the brain to move the feet. This may get him into trouble; he may fail to take account of the irrational in politics. Not everyone he deals with sees things his way and he may find it hard to understand why.

Active-negative: The contradiction here is between relatively intense effort and relatively low emotional reward for that effort. The activity has a compulsive quality, as if the man were trying to make up for something or to escape from anxiety into hard work. He seems ambitious, striving upward, power-seeking. His stance toward the environment is aggressive and he has a persistent problem in managing his aggressive feelings. His self-image is vague and discontinuous. Life is a hard struggle to achieve and hold power, hampered by the condemnations of a perfectionistic conscience. Active-negative types pour energy into the political system, but it is an energy distorted from within.

Passive-positive: This is the receptive, compliant, other-directed character whose life is a search for affection as a reward for being agreeable and cooperative rather than personally assertive. The contradiction is between low self-esteem (on grounds of being unlovable, unattractive) and a superficial optimism. A hopeful attitude helps dispel doubt and elicits encouragement from others. Passive-positive types help soften the harsh edges of politics. But their dependence and the fragility of their hopes and enjoyments make disappointment in politics likely.

Passive-negative: The factors are consistent—but how are we to account for the man's *political* role-taking? Why is someone who does little in politics and enjoys it less there at all? The answer lies in the passive-negative's character-rooted orientation toward doing dutiful service; this compensates for low self-esteem based on a sense of uselessness. Passive-negative types are in politics because they think they ought to be. They may be well adapted to certain nonpolitical roles, but they lack the experience and flexibility to perform effectively as political leaders. Their tendency is to withdraw, to escape from the conflict and uncertainty of politics by emphasizing vague principles (especially prohibitions) and procedural arrangements. They become guardians of the right and proper way, above the sordid politicking of lesser men.

Active-positive Presidents want most to achieve results. Active-negatives aim to get and keep power. Passive-positives are after love. Passive-negatives emphasize their civic virtue. The relation of activity to enjoyment in a President thus tends to outline a cluster of characteristics, to set apart the adapted from the compulsive, compliant, and withdrawn types.

The first four Presidents of the United States, conveniently, ran through this gamut of character types. (Remember, we are talking about tendencies, broad directions; no individual man exactly fits a category.) George Washington—clearly the most important President in the pantheon—established the fundamental legitimacy of an American government at a time when this was a matter in considerable question. Washington's dignity, judiciousness, his aloof air of reserve and dedication to duty fit the passive-negative or withdrawing type best. Washington did not seek innovation, he sought stability. He longed to retire to Mount Vernon, but fortunately was persuaded to stay on through a second term, in which, by rising above the political conflict between Hamilton and Jefferson and inspiring confidence in his own integrity, he gave the nation time to develop the organized means for peaceful change.

John Adams followed, a dour New England Puritan, much given to work and worry, an impatient and irascible man—an active-negative President, a compulsive type. Adams was far more partisan than Washington; the survival of the system through his Presidency demonstrated that the nation could tolerate, for a time, domination by one of its nascent political parties. As President, an angry Adams brought the United States to the brink of war with France, and presided over the new nation's first experiment in political repression: the Alien and Sedition Acts, forbidding, among other things, unlawful combinations "with intent to oppose any measure or measures of the government of the United States," or "any false, scandalous, and malicious writing or writings against the United States, or the President of the United States, with intent to defame . . . or to bring them or either of them, into contempt or disrepute."

Then came Jefferson. He too had his troubles and failures—in the design of national defense, for example. As for his Presidential character (only one element in success or failure), Jefferson was clearly active-positive. A child of the Enlightment, he applies his reason to organizing connections with Congress aimed at strengthening the more popular forces. A man of catholic interests and delightful humor, Jefferson combined a clear and open vision of what the country could be with a profound political sense, expressed in his famous phrase, "Every difference of opinion is not a difference of principle."

The fourth President was James Madison, "Little Jemmy," the constitutional philosopher thrown into the White House at a time of great international turmoil. Madison comes closest to the passive-positive, or compliant, type; he suffered from irresolution, tried to compromise his way out, and gave in too readily to the "warhawks" urging combat with Britain. The nation drifted into war, and Madison wound up ineptly commanding his collection of amateur generals in the streets of Washington. General Jackson's victory at New Orleans saved the Madison administration's historical reputation; but he left the Presidency with the United States close to bankruptcy and secession.

These four Presidents—like all Presidents—were persons trying to cope with the roles they had won by using the equipment they had built over a lifetime. The President is not some shapeless organism in a flood of novelties, but a man with a memory in a system with a history. Like all of us, he draws on his past to shape his future. The pathetic hope that the White House will turn a Caligula into a Marcus Aurelius is as naive as the fear that ultimate power inevitably corrupts. The problem is to understand—and to state understandably—what in the personal past foreshadows the Presidential future. ■

THE PSYCHOLOGICAL PRESIDENCY
Michael Nelson

The primary danger of the Nixon administration will be that the President will grasp some line of policy or method of operation and pursue it in spite of its failure. . . . How will Nixon respond to challenges to the morality of his regime, to charges of scandal and/or corruption? First such charges strike a raw nerve, not only from the Checkers business, but also from deep within the personality in which the demands of the superego are so harsh and hard. . . . The first impulse will be to hush it up, to conceal it, bring down the blinds. If it breaks open and Nixon cannot avoid commenting on it, there is a real setup here for another crisis. . . .

James David Barber is more than a little proud of that prediction, primarily because he made it in a talk he gave at Stanford University on January 19, 1969, the eve of Richard Nixon's first inauguration. It was among the first in a series of speeches, papers, and articles whose purpose was to explain his theory of presidential personality and how to predict it, always with his forecast for Nixon's future prominently, and thus riskily, displayed. The theory received its fullest statement in *The Presidential Character.*

"Character," in Barber's usage, is not quite a synonym for personality. A politician's psychological constitution also includes two other components: his adolescence-born "world view," which Barber defines as his "primary, politically relevant beliefs, particularly his conceptions of social causality, human nature, and the central moral conflicts of the time"; and his "style," or "habitual way of performing three political roles: rhetoric, personal relations, and homework," which develops in early adulthood. But clearly Barber regards character, which forms in childhood and shapes the later development of style and world view, to be "the most important thing to know about a president or candidate." As he defines the term, "character is the way the President orients himself toward life— not for the moment, but enduringly." It "grows out of the child's experiments in relating to parents, brothers and sisters, and peers at play and in school, as well as to his own body and the objects around it." Through these experiences, the child—and thus the man to be—arrives subconsciously at a deep and private understanding of his fundamental worth.

For some, this process results in high self-esteem, the vital ingredient for psychological health and political productiveness. Others must search outside themselves for evidence of worth that at best will be a partial substitute. Depending on the source and nature of their limited self-esteem, Barber suggests, they will concentrate their search in one of three areas: the affection from others that compliant and agreeable behavior brings, the sense of usefulness that comes from performing a widely respected duty, or the deference attendant with dominance and control over other people. Because politics is a vocation rich in opportunities to find all three of these things—affection from cheering crowds and backslapping colleagues, usefulness from public service in a civic cause, dominance through official power—it is not surprising that some insecure people are attracted to a political career.

This makes for a problem, Barber argues: if public officials, especially presidents, use their office to compensate for private doubts and demons, it follows that they will not always use it for public purposes. Affection-seekers will be so concerned with preserving the good will of those around them that they rarely will challenge the status quo or otherwise rock the boat. The duty-doers will be similarly inert, although in their case inertia will result from their feeling that to be "useful" they must be diligent guardians of time-honored practices and procedures. Passive presidents of both kinds may provide the nation with "breathing spells, times of recovery in our frantic political life," or even "a refreshing hopefulness and at least some sense of sharing and caring." Still, in Barber's view, their main effect is to "divert popular attention from the hard realities of politics," thus leaving the country to "drift." And "what passive presidents ignore, active president inherit."

Power-driven presidents pose the greatest danger. They will seek their psychological compensation not in inaction but in intense efforts to maintain or extend their personal sense of domination and control through public channels. When things are going well for the power-driven president and he feels that he has the upper hand on his political opponents, there may be no problem. But when things cease to go his way, as eventually they must in a democratic system, such a president's response almost certainly will take destructive forms, such as rigid defensiveness or aggression against opponents. Only those with high self-esteem will be secure enough to lead as democratic political leaders must lead, with persuasion and flexibility as well as action and initiative.

Perhaps more important than the theoretical underpinnings of Barber's character analysis is the practical purpose that animates *The Presidential Character:* to help citizens choose their presidents wisely. . . .

How, though, in the heat and haste of a presidential election, with candidates notably unwilling to bare their souls publicly for psychoanalytical inspection, are we to find out what they are really like? Easy enough, argues Barber: to answer the difficult question of what motivates a political man, just answer two simpler ones in its stead: Is he active or passive? ("How much energy does the man invest in his presidency?"); and is he positive or negative? ("Relatively speaking, does he seem to experience his political life as happy or sad, enjoyable or discouraging, positive or negative in its main effect?") According to Barber, the four possible combinations of answers to these questions turn out to be almost synonymous with the four psychological strategies people use to enhance self-esteem. The "active-positive" is the healthy one in the group. His high sense of self-worth enables him to work hard at politics, have fun at what he does, and thus be fairly good at it. Of the four eighteenth- and nineteenth-century presidents and 14 twentieth-century presidents whom Barber has "typed," he places Thomas Jefferson, Franklin D. Roosevelt, Harry S. Truman, Kennedy, Ford, and Carter in this category. The "passive-positive" (James Madison, William Howard Taft, Warren Harding, Ronald Reagan) is the affection-seeker; although not especially hard-working in office, he enjoys it. The "passive-negative" (Washington, Calvin Coolidge, Eisenhower) neither works nor plays; it is duty, not pleasure or zest, that gets him into politics. Finally, there is the power-seeking "active-negative," who compulsively throws himself into his presidential chores with little satisfaction. In Barber's view, active-negative Presidents John Adams, Woodrow Wilson, Herbert Hoover, Johnson, and Nixon all shared one important personality-rooted quality: they persisted in disastrous courses of action (Adam's repressive Alien and Sedition Acts, Wilson's League of Nations battle, Hoover's depression policy, Johnson's Vietnam, Nixon's Watergate) because to have conceded that they were wrong would have been to cede their sense of control, something their psychological constitutions could not allow. . . .

Not surprisingly, *The Presidential Character* was extremely controversial when it came out in 1972. Many argued that Barber's theory was too simple, that his four types did not begin to cover the range of human complexity. At one level, this criticism is as trivial as it is true. In spelling out his theory, Barber states very clearly that "we are talking about tendencies, broad directions; no individual man exactly fits a category." His typology is offered as a method for sizing up potential presidents, not for diagnosing and treating them. Given the nature of election campaigning, a reasonably accurate shorthand device is about all we can hope for. The real question, then, is whether Barber's shorthand device is reasonably accurate.

Barber's intellectual defense of his typology's soundness, quoted here in full, is not altogether comforting:

> Why might we expect these two simple dimensions [active-passive, positive-negative] to outline the main character types? Because they stand for two central features of anyone's orientation toward life. In nearly every study of per-

Barber's Character Typology, with Presidents
Categorized According to Type*

Affect Toward the Presidency

	POSITIVE	NEGATIVE
ACTIVE	Thomas Jefferson Franklin Roosevelt Harry Truman John Kennedy Gerald Ford Jimmy Carter "consistency between much activity and the enjoyment of it, indicating relatively high self-esteem and relative success in relating to the environment . . . shows an orientation to productiveness as a value and an ability to use his styles flexibly, adaptively"	John Adams Woodrow Wilson Herbert Hoover Lyndon Johnson Richard Nixon "activity has a compulsive quality, as if the man were trying to make up for something or escape from anxiety into hard work . . . seems ambitious, striving upward, power-seeking . . . stance toward the environment is aggressive and has a problem in managing his aggressive feelings."
PASSIVE	James Madison William Taft Warren Harding Ronald Reagan "receptive, compliant, other-directed character whose life is a search for affection as a reward for being agreeable and cooperative . . . low self-esteem (on grounds of being unlovable)"	George Washington Calvin Coolidge Dwight Eisenhower "low self-esteem based on a sense of uselessness . . . in politics because they think they ought to be . . . tendency is to withdraw, to escape from the conflict and uncertainty of politics by emphasizing vague principles (especially prohibitions) and procedural arrangements."

Energy Directed Toward the Presidency

* SOURCE: Barber's discussion of all presidents but Ford, Carter, and Reagan are in *The Presidential Character: Predicting Performance in the White House* (Englewood Cliffs, N.J.: Prentice-Hall, 1972). For Ford and Carter, see "After Eight Months in Office—How Ford Rates Now," *U.S. News & World Report,* April 28, 1975, and James David Barber, "An Active-Positive Character," *Time,* January 3, 1977, 17. For Reagan, see James David Barber, "Worrying About Reagan," *The New York Times,* September 8, 1980, 19.

sonality, some form of the active-passive contrast is critical; the general tendency to act or be acted upon is evident in such concepts as dominance-submission, extraversion-introversion, aggression-timidity, attack-defense, fight-flight, engagement-withdrawal, approach-avoidance. In every life we sense quickly the general energy output of the people we deal with. Similarly we catch on fairly quickly to the affect dimension—whether the person seems to be optimistic or pessimistic, hopeful or skeptical, happy or sad. The two baselines are clear and they are also independent of one another: all of us know people who are very active but seem discouraged, others who are quite passive but seem happy, and so forth. The activity baseline refers to what one does, the affect baseline to how one feels about what he does.

Both are crude clues to character. They are leads into four basic character patterns long familiar in psychological research.[10]

In the library copy of *The Presidential Character* from which I copied this passage, there is a handwritten note in the margin: "Footnote, man!" But there is no footnote to the psychological literature, here or anywhere else in the book. Casual readers might take this to mean that none is necessary, and they would be right if Barber's types really were "long familiar in psychological research" and "appeared in nearly every study of personality." But they aren't and they don't; as Alexander George has pointed out, personality theory itself is a "quagmire" in which "the term 'character' in practice is applied loosely and means many different things."[11] Barber's real defense of his theory—that it works; witness Nixon—is not to be dismissed, but one wishes he had explained better why he thinks it works.

Interestingly, Barber's typology also has been criticized for not being simple enough, at least not for purposes of accurate preelection application. Where, exactly, is one to look to decide if Candidate Jones is, deep down, the energetic, buoyant fellow his image-makers say he is. Barber is quite right in warning analysts away from their usual hunting ground—the candidate's recent performances in other high offices. These offices "are all much more restrictive than the Presidency is, much more set by institutional requirements," and thus much less fertile cultures for psychopathologies to grow in. (This is Barber's only real mention of what might be considered a third, coequal component of the psychological presidency: the rarefied, court-like atmosphere—so well described in George Reedy's *The Twilight of the Presidency*—that surrounds presidents and allows those whose psychological constitutions so move them to seal themselves off from harsh political realities.)

Barber's alternative—a study of the candidate's "first independent political success," or "fips," in which he found his personal formula for success in politics—is not very helpful either. How, for example, is one to tell which "ips" was first? According to Barber's appropriately broad definition of "political," Johnson's first success was not his election to Congress, but his work as a student assistant to his college president. Hoover's was his incumbency as student body treasurer at Stanford. Sorting through someone's life with the thoroughness necessary to

Founding Fathers—portraits in oil or pen and ink, busts of marble—were done for posterity, not for political impact.

So it was when Presidents and former Presidents first confronted photography.

A photographic likeness partakes of reality, *seeming* to communicate a spirit of fact. And every photograph does freeze a moment in time.

During the early 1840s, hoping to capitalize on public fascination with newly developed camera images, American daguerreotypers rushed to capture the likenesses of former Presidents. John Quincy Adams, by then in his 70s, sat for posterity, though he thought the camera made him look "hideous." Walt Whitman, studying a picture of Adams, thought otherwise: "those eyes of individual but still quenchless fire."

Today, it is a rare college history survey text that does not include a daguerreotype of Adams, sitting in his parlor, in Quincy, Massachusetts, a few months before his death. The intensity of Adams' gaze, so in keeping with his record of advocacy, seems a sign of the inner man.

Surviving dguerreotypes of Andrew Jackson, taken in 1845, are less kind. We see a dying man propped up in his chair, a camera portrait which intrudes upon final private moments, not a representation of character. And, if James Polk was the first President to have his camera portrait taken while in the White House, the surviving image merely reflects the mask Polk always displayed to the outside world (he was dubbed by his critics "Polk the mendacious").

Yet, in a way that is hard to explain, the very fact that his features, and those of Jackson and Adams, are preserved photographically is important. The photographs change our perceptions, perhaps make these men seem more "real" than do monumental busts and oil portraits of their predecessors.

The President whom the camera best revealed was surely Abraham Lincoln. The noted portrait taken by Alexander Gardner is considered by the specialists to be the most significant photograph of Lincoln (more than 100 likenesses survive). In my view, it is the most valuable American photograph ever taken.

The story behind the photograph partakes of legend. Lincoln sat for a number of small portraits by Gardner in the latter's Washington studio on April 10, 1865, the day after Appomattox and four days before the assassination. At the conclusion of this session, Gardner moved his camera closer for a final large image. When he developed the picture, the glass plate cracked. In spite of this, Gardner managed to make a single oversized print before tossing away the glass negative. (Historian Lloyd Ostendorf believes the story not only partakes of legend but *is* legend—insofar as the date is concerned, at any rate, which he places in February. The matter remains in dispute.)

What does this photograph reveal? First, of course, it tells us that Lincoln was not just homely, but of surpassing ugliness. Historical context heightens the meaning of the picture: the last image before death. Yet we see not a man a few days from martyrdom but one dying of sadness, wearing a deathlike mask, a deeply etched weariness from directing one part of the country's conquest of another. In the words of poet Wilfred Owen, the President's expression seems to be saying: "My subject is War, and the pity of War."

WILD PERFUME

Walt Whitman was fascinated by photographs in general and by Lincoln's appearance in particular. He wrote that he had observed Lincoln at close hand 20 or 30 times during the Civil War years. In 1963 he described the "dark brown face, with the deep-cut lines, the eyes, always to me with a deep latent sadness." He later complained that no portrait, photographic or otherwise, "has caught the deep, though subtle and indirect expression of this man's face," though I think he was wrong. Whitman noted that there was no good portrait of Lincoln, but that some faces, "behind their homeliness, or even ugliness, held superior points so subtle, yet so palpable, making the real life of their faces almost as impossible to depict as wild perfume."

Lincoln is the true beginning of the "visual Presidency," for his symbolic meaning to all of us depends heavily on photographic detail. As perhaps our greatest President, Lincoln demands iconic uniqueness, a symbol of martyrdom based on assassination but defined through photography. Contrast the pallid imagery of the Lincoln penny, itself based on a photographic likeness. The penny provides a general outline, but nothing of the suffering that Lincoln's symbolic image must convey. As Whitman noted, "I should say the invisible foundations and vertebra of his character, more than any man's in history, were mystical, abstract, moral and spiritual."

As printing improved and drawings and photographs got into the newspapers, Presidents began to be worried about the impression they made, via pictures, on the public. The first was Theodore Roosevelt. To the delight of photographers and cartoonists, Roosevelt in real life was a caricature: the oversized teeth, the thick glasses reflecting light, the bristling moustache, the substantial paunch despite all the talk about fitness. Roosevelt loved being President; he was always on stage, a natural ham.

FROM TR TO FDR

. . . Roosevelt was the first President to seem warm and affectionate to a mass public and the first to be known by his initials. Yet TR was careful about photographers and warned his bulky successor, William Howard Taft, about being shown playing golf (in a pre-Eisenhower age, the game connoted aristocratic tendencies): "I'm careful about that; photographs on horseback, yes; tennis, no. And golf is fatal."

TR's term of office marks the end of visual innocence: Presidents had become self-conscious about being "caught" by the camera.

Ahead of his own time was Franklin Roosevelt, whose understanding of publicity and persuasion remains unsurpassed. Roosevelt, the ablest political speaker of his generation, had an instinctive understanding of radio, the new medium, which explained much of his enduring popularity. Voters knew that his legs were crippled by polio, but it seemed impossible that one who sounded so vigorous could be seriously handicapped.

Careful, defensive management of the "visual" helps to explain why. The

White House discouraged the publication of photographs showing FDR from the waist down—and few such photographs appeared in print. Roosevelt's patrician artifices—the pince-nez and the cigarette holder—helped to make him look supremely self-confident.

In our pictures of Roosevelt, we see a man so sure of himself that his vitality bursts out of the frame. The props help: that so-called fighting jaw, the angle of the cigarette holder, the rumpled hat. Roosevelt was our modern presidential salesman, the man who knew how to flatter and cajole.

Today, as during the 1930s and '40s, we can look, we can admire, but we cannot see inside. Turn back to Lincoln. Photographs invite us to examine the inner Lincoln; nobody ever saw the inner Roosevelt.

NIXON AND JOHNSON

Dwight Eisenhower was, in his way, no less artful than FDR. World War II newsreels showed a serious General Eisenhower urging continuing sacrifice; the 1952 election campaign against Adlai Stevenson demanded beaming self-confidence. The newspaper photograph defined Ike's notable campaign asset, the grin, conveying a simple image of humanity and trustworthiness. That grin masked a shrewd, seasoned manager of men, but Eisenhower's photographs, then as later, never penetrated the genial exterior.

In 1953, Helen Keller, blind, deaf, and dumb almost from birth, asked to visit the White House so that she could "see" Eisenhower's smile. The image captures the pleasure of Miss Keller, who, unable to see, did not know how to appear shy in front of the camera. Eisenhower humanized himself by allowing Helen Keller to touch his face as he grinned. One can barely see the smile, but Ike's eyes and the laugh lines around his eyes and on his forehead all suggest it powerfully.

With Richard Nixon, as Eisenhower's running mate, television became part of our concept of "visual" politics and the "visual" candidacy. His famed "Checkers speech" of September 23, 1952, was an emotional rebuttal to Democratic charges of misappropriating campaign funds. Nixon's cocker spaniel, Checkers, was a supporting actor. Drawing an avalanche of favorable telegrams from the public, Nixon showed every politician how the new visual medium could inform and affect the American people directly. (Lyndon Johnson touched on the legacy of the Checkers speech when he told a network producer shortly before his death, "You guys. All you guys in the media. All of politics has changed because of you. You've broken all the machines and the ties between us in Congress and the city machines.")

Television images differ from still pictures, which allow time for study and reflection.

We [saw] a photograph taken off a television monitor during the Checkers speech just before Nixon says, "One other thing I probably should tell you, because if I don't they'll probably be saying this about me too. . . . Our little girl— Trisha, the six-year-old, named it Checkers." I studied a kinescope of the Checkers speech frame-by-frame, looking for any evidence of Nixon's character. There wasn't much. But just before he introduces Checkers, he momentarily touches his nose with his hand, and then his face fleetingly takes on an unhappy, almost haunted expression.

Television served Nixon in 1952 and, with elaborate White House staging, through most of his Presidency. Nixon served television on August 9, 1974, when he made a farewell speech to his White Hous staff after formally resigning. His rambling talk will continue to interest scholars because of how Nixon looked and what his appearance seemed to say about the impact of, and responsibility for, Watergate.

Our TV image, also of poor quality, shows the moment when Nixon cries as he speaks of his mother: "Yes, she will have no books written about her. But she was a saint." In his *Memoirs*, Nixon says "the memory of that scene for me is like a frame of film forever frozen."

What does Nixon mean? That he remembers crying? And what does this image tell us? Nixon speaks of tragedy and suffering. Look one more time at the Lincoln photograph, then at this. Above all, Nixon's shows us failure; Lincoln's, sadness. No longer able to "shape" his image, Nixon stood humiliated before his favorite enemy, the news media, and admitted, to the extent that he was capable, that his quest for his mother's approval—his quest for a role in history—would not gain what he had sought.

What about Lyndon Johnson, the U.S. President most fascinated by the media? "Television and radios were his constant companions," biographer Doris Kearns tells us. "Hugging a transistor radio to his ear as he walked through the fields of his ranch or around the grounds of the White House, Johnson was a presidential teenager, listening not for music but for news."

His obsession with what others were saying stemmed from an inordinate concern with his own image, both aural and visual.

LBJ VS. JFK

Johnson seldom sounded convincing in public. Senator Paul Douglas (D.-Ill.) once observed that "[I] never saw Lyndon Johnson win a debate conclusively on the Senate floor, and I never heard him lose one in the cloak room." Johnson said that he felt uncomfortable before the TV camera because it allowed viewers to focus on his awkward physical appearance rather than on the substance of what he said.

Television also emphasized the way he spoke. Johnson's rise to prominence in the U.S. Senate coincided with the emergence of civil rights as a major issue. To talk "corn pone," he felt, ruined his attempt to sound credible on this issue to Northerners.

No device, whether new glasses, a new TelePrompter, a shirt of a different color, or a new backdrop, could turn Johnson into a winsome performer on television. Johnson's great skills in wheeling and dealing, however important in getting major legislation through Congress, failed to inspire confidence in him as the Man in the Oval Office, his critics wrote. Johnson was the old dog who just could not learn new tricks. And his Texas accent and garbled syntax betrayed him, he thought, when he talked in public in anything like the same manner that he employed on the telephone or in private. The architect of the Great Society did not look or sound statesmanlike—he looked like a politican.

Johnson felt particular uneasiness over the endless unflattering comparisons, real or imagined, between him and his handsome predecessor, John Kennedy.

A New England accent, good looks, and playful banter during televised news conferences went a long way toward creating Kennedy's image of youthful vigorous leadership. Kennedy looked and sounded as though he could get results. He was photogenic (imagine Lyndon Johnson running along a beach), and his 1960 campaign speech (defending himself as a Catholic candidate) to the Greater Houston Ministerial Association looks good on film today. Yet Johnson ignored one fact: Just before his death, judging by the polls, Kennedy was no more popular than any other President, including LBJ, after 1,000 days in office.

CARTER'S CARDIGAN

Johnson was the first President to use video tape playback equipment to record TV broadcasts for later viewing. In our picture, he studies a replay of his November 17, 1967, press conference, in which he used a lavaliere microphone so he could walk about the room. His aide, Walt Rostow, termed Johnson's performance "electrifying." But Johnson told his assistant press secretary, Robert Fleming, "You're trying to make me into an actor, and I'm not an actor, I'm a President. I won't wear that god-damned microphone again." And he didn't.

Johnson's presidential image converged in photographs and cartoons, memorably in the notorious scar photograph of October 20, 1965, which fixed a portrait of Johnson as lacking Kennedy's elegance and presidential stature. The UPI caption read "President Johnson, in good spirits after a walk around the hospital grounds and buoyed by the thought of leaving the hospital [after a gall bladder operation], pulls up the tails of his sport shirt to show his surgical bandage and to illustrate just where it was that the surgeons 'messed around' in his abdomen." The photograph appeared the next day in newspapers across America, in some instances with an enlargement of the scar "transmitted in answer to requests." Thousands wrote to protest the photograph's poor taste. What possessed Johnson to pull up his shirt remains a mystery.

The photograph later inspired David Levine's best-known cartoon. Levine exaggerated the size of the President's ears, the length of his nose (Pinocchio-like), the thinness of his hair, and gave him a pronounced double chin, along with watchful, shifty eyes. Levine's cartoon presumed a collective memory of the scar photograph and made the scar into a symbol of Johnson's Vietnam policies and the "credibility gap" plaguing his administration. In May 1968, Johnson told a group of editorial cartoonists, "Thank goodness [columnist] Walter Lippmann never learned to draw."

Johnson tried assiduously—and in vain—to create a flattering visual image of himself. Staff photographers took more than 500,000 photographs during the White House years. A weekly 30-minute color film, *The President,* was produced at his orders from 1966 to 1969. The President regularly gave away inscribed pictures and had albums of White House activities prepared for visiting dignitaries.

He examined himself in picture after picture, looking for indications of credibility and Eastern urbanity. His aide, Harry McPherson, tells of a conversation with the President about one photograph. "God, look at that photograph," Johnson said.

> It had what I call his John Wayne look—you know, the smile as we look into the Western sunset with Old Paint. It's the inverted "V's" in the brows and smile on the face: weathered, troubled, but still philosophical, Uncle Lyndon looks to the West. And he said, 'Have you ever seen anything phonier in your life?' And I said, 'No, I haven't.'
>
> He had one of those smiles on, standing next to somebody, and he said, 'I didn't want to be there with that guy. I don't care anything about him; I didn't want to be there with the picture, and I knew that would show. So I tried to put on a smile. And every time I try to do that, I look phonier. It all comes through and I can't break it.'

Johnson finally got the photograph he was looking for after he left the White House. Taken at the LBJ ranch, it is filed at the Johnson Library in Austin under "John Wayne Photo." The photographer, Frank Wolfe, explains what Johnson liked abbut the image: the cowboy hat and shirt gave an "earthy look," making him appear "tall and robust." It is the image of a man who comes from the land—tough, grizzled, dependable, not given to boasting—the heroic figure John Wayne played in so many Hollywood productions. Apparently, Johnson decided that being an actor was not so bad after all.

That Lyndon Johnson was obsessed with his "image" tells us more about the man than it does about the impact of TV or photography. So do the calculations of the Nixon White House; returning from Peking in 1972, President Nixon sat in Air Force One for nine hours in Anchorage, Alaska, so that he could arrive home triumphantly in prime time. So do President Carter's revival of the fireside chat to discuss energy problems, dressed in a cardigan, and his early effort to show himself as a populist Chief Executive by spending the night with an ordinary family in Clinton, Massachusetts.

Oddly enough, Ronald Reagan, the first President to have been a professional actor, has largely eschewed such elaborate image-making, confining himself, Truman-like, to quips and fairly conventional political gestures. Indeed, he seems hardly to notice that he is on camera.

The modern Presidency, in fact, does not require an actor. It does require someone who is not terrified by television and able to make a coherent speech to rally public support for his programs. Photographs and TV coverage provide reminders of his role as our Chief Executive, and the President is expected to keep his shirt-tail tucked in. But the "image" in people's heads does not necessarily correspond to the pictures of the Man in the White House seen on television.

The perceived effects of presidential words or decisions (or indecision) soon tend to create their own popular images—and every President in the Age of Television has suffered almost the same steady erosion of popularity in the polls over time, regardless of White House "media events." In truth, presidential images are what *we* make of them. ■

THE PRESS AND THE PRESIDENT
George E. Reedy

To the leisurely observer of the Washington scene, there is a distinct charm in the startled air of discovery with which the press greets each step in the entirely predictable course of its relationship with the president and the White House staff.

Actually, the patterns are as well-established and as foreseeable as the movements of a Javanese temple dance. The timing will vary as will the alternating degrees of adoration and bitterness. But the sequence of events, at least in modern times, appears to be inexorable. It is only the determination of the press to treat each new day as unprecedented that makes the specific events seem to be news.

Seen from a little distance, cries of outrage from the press over the discovery that Mr. Reagan seeks to "manage the news" have the flavor of an Ed Sullivan rerun show on after-midnight television. They are reminiscent of similar protests in the administrations of Presidents Carter, Nixon, Johnson, Kennedy, Eisenhower, Truman, and Roosevelt. Presidents before that do not offer much material for discussion simply because they served prior to the FDR era, when press-White House relations were put on a daily-contact basis for the first time in history.

The charge of management is a familiar one because it has a strong element of truth. All presidents seek to manage the news and all are successful to a degree. What is not taken into account is that legitimate management of the news from the White House is inescapable and, human nature being what it is, it is hardly surprising that presidents try to bend this necessity for their own ends. Few men will decline an opportunity to recommend themselves highly.

The press would not be happy with a White House that ended all efforts at news management and either threw the mansion wide open for coverage or closed it to outsiders altogether and told journalists to get facts any way they could. Since the early days of the New Deal, reporters have been relying on daily press briefings, prearranged press conferences, and press pools when the president travels. There would be chaos should all this come to an end.

The point is that the White House is covered by journalists through highly developed and formal organizational structures. It is inherent in the nature of such structures that they must be managed by somebody, and the president's office is no exception. Management technique is employed every time the president decides what stories will be released on Monday and what stories will be released on Saturday; every time he decides that some meetings will be open to press coverage and others will not; every time he decides that some visitors will be fed to the press as they walk out of the Oval Office and others will not. Anybody who believes that he will make decisions on the basis of what makes him look bad will believe a hundred impossible things before breakfast.

There are actually times when the press literally does not want news. This became very clear early in the administration of Lyndon Johnson when he inaugurated the custom of unexpected Saturday morning news conferences. This meant disruption of newspaper production shcedules all over the United States. Printing pressmen had to be recalled from weekend holidays to work at exorbitant rates; front pages that had been planned in leisurely fashion in the morning had to be scrapped for new layouts; rewrite men who had looked forward to quiet afternoons with their families worked into the evening hours. It was a mess.

After two such conferences, I began getting calls from top bureau chiefs in Washington pleading with me to put an end to them. They made it clear they wanted stories timed so that they would fit conveniently into news slots. It took some doing on my part; Johnson would have enjoyed the discovery that he was putting newspaper publishers to so much expense and trouble. (I think he started these conferences simply because he became lonely on Saturday mornings when there was little to do.) I talked him into dropping the custom by producing figures which showed that the weekend audiences were not large enough to justify the effort.

While it was actually going on, the episode struck me as just another example of the Johnsonian inability to comprehend the press. It was not until later that I realized the deeper significance. The press had not only acquiesced in news management but had actually asked that it be instituted. The fact that nothing was involved except timing was irrelevant. The ability to control the timing of news is the most potent weapon that any would-be news manipulator can have. No absolute line can be drawn between the occasions when he should have it and those when he should not.

This may well account for the indifference of the public to the periodic campaigns against news management. Even to an unsophisticated audience it is apparent that journalists are not objecting to news management per se but only to the kind of news management that makes their professional lives more difficult. However it may look in Washington, at a distance the issue appears as a dispute over control of the news for the convenience of the president or for the convenience of the press. In such a situation, Americans tend to come down on the side of the president.

Of course, if the president is caught in an outright lie—a lie about something in which the public is really concerned—the public will mobilize against him swiftly. But many charges of news management are directed at statements that Americans do not regard as outright lies. Americans have become so accustomed to the kind of exaggeration and misleading facts that are used to sell products on nightly television that a little White House puffery seems quite natural.

There is, of course, another side to the coin. While presidents always try to manipulate the news—and all too often succeed—there is a very real doubt whether the manipulation performs any real service for them, even in the crassest image-building sense. The presidency is a strange institution. The occupant must accept never-ending responsibilities and must act on never-ending problems. It may well be that what a president does speaks so much more loudly than anything he can say that the normal techniques of public relations are completely futile.

In the first place, a president may be able to time his public appearances but he cannot time his acts. He *is* the United States and anything that affects the United States must have a presidential response. He must react to internationl crises, to domestic disasters, to unemployment, and to inflation; if he chooses to do nothing in any of these instances his inaction will be writ large in the public media.

In the second place, a president may be able to keep his thoughts to himself but he cannot act in any direction without causing waves that sweep through the Washington community. The federal bureaucracy is shot through with holdovers from previous administrations who do not like him; the Congress is loaded with political opponents with whom he must deal; the lobbying offices of the capital are staffed by skilled president-watchers who can interpret his every act and who have sympathetic journalistic listeners.

Finally, there is the overwhelming fact that the president has a direct impact on the lives of every citizen and there is a limit to his capacity to mislead. He cannot convince men and women that there is peace when their sons are dying in a war. He cannot hold up images of prosperity (although he will try) when men and women are out of work. He cannot persuade constituents that there is peace and harmony when there is rioting in the streets. There may be instances when he can escape the blame but only when his political opposition is not on its toes.

Against this background the efficacy of manipulation is dubious at best. It may have a favorable impact on public opinion in the short run. But I know of no persuasive evidence that it helps to build the long-term support a politician needs. Every instance I have studied bears a close parallel to what happened when Lyndon Johnson held his meaningless meeting with the late Soviet premier Alexei Kosygin at Glassboro, New Jersey, in 1967. He was able to maneuver the press into treating it as a major summit conference for a few days, and his poll ratings rose accordingly. But it soon became clear that the meeting had produced nothing of substance and that there had been no reason to expect that it would. The poll ratings went right back down again.

On the other hand, efforts at manipulation invariably challenge the press to dig deeper than journalists ordinarily would. The stories they write about manipulation have little effect. But the stories they write as a result of the digging may have the kind of substance that does make an impact. The whole exercise can well be merely an invitation to trouble on the part of the president.

The bottom line can be simply stated. The president can, within limits, manipulate that part of the press which covers the White House. But he cannot manipulate the press as a whole, and it is probable that his efforts to do so will always backfire. ■

THE PRESIDENTIAL PRESS CONFERENCE
Wayne King

It . . .[was] a quarter of a century Saturday, but like almost everything else the young President did, it seems a moment frozen in time.

John F. Kennedy was 43 years old and it was his first news conference as President of the United States.

Perhaps more important from a historical perspective—Kennedy would be 68 today, just a few years younger than Ronald Reagan—it was also the very first time a President had held a full-blown, formal news conference before live television cameras.

The new President, a figure of special grace and a black belt in Irish wit, emerged from the encounter, as Russell Baker of The New York Times put it the next day, as "a new star with a tremendous national appeal, the skill of a consummate showman."

For better or worse, Presidential news conferences have never been the same.

At the same time that the televised news conference exposes the President to the people, it sometimes becomes a vehicle for self-promotion, a stage-managed political commercial imparting not information but image.

True, reporters ask questions, but the President can call on whom he likes, often with a fine sense of who might provide relief and who anguish. He can, and does, ignore questions and give speeches instead.

Reporters, on the other hand, become players in the drama, argue at times and sometimes posture rather than inquire. Are you running for something, Mr. Rather? No, Mr. President, are you?

In truth it was an evolution rather than a quantum leap into the new technology. President Eisenhower had allowed filming of his exchanges with the capital press corps, but never before had it been live.

With Kennedy, for the first time, the mad rush to a telephone the moment the pressroom doors flung open was superfluous. Everybody already knew what the President had said—about U-2 spyplanes, a possible visit by Khrushchev and reciprocal trade agreements.

James Hagerty, the press secretary who had persuaded Eisenhower to allow the cameras for the first time, nonetheless balked at going live lest his boss, who seemed occasionally to wander in a verbal thicket, should lose his way entirely and "misspeak himself."

It was Eisenhower who, asked in his 190th news conference on Aug. 24, 1960, for just one "major idea" instigated by his Vice President, Richard Nixon, replied: "If you give me a week, I might think of one. I don't remember."

More recently, just this month, President Reagan managed to call the Vienna airport the Vietnam airport, misidentified one of the victims of a terrorist attack, flubbed the numbers of two key United Nations resolutions on the Mideast and incorrectly evaluated tax revenue in comparison with the gross national product. But nobody paid much attention because he described the Libyan leader, Col. Muammar el-Qaddafi, as "flaky." It was a piece of verbal footwork before the lights worthy of Mr. Kennedy, whose style Mr. Reagan admires.

The Presidential news conference is fundamentally a phenomenon of the 20th century, traceable, according to a Commission on Presidential Press Conferences, to Theodore Roosevelt's habit of summoning reporters to the White House for occasional briefings, often while he was being shaved in the morning.

Taft abandoned the practice, perhaps aware of John Adams's admonition about the press that "mankind cannot now be governed without it, nor at present with it," but it was reinstituted and institutionalized under Woodrow Wilson in 1913 and has been a part of every administration ever since.

President Wilson held regular meetings with reporters with a fair amount of verbal give and take, but successors Harding, Coolidge and Hoover required that questions be put in writing in advance.

Franklin Roosevelt, at his first news session on March 8, 1933, told assembled reporters he hoped "these conferences are going to be merely enlarged editions of the kind of very delightful family conferences I have been holding in Albany for the last four years."

The sessions were frequent, informal, largely off the record (reporters were forbidden to discuss sensitive material even with their editors) and there was no direct quotation of the President, who made the refreshing concession at the outset that "there will be a great many questions you will ask that I do not know enough about to answer"– a mere quibble to modern masters who simply answer another question altogether.

Roosevelt's questioners simply clustered around his desk. The explosive growth of the press corps after World War II meant a more formal arrangement with Truman standing in front of a room full of reporters.

Taping and filming eliminated off-the-record answers and Kennedy's decision for live cameras made immediate answers mandatory. No longer could a President simply say, "Hold on, I'll need a minute to call the Secretary of State on that."

Thus, say critics, the air of immediacy and give-and-take given by live televised news conferences is largely illusory.

Too, said the private panel that studied news conferences in 1981, "What many in the press regarded as deceptions, as with Lyndon Johnson's reports about the Vietnam War and Richard Nixon's duplicities about Watergate, raised a curtain of distrust between the President and the press. If the role of the news media in their relationship to the White House had hitherto been adversarial, it now became downright antagonistic."

Thus, while Presidents seem more visible, they are less accessible. President Roosevelt averaged 6.9 news conferences a month, Truman 3.4, Eisenhower 2, Kennedy 1.9, Johnson 2.2, Nixon 0.5, Ford 1.3, Carter 1.2 and Reagan 0.5.

When Jimmy Carter left office, he observed that two things he had no trouble bequeathing to Ronald Reagan were Menachem Begin and Sam Donaldson. ■

CHAPTER 10

The Bureaucracy

Bureaucracy is a formally established administrative system characterized by job specialization, a hierarchy of authority, a system of rules, and impersonality. Bureaucracy is not, of course, confined to government; there is bureaucracy in any large corporation, for example. Within government, it is not just found at the federal level; most governmental bureaucracy exists at the state and local levels.

Here, however, we are particularly interested in the *federal* bureaucracy. But, before going further, we should dispel certain myths about the federal bureaucracy. It has *not* experienced runaway growth in modern times; growth in its employee numbers has been relatively flat in recent years, while the number of state and local employees has risen fairly sharply. Most federal employees do *not* live and work in Washington; only about 12 percent do. Most federal workers are *not* employed in social welfare agencies; only about 15 percent are.

The bureaucracy of the federal executive branch is found in the Executive Office of the President (including, for example, the Council of Economic Advisers and the Office of Management and Budget), the Cabinet departments (such as the Department of Defense and the Department of Interior), independent agencies (such as the Central Intelligence Agency and the National Aeronautics and Space Agency), and the regulatory bodies (which include the Interstate Commerce Commission and the Securities Exchange Commission, for example).

The fundamental responsibility of the federal bureaucracy is to administer and implement policy. But it does much more. Even its central function of administration and implementation involves considerable discretion—and, in practice, therefore, the making of policy. But many agencies actually make law and policy directly. For example, when the Department of Agriculture or the Federal Trade Commission—or any number of other federal departments, agencies, or commissions—publishes binding rules and regulations under authority delegated to them by Congress, they are exercising legislative power. Further, when agencies—such as the Federal Communications Commission or the Internal Revenue Service, for example—hold hearings and issue orders interpreting and enforcing law and policy, they are exercising judicial power. And, many times, federal bureaucracies act as interest groups, seeking to influence other government policymakers.

Though a part of the executive branch, the federal bureaucracy has been called the "fourth branch" of government (in addition to the executive, legislative, and judicial branches, of course). This is partly because of the bureaucracy's importance and permanence. The "fourth branch" designation also results from the fact that, though operating under the direction and management of the president and the oversight of the Congress, the federal bureaucracy often acts with a degree of independence.

In this chapter, we will first give attention to the historical development of the federal bureaucracy. Then, we will consider defenses of the federal bureaucracy, including answers to criticisms of it and suggestions for improving it.

HISTORICAL DEVELOPMENT

The federal Civil Service—permanent employees hired and promoted on merit and removable only for cause—was adopted by Congress in the emotional aftermath of the assassination of President James A. Garfield by a disappointed jobseeker.

The federal bureaucracy goes back much further, of course. Alexander Hamilton, in *Federalist 72*, expected a straightforward system of appointment and management of the bureaucracy by the President. "The persons, therefore, to whose immediate management the different administrative matters are committed," he wrote, "ought to be considered as Assistants or Deputies of the Chief Magistrate, and on this account, they ought to derive their offices from his appointment, at least from his nomination, and ought to be subject to his superintendence."

In the excerpted selection that follows, by Michael Nelson, we see that the federal bureaucracy, what it does, and the way it is selected have become considerably more complex. Nelson also interestingly maintains that the historical developments of the federal bureaucracy have been ironic, in that reforms of it have often produced unintended consequences.

THE IRONIC HISTORY OF BUREAUCRACY
Michael Nelson

The history of American national bureaucracy, if not untold, certainly is unsung. Political scientists seem to have assumed that for most purposes the federal bureaucracy became a subject worth studying only with the coming of the New Deal, and then only in its contemporary form. . . .

Although American national bureaucracy did not spring full-grown from the head of the First Continental Congress in 1775, its fundamental nature, and structure began to develop then and substantially were formed well before the New Deal. Further, at almost every critical turn in American bureaucratic history, the efforts of public officials and organized political groups to enhance popular control of government inadvertently planted the seeds of modern bureaucratic power. . . .

Seven particular ironies of pre-1933 American bureaucratic history—ironies of "Revolution," of "Jacksonian Democracy," of "Reform," and of "Representation"—form the heart of this essay. The concluding section offers some notes toward a theory of the "hidden relationship" that underlies the grand irony of American bureaucracy.

IRONIES OF REVOLUTION: 1775-1828

The country was conceived as much in anger as in liberty, with much of that anger directed at perceived abuses by the British administration. As James Q. Wilson has observed, even a cursory review of the particulars of the revolutionaries' indictment of British colonial rule, for "the weakening of the independence of the judiciary, the stationing of standing armies, and the extensive use of royal patronage to reward office-seekers at colonial expense," reveals that "almost all of their complaints involved the abuse of *administrative* powers."[1] "He [King George] has erected a multitude of new offices," charged the Declaration of Independence, "and sent hither swarms of officers to harass our people and eat out their subsistence."

The colonies' distasteful experience with British executive power caused many Americans to reject all executive forms as potentially tyrannical. Thus, though the sole task of the provisional government established by the First Continental Congress in 1775 was an executive one—to raise, support, and direct an army of revolution—it was made purely legislative in structure. Not only did Congress omit a chief executive, it followed the recommendation of what Francis Wharton called the "liberative-expulsive" school, led by Sam Adams, and deter-

---

1. James Q. Wilson, "The Rise of the Bureaucratic State," in *The American Commonwealth,* eds. Nathan Glazer and Irving Kristol (New York: Basic Books, 1976), 101.

mined that there would be no departments to serve as adjuncts of Congress. Congress instead created committees from its members to make administrative decicions, however minor, by itself. John Adams, who originally had supported his cousin's proposal for legislative government, found himself working eighteen-hour days just to keep up with the business of the ninety committees on which he served. In one typical case, Congress formed a three-member committee "to prepare a plan for intercepting two [enemy supply] vessels" that were en route to America.

This form of decisionmaking doubtless comforted British sea captains, but it exasperated almost everyone else. "Inefficiency and waste, if not downright peculation and corruption" were the rule, writes Charles Thach; General George Washington complained that ". . . . there is a vital and inherent Principle of Delay incompatible with military service in transacting business thro' such numerous and different channels."[2] After much debate, Congress first created boards, embryonic departments made up of congressmen, such as the Board of War and Ordnance; later, it added outside officials to the boards; and finally, in 1781 it established separate departments of Foreign Affairs, War, Marine, and Finance (later Treasury). They were headed by single executives, elected by and accountable to Congress, but otherwise in full control of their jurisdictions, at least until war's end. . . .

In creating the departments, following a pattern which would become typical, Congress inaugurated the First Irony of American bureaucratic history, by which *the revolt against the old administrative order planted the seeds of a new administrative order.* The political goal of securing American independence from British administrative power led Congress to give to the new country administrative institutions of its own. . . .

To be sure, this first irony was an irony of necessity. State administration of some sort is virtually inherent to societies more complex than the agricultural village. Certainly, too, the executive departments were, as had been hoped, vastly more efficient than the boards and committees that had preceded them. Their examples, as well as George Washington's model of "energy, probity, disinterestedness, and a magnificent tactfulness" in his career as the country's chief military executive, and the bitter experiences of those states that continued through the mid-1780s to experiment with almost purely legislative government, helped to allay popular doubts about executive powers. But they did not end those doubts; memories of the royal governors and their agents were too fresh.

Inevitably, the Constitutional Convention of 1787 took this popular ambivalence into account. The framers' purpose, after all, was to write a plan of government that was sellable as well as workable. They had no desire to wave red flags at the still-powerful champions of legislative supremacy. That there would be departments headed by single officials appointed by the president with the advice and consent of the Senate was desired by the framers and allowed by prece-

---

2. Charles C. Thach, Jr., *The Creation of the Presidency, 1775–1789* (Baltimore: Johns Hopkins University Press, 1923), pp. 59, 62, 63.

dent. But the convention debates were almost silent on the issues of who would control the government's administrative apparatus. Not surprisingly, the Constitution produced by those debates is equally unhelpful.

It never has been clear to whom the administrative agencies are to be constitutionally accountable. Presidential scholars have made much of *Federalist* No. 72, which refers to civil servants as "assistants or deputies of the chief magistrate, . . . subject to his superintendence," and of the First Congress's decision in 1789, when it re-created the State, War, and Treasury departments, to vest the president with the power to remove administrative officials unilaterally. They argue that the presence in that Congress of so many of the framers indicates that the Convention's real, though unstated, intent was to place government agencies under presidential control. And in truth, although Congress concerned itself from the first with patronage (John Adams admitted that he had to clear his appointments with the Senate prior to their nomination if he hoped to see them approved) and pork (e.g., the laying of post roads), Presidents Washington, Adams, and Jefferson were not far from being the "undisputed master" of their house.

. . . The Jeffersonians, who dominated government from 1801–1829, were much more congressionally minded than the pro-executive Federalists who preceded them. But institutional history explains more. In particular, the birth in 1800 of the congressional caucus method of nominating candidates for president started a vicious cycle in presidential politics that sometimes made department heads as responsive to Congress, which could advance their own presidential ambitions, as to the president who could not. James Monroe, for example, spent much of his time as President James Madison's Secretary of State currying favor on Capitol Hill. (Madison often had to find sympathetic legislators to introduce bills his department heads refused to press.) After the caucus made Monroe president, he, of course, was obliged to reward his leading supporters with cabinet posts. The new department heads, John Quincy Adams (State), John C. Calhoun (War), and William Crawford (Treasury), soon began to conduct their own campaigns in Congress, turning their backs on Monroe in the process. They also plotted against each other. Crawford, for example, spread rumors that Adams had appeared barefoot in church and forged changes in the original copy of the Constitution, which was in State's custody. Crawford, in turn, was accused of mental incompetence and of using his office to pry into the financial affairs of his cabinet colleagues. Adams, whose election in 1824 marked the end of the caucus system, deplored its effects on government in his *Memoirs:*

> The only possible chance for a head of Department to attain the Presidency is by ingratiating himself personally with the members of Congress; . . . [This is] one of the numerous evils consequent upon the practice which has grown up under this Constitution, but contrary to its spirit, by which the members of Congress meet in caucus and determine . . . upon the candidate for the Presidency . . . a practice which . . . leads to a thousand corrupt cabals between the members of Congress and the heads of the Departments, who are thus almost necessarily made rival pretenders to the succession.[3]

---

3. John Quincy Adams, *Memoirs*, Charles F. Adams, ed. (Philadelphia: J. B. Lippincott, 1874–75), Vol. IV, pp. 242.

If presidents in this period could not fully control their secretaries, those secretaries could not exercise unfettered control of their departments. Beginning in earnest during the War of 1812, Congress had organized itself into specialized committees that corresponded functionally to the departments and whose purpose was to direct and oversee them. . . .

Through the committee system, Congress used its clear constitutional powers, such as investigation, to dominate administration, and claimed near-monopolistic control over the statute-writing and appropriations powers shared with the president. Even the president's specific constitutional authority was undercut by Congress in this period. Jefferson found that only 600 of the federal government's 2,700 civilian positions were his alone to fill—Congress had entrusted the Postmaster-General with more appointees than the president. . . . The best jobs, department heads, United States attorneys, territorial governors, and ambassadors, required Senate confirmation, which meant realistically that most diplomatic and secretarial appointments went to congressmen or ex-congressmen, and the others usually were awarded to their friends. Once, after Monroe expressed reservations about some of Crawford's nominations for customs officers, the secretary raised his cane and called him a "damned infernal old scoundrel," causing Monroe to grab the fireplace tongs in self-defense and order him out, the last time the two men met. When Monroe invoked his constitutional power to "require the opinion in writing" of his department heads and asked a cabinet meeting not to send departmental messages to Capitol Hill before clearing them with him, he was greeted with general silence, then told by a secretary that the practice had existed "ever since the establisment of Government" and presumably would continue. Secretary of War Calhoun, for one, continued to urge internal improvements legislation that Monroe opposed.

Yet Henry Clay, whose "American System" would explicitly have strengthened national administration under congressional control, ultimately was as unsuccessful as Hamilton, who would have done so under the direction of the president. Agencies, forced to live with the ambiguities of control from both elected branches, set about developing power resources of their own. The "secretarial salons" were born—lavish entertainments (in an entertainment-starved city) at which the host cabinet member would woo congressmen with good wine, attractive if decorous women, and fine music. In all this, there was a Second Irony: *the system of dual control of administration became one of limited control.* The Constitutional Convention, in loosing the agencies from their old legislative moorings (politically necessary if the support of executive power adherents was to be won) without tying them securely to the presidency (equally politic if antifederalist support was to be kept) forced agencies to find and exercise relatively independent power. Agencies began to learn to play one branch off against the other; if neither president nor Congress was supreme, then law was, and the agencies interpreted and implemented the law.

The status of administration as a locus of political power in national government was, of course, still nascent in the early nineteenth century. Though the government of this period was responsive to the limited demands placed upon it . . . the "runaway bureaucracy" or pre-Jacksonian America was small and its functions were modest, essentially to collect customs and excise taxes and to deliver the mail. (The Post Office was created in 1792.) A Navy Department was added to War in 1793, the last new department until well into the nineteeth century, but national defense was entrusted primarily to the state militia. The tiny regular army consisted of the corps of engineers and a few frontier patrols. Congressmen outnumbered civil servants in Washington until the 1820s; the Attorney-General (there was no Justice Department) was a private lawyer for whom the government was one client. The president had no staff at all; Washington was known to call department heads in for dictation, which made them secretaries in both senses of the word.

Equally important, administrative agencies at this time were not organized bureaucratically. . . . In other words, congressional or presidential interference aside, the idea was that agencies were to be run in the same way as the law firms, small businesses, plantations, and military units that agency chieftains came from. The standard rule of management was that the boss should direct the show as he saw fit: choose his subordinates for their personal loyalty and "fitness of character," tell them what to do, and keep an eye out to see that it was done. As Jeffersonian America was a country of shopkeepers, so was its government a collection of shops. But, due inadvertently to the efforts of political leaders to forge a new government, they were distinct shops and on the way to becoming independent ones.

IRONIES OF JACKSONIAN DEMOCRACY: 1829–1860

The mass political movement that raised Andrew Jackson to the presidency was fueled by popular resentment of the emerging administrative independence, specifically of the social privilege associated with agency staffing and the corruption that were by-products of this independence. Both of these ills spurred remedial action by the Jackson administration to enhance political branch control of the departments. Yet both sets of remedies planted seeds of irony that later would contribute to the rise of bureaucratic power in America.

Privilege

. . . Washington clearly regarded good appointments as a fundamental task of his presidency. . . . His "primary object" was to appoint men imbued with "fitness of character."

. . . "Expertise" counted for little (not a single appointee to the State Department, for example, other than Secretary Jefferson, had any training or experience in foreign affairs); standing in "the gentry" counted for much. Adams continued and defended this policy . . . Even President Jefferson and his Republican successors tended to equate fitness of character with fitness of family; if 70 percent of Adams's higher civil service appointments had been to men whose fathers had high-status occupations and 92 percent, to men who held such occupations themselves, the comparable figures for the Jefferson administration were 60 percent and 93 percent, respectively. . . .

Kinship as well as class helped to assure the elite character of the early civil service. No fewer than sixteen members of the Livingston/Clinton family held positions in the federal government of 1804. Forty percent of Adams's high-level appointees were relatives of other high-level appointees in his or Washington's administration, and though Jefferson made a point of selecting Republicans, so were 34 percent of his, including 22 percent who shared common kinship with earlier Federalist appointees. Some subsecretarial American civil servants, like their British counterparts, asserted not only a property right to their offices, but a right of inheritance as well. Henry Dearborn, William Ellery, Abraham Bishop, and John Page were among those succeeded in office by their sons, a practice so widespread that John C. Calhoun wrote President Monroe to note its cause and warn of its effects . . . . Decades of administrative stalemate between president and Congress meant that few appointees ever were removed.

None of these sources of administrative privilege—the narrow definition of character rooted in an electorate that was property based until the 1820s, the sympathetic attitude toward patrician office holders and their orphaned sons, or the inter-branch stalemate over appointments and removals (such that almost a third of the cabinet members serving the Jeffersonian era were holdovers from previous administrations)—were very persuasive to the socially, geographically, and economically diverse voters of 1828. If the answer of disgruntled and newly enfranchised western farmers, eastern workers, and rising entrepreneurs of both regions was Jackson's election, Jackson's own answer was equally blunt. In his first annual message to Congress, the president attacked the "corruption," "perversion," and "indifference" of an administrative system in which ". . . office is considered a species of property, and government . . . a means of promoting individual interests," then made his fabled argument that, "The duties of all public officers are, or at least admit of being made, so plain and simple that men of intelligence may readily qualify themselves for their performance; and I cannot but believe that much more is lost by the long continuance of men in office than is generally to be gained by their experience."

Rotation in office was the elevated description of this philosophy, one which Jeremy Bentham told Jackson that he subscribed to as well. "To the victor belong the spoils of the enemy" was Democratic Senator William Marcy's blunt corollary. In eight years, Jackson removed 252 "presidential officers," more than his six predecessors combined had in forty years, even though the pool of offices so designated had dropped from 824 in 1816 to 610 in 1829. Although no more than 20 percent of the total civil service were fired during the Jackson years, almost half of those firings took place in the first 18 months, thus setting the tone for the administration. Many more resigned in anticipation of removal, and spoils were the formula for filling new posts created while Jackson was president . . .

The conventional wisdom, familiar to every schoolchild, is that rotation represented the ultimate politicization of administration, the opposite of modern technocratic bureaucracy. Nothing could be less accurate; indeed, it is the Third Irony of American bureaucratic history that *spoils bred bureaucracy:* Jackson's patronage system helped to hasten the reorganization of federal administrative agencies along bureaucratic lines.

One source of this ironic bureaucratization was the changing nature of party politics. As historian Lynn Marshall points out, Jackson's Democrats were the world's first mass-based political party. Their "whole structure was firmly cemented by the award of federal offices," especially local postmasterships.⁴ But government jobs, though less technical then than now, still were not so simple that any backwoods party stalwart could perform them at a moment's notice. Thus, the Democrats' dilemma: satisfaction of the party faithful seemed to require the appointment of incompetent officials whose poor performance eventually might bring on a popular backlash fatal to the party. After all, more voters send mail than deliver it.

Jackson's remedy lay in the key phrase of his message to Congress: federal jobs "admit of being made" so simple that any intelligent person could do them. "The Jacksonians proposed to organize the executive department as a rationalized complex of offices," writes Marshall, "ordered by function, and defined by rules and regulations." Labor was to be divided, tasks defined, jobs simplified. "In this system, individuals could be placed or replaced [after an election] without upsetting the integrity of the whole. . . . It was the administrative counterpart of the interchangeability of machine parts."⁵ Consequently, it also was an impetus, however inadvertent, to bureaucratic organization in American government.

Corruption

The second source of the bureaucratization of administration that took place under Andrew Jackson also was the second of his supporters' expressly governmental concerns: rampant corruption in the executive agencies. Westward expansion in the 1820s and the new temptations it had spawned for land and currency speculation had subverted occupational morality in almost every sector of society, including government. The extension of agency branch officers, particularly those of the Post Office and the Treasury Department's General Land Office, into new and distant states and territories made administrators' efforts to supervise field agents precatory at best.

Jackson tried at first to infuse the existing "personal organization" mode of administration with new life. Its unity-of-command principle fit nicely with his military background and, for that matter, with the experience of his department heads running civilian enterprises. But for the agency chief to run a clean shop required that one of two conditions pertain: either he and his employees all were able and honest men who could be left on their own, or, if the chief alone was honest, his employees were few enough in number and compact enough in location so that he could monitor their actions personally. Neither of these conditions existed any longer in the rapidly and raucously expanding United States of the mid-nineteenth century. Jackson learned this the hard way, as, for example, when his customs collector in New York City, Samuel Swartwout, sailed off to Europe with $1.25 million in his satchel—a sum equal to more than five

4. Lynn Marshall, "The Strange Stillbirth of the Whig Party," *American Historical Review,* LXXII (January 1967), 450.

5. *Ibid.,* 455–56.

percent of the federal budget! – leaving "swartwouting" to the national vocabulary as a synonym for embezzlement. . . .

The decision to shape federal offices for the purpose of preventing corruption did not come without cost. Form follows function in bureaucracy; agencies designed to prevent internal fraud look and act differently from those designed to promote efficiency, coordination, responsiveness, or some other value. All those internal checks and balances took time. For example, when the House Ways and Means Committee convened in 1836 to investigate complaints about the Treasury Department's excruciating slowness in releasing funds, it found that in order to prevent embezzlement five internal clearances had to be made prior to any departmental financial transaction – hence, the Fourth Irony: *agencies organized to avoid evil became that much less able to do good.* The popular political demand for honest bureaucracy restricted the possibility for efficient and responsive bureaucracy that could satisfactorily meet other, later popular political demands. . . .

AN IRONY OF REFORM: 1861–1932

The lessons of the Fourth Irony were not immediately apparent. Indeed, mid-nineteenth-century advocates of a merit-selected civil service sold their proposal with the argument that honest administration and efficient, politically responsive administration were one and the same. . . .

Admittedly, spoils had become an easy target in the years after Jackson. Rapid turnover made continuity in government difficult to maintain. As the House Committee on Retrenchment noted in 1842, ". . . it very often happens that individuals are brought from a distance, perfect strangers to the duties and details of their offices, installed in bureaus or clerkships with which they never become familiar until in their turn they have to give place to others equally ignorant with themselves." Also, despite the success of the new bureaucratic checks and balances at reducing internal peculation, there was wide corruption at the hiring stage. The "Wanted-Situations" columns of Washington newspapers sometimes carried advertisements like this one from the *Star*: "$100 Cash and 10 per cent of salary for one year, will be given for a Position in any of the Departments." And some political leaders were known to featherbed agencies in order to free employees' time for party labors. Gideon G. Westcott's half-year paid "leave of absence" from his position as an appraiser in the Philadelphia customhouse to serve on Pennsylvania's Democratic Central Committee during the 1856 election campaign was not wholly atypical. . . .

In hindsight, the case for spoils is a powerful one. By democratizing the public service, it helped to legitimate the national government among the new classes of Jacksonian America and assimilate those that emerged later. . . . The actual proportion of swindlers probably was not much higher than it had been before spoils, however conspicuous the exceptions. For very sound electoral resons, "neither party welcomed scoundrels or irresponsibles in public office;" President John Tyler, for example, reported as he left office that during the preceding four years only two cases of embezzlement had been found. As for the Civil War, spoils had no greater triumph. Without patronage to bargain with,

Abraham Lincoln—no president ever used spoils more extensively than he—would have been hard-pressed to keep sullen northern congressmen on board through the military setbacks of 1861 and 1862. And had federal agencies been staffed by tenure-protected employees before secession, the government might have had to prosecute the war half-full of southern sympathizers, a house divided in the most literal sense.

But whatever its retrospective value, spoils' fate was sealed during the administration of James Garfield. Garfield let it be known that he had little liking for the distribution of patronage. Shortly after he entered the White House he complained to James G. Blaine: "All these years I have been dealing with ideas, and here I am . . . considering all day whether A or B should be appointed to this or that office. It was, however, the deceased Garfield, assassinated in 1881 by Charles Guiteau, the campaign worker since immortalized as a "disappointed office seeker," who did the cause of civil service reform the most good. Shortly after the assassination, it was revealed that in one of his many letters to Garfield, Guiteau had written: "The men that did the business last fall are the ones to be remembered." The shock value of this remark, then and now, is evidenced by this dark, decades-later assessment in the Civil Service Commission's official history: "No more revealing description of the spoils system had ever been penned." The Pendleton Act passed soon after, in 1883, giving birth to the modern civil service.

In the half-century that followed, a Fifth Irony emerged: *reformers' efforts to make the civil service more responsive to the political branches made it less responsive.* This was true in part because, as Richard Schott states, the new civil service's "emphasis on merit in hiring promoted the development of a professional, specialized bureaucracy whose expertise [could] not be matched either by president or Congress. Its emphasis on tenure and permanence in office built into this bureaucracy an insensitivity toward and protection from direct overhead political control."[6]

Also, tenured public employees, unlike eunuchs or hammers, developed interests of their own that impeded the efforts of elected officials to have their decisions implemented faithfully. This was possible because the Act was unclear as to which political branch the new Civil Service Commission was to be primarily responsive. When Presidents Theodore Roosevelt and William Howard Taft tried to increase presidential control over federal employees by, among other things, making dismissals for cause easier to obtain, employee unions played on Congress's jealousy of its institutional power to beat their efforts back. Soon after, the unions were able to play the power of President Woodrow Wilson off against Congress when that institution sought to bind the civil service more closely to it; "the federal employees and the American Federation of Labor were two groups that Wilson could not afford to antagonize in undertaking war preparations." These and future efforts by one or the other political branches left the civil service more autonomous, prosperous, and unionized than it had been before. The result, according to Nicholas Lemann, was that ". . . as it grew, the purpose of the civil

---

6. Lawrence C. Dodd and Richard L. Schott, *Congress and the Administrative State* (New York: John Wiley & Sons, 1979), 25.

service system changed somewhat . . . Reforms such as pay raises, improved working conditions, and insurance protection didn't directly make the government more honest or efficient, but they did make working for it more rewarding."

Compounding the Fifth Irony is the manner in which the merit civil service grew. The Pendleton Act itself placed only 13,900 federal jobs, some ten percent under the merit system, but presidents were empowered to extend its coverage by executive order. This they did—almost every nineteenth-century executive order subsequent to passage of the Act dealt with coverage extension—and for the purest of partisan motives. When Grover Cleveland took office in 1885, he vigorously fired Republicans and appointed Democrats to "redress the balance" of twenty-four years of Republican rule, then blanketed in 11,757 of their jobs to prevent them from being fired. Republican Benjamin Harrison, who defeated Cleveland in 1888, added the jobs of 10,535 of his copartisans to the merit-protected list shortly before Cleveland returned to the White House in 1893, then watched as Cleveland upped the ante by blanketing in 49,179 jobs prior to turning the office over to another newly elected Republican, William McKinley. All this raised the number of merit-selected jobs to 87,044, nearly 50 percent of the federal work force. By the time of Franklin Roosevelt's election in 1932, that figure had risen to 80 percent—Taft, a lame-duck in 1912, alone accounted for 52,236 blanketed-in jobs. Nor surprisingly, many of the laws that Roosevelt proposed for the creation of New Deal programs also called for new agencies, temporarily free from civil service domination, to carry them out.

IRONIES OF REPRESENTATION: 1861–1932

Though the size of the federal government grew through the early and middle decades of the nineteenth century, its functions really did not. The only new department created in this period was Interior in 1849, and it consisted almost entirely of already-existing agencies such as the Patent Office and the Office of Indian Affairs that were grouped together because their previous departmental custodians "had grown tired of them." Of the almost eight-fold increase in federal employment between 1816 and 1861, 86 percent were in the Post Office, which simply had a larger country to serve.

The next seventy years were different. New agencies proliferated, seemingly without pattern. By 1887, Woodrow Wilson reasonably could compare American administration to a "lusty child" that "has expanded in nature and grown great in stature, but has also become awkward in movement. The vigor and increase of its life has been altogether out of proportion to its skill in living." The President's Committee on Administrative Management, the oft-cited Brownlow Commission, concluded a half-century later that bureaucracy in this period grew like a farm: a wing added to the house now, a barn put up later, a shed built at some other time, a silo at one stage, a corn crib at another, until it was spread over the landscape in a haphazard and thoroughly confusing way.

But as with most farms, there was an underlying order to bureaucracy's apparent chaos. The United States had been changing rapidly, from a rural society, individualist in its values yet rather homogeneous in composition, to one that was urban, industrial, and highly diverse. The rise of a national market economy produced new demands on government for "clientele" agencies that would represent and support society's increasingly distinct economic groups. It also generated a second set of demands for regulation, in part to protect weak, albeit large, groups from more powerful ones.

None of this came easily, not in a political system invested with all the qualities of Newton's First Law of Motion. American government at rest tends to stay at rest; except in unusual times, its inertial resistance is overcome only when a powerful group is able to press the kind of claim on government that other powerful groups do not strenuously oppose. Such was the birth of the federal government's first important clientele agency, the Agriculture Department, in 1862. Farmers had organized a lobby, the United States Agricultural Society, to press for the creation of a department that would represent their interests in the administrative realm. Powerful congressmen, mindful of the farm vote, and President Lincoln and former presidents back to Millard Fillmore were enrolled as honorary members. The specific proposal the Society advanced seemed modest—a new department that merely would sponsor agricultural research and collect useful data. Who could object?

The story of what happened will sound familiar to observers of modern bureaucracy, but it doubtless astonished the political Newtonians of the day. For, once in motion, the new Department of Agriculture not only stayed in motion but accelerated, snowballing in size and eventually in function. By 1901 it had added divisions of Forestry, Animal Husbandry, Entomology, Pomology, Ornithology, and Mammalogy, and Plant Industry, as well as the Weather Bureau and an Office of Experiment Stations. The politics of this process were as follows: the new department was staffed, for obvious and entirely innocent reasons, by friends of agriculture. The legislative committees with jurisdiction over the department attracted sympathetic congressmen from farm districts, eager to advance their constituents' and thus the department's interests. The agriculture lobby grew in influence; its new power in Washington made it more powerful with the folks back home; the latter's support made it even more influential in Washington, and so on. . . .

Other groups followed agriculture's lead and demanded agencies of their own. In 1869, education interests obtained the establishment by Congress of a Bureau of Education, the forerunner of the Office of Education and later the Department of Education, in the Interior Department. The Knights of Labor and other unions persuaded Congress to begin a Bureau of Labor in Interior in 1884, and, as union power grew, a full-fledged Labor department in 1913. Samuel Gompers, president of the American Federation of Labor, may have been embarrassingly blunt when he hailed the new department as "Labor's Voice in the Cabinet," but the department's legal definition of purpose was not much different: to "foster, promote, and develop the welfare of wage earners of the United States, to improve their working conditions, and to advance their opportunities for profitable employment." In deference to business and commercial interests, Congress also created a Department of Commerce in 1913; one of its first actions was to help found the U.S. Chamber of Commerce.

The largest clientele agency of the period, however, was the Bureau of Pensions, precursor to the modern Veterans Administration. Originally created in 1833, its clients as the nineteenth century wore on were civil war veterans and the Grand Army of the Republic, the largest of the interest groups that represented them. As the GAR grew in size from 60,678 to 427,981 and correspondingly, in political influence, Congress responded by loosening the terms of eligibility for veterans benefits. The original idea had been to give pensions to those who had been injured on the battlefield. "The Pension Act of 1890," observes Keller, "made almost every northern Civil war veteran and his dependents eligible." In 1891, the Pension Office spent 34 percent of the federal budget.

A century ago, the creation of client agencies must have seemed like democracy at its best—worthy groups in society demanding government responding—but once again things turned out less than happily. The Sixth Irony of American bureaucratic history, in fact, is that *client agencies, created to enhance political representation in government, often became almost independent from general political branch control.* "Subgovernments" consisting of constituencies, agencies, and committees grew secure from the direction of either distracted presidents or apathetic majorities of congressmen, whose districts directed their attention to the advancement of other interests, perhaps through subgovernments of their own.

The other set of demands born of the rise of a national industrial economy was for the restriction of economic power; it resulted in the creation of the first independent regulatory agencies. Railroads, which not only were the fastest growing enterprise in the new interregional commerce but its very foundation, also were the first objects of federal regulation. The politics of the Interstate Commerce Act of 1887 and of the Interstate Commerce Commission it established set the pattern for the regulatory explosion that followed,

The railroad system that emerged in the post-Civil War period operated on two planes. The five great trunk lines, the Grand Trunk, New York Central, Erie, Pennsylvania, and Baltimore and Ohio, competed on longhaul runs, but they and their affiliates each enjoyed monopoly control within some region or state. The railroads' correspondingly two-pronged economic strategy, first, was to charge high rates at the local level to make up for the lower-rates competition occasionally forced them to charge on the longhaul runs; and, second, to try to keep longhaul rates high by means of cartel-style "pooling," that is, by informally agreeing among themselves not to compete on the basis of price.

Both these practices enraged the Grange-represented dirt farmers, western merchants, Pennsylvania independent oil producers and reflners, New York businessmen, and others who shipped their products by rail. Each group's protests have been singled out by one scholar or another as the reason Congress eventually passed regulatory legislation. In truth, writes Edward Purcell, ". . . It was neither "the people," nor "the farmers," nor even "the businessmen" who were responsible for the government's regulation of the railroads. Rather it was many diverse economic groups in combination throughout the nation who felt threatened by the new national economy and sought to protect their interests through the federal government."

To mute these mass protests, Congress created the ICC and charged it to block pooling and to regulate rates. Then, in the familiar manner of "majoritarian politics," the triumphant small shippers, rendered "quiescent" by their legislative victory . . . happily abandoned political affairs and went on about their business. Who was left to provide the new commission with the political support it needed to survive? Who was to influence its staffing and monitor its activities? Who, aided by a sympathetic Supreme Court, was to dominate its legalistic rate-setting proceedings? The railroad lobby that had "lost" the war found the peace that followed to be its for the asking. By the time of its second annual report, the Commission already was saying—the Commerce Act and the new Sherman Anti-Trust Act notwithstanding—that pooling was permissible in its eyes. The annual report for 1898 went even further, asking Congress to recognize the railroad industry as a natural monopoly. In 1920, Congress succumbed; the Transportation Act passed that year authorized the ICC to approve such proposals for railroad pooling as it deemed desirable. As for rates, the Commission now was authorized to set minimum as well as maximum limits.

Thus, the Seventh, and familiar, Irony is *regulatory agencies created in response to popular political movements often became, in effect, client agencies of the regulated.* The Food and Drug Administration, established (under a different name) in 1906 to protect customers from unsafe "medicines," soon became highly lenient in approving new drug applications from pharmaceutical companies. . . .

GRAND IRONY, UNINTENDED CONSEQUENCES, AND THE "HIDDEN RELATIONSHIP"

Sorting out the relative importance of historical influences on contemporary bureaucracy from newer ones is no easy task. Clearly, modern American bureaucracy has taken shape in ways that were indicated in the pre-New Deal period. To say this, however, is not to say that the bureaucracy of today is identical, but in size, to the bureaucracy of 1932. That would be foolish in the same way a statement that only size distinguishes the adult from the child would be foolish.

The clientist ironies of representation illustrate the problem. Clientism began its full flowering with the New Deal. New clientele agencies of the 1930s, such as the National Recovery Administration and the Tennessee Valley Authority, delegated public power as well as services and subsidies to affected groups, and some existing agencies, like the Agriculture Department, saw their charters revised for the same purpose. New-style regulatory agencies, such as the Civil Aeronautics Board, the Federal Communications Commission, and the federal Maritime Commission, were enjoyed by their authorizing statutes to promote as well as regulate the industries in their jurisdictions. And in the early and mid-1960s, grant-in-aid poverty programs blossomed, whose purpose actually was to create organized clientele where none really existed.

The late 1960s and early 1970s, however witnessed a series of developments that, in the opinion of some observers, marked the end of client-oriented government. The rise of activist courts, "public interest" lobbies, and congressional staffs were cited as evidence for this proposition, as were new economic cleavages that produced countervailing political forces within most policy areas and the shift in political campaigning toward television and direct mail, which placed a premium on the sharp definition of issues. These developments, it was said, altered dramatically the behavior of such agencies as the CAB, whose staff led the way for airline deregulation in the face of client opposition, and the FDA, which began rendering decisions that much displeased the pharmaceutical companies.

Such evidence is interesting, but not yet persuasive. Already the 1980s show signs of bringing a return to normalcy in subgovernment politics. The swift and severe chastening recently received by the FTC, the Interior Department, and other agencies when they strayed from their traditionally generous policies toward the commercial interests in their constituencies may indicate that we are back to clientist politics as usual. The point is that we just do not know, and neither history nor journalism alone can tell us.

Yet, in at least one area of surpassing modern concern, the past seems to speak convincingly. "Unintended consequences" are the bane of the modern policy process: programs are established by law with certain purposes in mind; their actual effects, however, are not (or are not only) those that were intended. Welfare programs that subvert family life, school integration plans that lead to greater segregation, technologically advanced weapons systems that reduce national security are among the familiar examples. The prevalence of unintended consequences concerns not just policy theorists but democratic theorists as well. After all, even a strong connection between the electorate and its representatives is inconsequential if the demands made by the former and enacted into law by the latter still are not satisfied.

Most efforts to account for these breakdowns in the policy process come in two parts: first, the self-interest of implementing agencies, which adds goals of organizational preservation and growth to those provided by the program statute; and second, the lack of care and specificity characteristic of many such statutes themselves. But the questions again are why? Why is the organizational self-interest of bureaucratic agencies such a powerful force in the American policy process? Why are American legislators and political executives so inattentive to program design?

It is possible that history offers the answers to these questions. If nothing else, history shows that unintended consequences are nothing new; the evolution of American bureaucracy has been marked by one ironic failure after another, the "grand irony" of which is that repeated efforts to bring government under political branch control have enhanced the power of bureaucracy. In particular, I would argue that clues to the nature of the "hidden relationship" discussed in the introduction to this essay that causes this irony are to be found in historical *sequence,* the order in which things happened in the country's political development.

The importance of historical sequence becomes apparent through comparison. In Western Eruope, a monarchical past meant that the democratization of national political systems occurred long after their bureaucratization. Because the legitimate presence and power of bureaucratic organizations were given by the time democracy came along, the primary democratic task was to control and direct their activities to popular ends. One of the reasons that European political parties developed as programmatic, disciplined organizations was to provide the kinds of clear, sustained external direction that bureaucratic agencies need if their organizational goals are to be overcome. The strict internal hierarchy of these agencies, a carry-over from pre-democratic days, facilitated this effort: to appoint or control the agency heads was a giant step toward controlling the agency.

In the United States, however, the establishment of democratic political institutions *preceded* the establishment of administrative ones. The latter, which were resisted strenuously in the Continental Congress and scarcely mentioned in the Constitution, have remained somewhat illegitimate in American political culture ever since. From the start, this has forced bureaucratic agencies to build independent political bases to provide sustenance to their pursuit of organizational goals, an endeavor encouraged by the constitutional system of divided political control. . . .

The order of American political development (democracy before bureaucracy) also affected the country's political parties (which, in turn, affected the later development of national bureaucracy which, in turn, affected the parties, and so on). Early American parties, quite understandably, had little of the European concern for curbing and directing bureaucratic power. To them, administrative agencies were sources of bounty (pork and patronage), not loci of power in need of control; indeed, Jackson's Democrats fostered the process of bureaucratization in order to reap the harvest of spoils such organizational changes allowed. In part, because bureaucracy was looked at this way, parties also had no incentive to develop as programmatic organizations. This meant, for example, that unlike Great Britain where civil service reform followed the establishment of central party leadership and really did turn British bureaucracy into a "hammer and saw" for the elected government, the American civil service took shape with no vision at all from the parties as to what policy purposes it should serve. This made it a good deal easier for it to foster purposes of its own.

In recent years, as the size and complexity of governmental tasks have increased, the technical expertise to handle them has become an added source of power for bureaucratic agencies. The challenge to party control thus has become more formidable even if a) the party organizations were strong, and b) the will was there. Actually, neither of these conditions obtain. Parties are unprecedentedly weak, in no small measure because bureaucracy now distributes the jobs and welfare that once were the parties' main appeals to their members. Legislators, interested as never before in Congress as a vocation, pay less attention to the politically unrewarding task of writing clear, careful legislation and more to its symbolic and distributive aspects. Presidents . . . also neglect program implementation because their desire for re-election and a place in history leads them to emphasize the "dramatic achievement" of "dramatic goals." Without clear policy direction from the parties or their elected officials, organizational self-interest has been able to thrive. And so have unintended consequences.

CONCLUSION

If there is a pertinent lesson to be learned from the ironic history that has helped to shape the current period, it might be one that justifies despair: a lesson in the pitfalls of political reform. Time and time again, major efforts to make administration more responsive to political control have had the opposite effect.

It is enough to chasten even the boldest reformer if, like the sorcerer's apprentice, his every assault on his tormenters doubles their strength.

Is it enough, though, to convince us that modern bureaucracy as we know it is inevitable in the United States? After all, British, Russian, and private bureaucracies share many of the characteristics and draw many of the same complaints. Does bureaucracy evolve, then, purely in response to its own imperatives, reinforced in the American experience by the vagaries of historical evolution, until it ineluctably overpowers what Weber sardonically called its "political master"?

Only in part. For if it was inevitable, and certainly it was, that the federal government would establish a separate executive apparatus, its continued constitutional removal from unambiguous control by Congress, the president, or anyone else is not. If it was inevitable that technical skills and other evidence of "merit" would become the standard for staffing bureaucracy, there still is no compelling reason not to restore rotation in office, while simply raising the qualifications of those rotated.

The list goes on. Were clientele agencies of some sort inevitable? Probably; the proliferation of distinctive economic interests in society mandated some corresponding response in government. But the subgovernments that frequently safeguard them from general political control—an artifact of our divided system of powers—surely are not. And though the departments of government necessarily had to assume some form of bureaucratic organization, it hardly is ordained that the form chosen must be one designed not to promote efficiency or sensitivity, but to prevent fraud.

Despair, then, is not justified, at least not by this account. To paraphrase Santayana, history repeats itself not when we understand it, but rather when we do not. ■

IN DEFENSE OF THE BUREAUCRACY

Through the years, a good many observers have been concerned about the fact that in a democracy, considerable power is exercised by an unelected bureaucracy. There have been a good many criticisms, too, of bureaucrats, bureaucracy, and "red tape."

In the James W. Fesler article excerpted in this chapter, we focus on the interplay between senior civil servants and political appointees in the federal executive branch. Fesler takes the position that the operation of the bureaucracy would be improved if more of the top positions in the executive branch were a part of the Civil Service, rather than being appointive. In the process, Fesler also answers criticisms that the federal bureaucracy has grown too much and is unresponsive to administrative control and that bureaucrats are unrepresentative of the public, in party affiliation and ideology.

POLITICS, POLICY, AND BUREAUCRACY AT THE TOP
James W. Fesler

. . . The upper reaches of the executive branch are a curious mélange. They include roughly 9000 officials: about 100 in the White House and other parts of the Executive Office of the President; about 700 cabinet and subcabinet posts, commissionerships, and bureau chiefships filled by presidential appointment, usually with the advice and consent of the Senate; some 7000 members of the Senior Executive Service, of whom 700 are political appointees and 6300 are senior civil servants; and about 1200 scientists and other specialists without managerial responsibilities. Altogether these top officials amount to four-tenths of one percent of total federal civilian employment.

Except immediately under the cabinet, no line can be drawn across the executive branch, or across a single department, above which all senior officials are political executives and below which all are civil-service careerists. By law, some bureau chiefs are presidential appointees confirmed by the Senate, some are noncareer appointees of a cabinet member, and some are career appointees. A further complexity is that some civil-service careerists accept appointment as political executives, though until recently they thereby lost civil-service status, including tenure.

The United States outdoes all other modern democracies in its provision for change when party control of the executive branch shifts. About 1600 higher positions are filled by political appointment. This contrasts with the approximately 100 top officials in Britain and 360 in France—though 85 percent of France's are drawn from the civil service—that a new administration is entitled to choose afresh. In a typical American department, the secretary, deputy and under secretaries, assistant and deputy assistant secretaries, administrators of large aggregates, chiefs of several bureaus, and regional directors are replaced by a new set of officials. In the Department of Commerce, 93 high political incumbents can be displaced; in the Department of Agriculture, 65.

For three decades the number of politically filled posts has increased. This occurred partly by interposition of new layers of political appointees and partly by multiplication of executives' staff assistants. But existing positions were also shifted from the career service to political appointment; examples are department's assistant secretaries for administration and regional directors. If political executives are the principal means by which a president and a department head can grasp control of the bureaucracy and institute changes in policy and program, the United States has abundantly provided for it.

From James Fesler, "Politics, Policy, and Bureaucracy at the Top," *The Annals of the American Academy of Political and Social Science,* Volume 466, March 1983, p. 23–41. Copyright © 1983 by The American Academy of Political and Social Science. Reprinted with permission of Sage Publications, Inc. and the author.

THE PRESIDENT'S ENTOURAGE

Nearest the president are the White House staff and the agencies housed in the Executive Office of the President, especially the mostly career-staffed Office of Management and Budget (OMB). Between them one might expect a happy melding of short-term political and long-term careerist points of view in service of the president's policy and management responsibilities.

The White House Staff

Every president needs near him a few intimate advisers who are politically astute and personally loyal. He turns to those with whom he has been closely associated in the campaigns for nomination and election and to friends in his home state. The problem that arises is twofold. One is that his closest advisers are often poorly qualified for the responsible governmental roles in which they are suddenly cast, roles that have become magnified by the centripetal pull of policy and short-term decision making to the White House and by the president's delegation of the tangle of domestic affairs to his aides as he increasingly becomes absorbed in foreign affairs.

The other form of the problem is extension downward in White House staffing of the same recruitment criteria, except for prior intimacy with the president: personal loyalty, campaign service, and congruence of substantive policy views, if any, with those voiced in the election campaign. In 1981, runs one report, "with few exceptions, the professionals on the policy development staff were active in Reagan's 1980 campaign for the presidency." Two of them, in their mid-twenties, had been campaign speech writers. In the Carter administration, the then associate OMB director recalls, "OMB felt that the Domestic Policy Staff was too pervasive, too concerned with short-term political considerations and that some of its junior people were not too capable."[7]

Characterizations of the presidential assistants constituting the White House staff vary more in tone than in essentials. One, kinder than most, reads, "They tend to be young, highly intelligent, and unashamedly on the make. They take chances, they cut corners, and unlike most politicians they sometimes have a little spontaneity and irreverence left in them. This accounts for much of their charm and most of their problems."[8] The words are from Patrick Anderson's study of assistants serving presidents from Roosevelt to Johnson. Characterizations of assistants to Nixon, Ford, Carter, and Reagan have a darker cast.

Efforts to strengthen the president by furnishing him with a staff of several hundred creates more problems than it solves. The White House itself becomes a complex, layered bureaucracy that is difficult to manage. The number of aides with the ready access to the president that propinquity promotes reduces his op-

---

7. W. Bowman Cutter, quoted in Dick Kirschten, "Decision Making in the White House: How Well Does It Serve the President?" *National Journal*, 14:584–89, 588 (3 Apr. 1982).

8. Patrick Anderson, *The President's Men: White House Assistants of Franklin D. Roosevelt . . . Lyndon Johnson* (Garden City, NY: Doubleday, Anchor Books, 1969) p. 469. In the 1976 campaign, Anderson was a speech writer for Jimmy Carter; he declined appointment to the White House staff.

portunities for conferring with cabinet members and seeking counsel from knowledgeable persons outside the government. The number, energy, and policy-area assignments of lower-level aides draw business to the White House that might well be left to cabinet departments. Such aides' intrusiveness into departmental affairs often bypasses department heads, thus weakening the prestige of those on whom the president depends for departmental management. The policy-formation process is slowed and complicated by in-house clearance procedures and by substantive and personal controversies among aides. The White House contribution, then, becomes not the comprehensive, long-range view of policy and honest brokering of conflicting departmental advocacy positions, but often a poorly coordinated battle for the president's mind among his own assistants.

The Office of Management and Budget

Established in 1921 and brought into the new Executive Office in 1939, the Bureau of the Budget was a major resource for management of much of the presidential-level policy-formation process. It was staffed with unusually able careerists and generally headed by a well-qualified presidential appointee. Its skeptical review of departments' budget requests gave it control, under the president's direction, over one of the two major presidential policy instruments: the budget and the State of the Union Message. Additionally, its legislative clearance role enabled it to review all departments' legislative proposals and positions in support of or opposition to pending legislation, all with a view to advising whether they were in accord with the president's program. And its review of bills passed by Congress, including gathering of concerned departments' reactions, gave it a key role in advising the president whether to approve or veto the bills. Its administrative management staff had broad responsibility for improving the organization and efficiency of executive agencies.

Aftr 1960, while its budgetary power did not decline, presidential aides largely superseded the bureau's policy-level role in legislative clearance and review of enrolled congressional bills. And its work on administrative management declined as the budgetary staff gained dominance, so much so that it could not monitor compliance with its own administrative directives.

Despite Nixon's change of its name, in 1970, to the Office of Management and Budget, and despite its sizable staff, now about 600, these tendencies have persisted and new tendencies have appeared. Appointees to director and deputy director positions are more often political men, closely associated with the president, lobbying with Congress, and soliciting public support of his policies. A layer of noncareer appointees has been inserted between the director and the civil servants on the staff. New presidents and their aides initially distrust the bureaucrats in OMB, so that its rich fund of knowledge about the executive branch, the fate of earlier presidential initiatives, and the policy-affecting potential of the budget process are rarely tapped in the crucial first year. Though OMB mounts specific administrative management undertakings for particular presidents — as in executive branch reorganization, regulatory review, and paperwork management—the management staff for longer-range responsibilities has been successively cut, most recently, in mid-1982. Informed observers believe that OMB needs reinvigoration, greater high-level participation by senior careerists, and either strengthening of its nonbudgetary activities or transfer of them to a new staff agency.

CABINET MEMBERS

The initial selection of members of the cabinet receives more personal attention by the president-elect than that of any other set of political executives, save his few top aides. Recent presidents have had such confidence in those they select as to assert an intention to institute cabinet government, meaning reliance on cabinet members for counsel and for the staffing and running of their departments.

Cabinet members are an abler lot than the conspicuous exceptions lead us to believe. Many have achieved distinction in their careers and, for good or ill, are members of the establishment. Eisenhower appointed nine millionaires and Reagan at least eight. Carter's 1977 cabinet included five members with Ph.D.s and five who were lawyers. Most have had federal government experience. From 1953 to 1976, this was true of 55 percent of the initial appointees and of 85 percent of replacement appointees. They often are generalists who have served in other cabinet posts, at the subcabinet level in the same or other departments, or as top presidential aides. Early exemplars of the pattern are George Marshall, Dean Acheson, Robert Lovett, Averell Harriman, and Douglas Dillon. Later ones are Elliot Richardson, James Schlesinger, Cyrus Vance, Harold Brown, Joseph Califano, Alexander Haig, Caspar Weinberger, and George Shultz. Many are highly qualified, whether by public or private experience, for the processes of advocacy, negotiation , and compromise that are at the heart of governmental policy-making—laywers more so, corporate executives and academics somewhat less so, the few ideologues not at all.

However able and experienced they are, the president's early promise of cabinet government soon evaporates. Why should this be so? A too easy explanation, favored by White House aides, is that cabinet members "marry the natives"; each, headquarteed in his department, is captured by the bureaucracy and by the clientele groups in the department's immediate environment. Responsiveness to the president, and to his aides, lapses.

An explanation that receives too little attention is that each cabinet member, as department head, is obligated to see to the faithful execution of the laws that fall within his department's jurisdiction. In most of its statutes, Congress vests authority directly in departments and their heads, not in the president. A department head is bound to resist White House aides' urging that he neglect or distort any of his principal statutory responsibilities. Should he not resist, he will alienate his career executives and will have to answer to clientele groups, congressional committees, and the courts.

A political element helps to poison the well. Though the president may initially promise cabinet members free hands in filling their subcabinet and other executives posts, this commitment eventually yields to the White House staff's insistence on clearance of nominees and, often, appointment of candidates centrally identified and preferred.

A variety of factors set cabinet members and White House aides on a collision course. In addition to those mentioned, petty and not-so-petty behaviors play their part. Cabinet members' access to the president is denied, White House aides fail to return cabinet members' telephone calls, and deliberate slights of protocol signal that individual members are out of favor. President Carter's purge of his cabinet in 1979 focused on those who had incurred White House aides' displeasure.

Joseph Califano quotes from his exit interview with Carter: " 'Your performance as Secretary has been outstanding,' the President said. 'You have put the Department in better shape than it has ever been before. You've been the best Secretary of HEW. . . . The problem is the friction with the White House staff. The same qualities and drive and managerial ability that make you such a superb Secretary create problems with the White House staff.' "[9] The secretary must have sensed an odd reversal of role, for in the Johnson White House, "serving as the chief expediter for an impatient and demanding President, Califano made many enemies," some among cabinet members. "Time and again . . . Califano fought to impose Johnson's interests over the narrower interests of the departments of government."[10]

Whether by their own or the president's choice, cabinet members' median term since World War II has been barely more than two years. Over one-fifth of the secretaries were in place for less than 11 months. From 1953 through 1976, there were 5 presidents, but 12 secretaries of commerce, 11 secretaries of HEW, 10 attorneys general, 9 secretaries of labor and of the treasury, and 8 secretaries of defense.

Brevity of tenure, perhaps because it is not anticipated, does not deflect cabinet members from according highest priority to the making and influencing of policy. This is no doubt appropriate, but there is a price to pay. Many give very low priority to departmental management, which is the key to assuring responsiveness and effectiveness of the bureaucracy. This is as true of able corporate executives as of their colleagues from other walks of life. Secretary of the Treasury Michael Blumenthal, formerly head of the Bendix Corporation, made the pont: "You learn very quickly that you do not go down in history as a good or bad Secretary in terms of how well you ran the place, whether you're a good administrator or not. You're perceived to be a good Secretary in terms of whether the policies for which you are responsible are adjudged successful or not. . . . But that's not true in a company. In a company it's how well you run the place."[11]

---

9. Joseph A. Califano, Jr., *Governing America: An Insider's Report from the White House and the Cabinet* (New York: Simon & Schuster, 1981), pp. 434–35.

10. Anderson, *The President's Men*, pp. 443, 446.

11. W. Michael Blumenthal, "Candid Reflections of a Businessman in Washington," *Fortune*, 99(2):36ff., 39 (Jan. 1979).

POLITICAL EXECUTIVES

Below cabinet members and other major agencies' heads are most of the 1600 political executives. A president intent on effecting change within the executive branch normally transmits his intentions through these appointees and, at least in theory, should be able to rely on them for vigorous translation of intentions into action. Yet the multiplicity, qualifications, and tenure of political executives probably hamper the effecting of change more than does any obduracy of the permanent bureaucracy.

Numbers

The large number of political appointments available guarantees that errors of choice will be made, and the earlier the more. In the 10-week post-election rush, self-nomination, others' recommendations, the old-boy network, the BOGSAT technique ("a bunch of guys sitting around a table"), and a variety of other means provide the large pool of candidates and the disorderly modes of selection.

The numbers also account for how deeply political appointments extend into the bowels of departmental administration. The proliferation of subcabinet posts, strictly defined, affords one clue. These positions—of under secretary, deputy under secretary, and assistant secretary—increased from 55 in 1950 to 84 in 1960, 113 in 1970, and 145 in 1978. The secretary may have as many as 15 politically appointed assistants attached to his own office, and the subcabinet officials may average two such assistants apiece. Below the subcabinet level are a number of political appointees with such titles as deputy assistant secretary, bureau chief, deputy bureau chief, and regional director.

The large number of political executives and their penetration of departments, bureaus, and the field service distance able careerists from the centers of decision making. Their rich potential remains untapped, especially in the early period when the administration's and departments' major policy proposals are formulated.

Qualifications

By most standard criteria, especially educational level and subject-matter knowledge relevant to their particular program-area responsibilities, political executives are a well-qualified elite. Three other criteria concern us here. These are partisan and policy compatibility with the president, governmental experience, and capacity to manage large organizations.

Political executives are less partisan than their designation suggests. From 1961 to 1978, members of the president's party averaged only 58 percent among the four administrations' sets of political appointees, with a range of 47 percent under Johnson to 65 percent under Nixon. Within cabinet departments, two-thirds of the political appointees, on average, belonged to the president's party, with State and Defense on the low side (44 and 47 percent) and Housing and Urban Development and Agriculture (89 and 86 percent) on the high side.

Old images of party patronage have largely ceased to reflect reality. White House personnel staffs try to deflect partisan pressures by rewarding large financial contributors and taking care of defeated candidates for electoral office by minor, though sometimes major, ambassadorships; membership in multimember bodies — regulatory boards and commissions, presidential advisory commissions, and departmental advisory committees — and invitations to White House galas for foreign dignitaries.

The politics of policy, if not of party, plays a large role in recruitment. This politics takes two forms: loyalty to the president and his policies throughout his term, including the possibility of his changing course, and inflexible loyalty to particular policies, most of them compatible with the president's campaign rhetoric but selectively erosive during his term. The second kind of loyalty can turn antipresidential. Initial selection of subcabinet and subordinate executives depends heavily on nominations and recommendations from the economic and professional communities interested in particular programs. A number of those chosen are likely to be drawn from interest groups, single-cause movements, conservative or liberal think tanks, and congressional staff members who share the president's initial orientation. Many such are advocates, with agendas of their own. There is little assurance that such political appointees will flexibly respond to the president's initiatives for change rather than firmly adhere to their convictions, constituencies, political patrons. Yet they are arrayed in many layers between the good to be done, as the president perceives it, and those who can do it, the career executives in closest touch with implementation.

Advocates, it is true, have a strong impulse to innovate, whether to turn the clock forward or backward. But innovations can be good or bad, well timed or ill timed, contributors or embarrassments to a larger strategy of change. Advocacy-oriented political executives are not the president's men and women. They march to a different drummer.

Prior experience in the federal government is a criterion closely linked to political executives' performance. Looking back, former appointees confess that they were poorly prepared for the Washington setting of interest groups, congressional committees, the White House staff, the goldfish-bowl exposure to the media, the budget process, and the permanent bureaucracy. In 1970 over two-thirds of presidential and two-fifths of departmental political appointees had less than two years of federal governmental experience. Another two-fifths of the departmentally appointed political officials had over 10 years of federal experience and, like the top civil servants, were better prepared. Hugh Heclo notes the anomaly, that "unlike the situation in most private organizations, in the U.S. executive branch those in the top positions of formal authority [that is, presidential appointees] are likely to be substantially less familiar with their working environment than both their civil service and political subordinates."[12]

Capability for the management of large organizations or for operating in

---

12. Hugh Heclo, *A Government of Strangers: Executive Politics in Washington, D.C.:* Brookings Institution, 1977), p. 101.

them is a third criterion of executives' effectiveness. Few of the political executives who are lawyers or who are recruited from universities and research institutes, interest-group organizations, congressional staffs, and small business firms have had experience that prepares them for running a bureau of 5000 employees, let alone for operating in one of the cabinet departments, which range from 15,000 to one million employees. Sometimes, as Dean Acheson and George W. Ball have noted, even the head of a major corporation may have served only an ornamental function there and can do no more in government.

Tenure

Independently of other attributes, the brief tenure of political executives suffices to explain the marginality of their impact. In the period of 1960 to 1972, over half of the under secretaries and assistant secretaries moved out within less than two years, including a fifth who left in less than one year. How much time does a new political executive need to achieve effectiveness? Maurice Stans, former secretary of commerce, said, "A business executive needs at least two years to become effective in government, to understand the intricacies of his programs, and to make beneficial changes."[13]

Rapid turnover not only reduces individual effectiveness, it impairs three relationships that are at the heart of the administration's effectiveness. First, it complicates a department head's effort to establish teamwork among his principal subordinates, for they are ever changing. Second, rapid turnover near the top recurrently breaks up interdepartmental networks of political executives sharing concern with, and perhaps having divergent views on, particular policy and program areas extending across several departments. For these, especially, there need to be what Heclo terms "relationships of confidence and trust." The chemistry involved in these interpersonal relations takes time to develop and is upset if new elements are constantly being introduced. Third, top civil servants' relations with political superiors that are here today and gone tomorrow cannot faithfully follow copybook maxims. Some careerists, if called on, will patiently tutor one after another political executive to speed his learning process. Others, particularly those in charge of bureaus and programs, will take protective measures to minimize the damage an ill-prepared and very temporary political executive can do.

Political executives share a number of attributes that limit their effectiveness as the president's agents of change. Their number is too large. Partisanship is too weak to make them a cohesive group. In its place is the politics of policy. For some this means a commitment to support the president and, so, to adapt flexibly to his changing policy agenda and priorities. But for many it means tenacious devotion to particular program areas and particular policies, whether or not they comport with the president's strategic emphases. Too few political executives have prior governmental experience; fewer know how to run a large

---

13. Arch Patton, "Government's Revolving Door," *Business Week,* Sept. 1973, pp. 12–13.

organization well. Finally, political appointees' stay is short and their comings and goings erratic.

CAREER EXECUTIVES

Recent presidents campaigned against the bureaucracy and complained during their terms of the unresponsiveness of the bureaucracy. Most political appointees enter office with a stereotypical view of bureaucrats. This inhibits their seeking a collaborative relation with those best informed on departmental programs and best prepared to warn inexperienced superiors of minefields in the surrounding terrain. The three elements of the president's and political executives' stance are an assumption that the bureaucracy is swollen, a doubt of careerists' competence, and an expectation of their unresponsiveness to the administration in power. The first is quickly disposed of. For three decades the number of federal civilian employees has been substantially stable, in contrast to increases in the nation's population, its employed labor force, and the range of governmental responsibilities.

Doubt of careerists' competence is ill founded. Elmer Staats, after a distinguished career in politically appointive posts, said on ending his term as the comptroller general of the United States that ever since World War II days, "I have worked with business people who have been in the government. . . . And I have yet to find a single one of those business executives after their experience here who doesn't go out and have nothing but praise for the calibre and the hard work of the people in the government."[14] And Alan K. Campbell, an executive vice-president of ARA Services, Inc.—and earlier a Carter appointee—reports that "the quality of top managers I knew in the federal government . . . is every bit as high as we have at ARA; and on the whole, the people at ARA are paid from 1½ to 3 times more than their public sector counterparts."[15]

An expectation that the bureaucracy will be unresponsive to the administration in power is too simplistic to fit comfortably with the complexity of factors determining senior civil servants' behavior. Top careerists are remarkably diverse in ideological orientation and in party identification. On a scale of attitudes ranging from state intervention to free enterprise, Joel D. Aberbach and his colleagues found that their sample of such American careerists was "more heterogeneous than any of the European bureaucratic samples." The basic picture is a distribution of attitudes that is not only wide but substantially congruent with the distribution pattern in Congress.

Party affiliations of careerists are weaker predictors of behavior. In social-service agencies in 1970, "even Republican administrators . . . were not wholly sympathetic to the social service retrenchments sought by the Nixon administration."[16] Sample surveys in 1970 and 1976 found that top careerists were 47 per-

14. Transcript, *The MacNeil/Lehrer Report: Elmer Staats Interview,* 6 Mar. 1981, pp. 6–7.

15. Alan K. Campbell, in a symposium. "The Public Service as Institution," *Public Administration Review,* 42:304–20, 315 (July–Aug. 1982).

16. Joel D. Aberbach and Bert A. Rockman, "Clashing Beliefs Within the Executive Branch: The Nixon Administration Bureaucracy," *American Political Science Review,* 70:456–68, 467 (June 1976).

cent Democratic (38 percent in 1976), 36 percent Independent (48 percent in 1976), and 17 percent Republican (16 percent in 1976). Using different tests of Independents' leanings, the surveyors drew different conclusions. For 1970, Joel Aberbach and Bert Rockman held that "the belief that a Republican administration does not have natural political allies within the federal bureaucracy seems well-justified."[17] For 1976, Richard Cole and David Caputo believed that "Independents and party identifiers combined assure either a Republican or a Democratic president substantial support at the senior career levels of the federal bureaucracy."[18]

Beyond ideologies and party affiliations, and often overriding them, is another attitudinal orientation. Most careerists perceive their role as one entailing the obligation to serve loyally the people's choice as president. Because senior careerists have served through several changes in administration, this is a well-internalized commitment. It is qualified, to be sure, by resistance to illegality, a resistance that served the nation well in the Watergate era.

This basic commitment, however, can be attenuated by another attitude toward role performance. Typically, senior civil servants identify with their agency and its responsibilities. Their finding fulfillment in achieving the purposes of statutes entrusted to them, instead of being passively neutral, generally strengthens the faithful execution of the laws. But it lures some into bureaucratic politics — protection of the agency's turf, development of a degree of autonomy, and mobilization of allies in Congress and clientele groups.

How responsive careerists are to presidential policy shifts is a complex product of ideologies, party affiliations, the civil-service doctrine of loyalty to the incumbent president, and devotion to particular programs and agencies. The relative weights of these factors vary with circumstances. The most negative reactions can be expected when the president orders termination of an agency or of well-established programs, reduction of funds, or slashing of staff. Yet when, by President Reagan's order, the Community Services Administration, an antipoverty agency, was dismantled in three months, the agency director reports, "The career service had demonstrated in a dramatic way the best of professional integrity in executing a difficult assignment most of them opposed." It shows, he adds, that "the mythology of an untrustworthy bureaucracy poised to undermine a policy with which it disagreed was simply not true."[19]

THE SHARED WORLD OF POLITICAL AND CAREER EXECUTIVES

Though political and career executives differ in important regards, the considerable degree of congruence of orientations permits expectation that they might harmoniously collaborate in their shared world. The recent institution of the Senior Executive Service is designed to facilitate such collaboration. Yet careerists'

---

17. Ibid., p. 458.

18. Richard L. Cole and David A. Caputo, "Presidential Control of the Senior Civil Service: Assessing the Strategies of the Nixon Years," *American Political Science Review*, 73:399–413, 412 (June 1979).

19. Dwight Ink, "CSA Closedown—A Myth Challenged," *Bureaucrat*, 11:39–43, 39, 43 (Summer 1982).

morale has fallen to perhaps its lowest point, and their career paths often poorly prepare them for engagement in the fashioning of broad policy.

Some Congruent Orientations

Political executives and top careerists have a good deal in common. Both groups are highly educated; more than half the members of each hold graduate or professional degrees. However, more of the senior civil servants, 40 percent, majored in technology and natural science; only 10 percent of political executives did so. Members of the two groups do not differ substantially in the proportions that see their role, or roles, as that of advocate, legalist, broker, trustee, facilitator, policymaker, or ombudsman. The civil servants, though, are twice as likely as political executives to have a technician-role focus, and half as likely to have a partisan-role focus. Their external activities disclose a common pattern: nearly two-thirds of each group have regular contacts with members of Congress; over 90 percent of each have regular contacts with representatives of clientele groups. Internally, not surprisingly, political executives have about twice as much contact with their department heads as do senior civil servants. But, if not surprising, it indicates exclusion or filtering of counsel from members of the permanent government.

Top careerists share political executives' frustrations with bureaucratic obstacles to effective performance, particularly the pervasiveness of red tape and the constricting personnel system. At least two-thirds of those sampled in 1981 answered no when asked whether "the administrative support systems" provide a pool of qualified professional and managerial talent to hire from, make it easy to hire employees, or make it easy to fire or to apply lesser sanctions against poorly performing employees.

Finally, the infiltration of political-executive ranks by career civil servants fosters congruence of outlook with those continuing in civil-service status. Former careerists filled 25 percent of assistant secretaryships in the 1933–61 period—an average for the three presidencies. In the mid-1970s they held nearly half of such posts, and in 1978, under Carter, 61 percent. Below the assistant secretaries, Heclo reports, "one-third to one-half of the noncareer . . . posts . . . are usually filled by career civil servants."[20] In the period Heclo deals with, such cooptation by the incumbent administration required sacrifice of civil-service status and possible dismissal from government service by the next administration. This has changed.

The Senior Executive Service

The 1978 Civil Service Reform Act pooled most political executives and top career executives in a Senior Executive Service (SES). The service currently includes about 7000 executives, 90 percent of them careerists and 10 percent

---

20. Heclo, *A Government of Strangers*, p.131.

political appointees. This is a specified governmentwide ratio; within it an individual agency's political appointees may rise as high as 25 percent. Except for presidential appointees requiring senatorial confirmation, or requiring White House clearance, a department head freely chooses political appointees who meet his previously established qualification standards. In making career appointments to the SES, he must adhere to competitive merit principles.

The key feature is the new flexibility with which the department head can assign and reassign SES members, whether political or career, to particular positions. Only two restrictions apply. A careerist is protected against involuntary reassignment for the first 120 days after appointment of a new department head, or of a political executive with reassignment authority. And in about 45 percent of the positions, the department head can assign and reassign only careerists, not political appointees. These are posts reserved for civil servants "to ensure impartiality, or the public's confidence in the impartiality of the Government," as the statute phrases it.[21]

These necessary protections accounted for, the system is one in which the department head can assemble his large management team, mixing political and career executives as suits his purpose. Additionally, advised by performance-review boards, he can at any time remove from SES a career member rated "less than fully successful."

Morale

The Senior Executive Service had a troubled start.[22] Pay was a major problem. Though the Reform Act directs the president to establish SES pay levels, Congress later set a pay ceiling that in 1982 put 84 percent of SES members at the same pay, $6000 below the president's top pay level. The performance awards and substantial bonuses for abler SES careerists, provided in the act, were also later curtailed. The most basic problem was eased when, at the end of 1982, Congress authorized pay increases of up to 15 percent for some 32,000 senior government employees.

For nonpay reasons, too, the morale of SES career members fell to a lamentably low point. They tired of being flayed as bureaucrats by the succession of recent administrations. They believed that "the quality of political leadership in the agencies has been declining" in the last several years, so that "career staffs are being directed by persons who are simply not capable of providing the kind of leadership and guidance that the programs of agencies and the public deserve."[23] They were disturbed by political executives' short time frames. In 1981 over three-fifths of top careerists sampled said that rapid turnover of political appointees made long-term planning difficult, and that such appointees focus on short-term

21. *U.S. Code,* Title V, secs. 3395, 3132 (b).

22. Panel on the Public Service, National Academy of Public Administration, *The Senior Executive Service: An Interim Report, October 1981* (Walshington, DC: National Academy of Public Administration, 1981).

23. Ibid., pp. 34–35.

projects "nearly all the time" or "rather often." And, rightly or wrongly, they reacted negatively to the reversal of programs by foxes in the chicken coop.

Whatever the causes, an alarming exodus of top careerists occurred. About 1600 career executives left the federal service between July 1979 and June 1981. In 1981 about 95 percent of the most experienced senior careerists, those eligible for voluntary retirement at ages 55 to 59, with 30 years' service, were deciding to leave, compared to about 18 percent in 1978.

Career Paths

Two features of the careers of senior civil servants weaken their potential contribution to high-level policymaking and management. Most were initially recruited in their twenties and thirties as specialists—scientists, engineers, economists, and the like. What they know about public affairs and the management of large organizations must, therefore, be haphazardly acquired as they move forward in their careers. The second career feature is confinement of most of their experience to one agency. The two specializations, by discipline and by agency, reinforce each other. Top careerists, therefore, have depth of expertness but not the breadth of training and experience that in other countries produces generalist administrators. For the same reasons, many American senior civil servants develop a myopic loyalty to particular agencies and programs.

These disabilities are not necessarily compensated for by political executives. Many of them qualify for particular political positions because their professional specialties and private-sector activities closely relate to the programs they are to administer. Though this may make for some congruence of outlook with that of top careerists, it also imposes blinders that remove much of the world from their field of vision.

POLICYMAKING PROBLEMS

Formation and effectuation of an administration's policies are plagued by two major problems. One is the counterpull of centrifugal and centripetal forces. The other is the prevalence of short time perspectives.

Centrifugal and Centripetal Forces

The multiplication of governmental responsibilities has generated a geometrical growth of interrelations among programs and among departments. Whether the focus is on reduction of poverty, environmental protection, or foreign policy, the range of relevant factors and of concerned departments casts a shadow of quaintness on classic organizational doctrines of compartmentalization of authority and responsibility. Everything seems to be connected with everything else. Yet centrifugal forces create narrowly oriented, substantially autonomous policy communities in the governmental system.

George P. Shultz and Kenneth W. Dam, before becoming the secretary and deputy secretary of state, wrote of the costs of such partitioning: "In a balkanized executive branch, policymaking is necessarily a piecemeal affair; policymakers are under the constraint that they are not permitted to view problems whole."[24] Many share their concern that "the trend of events is toward greater fragmentation" and inveigh against iron triangles—enduring alliances of bureau, relevant congressional committees, and special-interest groups concerned with the bureau's programs. Joseph Califano believes that "the severest threat to governing for all the people" comes from the pernicious fact that "we have institutionalized, in law and bureaucracy, single-interest organizations that can accede only in the narrow interest and are incapable of adjudicating in the national interest." "We must," he says, "have people and institutions . . . that will render national policy more than the sum of the atomistic interests. We must design bureaucratic structures that permit and encourage top government officials to assess special interests, rather than pander to them."[25]

How to counter these tendencies is a problem far from solution. The principal, though problematic, counterstrategy is the centripetal pull to the White House of matters that earlier might have been left for resolution within individual departments. Elliot Richardson, holder of four cabinet posts, writes that "the delegation of responsibilities and their interposition between the President and department or agency heads are symptoms, not causes. The fundamental problems are the growth of Presidential tasks and the inescapable burdens of interrelatedness which lead inexorably to the enlargement of staff functions." White House assistants, we have seen, are weakly prepared for the formulation of broad, long-range policies.

A hazard that attends the centripetal tendency is the swamping of deliberative policymaking at the top by strong pressures on the White House for quick decisions on myriad problems, which arise seriatim in no discernible pattern and are mistakenly thought to be discrete. Responses to sudden surprises can rarely be tested for compatibility with recent and pending actions or checked for consistency with long-range policy. Shultz and Dam attest to the phenomenon: "Most decisions in government . . . are made . . . in the day-to-day process of responding to crises of the moment. The danger is that this daily firefighting leaves the policymaker further and further from his goal. . . . Many of the failures of government in dealing with the economy can be traced to an attempt to solve minor problems piecemeal."[26]

Efforts are made, of course, to involve cabinet members in top-level policymaking. The Reagan administration, with six Cabinet Councils, was not the first to assemble cabinet members concerned with the same policy area in hopes of a coordinated approach to policy formation. But, as Richardson says, "Interdepartmental committees cannot do the job alone because their

---

24. George P. Schultz and Kenneth W. Dam, *Economic Policy Beyond the Headlines* (New York: W. W. Norton, 1977), p. 173.

25. Califano, *Governing America,* pp. 451, 452. "Government by advocacy" (Shultz and Dam's term) has invaded the White House itself. Charged with "public liaison" are assistants and deputy assistants to the president for the elderly, youth, women, consumers, Hispanics, Blacks, the Jewish community, and other groups.

26. Schultz and Dam, *Economic Policy,* p. 18.

disagreements can all too easily end in deadlock. To prevent deadlocks some external authority is needed—and here is a role that invites reliance on the anonymous Presidential staff."[27] Furthermore, cabinet-level committees, including the Reagan Cabinet Councils, though they were staffed by White House aides, do not monopolize policymaking channels. In 1981 and 1982, major presidential policy decisions and proposals emerged without cabinet input.

Time Perspectives

George W. Ball, the under secretary of state under Kennedy, recalls, "When one tried to point out the long-range implications of a current problem or how it meshed or collided with other major national interests, Kennedy would often say, politely but impatiently, 'Let's not worry about five years from now, what do we do tomorrow?' "[28] This attitude pervades the White House staff, is less operative among cabinet members and their deputy and under secretaries, gets strongly reinforced among assistant secretaries and other political executives, and is the despair of career civil servants. Systematic factors, not personal quirkiness, account for its prevalence.

The president's major opportunity for formulating his major policies with an expectation of favorable congressional action falls in the period between the popular election and the end of his first six months in office. He can, or does, claim a mandate for change, his public-approval ratings quickly register 70 percent or so, Congress grants a honeymoon period, the president can usually focus on domestic rather than principally foreign policies, and his cabinet members are not yet alienated by the White House staff.

Most presidents seize the opportunity offered. They initiate more requests for legislation in the first than in any later year. If wise, they act early in that year, for, Paul C. Light reports, 72 percent of requests introduced in January to March of the first year are eventually enacted, but only 25 percent of third- and fourth-quarter requests are so successful.[29]

The period of greatest opportunity is also the period when the administration may be least capable of carefully fashioning a policy program. Legislative proposals advanced in the first three months are largely products of the campaign staff and pro tem transition advisers. Though the cabinet is completed in December, appointment of subcabinet and other political executives stretches through several months. The permanent bureaucracy is not fully available in the preinaugural period. After the inauguration the bureaucracy is not trusted. So the new administration deprives itself of data, expertness, sophisticated

27. Elliot Richardson, *The Creative Balance: Government, Politics, and the Individual in America's Third Century* (New York: Holt, Rinehart & Winston, 1976), p. 73.

28. George W. Ball, *The Past Has Another Pattern: Memoirs* (New York: W. W. Norton, 1982), p. 167.

29. Paul C. Light, *The President's Agenda: Domestic Policy Choice from Kennedy to Carter* (Baltimore: Johns Hopkins University Press, 1982), pp. 44–45.

understanding of the Washington environment, and longer time perspectives, all of which could strengthen the policy-formation process.

Coming elections, congressional and presidential, soon cast their shadows. That, together with the presdient's increasing absorption in foreign affairs, explains why, as John Helmer writes, "for only one year, the first for a one-term president, can it be said that he has time and some political incentive to consider longer-term problems and to make decisions and commitments whose results may not be immediately apparent."[30] In the second year, seeking to minimize loss of his party's congressional seats, he and his aides prefer initiatives with quick impact. The presidential reelection campaign begins in the third year and becomes all-important in the fourth year. Furthermore, neither congress nor foreign governments welcome major policy proposals for which negotiation must bridge the current and a possibly different successor administration.

The irony is that by the second half of the presidential term, the administration has become better equipped to formulate long-range policies. The White House usually has achieved a clearer structure and more orderly processes, though it may have increased friction with cabinet members. Half the initial political appointees have left their posts and replacements have been more prudently chosen, often by promotion or transfer of able and responsive political executives and by promotion of careerists. Continuing political executives have acquired Washington experience, discovered that civil servants are colleagues, not enemies, and learned that the designing of policies needs to take account of their implementability. Regrettably, these resources cannot be exploited in a period dominated by short time perspectives.

A MODEST PROPOSAL

Deficiencies in the making and implementing of policy at the top levels of the executive branch derive from many sources. Some of the most basic lie outside the scope of this article. Within our framework one thing is clear: exhorting officials to behave differently than they do is profitless unless incentives are created that will alter their behavior. That daunting task might be circumvented by changing the mix of top executives.

Reducing the number of political executives would permit greater care in their selection and would open opportunities for experienced careerists, with their longer time perspectives, to contribute to the design and implementation of programs that embody the administration's innovative policies. Surprisingly, this is strongly advocated by President Nixon's top political recruiter. Frederick Malek writes,

30. John Helmer, "The Presidential Office: Velvet Fist in an Iron Glove," in *The Illusion of Presidential Government*, eds. Hugh Heclo and Lester M. Salamon (Boulder, CO: Westview Press, for the National Academy of Public Administration, 1981), pp. 78–79.

The solution to problems of rigidity and resistance to change in government is *not* to increase the number of appointive positions at the top, as so many politicians are wont to do. . . . An optimum balance between the number of career and noncareer appointments . . . should be struck in favor of fewer political appointees, not more. In many cases, the effectiveness of an agency would be improved and political appointments would be reduced by roughly 25 percent if line positions beneath the assistant secretary level were reserved for career officials.[31]

If his prescription were followed, top careerists would play a more significant role, one that is common in Europe and one that would bolster their morale and reduce the rate of prime-age resignations and retirements.

James L. Sundquist compared the policymaking capacity of the United States with that of five Western European countries that successfully developed and applied policies to influence the regional distribution of their populations—largely a matter of incentives for private investment in declining areas and disincentives for investment in regions growing too rapidly. By 1970 the United States had a clear national policy, in principle. It was embraced in both major parties' platforms, was frequently set forth by President Nixon, and was partially reflected in two congressional statutes. But, in contrast to European countries, "the institutional structure in the United States did not respond to the political directives."[32] Why not?

Among several reasons, Sundquist emphasizes the "gulf between the career bureaucracy, which was familiar with the data and had some degree of competence to analyze it, and the [White House] staff advisers who had responsibility for developing policy recommendations." In Europe a typical participant "was at the same time the long-time career civil servant and the respected policy adviser." In the United States, "many of the most competent and ambitious of the career officials—the kind that rise to the top in European civil services—find themselves excluded from the inner policy-making circles, or subordinated to younger, less experienced political appointees, and so depart. The capability of the career service is reduced, which leads to pressures for further politicization, in a vicious circle."[33]

If the quality of senior civil servants has been declining and if the policymaking process needs greater participation by careerists, we urgently need to repair the damage and strengthen careerists' capabilities for high-level responsibilities. Raising the level of positions to which able careerists can aspire will help. Beyond that, the top civil service needs strengthening of executive develop-

31. Frederick V. Malek, *Washington's Hidden Tragedy* (New York: MacMillan, 1978), pp. 102–103.

32. James L. Sundquist, "A Comparison of Policy-Making Capacity in the United States and Five European Countries: The Case of Population Distribution," in Michael E. Kraft and Mark Schneider, eds., *Population Policy Analysis* (Lexington, Mass.: D.C. Heath, 1978), pp. 67–80.

33. Ibid., p. 73. The theme is more fully developed in James L. Sundquist, "Jimmy Carter as Public Administrator: An Appraisal at Mid-Term," *Public Administration Review,* 39:3–11, 6–8 (Jan–Feb. 1979).

ment programs. These are a mix of identifying the comers, moving them among a variety of broadening assignments, and providing sabbatical-leave years in university graduate programs and shorter training periods at federal academies such as the Federal Executive Institute. Such leaves and training opportunities should come at the career point when a careerist's special professional discipline and narrow, single-agency experience are inadequate preparation for the work that lies ahead. This includes management of large organizations, negotiations with other agencies, the White House, Congress, and interest groups, shaping of legislative and presidential-directive drafts to assure successful implementation, and relating of policy ideas to one another and to the social fabric of America.

From 1953 on, says Sundquist, "no administration devoted any appreciable attention to training and developing a new generation of career managers, or even seemed to care."[34] The reason is a familiar one. This requires a long time perspective and yields no credit for an administration in its short life. ■

---

34. Sundquist, "Jimmy Carter as Public Administrator," p. 8.

CHAPTER 11

The Courts

In our separation-of-powers system, the principal judicial power, the power to interpret the law and apply it, is vested in courts and judges. Legislative, executive, and judicial powers are not rigidly separated, however. There is some overlapping—to the degree that it has even been argued that federal institutions are, indeed, separated, but powers are shared.

In our federal government, the principal legislative powers are, of course, exercised by Congress. But federal courts and judges also make law and policy. When, for example, the U. S. Supreme Court, in *Brown* v. *Board of Education*, reversed an older decision in *Plessy* v. *Ferguson* and held that "separate but equal" public facilities were inherently unconstitutional, the Court was clearly making law. There had been no amendment of the Constitution in the meantime, no new act passed by Congress.

The federal judiciary—courts and judges—is an independent branch of the national government. One way this independence is assured is through shared appointive powers—the president appoints, but judges or justices cannot take office until their appointments have been confirmed by the Senate. Judicial independence is also safeguarded by the fact that federal judges (and justices) are, in effect, appointed for life.

In this chapter, we will first consider the constitutional background of the judiciary and the concept of "judicial review." We will then focus on the way in which the Supreme Court makes decisions. After that, recognizing that courts are made up of individuals, we will give our attention to the members of the Supreme Court, who they are and have been, and, finally, to the effect of the Reagan presidency on the federal judiciary.

JUDICIAL REVIEW

The U. S. Constitution is clear in specifying—in the so-called "Supremacy Clause"—that the Constitution, as well as treaties and acts of Congress consistent with it, are the supreme law of the land. State judges are required to abide by this supreme law, and state laws that conflict with it must fall. All this is provided in the second paragraph of Article VI:

> This Constitution, and the Laws of the United States which shall be made in pursuance thereof; and all treaties made, or which shall be made, under the authority of the United States, shall be the supreme Law of the Land; and the judges in every state shall be bound thereby, any Thing in the Constitution or Laws of any state to the Contrary notwithstanding.

The Constitution is silent on the question of what official or branch can decide whether an act or treaty is, or is not, consistent with the Constitution. But, for Alexander Hamilton at least, there was no doubt that this was to be a part of the judicial function, a power of the courts. We know that because of what he wrote on the subject in *Federalist 78*, which is excerpted here.

It was not until 1803, however, that the doctrine of "judicial review," the power of the courts to hold state laws and acts of Congress unconstitutional, was spelled out. This came in a decision of the U.S. Supreme Court itself in the case of *Marbury* v. *Madison*, which we have reprinted here in part. The "Marbury" of this case was a man who had been appointed to a new judgeship by President John Adams (and confirmed by the Senate). But before Marbury was issued his commission by the Secretary of State, President Adams was replaced by Thomas Jefferson. The "Madison" of this case was James Madison, Jefferson's Secretary of State. Madison and Jefferson decided against giving Marbury, a member of the political opposition, his commission. Marbury sued. The act creating the judgeship (and others) had provided that such a suit could be filed directly in the U. S. Supreme Court, thus attempting to expand the original jurisdiction of the Court as specified in the Constitution.

Suppose that Chief Justice John Marshall, not a friend of Madison and Jefferson, had issued an order to Madison, and Madison (and Jefferson) had refused to obey it. This could have produced a severe constitutional crisis. As you will see in the opinion in the case, written by Marshall, a solution was decided upon which, at one and the same time, avoided the constitutional crisis and enhanced the power of the Supreme Court: the Court held that the power of "judicial review" was a power of the courts and that the part of the act that sought to expand the original jurisdiction of the Court was unconstitutional.

There are those who feel that the U. S. Supreme Court and other unelected courts have too much power in our system. But in an article excerpted here, Chief Justic Warren E. Burger argues that "someone must decide" and that that someone is properly the judiciary.

FEDERALIST 78

We proceed now to an examination of the judiciary department of the proposed government.

In unfolding the defects of the existing confederation, the utility and necessity of a federal judicature have been clearly pointed out. It is the less necessary to recapitulate the considerations there urged; as the proprietary of the institution in the abstract is not disputed: The only questions which have been raised being relative to the manner of constituting it, and to its extent. To these points therefore our observations shall be confined.

The manner of constituting it seems to embrace these several objects—1st. The mode of appointing the judges. 2d. The tenure by which they are to hold their places. 3rd. The partition of the judiciary authority between different courts, and their relations to each other.

First. As to the mode of appointing the judges: This is the same with that of appointing the officers of the union in general and has been so fully discussed . . . that nothing can be said here which would not be useless repetition.

Second. As to the tenure by which the judges are to hold their places: This chiefly concerns their duration in office; the provisions for their support; and the precautions for their responsibility.

According to the plan of the convention, all the judges who may be appointed by the United States are to hold their offices *during good behaviour,* which is conformable to the most approved of the state constitutions; and among the rest, to that of this state. Its propriety having been drawn into question by the adversaries of that plan, is no light symptom of the rage for objection which disorders their imaginations and judgments. The standard of good behaviour for the continuance in office of the judicial magistracy is certainly one of the most valuable of the modern improvements in the practice of government. In a monarchy it is an excellent barrier to the despotism of the prince: In a republic it is a no less excellent barrier to the encroachments and oppressions of the representative body. And it is the best expedient which can be devised in any government, to secure a steady, upright and impartial administration of the laws.

Whoever attentively considers the different departments of power must perceive, that in a government in which they are separated from each other, the judiciary, from the nature of its functions, will always be the least dangerous to the political rights of the constitution; because it will be least in a capacity to annoy or injure them. The executive not only dispenses the honors, but holds the sword of the community. The legislature not only commands the purse, but prescribes the rules by which the duties and rights of every citizen are to be regulated. The judiciary on the contrary has no influence over either the sword or the purse, no direction either of the strength or of the wealth of the society, and can take no active resolution whatever. It may truly be said to have neither Force nor Will, but merely judgment; and must ultimately depend upon the aid of the executive arm even for the efficacy of its judgments.

This simple view of the matter suggest several important consequences. It proves incontestibly that the judiciary is beyond comparison the weakest of the three departments of power; that it can never attack with success either of the other two; and that all possible care is requisite to enable it to defend itself against their attacks. It equally proves, that though individual oppression may now and then proceed from the courts of justice, the general liberty of the people can never be endangered from that quarter: I mean, so long as the judiciary remains truly distinct from both the legislative and executive. For I agree that "there is no liberty, if the power of judging be not separated from the legislative and executive powers." And it proves, in the last place, that as liberty can have nothing to fear from the judiciary alone, but would have every thing to fear from its union with either of the other departments; that as all the effects of such an union must ensue from a dependence of the former on the latter, notwithstanding a nominal and apparent separation; that as from the natural feebleness of the judiciary, it is in continual jeopardy of being overpowered, awed or influenced by its coordinate branches; and that as nothing can contribute so much to its firmness and independence, as permanency in office, this quality may therefore be justly regarded as an indispensable ingredient in its constitution; and in a great measure as the citadel of the public justice and the public security.

The complete independence of the courts of justice is peculiarly essential in a limited constitution. By a limited constitution I understand one which contains certain specified exceptions to the legislative authority; such for instance as that it shall pass no bill of attainder, no *ex post facto* laws, and the like. Limitations of this kind can be preserved in practice no other way than through the medium of the courts of justice; whose duty it must be to declare all acts contrary to the manifest tenor of the constitution void. Without this, all the reservations of particular rights or privileges would amount to nothing.

Some perplexity respecting the right of the courts to pronounce legislative acts void, because contrary to the constitution, has arisen from an imagination that the doctrine would imply a superiority of the judiciary to the legislative power. It is urged that the authority which can declare the acts of another void, must necessarily be superior to the one whose acts may be declared void. As this doctrine is of great importance in all the American constitutions, a brief discussion of the grounds on which it rests cannot be unacceptable.

There is no position which depends on clearer principles, than that every act of a delegated authority, contrary to the tenor of the commission under which it is exercised, is void. No legislative act therefore contrary to the constitution can be valid. To deny this would be to affirm that the deputy is greater than his principal; that the servant is above his master; that the representatives of the people are superior to the people themselves; that men acting by virtue of powers may do not only what their powers do not authorize, but what they forbid.

If it be said that the legislative body are themselves the constitutional judges of their own powers, and that the construction they put upon them is conclusive upon the other departments, it may be answered, that this cannot be the natural presumption, where it is not to be collected from any particular provisions in the constitution. It is not otherwise to be supposed that the constitution could intend to enable the representatives of the people to substitute their *will* to that of their constituents. It is far more rational to suppose that the courts were designed to be an intermediate body between the people and the legislature, in order, among other things, to keep the latter within the limits assigned to their authority. The interpretation of the laws is the proper and peculiar province of the courts. A constitution is in fact, and must be, regarded by the judges as a fundamental law. It therefore belongs to them to ascertain its meaning as well as the meaning of any particular act proceeding from the legislative body. If there should happen to be an irreconcileable variance between the two, that which has the superior obligation and validity ought of course to be preferred; or in other words, the constitution ought to be preferred to the statute, the intention of the people to the intention of their agents.

Nor does this conclusion by any means suppose a superiority of the judicial to the legislative power. It only supposes that the power of the people is superior to both; and that where the will of the legislature declared in its statutes, stands in opposition to that of the people declared in the constitution, the judges ought to be governed by the latter, rather than the former. They ought to regulate their decisions by the fundamental laws, rather than by those which are not fundamental. . . .

It can be of no weight to say, that the courts on the pretence of repugnancy, may substitute their own pleasure to the constitutional intentions of the legislature. This might as well happen in the case of two contradictory statutes; or it might as well happen in every adjudication upon any single statute. The courts must declare the sense of the law; and if they should be disposed to exercise WILL instead of JUDGMENT, the consequence would equally be the substitution of their pleasure to that of the legislative body. The observation, if it proved any thing, would prove that there ought to be no judges distinct from that body.

If then the courts of justice are to be considered as the bulwarks of a limited constitution against legislative encroachments, this consideration will afford a strong argument for the permanent tenure of judicial offices, since nothing will contribute so much as this to that independent spirit in the judges, which must be essential to the faithful performance of so arduous a duty.

This independence of the judges is equally requisite to guard the constitution and the rights of individuals from the effects of those ill humours which the arts of designing men, or the influence of particular conjunctures, sometimes disseminate among the people themselves, and which, though they speedily give place to better information and more deliberate reflection, have a tendency in the mean time to occasion dangerous innovations in the government, and serious oppressions of the minor party in the community. . . . Until the people have by some solemn and authoritative act annulled or changed the established form, it is binding upon themselves collectively, as well as individually; and no presumption, or even knowledge of their sentiments, can warrant their representatives in a departure from it, prior to such an act. But it is easy to see that it would require an uncommon portion of fortitude in the judges to do their duty as faithful guardians of the constitution, where legislative invasions of it had been instigated by the major voice of the community.

But it is not with a view to infractions of the constitution only that the independence of the judges may be an essential safeguard against the effects of occasional ill humours in the society. These sometimes extend no farther than to the injury of the private rights of particular classes of citizens, by unjust and partial laws. Here also the firmness of the judicial magistracy is of vast importance in mitigating the severity, and confining the operation of such laws. It not only serves to moderate the immediate mischiefs of those which may have been passed, but it operates as a check upon the legislative body in passing them; who, perceiving that obstacles to the success of the courts, are in a manner compelled by the very motives of the injustice they meditate, to qualify their attempts. . . .

That inflexible and uniform adherence to the rights of the constitution and of individuals, which we perceive to be indispensable in the courts of justice, can certainly not be expected from judges who hold their offices by a temporary commission. Periodical appointments, however regulated, or by whomsoever made, would in some way or other be fatal to their necessary independence. If the power of making them was committed either to the executive or legislature, there would be danger of an improper complaisance to the branch which possessed it; it to both, there would be an unwillingness to hazard the displeasure of either; if to the people, or to persons chosen by them for the special purpose, there would be too great a disposition to consult popularity, to justify a reliance that nothing would be consulted but the constitution and the laws.

There is yet a further and a weighty reason for the permanency of the judicial offices; which is deducible from the nature of the qualifications they require. It has been frequently remarked with great propriety, that a voluminous code of laws is one of the inconveniences necessarily connected with the advantages of a free government. To avoid an arbitrary discretion in the courts, it is indispensable that they should be bound down by strict rules and precedents, which serve to define and point out their duty in every particular case that comes before them; and it will readily be conceived from the variety of controversies which grow out of the folly and wickedness of mankind, that the records of those precedents must unavoidably swell to a very considerable bulk, and must demand long and laborious study to acquire a competent knowledge of them. Hence it is that there can be but few men in the society, who will have sufficient skill in the laws to qualify them for the stations of judges. And making the proper deductions for the ordinary depravity of human nature, the number must be still smaller of those who unite the requisite integrity with the requisite knowledge. . . .   ■

MARBURY V. MADISON*

At the last term, viz., December term, 1801, William Marbury, Dennis Harper, by their counsel, Charles Lee, Esq. late attorney general of the United States, severally moved the court for a rule to James Madison, Secretary of State of the United States, to show cause why a mandamus should not issue commanding him to cause to be delivered to them respectively their several commissions as justices of the peace in the District of Columbia. This motion was supported by affidavits of the following facts; that notice of this motion had been given to Mr. Madison; that Mr. Adams, the late President of the United States, nominated the applicants to the senate for their advice and consent to be appointed justices of the peace of the District of Columbia; that the senate advised and consented to the appointments; that commissions in due form were signed by the said President appointing them justices, &c.; and that the seal of the United States was in due form affixed to the said commissions by the Secretary of State; that the applicants have requested Mr. Madison to deliver them their said commissions, who has not complied with that request; and that their said commissions are withheld from them; that the applicants have made application to Mr. Madison, as Secretary of State of the United States, at his office, for information whether the commmissions were signed and sealed as aforesaid; that explicit and satisfactory information has not been given in answer to that inquiry, either by the Secretary of State or any officer in the department of state; that application has been made to the secretary of the senate for a certificate of the nomination of the applicants, and of the advice and consent of the senate, who has declined giving such a certificate; whereupon a rule laid to show cause on the fourth day of this term. . . .

The act [Judiciary Act of 1789] to establish the judicial courts of the United States authorizes the Supreme Court "to issue writs of mandamus in cases warranted by the principles and usages of law, to any courts appointed, or persons holding office, under the authority of the United States." . . .

The constitution vests the whole judicial power of the United States in one

* 1 Cranch 137 (1803).

Supreme Court, and such inferior courts as congress shall, from time to time, ordain and establish. This power is expressly extended to all cases arising under the laws of the United States; and, consequently, in some form, may be exercised over the present case; because the right claimed is given by a law of the United States.

In the distribution of this power it is declared that "the Supreme Court shall have original jurisdiction in all cases affecting ambassadors, other public ministers and consuls, and those in which a state shall be a party. In all other cases, the Supreme Court shall have appellate jurisdiction." . . .

If it had been intended to leave it in the discretion of the legislature to apportion the judicial power between the supreme and inferior courts according to the will of that body, it would certainly have been useless to have proceded further than to have defined the judicial power, and the tribunals in which it should be vested. The subsequent part of the section is mere surplusage, is entirely without meaning, if such is to be the construction. If congress remains at liberty to give this court appellate jurisdiction, where the constitution has declared their jurisdiction shall be original; and original jurisdiction where the constitution has declared it shall be appellate; the distribution of jurisdiction, made in the constitution, is form without substance. . . .

The authority, therefore, given to the Supreme Court, by the act establishing the judicial courts of the United States, to issue writs of mandamus to public officers, appears not to be warranted by the constitution; and it becomes necessary to inquire whether a jursidiction so conferred can be exercised.

The question, whether an act, repugnant to the constitution, can become the law of the land, is a question deeply interesting to the United States; but, happily, not of an intricacy proportioned to its interest. It seems only necessary to recognize certain principles, supposed to have been long and well established, to decide it.

That the people have an original right to establish, for their future government, such principles, as, in their opinion, shall most conduce to their own happiness is the basis on which the whole American fabric has been erected. The exercise of this original right is a very great exertion; nor can it, nor ought it, to be frequently repeated. The principles, therefore, so established, are deemed fundamental. And as the authority from which they proceed is supreme, and can seldom act, they are designed to be permanent.

This original and supreme will organizes the government, and assigns to different departments their respective powers. It may either stop here, or establish certain limits not to be transcended by those departments.

The government of the United States is of the latter description. The powers of the legislature are defined and limited; and that those limits may not be mistaken, or forgotten, the constitution is written. To what purpose are powers limited, and to what purpose is that limitation committed to writing, if these limits may, at any time, be passed by those intended to be restrained? The distinction between a government with limited and unlimited powers is abolished, if those limits do not confine the persons on whom they are imposed, and if acts prohibited and acts allowed, are of equal obligation. It is a proposition too plain to be contested, that the constitution controls any legislative act repugnant to it; or, that the legislature may alter the constitution by an ordinary act.

Between these alternatives there is no middle ground. The constitution is either a superior paramount law, unchangeable by ordinary means, or it is on a level with ordinary legislative acts, and, like other acts, is alterable when the legislature shall please to alter it.

If the former part of the alternative be true, then a legislative act contrary to the constitution is not law: if the latter part be true, then written constitutions are absurd attempts, on the part of the people, to limit a power in its own nature illimitable.

Certainly all those who have framed written constitutions contemplate them as forming the fundamental and paramount law of the nation, and, consequently, the theory of every such government must be, that an act of the legislature, repugnant to the constitution, is void.

This theory is essentially attached to a written constitution, and, is consequently, to be considered, by this court, as one of the fundamental principles of our society. It is not therefore to be lost sight of in the further consideration of this subject.

If an act of the legislature, repugnant to the constitution, is void, does it, nothwithstanding its invalidity, bind the courts, and oblige them to give it effect? Or, in other words, though it be not law, does it constitute a rule as operative as if it was a law? This would be to overthrow in fact what was established in theory; and would seem, at first view, an absurdity too gross to be insisted on. It shall, however, receive a more attentive consideration.

It is emphatically the province and duty of the judicial department to say what the law is. Those who apply the rule to particular cases, must of necessity expound and interpret that rule. If two laws conflict with each other, the courts must decide on the operation of each.

So if a law be in opposition to the constitution; if both the law and the constitution apply to a particular case, so that the court must either decide that case conformably to the law, disregarding the constitution; or conformably to the constitution, disregarding the law; the court must determine which of these conflicting rules governs the case. This is of the very essence of judicial duty.

If, then, the courts are to regard the constitution, and the constitution is superior to any ordinary act of the legislature, the constitution, and not such ordinary act, must govern the case to which they both apply.

Those, then, who controvert the principle that the constitution is to be considered, in court, as a paramount law, are reduced to the necessity of maintaining that courts must close their eyes on the constitution, and see only the law.

This doctrine would subvert the very foundation of all written constitutions. It would declare that an act which, according to the principles and theory of our government, is entirely void, is yet, in practice, completely obligatory. It would declare that if the legislature shall do what is expressly forbidden, such act, notwithstanding the express prohibition, is in reality effectual. It would be given to the legislature a practical and real omnipotence, with the same breath which professes to restrict their powers within narrow limits. It is prescribing limits, and declaring that those limits may be passed at pleasure.

That it thus reduces to nothing what we have deemed the greatest improvement on political institutions, a written constitution, would of itself be sufficient, in America, where written constitutions have been viewed with so much reverence, for rejecting the construction. But the peculiar expressions of the constitution of the United States furnish additional arguments in favour of its rejection.

The judicial power of the United States is extended to all cases arising under the constitution.

Could it be the intention of those who gave this power, to say that in using it the constitution should not be looked into? That a case arising under the constitution should be decided without examining the instrument under which it arises?

This is too extravagant to be maintained.

In some cases, then, the constitution must be looked into by the judges. And if they can open it at all, what part of it are they forbidden to read or to obey?

There are many other parts of the constitution which serve to illustrate this subject.

It is declared that "no tax or duty shall be laid on articles exported from any state." Suppose a duty on the export of cotton, of tobacco, or of flour; and a suit instituted to recover it. Ought judgment to be rendered in such a case? Ought the judges to close their eyes on the constitution, and only see the law?

The constitution declares "that no bill of attainder or ex post facto law shall be passed."

If, however, such a bill should be passed, and a person should be prosecuted under it; must the court condemn to death those victims whom the constitution endeavors to preserve?

"No person," says the constitution, "shall be convicted of treason unless on the testimony of two witnesses to the same overt act, or on confession in open court."

Here the language of the constitution is addressed especially to the courts. It prescribes, directly for them, a rule of evidence not to be departed from. If the legislature should change that rule, and declare one witness, or a confession out of court, sufficient for conviction, must the constitutional principle yield to the legislative act?

From these, and many other selections which might be made, it is apparent, that the framers of the constitution contemplated that instrument as a rule for the government of courts, as well as of the legislature.

Why otherwise does it direct the judges to take an oath to support it? This oath certainly applies in an especial manner, to their conduct in their official character. How immoral to impose it on them, if they were to be used as the instruments, and the knowing instruments, for violating what they swear to support!

The oath of office, too, imposed by the legislature, is completely demonstrative of the legislative opinion on this subject. It is in these words: "I do solemnly swear that I will administer justice without respect to persons, and do equal right to the poor and to the rich; and that I will faithfully and impartially discharge all the duties incumbent on me as _____, according to the best of my abilities and understanding agreeably to the constitution and laws of the United States."

Why does a judge swear to discharge his duties agreeably to the constitution of the United States, if that constitution forms no rule for his government? if it is closed upon him, and cannot be inspected by him?

If such be the real state of things, this is worse than solemn mockery. To prescribe, or to take this oath, becomes equally a crime.

It is also not entirely unworthy of observation, that in declaring what shall be the supreme law of the land, the constitution itself is first mentioned; and not the laws of the United States generally, but those only which shall be made in pursuance of the constitution, have that rank.

Thus, the particular phraseology of the constitution of the United States confirms and strengthens the principle, supposed to be essential to all written constitutions, that a law repugnant to the constitution is void; and that courts, as well as other departments, are bound by that instrument.

The rule must be discharged. ■

SOMEONE MUST DECIDE
Warren E. Burger

. . . The story is too well known to be chronicled in detail. Marbury was one of those whose commission as justice of the peace was signed by President Adams and attested to by Marshall, who was still acting as President Adams's Secretary of State even after being appointed chief justice and confirmed by the Senate. But Marbury's commission was not delivered.

Marbury then sought mandamus in the Supreme Court against Madison, Jefferson's Secretary of State, to compel what Marbury claimed was the purely ministerial act of delivering the commissions. In the Supreme Court the first reaction may well have been, "of course," since the Judiciary Act provided that precise remedy.

But if, as no one had even remotely suspected up to that time, Congress could not constitutionally grant original jurisdiction to the Supreme Court in any cases except those specifically recited in Article III, then the Court could say, "Yes, Marbury was duly confirmed"; and "Yes, the Commission was duly signed and sealed"; and "Yes, this Court may examine the manner in which the executive conducts its affairs"; and "Yes, delivery is a purely ministerial act"; and "Yes, it is improper that the new administration will not perform the simple ministerial act of delivery"; but the Court could also say, "However, this Court has no power under the Constitution to entertain any original action except those specified in Article III, and this case is not one of them. That being so, Section

13 of the Judiciary Act of 1789 purporting to give the Supreme Court such authority would be invalid and any action to compel the executive to deliver the commission to Marbury could not be entertained as an original action." This, in essence, is what Marshall wrote.

Jefferson and Madison had won the lawsuit—the battle; Marbury, the Federalist, had lost; but the real war, the great "war" over the supremacy of the Supreme Court in constitutional adjudication, had been won by the Court—and by the country. Not for fifty-four years after *Marbury* did the Court hold another act of Congress unconstitutional, although in *Marin* v. *Hunter's Lessee* (1816), Justice Joseph Story for the Court firmly asserted the power of the Supreme Court to invalidate a state statute contrary to the federal Constitution.

As with so many great conceptions, the idea of judicial review of legislation now seems simple and inevitable in the perspective of history. The people of the states delegated certain powers to the national government and placed limits on those powers by specific and general reservations. After having flatly stated certain guarantees relating to religious freedom, to speech, to searches, seizures, and arrests, would it be reasonable to think that Congress and the executive could alter those rights? Standing alone, the explicit procedures carefully providing for constitutional amendments negate the idea that a written constitution could be altered by legislative or executive action. The language of Article III vesting judicial power "in one Supreme Court" for "all Cases, in Law and Equity, *arising under this Constitution, the Laws* of the United States, and Treaties. . ." would be sterile indeed if the Supreme Court could not exercise that judicial power by deciding cases involving conflicts between the Constitution, federal laws, and treaties on the one hand, and acts of Congress, the executive or states on the other.

Given the extraordinary power that judicial review vests in the judiciary, the question may be raised: Who will watch the watchmen? This was a concern to some of those who opposed ratification of the Constitution. Anti-Federalist commentator "Brutus" argued that "this power in the judicial, will enable them to move the government into almost any shape they please." Another Anti-Federalist, "A Columbia Patriot," similarly wrote: "There are no well-defined limits of the Judicial Powers, they seem to be left as a boundless ocean."

It is clear that when Congress disagrees with the judicial interpretation of a statute, Congress can enact a new statute that supersedes that judicial interpretation. Congress has done this many times in our history. Similarly, in four instances Congress and the state legislatures have overridden a Supreme Court opinion through constitutional amendment. Furthermore, when appointments are made to the Supreme Court, it is surely not unnatural that presidents try to appoint, subject to Senate confirmation, justices who they hope will interpret the Constitution "properly." President Franklin D. Roosevelt failed in his effort to control the Supreme Court by seeking to increase it to fifteen justices; yet in his four terms, he appointed eight justices.

It is true that in the tenure of office of all federal judges, so essential to their independence, there is risk that power can be abused, but three tiers of federal courts have mitigated that risk, although not always to every person's satisfaction. The Draftsmen were aware of those risks, but the risks were unavoidable, since "someone must decide."

Chief Justice Harlan Fiske Stone reminded all federal judges that "the only check upon our own exercise of power is our own sense of self-restraint." ■

SUPREME COURT DECISIONMAKING

The courts make law and policy when they interpret and apply the law in actual cases. This requires the exercise of discretion. Appellate courts make law and policy, too, when they say what the law is. The "court of last resort" on a federal question is, of course, the U. S. Supreme Court. Its power to have the final say in cases involving constitutional questions has been characterized as resulting in the rule that "the Constitution means what the Supreme Court says it means."

The Supreme Court, made up of a Chief Justice and eight Associate Justices—nine in all, then—decides cases by majority vote. The "majority opinion" is binding in the particular case decided, and it also applies to similar future cases. It is the law. (A "dissenting opinion" is not the law, but states the views of one or more justices who disagree with the majority in the case. Neither is a "concurring opinion" the law. It states the views of one or more justices who agree with the majority result in the case, but disagree as to the reasons.)

The Supreme Court does not *make* its decisions in public. It only *announces* its decisions in public. No statement is ever made, or press release issued, by the Court—or by its individual members—explaining from an insider's point of view how much argument there was among the justices on a particular question, for example, or how a majority position was developed. A bestselling 1979 book by Bob Woodward and Scott Armstrong, *The Brethren: Inside the Supreme Court*,[1] created somewhat of a sensation when it first appeared. As its name indicates, the book resulted from extensive, off-the-record insider interviews. It attempted to show how the Court really operates and how it had decided certain recent famous cases.

Less detailed and sensational are writings about the Court by members and former members. Reprinted here is a very informative article by Justice William J. Brennan, Jr., who gives a generalized inside view of the Court and its operation. Following that is an excerpt from the memoirs of the late Chief Justice Earl Warren. Warren was one of the towering figures in Court history, and he presided over a great number of really important, or "landmark," Supreme Court decisions—including, for example, those dealing with desegregation, reapportionment, prayer in the schools, abortion, and the rights of a person accused of a crime. In this excerpt, he especially deals with the public controversy which resulted from many of these decisions.

---

1. Bob Woodward and Scott Armstrong, *The Brethren: Inside the Supreme Court* (New York: Avon Books, 1979).

AN INSIDE VIEW OF THE SUPREME COURT
William J. Brennan, Jr.

Throughout its history the Supreme Court has been called upon to face many of the dominant social, political, economic and even philosophical issues that confront the nation. But Solicitor General Cox only recently reminded us that this does not mean that the Court is charged with making social, political, economic, or philosophical decisions. Quite the contrary. The Court is not a council of Platonic guardians for deciding our most difficult and emotional questions according to the Justices' own notions of what is just or wise or politic. To the extent that this is a governmental function at all, it is the function of the people's elected representatives.

The Justices are charged with deciding according to law. Because the issues arise in the framework of concrete litigation they must be decided on facts embalmed in a record made by some lower court or administrative agency. And while the Justices may and do consult history and the other disciplines as aids to constitutional decision, the text of the Constitution and relevant precedents dealing with that text are their primary tools.

It is indeed true, as Judge Learned Hand once said, that the judge's authority "depends upon the assumption that he speaks with the mouth of others: the momentum of his utterances must be greater than any which his personal reputation and character can command; if it is to do the work assigned to it—if it is to stand against the passionate resentments arising out of the interests he must frustrate—he must preserve his authority by cloaking himself in the majesty of an overshadowing past, but he must discover some composition with the dominant trends of his times."

However, we must keep in mind that, while the words of the Constitution are binding, their application to specific problems is not often easy. The Founding Fathers knew better than to pin down their descendants too closely. Enduring principles rather than petty details were what they sought. Thus the Constitution does not take the form of a litany of specifics. There are, therefore, very few cases where the constitutional answers are clear, all one way or all the other, and this is also true of the current cases raising conflicts between the individual and governmental power—an area increasingly requiring the Court's attention.

Ultimately, of course, the Court must resolve the conflicts of competing interests in these cases, but all Americans should keep in mind how intense and troubling these conflicts can be. Where one man claims a right to speak and the other man claims the right to be protected from abusive or dangerously provocative remarks the conflict is inescapable. Where the police have ample external evidence of a man's guilt, but to be sure of their case put into evidence a confession obtained through coercion, the conflict arises between his right to a fair prosecution and society's right to protection against his depravity. Where the orthodox Jew wishes to open his shop and do business on the day which non-Jews have chosen, and the Legislature has sanctioned, as a day of rest, the

Court cannot escape a difficult problem of reconciling opposed interests. Finally, the claims of the Negro citizen, to borrow Solicitor General Cox's words, present a "conflict between the ideal of liberty and equality expressed in the Declaration of Independence, on the one hand, and, on the other hand, a way of life rooted in the customs of many of our people."

If all segments of our society can be made to appreciate that there are such conflicts, and that cases which involve constitutional rights often require difficult choices, if this alone is accomplished, we will have immeasurably enriched our common understanding of the meaning and significance of our freedoms. And we will have a better appreciation of the Court's function and its difficulties.

How conflicts such as these ought to be resolved constantly troubles our whole society. There should be no surprise, then, that how properly to resolve them often produces sharp division within the Court itself. When problems are so fundamental, the claims of the competing interests are often nicely balanced, and close divisions are almost inevitable.

Supreme Court cases are usually one of three kinds: the "original" action brought directly in the Court by one state against another state or states, or between a state or states and the Federal Government. Only a handful of such cases arise each year, but they are an important handful. A recent example was the contest between Arizona and California over the waters of the lower basin of the Colorado River. Another was the contest between the Federal Government and the newest state of Hawaii over the ownership of lands in Hawaii.

The second kind of case seeks review of the decisions of a Federal Court of Appeals—there are 11 such courts—or of a decision of a Federal District Court in each of the 50 states.

The third kind of case comes from a state court—the Court may review a state court judgment by the highest court of any of the 50 states, if the judgment rests on the decision of a Federal question.

COURT PROCEDURE

When I came to the Court seven years ago the aggregate of the cases in the three classes was 1,600. In the term just completed there were 2,800, an increase of 75 percent in seven years. Obviously, the volume will have doubled before I complete 10 years of service. How is it possible to manage such a huge volume of cases? The answer is that we have the authority to screen them and select for argument and decision only those which in our judgment, guided by pertinent criteria, raise the most important and far-reaching questions. By that device we select annually around 6 percent—between 150 and 170 cases—for decision. That screening process works like this: When nine Justices sit, it takes five to decide a case on the merits. But it takes only the votes of four of the nine to put a case on the argument calendar for argument and the decision. Those four votes are hard to come by—only an exceptional case raising a significant Federal question commands them.

Each application for review is usually in the form of a short petition, attached to which are any opinions of the lower courts in the case. The adversary may file a response—also, in practice, usually short. Both the petition and response identify the Federal questions allegedly involved, argue their substantiality, and whether they were properly raised in the lower courts. Each Justice receives copies of the petition and response and such parts of the record as the parties may submit. Each Justice then, without any consultation at this stage with the others, reaches his own tentative conclusion whether the application should be granted or denied.

The first consultation about the case comes at the Court conference at which the case is listed on the agenda for discussion. We sit in conference almost every Friday during the term. Conferences begin at 10 in the morning and often continue until 6, except for a half-hour recess for lunch. Only the Justices are present. There are no law clerks, no stenographers, no secretaries, no pages—just the nine of us. The junior Justice acts as guardian of the door, receiving and delivering any messages that come in or go from the conference.

The conference room is a beautifully oak-paneled chamber with one side lined with books from floor to ceiling. Over the mantel of the exquisite marble fireplace at one end hangs the only adornment in the chamber—a portrait of Chief Justice John Marshall. In the middle of the room stands a rectangular table, not too large but large enough for the nine of us comfortable to gather around it. The Chief Justice sists at the south end and Mr. Justice Black, the senior Associate Justice, at the north end. Along the side to the left of the Chief Justice sit Justices Stewart Goldberg, White and Harlan. On the right side sit Justice Clark, myself and Justice Douglas in that order.

We are summoned to conference by a buzzer which rings in our several chambers five minutes before the hour. Upon entering the conference room each of us shakes hands with his colleagues. The handshake tradition originated when Chief Justice Fuller presided many decades ago. It is a symbol that harmony of aims if not of views is the Court's guiding principle.

Each of us has his copy of the agenda of the day's cases before him. The agenda lists the cases applying for review. Each of us before coming to the conference has noted on his copy his tentative view whether or not review should be granted in each case.

The Chief Justice begins the discussion of each case. He then yields to the senior Associate Justice and discussion proceeds down the line in order of seniority until each Justice has spoken. Voting goes the other way. The junior Justice votes first and voting then proceeds up the line to the Chief Justice who votes last. Each of us has a docket containing a sheet for each case with appropriate places for recording the votes. When any case receives four votes for review, that case is transferred to the oral argument list. Applications in which none of us sees merit may be passed over without discussion.

Now how do we process the decision we agree to review? There are rare occasions when the question is so clearly controlled by an earlier decision of the Court that a reversal of the lower court judgment is inevitable. In these rare instances we may summarily reverse without oral argument. The case must very clearly justify summary disposition, however, because our ordinary practice is not to reverse a decision without oral argument. Indeed, oral argument of cases taken for review, whether from the state or Federal courts, is the usual practice. We rarely accept submissions of cases on briefs.

Oral argument ordinarily occurs about four months after the application for review is granted. Each party is usually allowed one hour, but in recent years we have limited oral argument to a half-hour in cases thought to involve issues not requiring longer argument. Counsel submit their briefs and record in sufficient time for the distribution of one set to each Justice two or three weeks before the oral argument. Most of the members of the present Court follow the practice of reading the briefs before the argument. Some of us often have a bench memorandum prepared before the argument. This memorandum digests the facts and the arguments of both sides, highlighting the matters about which we may want to question counsel at the argument. Often I have independent research done in advance of argument and incorporate the results in the bench memorandum.

We follow a schedule of two weeks of arguments from Monday through Thursday, followed by two weeks of recess for opinion writing and the study of petitions for review. The argued cases are listed on the conference agenda on the Friday following argument. Conference discussion follows the same procedure I have described for the discussion of certiorari petitions. Of course, it is much more extended. Not infrequently discussion of particular cases may be spread over two or more conferences.

Not until the discussion is completed and a vote taken is the opinion assigned. The assignment is not made at the conference but formally in writing some few days after the conference. The Chief Justice assigns the opinions in those cases in which he has voted with the majority. The senior Associate Justice voting with the majority assigns the opinions in the other cases. The dissenters agree among themselves who shall write the dissenting opinion. Of course, each Justice is free to write his own opinion, concurring or dissenting.

WRITING THE OPINION

The writing of an opinion always takes weeks and sometimes months. The most painstaking research and care are involved. Research, of course, concentrates on relevant legal materials—precedents particularly. But Supreme Court cases often require some familiarity with history, economics, the social and other sciences, and authorities in these areas, too, are consulted when necessary.

When the author of an opinion feels he has an unanswerable document he sends it to a print shop, which we maintain in the building. The printed draft may be revised several times before his proposed opinion is circulated among the other Justices. Copies are sent to each member of the Court, those in the dissent as well as those in the majority.

Now the author often discovers that his work has only begun. He receives a return, ordinarily in writing, from each Justice who voted with him and sometimes also from the Justices who voted the other way. He learns who will write the dissent if one is to be written. But his particular concern is whether those who voted with him are still of his view and what they have to say about his proposed opinion. Often some who voted with him at conference will advise that they reserve final judgment pending the circulation of the dissent. It is a common experience that dissents change votes, even enough votes to become the majority. I have had to convert more than one of my proposed majority opinions into a dissent before the final decision was announced. I have also, however, had the more satisfying experience of rewriting a dissent as a majority opinion for the Court.

Before everyone has finally made up his mind a constant interchange by memoranda, by telephone, at the lunch table, continues while we hammer out the final form of the opinion. I had one case during the past term in which I circulated 10 printed drafts before one was approved as the Court opinion.

The point of this procedure is that each Justice, unless he disqualifies himself in a particular case, passes on every piece of business coming to the Court. The Court does not function by means of committees or panels. Each Justice passes on each petition, each item, no matter how drawn, in longhand, by typewriter, or on a press. Our Constitution vests the judicial power in only one Supreme Court. This does not permit Supreme Court action by committees, panels, or sections.

The method that the Justices use in meeting an enormous caseload varies. There is one uniform rule: Judging is not delegated. Each Justice studies each case in sufficient detail to resolve the question for himself. In a very real sense, each decision is an individual decision of every Justice. The process can be a lonely, troubling experience for fallible human beings conscious that their best may not be adequate to the challenge. "We are not unaware," the late Justice Jackson said, "that we are not final because we are infallible; we know that we are infallible only because we are final." One does not forget how much may depend on his decision. He knows that usually more than the litigants may be affected, that the course of vital social, economic and political currents may be directed.

This then is the decisional process in the Supreme Court. It is not without its tensions of course—indeed, quite agonizing tensions at times. I would particularly emphasize that, unlike the case of a Congressional or White House decision, Americans demand of their Supreme Court judges that they produce a written opinion, the collective expression of the judges subscribing to it, setting forth the reasons which led them to the decision. These opinions are the exposition, not just to lawyers, legal scholars and other judges, but to our whole society, of the bases upon which a particular result rests—why a problem: looked at as disinterestedly and dispassionately as nine human beings trained in a tradition of the disinterested and dispassionate approach can look at it, is answered as it is.

CONTROVERSIAL DECISIONS

It is inevitable, however, that Supreme Court decisions—and the Justices themselves—should be caught up in public debate and be the subjects of bitter controversy. An editorial in The Washington Post did not miss the mark by much in saying that this was so because "one of the primary functions of the Supreme Court is to keep the people of the country from doing what they would like to do—at times when what they would like to do runs counter to the Constitution . . . . The function of the Supreme Court is not to count constituents; it is to interpret a fundamental charter which imposes restraints on constituents. Independence and integrity, not popularity, must be its standards."

Certainly controversy over its work has attended the Court throughout its history. As Professor Paul A. Freund of Harvard remarked, this has been true almost since the Court's first decision:

"When the Court held, in 1793, that the State of Georgia could be sued on a contract in the Federal courts, the outraged Assembly of that state passed a bill declaring that any Federal marshal who should try to collect the judgment would be guilty of a felony and would suffer death, without benefit of clergy, by being hanged. When the Court decided that state criminal convictions could be reviewed in the Supreme Court, Chief Justice Roane of Virginia exploded, calling it a 'most monstrous and unexampled decision. It can only be accounted for by that love of power which history informs us infects and corrupts all who possess it, and from which even the eminent and upright judges are not exempt.'"

But public understanding has not always been lacking in the past. Perhaps it exists today. But surely a more informed knowledge of the decisional process should aid a better undersanding.

It is not agreement with the Court's decisions that I urge. Our law is the richer and the wiser because academic and informed lay criticism is part of the stream of development. It is only a greater awareness of the nature and limits of the Supreme Court's function that I seek. I agree fully with the Solicitor General: It is essential, just because the public questions which the Court faces are pressing and divisive, that they be thoroughly canvassed in public, each step at a time, while the Court is evolving new principles. The ultimate resolution of questions fundamental to the whole community must be based on a common consensus of understanding of the unique responsibility assigned to the Supreme Court in our society.

The lack of that understanding led Mr. Justice Holmes to say 50 years ago:

"We are very quiet there, but it is the quiet of a storm center, as we all know. Science has taught the world skepticism and has made it legitimate to put everything to the test of proof. Many beautiful and noble reverences are impaired, but in these days no one can complain if any institution, system, or belief is called on to justify its continuance in life. Of course we are not excepted and have not escaped. Doubts are expressed that go to our very being. Not only are we told that when Marshall pronounced an Act of Congress unconstitutional he usurped a power that the Constitution did not give, but we are told that we are the representatives of a class—a tool of the money power. I get letters, not always anonymous, intimating that we are corrupt. Well, gentlemen, I admit that it makes my heart ache. It is very painful, when one spends all the energies of one's soul in trying to do good work, with no thought but that of solving a problem according to the rules by which one is bound, to know that many see sinister motives and would be glad of evidence that one was consciously bad. But we must take such things philosophically and try to see what we can learn from hatred and distrust and whether behind them there may not be a germ of inarticulate truth.

"The attacks upon the Court are merely an expression of the unrest that seems to wonder vaguely whether law and order pay. When the ignorant are taught to doubt they do not know what they safely may believe. And it seems to me that at this time we need education in the obvious more than investigation of the obscure." ■

THE SUPREME COURT AND CONTROVERSIAL DECISIONS
Earl Warren

In a matter of hours after first coming to the Court, I learned more about the important cases previously mentioned to me by some of its members. They called for a full Court at the opening of the term and were lumped as the school desegregation cases.

There were five of them, from Kansas, Virginia, South Carolina, Delaware, and the District of Columbia. While the latter was in a somewhat different setting because it did not involve a state law, they all involved the so-called "separate but equal" doctrine as established by the Supreme Court in the case of *Plessy* v. *Ferguson* (1896). That decision declined to prohibit separate railroad accommodations for blacks and whites. It sought to justify racial segragation for almost every movement or gathering so long as "separate but equal" facilities were provided and became known as the "Jim Crow" doctrine. The central issue in each of these school cases was:

> Does segregation of children in public schools solely on the basis of race, even though the physical facilities and other "tangible" factors may be equal, deprive the children of the minority group of equal educational opportunities?

The five cases had been argued during the 1952 term before I came to the Court but had not been decided and had been put over for reargument, with a set of specific questions for discussion.

The United States Government, through Assistant Attorney General J. Lee Rankin, supported by a brief signed also by Attorney General Herbert Brownell and other Justice Department attorneys, argued as a friend of the Court in favor of the positions maintained by the black students' lawyers. The first case was argued December 7, 1953, and it was easy to understand why the Court felt it necessary to have a full complement of Justices. The case had been first argued exactly a year before, and failure to reach an agreement had caused resubmission for argument. This would normally indicate a difference of opinion within the Court but without any knowledge by the outside world as to the degree or nature of the disagreement. In these circumstances, there is always the danger of an evenly divided four-to-four Court if any member is absent or disqualifies himself, which means the decision of the Court below is affirmed without opinion from the Supreme Court and without any precedential value.

Some of the cases under review had been decided against the black petitioners in the lower courts on the authority of the much eroded "separate but equal" doctrine of *Plessy* v. *Ferguson*.

To have affirmed these cases without decision and with the mere statement that it was being done by an equally divided Court, if such had been the case, would have aborted the judicial process and resulted in public frustration and disrespect for the Court. The Court was thoroughly conscious of the importance of the decision to be arrived at and the impact it would have on the nation. With this went realization of the necessity for secrecy in our deliberations and for achieving unity, if possible. Accordingly, we proceeded in a manner somewhat different from that in the average case. Perhaps it might be well to outline our normal way of proceeding in the conference. That procedure is not a secret, though what is said and done beyond the final results as given in the United States Reports is confidential and should not be disclosed.

PROCEDURE

Our usual manner of proceeding was as follows: When the briefs of the parties were all filed, the case was placed on our calendar for argument. Enough cases were listed for two weeks because throughout the year we heard arguments for that period of time and then recessed for two weeks to work on the opinions that were assigned to us for writing. When I assumed office, we heard cases argued Monday through Friday; later I changed the schedule to Monday through Thursday. On Saturday morning, we held a conference on the cases heard during the week. The procedure was very simple. In each case, the Chief Justice would, in a few sentences, state how the case appeared to him, and how he was inclined to decide it. Then, beginning with Justice Black, the senior Justice, each would speak his mind in a similar manner. He might only say, "I look at it the same way the Chief does and come to the same conclusion," or he might say, "I view the case differently. It seems to me this is the real issue, etc.," defining it. Or, "I believe it is controlled by the case of *So-and-So* v. *So-and-So* (citing precedent), and that brings me out the other way." Then we proceeded down the line until everyone had spoken briefly in this informal manner. During all of this, nobody was interrupted, and there was not debate. If we were all of one mind and no one desired to say anything more, the case was ready for assignment for the writing of the opinion. The Chief Justice always assigned the opinion to be written if he were with the majority. If he were not, the senior Justice who was with the majority made the assignment. If, after the first canvassing of the Court, as I have described it, there was a difference of opinion, the case was open for debate. We did not observe Robert's Rules of Order or any other definite procedure. It was a self-disciplined affair, each Justice deferring to the speaker until he was finished. The discussion proceeded in an orderly manner until all had spoken as much as they desired. If they were ready to vote, we did so at that time. In voting, we reversed the process and first called upon the junior member, going up the ladder with the Chief Justice voting last. I have tried diligently to learn when and why this procedure was first adopted, but without success. It is one of those things that grew up in the dim past and has been carried on without question. The reason assigned by some is that by voting first the junior member is relieved of casting the deciding vote when the other eight members are in a four-to-four deadlock. I suppose that is as good as any other reason. We then moved from case to case in this manner until all had been decided. The conference started at ten o'clock, and, with the exception of a half hour for lunch, which had been ordered beforehand and was always on the table in our dining room directly above the Conference Room, we continued throughout the day until we had discussed all our cases. Usually we adjourned shortly after five, but often not until after six. On rare occasions we recessed until Monday morning to complete our work.

During these conferences, no one was in the room except the Justices—not a secretary, a law clerk, or even a messenger. If it were necessary for anyone to contact us, it was done by written message and a knock on the door. When there was a knock, the junior member of the Court answered it unless he was speaking at the time, in which case some other Justice would respond. We had a telephone in the room, but I have no recollection of its ever having been used during a conference while I was on the Court.

The Justice to whom a case had been assigned for the writing of an opinion would, on his own time, prepare a draft, have it printed in our own print shop in the building, and distribute it to all the members of the Court. If they all agreed, it would be reported in open Court at the next session by the opinion writer, who might read or summarize it as he chose. If any Justice desired to dissent, he prepared his draft and circulated it to all the members, any of whom might join it or, if they desired, write and distribute their own dissent. Also, we had what is known as a concurring opinion. Often Justices arrived at the same conclusion as the majority, but reached it by different routes. They, too, might write an opinion and have it recorded with the others. When all the Justices had either written or joined an opinion, but not before, the case was ready to be announced to the public. If a Justice should, for any reason, feel disqualified, he could recuse himself and that action was also reported with the opinion.

This whole procedure is substantially the one still followed today. . . .

SCHOOL SEGREGATION CASES

To return to our method of handling the school segragation cases, we were all impressed with their importance and the desirability of achieving unanimity if possible. Realizing that when a person once announces he has reached a conclusion it is more difficult for him to change his thinking, we decided that we would dispense with our usual custom of formally expressing ourselves for a time to informal discussion of the briefs, the arguments made at the hearing, and our own independent research on each conference day, reserving our final opinions until the discussions were concluded.

We followed this plan until the following February, when it was agreed that we were ready to vote. On the first vote, we unanimously agreed that the "separate but equal" doctrine had no place in public education. The question then arose as to how this view should be written—as a *per curiam* (by the Court) or as a signed, individualized opinion. We decided that it would carry more force if done through a signed opinion, and, at the suggestion of some of the Justices, it was thought that it should bear the signature of the Chief Justice. I consented to this, and then the importance of secrecy was discussed. We agreed that only my law clerks should be involved, and that any writing between my office and those of the other Justices would be delivered to the Justices personally. This practice was followed throughout and this was the only time it was required in my years on the Court. It was not done because of suspicion of anyone, but because of the sensitiveness of the school segregation matter and the prying for inside information that surrounded the cases. It was thought wise to confine our communications to the fewest people as a matter of security. Headway being made in conference was discussed informally from time to time, and on occasion I would visit with Mr. Justice Jackson, who was confined to the hospital, to inform him of our progress. Finally, at our conference on May 15, we agreed to announce our opinion the following Monday, subject to the approval of Mr. Justice Jackson, who was still recuperating from a heart attack which had incapacitated him for some time. I went to the hospital early Monday morning, May 17, and showed the Justice a copy of the proposed opinion as it was to be released. He agreed to it, and to my alarm insisted on attending the Court that day in order to demonstrate our solidarity. I suggested that it was unecessary, but he insisted, and was there at the appointed time.

It was a momentous courtoom event and, unlike many other such events, it has not lost that character to this day. . . .

With courage drawn from this profession of faith in white supremacy by practically every Southern member of Congress, together with oft-repeated congressional speeches and statements to the effect that no nine honest men could possibly have come to the conclusion reached by the Court in *Brown* v. *Board of Educa-*

The inquiry was to show that he had fraternized with students who were said to have been Communists at that distant time.

I mention this example to show the extent of overzealousness that was rife in those days, and something of the human suffering it could cause.

Yet we continued to be assailed from every quarter for the Court's stand against such abuses. There was even legislation proposed, sponsored by Senator William Jenner of Indiana and later by Senator John M. Butler of Maryland, which was designed to divest the Supreme Court of jurisdiction in some of the "subversive activities" fields in which the McCarthy group was most interested. Some of this legislation, evoking as it did the atmosphere of Cold War hysteria, came dangerously close to passing. . . .

We also were heavily attacked by many people, particularly legislators, when we declared compulsory prayers in the public schools to be unconstitutional. I vividly remember one bold newspaper headline saying, "Court outlaws God." Many religious denominations in this same spirit condemned the Court, although most of them have receded from that position. Scores of Constitutional Amendments and legislative bills were proposed in the Congress to circumvent the decision but were later abandoned when the public came to recognize that the ruling was not an irreligious one. Rather it tried to maintain the separation of church and state guaranteed by the First Amendment. . . .

Because the Court, over the years, sought to make our criminal procedures conform to the relevant provisions of the Constitution and be a reality for the poor as well as the rich, it was made the target for widespread abuse. Many of these cases dislodged old law enforcement practices that had become tarnished with brutal intimidation of prisoners and suspects along with other injustices. Because police and indignant citizens were overwhelmed with the wave of violence that flooded the land, they found in the Court a stationary target and made us responsible for the increasing crime rate. We were "soft on criminals," they said.

Their attack centered on the case of *Miranda* v. *Arizona,* in which we held that before a prisoner—as distinguished from one who is being questioned in the merely investigative process—can be interrogated by police, he must be informed of his constitutional rights as to the purpose of the arrest and of the fact that he is entitled to have a lawyer present during questioning if he desires one. We also declared that the defendant must be told that if he cannot afford counsel, the state will provide same free of charge, and that he cannot be compelled to talk, but that if he does, anything said can be used against him. There was really nothing new in this except to require police and prosecutors to advise the poor, the ignorant, and the unwary of a basic constitutional right in a manner which had been followed by Federal Bureau of Investigation procedures for many years. It was of no assistance to hardened underworld types because they already know what their rights are and demand them. And so it is with all sophisticated criminals and affluent prisoners who had ready access to their lawyers. However, because so many people who are arrested are poor and illiterate, short-cut methods and often cruelties are perpetrated to obtain convictions. Hence a large percentage of police officers and prosecutors rebelled against such an articulation of a defendant's rights by Supreme Court.

A sizeable proportion of the American people, too, groping for a reason for so much criminal activity in our disturbed society but overlooking the root causes the crime—such as the degradation of slum life in the ghettos, ignorance, poverty, the drug traffic, unemployment, and organized crime (often made possible by the corruption of law enforcement officials)—joined in placing the blame on the courts and particularly on the Supreme Court. This formed part of the basis for the so-called "law and order" campaign of 1968. It was a one-sided affair because courts cannot debate the wisdom or propriety of their decisions, and the wildest and most emotional charges often go unchallenged.

This resulted in much proposed legislation in the Congress, and a great deal of castigation of the courts in congressional committees and on the floor. . . .

I have enumerated these different areas of decision and the enemies they have created for the Court, not as a complaint against their disapproval of us, but merely to show that the Supreme Court, if it defies the status quo, is bound to build up a formidable array of dissenters in powerful places. I hope the Court can always be criticized as publicly and as forcibly as desired. Justices must live with their judgments and be judged by them, not only at the time of their rendition, but through the indefinite future. . . .

The Supreme Court is particularly subject to criticism because most of its decisions are, as they say in athletic events, "close calls" and "judgment calls." Also, as a case wends its way to the Supreme Court, it becomes charged with emotion from the publicity given it and the discussion that follows. In addition, the questions presented to the Court are public questions which normally affect large groups of people. Add to these things the fact that its decisions are final, and one can easily see why the Supreme Court would attract more criticism than other courts. Also, the criticism becomes effective because it is a one-sided affair. Justices must take it in silence, leaving it to the people to form their own opinions concerning the Court's actions. This limitation and others make the life of a Justice of the Supreme Court an austere one, yet I could generally accept denunciation as a part of the job without resentment. . . .   ∎

MEMBERS OF THE SUPREME COURT

As with Congress, of course, the U. S. Supreme Court is not only an institution; it is also a collection of individuals. The Chief Justice and each of the Associate Justices must be appointed by the President and confirmed by the U.S. Senate.

What are the qualifications a President looks for in making appointments to the highest court? In an article excerpted here, political scientist Henry Abraham focuses on that question. He gives us a description of the 101 men and one woman who had served on the Supreme Court until 1986. Objective merit, personal and political friendship, and balancing representativeness have all been factors in Supreme Court appointments, Abraham says, and he assures us that the results have been very good for the country.

Next, an article from *Newsweek* examines the newest Reagan appointment to the Court, Antonin Scalia, and his appointment to fill the vacancy left by the resignation of Chief Justice Warren Burger, Justice William Rehnquist.

Finally, a *Time* magazine article assesses the record of the Burger Court following the June 1986 announcement of Chief Justice Burger's resignation.

THE SELECTION OF SUPREME COURT JUSTICES
Henry Abraham

A total of only 102 individuals have served to date on the Supreme Court of the United States, evincing an average longevity exceeded only by symphony orchestra conductors. I cannot speak to the latter, but what of the former's quantifiable characteristics? The 101 men and the one woman were nominated by 35 presidents, with three—W. H. Harrison, Taylor, and Carter—having no opportunity to choose anyone at all, and one, Andrew Johnson, seeing his efforts frustrated by a hostile Senate. Not counting a mere refusal to act on nominations—of which there were several—that constitutional partner in the appointment process has so far formally rejected 26 presidential nominations to the Court, all but four of these (namely, lower federal court judges Parker, Haynsworth, and Carswell, and the aborted promotion of Justice Fortas to Chief Justice) coming in the nineteenth century.

The total rejection figure comprises a remarkable but contemporary unthinkable 23 percent! Why were so many rejected by the Senate? Among the reasons, seven seem to be most compelling:

• Opposition to the nominating President, not necessarily the nominee— e.g., President John Quincy Adams' nomination of sometime United States Senator from Kentucky, John J. Crittenden, in 1828.

• The nominee's involvement with a visible or contentious issue of public policy—e.g., President George Washington's nomination of South Carolina's then Chief Justice, John Rutledge, as Chief Justice of the United States in 1795, because of the outspoken nominee's vigorous opposition to the Jay Treaty of 1794.

- Senatorial opposition to the record of the incumbent Court which the nominee seemed to support—e.g., President Ulysses S. Grant's selection of his own Attorney General, Ebenizer R. Hoar, in 1870.
- Senatorial courtesy, closely linked to the presumed consultative nominating process—e.g., President Grover Cleveland's choices of William B. Hornblower and Wheeler S. Peckham in 1893 and 1894, respectively, both ardently opposed by their fellow New Yorker, Democratic Senator David B. Hill.
- A perceived "political unreliability" of the nominee—e.g., another unsuccessful Grant nomination, this one of his one-time Attorney General Caleb Cushing, to the Chief Justiceship in 1874.
- An alleged lack of qualification or limited ability on the nominee's part—e.g., President James Madison's selection of Connecticut attorney and ex-United States Collector of Customs, Alexander Wolcott, in 1811.
- Powerful opposition to an otherwise patently qualified nominee by special issue interest or pressure groups—e.g., President Herbert Hoover's attempted promotion of United States District Court Judge John R. Parker of North Carolina in 1930.

Not at all infrequently, more than one of these seven reasons has combined to bring about an individual's rejection. The unenviable record of having more nominees rejected than any other President (five) is held by John Tyler.

THE SUCCESSFUL APPOINTEES

The 102 successful lawyer-appointees have come from 10 major professional subgroups, with 22 each from three of these, i.e., the lower federal judiciary, the state judiciary, and from diverse posts in the federal executive/administrative branch. Upon ascending to the high bench they resided in 31 different states, headed by 15 from New York, nine from Ohio, eight from Massachusetts, and seven from Virginia; 10 states have sent one; 19 none at all. The latter fact of political life prompted Republican Senator William ("Wild Bill") Langer of North Dakota, then a senior member of the Senate's Committee on the Judiciary, to commence in 1953 a campaign of opposition to any and all presidential nominees to the Court until his home state received a Supreme Court nomination. He went to his grave in 1959, his wish still unrealized—as it is to this day.

The acknowledged religious preferences of the 102 individual jurists fall into 12 different groups, the only ones in "double-digit-figures" being 27 Episcopalians, 25 avowedly unspecified Protestants, and 17 Presbyterians; there have been six Roman Catholics, five Jews, and the balance have been specified other Protestant adherents. Five professed political party designations characterize the successful nominees, including one Whig, one Independent, 12 Federalists, 40 Republicans, and 48 Democrats—hence, it is difficult to categorize an overwhelming partisan flavor to the bench.

Such a flavor unmistakably, however, has informed the selection of nominees in terms of their political affiliation in concord with that of the nominating president: the lowest partisan percentage to date—and now necessarily counting *all* federal judges—having been earned by President Ford (81.3 percent Republican), the highest by President Washington (100 percent Federalist). The lowest partisan-correlation nomination percentage in this century for all federal judges is still

President Ford's aforementioned 81.2 (President Taft's 82.2 being a close second), the highest that by the sole Ph.D. in political science so far to occupy the White House, Woodrow Wilson, who amassed a near perfect 98.6 percent score of Democratic appointees. More or less tied for the second highest correlative slot are presidents Carter and Harding, with 97.8 Democratic and 97.7 Republican indentifications, respectively.

Indubitably the profile and statistics just cited point to a broad-gauged commitment to a "representative" philosophy for judicial appointments. Whether that is wise may be put aside for the moment in favor of an examination of the intention of the Founding Fathers on that always so lively controversial issue. The conclusion is as crystal clear as it is inevitable that "representativeness" was not even considered, let alone advocated. Merit was the sole criterion on the mind of the delegates, "representativeness" being reserved to the legislature.

METHODOLOGY, NOT QUALIFICATIONS

Monday, May 14, 1787, was the date agreed upon for the opening of the Federal Constitutional Convention in the Old Independence Hall, called the State House, down on Fifth and Chestnut Streets in Philadelphia. But since only two states — Virginia and Pennsylvania — were represented on that historic day, the Convention was compelled to adjourn for lack of a quorum. This procedure continued daily, until Friday, May 25, at last saw the requisite majority of the 13 constituent states in their seats. Some five months later, on Tuesday, September 17, 1787, the Convention adjourned, having signed the historic document, the nascent Constitution of the United States, on the preceding day, highlighted by Dr. Franklin's magnificent closing address to the assemblage (which was read for him by his fellow-Pennsylvanian, James Wilson). As the most authoritative accounts, records, and interpretations of the events of that historic period demonstrate reliably, . . . while the question of the methodology to be employed for judicial appointments was subjected to intensive floor debate during 12 days in June, July, August and September, *criteria* for such appointments were neither debated nor did they appear to loom as a matter of either significance or puzzlement.

Those few delegates who vocalized the issue of *criteria* at all did so by assuming *viva voce* and *sub silentio* that *merit*, as opposed to favoritism, should, and indeed would, govern naturally. The central issue *cum* controversy concerned the degree of power to be vested in the executive and/or the degree of legislative participation. The provision finally agreed upon as a result of debates on September 6, 7 and 15, represented a compromise between those who, like Benjamin Franklin, James Madison, and John Rutledge, feared "monarchical" tendencies in strong solo executive prerogatives on the issue and called for a potent legislative role; and those who, like James Wilson, Alexander Hamilton, and Gouverneur Morris favored broadly independent executive appointive powers. It was the latter group that did most of the compromising, resulting in the largely James Madison-fashioned ultimate adoption of Article II, Section 2, as we know that provision today. . . . Delegates simply assumed, perhaps a mite naively, albeit quite understandably, that those selected as federal jurists would be chosen on the basis of merit. Period.

It is thus clear—with convenient 20/20 hindsight—that the Founding Fathers did not foresee the role political parties would soon come to play in the appointment process. Only John Adams among the notable contemporary statesmen— and he, of course, was not a member of the Constitutional Convention—visualized clearly the future rise of political parties and, as Harris put it well, "that partisan considerations rather than the fitness of nominees would often be the controlling consideration of the Senate in passing on nominations."

MERIT OVER POLITICS

Little attention was given to the matter of judicial appointments in the debate surrounding the ensuing state ratifying conventions. It was assumed as a matter of course that merit would govern. Alexander Hamilton did address the appointment power in *The Federalist, Nos. 66, 72, 76,* and *77,* which render patently evident that even that supreme political cognoscenti verily championed merit. Thus, in his *No. 66* he expressed full confidence that the Senate, whatever its stance on a particular nominee might be, would be guided by a candidate's *merit.* In his famed *No. 76,* in which he so trenchantly and approbatively elucidated the judicial funcion, he lauded the Senate's putative role as "an excellent check upon a spirit of favoritism in the President . . . [one that] would tend greatly to prevent the appointment of unfit character from State prejudice, from family connection, from personal attachment, or from a view of popularity."

And his *No. 77* assumed without self-doubt—and, of course, quite erroneously— that individual senators would not exert influence on presidential nominations. For he, too, quite unlike Adams, failed to foresee the influence that political parties would exert on appointments; the leverage they would provide thereby to an assertive chief executive; and the prominent role senators would soon play in dictating nominations. In sum, and notwithstanding Hamilton's interest and concerns, the debates in the state constitutional conventions paid but passing heed, if any, to the appointive arrangements, in general, and judicial ones, in particular. Engaged by issues of far more moment to them in their crucial decison whether or not to ratify the handiwork of the Founding Fathers, they assumed that those appointed to the bench would be qualified. Merit was assumed; "representativeness" did not even surface as an academic question.

REPRESENTATIVENESS AS AN ISSUE

Yet if it was not an issue then, it has assuredly become one—and increasingly so in modern mold. Indeed, it has become a demonstrable fact of the life of government and politics that so-called "equitable considerations" in the selection and nominations to the bench are not only omnipresent, but arguably omnipotent, in the decisional processes leading to selection, nomination, and appointment. And whereas initially these commitments were perhaps confined largely to the components of political persuasion and geography, the passing parade of the century in which we live has witnessed the insistent adoption and adaption of such additional expectations and requirements as contemporarily inform the "representation" of race, gender, religion, and perhaps even age. Whatever the Framer's ascertainable intentions may have been, the notion of the entitlement to a "peer model" has become all but pervasive in judicial staffing today. . . .

Is the nation, is the citizenry, served better, served more appropriately, if "representativeness" is rendered a prolegomenum for judicial selection, nomination, and appointment?

The attempted answer has evoked lively, often bitter, debate for close to half-a-century now, reaching a crescendo during the past generation. . . . I suspect that the verdict is in: if something can be "more or less" *res judicata,* it is obvious that the political branches have embraced "representativeness." That the pages of history demonstrate beyond any shadow of a doubt that the Founding Fathers did not ponder the issue does not necessarily determine its wisdom or desirability. But it is on those frontiers that an opinion opting for the sole criterion of *merit* as *the* irreducible imperative basic threshold requirement may be respectfully submitted, joined to the plea *cum* conviction that any "plus" considerations in behalf of "representativeness" must be wholly dependent upon the demonstrable presence of merit at the threshold.

THE CONCEPT OF MERIT

The concept, the phenomenon, of merit unfortunately defies universal definition; it is neither axion nor theorem. It may even lie entirely in the eye and mind of the beholder—but it need not do so. It is possible to suggest a merit model, and I should like to suggest one—eschewing any claim to originality. A sextet, the model comprises the following self-evident components (in no particular order of significance):

One: demonstrated judicial temperament.
Two: professional expertise and competence.
Three: absolute personal as well as professional integrity.
Four: an able, agile, lucid mind.
Five: appropriate professional educational background or training.
Six: the ability to communicate clearly, both orally and in writing, especially the latter.

Not only are these attainable components, but the history of our Supreme Court has demonstrated their presence amply. If the Holmesian tongue-in-cheek aphorism that the job of a jurist requires a "combination of Justinian, Jesus Christ, and John Marshall"[2] may not always have been attainable—it is apposite to note that with one possible exception even that trio may not have been perfect! If political party affiliation has almost always played a role—well, there are but nine positions on the highest bench, and there are unquestionably just as many qualified Republicans as there are qualified Democrats, and as many qualified Democrats as there are qualified Republicans. Nor is there any gainsaying a nominator's resolve to select a nominee with whom he is ideologicaly and

---

2. As quoted by Judge Irving R. Kaufman, *Charting a Judicial Pedigree,* The New York Times, January 24, 1981, p. 23.

jurisprudentially comfortable. You would, and I would, act similarly, always assuming the presence of threshold merit.

At any rate, as president after president has found out, without any particular degree of amusement, if there is anything certain about his nominees' on-bench performance in jurisprudential terms, it is that it is hardly predictable with accuracy, let alone certainty—which, to a very considerable degree, is a comforting fact of the judicial process. "You shoot an arrow into a far-distant future," wrote Alexander M. Bickel not long before his untimely death, "when you appoint a justice and not the man himself can tell you what he will think about some of the problems he will face."[3]

That is, of course, why such wise politicians as that All-American boy President Theodore Roosevelt, in a famed exchange with Connecticut's United States Senator Henry Cabot Lodge regarding the potential candidacy of Democrat Horace H. Lurton in 1906, wrote his objecting fellow-Republican that "the nominal politics of the man has nothing to do with his actions on the bench. His *real* politics are all important . . ." And T.R. lauded Lurton's position on sundry policies "in which you and I believe." Lodge concurred in substance, but replied that he saw no reason "why Republicans cannot be found who hold these opinions as well as Democrats." . . .

1. OBJECTIVE MERIT

A classic example of presidential selection based purely on . . . objective merit, *qua* merit, is that of Democrat Benjamin Nathan Cardozo by Republican Herbert Hoover to succeed Justice Holmes early in 1932. The two were neither personal nor professional friends: they were hardly, not even arguably, politically or ideologically compatible; and there was no question of "balancing representation." If anything, as Hoover would soon make clear, his reluctance to appoint the long-time, great New York appellate jurist was at least partly due to the fact that two other distinguished New Yorkers already were ornaments of the bench, namely Justices Stone and Hughes, and Cardozo's religious faith—he was a Sephardic Jew—was "represented" by Justice Brandeis. Yet if ever a nomination was forced upon a president by all but unanimous public and private acclaim, this was it. . . .

2. PERSONAL AND POLITICAL FRIENDSHIP

Examples that point to personal and political friendship as the overriding causation for presidential choice are legion—although in most instances other considerations loomed as contributory, if perhaps either as buttressing or subsidiary reasons. One of the several illustrations that quickly come to mind, and that unquestionably were characterized by the threshold presence of merit, is President Andrew Jackson's selection—or, more accurately, selections—of Roger Brooke

---

3. *Time* (May 23, 1969), p. 24.

Taney upon the resignation from the Court of the octogenarian Justice Gabriel Duval of Maryland.

The worst apprehensions of contemporary Whigs and Calhounians were promptly confirmed when Jackson nominated his close friend, long-time loyal adviser and supporter, to the seat. Taney, now 58, had successfully navigated the political shoals from the localism of Maryland politics to national prominence, having served as chairman of the Jackson Central Committee of Maryland in 1828, as Jackson's attorney general and, on a recess appointment, as secretary of the treasury after the Cabinet reorganization of 1832. . . . The Senate thwarted him [Jackson] by "postponing" the nomination on the last day of its session—but not before it had voted to do away with the vacant seat entirely, a manuever that failed of enactment, however, in the House of Representatives.

Enraged, Jackson refused to make another nomination and resolved to try Taney again. Fate played into his hands. On July 6, 1835, after almost 35 years on the bench, Mr. Chief Justice John Marshall died in Philadelphia. Jackson now had two vacancies to fill. That one of them would go to Taney was a foregone conclusion. . . .

"Judge Story thinks the Supreme Court is gone, and I think so too," Daniel Webster had written on hearing of Taney's selection. The remarkable chief justiceship of Taney would prove both men wrong, indeed. But first Jackson's favorite nominee would have to run the gauntlet of a hostile and powerful group of senators. For close to three months the battle raged in the upper house, but when the vote finally came it was not nearly so close as the bitter debates had led the country to believe. Taney won the nomination by a 14-vote margin, 29–15, opposed to the last by such powerful and influential Senate leaders as Calhoun, Clay, and Webster, who later would come to respect the superb performance of the man they had so ardently opposed. . . .

3. BALANCING REPRESENTATION

Although demonstrated professional merit was indubitably present, a case of presidential choice committed patently to what I have categorized as the balancing of "representation," and in this instance that of *geography,* was F.D.R.'s early 1943 selection of Wiley Blount Rutledge of Iowa. Roosevelt had appointed eight justices in less than four years between 1937 and 1941. Barring unforeseeable illness or resignations, that certainly would presumably be the end of the line. Yet in October 1942 came Justice Byrne's resignation from the Court and the ninth vacancy! This time there was no obvious successor, no obvious political debt to be paid. Such major New Deal supporters as Messrs. Black, Reed, Frankfurter, Douglas, Murphy, Jackson, and Byrnes had been sent to the Court; others, such as Attorney General Francis Biddle, were not interested. At last F.D.R. might indulge his repeatedly expressed desire to nominate someone from west of the Mississippi.

There was no rush as far as he was concerned, and he asked Biddle to look around carefully for a likely candidate. The ultimate nominee, pressed on the Administration by Biddle as well as by such allies as Senator Norris of Nebraska,

Justices Murphy and Douglas—Frankfurter and Stone still asked for Learned Hand—and particularly by the influential *Des Moines Register* and *Chicago Sun* journalist Irving Brant, was perhaps a rather "marginal" Westerner, but with identifiable claims to that region: 49-year-old Judge Wiley Rutledge of the United States Court of Appeals for the District of Columbia. Rutledge would be the only Roosevelt appointee with federal judicial experience (four years) and one of only three with any judicial background—the other two being Black and Murphy. F.D.R. was not personally acquainted with Rutledge, but after chatting with him at the White House, and being assured by Biddle that the candidate was a bona fide libertarian, an early and solid New Dealer who ardently championed the Court-packing plan, and a judge whose opinions demonstrated a solid commitment to the presidential philosophy, he nominated him in February 1943. "Wiley, you have geography," F.D.R. beamed at his happy selectee. Confirmation came readily without a formal roll call by the Senate. . . .

During his scant six and a half years on the bench Rutledge's scholarship, his mastery of law, his articulate explication of difficult issues, and his prodigious workmanship combined to establish him as an all but universally respected jurist. . . .

4. POLITICAL/IDEOLOGICAL COMPATIBILITY

The last of my suggested quartet of historically demonstrable major motivations in the presidential selection process of future justices of the Supreme Court is that of "real" political and ideological compatibility. My chosen example again points to the salutary fact that, notwithstanding the identifiable commitment to one or more of the quartet, threshold merit is prolegomenum or accompanist. Thus, it was patently true, too, of President Harding's Chief Justice Taft-inspired selection of George Sutherland of Utah in 1922.

That September 4, Justice John Hessin Clarke of Ohio had resigned after less than six years of service. The following day the president nominated the then 60-year-old Sutherland, and the Senate confirmed its two-term ex-fellow senator on the very same day, thereby establishing a speed record in the appointment process. Seldom in the history of the Court had, or indeed has, a successor-candidate been so universally obvious: a close personal and political ally of the president, Sutherland was insistently and enthusiastically backed by Taft, who earlier had written to the nominee: "I look forward to having you on the bench with me. I know, as you do, that the president intends to put you there." Sutherland was the first (and to date the only) Supreme Court justice from Utah and one of the very few of foreign birth (England) to reach the Court. . . .

Once he attained the high tribunal, George Sutherland demonstrated that the evaluation of his supporters had been entirely correct: he not only proved himself to be the judicial conservative everyone knew him to be, but he soon became the lucid and articulate spokesman for the Court's so-called Darwin-Spencer wing (also consisting of his colleagues Van Devanter, McReynolds, and Butler). The jurist whom his biographer characterized aptly as "A Man Against the State" spent 16 years on the Court as the personification of those against whom Holmes had railed in his anguished *Lochner* dissent, exclaiming that "The Fourteenth Amendment does not enact Mr. Herbert Spencer's Social Statics." Yet to

Sutherland, the Fourteenth Amendment meant "keep-your-hands-off, government!" and in the libertarian as well as the proprietarian sense. . . .

In the 1930s he became the scourge of the New Deal, heading a majority that struck down more than a dozen pieces of domestic legislation fundamental to the New Deal in 1935–36. Yet he was not blindly opposed to the exercise of governmental power, particularly in the realm of foreign relations. One of the most significant opinions in support of Presidential authority, *United States v. Curtiss-Wright Export Corporation,* was from his pen. It is only just that no matter how many of them have disapproved of his philosophical imperatives, leading students of the Court have never hesitated to accord him the high regard and rating history has so deservedly bestowed upon him.

■ ■ ■

The four illustrations selected almost at random, as well as the numerous others alluded to with affection and admiration throughout these refllections, testify to the rich mine of giants that have served so remarkably well on the Court in its now almost two centuries of life. They provide proof positive of promises fulfilled and achievevemts rendered. Indeed, notwithstanding the often tiresome, and not infrequently self-serving—albeit exasperating—sniping that has charcterized the Court's existence, sniping that has regrettably, although not surprisingly, emanated most loudly from prestigious centers of learning located near bodies of water on both the East and West Coasts, it has, I submit with conviction, truly been, in James Madison's words, a "bench happily filled." His wish *cum* plea, expressed in 1787, has stood the test of time admirably.   ■

A PAIR FOR THE COURT
Larry Martz

W hat does it take to make a good judge? William Rehnquist asked that question in a speech a few years ago, and answered it: a judge should be at least "a pretty good lawyer," with a concern for how people are governed, a feel for legal tradition and a common-sense knowledge of human nature. A judge should also be a good writer, he added, and the chief justice especially should be able "to keep eight prima donnas on some sort of a leash." It remains to be seen whether Rehnquist can perform that trick in his new role, but the rest of the specs clearly describe him—and to a surprising degree, his prospective new colleague, Antonin Scalia, as well. Predictions of Supreme Court votes are notoriously tricky, but students of judicial form charts see the two as remarkably similar in background and temperament, with impressive brains, incisive prose styles and driving but affable personalities.

Both are strivers from immigrant stock. Rehnquist, son of a first-generation Swedish-American salesman from suburban Milwaukee, served in the Army Air Corps in World War II and used his veteran's benefits and part-time jobs to work himself onto the fast track: he graduated first in his class from Stanford Law School, clerked for Supreme Court Justice Robert H. Jackson, set up a law practice in Phoenix and went to Washington as assistant attorney general in the Nixon administration. Richard Nixon himself knew so little of Rehnquist that he was heard on the Watergate tapes referring to "Renchburg" as one of a "group of clowns" in the Justice Department. But after two Nixon nominees for the high court ran into fire in the Senate, Rehnquist got the job. He was only 47.

Scalia, now 50, son of an Italian-born teacher at Brooklyn College, topped his class at Georgetown University and went on to be a law review editor at Harvard. After a stint in a Cleveland law firm, he too left for the East and eventually a job as the head of Gerald Ford's office of legal counsel. Jimmy Carter's victory sent him to teaching at the University of Chicago for six years before Ronald Reagan named him to the federal appellate court in the District of Columbia Circuit. He was an instant star.

Like other self-made men, both Rehnquist and Scalia have a tory respect for authority and generally vote to defend it; they tend to be impatient with the complaints of those who have failed to match their own achievements. As a clerk, Rehnquist wrote several memos to Jackson arguing for the constitutionality of segregation laws, and he has consistently voted against expanded rights for blacks, women and criminal defendants. Similarly, Scalia conceded in a 1979 article that his views opposing affirmative action could open him to charges of bigotry. But he argued vigorously that the realities of quotas would taint the achievements of truly gifted minorities. He went on to propose his own satiric solution to racial inequities: a "restorative justice handicapping system," under which penalty points would be assigned to U.S. citizens in proportion to their ancestors' date of arrival and their own consequent racial guilt. That would be difficult, he conceded, but he added sarcastically that a Supreme Court that had reached the *Roe v. Wade* abortion decision "would not shrink from the task."

If both men hungered for success, they did not measure it in financial terms. "Bill is astonishingly uninterested in making money," said Rehnquist's former law partner, James Powers, when he was named to the court. These days, top Washington hands who aren't millionaires simply aren't trying. But last year Rehnquist officially disclosed that his net worth, apart from real estate, was still less than $150,000. Scalia, a devout Catholic, accumulated so little wealth from teaching and government work that when he left Washington, friends say he chose the University of Chicago at least in part because it would pay tuition for his nine children. But he was interested in power and the proximity to it; he turned down an appointment to the Seventh Circuit Court of Appeals, based in Chicago, to hold out for the Washington bench.

Poker games: And while both men are conservative, neither fits the stereotype of the right-wing sourpuss. They are storytellers, kibitzers, outdoorsmen. "Nino" Scalia gets his judicial colleagues to sing along at the piano and shows a relaxed tolerance as a family man. One Chicago dinner partner recalls him joking about his eldest son, who was not following the traditional path to college. In a big family, he said, "The first child is kind of like the first pancake. If it's not perfect, that's okay, there are a lot more coming along." He and Rehnquist both have the gift of persuasion and an unpretentious lifestyle. Justice Sandra Day O'Connor, who sometimes dated Rehnquist at Stanford, has described him piloting an old Studebaker that he had to fix "with chewing gum"; to this day he drives a Volkswagen Rabbit and ambles around the court in slacks, desert boots and a tweed jacket. He and Scalia are regular players in a monthly nickel-and-dime poker game. Rehnquist's style of play was described by The Wall Street Journal last week as subdued and canny, Scalia's as intuitive and ebullient.

They have a formidable capacity for work. In weighing cases, neither follows the usual practice of ordering clerks to prepare bench summaries of the opposing arguments. Scalia reads all the briefs, engages his clerks in role-playing debates on each case and terrifies lawyers who aren't thoroughly prepared for oral arguments. (A former student at Chicago recalls that his classes were enjoyable, but only when students came prepared; once, when four in a row didn't know an answer, Scalia walked out.) He writes many of his own decisions, on a word processor without preliminary drafts from the clerks. Rehnquist sorts out his arguments in brisk walking debates with his clerks and writes opinions in quick, often pungent prose: the First Amendment, he said once, is not "some sort of constitutional 'sunshine law'." He is so efficient he usually manages to leave the court by 3 p.m.

Each of the two brings a common-sense approach to legal issues. In one scathing opinion, Scalia dissented from a liberal ruling that lethal injections for condemned prisoners had to meet FDA standards of safety: "The condemned prisoner executed by injection is no more the 'consumer' of the drug than is the prisoner executed by firing squad a consumer of the bullets." Both men are credited with intellectual rigor, but both have been criticized for tempering their views on occasion. Rehnquist it is said, sometimes even twists facts; a clerk once apologized for participating in writing a decision that Rehnquist refused to revise to reflect the true history of the federal welfare program. And Scalia's professed devotion to judicial restraint sometimes yields to his zeal for a cause. Last February's decision overturning the Gramm-Rudman budget-balancing law, for instance, was assailed by Michael Kinsley in The Wall Street Journal as a textbook case of judicial activism that strained logic, went unnecessarily far and opened a Pandora's box of mischievous precedents.

The court will surely change Scalia, as it has changed almost every talented judge in its long history. But nobody can foretell how. As for Rehnquist, he is 14 years into the process. When he came to the court, he told The New York Times last year, he thought his job was to counterbalance the liberal trend of the Warren court, "to kind of lean the other way" with a series of fierce dissents. He spoke for himself so often that his clerks presented him with a Lone Ranger doll that still perches on his mantelpiece. Lately, he went on, "I think I see it quite differently . . . there probably are things to be said on both sides of issues that I perhaps didn't always think there were." Rehnquist had been talking in recent months about looking for a new job with new challenges when he reached 65. He has beaten that schedule by four years, and this job looks big enough even for him. ■

THE COURT THAT TILTED AND VEERED
Richard Lacayo

When Warren Burger was made Chief Justice in 1969, there were those who saw the potential for a revolution against the activism of the Earl Warren Court. Seventeen years and five more Republican appointments later, the Burger Court has not undone the Warren legacies so much as consolidated them, affirming the earlier rulings even as it modified and diluted them. It was a court that could move boldly when it needed to. It upheld the right of the press to publish the Pentagon papers. It ruled unanimously that Richard Nixon could not withhold the damning White House tapes sought by the Watergate special prosecutor. But it did not reverse outright a single one of the major Warren doctrines.

"The Burger Court will be remembered, if it's remembered at all, as a moderate court, neither retrenching nor avant-garde," says Duke University Law Professor William Van Alstyne. Its prudence derived from the respect it, like previous courts, accorded to the precedents set by predecessors. Thus the Warren rulings became the basis upon which the Burger Court built its reasonings. It left standing the chief emblem of the Warren era's expansion of defendants' rights, the Miranda decision, which requires police to inform suspects of their rights before interrogation. But it allowed police to dispense with Miranda warnings in emergency situations, weakened the rights of suspects during pretrial procedures and identified some circumstances in which illegally obtained evidence could be admitted in court.

The Burger Court was expected to apply the provisions of the Constitution narrowly rather than find in them an opportunity to mandate its own far-reaching solutions to social problems. Even so, it practiced its share of judicial activism. It upheld busing as a legitimate tool for desegregating schools and overturned laws that discriminated on the basis of sex. In its most difficult advance into new territory, it ruled that women have a right to abortion. "This court has moved into areas the Warren Court never came near," says American University Law Professor Herman Schwartz.

Yet when it moved, it was typically with a lumbering tread, tilting and veering with the shifts of the Justices at its center: Blackmun, Powell, Stevens, White and the late Potter Stewart. The Burger era may be remembered as one in which the centrists played the crucial role as swing votes in a court that was always swaying. But durable voting blocs were hard to forge among Justices who faced the divisive task of implementing broad principles that the Warren Court had merely sketched out: first the agreeable axions of equality, then the vexing arithmetic of affirmative action. So in the landmark Bakke case, five Justices voted to invalidate a racial quota at a California medical school but five (Powell was in both camps) also approved the use of some race-conscious affirmative-action programs. In a string of decisions since then, the shifting coalitions on the court have tilted back and forth on when and how affirmative action can be applied.

The Burger Court also tinkered with the barrier between church and state, though again in ways that left both sides dissatisfied. The same is true of its mixed treatment of free speech and the press. But after the announcement of his resignation last week, the Chief Justice told reporters that he had written more opinions favorable to the press than any other Justice: "The First Amendment isn't one damn bit more important to you than it is to me."

"This court had a couple of Justices with vision," says University of Michigan Law Professor Yale Kamisar. "Brennan on the left and Rehnquist on the right. But nobody had the votes." As a result, the legacy of the Burger Court, insofar as it makes sense to speak of a Burger Court, lies mainly in the details. "It met the hard cases, decided the finger points and didn't push things along any further," says University of Texas Law Professor Scot Powe. For an era of rapid and thus often heated social change, that amounts to a respectable epitaph.   ■

PRESIDENT REAGAN AND THE FEDERAL COURTS

There are two important ways by which presidents may seek to affect federal court decisions. They can use their appointive power to name judges who share their views. And, by taking sides in actual cases, they and their administration officials can try to influence courts and judges directly.

Members of the U. S. Supreme Court, as well as judges of the U. S. Courts of Appeal and District Courts, serve on "good behavior," or, in effect, for life (unless, quite rarely, they are removed through the impeachment process). Every president, then, has some opportunity to shape the federal judiciary for years to come.

An article by Sheldon Goldman, excerpted here, points out that by the end of his second term, President Ronald Reagan—matched in this century only by Franklin D. Roosevelt and Dwight Eisenhower—will have named a majority of the active lower federal judges. (Since, at the beginning of Reagan's second term, five of the nine members of the Supreme Court were over 70 years of age, it was possible that he might have an opportunity to appoint a majority of the members of that body, too). To estimate the effect of President Reagan's two-term judicial appointments, Goldman surveys his first-term appointments. He categorizes them on the basis of occupation, experience, education, race, and sex. President Reagan, Goldman says, instituted the most thorough ideological screening of judicial candidates since Franklin Roosevelt. His fairly good record in regard to the appointment of women judges has not been matched by his record in regards to blacks, a record which is the worst of any president since Einsenhower.

Next, an article reprinted from *U. S. News & World Report* shows further how President Reagan and Attorney General Edwin Meese have put their stamps on federal law through the appointment of federal judges.

REAGAN RESHAPES THE FEDERAL BENCH
Sheldon Goldman

Ronald Reagan's reelection by a landslide victory in 1984 was hailed by some observers as a significant political event comparable to Franklin Roosevelt's reelection in 1936. Both presidents received overwhelming electoral approval, which was widely interpreted as a mandate to continue along the course set in the first term. Both were enormously popular with the large majority of the populace, although both stimulated considerable antipathy and even denigration from a vocal minority opposed to Administration philosophy and policy. Both elections could be seen as confitrming a new electoral era in national politics and new voting patterns among young voters and other population groups.

In addition, both presidents had spent their first terms dealing with economic crises and both used Keynesian economics (without credit to Keynes in the latter instance) to nurse the economy back to health. Both presidents had a view of the role of government, including the courts, that was radically different from their immediate predecessors in office. Indeed, both sought to change the direction of government, saw the courts as frustrating their policy agendas, and self-consciously attempted to use the power of judicial appointment to place on the bench judges sharing their general philosophy. And with both, their presidential campaigns saw the courts and judicial appointments emerge as issues.

Franklin Roosevelt left a major legacy with his court appointments that fundamentally reshaped constitutional law and whose judges numerically dominated the lower federal courts for close to a decade after his presidency. Ronald Reagan has already begun the groundwork for his judicial legacy. With just two terms in office as compared to Roosevelt's three plus, Reagan will accomplish what only Roosevelt and Eisenhower accomplished during the last half century—naming a majority of the lower federal judiciary in active service. This makes it all the more significant to inquire what has been the Reagan first term record in the realm of judicial selection. What changes have occurred in the selection process? What is the professional, demographic, and attribute profile of the Reagan appointees and how do they compare with appointees of previous administrations? Has the Administration been successful in placing on the bench those in harmony with Administration philosophy? What can we expect in the second term? These are the questions that this article confronts. . . .

The findings and analyses presented here concern all lifetime federal district and courts of appeals judges confirmed by the U.S. Senate of the 97th and 98th Congresses. The courts of appeals judges analyzed were only those appointed to the 11 numbered circuits and the Court of Appeals for the District of Columbia. Appointments to the Court of Appeals for the Federal Circuit, a court of specialized as opposed to general jurisdiction, were not included. The findings for the Reagan first term appointments are compared to those for the Johnson, Nixon, Ford, and Carter lifetime appointments to courts of general jurisdiction. During his first term Reagan named 129 to the district courts and 31 to the appeals courts.

SELECTION UNDER REAGAN

A striking characteristic of the judicial selection process in the Reagan Administration has been the formalization of the process by institutionalizing interaction patterns and job tasks that in previous administrations were more informal and fluid. There have also been changes of more substantive import.

The center of judicial selection activity in previous administrations was the Deputy Attorney General's Office, with an assistant to the deptuy responsible for the details, and at times negotiations, associated with the selection process. During the Reagan Adminstration these responsibilities have shifted to the Office of Legal Policy. The Assistant Attorney General heading that office reports to the Deputy Attorney General but also has an independent role as a member of the President's Federal Judicial Selection Committee. Assisting the head of the Legal Policy division in matters concerning judicial selection is the Special Counsel for Judicial Selection, a post formally established in September of 1984. The Attorney General, Deputy Attorney General, the Assistant Attorney General for Legal Policy, the Special Counsel for Judicial Selection, and some of their assistants meet to make specific recommendations for judgeships to the President's Committee on Federal Judicial Selection.

The major substantive innovation in the selection process made by the Reagan Administration is the creation of the President's Committee on Federal Judicial Selection. This nine-member committee institutionalizes and formalizes an active White House role in judicial selection. Members of the Committee from the White House during the first term included presidential counselor Edwin Meese III, White House chief of staff James A. Baker III, John S. Herrington, assistant to the President for personnel, M. B. Oglesby, assistant to the President for legislative affairs, and presidential counsel Fred Fielding, who serves as chair of the Committee. From the Justice Department are the Attorney General, Deputy Attorney General, Associate Attorney General, and the Assistant Attorney General for Legal Policy.

The highest levels of the White House staff have played a continuing active role in the selection of judges. Legislative, patronage, political, and policy considerations are considered to an extent never before so systematically taken into account. This has assured policy coordination between the White House and the Justice Department, as well as White House staff supervision of judicial appointments.

The Committee does not merely react to the Justice Department's recommendations; it is also a source of names of potential candidacies and a vehicle for the exchange of important and relevant information. Furthermore, the president's personnel office conducts an investigation of prospective nominees *independent* of the Justice Department's investigation. It is perhaps not an overstatement to observe that the formal mechanism of the Committee has resulted in the most consistent ideological or policy-orientation screening of judicial candidates since the first term of Franklin Roosevelt.

It is also relevant to observe that this selection process innovation potentially contains an inherent source of tension as the perspective from the Justice Department can be quite different from that of the White House. The cooptation of judicial selection by the Reagan White House has now been completed with former presidential counsel Edwin Meese III now serving as Attorney General.

Although the consequences of this shift is immediately apparent in terms of the screening of candidates, in the hands of a less ideologically oriented administration partisan patronage considerations could conceivably become the principal selection criterion. Professional credentials would then be minimized, resulting in a lower quality federal bench. This is not meant to fault the Reagan Administration for its innovations in the selection process. Indeed, from the standpoint of achieving Administration goals, those innovations are rational and functional. But there may be unintended consequences from these changes that should be watched by those who are concerned with the administration of justice.

Another change in the process worthy of note is that the Reagan Administration is the first Republican Administration in 30 years in which the American Bar Association Standing Committee on Federal Judiciary was not actively utilized and consulted in the prenomination stage. From the Eisenhower Administration through the Ford Administration, Justice Department officials sounded out the ABA Standing Committee for tentative preliminary ratings of the leading candidates for a specific judgeship. These informal reports could be used by Justice officials in negotiations with senators and other officials of the president's party. At times they influenced the justice officials' final selection. During the Carter Administration, however, this close working relationship ended as the Administration established its own judicial selection commission for appeals court appointments and most Democratic senators established analogous commissions for district court positions.

The Reagan Administration abolished the selection commission but has, with few exceptions, maintained a more formal relationship with the ABA Standing Committee and has not sought preliminary ratings on anyone but the individual the Administration has already settled on to nominate. This has also meant that unlike previous Republican Administrations which pledged not to nominate any person rated "Not Qualified" by the ABA Standing Committee, this Administration has made no such pledge and is willing, if not persuaded by the Committee, to nominate the person of its choice even were the nominee rated "Not Qualified."

This is not to suggest that relations were cool with the ABA Committee. Senate Judiciary Committee hearings on the nomination of J. Harvie Wilkinson to the Fourth Circuit revealed a close working relationship, but that relationship occurred *after* the Administration had decided on Wilkinson, not before. Of course, the Administration has been concerned that its nominees receive high ABA ratings, but evidently it has not been willing to give the ABA Standing Committee an opportunity to influence the selection during the more fluid pre-nomination stage.

One further observation about the selection process is in order. The Reagan Administration repudiated the selection commission concept and in so doing abandoned the most potentially effective mechanism for expanding the net of possible judicial candidates to include women and racial minorities, groupings historically excluded from the judiciary. The Carter Administration's record in this regard was unprecedented, with Carter naming to the courts of appeals 11 women, nine black Americans (including one black woman), two Hispanics, and the first person of Asian ancestry (out of a total of 56 appointments). The Reagan record with regard to the appeals courts, as will be discussed shortly, falls markedly short of that.

DISTRICT COURT APPOINTMENTS

Occupation: If we look at the occupation [of Reagan, Carter, Ford, Nixon, and Johnson appointees] at time of appointment we find that about 40 per cent were members of the judiciary on the state bench or, in several instances, U.S. magistrates or bankruptcy judges. Only the Carter Administration of the past five administrations had a higher proportion of those who were serving as judges at the time they were chosen for the federal district bench. About eight per cent of the Reagan district court appointees were in politics or governmental positions but few of these were U.S. Attorneys; this also had been true for the Carter appointees but not for the appointees of previous administrations. It would appear, for whatever the reason, that the U.S. Attorney position is not the direct stepping-stone to a federal judgeship it once was, although both federal and state prosecutorial experience was prominent in the backgrounds of the judges. Also of note is that few law school professors were appointed, in contrast to the Reagan record for the courts of appeals. The Carter, Nixon, and Johnson Administrations appointed proportionately more law school professors that did Reagan in his first term.

Private law practice was the occupation at time of appointment for close to half the Reagan appointees. The range of the size of firm varied considerably, with close to 12 per cent affiliated with large firms (with 25 or more partners and/or associates) and a slightly lower proportion at the other end of the spectrum practicing in firms with four or fewer members or associates. This is roughly comparable to the distribution of the Carter appointees. Since the Johnson Administration, proportionately fewer of those in a small practice have been chosen. Close to one out of four Johnson appointees, but only about one in seven Carter and one in ten Reagan first term appointees came from a small practice. Perhaps this is a reflection of the changing nature of the practice of law.

Experience: Over 70 per cent of the first term Reagan district court appointments had either judicial or prosecutorial experience, a proportion comparable to the appointees of the Carter Administration, and the second highest of all five administrations' appointees. Of special interest and importance is that the proportion of those with judicial experience exceeded the proportion of those with prosecutorial experience—a trend begun only in the Carter Administration. Before Carter, prosecutorial experience was more frequent.

Why the shift toward a greater emphasis on judicial experience? The reasons may be two-fold. First, to the extent that judicial selection commissions are involved in judicial selection, and as many as 18 Republican senators in 14 states have employed them during Reagan's first term, judicial experience will be seen as a desirable and relevant credential. Commissions have been concerned with the professional quality of prospective nominees, and those with judicial experience have a professional track record that can be evaluated. Second, such track records can also be scrutinized by Justice Department officials to determine if the candidate shares the Administration's judicial philosphy and ideological outlook. The result of this recent emphasis on judicial experience may be the growing professionalization of the American judiciary.

Education: The educational background of a majority of Reagan appointments to the district courts . . . was private school including the highly prestigious Ivy League schools. Only about one-third of Reagan appointees attended a public university for undergraduate work, whereas over 57 per cent of the Carter appointees attended public colleges—perhaps a reflection of poorer socioeconomic roots of a substantial segment of the Carter judges. Again, with law school education, the majority of the Reagan appointees attended private law schools while a bare majority of the Carter appointees attended public-supported law schools.

Although there are some problems with equating being able to attend a private undergraduate college with socioeconomic status, the argument can be made that it is a rough indicator. The findings for the Reagan appointees are consistent with earlier findings and compatible with findings from other studies suggesting that the socioeconomic differences between the Republican and Democratic electorates are mirrored to some degree in the appointments of Republican and Democratic Administrations. This has particular persuasiveness in light of the net work findings . . . . In sum, we can observe that with relatively few exceptions, there is a tendency for the typical Republican appointee to be of a higher socioeconomic status than the typical Democratic appointee.

A word about the professional education of the appointees is in order. A study of the Reagan appointees at mid-term tentatively concluded that as a group the Reagan appointees might have had a marginally less distinguished legal education than the appointees of the four previous presidents. This was based on the relatively small proportion of appointees with an Ivy League law school education, the smallest proportion over the past five administrations. The proportion has remained constant for the entire first term appointments. However, the same caveat noted earlier must be repeated here—that is, that a number of Reagan appointees as well as appointees of other presidents attended distinguished non-Ivy League schools including Michigan, Virginia, Berkeley, Stanford, and N.Y.U. Interestingly, a study conducted by Fowler found that a smaller proportion of the Reagan appointees than the Carter appointees attended "prestige" law schools, which supports the earlier conclusion that the Reagan appointees' legal education, on the whole, was marginally less distinguished than the appointees of previous presidents.

Affirmative action: The record of the Reagan first term district court appointments is a mixed one with regard to gender and race/ethnicity. The Reagan Administration was, of course, responsible for the historic appointment of the first woman to the Supreme Court. At the district court level, the record . . . shows that the Reagan Administration's appointment of women was second only to the Carter Administration. Over nine per cent of the appointments went to women, and this suggests that the Administration, as well as some Republican senators, made an effort to recruit well qualified women. While it is true that the large majority of all appointees of all five administrations have been male, the Reagan Administration must be given credit for continuing the push for sexual equality in the recruitment of federal district judges. It is also significant to note that by the end of the first term two women held important Justice Department positions that are concerned with judicial selection: Carole Dinkins as Deputy Attorney General and Jane Swift as Special Counsel for Judicial Selection in the Office of Legal Policy. It is likely that women in key Justice Department positions will be sensitive to sexual discrimination in the judicial selection process.

The record as to black appointments, however, is markedly different. The Reagan first term record is not only the worst of all five administrations, . . . it is the worst since the Eisenhower Administration in which no blacks were appointed to life-time district court positions. Justice Department officials are aware of this poor record and have said they would like it to improve, but feel that it is extraordinarily difficult to find well qualified blacks who share the President's philosophy and are also willing to serve. Critics respond that the Administration has not made the recruitment of blacks a high priority in part because the black electorate votes overwhelmingly Democratic, and there is little political payoff in the appointment of blacks. In contrast, the proportion of Hispanics was second only to that of the Carter Administraton. Some observers link that fact to the Republican Party effort to woo Hispanic voters in the 1984 election.

ABA ratings and other factors: When we examine the ratings of the ABA Standing Committee on Federal Judiciary we find that about seven per cent of the Reagan first term apointees to the district courts received the highest rating, that of Exceptionally Well Qualified. This is the best record since the Johnson Administration. The next highest rating, that of Well Qualified, was received by about 43 per cent, which means that half the Reagan appointees were in the top two categories. The Carter appointees received proportionately more Well Qualified ratings than did the Reagan appointees but fewer Exceptionally Well Qualified ratings. However, when the top two ratings are combined, 51 per cent of the Carter appointees fell into those categories – about the same as the Reagan appointees. If the ABA ratings are taken as a rough measure of "quality," the Reagan appointments may be seen as equaling the Carter appointees in quality and marginally surpassing the appointments of Ford, Nixon, and Johnson.

In terms of party affiliation of district court appointees, approximately 97 per cent of the Reagan appointees were Republican, the highest partisanship level of all five administrations and the highest proportion of a president choosing members of his own party since Woodrow Wilson. The figures for previous prominent party activism suggest that the Reagan appointees had the highest proportion of all five administrations. However, there is no suggestion that the Reagan appointees with a record of party activism received their appointments solely because of their political activities. Instead, it must be recognized that a history of party activity is helpful to a judicial candidacy only when other factors are present such as distinguished legal credentials, and, particularly as far as the Reagan Administration is concerned, a judicial philosophy in harmony with that of the Administration. Suffice it to note that many of the Reagan appointees to both the district and appeals courts had impressive legal credentials as well as a background of partisan activism. . . . Also observe that about four out of ten Reagan appointees did *not* have a record of prominent partisan activism, although they of course had to receive sufficient political backing or clearance in order to have been nominated.

The religious origins or religious affiliation of the Reagan first term district court appointees differed markedly from the appointees of previous Republican administrations; Reagan appointed more Catholics and fewer Protestants – proportions similar to those of Democratic administrations. In fact, . . . the Republican Reagan Administration appointed proportionately more Catholics than did the Democratic Carter and Johnson Administrations. In the past, Republican administrations appointed more Protestants and fewer Catholics and Jews than did Democratic administrations; this could be attributed to the fact that the religious composition or mix of the parties was different and thus, to a large extent, so was the pool of potential judicial candidates from both parties. The finding for the Reagan appointees does not mean that the Administration gave greater preference to Catholics because of their religion than did previous Republican administrations, but rather than more Catholics have entered the potential pool from which Republican judicial nominees emerge thus increasing their proportion of appointees. This is consistent with the relatively heavy Catholic vote for Reagan in 1980 and especially 1984.

The average age of the Reagan appointees was about that of the Carter appointees and similar to that of the appointees of the previous three presidents.

The net worth of the Reagan appointees as compared to the Carter appointees . . . [indicates] differences in degree at both ends of the financial spectrum. There were proportionately more millionaires among the Reagan district court appointees, over five times as many as the Carter appointees, and proportionately fewer Reagan appointees at the lower end of the economic spectrum. This suggests, along the lines reported in the 1983 study of Reagan appointees, that there is somewhat of a class difference between the Republican and Democratic appointees on the whole that is analogous to the socioeconomic differences among the electorates of the two parties. However, the findings also suggest that the Reagan and Carter appointees were for the most part drawn from the middle to upper classes.

APPEALS COURT APPOINTMENTS

Traditionally, senators of the president's party have had considerably less influence in the selection of appeals court as distinct from district court judges. This has meant that administrations have had more of an opportunity to pursue their policy agendas (such as they may have them) by way of recruiting appeals judges who are thought to be philosophically sympathetic with such agendas. We can so view the 31 first term Reagan appointments to the courts of appeals with general jurisdiction as compared to the 56 Carter, 12 Ford, 45 Nixon and 40 Johnson appointees. Because there are fewer appeals judges than district judge appointments, differences in percentages, . . . must be treated with caution.

Occupation and experience: A striking finding is that three out of five Reagan appeals court appointees and over half the Ford, Nixon, and Johnson appointees were already serving in the judiciary at the time of their appointment to the courts of appeals. Of the 19 Reagan appointees who were judges at the time of appointment, 16 were serving as federal district judges and the remaining three on the state bench. Just as with the selection of federal district judges, Justice Department officials felt more secure evaluating the candidacies of those with judicial track records. The Reagan Administration was particularly concerned not only with the professional quality of prospective nominees, but also with their judicial philosophy. As presidential counsel Fred F. Fielding noted, "We have an opportunity to restore a philosophical balance that you don't have across the board right now."

The promotion of a lower court judge to a higher court can also be seen as furthering the concept of a professional judiciary, although it does not appear that pure merit was the governing factor with the Reagan first term elevations. The same undoubtedly holds true for the appointments of other administrations. Politically, the elevation of a federal district judge enables an administration to make two appointments: the elevation that fills the appeals court position; and the appointment to fill the vacancy thus created on the federal district bench.

Another striking finding . . . is the proportion of Reagan appeals court appointees who were law school professors at the time of appointment. Because Robert Bork had left his professorship at Yale Law School some six months before and at the time of selection was a senior partner in the Washington, D.C. firm of Kirkland & Ellis, he was not counted in the professor of law category. Were he counted, the proportion of professors of law would be about one out of five Reagan appeals court appointees, a modern record.

Bork, as well as the five other law professors, were all known as conservative thinkers and advocates of judicial restraint with a tendency toward deference to government in matters of alleged civil liberties or civil rights violations. These appointees also had a track record of published works so that their candidacies could be evaluated as to their compatibility with the Administration's vision of the role of the courts. Further, the appointment of academics was expected to provide intellectual leadership on the circuits and a potential pool of candidates for vacancies that might occur on the Supreme Court. It will be of more than academic interest to see whether the second term appointments will draw as heavily from the law schools as did those from the first term. Over the last 20 years (and excluding the small number of Ford appointees), the Reagan Administration drew the least from the ranks of those in private practice.

In terms of experience, about three out of four Reagan appointees had judicial or prosecutorial experience in their backgrounds, with judicial experience being the most prominent. Indeed, over three times as many appeals court appointees had judicial experience as had prosecutorial experience, and the proportion with prosecutorial experience was the lowest of the five administations. This also supports the suggestion that Justice officials were more concerned with judicial track records in evaluating ideological compatibility than with prosecutorial track records.

Education and affirmative action: The majority of the Reagan appointees as well as the Carter, Nixon, and Johnson appointees attended private schools for both their undergraduate and law school training. About one out of four Reagan appointees had an Ivy League undergraduate education, the highest proportion of the appointees of the five administrations. However, the proportion of Reagan appointees with an Ivy League law school education was the *lowest* of all five administrations. Although some of the appointees attended prestigious non-Ivy League law schools both public and private, it may be that the quality of legal education of the Reagan appeals court appointees, like that of the district court appointees, was on the whole somewhat lower than the Carter appointees, a finding also reported by Fowler.

In terms of appointments of women and minorities, the first term Reagan record for the appeals courts can be seen as a dramatic retreat from the Carter record. Of 31 appeals court appointees only one was a woman, only one was black, and only one was Hispanic. Whether the participation of Carole Dinkins (until her departure from the Justice Department in March 1985) and Jane Swift in the selection process will result in the active consideration and recruitment of women to the appeals courts will be something to watch for during the second term. It may be that the male dominated selection process is such that there is greater willingness to recruit women for the district bench than for the more important and prestigious appeals courts. The Administration may also want their women appointees to the district courts to prove themselves on the bench before being actively considered for promotion.

ABA ratings and other factors: The proportion of Reagan appointees with the highest ABA rating, that of Exceptionally Well Qualified, was the highest since the Johnson Administration. However, the Reagan appointees also had the highest proportion of all five administrations of those with the lowest Qualified rating. Interestingly, all five who were professors of law at the time of their nominations were only rated Qualified despite their distinguished legal scholarly achievements. This suggests that the ABA ratings are biased against legal academics who are not active practitioners. Had Robert Bork remained on the Yale Law School faculty rather than joining Kirkland & Ellis, it is a matter of conjecture whether he would have received the Exceptionally Well Qualified rating he in fact received as a senior partner of that prestigious District of Columbia firm.

None of the Reagan first term appointees to the appeals courts were Democrats. The absence of any appointees affiliated with the opposition political party last occurred in the Administration of Warren Harding. As for prominent past partisan activism, however, the proportion is lower than that for the Carter appointees and comparable to that of the Ford, Nixon, and Johnson appointees. . . .

As for religious origin or affiliation, the Reagan appeals court appointments were somewhat similar to his district court appointments with the proportion of Catholics akin to that of the previous Democratic Administrations of Carter and Johnson.

Given the importance of the appeals courts and the desire of the Reagan Administration to place on the bench those with a judicial philosophy compatible with that of the Administration, one might expect that there would be an active effort to recruit younger people who could be expected to remain on the bench longer. There is a hint that this may have occurred. The average age of the Reagan appointees was 51.5, the lowest for all five administrations.

The net worth of the Reagan appointees compared to the Carter appointees [shows that] the differences between both groups of appointees are similar to those for the district court appointees. Over one in five Reagan appointees were millionaires as compared to one in ten Carter appointees. Two-thirds had a net worth between $200,000 and under $1 million, compared to 56 per cent of the Carter appointees. At the lowest end of the net worth continuum, one in ten Reagan appointees had a net worth of under $200,000, compared to one in three of the Carter appointees.

The net worth findings for the appeals courts, as well as the district courts, underscore the importance of Chief Justice Warren Burger's urgent request that Congress dramatically increase the pay of the federal judiciary. The Chief Justice observed that since he became Chief Justice 30 of the 43 resignations from the federal bench were due in part to financial reasons. Although there are differences in degree between the Carter and Reagan appointees' wealth that may mirror to some extent different constituencies of the parties, there is a very real danger that the federal courts will soon become the preserve of the wealthy for only they will be able to afford the assumption of judicial office. If it is considered desirable that monetary considerations not affect judicial recruitment, then judicial salaries will have to be increased significantly.

IDEOLOGICAL SUCCESS?

We have thus far seen how the Reagan Administration has to some extent reshaped the judicial selection process, and we have examined the demographic and attribute profiles of the Reagan district and appeals court appointees as compared to those of four previous presidents. The questions remain, have the Reagan appointees met the expectations of the Administration? Have the Reagan appointees begun to shift the ideological balance on the lower courts?

The answers to these questions must await systematic empirical analysis; there is fragmentary evidence that has begun to emerge, however, that suggests that the Reagan Administration on the whole is satisfied. For example, a study by the Center for Judicial Studies of every decision published by every Reagan appointee serving during the first two years of Reagan's first term concluded that the overwhelming majority of appointees demonstrated judicial restraint along the lines favored by the Administration.

Students in a seminar at the University of Massachusetts-Amherst conducted a class project in which published decisions of selected appeals courts and Reagan appointees were analyzed. Although these analyses were exploratory and their findings must be interpreted with caution, here, too, it would appear that, with few exceptions, the Reagan appointees have joined the more conservative wings of their courts particularly on issues of alleged violations of civil liberties. Another finding that emerged was that the differences that occurred between the Reagan appointees and the Carter (and other Democratic) appointees were differences of degree and that it was rare for there to be the sort of dramatic cleavages on the appeals courts as is found on the Supreme Court. Nevertheless, the Reagan appointees appear to be making their imprint.

Other accounts of the Reagan appointees on the courts have also focused on the appeals courts. In one, Jonathan Rose, the former Assistant Attorney General for Legal Policy during the first three years of Reagan's first term, was quoted as being "tremendously pleased" with the records of the law professors chosen by the Administration for the appeals courts. An extensive analysis of Robert Bork's record and more anecdotal accounts of other appointees also provide additional evidence on this point.

At the Supreme Court level there is reason for the Administration to be pleased with its appointee Justice Sandra Day O'Connor. O'Connor was either the second or third most conservative justice in matters of civil liberties, rejecting the civil liberties claim in 71 per cent of the cases decided with full opinion in the 1981 term, and in the 1982 and 1983 terms rejecting 75 percent of such civil liberties arguments. Her opinions, whether for the majority, concurrences, or dissents on a variety of issues ranging from abortion to criminal procedures were surely, with few exceptions, a source of satisfaction to the Administration.

Although political party platforms are notorious for being treated as merely campaign rhetoric, the 1984 Republican Party platform can be seen as containing a good summary of the Reaganizing philosophy for the judiciary that also points the way for the second term. The platform reads in part:

> Judicial power must be exercised with deference towards state and local officials . . . . It is not a judicial function to reorder the economic, political, and social priorities of our nation . . . . We commend the President for appointing federal judges committed to the rights of law-abiding citizens and traditional family values . . . . In his second term, President Reagan will continue to appoint Supreme Court and other federal judges who share our commitment to judicial restraint.[4]

FUTURE APPOINTMENTS

Although the above quote from the 1984 Republican Party platform does suggest the ideological or philosophical outlook of the people the Administration will be seeking for judgeships during the second term, we can also offer some projections as to the likely makeup of the demographic and attribute profiles of second term appointees. Central to this undertaking is the realization that just as there was no indication at the start of the second term that there would be sharp alterations in other areas of public policy, so with the judiciary there is no reason to anticipate a shift in the course already set during the first term. What this means is that second term appointees will continue to be predominantly white male Republicans, many of whom are at the upper end of the socioeconomic spectrum. Women will likely continue to receive appointments at a level comparable to that for the first term, which will place the Reagan Administration second only to the Carter Administration in terms of appointments to women. As for black Americans, there is no reason to believe that there will be a marked change from the poor record of the first term during the second term.

Judicial experience should continue to be important for the Administration and used to assess the track record of prospective appointees. For the courts of appeals, law school professors will likely continue to hold some attraction for the Administration, both because of the relative ease of identifying a judicial philosophy from published writings and the desire to place conservative intellectual leaders on these important collegial courts.

---

4. See the text of the 1984 Republican Party platform and in particular the quoted material in 42 CONGRESSIONAL QUARTERLY WEEKLY REPORT 2110 (August 25, 1984).

It will be of interest to see whether the Administration broadens its recruitments efforts, particularly at the appeals court level, to find Democrats who share the Administration's outlook or whether the extreme partisanship discussed previously will prevail during the second term.

Of major interest during the second term will be the filling of any Supreme Court vacancies that occur. There is frequent speculation along these lines in the media. How a Supreme Court vacancy is filled will signal the seriousness of the Administration's ideological goals. If the Administration turns to a conservative personal friend of the President's not known for intellectual brilliance instead of one of the conservative intellectual leaders on the appeals courts, it may be interpreted as a failure to fully utilize the power of appointment to most effectively reshape judicial policy.

There has also been speculation about the Chief Justiceship. If the Chief Justiceship becomes vacant, it is possible that Justice O'Connor would be elevated to that position, thus enabling the Administration to make another historic appointment and at the same time have an associate justiceship to fill. But even if the President makes *no* Supreme Court appointments, the Reagan Administration will have left an indelible mark on the judiciary and the course of American law with its lower court appointments.

Ours is a historic political era that in the pendulum of American politics has come every 30 to 40 years. The era of New Deal Democratic political domination of American politics ended with the election of 1968. In all likelihood, were it not for Watergate, the new conservative Republican era would then have been firmly established. It took Ronald Reagan and his Administration to seize the historic opportunity to reshape American politics. Barring economic or military catastrophies, the cycle of conservative Republican domination may well last until the turn of the century. The Reagan Administration correctly sees the courts as having the power to further or hinder Administration goals; thus judicial appointments are of major importance for this Administration in its attempt to reshape public policy. How successful the Administration will ultimately be must await more extensive analysis of the judicial decisionmaking of the first and second term appointments.

The Roosevelt Administration was successful in its struggle with the federal judiciary and the federal courts abandoned or modified interpretations of the Constittution that, in the name of economic liberty, had prevented government from acting in certain areas of economic and social welfare policy. The crucial question now is will the Reagan Administration be successful in its struggle with the federal judiciary to have the federal courts abandon or modify interpretations of the Constitution that, in the name of civil liberty, place restraints on government when acting in certain areas concerning protection from criminals, public morality, and social policy? It is no surprise that students of the courts will be intently watching judicial appointments by a second term Reagan Administration.   ■

FEDERAL LAW GETS A REAGAN-MEESE STAMP

Stewart Powell

President Reagan's changes on the Supreme Court highlight a sweeping effort to recast the federal legal system from top to bottom before his administration's time runs out.

Orchestrated by Atty. Gen. Edwin Meese, the second-term White House is also putting a lasting conservative imprint on the lower federal courts and significantly reordering federal law-enforcement priorities. Proposed lifetime appointments for William Rehnquist as Chief Justice and Antonin Scalia as Associate Justice are only the most vivid examples of a campaign designed, as one Reagan aide puts it, to make sure that "it's going to be a longer [Reagan] revolution."

Indeed, Congress has balked at many of the key social issues on conservatives' wish lists—measures to permit prayer in public school, restrict abortion, tighten anti-pornography laws and ban school busing for desegregation. Democrats in November could regain control of the Senate, making legislative action even less likely. Conceded White House Communications Director Patrick Buchanan in March: Naming just two Justices to the Supreme Court "could do more to advance the social agenda . . . . than anything Congress can accomplish in 20 years."

No one is better suited to secure the President's political legacy than an Attorney General with the closest ties to the White House since Robert Kennedy served his brother John in the 1960s. Meese, 54, a graduate of Yale and the University of California's Law School at Berkeley, sees Reagan at will, chairs the Domestic Policy Council and sits on the National Security Council. "He's very controversial," says American Bar Association President William Falsgraf, "and depending on how you feel about an issue, you view him as either hero or devil."

To supporters, Meese is an easygoing ex-prosecutor who lends support to hard-pressed police departments, favors victims' rights over criminals' and carries the Reagan mandate into every corner of the bureaucracy. "Law enforcement," says the ABA president, "is as efficient and aggressive as it's ever been."

To detractors, the Reagan insider is a legal vigilante ready to rid states of the burden of abiding by the Bill of Rights, to limit free expression and threaten federal employees with drug testing. The Democratic Senatorial Campaign Committee recently used the specter of Meese himself being "only a heartbeat away" from appointment to the Supreme Court to raise money in a direct-mail drive—though Meese has said for many months that he does not want to be a Justice.

Controversy notwithstanding, Meese is fast becoming known around

Washington as the man who makes the judges. He "did have a considerable amount of research already done" on candidates for the Supreme Court when vacancies opened, says a White House insider. Meese "played an equal role" with Chief of Staff Donald Regan in selecting Rehnquist and Scalia.

Meese has led the way in selecting many of the 281 federal judges that Reagan has named to the 761-member federal judiciary since taking office. The President soon will have named majorities on at least five of the 13 U.S. courts of appeal, including the influential appeals tribunal in Washington, D.C., considered second only to the Supreme Court in clout. Fifty-seven more vacancies in coming months will insure Meese's continuing role in shaping the judiciary. It is expected that by the end of Reagan's second term in 1989, he will have named half the judges on the federal bench.

With many appointees in their middle years, the Reagan judges have long careers ahead and will be in a good position to succeed to higher courts under future Republican Presidents.

Federal judges handle nearly 330,000 cases a year. Appeals courts are becoming more crucial for clarifying Supreme Court rulings in which even the majority is split on the reasoning. Reagan's appointees to lower courts already have influenced everything from discrimination suits to the death penalty. Fewer stays of execution have made possible 27 executions in the past 18 months—vs. eight in the seven previous years. The length of average federal sentences has risen 12 percent since 1980.

Meese is complementing installation of conservative jurists with a coordinated drive to set new priorities for the Justice Department. A 46 percent increase in annual funds since 1980 has stiffened enforcement of criminal statutes, with agencies such as the Federal Bureau of Investigation reaping as much as a 95 percent increase. Antitrust cases have dropped 63 percent since 1980 as the administration "gets off the back" of business. Money for prosecution of tax cases has trailed increases elsewhere.

Government lawyers are attempting to reverse many of the civil-rights milestones of recent years, from legalized abortion to affirmative action. The Attorney General seeks to weaken a 1965 executive order that now requires promotion of women and minorities at 15,000 firms employing 23 million people. And his department has used a Supreme Court decision stemming from a dispute in Memphis to urge 51 other localities to rescind affirmative-action programs that set numerical goals. It also seeks to curtail busing. Many of these changes are being challenged in a federal court system in which already 37 percent of the judges have been named by the President. "Meese's accomplishments are yet to come," declares Alan Dershowitz of Harvard Law School. "He has been building an edifice brick by brick and that takes time."

Some think that with the predicted tilt to the right by the Supreme Court, lower court judges may feel freer to test precedents set in earlier years by the Justices.

As the battle shifts to the courtroom, the age-old debate of judges' politics vs. qualifications is erupting anew. No "litmus test" exists for conservatism, insists Meese, only the understanding that judges exercise restraint by not setting public policy. Review of prospective judges is vital, says Bruce Fein, who screened candidates while at the Justice Department. "When you have a judiciary that is as powerful as ours and appointed for life, this is your one chance."

Critics accuse Meese of being too concerned with candidates' politics. "His idea of checks and balances," says Anthony Podesta, president of the 250,000-member People for the American Way, "is to check with the [conservative] Heritage Foundation first and then to balance their recommendations with" those of TV evangelist Pat Robertson and conservative Senator Jesse Helms (R-N.C.).

Increasingly, nominees' qualifications are coming under vigorous scrutiny. The American Bar Association, which has reviewed nominees since the 1950s, has given 13 of Reagan's last 60 appeals-court nominations the compromise "qualified/unqualified" rating, compared with three of Jimmy Carter's 56 appeals-court nominations. Says Sheldon Goldman of the University of Massachusetts: "We now have the danger of ideological hacks on the bench."

Counters ABA President Falsgraf: "Ideology is always a factor for a President. Putting that aside, the appointments have been of the highest caliber."

The GOP-controlled Senate balked at two recent nominees. The Senate Judiciary Committee rejected Jefferson Sessions as a district-court judge for Alabama, citing alleged racial insensitivity. It sent to the Senate floor without recommendation the nomination of Daniel Manion for an appeals court in Chicago, after critics branded Manion's legal skills worse than mediocre. The White House is pressing the Senate for approval of Manion before the July 4 recess to clear the way for summer confirmation hearings on Rehnquist and then Scalia. The Manion fight is touch and go.

For lower-court appointments, insiders said, the White House may now turn to candidates less controversial than Sessions and Manion. "It's much more contentious, adversarial and partisan on the Hill now," says Jonathan Rose, a Washington lawyer who supervised judicial selection in the first term. "It's a venomous atmosphere."

With stakes so high and controversy building, Senate confirmation proceedings are bound to focus public attention once again on the delicate balance of politics and qualifications that accompanies appointment of the men and women who interpret the law long after Presidents have come and gone.   ■

Library of Congress

PART IV

Public Policy

H ow America's government carries out its broad responsibilities—the goals and assumptions underlying the laws it passes, the programs it establishes, and the other actions it takes—are called public policy. Policymaking means that government must make choices. It has limited resources, and it cannot do everything at once.

The policymaking process involves agenda-building, formulation, adoption, implementation, and evaluation. Issues must get on the agenda before they can be acted upon. This may come about through the influence of events, or actors, or both. In the formulation stage, a proposal is developed for remedying the problem posed by the issue. Policy adoption (and rejection) takes place when policymakers make decisions about alternative solutions. The policies adopted are the "outputs" of the system, and they are put into operation in the implementation stage, assessed as to their real effects in the evaluation stage. These are not totally separate stages, though. They overlap and are interactive.

In Part IV, our purpose is to consider the policy process and policy outputs, particularly in two fields, two of the most important among those dealt with by our federal government. Chapter 12 deals with national economic policy. Chapter 13 focuses on the subject of foreign policy and national security.

Economic Policy

Political science and economics were once parts of the same discipline. Today, quite obviously, what happens in the economy affects politics and government, just as what happens in politics and government affects the economy.

Ours is a *capitalist* economy—that is, the means of production are privately, rather than publicly, owned. Yet, the federal government intervenes in the market place. It regulates business and industry in regard to such matters as wages and working conditions, pollution, product standards, prevention of monopoly, and sometimes, and in some instances, prices.

The federal government also seeks to manage the national economy. The aims of federal economic policy include the stimulation of economic growth and job creation, the maintenance of moderate interest rates and a low level of inflation and unemployment, and the assurance of at least a minimum standard of living for all.

Federal economic management uses both *fiscal policy* and *monetary policy*. Fiscal policy—what is done in regard to taxes, spending. and borrowing—is the shared province of the Congress (and its powerful appropriations, tax, and budget committees) and the president and the Executive Department (including, particularly, the Office of Management and Budget, the Treasury Department, and the Council of Economic Advisers). Monetary policy—which can expand or contract the supply of money and thus affect the level of interest rates—is mostly within the province of the largely independent Federal Reserve Bank.

Economics is far from an exact science. Economists of different theoretical schools disagree about what the nation's economic policy should be. But no one would say today that the government should keep its hands off the economy and let things happen—to unemployment, inflation, interest rates— as they might.

Economic policy, then, is a centrally important output of government. How is it made? What should be its goals? How effective is it in attaining those goals? In this chapter, we will first discuss fiscal policy and the federal budget process. Then, we will turn our attention to the consideration of wealth and poverty in the United States. How well our welfare and antipoverty programs work will be our next concern. And, finally we will focus on the goals of economic policy, with a discussion of the Catholic Bishops' letter on this subject.

FISCAL POLICY AND THE BUDGET PROCESS

Sometimes the federal government has run a deficit—spent more than it has taken in—on purpose. Sometimes the federal government has appeared unable to keep from it. During President Reagan's first term, the national debt went from one trillion dollars to *two* trillion dollars!

How did this happen? Was it bad? Was the so-called "Gramm-Rudman" approach adopted by Congress in 1985 a good one? Was it workable? Was it constitutional? These are some of the questions that are taken up in the article that follows.

DEFICITS, DEBT—AND GRAMM-RUDMAN
Fred R. Harris

In the first flush of victory, after President Reagan, in December of 1985, had signed the radical new Gramm-Rudman budget balancing act into law, reporters were encouraged to call it Gramm-Rudman-Hollings. This was to give a coauthor, Senator Ernest Hollings, equal credit for it. But critics said that as soon as the automatic, across-the-board budget-cutting measure went into effect, it would become so unpopular that Hollings would be glad that his name was usually left off in references to it.

When the government takes in less than enough to cover what it spends, this *deficit* must be made up by borrowing—from banks and other private lenders. From time to time, Congress has to pass a law, increasing the limit on the total national debt allowed—the total amount the federal government can owe. There's always a lot of political and partisan debate each time the debt limit question comes up. But, finally, the limit is always raised—because, of course, the government has to pay the debts it has already incurred.

THE NATIONAL DEBT

The first serious increase in the national debt came during World War I, but only up to $25 billion. Afterwards, the debt was whittled back down. World War II's military spending again produced federal deficits and increases in the national debt. The debt stood at $49 billion in 1946, but it went back down a little during the postwar years of President Truman. In the Eisenhower years of the 1950s, the national debt inched upward, and this trend continued during John Kennedy's New Frontier years, which began in 1960 and were cut short by his assassination. Deficits and debt continued to increase during the late 1960s Great Society-Vietnam War years of Lyndon Johnson. He asked Congress for both "guns and butter," as reporters put it, without new taxes to pay for them. Still, as noted earlier, President Johnson was able to balance the budget in fiscal 1969.

Up to that time, deficits had primarily been caused by *overspending*. During the early 1970s (the years of President Nixon) there was a huge jump in federal deficits and a corresponding increase in the national debt because of *undercollection, a drop in federal revenues*. Nixon's economic policies, intended to fight inflation, produced a recession. People were put out of work. Factories were shut down or slowed down. When people are out of work, of course, they don't pay much income tax. So, federal collections went way down. And, incidentally, federal unemployment and welfare expenditures went up, as they always do when people are out of work. What was the result? The largest federal deficits ever. But *these* deficits were almost nothing compared to the really huge deficits and enormous increases in the national debt that were to come during the first term of President Reagan, which began in 1981.

It took more than 190 years—from George Washington's inauguration until the first months of Ronald Reagan's presidency—for the national debt to reach one trillion dollars. How much *is* a trillion dollars? When the national debt hit that figure in 1981, President Reagan called it an "incomprehensible" amount. "If you had a stack of $1,000 bills in your hand only 4 inches high," he said, "you'd be a millionaire." And he added, "A trillion dollars would be a stack of $1,000 bills 67 miles high." Just a little over four years later in his administration, in 1985, that symbolic stack President Reagan spoke about was twice as high. During that short period, the national debt had doubled—to *two* trillion dollars!

THE REAGAN DEFICITS

How had the deficits and the debt grown so unbelievably rapidly? Deficits, as we have seen, can result from overspending or undercollection, or both. In President Reagan's case, it was both. Running for president in 1984, candidate Ronald Reagan had called for great increases in defense spending, cuts in domestic spending, cuts in taxes, and a balanced budget. George Bush, while he was an opponent of Ronald Reagan for the Republican nomination and before he joined him on the ticket, called this "voodoo economics."

Riding a crest of popularity and, some said, a popular mandate to carry out his promises, President Reagan pretty much had his way with Congress after taking office in 1981. He got the great increase in defense spending he wanted. From 1980 to 1985, defense authorizations more than doubled—from $141 billion to $283 billion. Defense grew to 28 percent of the total federal budget—the highest level in peace-time history, even after adjusting for inflation, according to the Congressional Budget Office.

The president got a decline in expenditures for social programs as a percentage of Gross National Product (that is, the total of all goods and services annually produced in the country). President Reagan did not push for a decrease in so-called "entitlements," which include such things as Social Security and veterans' pensions—and these continued to increase sharply.

The president got an unprecedented tax cut, the largest in history. During the five-year period from 1982 to 1986, federal revenues were cut by about $700 billion. Tight money policies helped bring on a recession in 1981 and 1982, and, as in the Nixon recession, this helped worsen the deficit.

So, the president got his increase in defense spending, and he got a cut in the rate of growth in social programs. President Reagan also got his tax cut. But what he didn't get, of course, was a balanced budget. Just the opposite. And, as the debt mushroomed, so did the amount that the government had to pay for interest on it. In 1986 alone, interest on the national debt cost the federal government $136 billion, almost as big by itself as the annual federal deficit, which was running at something over $200 billion.

On the tax cut, the president was following the advice of economists and others, including Representative Jack Kemp of New York, who advocated what was called "supply-side" economics. The idea was to stimulate investment through a tax cut, especially for business and investors, so that the resultant increase in economic activity would result in increased tax revenues, rather than increased deficits. Supply-siders pointed to the tax cut early in the administration of President Kennedy that had that effect. But, back then, there was not the level of idle, or unused, plant capacity there was in 1981. New equipment in the early 1960s could be used to increase production. New equipment in 1981 could not, because plants were producing far less than they were *already* able to with the equipment they *already* had. Some supply-siders said Reagan didn't give supply-side economics a fair chance because his tight money policies and high interest rates caused an intervening recession. The fact was, though, that Reagan policies did *not* greatly increase production and tax revenues; instead, they produced greatly increased *deficits* and national debt.

THE MEANING OF DEBT AND DEFICITS

How alarmed should we be about the size of the annual deficits and the national debt? Should taxpayers be jumping off buildings? No. The amounts are worrisome, but they are not yet disastrous.

Some people say that we should run the government like a business. Others say, "My family has to live within its means. Why shouldn't the government?" Good questions. But, in a way, the federal government *is* run like a business—at least in regard to borrowing. No business could exist without going into debt, and, for most, like the Bell Telephone companies, for example, the amount of the debt keeps increasing as improvements are made to the system. Most families could not make it, either, withoutout borrowing, especially to buy a car or a home.

When you go to the bank to borrow money, one thing the bank wants to know is whether the collateral you're using as security for the loan—the car or the house, for example—is worth at least as much as the loan amount. The bank also asks for a financial statement showing your assets (what you own) and your liabilities (what you owe). But the federal government is an unusual borrower. It lists only its liabilities—the national debt. It doesn't list its assets—its national parks, cars, guns, military bases, government buildings, or government enterprises, such as the Federal Housing Administration or the Bonneville Power Authority. This is just as well, because we are not going to sell most of this stuff anyway (although President Reagan has said he wants to sell off some of the enterprises).

A bank making a private loan primarily wants to know about your *ability to pay*—will you have enough left over to pay the loan payments after you subtract present obligations from your income? And that's what's important about government borrowing, too—the ability to pay.

Some people have pointed out that if the national debt were required to be paid off immediately by dividing it up equally among all Americans, the share of an American family of four would be $34,675. But such examples are not very helpful, because no such requirement is ever going to be made. And comparing the dollar amount of the debt now with, say, the dollar amount in 1946 is not very helpful either. A dollar owed today is much less than a dollar owed then because of inflation, the decrease in what the dollar buys.

A useful way to measure the federal government's ability to pay is to look at the relationship between the national debt and the Gross National Product, the total value of goods and services produced in the United States each year. Why is this important? Because it tells us something about the general strength and health of the national economy—and that is what federal taxes are collected on. Back in 1946, the national debt was over 134 percent of the Gross National Product. Then the percentage began to drop—down to around 82 percent in 1951, on down to about 66 in 1956, to about 40 in 1971, and further down to around 35 percent in 1981, when President Reagan took office. Since then, the national debt has not only climbed in total dollars. It has also climbed as a percentage of Gross National Product—back up to 49.4 percent in 1986. This percentage is not as high, of course, as it was in 1961 and earlier.

But many economists are worried because expenditures have been greatly increased for defense and entitlement programs and there have been big cuts in taxes. By the end of 1985, the federal government was spending $24 for every $19 it took in. And the debt was growing faster than the Gross National Product. Does the federal government have the ability to pay? Yes. Is our debt a larger percentage of Gross National Product than, say, Japan's? Yes, a little. Than West Germany's or Canada's? Yes, a lot. Is the percentage too high? Not yet. Does the federal government still have sufficient ability to pay? Sure.

What's the worry, then? Some people say that interest rates will never come down to what they used to be until we get the deficits down. But the fact is that during the Reagan administration, interest rates have been coming steadily down even as the deficits and debt have been zooming up. A stickier problem is that of the *trade* deficit. We're buying from suppliers in other countries a lot more than we're selling there—and that means fewer jobs here for our people, among other things. A major reason is that the dollar is valued too high in comparison to other currencies, like the British pound or the Japanese yen. We're hurt, therefore, by the fact that our goods offered abroad cost too much, while what foreigners sell here is relatively cheap. This will change, it is said, and the danger of renewed inflation will be lessened if federal deficits are reduced, over time, and then eliminated.

Some liberal economists, who advocate a kind of neo-Keynesianism, say that the large deficits we've been running have actually been good for us, that they have fueled the recovery that brought us out of recession and cut the rate of unemployment in the country. By early 1986, the rate of unemployment had come down to its lowest level since President Reagan took office.

English economist John Maynard Keynes, writing back in 1936, argued, among other things, that unemployment results from inadequate *spending*—by consumers, investors, and government. His remedy, then, for recession and unemployment was greater spending—by government directly or by tax cuts, in order to leave more money in the hands of consumers and investors for spending by them, or both. For many years—with Democratic presidents like Kennedy and Republicans like Nixon—the United States practiced Keynesian economics—borrowing and spending when it was felt necessary to stimulate the economy, even if this meant a greater national debt. Conservatives, led by Ronald Reagan and others, began increasingly to attack this kind of government spending and call for a balanced budget.

But, in the midst of the deep recession during his first term, President Reagan and his then Treasury Secretary, Donald Regan, changed and seemed to adopt a kind of Keynesian line, declaring that deficits were not all that bad after all. They financed an economic recovery through government spending and un- precedentedly high government borrowing. In a kind of political switch, the Democrats in the Congress began to complain about the national debt. So did that party's 1984 presidential candidate, Walter Mondale. His forthright advocacy of a tax increase to help balance the budget probably cost him support at the polls, especially after President Reagan took an increasingly adamant stand against new taxes.

The liberal economists who said that, actually, the deficits of recent years had been good, had brought us out of inflation and cut unemployment, just as Lord Keynes advocated, quarreled with the *purposes* of President Reagan's increased spending. They said that instead of a huge military buildup, the spending should have been directed toward domestic goals that would improve the quality of American life.

BALANCED BUDGET EFFORTS

Still, political leadership of both parties—and public opinion—put a balanced budget high on the national agenda for action. The U. S. Senate passed a proposed constitutional amendment to require that the federal government balance its budget, as most states are required to do. But critics of this plan pointed out that states don't have to worry about spending for national security, nor are they called upon, individually, to take economic measures from time to time to affect national rates of unemployment and inflation. A constitutional amendment requiring a balanced federal budget, critics said, would have to have so many exceptions in it that it would be meaningless. The proposal failed to get the necessary two-thirds vote in the House of Representatives.

Some issues—like the federal budget and the debt limit—are automatically and regularly on the congressional agenda for action. Normally, they are dealt with on an *incremental* basis—that is, the basic concepts are not touched; changes are relatively small and are patched on to the existing framework. There is usually little invention and innovation and no starting from scratch. But that was not the case when Congress, in December of 1985, adopted the radical Gramm-Rudman budget-balancing act.

Earlier, in 1974, Congress had adopted a reformed system for dealing with the budget, creating separate new budget committees in each house and establishing the Congressional Budget Office to do the staff work. The idea was to give the Congress a unified way to deal with the whole budget (rather than have the various committees and subcommittees deal with it piecemeal), to set priorities on spending, and to adopt, each session, overall limits on taxing, spending, and borrowing. But the process did not work very well. Year after year, the Congress fell further behind in trying to agree to overall budget resolutions. Critics of the system pointed to its impotence in the face of rising deficits.

So, members of Congress felt increasingly frustrated about rising deficits. A Gallup poll in mid-1985 showed that 58 percent of Americans thought deficits were a "very serious" national problem, and another 23 percent thought they were at least "fairly serious." To deal with the deficits, should Congress cut spending, or raise taxes, or both? A majority in Congress was probably ready to raise taxes, but President Reagan, in promising a sure veto of any such move, said, in Dirty Harry's words, "Go ahead: make my day." That left only spending cuts. The Gallup poll showed that cutting entitlement programs, like Social Security, would be the *least* popular means of reducing the deficit. Politically, members of Congress knew that that route was closed. Two-thirds of Americans favored cuts in defense spending. But again, President Reagan had declared that national security required a three percent annual increase in defense appropriations, over and above inflation. And, any time the Congress debated *individual* program cuts, they seemed to get in hopeless tangles, and they were inundated by interest-group and other counter-lobbying.

This, then was the setting for Gramm-Rudman, or, sometimes, Gramm-Rudman-Hollings — named for its principal authors, Senator Phil Gramm, a conservative Texan, new both to the Senate and to the Republican Party, Senator Warren Rudman, a Republican from Minnesota, and Senator Ernest Hollings, a fically conservative Democrat from South Carolina. Their plan was to put the budget on automatic pilot, as Senator Gary Hart, an opponent of Gramm-Rudman, charged.

GRAMM-RUDMAN

The plan, as eventually written into law, sets a declining limit on the deficit each year, until it reaches zero in fiscal 1991. In August of every year, after regular congressional budget action, the Congressional Budget Office and the President's Office of Management and Budget must make an estimate of the deficit. Then, with this report, the General Accounting Office was required to draft an order for the President's signature, automatically cutting spending across the board. Fifty percent of the cuts had to come from the military budget (with exceptions for multiyear procurement contracts) and fifty percent from the nonmilitary programs (with exceptions for Social Security, Medicaid, Aid to Families with Dependent Children, interest on the national debt, veterans' compensation, and certain programs for the poor). These automatic cuts were to be forestalled in any year only if Congress itself agreed upon a budget within the deficit limits.

Gramm-Rudman was never introduced as a bill, never considered in a congressional committee. It was offered as an amendment, a rider, on the Senate floor. The horse for this rider was the bill to increase the national debt limit to $2.079 trillion. With Gramm-Rudman in the saddle, the debt-limit horse took off. Many Democrats joined Republicans in support. Reagan endorsed Gramm-Rudman, though the plan was a much a surprise to the White House as to the Senate. Nobody could quite be sure what it would do. For example, New York Democratic Senator Daniel Patrick Moynihan opposed Gramm-Rudman because it would, he said, cut defense too severely. But Georgia's Senator Sam Nunn, also a Democrat and a supporter of a strong U. S. defense, supported it. Gary Hart called Gramm-Rudman a "fraud," a "mindless" surrender of the constitutional responsibility of Congress. "We are lacing ourselves into a fiscal straitjacket — as if to say, 'stop me before I kill again,' " he said. But Democrat Edward Kennedy voted for the plan, claiming it was the only way to save the Democratic social programs he supported. He and others hoped that the deficit limits would, at long last, force President Reagan to agree to a tax increase and to defense cuts.

Oddly, there was little overt lobbying for or against the legislation, except for last-minute objections from the Defense Department. House Democrats agreed to go along with Gramm-Rudman after making some changes in conference. Their support, a critic said, was based on "abject fear that they're not going to be able to explain in a 20-second TV spot next fall why they voted against Gramm-Rudman."

And, so, it became law. Many, if not most, knowledgeable observers, thought it was bad law. How can anyone know in advance, they asked, how much of a deficit will be appropriate for economic conditions during each of the next six years? Why does Gramm-Rudman rely only on cuts in spending to reduce the deficits? Why not also consider some increase in taxes? How can Congress abdicate its responsibility to establish spending priorities?

A lawsuit was filed at once by members of Congress and was headed for the Supreme Court to question the constitutionality of the new law. The Supreme Court ruled unconstitutional the automatic triggering of across-the-board cuts because this provision sought to give executive responsibilities to an agency, the General Accounting Office.

The weeping and gnashing of teeth started at once, too, as the first year's cuts—4.3 percent for domestic agencies and 4.9 percent for the military—began to be put into effect in early 1986. Would Congress simply evade the law it had so recently passed? Would Gramm-Rudman's strictures be followed even though not automatically triggered? Would Congress and the president get together on a deficit-reduction plan that included defense cuts and tax increases in order to avoid Gramm-Rudman's harsh strictures? Nobody knew for sure. But, as the Chair of the Senate Budget Committee, Republican Senator Pete Domenici of New Mexico, said, "I don't think anybody can predict how the way we do business will change. But it will be dramatic." ∎

WEALTH AND POVERTY IN AMERICA

The economic policy of the United States affects the distribution of wealth and income in the country. Among other goals of this policy is one of putting some floor under income to ameliorate poverty and its effects.

What is the extent of wealth and income in America and what do we think about the subject? Excerpted here, first, is a brief essay by economist Lester C. Thurow about the extensiveness and influence of wealth in the United States. Next, we reprint a short piece by another well-known economist, John Kenneth Galbraith, who outlines past and present approaches to, as he puts it, "get the poor off our conscience."

Lastly, there follows an article by I. A. Lewis and William Schneider that details and discusses a recent public opinion poll showing what Americans, including poor people, think about poverty.

THE LEVERAGE OF WEALTH
Lester C. Thurow

At a trivial level, it is almost impossible not to be interested in Forbes magazine's annual list of the 400 wealthiest individuals, minimum net worth $150 million, and 82 wealthiest families, minimum net worth $200 million. Subconsciously, we read their biographies hoping to find the elixir that will add us to the list. While the elixir—a rich father—is to be found (all of the 82 families and 241 of the 400 wealthiest individuals inherited all or a major part of their fortunes), it doesn't help most of us to point this out to our fathers.

Certainly, the Forbes 400 proves that America is still the land of economic opportunity—there are 159 entirely self-made individuals and one is only 29 years old. Yet the list also reveals a concentration of wealth that should trouble anyone concerned about the accumulation of economic power in the hands of a few.

How extensive is the wealth of America's wealthiest people? The combined net worth of Forbes's 482 individuals and families is at least $166 billion in business investment assets.

The influence of one's wealth, however, is not limited to one's net worth. Funds can be borrowed to expand that influence. Depending upon their line of business, Forbes's wealthy will have borrowed very different amounts. But let's assume, conservatively, that the average person on the Forbes list has borrowed an amount, or controls a family foundation with assets, equal to their net worth.

In most investment situations, one need not own 100 percent of a company's equity to control it. While the founders of large manufacturing firms will own large equity stakes, the old wealthy will control firms with small fractions of total equity. For instance, the Pew family (net worth $350 million) owns 6 percent of Sun, the oil company, but controls 7 family foundations ($1.8 billion in assets not counted by Forbes) that vote another 25 percent of the equity. Now make another very conservative assumption that on average it takes a 15 percent equity stake to have effective control.

Put these two assumptions together and the $166 billion in business net worth held by Forbes's 482 individuals and families leads to control over $2,200 billion in business assets—about 40 percent of all fixed nonresidential private capital in the United States.

Why should this concern us? Standard economics, after all, assumes that people accumulate wealth solely to provide future consumption privileges for themselves and their children. If this were not correct, we would have no grounds for concern.

But the standard assumption is incorrect. Future consumption is not the motive that leads to large accumulations of wealth. If the 12 billionaires on the Forbes list were to treat their wealth as an annuity to be consumed before death, they would have to spend $630,000 a day for the rest of their lives. Clearly they do not have enough time left to spend their money, much less enjoy it.

Great wealth is accumulated to acquire economic power. Wealth makes you an economic mover and shaker. Projects will happen, or not happen, depending upon your decisions. It allows you to influence the political process—elect yourself or others—and remold society in accordance with your views. It makes you an important person, courted by people inside and outside your family. Perhaps this explains why some people try to persuade Forbes that they are wealthy enough to merit inclusion.

Economic power is a source of social concern because power entails the ability to order others about. With great inequalities in the distribution of economic power, it is also hard to maintain the equality of influence that is the backbone of democracy.

The distribution of wealth was last measured officially in 1962. At that time, the bottom 25 percent of the population had no net worth, the top 19 percent had 76 percent of total net worth and the middle 56 percent had 24 percent of total net worth.

The distribution of wealth probably has become somewhat less unequal since 1962, mostly because home values have risen far more rapidly than the value of corporate securities. If one is concerned about economic power, however, it is a mistake to include home values in distributional measurements—they are not a source of wealth that can be used to control others.

To say that great wealth controls much of business America is not an exaggeration. To say whether this degree of control is good or bad goes far beyond a simple listing of the very rich. But it is a topic that merits more public discussion. ■

HOW TO GET THE POOR OFF OUR CONSCIENCE
John Kenneth Galbraith

I would like to reflect on one of the oldest of human exercises, the process by which over the years, and indeed over the centuries, we have undertaken to get the poor off our conscience.

Rich and poor have lived together, always uncomfortably and sometimes perilously, since the beginning of time. Plutarch was led to say: "An imbalance between the rich and poor is the oldest and most fatal ailment of republics." And the problems that arise from the continuing coexistence of affluence and poverty—and particularly the process by which good fortune is justified in the presence of the ill fortune of others—have been an intellectual preoccupation for centuries. They continue to be so in our own time.

One begins with the solution proposed in the Bible: the poor suffer in this world but are wonderfully rewarded in the next. Their poverty is a temporary misfortune; if they are poor and also meek, they eventually will inherit the earth. This is, in some ways, an admirable solution. It allows the rich to enjoy their wealth while envying the poor their future fortune.

Much, much later, in the twenty or thirty years following the publication in 1776 of *The Wealth of Nations*— the late dawn of the Industrial Revolution in Britain—the problem and its solution began to take on their modern form. Jeremy Bentham, a near contemporary of Adam Smith, came up with the formula that for perhaps fifty years was extraordinarily influential in British and, to some degree, American thought. This was utilitarianism. "By the principle of utility," Bentham said in 1789, "is meant the principle which approves or disapproves of every action whatsoever according to the tendency which it appears to have to augment or diminish the happiness of the party whose interest is in question." Virtue is, indeed must be, self-centered. While there were people with great good fortune and many more with great ill fortune, the social problem was solved as long as, again in Bentham's words, there was "the greatest good for the greatest number." Society did its best for the largest possible number of people; one accepted that the result might be sadly unpleasant for the many whose happiness was not served.

In the 1830s a new formula, influential in no slight degree to this day, became available for getting the poor off the public conscience. This is associated with the names of David Ricardo, a stockbroker, and Thomas Robert Malthus, a divine. The essentials are familiar: the poverty of the poor was the fault of the poor. And it was so because it was a product of their excessive fecundity: their grievously uncontrolled lust caused them to breed up to the full limits of the available subsistence.

This was Malthusianism. Poverty being caused in the bed meant that the rich were not responsible for either its creation or its amelioration. However, Malthus was himself not without a certain feeling of responsibility: he urged that the marriage ceremony contain a warning against undue and irresponsible sexual intercourse—a warning, it is fair to say, that has not been accepted as a fully effective method of birth control. In more recent times, Ronald Reagan has said that the best form of population control emerges from the market. (Couples in love should repair to R. H. Macy's, not their bedrooms.) Malthus, it must be said, was at least as relevant.

By the middle of the nineteenth century, a new form of denial achieved great influence, especially in the United States. The new doctrine, associated with the name of Herbert Spencer, was Social Darwinism. In economic life, as in biological development, the overriding rule was survival of the fittest. That phrase—"survial of the fittest"—came, in fact, not from Charles Darwin but from Spencer, and expressed his view of economic life. The elimination of the poor is nature's way of improving the race. The weak and unfortunate being extruded, the quality of the human family is thus strengthened.

One of the most notable American spokespersons of Social Darwinism was John D. Rockefeller—the first Rockefeller—who said in a famous speech: "The American Beauty rose can be produced in the splendor and fragrance which bring cheer to its beholder only by sacrificing the early buds which grow up around it. And so it is in economic life. It is merely the working out of a law of nature and a law of God."

In the course of the present century, however, Social Darwinism came to be considered a bit too cruel. It declined in popularity, and references to it acquired a condemnatory tone. We passed on to the more amorphous denial of poverty associated with Calvin Coolidge and Herbert Hoover. They held that public assistance to the poor interfered with the effective operation of the economic system—that such assistance was inconsistent with the economic design that had come to serve most people very well. The notion that there is something economically damaging about helping the poor remains with us to this day as one of the ways by which we get them off our conscience.

With the Roosevelt revolution (as previously with that of Lloyd George in Britain), a specific responsibility was assumed by the government for the least fortunate people in the republic. Roosevelt and the presidents who followed him accepted a substantial measure of responsibility for the old through Social Security, for the unemployed through unemployment insurance, for the unemployable and the handicapped through direct relief, and for the sick through Medicare and Medicaid. This was a truly great change, and for a time, the age-old tendency to avoid thinking about the poor gave way to the feeling that we didn't need to try—that we were, indeed, doing something about them.

In recent years, however, it has become clear that the search for a way of getting the poor off our conscience was not at an end; it was only suspended. And so we are now again engaged in this search in a highly energetic way. It has again become a major philosophical, literary, and rhetorical preoccupation, and an economically not unrewarding enterprise.

Of the four, maybe five, current designs we have to get the poor off our conscience, the first proceeds from the inescapable fact that most of the things that must be done on behalf of the poor must be done in one way or another by the government. It is then argued that the government is inherently incompetent, except as regards weapons design and procurement and the overall management of the Pentagon. Being incompetent and ineffective, it must not be asked to succor the poor; it will only louse things up or make things worse.

The allegation of government incompetence is associated in our time with the general condemnation of the bureaucrat—again excluding those concerned with national defense. The only form of discrimination that is still permissible—that is, still officially encouraged in the United States today—is discrimination against people who work for the federal government, especially on social welfare activities. We have great corporate bureaucracies replete with corporate bureaucrats, but they are good; only public bureaucracy and government servants are bad. In fact, we have in the United States an extraordinary good public service—one made up of talented and dedicated people who are overwhelmingly honest and only rarely given to overpaying for monkey wrenches, flashlights, coffee makers, and toilet seats. (When these aberrations have occurred, they have, oddly enough, all been in the Pentagon.) We have nearly abolished poverty among the old, greatly democratized health care, assured minorities of their civil rights, and vastly enhanced educational oportunity. All this would seem a considerable achievement for incompetent and otherwise ineffective people. We must recognize that the present condemnation of government and government administration is really part of the continuing design for avoiding responsibility for the poor.

The second design in this great centuries-old tradition is to argue that any form of public help to the poor only hurts the poor. It destroys morale. It seduces people away from gainful employment. It breaks up marriages, since women can seek welfare for themselves and their children once they are without their husbands.

There is no proof of this—none, certainly that compares that damage with the damage that would be inflicted by the loss of public assistance. Still, the case is made—and believed—that there is something gravely damaging about aid to the unfortunate. This is perhaps our most highly influential piece of fiction.

The third, and closely related, design for relieving ourselves of responsibility for the poor is the argument that public-assistance measures have an adverse effect on incentive. They transfer income from the diligent to the idle and feckless, thus reducing the effort of the diligent and encouraging the idleness of the idle. The modern manifestation of this is supply-side economics. Supply-side economics holds that the rich in the United States have not been working because they have too little income. So, by taking money from the poor and giving it to the rich, we increase effort and stimulate the economy. Can we really believe that any considerable number of the poor prefer welfare to a good job? Or that business people—corporate executives, the key figures in our time—are idling away their hours because of the insufficiency of their pay? This is a scandalous charge against the American businessperson, notably a hard worker. Belief can be the servant of truth—but even more of convenience.

The fourth design for getting the poor off our conscience is to point to the presumed adverse effect on freedom of taking responsibility for them. Freedom consists of the right to spend a maximum of one's money by one's own choice, and to see a minimum taken and spent by the government. (Again, expenditure on national defense is excepted.) In the enduring words of Professor Milton Friedman, people must be "free to choose."

This is possibly the most transparent of all of the designs; no mention is ordinarily made of the relation of income to the freedom of the poor. (Professor Friedman is here an exception; through the negative income tax, he would assure everyone a basic income.) There is, we can surely agree, no form of oppression that is quite so great, no constriction on thought and effort quite so comprehensive, as that which comes from having no money at all. Though we hear much about the limitation on the freedom of the affluent when their income is reduced through taxes, we hear nothing of the extraordinary enhancement of the freedom of the poor from having some money of their own to spend. Yet the loss of freedom from taxation to the rich is a small thing as compared with the gain in freedom from providing some income to the impoverished. Freedom we rightly cherish. Cherishing it, we should not use it as a cover for denying freedom to those in need.

Finally, when all else fails, we resort to simple psychological denial. This is a psychic tendency that in various manifestations is common to us all. It causes us to avoid thinking about death. It causes a great many people to avoid thought of the arms race and the consequent rush toward a highly probable extinction. By the same process of psychological denial, we decline to think of the poor. Whether they be in Ethiopia, the South Bronx, or even in such an Elysium as Los Angeles, we resolve to keep them off our minds. Think, we are often advised, of something pleasant.

These are the modern designs by which we escape concern for the poor. All, save perhaps the last, are in great inventive descent from Bentham, Malthus, and Spencer. Ronald Reagan and his colleagues are clearly in a notable tradition—at the end of a long history of effort to escape responsibility for one's fellow beings. So are the philosophers now celebrated in Washington: George Gilder, a greatly favored figure of the recent past, who tells to much applause that the poor must have the cruel spur of their own suffering to ensure effort; Charles Murray, who, to greater cheers, contemplates "scrapping the entire federal welfare and income-support structure for working and aged persons, including A.F.D.C., Medicaid, food stamps, unemployment insurance, Workers' Compensation, subsidized housing, disability insurance, and," he adds, "the rest. Cut the knot, for there is no way to untie it." By a triage, the worthy would be selected to survive; the loss of the rest is the penalty we should pay. Murray is the voice of Spencer in our time; he is enjoying, as indicated, unparalleled popularity in high Washington circles.

Compassion, along with the associated public effort, is the least comfortable, the least convenient, course of behavior and action in our time. But it remains the only one that is consistent with a totally civilized life. Also, it is, in the end, the most truly conservative course. There is no paradox here. Civil discontent and its consequences do not come from contented people—an obvious point. To the extent that we can make contentment as nearly universal as possible, we will preserve and enlarge the social and political tranquillity for which conservatives, above all, should yearn.   ∎

PUBLIC OPINION ON POVERTY
I. A. Lewis and William Schneider

In April, the *Los Angeles Times* interviewed 2,444 people, including an oversample of 272 individuals who, according to federal government guidelines, were living in poverty. The poll found precious little evidence of "a new selfishness" in American culture. On one hand, the American public has an enormous reserve of sympathy for the poor and for their plight. On the other hand, there is plenty of cynicism and even fatalism about government efforts to eliminate poverty. Those attempts haven't worked in the past, people feel, and they are not likely to work in the future. The poor themselves are inclined to agree with this assessment.

The Reagan administration shares the public view that many of these programs have failed, and it has tried to translate that aspect of the public's critique into policy. While the safety net for the most destitute has been preserved, the vigor with which past administrations approached anti-poverty programs has been missing in this one. The centerpieces of this administration have been efforts to get inflation and government spending under control. Supply-siders optimistically projected that a rising economic tide would lift all boats, even those under water.

According to the poll, the public does not buy this argument. Americans believe that it is proper and necessary for the federal government to take action to help the poor, even if its record in this area is not encouraging. That is essentially a moral conviction, and it overrides what people know to be the practical difficulties of mounting a war on poverty. People think that a lot of the money we have spent on behalf of the poor has been wasted or intercepted; the poor agree. People also acknowledge that we really don't know how to solve the poverty problem; the poor also agree with that. But neither of these practical considerations reverses the basic moral consensus that it is a primary responsibility of government to fight poverty. The fact that the government does not do it particularly well does not mean it shouldn't do it at all. On that point, the poor and the nonpoor resoundingly agree.

One of the clearest examples of sympathy for the poor in this study is the conviction that money and wealth ought to be more evenly shared by a larger percentage of the population. Income redistribution is supported by every income group, including those who make more than $75,000 a year. Nationwide, the public favors a more even distribution by two to one.

Also, a majority of Americans do not believe that poor people prefer to stay on welfare. By better than two to one (63 to 25 percent), they say the opposite is true: that poor people would rather earn their own living. And fewer than one American in four believes that we are "coddling" the poor. In fact, two out of three Americans believe that the poor can hardly get by on what the government gives them.

Whether the poor contribute as much as they take from society may be disputed by some, but there is little doubt about it among the majority of the public. Only 21 percent say that the poor don't pay their fair share of taxes, while 75 percent reject that view.

Moreover, by better than two to one, the public rejects the idea that poor people are worse off because they have less inborn ability to get ahead. Only 29 percent support that view, while fully 62 percent disagree.

Sympathy for the poor may be associated with the view that people who live in poverty don't hold steady jobs. After all, isn't that why they're in poverty? Only 28 percent think a large proportion of poor people hold steady jobs. Among poor people, however, 40 percent think that is the case. Their opinions seem closer to the truth. In fact, 44 percent of the poor people who responded to this study report that they do indeed work: 33 percent hold full-time jobs, 7 percent work part time, and 4 percent are self-employed. Apparently about a third of the poor hold steady jobs that are so low-paying that they don't provide an escape from poverty.

Not only are Americans sympathetic to the poor, but they are also willing to dig into their pockets to help. A clear majority of Americans would, in principle, favor an additional one-cent-a-dollar sales tax to be used to help the poor. The idea is supported by most demographic groups (people over sixty-five are one exception). Understandably, the poor themselves support the tax somewhat more enthusiastically (68 percent) than do others (56 percent).

It may come as no surprise that a substantial portion of the general public thinks poor people are lazy: 25 percent of the respondents in the *Los Angeles Times* poll express that opinion, and about the same percentage (23 percent) say they're not sure if that is the case. Together these two groups nearly equal the half who are convinced that the poor are hard-working. What may be surprisng to some, however, are the numbers of poor people who agree with this evaluation. More than a third of the poor say either that poor people are lazy or that one can't be sure about it.

As can be seen, . . . sympathy for the poor is notably stronger among women than among men. Women are more likely to see poverty as a long-term condition, to feel that the poor lack basic social and occupational skills, and to believe that conditions for those living in poverty are bad. The difference between men and women appears to be linked to a fatalistic view prevalent among women, particularly women who are not poor. Here is what happened, for instance, when respondents were asked whether most poor people remain poor for a long time and whether government knows how to solve poverty.

	Most poor remain poor	*Government doesn't know how to solve poverty*
Nonpoor women	79%	80%
Nonpoor men	68	66

Poor women are strongly supportive of more direct forms of aid; they are more likely than poor men to say that the purpose of the welfare system is to provide for the immediate needs of poor people rather than to help them get back on their feet again, and to favor spending money on direct aid rather than "trying to eliminate the causes of poverty."

One of the most striking findings of the *Los Angeles Times* poll is the widespread conviction that the federal government must take responsibility for the poor and must play a vigorous role in combatting poverty. Seventy-three percent of the American public favor federal government actions on behalf of the poor, while only 18 percent oppose such actions. Moreover, only 14 percent accept the view that poverty in the United States can be handled mainly by volunteer efforts; no less than 78 percent feel that there must be "substantial government involvement."

By two to one, those interviewed feel that the government ought to spend more rather than less money on poverty programs. When given a list and asked who on it should have the greatest responsibility for helping the poor, one-third said the government, far more than said churches (17 percent), families and relatives (12 percent), or voluntary charities (7 percent). Twenty-one percent said "the poor themselves," which still fell behind the proportion who said the government. Interestingly, the poor and the nonpoor both place the government first on the list (34 percent and 33 percent, respectively). The poor, however, are somewhat more likely to give primary responsibility to the poor themselves and to churches.

Still, when asked directly whether "government is responsible for the well-being of all its citizens and has an obligation to take care of them," or whether "people are responsible for their own well-being, and have an obligation to take care of themselves," public sentiment tips strongly toward the latter view. In fact, the poor and the nonpoor are no different on this issue. The same basic values are shared by the poor and the nonpoor: People are ultimately responsible for their own well-being, but government bears the primary responsibility for helping people when they need it.

GOVERNMENT AND THE NEEDY

Among the nonpoor, both women and blacks tend to be more supportive of an active government role. But it is among the black poor that one finds a constituency with a high degree of confidence in government action. A majority of the black poor believe that government, rather than people themselves, are responsible for citizens' well-being; the figure is 30 percent among nonpoor blacks, 25 percent for the female poor, and 12 percent for the white poor. A majority of the black poor names the government as having greatest responsibility for helping the poor, compared to 38 percent among nonpoor blacks, 36 percent among the female poor, and 23 percent among the white poor. Most striking is that no less than 60 percent of poor blacks believe that the government knows how to eliminate poverty, which is more than twice the proportion who feel that it is the case among the female poor and among nonpoor blacks (both 27 percent).

Ronald Reagan once said, "In the war on poverty, poverty won." Americans are inclined to agree. Forty-five percent are of the opinion that the efforts of the Kennedy and Johnson administrations made things "somewhat better" for the poor; only 10 percent say they made things "much better." Seventeen percent believe the war on poverty had no impact, and 11 percent say it made matters worse. Even among the poor, only 14 percent felt the war on poverty made things much better. The figure among poor blacks, however, was 31 percent.

Giving money to the poor outright is surely one way to lift people out of poverty. As a matter of fact, that method has a fairly good track record. Medicare, social security, and similar transfer programs have been among the most effective poverty programs over the past thirty years, even though they are not aimed specifically at the poor. Meanwhile, programs designed to strike at the roots of poverty have not been spectacularly successful. Nevertheless, the public insists, two to one, that poverty funds should be directed toward eliminating the causes of poverty rather than giving money to poor people directly.

Eighty-nine percent of the nation is convinced that poverty will always be a major problem for our society. Only 8 percent think it is a problem that will be solved. Moreover, there is no clear consensus about the objectives of anti-poverty programs. About half of the nation thinks they should be rehabilitation programs, designed to help poor people get back on their feet. But the other half thinks they are simply maintenance programs that should provide for the needs of poor people while they are poor. And finally, Americans are not convinced that we know how to set things right. Seventy percent believe the government doesn't know enough about how to eliminate poverty in the United States. Only 22 percent think it does.

WHY POVERTY PROGRAMS FAIL

If Americans sometimes seem impatient with the poor, it is because they feel that little we have done in the past has actually worked: 58 percent think anti-poverty programs have seldom worked, but only 32 percent think they have often worked. This assessment is shared by poor people, who arrive at nearly the same conclusion (56 percent to 31 percent negative).

Most people feel the reason for the failure of anti-poverty programs is either that the money was wasted on useless projects that didn't help poor people or that the money never filtered through to the poor who needed it. Among poor people themselves, the feeling is even stronger that poverty money was intercepted before it got to them. Anti-poverty programs haven't worked very well because we don't know enough about how to make them work.

Part of the frustration about poverty can be summed up in the widespread conviction that, far from fostering independence and a desire to escape from poverty, current programs make poor people even more dependent on welfare and encourage them to remain in their present condition. Nearly three out of five think that, while only one in five says that welfare benefits give people a chance to stand on their own two feet and get started again. This conviction is not so strongly held by the poor themselves, however, with 31 percent saying that poverty programs give poor people a chance, and only 43 percent saying that they make them more dependent.

As to specifics, it is widely believed that welfare encourages husbands to avoid their family responsibilities. Sixty-one percent of respondents said that welfare often encourages fathers to leave home because, if they do, it is easier for wives to collect welfare. (The principal federal welfare program is Aid to Families with Dependent Children.) Only 33 percent said that seldom happens. Some support is lent to this view by the attitudes of people in poverty, which are nearly identical on this question (60 percent to 32 percent think it often happens).

On the question of whether poor young women have babies so they can collect welare, our sample is undecided: 48 percent say it happens often, and 46 percent say it happens seldom. But for poor people, there seems to be little doubt.

Sixty-four percent of the people who live in poverty say that poor women often have babies to get welfare. And better than three out of four (78 percent) poor women who have babies say that often happens.

THE WORK ETHIC AND THE POOR

Who should get the most help? There is clear agreement among the public at large and also among the poor: Children and the handicapped need help, and also able-bodied men who can't find work. Less deserving of consideration, in the public's view, are old people who are poor, the working poor, poor people without job skills, and least of all, poor unwed mothers. There is an indication here that the public differentiates between those who are poor because of circumstances beyond their control (children, the handicapped, those who can't find work) and those whose poverty is at least to some extent their own fault.

In fact, the work ethic is alive and well among the poor. When people who live in poverty are asked, "Which do you think is more important in life: working hard and doing what is expected of you, or doing the things that give you personal satisfaction and pleasure?" 78 percent subscribe to the idea of hard work while only 16 percent choose personal satisfaction and pleasure. That is a stronger commitment to the work ethic than one finds among the nonpoor; they endorse "working hard and doing what is expected of you" by 65 to 28 percent.

When asked their opinion of "workfare—the government program that requires poor people to work, if they are physically able to, before they can receive poverty benefits" the poor favored the idea by a 59-to-3 percent margin (the rest had not heard anything about workfare or were not sure how the felt about it). That is a slightly stronger endorsement than workfare received from the nonpoor, who favored it 51 to 4 percent.

The poor clearly share the same values and attitudes as other Americans. Where they differ, sometimes, is in their view of the circumstances of poverty. On this subject, we may accept the assessments of poor people as more realistic, or at least more likely to be informed by experience.

Many Americans, for example, are convinced that jobs are available for anyone willing to work. Indeed, 54 percent say so, with only 43 percent taking the opposite point of view. But among poor people, the perception is different. Fifty-nine percent think poor people find it very hard to get work, and only 31 prcent think there are jobs available to anyone who wants them.

Most Americans are sure that welfare benefits make poor people even more dependent and encourage them to remain in poverty. People who live in poverty are less convinced. Thus, 16 percent of the nonpoor and 31 percent of the poor believe that welfare benefits give poor people a chance to stand on their own two feet and get started again.

Both the rich and the poor consider unemployment one of our country's most important national problems. But three times as many poor people as nonpoor people say that inflation is a major problem. In fact, among the poor, inflation is about equal to unemployment in importance, 19 to 17 percent, whereas unemployment outweights inflation among the nonpoor by 16 to 6 percent. To poor people, many of them on a fixed income, even the smallest rise in prices can be catastrophic.

Consider also the notion that a permanent underclass of poor people is emerging in the United States. By better than three to one, nonpoor respondents say that most poor people have been poor for a long time and will probably remain that way. But once again, the attitudes of poor people themselves are instructive. Poor people are twice as likely to report that they move into and out of poverty in a relatively brief time. And, indeed, some recent studies suggest that less than 10 percent of poor people remain in poverty for as long as ten years.

The public at large splits, 49 to 44 percent, over whether poor people lack basic social and occupational skills and thus belong to a newly developing underclass. Poor people, however, reject that opinion—52 percent say their abilities are not all that much different from other Americans, while 40 percent think they lack basic skills.

REAGAN AND THE POOR

The public clearly believes that the poverty problem is difficult, if not intractable. And it is not encouraged by the record of government action in the past. But none of this means that the government should abandon its commitment to helping the poor. That commitment is based on moral, not practical, considerations. And the survey makes it clear that many Americans are doubtful that the Reagan administration shares that moral commitment.

Despite President Reagan's generally high overall job rating at the time the poll was taken (62 to 31 percent positive), his handling of the poverty problem got very low marks (58 to 34 percent negative), with the sharpest distinction made by members of the baby boom generation (65 to 31 positive overall versus 65 to 28 percent negative on poverty). People who live in poverty split evenly on Reagan's overall job rating and rate him almost three-to-one negative on his handling of poverty.

As has been the case since the fall of 1981, a majority of Americans are convinced that Ronald Reagan cares more about the rich, compared with 30 percent who think he cares about all income groups equally. Very few think he cares more about poor people. (See page 31.) Moreover, the nation is not convinced that his management of poverty programs protects the truly needy; only 40 percent feel the "safety net" for the poor is still in place, while 50 percent think the poor have been left unprotected. Among the poor themselves, this conviction is held by nearly a three-to-one margin.

In short, while practical judgments about what government can do to fight poverty may have changed, the moral consensus has not. The public shares the Reagan administration's assessment that the federal government has done badly in the past. And they are skeptical that much can be done in the future. But they do not feel this justifies abandoning the effort. Many Americans, and most poor people, are convinced that the Reagan administration has done just that. ■

HAVE WELFARE AND ANTIPOVERTY PROGRAMS WORKED?

The New Deal programs of Franklin Roosevelt and the Great Society programs of Lyndon Johnson greatly expanded the federal role in the alleviation of unemployment and poverty in America. Just how effective have these programs been?

A controversial 1984 book by Charles Murray, *Losing Ground: American Social Policy 1950–1980,* put forward the startling conclusion that despite all government efforts to the contrary, things took a turn for the worse for poor people in the 1960s. Needless to say, this assertion, which has also been made by some other conservative writers, was hotly contested.

Reprinted here is a later article by Charles Murray. In it, he reiterates and explains the contentions of *Losing Ground* and then attempts to answer criticisms of the book. Following that is an essay by one of Murray's numerous critics, economist Sar A. Levitan, who maintains that America's welfare system has, indeed, worked, that it has done a great deal to promote economic security for America's people.

The question addressed by these two essays, then is: Have America's welfare and antipoverty programs worked?

NO, WE'VE LOST GROUND
Charles Murray

In the year since it was published, *Losing Ground* has become a political football in the debate about social policy toward the poor, and many of the substantive issues it raises have gotten lost in the melee. What follows recapitulates some of the major sources of controversy as of this writing (April 1985) and my response to them. I should emphasize at the outset that this is not an attempt to prove that *Losing Ground* is "right." The book covers too much ground and makes too many speculative interpretations to lend itself to airtight proof. What can be done at this point is to present reasons why the attempts to prove it is "wrong" are inadequate and to identify some of the gaps in knowledge that need to be filled in.

Let me begin by stating the core contentions of *Losing Ground.* The first is an assertion of fact:

Basic indicators of well-being took a turn for the worse in the 1960s, most consistently and most drastically for the poor. In some cases, earlier progress slowed; in other cases mild deterioration accelerated; in a few instances advance turned into retreat.[1]

The book documents this assertion in the areas of poverty, employment, education, crime, and family structure.

The second is a causal argument that the governmental reforms of the 1960s were responsible for some unknown but large portion of this turn for the worse. The basic mechanism was summarized as follows:

A government's social policy helps set the rules of the game—the stakes, the risks, the payoffs, the tradeoffs, and the strategies for making a living, raising a family, having fun, defining what "winning" and "success" mean. The more vulnerable a population and the fewer its independent resources, the more decisive is the effect of the rules imposed from above. The most compelling explanation for the marked shift in the fortunes of the poor is that they continue to respond, as they always had, to the world as they found it, but that we—meaning the not-poor and the un-disadvantaged—had changed the rules of their world. . . . The first effect of the new rules was to make it profitable for the poor to behave in the short term in ways that were destructive in the long term. Their second effect was to mask these long-term losses—to subsidize irretrievable mistakes.[2]

These reforms include the Great Society legislation of 1964–66, but also court decisions, changes in bureaucratic regulations, and changes in the intellectual elite wisdom that both preceded and followed the Lyndon Johnson years. In one way or another, the critiques of *Losing Ground* have attempted to demonstrate why these contentions are inaccurate. I group the criticisms under four headings.

The problems are overstated. The book is really talking about black youths, who are a small proportion of the population. Or, another version: welfare dependency is not a major problem.

Forces beyond our control caused the problems. The changes that *Losing Ground* recounts are explained by macroeconomic, demographic, and social trends.

The reforms worked. The job-training and educational programs helped. Medicaid improved the health of the poor. The income transfers have kept people out of poverty.

The causal analysis is contradicted by the available evidence. It has already been demonstrated that the reforms did not lead to illegitimacy and chronic unemployment.

1. Charles Murray, *Losing Ground: American Social Policy 1950–1980* (New York: Basic Books, 1984), pp. 8–9.
2. Ibid., p. 9.

AN OVERSTATED PROBLEM

It has been proposed that the problems *Losing Ground* describes are not as serious as they seem. One such contention is that *Losing Ground* is, in effect, about problems of black youth. Black youths constitute a small fraction of the population; therefore, it is inappropriate to use them as a basis for indicting social policy as a whole. The point of *Losing Ground*, however, is that the statistics on blacks are in large part a proxy measure of trends among poor people of all races. Whenever the data permit us to disaggregate by both race and economic class, as in the case of single-parent families and crime victimization, the behavior and trends we too easily have considered characteristic of blacks turn out to be characteristic of poor whites as well. The alarm expressed in *Losing Ground* is not just that poor blacks are suffering extremely serious problems, but that these phenomena generalize to poor whites; not just that youth are involved, but that their behaviors are affecting life for much larger populations of people even now, and still larger ones in the future.

Others have argued that even when whites are included, the number of permanently poor and dependent people is small and that the existence of an "underclass" has been grossly exaggerated. The primary source for this conclusion is *Years of Poverty, Years of Plenty,* a report on analyses of the Panel Study of Income Dynamics (PSID), in which it is concluded that only 2.0 percent of the U.S. population is "persistently dependent" on welfare income.[3]

The figure is encouragingly low. It is also the result of a definitional artifact. The authors require that any family classified as "dependent" receive more than 50 percent of its income from welfare, *not* including housing assistance, Medicaid, child nutrition, and unemployment payments. Thus, for example, a family living in subsidized housing, receiving food stamps, paying for medical care through Medicaid, and relying on free school breakfasts and lunches for the children would not be classified as dependent if the earned income was greater than the size of the food stamp allowance. Only the food stamps would show up in the authors' calculation of the size of the welfare benefits received by the family. To be classified as "persistently dependent" requires that this condition obtain eight out of the ten years covered by the study. Given this definition, even a mother receiving long-term benefits from Aid to Families with Dependent Children (AFDC) was unlikely to qualify as "persistently dependent" on welfare if she moved in and out of the labor force periodically.

This extraordinarily restrictive conception has nothing to do with the problem of dependency described in *Losing Ground.* Apart from that, it masks a very troubling reality. Since the early 1970s, the United States has had a running population of more than 10 million people on AFDC. According to the PSID data, half the caseload on any given day, comprising more than five million people, are in the midst of a spell on AFDC that will last for at least eight years.

---

3. Greg J. Duncan et al., *Years of Poverty, Years of Plenty: The Changing Economic Fortunes of American Workers and Families* (Ann Arbor, Mich.: Survey Research Center, Institute for Social Research, 1984), pp. 75–78.

Illegitimacy among poor blacks in the early 1980s has been running at ratios of around 80 percent of all live births. The size of the adult male underclass is unknown but large. One clue to its dimensions is that, depending on the specific year one chooses, somewhere between a million and two and a half million healthy, working-aged men, not in school, have no work experience whatsoever.

These numbers are lower bounds, pointing primarily to the hard core. When one begins to add in the young woman who is on AFDC for only three years instead of eight, the young male who works for six weeks out of the year instead of zero, the teenager who does not give birth to an illegitimate child but who must grow up in a neighborhood without fathers, the numbers mushroom. They must be added in, for these people are just as much part of the problem described in *Losing Ground* as the hard core. The situation facing the working-aged poor has been obscured because it tends to exist where the white middle class does not often visit and because so many of its dimensions do not register on the economic indicators that have tended to preoccupy policy makers. But the urgency of the situation is not overstated in *Losing Ground*.

FORCES BEYOND OUR CONTROL

The Flooding of the Labor Market

Losing Ground focus on two measures, the gap in black and white labor force participation (LFP) and the black-white unemployment ratio, to argue that black youths lost ground to whites in the labor market.

The trends on both indicators, it has been objected, can be explained by the enormous changes that took place in the size of the labor force. John E. Schwarz, author of *America's Hidden Success,* writes that "Mr. Murray directs attention to the wrong cause. . . . Swollen by tidal waves of Baby Boomers, the number of Americans aged 16 to 34 looking for employment between 1963 and 1980 expanded by an extraordinary 26 million; a 14-fold increase over the 1947 to 1963 period when the same age group increased in the labor force by fewer than two million."[4] The causal mechanism whereby the baby boom or the influx of women into the labor force produce these effects is competition. More whites are in the job market. Given a choice, employers hire the more attractive candidates, who tend to be white—either because of superior preparation or simple racism. The job market is perceived as a queue in which blacks stand at the end.

Losing Ground argued that such explanations are inadequate because of the peculiar timing of the changes in behavior. The gap in labor force participation did not open up during a time of economic slowdown, but during the boom years of the 1960s, when jobs were being created faster than even the baby-boomers could enter the labor market. I also pointed out in the book that older blacks— who were disproportionately not only poorly educated and holding low-skill jobs,

---

4. John E. Schwarz, letter to the editor, *The Wilson Quarterly* 9 (Spring 1985): 172–3. See also the editorial "Losing More Ground," *New York Times,* 3 February 1985. Schwarz's full exposition of this view is in his *America's Hidden Success: A Reassessment of Twenty Years of Public Policy* (New York: W. W. Norton, 1983).

but also without even the benefits of youth and flexibility—should have been most vulnerable to a changing economy and to increased competition from the baby boom and women. But older blacks continued to improve their employment position through the early 1970s. None of the critiques published to date has explained how the swelling labor force hypothesis copes with these objections.

The swelling labor force hypothesis is susceptible, however, to more direct treatment than I presented in the book insofar as it implies that increases in the size of the labor force are associated with the deterioration in the employment position of black youths. Has this been the case? Have, in fact, increases in the number of persons competing for jobs been associated with the increase in the gap in black-white labor force participation or the increase in the black-white unemployment ratio?

If a relationship exists, it is not immediately apparent. From 1955–80, the labor force increased at a mean of 1.7 million persons annually, and the range of the annual increase was great, from a low of 155,000 in 1962 to a high of 3,242,000 in 1978. But there is no direct association between the size of the annual increases and the size of the annual changes in the unemployment and LFP gaps between blacks and whites. . . . Black teenagers did not experience greater employment problems in years with the larger increases in the labor force.

A more useful representation of change in labor force size is one that takes the job-creation performance of the economy into account. The indicator in this instance is "net work-seekers": the year's increase in the size of the labor force minus the year's change in the number of employed persons. A positive number thus represents more new work-seekers than jobs, and a negative number represents more new jobs than there were new workers to compete for them.

Again using the experience from 1955–80 for black and white teenagers (ages 16–19), the data do not fit the expectations that an excess of job seekers was associated with the deterioration in the employment situation of black youths. For example, in fourteen of those years, there were more new jobs than job seekers. Yet in eleven of those fourteen years, the gap in labor force participation increased. In eleven of those years, the unemployment ratio increased. . . .

We may also explore the hypothesis that it was specifically the increase in the number of teenagers, not general increases, that affected the indicators in question. Here too the bivariate relationships remain low. . . .

Space does not permit extension of these numbers to other age groups, nor will I attempt to develop more complex models here. I will leave it as an assertion (one that can be readily explored from data in the appendix of *Losing Ground*) that the weakness of the relationship between the increase in the labor force, size of the teenage cohorts, and the labor force behavior persists across age groups and across sexes. This does not mean that changes in these demographic variables had no effect at all. I would expect that they did and that a well-specified model will reveal such independent effects. The question is whether the relationships have much explanatory power, and to this the answer so far seems to be "no." The more complex modeling that has been done to date supports this conclusion.

Changes in the Job Market

Such relationships between labor force size and the experience of blacks relative to whites do not dispose of the argument that the swelling labor force had something to do with the deterioration of the black employment situation. The next hypothesis to examine is that the job creation was of a kind that was bound to leave blacks behind, and here we begin to touch on a second category of objections to the argument in *Losing Ground* having to do with the overall economic changes that affected the United States during the post-1965 period.

The Oil Shock. Let me first briefly comment on one set of arguments based on the changes brought about by the oil shock that occurred at the end of 1973. By that time, the trends that comprise the main portion of the indictment in *Losing Ground* were already established. By 1973, reductions in poverty among the working-aged had been stopped for three years. The gap in LFP among black and white teenagers had already grown to 16 percentage points. The unemployment ratio of black and white youth was at 2.4:1, compared with the ratio of 1.9:1 that had prevailed through the early 1960s. And the other noneconomic trends as well, in crime, education, and family structure, were already well-established. The oil shock of 1973 and the subsequent economic troubles we have come to associate with it undoubtedly affected a variety of employment and income trends. But trends in the post-1973 period are essentially irrelevant to the argument in *Losing Ground*. The problems it analyzes had begun much earlier.

If we consider the overall period, however, to what extent were blacks being caught in economic transformations that left them at a special disadvantage and that might, therefore, explain the statistics on labor force participation and unemployment relative to whites? From 1965 to 1980, the American economy created an unprecedented number of new jobs. White collar jobs were up 18.2 million. In the skilled blue-collar fields (crafts, operatives), a total of 3.8 million new jobs were created. In the low-skill areas (nonfarm labor, service), another 4.8 million new jobs were created. In farming, 1.3 million jobs were lost. How did blacks fare?

Farm Employment. We may begin with the diminishing number of farming jobs. Robert Greenstein has argued, using an article by John Cogan as his basis, that this explains away the problem: "Cogan . . . shows that virtually all of the decline in black teenage employment from 1950 to 1970 was caused by the disappearance of low-paying jobs in the South, as southern agriculture was mechanized."[5] One problem with extrapolating from the Cogan article to the argument in *Losing Ground* is that Cogan combined LFP and unemployment data, while the trends in these two indicators showed very different patterns. During the 1950s, while agricultural jobs were vanishing most rapidly and the unemploy-

---

5. Robert Greenstein, "Losing Faith in 'Losing Ground,'" *The New Republic*, 25 March 1985, 16; see also John Cogan, "The Decline in Black Teenage Employment: 1950–70," *The American Economic Review* 72 (September 1982): 621–38.

ment ratio was increasing, black teenage labor force participation nonetheless kept pace with that of whites, whereas it abruptly stopped doing so during the slower loss of agricultural jobs in the 1960s. Why should a weakening "cause" suddenly produce a new and very strong "effect"?

A second difficulty with Greenstein's interpretation is that Cogan was limited to decennial census data covering a time when the within-decade trends were changing rapidly. We know that the divergence in white and black economic indicators reported in *Losing Ground* occurred only in the last half of the 1960s; indeed, we know that during the first half of the 1960s the unemployment ratio was holding steady and the LFP gap was actually closing. We further know that the reductions in teenage agricultural employment in the 1960s were concentrated in the early 1960s—of the total loss of teenage agricultural jobs during the 1960s, 71 percent had occurred by 1965. By the last half of the 1960s, only a very small proportion of black teenagers in the labor force were still involved in the agricultural sector (only 8 percent of non-white teenagers in the labor force as of 1967, or 3 percent of the non-white teenage population). If reductions in agricultural employment are to explain the divergence in white and black teenage labor force behavior in the last half of the 1960s, why did they not have a similar effect in the first half of the 1960s?

Combining these observations with Cogan's analysis of the 1960–70 comparison, a specific prediction seems justified: If labor force data by urban versus rural locations for the 1960s are disaggregated by year, they must reveal a rapidly improving black teenage unemployment situation in urban areas during the first half of the 1960s, despite the indifferent performance of the economy during those years, and one that deteriorated just as rapidly during the last half of the 1960s, despite the boom.

Nonfarm Employment. Among nonagricultural jobs, the pie was expanding substantially in all job categories. Given the queue explanation—that blacks would tend to be selected after whites if both were available—of the deterioration in the employment of blacks, what proportions of these new jobs might be expected to have gone to blacks? Or to put it another way, for which of these job categories was the competition from the influx of white women and babyboomers most intense? . . .

"Blacks and others" constituted roughly 11 percent of the population in 1960 and 14 percent in 1980. Applying this information, it may be said that in the early 1960s blacks were acquiring at least their share of new jobs in non-farm labor, substantially more than their proportional share of the new skilled blue-collar jobs, and a very high proportion of the new service jobs. Insofar as the proportion of college graduates among blacks in 1960s was far lower than that of the white population, it may also be inferred that blacks were getting a disproportionate number of the new white-collar jobs.

After the mid 1960s, the same generalizations held true for the white-collar and skilled blue-collar occupations. For the low-skill job categories, the situation dramatically reversed. In nonfarm labor, blacks experienced a net *loss* of jobs from 1965 onward, from 966,000 such jobs in 1965 to 866,000 in 1970. By

1980, the figure had dropped to 752,000. During the same period, whites acquired a net of 984,000 additional nonfarm labor jobs. In the service sector, blacks went from an extremely high rate of job acquisition in the early 1960s to a net drop of 220,000 jobs from 1965–70. Only in the last half of the 1970s did blacks once again begin to acquire close to their proportional share of the new service jobs being created.

Losing Ground's explanation of this anomalous pattern is that young blacks changed their posture toward low-skill, low-paying jobs. The alternative proposition is that the extraordinary shift of low-skill jobs from blacks to whites reflects an influx of more qualified (or racially attractive) women and baby-boomers for these jobs. But consider the difficulties.

If discrimination is at issue, it must be remembered that women also had to fight discrimination, especially in the nonfarm labor sector. For nonfarm labor and service jobs involving heavy work, women were also at a competitive disadvantage because of size and strength. Nor can it be assumed that employers gave preference to job candidates who had extra academic or other credentials— overqualification can be as much of a handicap as other forms of discrimination. The notion that an employer, given the choice, would naturally rather hire a white woman or a college-educated white than a young, poorly educated black for low-skill labor is not self-evidently valid.

On the face of it, blacks competing for the skilled labor and white-collar positions would seem to have faced the most severe obstacles in a rapidly expanding labor force. The higher the skill, the more likely that licensing restrictions and union rules impeded black entrance into the workplace. Blacks seeking professional positions faced a burgeoning pool of white competitors who had gone to better colleges and had higher grades and test scores. Why then did blacks do so well in getting their share of the higher-skill jobs while doing so poorly in the lower-skill jobs? Affirmative action? But blacks were doing well in *all* job categories in the early 1960s, before the affirmative action legislation and court decisions were made, and continued to do well in the late 1960s in the higher-skill categories, before the Equal Employment Opportunity Commission had begun to wield enforcement powers.

It may well be that beginnning in the mid-1960s, employers did tend to favor whites, women, or Asians for positions that formerly tended to go to blacks, but not necessarily because white employers were waiting for the opportunity to express their racism. Rather, *Losing Ground* argues, job-seeking behaviors and on-the-job behavior were changing in ways that made the youths from working-class and middle-class families more attractive employees than youths from the poorest segments of the community. The explanation presented in *Losing Ground* implies another specific prediction: microeconomic analyses of the employment experience of black youths from blue-collar and middle-class families will reveal that they acquired and held low-paying jobs at rates approaching those of whites. Similar analyses of the experience of poor white youth will reveal that their patterns of low-skill employment are similar to those usually associated with black youth.

THE SUCCESSES OF THE GREAT SOCIETY

A third major theme of the critiques of *Losing Ground* is that the book ignores the successes of the Great Society. I will deal with this set of criticisms under three headings: the education and training programs, health and nutrition programs, and income transfer programs.

Education and training. The brunt of *Losing Ground's* argument is that education for blacks was improving until the mid-1960s. Thereafter, education for the population as a whole deteriorated substantially. While we do not have adequate longitudinal data to document what happened to blacks during this period, observation of what happened in inner-city schools suggests that the deterioration for blacks seems to have been as great or greater than for whites. This fundamental statement of trends is not especially controversial. Rather, it has been argued that evaluations of some of the specific programs, notably the job training programs, compensatory education, and Head Start, show some successes.

Losing Ground's review of these evaluations does not dispute this. Some programs produced evidence of progress; others did not. Most were ambiguous. Sometimes the results went the wrong way, and the evaluations had to explain why the students in the programs were doing worse than the control group. Making sense of this literature becomes even more difficult because of the widely varying quality of the research.

The point of *Losing Ground*, however, was not that the special educational programs failed, nor that the job training programs failed. They were not the culprit. On the contrary, I advocated more and better educational and training programs as one of our most promising routes for helping the disadvantaged. My criticism was, and remains, of the mind-set that permits one to scrutinize the data for small program-specific effects while ignoring that the desired overall state of affairs—good education, high employment—among the disadvantaged slipped further from reach.

Health. The conventional wisdom holds that the great success story of the Great Society for the non-aged was the dramatic improvement in health among the poor produced by Medicaid and the nutrition programs. Why were these ignored in *Losing Ground?* According to one critic, the reasons were sinister: "[Murray] never refers to any evidence about the health of blacks and the poor since the story there is exactly the reverse of the one he wants to tell."[6] As it happens, the allegation is half right. The original outline for *Losing Ground* included a chapter on health. The reasons that I finally decided to omit it are instructive.

In the field of health, there was every reason to expect that data would in fact tell a success story. Medical science has made major advances since Medicaid began, and access to medical science was surely made more available to the poor through Medicaid. Nor was there any reason to avoid telling of success. The intent of *Losing Ground* was not to claim that the government is powerless to

---

6. Paul Starr quoted by Greenstein, "Losing Faith," 17.

do good in any arena of life, but to try to discriminate the things that social policy can do (or has done) from the things that it cannot do (or has not done).

I examined four measures that seemed appropriate for tracking health of the poor over the period 1950–1980: infant mortality, maternal mortality, low birth-weight births (under 2,500 grams), and life expectancy (at age 20, to capture the quality of adult health care). The results were that infant mortality among blacks showed a sharp drop beginning in the late 1960s, maternal mortality showed an equally sharp drop beginning in the mid-1950s, life expectancy showed an increase in the 1970s for black men and an increase more or less throughout the entire three decades among black women, and low birth-weight births showed an increase through the mid-1960s and a slight decrease thereafter.

To what extent did these represent improvements that were occurring as medical science improved, and to what extent did they represent the kind of progress that I was investigating: blacks closing the gap with whites?

The year-by-year plots are even more ambiguous than the trends. . . . Consider, for example, the indicator most widely cited as evidence of the success of the Great Society health programs, the reduction in infant mortality among blacks. The raw reduction was large. Infant deaths among nonwhites fell from 43 per 1,000 live births in 1960, to 31 in 1970, and to 19 by 1980. But the large raw reduction was small in proportional terms—infant mortality fell for everyone, including blacks. But we may pursue the issue of causation further. Allen Matusow has compared infant mortality statistics during the period 1965–69 for states that had not implemented the Medicaid program during that period and found that the reductions in infant mortality were as large in the states without Medicaid as in those with a fully implemented program. Alabama and Mississippi had no Medicaid during that period, and their infant mortality rates fell by 14.8 and 21.5 percent respectively. Louisiana, a neighboring state with a comparable baseline, implemented the program in 1966 and its rate fell by 18.3 percent. Indiana had no Medicaid during the period, and its rate fell by 13.5 percent. Neighboring Illinois, with a comparable baseline rate, implemented Medicaid in 1966 and its rate fell by 6.3 percent.

I do not use these data to claim that the reductions in infant births were larger in the states without Medicaid, but to point to the extreme difficulty of documenting claims that Medicaid is the cause of substantial improvements. Much the same comments apply to the data purported to show improvements in nutrition among the poor, which I will not attempt to review here.

As I examined the data on health, it soon became clear that the correct answer to the question, "What has happened in health and nutrition?" was that we are not yet sure. To the extent that there has been progress in the health of the poor, it appears to have tracked with improvements among the affluent and was arguably no greater than would have occurred in the absence of the extremely expensive programs that were installed. Given the broad popular conception that substantial progress *has* been made, I decided that an argument otherwise should be made in a full-scale analysis, not in a single chapter of *Losing Ground.*

Poverty. Losing Ground presents trendlines for poverty showing that progress against poverty among the working-aged stopped in the late 1960s, ending progress that had continued, in tandem with economic growth, since the end of World War II. In refutation, it has been argued that given the rising unemployment rates of the 1970s, the income transfers were essential in preventing poverty from rising. The flat poverty rate for the working-aged from 1968 onward is evidence of success, not failure.

Neither side in the dispute can make its case in the absence of some crucial causal assumptions. If the decline in employment among black youths is caused by variables exogenous to social policy, and if the rise in female-headed households among blacks in caused by variables exogenous to social policy, then the conclusion is inescapable: without the increase in transfer payments, poverty among the working-aged would have risen substantially during the 1970s. If these phenomena were in part effects of social policy, then one may examine the massive job creation that occurred and ask why certain segments of the American population opted out of competition. One may ask why increasing numbers of blacks and poor people in general formed single-parent families that virtually guaranteed they would remain poor no matter what happened to the economy. It is the issue at the core of *Losing Ground's* argument: what is causing what?

CAUSES AND THE EMPIRICAL RECORD

The test of whether *Losing Ground* is "right" is still in the future. In the classic scientific paradigm, one presents a set of observations, advances a theory to explain them, then tests the theory against new data. *Losing Ground* in effect got through the first two of those steps.

The theory itself has little that is new. Martin Anderson, Edward Banfield, Milton Friedman, George Gilder, Thomas Sowell, and Walter Williams are just a few of the more prominent observers who have recently made similar points. And, as Gertrde Himmelfarb's *The Idea of Poverty* so elegantly describes, the underlying ideas in the debate over helping the poor in the late twentieth century were anticipated, often with more subtlety and rigor, by English intellectuals in the eighteenth and nineteenth centuries.

But while the ideas have been around for centuries, social scientists in the modern era have been slow to build testable models worthy of the theories. More bluntly, social scientists who have purported to test "conservative" theory regarding poverty and welfare—including that presented in *Losing Ground*—have seemed determined to cast such theory in terms of stereotypes that are easy to refute.

Illegitimacy. This is most apparent in the causal arguments regarding the illegitimacy rate. In 1984, David T. Ellwood and Mary Jo Bane of Harvard completed a study that has since been used as the stock refutation of the proposition that welfare causes illegitimate births. The conclusion is based on regression analyses of the effects of AFDC on divorce, separation, independent living arrangements, and illegitimacy. The analyses revealed that AFDC had substantial effects on living arrangements and lesser effects on separation and divorce. But they found no significant effect of AFDC on illegitimate births. The authors concluded that "[w]elfare simply does not appear to be the underlying cause of the dramatic changes in family structure of the past few decades."[7]

Now let us imagine the conditions under which two different levels of the "cause"– the dollar value of the AFDC payment– might have shown such an effect on illegitimate births. On consideration, it becomes apparent that the model will apply if poor young women accurately figure up the precise amount of the AFDC payment available to them and decide to get pregnant (or, being pregnant, decide to keep the baby) if the prospective welfare check is large enough, and otherwise not to do so. I submit that no serious observer of the phenomenon of rising illegitimate births accepts that stereotype; certainly not me.

Further, the model assumes that the existing range of welfare packages would reveal a causal impact of money payments. Why should this be so? To me, a more plausible model would posit a discontinuous function. At some very low level, welfare benefits have no causal effect on poor single women having and keeping babies. At some higher level (higher than any existing package) welfare benefits would make having a baby so economically beneficial for a poor person that it would in itself be a "cause" of such behavior. Between those two extremes, a break point exists at which the level of welfare benefits is sufficiently large that it permits an alternative to not having (or not keeping) the baby that would otherwise not exist. Once this break point is passed, welfare benefits become an enabling factor: they do not cause single women to decide to have a baby, but they enable women who are pregnant to make the decision to keep the baby. If in all states the package of benefits is already large enough to have passed the break point for a large proportion of the potential single mothers, then the effects on increases in the welfare package as measured by Ellwood and Bane will be very small.

How great is the range of welfare benefits? Ellwood and Bane open their report by stating that "the extreme variation in benefits across states seems to offer a marvellous natural experiment for testing the influence of welfare benefits," comparing Mississippi with its $60 monthly AFDC allowance to Michigan's $399. The study limits the independent variable to the value of AFDC, assuming that "total benefits are positively correlated with maximum AFDC benefits across states." But food stamps, Medicaid, and other important benefits are either invariant across states or subject to much less local discretion than the AFDC payment. As a result, while the correlation with the AFDC payment is surely "positive," the variation in the total welfare package is much narrower than a comparison of AFDC payments would lead one to expect. A study by the General Acounting Office estimated the value of welfare packages available as of 1978 and found that in a stingy location (New Orleans), the monthly dollar package amounted to $654 if housing benefits were obtained, $511 if they were not. In

---

7. David T. Ellwood and Mary Jo Bane, "The Impact of AFDC on Family Structure and Living Arrangements," Paper prepared for the U.S. Department of Health and Human Services under Grant No. 92A-82, March, 1984.

a generous location (San Francisco), the corresponding packages were $867 and $734. This is not a wide range. The package in New Orleans seems large enough to me to have passed the "break point." Then we correct for the difference in the cost of living in San Francisco and New Orleans, and the difference between the two cities is diminished. Correct for the differences in per capita income (to capture income relative to the local standard) and the welfare package in New Orleans puts the recipient at almost exactly the same relative level as the package in San Francisco. The young woman has to be a very precise calculator, extremely sensitive to small differences in real income, and indifferent to considerations of relative income, to figure out why it is sensible to give birth and keep the baby in San Francisco while it is not in New Orleans.

On these grounds alone, I would not expect the Ellwood and Bane approach to detect the effect of welfare on illegitimacy. But perhaps the more important point is that *Losing Ground* explicitly urges that a multidimensional model is essential to understanding illegitimacy rates, or increased unemployment among poor youth, or any of the other trends that the book deplores. It can be extremely important in a young woman's assessment of alternatives that she will be unable to live with the father of the child, or any other man (as was true before the Department of Health, Education and Welfare abandoned enforcement of the "man in the house rule" in the mid-1960s). It can be extremely important for her to know that she cannot supplement the welfare payment with any other income (as was true before the enactment of the "30 and a third" provision in 1967). These changes do not provide a cross-sectional "natural experiment"; they occurred nationwide.

Beyond these considerations, *Losing Ground* argues that the context in which the illegitimacy rate among poor women increased cannot be understood without understanding as well the importance of changes in crime, education, and status rewards — an interactive system that was described at length in the book and has scarcely been mentioned in any of the critiques. That "welfare," construed as the dollar payment for AFDC, does not cause higher illegitimacy rates is proven. The thesis in *Losing Ground* has barely been discussed, let alone tested.

Unemployment. Another caricature of *Losing Ground's* position involves the unemployed black youth. The stereotype says that black youths decide they can get more money on welfare than by taking a low-paying job. They are lured onto welfare rather than working for a living. Once on welfare, people become dependent on it and no longer seek work. The children of welfare recipients adopt the same slothful attitudes and themselves become dependent on welfare. This sequence of events is typical of welfare users.

This view is readily refuted by evidence that work pays more than welfare, by survey research that reveals black youths share middle-class aspirations for jobs and high income, and by evidence that most black youths are at least periodically employed, thereby demonstrating their allegiance to the job market. It can be further demonstrated that only small proportions of people who ever use welfare benefits remain on them for prolonged periods of time and that most of the children of welfare-dependent parents are not welfare-dependent as adults.

The argument in *Losing Ground* bears no relationship to the stereotype. *Los-*

ing Ground assumes that the typical poor youth aspires, just as middle-class youths do, to a high income. He or she knows that welfare will not provide a high income. This was as true in 1970 and 1980 as it was in 1950 to 1960. But for a person with limited education and talent, the most reliable way out of poverty is to acquire such a low-income job; keep working as steadily as possible through a succession of such jobs so as to acquire some skills and a good work record; and thereby eventually to move into a relatively secure job with a decent wage.

The reforms of the 1960s—as construed in *Losing Ground*, not reforms limited to "the Great Society"—discouraged poor young people, and especially poor males, from pursuing this slow, incremental approach in four ways. First, they increased the size of the welfare package and transformed the eligiblity rules so as to make welfare a more available and attractive *temporary* alternative to a job. Second, the reforms in law enforcement and criminal justice increased access to income from the underground economy. By the 1970s, illegal income (including that from dealing in drugs, gambling, and stolen goods, as well as direct predatory crime) had become a major source of income in poor communities. Third, the breakdown in inner-city education reduced job-readiness. Acculturation to the demands of the workplace—arriving every day at the same time, staying there, accepting the role of a subordinate—diminished as these behaviors were no longer required in the schoolroom. Fourth, the reforms diminished the stigma associated with welfare and simultaneously devalued the status associated with working at a menial, low-paying job—indeed, holding onto a menial job became in some poor communities a *source* of stigma.

All of these reasons, separately and interactively, encouraged young people at a critical phase of their lives to move in and out of the job market. The desire for high income remained; but the perceived means to it were more likely to be the "break," either through crime or the materialization of a "good" job. As I put it in *Losing Ground:* "The changes in welfare and changes in the risks attached to crime and changes in the educational environment reinforced each other. Together, they radically altered the incentive structure. I characterize these changes, taken together, as encouraging short cuts in some instances (get rich quick or not at all) and "no cuts" in others—meaning that the link between present behavior and future outcomes was obscured altogether."[8] As in the case of causation and illegitimacy, it is no exaggeration to say that the critiques of *Losing Ground* have not succeeded or failed in discrediting this argument, but rather have ignored it.

UNANSWERED QUESTIONS

In many respects, the chief subject of *Losing Ground's* indictment is not only the governmental reforms of the 1960s, but the inability, or reluctance, of modern social science to explore the issues it raises. *Losing Ground* examines the experience of the last thirty years of social policy and finds a variety of phenomena

---

8. Murray, *Losing Ground*, pp. 167–68.

that demand explanation. I put forward such an explanation, adducing a variety of evidence that the explanation is consistent with what is known. But to prove that I was right or wrong, or partly right, or to demonstrate what the alternative "truth" is, social science will have to develop new tools and ask new questions. Social scientists who leave behind their multiple-choice questionnaires and go out to talk with employers of low-skill labor will find that the reality of the employment problems among poor youth as described in *Losing Ground* are undeniable. How might this reality be calibrated and analyzed? If they talk to young single mothers and their neighbors—not in a formal interview, but in leisurely conversation—they will hear an account of the complicated role of the welfare alternative and its interaction with community norms, spun out openly and with surprising self-awareness. How might these insights be converted to data? Journalists and a few social scientists working in the anthropologists' tradition have shown that the information is out there and can be obtained. It is time that quantitative social scientists became more venturesome in taking advantage of such data to enrich our understanding of the dynamics that link social policy to the problems of the poor and disadvantaged.   ∎

YES, THE WELFARE SYSTEM PROMOTES ECONOMIC SECURITY
Sar A. Levitan

Underlying the New Deal, the Great Society, and related social legislation is an abiding trust in the potential greatness of American society. The designers of the evolving welfare system have assumed that our future is not predetermined, but can be molded by our energies, resources, and faith in the American future. They also have shared the belief that the United States is not condemned to passive acceptance of inequality of opportunity, poverty, urban blight, and economic booms and busts and that these social and economic ills could be alleviated and hopefully even eventually eradicated.

This vision of our future has been challenged and blunted by recent criticisms. It is ironic that the current most vociferous critics of the welfare system condemn the progress resulting from the social and economic initiatives taken by the New Deal and the Great Society while they accept the worst economic slump faced by the nation in four decades as an inevitable development.

Broadly defined, the American welfare system as it evolved over the past half century is the product of a sustained drive for guaranteeing individual civil rights and providing greater economic security for all income groups, and not merely a vehicle for assisting the poor. Through social insurance programs, tax expenditures, human capital investments, and proscribing discrimination, government aid and protection reach far into the ranks of middle- and upper-income America. Federal social welfare policies not only seek to prevent extreme deprivation among the most disadvantaged, but also attempt to cushion the impact of economic misfortune and uncertainty on more advantaged and affluent members of society. The resulting "safety net" has been remarkably successful in shielding diverse segments of the population from the full brunt of the vagaries and hardships implicit in a free market economy.*

THE ASSAULT ON THE WELFARE SYSTEM

Despite these achievements, however, the system has failed to gain universal acceptance. In recent years, attacks on the welfare system have grown more strident and shrill. Critics have sought to link rising incidences of crime, drug abuse, divorce, the problems that plague the educational system, and other social ills with federal social welfare interventions, and some have even claimed that the welfare system is the direct cause of an alleged unraveling of the American social fabric.

The detractors of the welfare system argue that these problems were largely due to the expansion of the welfare system during the late 1960s and 1970s to include not only the aged, disabled, and others who cannot work, but also the unemployed and the working poor as well. Charles Murray, for example, claims that beore 1964 welfare for the working poor was anathema, not to be mentioned in polite society. "We did not debate welfare for working people . . . " because "to have a job," he asserts, "was ipso facto to be self-supporting."[9] As long as the choice for able-bodied persons was between work and starvation, presumably they all worked. His assumption is that jobs were available and all able-bodied persons could find work. He ignores the fact that economic recessions were much deeper before the enactment of the New Deal regulatory agencies and that the Great Depression provided the initial impetus for welfare legislation when one of every four Americans was forced into idleness.

George Gilder carries this abiding belief in the availability of jobs even further. Following an old economic theorem that supply creates its own demand, Gilder contended that individuals can "create their own jobs" because "the supplies of work and human capital can engender their own demand."[10]

Variations on the theme of aid to the non-needy abound. Milton and Rose Friedman perceive waste and ineffectiveness as the inevitable result of bureaucrats "spending someone else's money," and they conclude that federal aid increases

---

* More specific analysis supporting the arguments prescribed in this article will be found in Sar A. Levitan and Clifford M. Johnson, *Beyond the Safety Net: Reviving the Promise of Opportunity in America* (Cambridge, Mass.: Ballinger, 1984). Other studies by the author that document the broad statements made in this article include: *The Great Society's Poor Law: A New Approach to Poverty* (Baltimore: The Johns Hopkins University Press, 1969); *Work and Welfare Go Together* (with Martin Rein and David Marwick) (Baltimore: The Johns Hopkins University Press, 1972, 1976); *The Promise of Greatness* (with Robert Taggart) (Cambridge, Mass.: Harvard University Press, 1976); *What's Happening to the American Family?* (with Richard Belous) (Baltimore: The Johns Hopkins University Press, 5th ed., 1985); *Programs in Aid of the Poor* (Baltimore: The Johns Hopkins University Press, 5th ed., 1985).

9. Charles Murray, *Losing Ground* (New York: Basic Books, 1984), p. 64.

10. George Gilder, *Wealth and Poverty* (New York: Basic Books, 1981), p. 158.

poverty by reasoning that "if you start paying people to be poor, you're going to have a lot of poor people."[11]

President Ronald Reagan seems to support these views. He perceives welfare as one of the major problems facing American society because it destroys "self-reliance, dignity and self-respect, the very substance of moral fibre."[12] At the heart of President Reagan's opposition to federal welfare initiatives lies the suspicion that the poor are morally different from the nonpoor — that they do not share the values and aspirations of working Americans, that they do not respond to the incentives and opportunities of the market in the same way as the more prosperous do. Although a very old idea, the association of poverty with deviance seems to acquire new life with every generation, as indicated by the preoccupation in recent years with the pronouncements of Milton and Rose Friedman, George Gilder, and Charles Murray, to single out four prominent representative critics of the welfare system and true believers in the operation of free markets.

As a result of the assaults on the welfare system by President Reagan and various scribes of diverse persuasions, the terms "welfare," "mess," and "crisis" have become virtually inseparable in contemporary public discourse. Liberals have found fault in the absence of federal standards for a comprehensive and universal system of income support and constraints on the more aggressive use of government powers to improve the quality of life. Conservatives contend that the welfare system has grown too large and unwieldy, frequently undermining the very objectives that it is designed to achieve. Under attack from all sides, the image of the welfare system as irrational, unmanageable, and in need of immediate and wholesale reform has come to dominate popular wisdom in the mid-1980s.

The notion of a "welfare crisis" is enhanced by tendencies to define the American welfare system narrowly as providing cash and in-kind assistance only to the poor. Without a perceived stake in the system, the middle class and affluent majority respond quickly to suggestions that "welfare" is a mess — too costly, mismanaged, unfair, and in many cases undeserved. When the welfare system is defined more realistically to include the host of entitlements and protections against economic insecurity available to the nonpoor, perceptions of crisis and prescriptions for sweeping retrenchment lose much of their appeal.

AN EVOLVING RATIONAL SYSTEM

A balanced and objective analysis would reveal that reports of a "welfare crisis" are greatly exaggerated. Removed from the distortions of budget battles and political ideologies, the record of federal social welfare interventions suggests that the system is a rational and necessary response to emerging societal needs and has functioned relatively well under the pressures of competing interests and conflicting demands.

Viewed in the context of societal goals first articulated half a century ago, the welfare system has nearly achieved its fundamental objectives. Most of the

---

11. Milton and Rose Friedman, *Free to Choose* (New York: Harcourt Brace Jovanovich, 1980), p. 108.
12. Ronald Reagan, *The Creative Society* (New York: Devin-Adair Company, 1968), p. 4.

destitute have been assured at least a meager stipend to meet basic needs, and the percentage of Americans living in poverty declined dramatically during the three decades following World War II. Social security and Medicare have removed the greatest threats to solvency in old age. Workers forced into idleness have gained temporary support through unemployment compensation programs, and disabled workers are protected by insurance that provides medical care and basic income. Tax expenditures and federally-sponsored financial institutions have enabled unprecedented numbers to purchase their own homes. Favorable tax policies have spurred the growth of private health insurance, and government regulations have guaranteed employees that their private pensions will be available upon retirement. Finally, substantial public investments in education, training, and employment have enabled millions to enter or remain in the mainstream of the U.S. economy, and thereby reaffirmed the promise of opportunity which lies at the heart of American society.

The role of the welfare system in enhancing economic security across diverse income groups is clearly reflected in its historical development. The cornerstone of the system, the Social Security Act of 1935, was crafted primarily to insure a basic income during the "golden years" or when forced idleness strikes and for persons incapable of self-support. Unemployment and old age insurance provided the bulk of protection against deprivation, while means-tested assistance to the poor was restricted to small numbers of widows and single mothers with dependent children, the aged, and the blind. Subsequent expansions of the social security system—including aid to dependent orphans in the waning days of the New Deal era, support for the disabled under Eisenhower, federally-financed health insurance under Johnson, and improved retirement and disability benefits under Nixon, Ford, and Carter—further increased the use of public funds to minimize economic insecurity without regard to personal income.

Contrary to today's view of the welfare system as synonymous with aid to the poor, public attention did not focus on the plight of the impoverished until the late 1950s, more than two decades after creation of the social security system. The welfare system's goals of expanded opportunity and reduced deprivation throughout the life cycle reflect the maturation of a productive and affluent society and offer a continuing agenda for progress toward a greater society.

Following World War II, social policy was preoccupied with helping veterans adjust to civilian life by subsidizing their health care, training and education, and, through Veterans Administration mortgages, their housing. The help was offered to all veterans without regard to their economic status. In the 1950s, amidst optimism that rapid economic growth during the postwar period could bring prosperity to the least advantaged, federal policy also focused on economic development efforts within depressed areas rather than direct assistance to those in need.

The persistence of poverty despite rising affluence during the 1960s prompted expansion of cash support under the Aid to Families with Dependent Children (AFDC) program for the non-aged poor, including liberalization of eligibility requirements and enhanced benefits that rose more rapidly than average earnings. The federal government also accepted responsibility for expanded direct aid to impoverished aged, blind, and disabled persons through the establishment of the Supplemental Security Income (SSI) program in 1972, and substantial additional help for the needy, including the working poor, was authorized with the creation of the food stamp program and its expansion during the recession in 1974. The working poor were also helped by wider coverage of the minimum wage and unemployment insurance laws during the Carter administration.

In-kind assistance has also been offered to low-income Americans when necessary to compensate for market inadequacies and to insure that public funds would be devoted to the fulfillment of basic human needs. Low-income housing programs were initiated when it became evident that income support alone would not serve as a short-term remedy for an inadequate private housing stock. Health care coverage under Medicaid represented further acknowledgment that cash stipends could not guarantee access to essential services in an efficient manner when individual needs are not directly related to income. In some cases it was easier to persuade Congress to provide in-kind help rather than cash assistance. For example, food stamps gained political support both as a response to the cry of hunger and malnutrition as well as a boost to the U.S. farm economy.

Because assistance to the poor is commonly viewed as "unearned," it attracts the greatest political attention and controversy. Yet means-tested aid constitutes only a sixth of the total transfer payments provided through the broader welfare system and less than a tenth of total federal outlays go to the poor. The federal share of the AFDC budget, commonly associated with "welfare," accounts for only about 2 percent of federal income transfers, and total outlays for the program (including state and local contributions) represent 0.5 percent of personal incomes in the United States. An analysis of in-kind benefits within the welfare system would yield similar results with large portions of aid (including the indirect subsidies) for housing, health care, and other supportive services directed to the nonpoor.

As a matter of policy as well as politics, the American welfare system has never identified income maintenance as an appropriate long-term response to economic misfortune and deprivation. The initiatives of the Great Society were founded upon the premise that only a *two-pronged* assault on poverty could lead to greater economic security for the poor: income support to meet immediate basic needs coupled with attempts to expand economic opportunities and change institutions in order to promote long-term self-sufficiency. Guided by this philosophy, the Great Society sought to stimulate public investments in education and training, seeking to open doors to permanent employment for the disadvantaged. During the late 1960s and 1970s, federal support for educational programs (ranging from primary and secondary schools to vocational and post-secondary education) and job training initiatives increased substantially. All segments of American society shared in the fruits of these investments, although they have not been sufficient to provide alternatives to long-term dependency for a minority of the nation's poor.

The development of diverse tax and sectoral policies not commonly associated with the welfare system further illustrates the extent to which federal social welfare policies have reduced economic insecurity for all income groups, rather than more narrowly aiding only the poor. Tax exemptions and expenditures are now designed to enhance personal economic security in areas ranging from home ownership to employee benefit programs and individual retirement accounts. A wide array of credit programs, supplemented by price supports for many agricultural commodities, also attempt to promote economic stability by aiding financially-troubled businesses. Disaster assistance routinely offers some measure of protection against natural calamities, while trade adjustment assistance and import restrictions have been employed to minimize economic disruptions associated with international trade. Certainly these federal interventions differ in important respects from the social investments and transfer programs typically linked with the welfare system. The point here is simply that a wide range of federal initiatives are part of a quest for economic security and well-being of all Americans and that it is this push for security, more than any narrower effort to help the poor, which defines and sustains the modern welfare system.

The broad layer of additional security provided by the welfare system and related federal initiatives has contributed to greater economic stability since World War II, even though periodic recessions persist. The American public's resistance to major retrenchments attests to the broad support from these reforms and virtually guarantees that an extensive welfare system serving as a buffer against economic uncertainty is here to stay. Indeed, some measure of protection against economic misfortune and some aid to the poor are rational and necessary responses to rising societal affluence. Just as private insurance to reduce financial risk becomes more affordable and attractive as personal income increases, government policies to spread or "socialize" the risks of a free market system become more prudent and popular with growing national wealth. Furthermore, the potential for humanitarian aid to relieve deprivation and for longer-term investments to help the deficiently educated, disabled, and discriminated-against become contributing members of society also increases with rising national income. In the absence of federal interventions through the welfare system, the gap between rich and poor would tend to widen in an advanced economy, generating unacceptable income disparities and straining the fabric of an open, free, and democratic society.

Even in the conservative political climate of the late 1970s and the 1980s, the welfare system has continued to respond to changing concepts of need and economic security amidst rising affluence. For example, in 1979 Congress enacted financial support for residential heating costs in response to rising energy prices. Subsidies for phone service in the wake of the American Telephone & Telegraph divestiture have been proposed as part of our definition of "basic needs" for low-income Americans. A parallel extension of the welfare system's scope has occurred in the realm of income security for the nonpoor with the adoption of new tax expenditures for individual retirement accounts. These changes are clear reminders that the welfare system is still evolving, responding to changing economic and social conditions, while also reflecting the higher expectations and aspirations of an increasingly affluent nation.

LESSONS OF THE PAST

What of the alleged failures of the modern welfare system? To be sure, federal interventions in the complex realm of social policy have brought their share of frustrations and excesses. Yet the more important issues are the extent to which social welfare policies and programs have been revised to reflect the lessons of the past, and the standards by which progress in the welfare system is measured. A balanced and reasonable assessment suggests that we have learned from our mistakes—some inevitable, others the result of overly ambitious efforts—during two decades of frequently bold innovation and that past gains have been generally encouraging in light of the ambitious and competing goals set out for the modern welfare system.

Varied strategies and multifaceted approaches needed to ameliorate poverty, discrimination, and related social ills. The designers of the emerging welfare system, from the New Deal to the founding of the Great Society, tended to underestimate the deep-seated problems associated with poverty. The authors of the Social Security Act in 1935 assumed that needs-tested public assistance would wither away as younger workers became fully covered by social insurance—an expectation that was shattered by changing demographics and steadily expanding welfare rolls and more generous benefits during the postwar period. Similarly, a central premise of President Lyndon B. Johnson's War on Poverty was that investments in education and training, civil rights protections, and community organizations representing the have-nots could dramatically lift this generation's poor out of deprivation and insure their children a decent life; but cycles of poverty and dependency have proved considerably more intractable. Yet it became increasingly clear that there are no easy answers or quick solutions to discrimination, economic deprivation, and other social ills. As some of the experiments turned out to be counterproductive as well as politically divisive, the ensuing disillusionment sorely taxed the nation's will to sustain the welfare system in pursuit of steady but incremental gains.

Because many social problems have proved more pervasive and persistent than originally believed, the welfare system has been forced to rely upon more varied and costly strategies for their long-term amelioration. Such comprehensive, long-term approaches frequently involved offering preferential treatment to targeted groups at the cost of the legitimate aspirations of those more fortunate. It has proven extremely difficult politically to defend these actions. Social programs requiring high initial investments and yielding delayed or cumulative benefits have often been abandoned, becoming victims of public resentment and insufficient commitments of funds over too brief a period of time. Furthermore, every solution to deep-seated social ills created new problems. Even when government interventions have achieved their intended results, the process of change in some instances has generated unwanted side effects and posed new problems for policy makers. One clear lesson provided by the experience of the past two decades is that the search for remedies to complex social problems is inherently difficult, particularly when the process involves helping the have-nots to compete effectively with those who have made it. In a democratic society, those who have gained privileged status generally have the clout to abort changes that would be contrary to their interests.

The experience of recent decades suggests that the federal government must proceed on several fronts simultaneously if it is to be successful in efforts to alleviate poverty. For example, training of low-income workers is unlikely to have a significant impact on overall poverty levels or welfare caseloads when provided amid high unemployment or in declining economic regions unless suitable employment and economic development programs are also initiated. In contrast, although income transfers address the immediate needs of the poor, they do not result in lasting improvements in earnings capacity and self-sufficiency unless complemented by public efforts to enhance the skills of recipients and to alter the institutions which trap them in poverty. The interdependence of these antipoverty strategies can create the appearance of failure when individual initiatives are viewed in isolation, particularly when concomitant interventions necessary for their success are not undertaken. At the same time, the benefits of comprehensive approaches are cumulative and can far exceed the potential of isolated efforts.

Income transfers are not enough to combat poverty. One of the clearest lessons arising out of America's experience with the welfare system is that poverty cannot be eliminated solely through a reliance upon income transfers. Income maintenance certainly is an essential component of any antipoverty effort, but a strategy relying upon transfers alone can neither enhance self-sufficiency nor avoid conflicts in labor markets.

In a society in which wages for millions of workers are too low to lift them out of poverty, the provision of adequate cash assistance to the nonworking poor, if unaccompanied by incentives to supplement assistance with earnings, inevitably raises serious questions of equity and generates strong political opposition among taxpayers. In addition, income transfers large enough to lift low-income households above the poverty threshold, if not tied to work effort, would trigger large drops in labor force participation or force massive public expenditures to the nonpoor in order to preserve acceptable work incentives. The political and economic realities have contributed to the demise of successive guaranteed income schemes during the past two decades and demonstrate the need for federal strategies that assist both the working and dependent poor.

The welfare system has neglected the expansion of economic opportunity. While the rhetoric of the Great Society and subsequent initiative often placed heavy emphasis on the expansion of economic opportunity for the less fortunate, this promise has never been fulfilled through a sustained and adequate commitment of societal resources. Many of the dilemmas posed by the modern welfare system — perverse incentives discouraging work by welfare recipients, neglect of the needs of the working poor, high youth and minority unemployment, and burgeoning costs of universal entitlements — arise from an inadequate emphasis on the extension of economic opportunity in current policies. Beyond fundamental guarantees of equal access and civil rights, the welfare system's attempts to broaden opportunity have relied upon relatively small and frequently sporadic investments in job training, public employment, compensatory education, and meaningful work incentives. These initiatives, despite yielding promising results, have fallen far short of their necessary role as equal partners with income maintenance in advancing the goals of the welfare system. To help the millions of the unskilled and deficiently educated, it is necessary to recognize that work and welfare go together as an appropriate public policy.

The difficulties associated with the expansion of economic opportunity through the welfare system are substantial, ranging from the technical and economic to the cultural and political. Certainly the heavy reliance upon transfer programs in recent years reflect the fact that assurances of income security tend to be less threatening to established interests and, therefore, easier to adopt than broader efforts to open avenues to self-support and economic advancement. Yet if the nation is to avoid the debilitating effects of its emphasis on income maintenance, there is no alternative to reviving the promise of opportunity in America. When the nation discards today's prevailing negativism it should turn to this urgent task of broadening access to opportunities for work and self-advancement for all Americans.

MAJOR CHALLENGES

Recognizing that the welfare system is here to stay and that it will continue to evolve, difficult questions and challenges for the future remain. Much concern is presently focused on the perceived inability of American society to afford the broad range of commitments to economic security already enacted at the federal level. The clamor to rein in public expenditures has profound implications for the political base and stability of the welfare system, generating lasting tensions between universal and means-tested provision of benefits. Finally, and perhaps most importantly, the appropriate roles of federal, state, and local governments, as well as the private sector, in the modern welfare system have been called into serious question in recent years, requiring establishment of a new consensus regarding the legitimacy and optimal scope of federal efforts to bolster the economic security of all Americans.

Maintaining an affordable system. The affordability of the welfare system is, except in the extreme, essentially a normative judgment reflecting society's wilingness to forego some measure of personal consumption and alternative public outlays in exchange for greater collective security. In some cases, the exchange of current income for future economic or national security is relatively direct—social insurance programs requiring prior contributions or investments in defense supported by higher taxes. In other instances the decision to sacrifice personal income represents a hedge against unforeseen misfortunes or hardships, an awareness that "there but for the grace of God, go I"—disaster relief, food stamps, and Medicaid. For the most targeted, means-tested initiatives, public expenditures are humanitarian attempts to relieve deprivation and enlightened acknowledgments of the broader societal benefits associated with reductions in poverty. All these societal choices are predicted on an awareness of societal affluence and on the belief that the nation can afford to defer a portion of today's consumption for tomorrow's economic or national security.

Without question, the potential for reasoned assessments of society's capacity to support social investments and protections has been diminished in recent years by the fiscal policies of the Reagan administration. By combining rapid increases in defense spending and deep reductions in the federal tax base, President Reagan has intentionally created budget conditions in which social welfare expenditures appear unaffordable. Both historical and international comparisons suggest that, with the adoption of responsible fiscal policies, the American welfare system has not exceeded the bounds of affordability. With the exception of Japan, the United States has devoted a smaller proportion of its gross national product to social programs than any other advanced industrialized nation.

The Reagan fiscal policy has failed to address the crucial legitimate issue regarding the future affordability of the welfare system. This issue concerns the optimal social investment or protection against economic uncertainty through entitlements and tax expenditures for the nonpoor, while still fulfilling our societal responsibilities to those in need. The rise of federal social welfare expenditures during the 1970s was primarily the result of dramatic increases in the cost of non-means-tested entitlements such as social security and Medicare. Between 1970 and 1984, means-tested programs accounted for one-seventh of the $337 billion rise in total transfer payments. Coupled with open-ended subsidies for middle- and upper-income groups through credit and tax policies ranging from student assistance to interest and retirement savings deductions, the principle of universal eligibility in many social welfare programs has clearly strained resources available for other components of the welfare system.

Burgeoning universal entitlements are gradually becoming a focus of potential spending cuts in the continuing budget difficulties precipitated by the Reagan administration. The current debate is hardly conducive to a thoughtful restructuring of the broader welfare system, framed as it is by the artificial pressures of misguided fiscal policies. Yet in some perverse fashion the problem of massive federal deficits may provide the political will for a much-needed reexamination of the balance between help for the needy and subsidies to the more fortunate in the welfare system. By curtailing expenditures for lower-priority initiatives aiding the nonpoor, the Reagan budget reductions of the mid-1980s may create opportunities for the emergence of a more efficient and effective welfare system in the years ahead.

Targeting v. universality. The conflict between goals of targeting and universality within the welfare system can never be fully resolved. Without question, universal provision of cash assistance and social services engenders broad public acceptance and a strong base of political support, as illustrated by the evolution of social security, Medicare, veteran, and college loan programs. Yet the extension of federal aid without regard to income necessarily expands vastly the costs of government interventions and dilutes their effectiveness in helping those most in need. On the other hand, as Wilbur Cohen, a prominent architect of the U.S. welfare system, has often remarked, programs which are narrowly targeted to serve poor people inevitably become poor programs. Thus, the challenge is to strike a balance between the goals of targeting and universality that gives every American a stake in the welfare system while still allocating the requisite resources for those who need them most with due regard to the dignity of recipients.

The Reagan administration's rhetorical crusade to focus federal aid on those with greatest need has not been unfounded. Despite the difficulty of judging the appropriate balance between targeting and universality, a strong case could be made by 1980 that too large a share of scarce federal resources was being diverted into benefits for the non-needy. Unfortunately, the administration's response to this imbalance has proven to be narrow, inequitable, and devoid of vision. Eligibility for programs aiding the poor has been restricted to the most needy as a means of slashing federal outlays. However, no broader effort to shift resources from universal entitlements or subsidies for the affluent to means-tested programs serving low-income Americans has been undertaken. Only this year, with opportunities, for significant budget savings from means-tested programs seemingly exhausted, has President Reagan challenged the flow of aid to middle- and upper-income households through the broader welfare system.

Principle of subsidiarity. The Reagan administration has similarly clouded the perennial debate over the appropriate sharing of social responsibilities among federal, state, and local governments, as well as the private sector. The Reagan program, under the banner of "New Federalism," has aggressively sought to shift responsibility for the administration and financing of social welfare initiatives to the states. The Reagan administration has also relied heavily upon the conviction that social welfare efforts, whenever feasible, should be left to private voluntary efforts. This perspective, founded on ideology rather than empirical evidence, has been useful in buttressing attempts to reduce federal expenditures, but it has precluded a balanced and reasoned assessment of appropriate public and private roles in the modern welfare system.

Taking the principle of subsidiarity (the belief that the federal government should not undertake functions that can be performed by lower levels of government or private groups) to the extreme, opponents of federal intervention seek to obscure the reasons why much of the responsibility for the welfare system has fallen upon the federal government. Contrary to idealized notions of community responsibility, state and local governments in prior decades consistently failed to marshal the will and the resources to alleviate poverty and expand economic opportunity for the most disadvantaged. By definition, the poorest states and localities faced the most severe problems while having the least capacity to redress them. Competition among states and localities also has discouraged responses to pressing social needs prior to federal intervention, as these smaller jurisdictions have attempted to attract new businesses and industries by holding down tax rates and public expenditures. Finally, because the federal government relies upon more equitable financing structures and a broader revenue base than state or local jurisdictions, its capacity to support large-scale income maintenance and human resource programs is far greater. For all these reasons, any effective welfare system must include a central federal role in setting national priorities, providing direction for equitable policies and program development, and generating the resources necessary to meet social welfare goals.

These principles are not inconsistent with the belief that decentralized program administration can be an appropriate response to regional diversity and bureaucratic inefficiency. In some realms, community decision making and program administration are crucial to the effectiveness of the welfare system, ensuring that interventions are tailored to local needs. Strategies for assisting the disadvantaged that are well suited for conditions in the South Bronx may have little relevance to the problems of rural Appalachia. The existing structure of federal programs in education, employment and training, economic development, and a host of other areas already reflects this need for local control over the specific form and substance of social welfare initiatives.

Given the unwillingness or inability of state and local governments to marshal adequate resources for the amelioration of social problems, the hope advanced by President Reagan that the private sector can fill the breach created by federal retrenchments appears even less credible. The nation's voluntary agencies and associations certainly have not proven able to compensate for losses in federal aid through greater reliance upon private philanthropy. As a detailed Urban Institute study of some 6,900 nonprofit organizations across the nation has documented, private social welfare agencies have fallen far short in their attempts to fill gaps left by domestic budget cuts. Furthermore, the business community is neither equipped nor inclined to accept responsibility for the wide array of problems confronting the nation's disadvantaged. Even in areas where the private sector presumably has a direct and immediate interest, such as occupational training under the Job Training Partnership Act, the evidence shows that industry molds social programs to serve its own profitability goals, insuring quick and efficient placements to minimize training costs to fill job vacancies, while investing little to develop skills among those most in need. The broader public interest cannot be either adequately protected or promoted through a reliance on private sector initiatives alone.

RENEWAL OF CONFIDENCE

The need for a strong federal role in the welfare system is clear, and yet public understanding of this federal responsibility had been undermined by the virulent antigovernment ideology of the New Right and nourished by President Reagan. Thus, the most pressing question for the future of the welfare system may rest upon the nation's ability to regain confidence in government responsibility for the welfare of the citizenry and belief in the legitimacy of collective action to meet societal needs. If America's political leadership continues to denigrate the federal government as a vehicle for advancing the common good, further progress in strengthening and improving the welfare system (as well as in other legitimate and proper realms of government responsibility ranging from protection of the environment to safety in the workplace) will remain stymied. However, through a clearer understanding of past experience, the nation can rekindle its faith in the ability of the welfare system to provide not only income for the poor but also greater opportunity and equity for all Americans. In this era of retrenchment, no challenge is more important than refreshing our memory of past accomplishments and refocusing our vision for the years ahead.

Progress has been made on various social and economic fronts. However, the advances will be halted, if not reversed, unless the challenge for greater social justice is renewed. Only dedicated pessimists and gainsayers can doubt our capacity to achieve further substantial improvements. As the nation prepares to celebrate the bicentennial of its Constitution, there is need for positivism, commitment, and compassion that still remain indispensable in the quest for a better society. We have the power if we have the will to forge an even better society and to promote the general welfare. ■

MORALITY AND ECONOMIC POLICY

Moral and ethical standards are certainly involved in the setting of goals for national economic policy. But such standards are seldom discussed and debated openly when economic policy decisions are being made.

To place such concerns on the national agenda, the National Conference of Catholic Bishops decided to issue a pastoral letter on the subject. Archbishop Rembert G. Weakland of Milwaukee was named as head of a panel to write it. Excerpted here is the second draft of that letter (issued October 7, 1985). In it, the bishops declared that the needs of the poor should have the "highest priority," that "people have a right to employment" and to organize unions with the right to strike, that the present disparities of wealth and income in America are "unacceptable," and that certain specific steps that they recommended should be taken to reform U. S. economic policy.

Almost as soon as the draft of the bishop's letter appeared, a group of conservatives, led by former Secretary of the Treasury William Simon and sociologist Michael Novak, issued their own response to it, attacking both its premises and its conclusions.

Reprinted here is an article by Peter Steinfels that takes on the critics of the bishops' letter. Steinfels argues that the pastoral letters recommendations, which Steinfels feels are actually moderate ones, have drawn the most criticism, when it should have been the premises, with which Steinfels agrees and which include the importance of the goal of a fair distribution of wealth and income, that drew the most fire.

PASTORAL LETTER ON CATHOLIC SOCIAL TEACHING AND THE U. S. ECONOMY
The National Conference of Catholic Bishops

Every perspective on economic life that is human, moral, and Christian must be shaped by three questions: What does the economy do *for* people? What does it do *to* people? And how do people *participate* in it? The economy is a human reality, formed by human decisions and actions. It is men and women working together, developing the gifts of God's creation and building a world more fit for human living. All this work must serve the material and spiritual well-being of people. It influences what people hope and believe about their destiny. It affects the way they live together. It touches their very faith in God. Concern for all these dimensions of economic life leads us to write this pastoral letter. . . .

The fulfillment of the basic needs of the poor is of the highest priority. Personal decisions, policies of private and public bodies, and power relationships must all be evaluated by their effects on those who lack the minimum necessities of nutrition, housing, education, and health care. In particular, this principle recognizes that meeting fundamental human needs must come before the fulfillment of desires for luxury consumer goods, for profits not conducive to the common good, and for unnecessary military hardware.

Increasing active participation in economic life by those who are presently excluded or vulnerable is a high social priority. The human dignity of all is realized when people gain the power to work together to improve their lives and to make their contribution to society. Basic justice calls for more than providing help *to* the poor and other vulnerable members of society. It recognizes the priority of policies and programs that enhance economic participation through employment. It challenges privileged economic power in favor of the well-being of all. It points to the need to improve the present situation of those unjustly discriminated against in the past. And it has very important implications for both the domestic and the international distribution of power.

The investment of wealth, talent, and human energy should be specially directed to benefit those who are poor or economically insecure. Achieving a more just economy in the United States and the world depends in part on increasing economic resources and productivity. Different sorts of investment of human and financial resources, however, can have very different outcomes for people even when they have similar rates of productivity. This priority presents a strong moral challenge to policies that put large amounts of talent and capital into the production of luxury consumer goods and military technology while failing to invest sufficiently in education, health, and the basic infrastructure of our society, or in economic sectors that produce urgently needed jobs, goods, and services.

These three priorities are not policies. They are norms which should guide the economic choices of all and shape economic institutions. They can help the United States move forward to fulfill the duties of justice and protect economic rights. They were strongly affirmed as implications of Catholic social teaching by Pope John Paul II during his visit to Canada in 1984: "The needs of the poor take priority over the desires of the rich; the rights of workers over the maximization of profits; the preservation of the environment over uncontrolled industrial expansion; production to meet social needs over production for military purposes." There will undoubtedly be disputes about the concrete applications of these priorities in our complex world. We do not seek to foreclose discussion about them. However, we believe, that an effort to move in the direction they indicate is urgently needed.

The economic challenge of today has many parallels with the political challenge that confronted the founders of our nation. In order to create a new form of political democracy they were compelled to develop ways of thinking and political institutions that had never existed before. Their efforts were arduous and their goals imperfectly realized, but they launched an experiment in the protection of civil and political rights that has prospered through the efforts of those who came after them. *We believe the time has come for a similar experiment in securing economic rights: the creation of an order that guarantees the minimum conditions of human dignity in the economic sphere for every person.* By drawing on the resources of the Catholic moral-religious tradition, we hope to make a contribution through this letter to such a new "American Experiment": a new venture to secure economic justice for all.

The economy of this nation has been built by the labor of human hands and minds. Its future will be forged by the ways persons direct all this work toward greater justice. The economy is not a machine that operates according to its own inexorable laws, and persons are not mere objects tossed about by economic forces. Pope John Paul II has stated that "human work is a key, probably the essential key, to the whole social question." . . .

WORKING PEOPLE AND LABOR UNIONS

Though John Paul II's understanding of work is a very inconclusive one, it fully applies to those customarily called "workers" or "labor" in the United States. Labor has great dignity, so great that all who are able to work are obligated to do so. The duty to work derives not only from God's command but from a responsibility to one's own humanity and to the common good. The virtue of industriousness is also an expression of a person's dignity and solidarity with others. All working people are called to contribute to the common good by seeking excellence in production and service.

Because work is this important, people have a right to employment. In addition, in return for their labor, workers have a right to wages and other benefits sufficient to sustain life in dignity. As Pope Leo XIII stated, every working person "has the right of securing things to sustain life." The way power is distributed in a free market economy frequently gives employers greater bargaining power than employees possess in the negotiation of wage agreements. Such unequal power may press workers into a choice between an inadequate wage and no wage at all. But justice, not charity, demands certain minimum guarantees. The provision of wages and other benefits sufficient to support a family in dignity is a basic necessity to prevent this exploitation of workers. The dignity of workers also requires adequate health care, security for old age or disability, unemployment compensation, healthful working conditions, weekly rest, periodic holidays for recreation and leisure, and reasonable security against arbitrary dismissal. These provisions are all essential if workers are to be treated as persons rather than simply as a "factor of production."

The Church fully supports the right of workers to form unions or other associations to secure their rights to fair wages and working conditions. This is a specific application of the more general right to associate. In the words of Pope John Paul II, "The experiece of history teaches that organizations of this type are an indispensable element of social life, especially in modern industrialized societies." Unions may also legitimately resort to strikes in situations where they are the only available means for pursuing the justice owed to workers. No one may deny the right to organize for purposes of collective bargaining without attacking human dignity itself. Therefore we firmly oppose organized efforts, such as those regrettably now seen in this country, to use intimidation and threats to break existing unions and prevent workers from organizing. Migrant agricultural workers today are particularly in need of the protection that unionization can provide. U. S. labor law reform is needed to meet these problems as well as to provide more timely and effective remedies for unfair labor practices. . . .

OWNERSHIP

The Catholic tradition has long defended the right to private ownership of productive property. This right is an important element in a just economic policy. It enlarges our capacity for creativity and initiative. Small and medium-sized farms, businesses, and entepreneurial enterprises are among the most creative and efficient sectors of our economy. They are highly valued by by people of the United States, as are land ownership and home ownership. Widespread distribution of property can help avoid excessive concentration of economic power. For these reasons ownership should be possible for a broad sector of our population.

This support of private ownership does not mean that anyone has the right to unlimited accumulation of wealth. There is a "social mortgage" on private property. "Private property does not constitute for anyone an absolute or unconditioned right. No one is justified in keeping for his exclusive use what he does not need, when others lack necessities."[13] In our increasingly complex economy, the common good may sometimes demand that the right to own cede to public involvement in the planning or ownership of certain sectors of the economy. The Church's teaching opposes collectivist and statist economic approaches. But it also rejects the notion that a free market automatically produces justice. Therefore, as Pope John Paul II has argued, "One cannot exclude the socialization, in suitable conditions, of certain means of production." The determination of when such conditions exist must be made on a case by case basis in light of the demands of the common good. . . .

SELECTED ECONOMIC POLICY ISSUES

The principles of Catholic social teaching help us to shape a moral vision of economic justice, a vision which guides us in our commitment to transform the economic and social world in which we live.

The Church is not bound to any particular economic, political, or social system or ideology. It has existed and will continue to exist in many different environments with different forms of economic and social organization. We must evaluate all these economic systems in terms of our moral and ethical principles. Our primary criterion in judging any economy is not adherence to a particular ideology but the impact it has on human beings. Does it promote or impede the realization of human dignity?

In this document we offer reflections on the particular reality that is the U. S. economy. In doing so we are aware of the need to address not only individual issues within the economy, but also the large question of the economic system itself. We situate our discussion within a context of diverse and competing views of how to understand the American economic system. One such analysis assumes that an unfettered free market economy—where owners, workers, and consumers are allowed to pursue their individual self-interest—provides the greatest possible liberty, material welfare, and equity. The policy implication of this view is to intervene in the economy as little as possible because it is such a delicate mechanism that any attempts to improve it are likely to have the opposite effect. A second view argues that current economic problems are inherent in the very nature of the capitalist system. In this view capitalism cannot be reformed, but must be replaced by a radically different system that abolishes private property and the market system.

Catholic social teaching has traditionally rejected both of these ideological extremes, for they are likely to produce results contrary to human dignity and economic justice. Nor is it the role of the Church to create or promote a "third way" or a specific new economic system. Starting with the assumption that the economy has been created by human beings and can be changed by them, the Church works for reforms in a variety of economic and political contexts.

---

13. The Vatican, "Charter of the Rights of the Family," *Origins*, 13:27 (December 15, 1983), p. 463.

Therefore, our approach in analyzing the U. S. economy is pragmatic and evolutionary in nature. We live in a "mixed" economic system which is the product of a long history of reform and adjustment. It is in the spirit of this American pragmatic tradition of reform that we seek to continue the search for a more just economy. Moreover, our nation has many assets to assist in this quest—vast economic, technological, and human resources and a vibrant system of political democracy through which we can help to shape economic decisions. . . .

EMPLOYMENT

Full employment is the foundation of a just economy. The most urgent priority for domestic economic policy is the creation of new jobs with adequate pay and decent working conditions. We must make it possible as a nation for every one who is seeking a job to find employment. Our emphasis on this goal is based on the conviction that human works has a special dignity and is a key to achieving justice in society.

Employment is a basic right, a right which protects the freedom of all to participate in the economic life of society. It is a right which flows from the principles of justice which we have outlined above. For most people employment is crucial to self-realization and essential to the fulfillment of material needs. Since so few in our economy own productive property, employment also forms the first line of defense against poverty. Jobs benefit society as well as workers, for they enable more people to contribute to the common good and to the productivity required for a healthy economy. . . .

Our own experiences with the individuals, families, and communities that suffer the burdens of unemployment compel us to the conviction that as a nation we simply cannot afford to have millions of able-bodied men and women unemployed. We cannot afford the economic costs, the social dislocation, and the enormous human tragedies caused by unemployment. In the end, however, what we can least afford is the assault on human dignity that occurs when millions are left without adequate employment. Therefore, we cannot but conclude that current levels of unemployment are morally unacceptable. . . .

We recommend that the nation makes a major new commitment to achieve full employment. At present there is nominal endorsement of the full employment ideal, but no firm commitment to bringing it about. If every effort were now being made to create the jobs required, one might argue that the situation today is the best we can do. But such is not the case. The country is doing far less than it might to generate employment. . . .

If we are to move toward full employment, we must first establish the right to a job for every American who wants to work. Then the burden is on all of us—policymakers, business, labor, and the general public—to create and implement the mechanisms to protect that right. We must work for the formation of a new national consensus and mobilize the necessary political will at all levels to make the goal of full employment a reality. . . .

The general or "macroeconomic" policies of the federal government are essential tools for encouraging the steady economic growth that produces more and better jobs in the economy. *We recommend that the fiscal and monetary policies of the nation should be coordinated in such a way that full employment is the number one goal.* Policies that reduce the federal deficit and contribute to the lowering of interest rates will be necessary if this goal is to be achieved. Tax policies can also be used to promote productive investment and to direct such investment toward the social goals that the nation seeks.

Any attempts to expand employment by general economic policies must deal directly with the problem of inflation. The risk of inflationary pressures resulting from high levels of employment is both real and serious. Our response to this risk, however, must not be to abandon the goal of full employment, but to develop specific policies that will attack the inflation problem directly. At the same time, we must seek to provide jobs in ways that produce as little inflationary pressure as possible.

While economic growth is an important and necessary condition for the reduction of unemployment, it is not sufficient in and of itself. More specific programs and policies targeted toward particular aspects of the unemployment problem are also necessary.

We recommend expansion of job-training and apprenticeship programs in the private sector which are administered and supported jointly by business, labor unions, and government. Any comprehensive employment strategy must include systematic means of developing the technical and professional skills needed for a dynamic and productive economy. Investment in a skilled workforce is a prerequisite both for sustaining economic growth and achieving greater justice in the United States. . . .

We recommend increased support for direct job creation programs targeted on the structurally unemployed. Such programs can take the form of direct public service employment and also of public subsidies for employment in the private sector. Both approaches would provide jobs for those with low skills less expensively and with less inflation than would general stimulation of the economy. The cost of providing jobs must also be balanced against the savings realized by the government through decreased welfare and unemployment insurance expenditures and increased revenues from the taxes paid by the newly employed. . . .

POVERTY

More than thirty-three million Americans—about one in every seven people in our nation—are poor by the government's official definition. The norms of human dignity and the preferential option for the poor compel us to confront this issue with a sense of urgency. Dealing with poverty is not a luxury to which our nation can attend when it finds the time and resources. Rather, it is an imperative of the highest priority.

Of particular concern is the fact that poverty has increased dramatically during the last decade. Since 1973 the poverty rate has increased by nearly a third. Although the recent recovery has brought a slight decline in the rate, it remains at a level that is higher than at almost any other time during the last two decades. . . .

Poverty is not a problem isolated among a small number of anonymous people in our central cities. Nor is it limited to a dependent underclass or to specific groups in the United States. It is a condition experienced at some time by many people in different walks of life and in different circumstances. Many poor people are working but at wages insufficient to lift them out of poverty. Others are unable to work and therefore dependent on outside sources of support. Still others are on the edge of poverty; although not officially defined as poor, they are economically insecure and at risk of falling into poverty.

While many of the poor manage to escape from beneath the official poverty line, others remain poor for extended periods of time. Long-term poverty is concentrated among racial minorities and families headed by women. It is also more likely to be found in rural areas and in the South. Of the long-term poor, most are either working at wages too low to bring them above the poverty line or are retired, disabled, or parents of pre-school children. Few are in a position to work more hours than they do now. . . .

ECONOMIC INEQUALITY

Important to our discussion of poverty in America is an understanding of the degree of economic inequality in our nation. Our economy is marked by a very uneven distribution of wealth and income. For example, it is estimated that 28 percent of the total net wealth is held by the richest 2 percent of families in the United States. The top 10 percent holds 57 percent of the net wealth. If homes and other real estate are excluded, the concentration of ownership of "financial wealth" is even more glaring. In 1983, 54 percent of the total net financial assets were held by 2 percent of all families, those whose annual income is over $125,000. Eighty-six percent of these assets were held by the top 10 percent of all families.

Although disparities in the distribution of income are less extreme, they are still striking. In 1984 the bottom 20 percent of American families received only 4.7 percent of the total income in the nation and the bottom 40 percent received only 15.7 percent, the lowest share on record. In contrast, the top one-fifth received 42.9 percent of the total income, the highest share since 1948. These figures are only partial and very imperfect measures of the inequality in our society, but they do suggest that the degree of inequality is quite large. In comparison with other industrialized nations, the United States is among the more unequal in terms of income distribution. Moreover, the gap between rich and poor in our nation has increased during the last decade.

Catholic social teaching does not suggest that absolute equality in the distribution of income and wealth is required. Some degree of inequality is not only acceptable, but may be considered desirable for economic and social reasons. However, unequal distribution should be evaluated in terms of several moral principles we have enunciated: the priority of meeting the basic needs of the poor and the importance of increasing the level of participation by all members of society in the economic life of the nation. These norms establish a strong presumption against extreme inequality of income and wealth as long as there are poor, hungry and homeless people in our midst. They also suggest that extreme inequalities are detrimental to the development of social solidarity and community, for large inequalities in the economic sphere mean that the degree of power and the level of participation in the political and social spheres is also very uneven. In view of these norms we find the disparities of income and wealth in the United States to be unacceptable. Justice requires that our society take the necessary steps to decrease these inequities. . . .

A key element in removing poverty is prevention through a healthy economy. The first lines of attack against poverty must be to build and sustain a healthy economy that provides employment opportunities at decent wages for all adults who are able to work. Poverty is intimately linked to the issue of employment. Millions are poor because they have lost their jobs or because their wages are too low. The persistent high levels of unemployment during the last decade are a major reason why poverty has increased in recent years. . . .

Vigorous action should be undertaken to remove barriers to full and equal employment for women and minorities. Too many women and minorities are locked into jobs with low pay, poor working conditions, and little opportunity for career advancement. So long as we tolerate a situation in which people can work full-time and still be below the poverty line—a situation common among those earning the minimum wage—we will continue to have many members of the "working poor." Concerted efforts must be made through job training, affirmative action, and other means to assist those now prevented from obtaining more lucrative jobs. Action should also be taken to upgrade poorer paying jobs and to correct wage differentials that discriminate unjustly against women.

Self-help efforts among the poor should be fostered by programs and policies in both the private and public sectors. We believe that an effective way to attack poverty is through programs that are small in scale, locally based, and oriented toward empowering the poor to become self-sufficient. Both private groups and the public sector can provide seed money, training and technical assistance, and organizational support for self-help projects in a wide variety of areas as low-income housing, credit unions, worker cooperatives, legal assistance, and neighborood and community organizations. Efforts that enable the poor to participate in the ownership and control of economic resources are especially important.

Poor people must take charge of their own futures and become responsible for their own economic advancement. Social reform is not enough; personal motivation and initiative are also necessary if individuals are to escape poverty. By taking advantage of opportunities for education, employment and training, and by working together for change, the poor empower themselves to be full participants in our economic, social and political life.

Reforms in the tax system should be implemented that would reduce the burden on the poor. We urge that two principles be incorporated in any tax reforms that are undertaken. First, such reforms should eliminate or offset the payment of taxes by those below the official poverty level. In recent years the tax burden of the poor has increased substantially while those at the top of the income scale have enjoyed significant reductions. Families below the official poverty line are, by definition, without sufficient resources to purchase the basic necessities of life. They should not be forced to bear the additional burden of paying taxes. Secondly, we urge that the principle of progressivity be a central guiding norm in any reforms of the tax system. Those with relatively greater financial resources should pay a higher rate of taxation—both in principle and in the actual or "effective" tax rates paid. The inclusion of such a principle in tax policies is an important means of reducing the severe inequalities of income and wealth in the nation.

Society should make a much stronger commitment to education for the poor. Any long-term solution to poverty in this country must pay serious attention to education, public and private, in school and out of school. Lack of adequate education prevents many people from escaping poverty. Illiteracy, a problem which affects an estimated 60 million Americans, condemns many to joblessness or chronically low wages. Moreover, it excludes them in many ways from sharing in the political and spiritual life of the community. . . .

Policies and programs at all levels should support the strength and stability of families, especially poor families. As a nation, we need to examine all aspects of economic life and assess their effects on families. Employment practices, health insurance policies, income security programs, tax policy, and service programs can either support or undermine the abilities of families to fulfill their roles in nurturing children and caring for infirm and dependent family members.

A thorough reform of the nation's welfare and income-support programs should be undertaken. For millions of poor Americans the only economic safety net is the public welfare system. The programs that make up this system should serve the needs of the poor in a manner that respects their dignity and provides adequate support. In our judgment the present welfare system does not adequately meet these criteria. We believe that several improvements can and should be made within the framework of existing welfare programs, but also that more far-reaching reforms should be given consideration in the future. Among the immediate improvements that could be made are the following:

Public assistance programs should be designed to assist recipients, wherever possible, to become self-sufficient through gainful employment. Individuals should not be worse off when they get jobs than if they relied only on public assistance. Under current rules, people who give up welfare benefits to work in low-paying jobs soon lose their Medicaid benefits. To help recipients become self-sufficient and reduce dependency on welfare, public assistance programs should work in tandem with job creation programs that include provisions for training, counseling, placement, and child care. Jobs for recipients of public assistance should be fairly compensated so that workers receive the full benefits and status associated with gainful employment.

Welfare programs should provide recipients with adequate levels of support. This support should cover basic needs in food, clothing, shelter, health care, and other essentials. At present only 4 percent of poor families with children receive enough cash welfare benefits to lift them out of poverty. The combined benefits of AFDC and Food Stamps typically come to less than three-fourths of the official poverty level. Those receiving public assistance should not face the prospect of hunger at the end of the month, homelessness, sending children to school in ragged clothing, or inadequate medical care.

National eligibility standards and a national minimum benefit level for public assistance programs should be established. Currently welfare eligibility and benefits vary greatly among states. In 1985 a family of three with no earnings had a maximum AFDC benefit of $96 a month in Mississippi and $558 a month in Vermont. To remedy these great disparities, which are far larger than the regional differences in the cost of living, and to assure a floor of benefits for all needy people, our nation should establish and fund national minimum benefit levels and eligibility standards in cash assistance programs. The benefits should also be indexed to reflect changes in the cost of living. These changes reflect standards that our nation has already put in place for aged and disabled people and veterans. Is it not possible to do the same for the children and their mothers who receive public assistance?

Welfare programs should be available to two-parent as well as single parent families. Most states now limit participation in AFDC to families headed by single parents, usually women. The coverage of this program should be extended to two-parent families so that fathers who are unemployed or poorly paid do not have to leave home in order for their children to receive help. . . .

THE ROLE OF THE UNITED STATES IN THE GLOBAL ECONOMY: CONSTRUCTIVE CHOICES:

In the absence of an international political authority, building a just world economic order demands that we and our governments promote public policies that increase the participation of poor nations and marginalized people in the global economy. We believe that this responsibility pertains especially to the United States, because no other nation's economic power matches ours.

In recent years, however, U. S. policy toward development in the Third World has become increasingly one of selective assistance based on an East-West assessment of a North-South set of problems, at the expense of basic human needs and economic development. Such a view makes the principal policy issue one of "national security." Developing countries have become largely test cases in the East-West struggle; they seem to have meaning or value only in terms of this larger geopolitical calculus. The result is that issues of human need and economic develop take second place to the political-strategic argument. We deplore this tendency.

Moreover, the U. S. performance in North-South negotiations seems often to cast us in the role of resisting developing-country proposals without advancing realistic ones of our own. The North-South dialogue is complex, protracted, and filled with symbolic and often unrealistic demands; but the situation has not reached the point where the rest of the world expects the United States to assume a reluctant, adversarial posture in such discussions. The U. S. approach to the developing countries needs urgently to be changed; a country of our size and with our resources and potential has a moral obligation to lead in helping to reduce poverty in the Third World.

We believe that U. S. policy toward the developing world should reflect our traditional regard for human rights and our concern for social progress. In the economic policy area, as we noted in our pastoral letter on nuclear war, the major international economic relationships of aid, trade, finance, and investment are interdependent among themselves and illustrate the range of interdependent issues facing U. S. policy. Each offers the United States the possibility of substantial, positive movement toward helping to increase social justice in the developing world; in each, regrettably, the United States falls short. It is urgent that immediate steps be taken to correct these deficiencies. . . .

CONCLUSION

None of the issues we have addressed in this chapter can be dealt with in isolation. They are interconnected, and their resolution requires difficult trade-offs among competing interests and values. The changing international economy, for example, greatly influences efforts to achieve full employment in the United States and to maintain a healthy farm sector. Similarly, as we have noted, policies and programs to reduce unemployment and poverty must not ignore the potential inflationary impact. These complexities and trade-offs are real and must be confronted, but they are not an excuse for inaction. They should not paralyze us in our search for a more just economy.

Many of the reforms we have suggested in this chapter would be expensive. At a time when the United States has annual deficits in the range of $200 billion per year, some might consider these costs too high. But this discussion must be set in the context of how our resources are allocated and the immmense human and social costs of failure to act on these pressing problems. We believe that the question of providing adequate revenues to meet the needs of our nation must be faced squarely and realistically. Reforms in the tax code which close loopholes and generate new revenues, for example, are among the steps that need to be examined in order to develop a federal budget that is both fiscally sound and socially responsible. The cost of meeting our social needs must also be weighed against the $300 billion a year allocated for defense. We have spent more than a trillion dollars on defense since 1980. Although some of these expenditures are necessary for the defense of the nation, some elements of the military budget are both wasteful and dangerous for world peace. Careful reductions should be made in these areas in order to free up funds for social and economic reforms. In the end, the question is not whether the United States can provide the necessary funds to meet our social needs, but whether we have the political will to do so. ■

THE BISHOPS AND THEIR CRITICS
Peter Steinfels

"Modern capitalism," wrote John Maynard Keynes, "is absolutely irreligious, without internal union, without much public spirit, often, though not always, a mere congeries of possessors and pursuers." Over 60 years ago, R. H. Tawney, who cited those lines from the young Keynes, set out to explore how this condition had come about. In *Religion and the Rise of Capitalism*, he examined the great "intellectual and moral conversion" of the 16th and 17th centuries. This period saw—

> the abdication of the Christian Churches from departments of economic conduct and social theory long claimed as their province [and] the general acceptance by thinkers of a scale of ethical values, which turned the desire for pecuniary gain from a perilous, if natural, frailty into the idol of philosophers and the mainspring of society.

In this "secularization of social and economic philosophy," a synthesis of values, presided over by religion, was—

> resolved into its elements—politics, business, and spiritual exercises; each assumes a separate and independent vitality and obeys the laws of its own being. . . . separate and parallel compartments, between which a due balance should be maintained, but which have no vital connection with each other.

Like other politically committed scholars, Tawney saw his historical investigations as intimately linked to contemporary concerns. In this case, it was his belief that—

> the philosophy which would keep economic interests and ethical idealism safely locked up in their separate compartments finds that each of the prisoners is increasingly restive. . . . Religious thought is no longer content to dismiss the transactions of business and the institutions of society as matters irrelevant to the life of the spirit. . . . The line of division between the spheres of religion and secular business . . . is shifting. . . . By common consent the treaty of partition has lapsed and the boundaries are once more in motion. . . . Rightly or wrongly, with wisdom or with its opposite, not only in England but on the Continent and in America, not only in one denomination but among Roman Catholics, Anglicans, and Nonconformists, an attempt is being made to restate the practical implications of the social ethics of the Christian faith, in a form sufficiently comprehensive to provide a standard by which to judge the collective actions and institutions of mankind, in the sphere both of international politics and social organization. . . . As in the analogous problem of relations between Church and State, issues which were thought to have been buried . . . have shown in our own day that they were not dead, but sleeping. . . .

Tawney's observations could have been written yesterday—which makes them both exhilarating and discouraging. Since he wrote, efforts to overcome the modern division between economics and morality have repeatedly grown dor-

mant and then stirred from slumber. And the reception afforded the latest effort—
the vigorous first draft of a pastoral letter on the economy by America's Catholic
bishops—shows how deep-seated are the opposing tendencies that Tawney studied
six decades ago.

The decision to write such a letter was made at the same 1980 meeting of
the bishops that also voted to prepare a pastoral letter addressing nuclear war.
(One observer, looking back at this double-barreled decision, remarked that the
bishops may be fiercely opposed to abortion and euthanasia but seem rather
favorably inclined toward suicide). Once the nuclear pastoral, which had been
given priority, turned out to directly challenge current armaments policy—and
in view of run-ins between national Catholic agencies and the Reagan administration over budget cutbacks affecting the poor—business circles grew uneasy about
what might be ticking away in the bishops' work on the economy. The bishops
seemed to be acting out the text of the classic Jewish telegram: "START WORRY-
ING. MESSAGE TO FOLLOW."

A few people did more than start worrying. A group of Catholics, headed
by William Simon and Michael Novak and heavily weighted with conservatives
and neoconservatives linked to the Nixon and Reagan administrations, began
preparing an alternative "lay" statement—an exercise, as one admirer described
it, in "preemptive damage control." The bishops did their best to be accommodating. The list of individuals with whom the bishops held formal consultations is heavy with business executives; they met once with representatives of
the Simon/Novak group and with Novak himself on several other occasions.

When the draft appeared last November 11, it did not disappoint. The contrast between its economic philosophy and that of an Administration that five
days earlier had won a massive vote of confidence was front-page news.

Where the Administration celebrated the successes of the American economy,
the bishops contrasted them with its persistent short-comings. Where the Administration exalted American individualism, the bishops emphasized "communal
solidarity." Where the Administration minimized—even derided—the economic
role of government, the bishops endorsed government efforts to guide the economy
and provide social welfare. Where the Administration prescribed inegalitarian
tax measures and the acceptance of the discipline of unemployment as necessary
steps toward properity, the bishops judged the existing level of socioeconomic
inequality in America as "morally unacceptable"; they called for a new national
commitment to full employment as the leading domestic priority; and they
declared that the litmus test of any society's economy was the way it treated the
poor and powerless. *Business Week* concluded that the letter's "comments on the
workings of the economy in four areas—unemployment, poverty, economic relations with developing nations, and economic planning—amount to a wide-ranging
critique of Reagan's less-is-more brand of governance."

Even a few of the president's supporters welcomed the letter. David Gergen,
former director of communications at the Reagan White House, wrote: "The
bishops have spoken up at exactly the right time and in the right way: at a moment when the nation is about to make crucial economic decisions, the bishops
have said we must focus again on the rising tide of poverty in America."

Most conservatives were not so generous. Jerry Falwell saw the letter as pointing the way to communism. So, in effect, did Norman Podhoretz. A columnist in the *National Review* called the draft "economically illiterate" and "an appeal to envy" while comparing the bishops to Lenin and declaring them "spiritually impoverished." The journal's editors labeled the letter "ecclesiastical Mondaleism"; the bishops were "off-the-wall utopians" engaged in "the evisceration of their own moral and intellectual authority" and inflicting "severe wounds on the credibility of their Church." William F. Buckley, Jr., was restrained by comparison, merely dismissing the bishops' draft as "an accumulation of lumpen clichés" and "a purée of . . . vapidity."

George F. Will outdid Buckley in disdain. The bishops, he began, had "discovered that God subscribed to the liberal agenda." And dripping sarcasm he continued, "But, then, in the mental world to which the bishops, in their flight from complexity, have immigrated, there are no intellectual difficulties, no insoluble problems; there are only shortages of good will." Their letter, he continued, springs from minds "marinated in conventional wisdom"; they never entertain "a doubt about government programs."

The same tone marked the criticism by the neoconservative Charles Krauthammer, an editor at the nominally liberal *New Republic*. Given the economic failings of Catholicism in the past, the bishops "might proceed with a touch of humility. That quality is difficult to find" in the letter. Michael Novak called the draft "whiney and ungenerous"; Andrew M. Greeley, having duly distanced himself from the "nervous neighings" of Novak, concluded that the letter was "inept and inadequate."

These critics' complaints can be summed up in a handful of propositions. The bishops are platitudinous: who is against the poor anyhow? The bishops are uninformed: all these questions are terribly complex. The bishops are partisan: as spiritual leaders they should stick to announcing broad norms rather than acting like the Democratic party at prayer. The bishops are unrealistic: they slight the strengths of the U.S. economy while putting demands on it that, cumulatively, would be crippling. The bishops are behind the times: their proposals date from Great Society days or derive from the mixed economies of Western Europe and, even when successful, both these economic models have now reached the limits of their possibilities.

Amid all these criticisms, there are of course some valid points as well as a number of contradictory ones. But what a surprise to turn from these strictures to the text of the draft itself! One wonders, in fact, how many of the critics did so. The bishops' text is bracketed by reflections on precisely the problem that Tawney addressed:

> We are well aware of the difficulties involved in relating moral and religious values to economic life [the bishops say at the beginning]. Modern society has become so complex and fragmented that people have difficulty sensing the relationships among the different dimensions of their lives, such as the economic, the moral, and the religious.

And at the close of letter:

> None of us can afford to live a spiritually schizophrenic existence in which our private lives are oriented toward Christian discipleship while our economic activities are devoid of these same values.

But the bishops do not assume naively that they can return to a premodern worldview dominated by religious faith alone. Citing a text from the Second Vatican Council, they agree that social and economic affairs "enjoy their own laws and values, which must be gradually deciphered, put to use and regulated by human beings." They have turned to experts out of their "conviction that earthly affairs have a rightful independence which the Church and we as bishops must respect."

The bishops' awareness of the difficulties of their task is reflected in the very structure of the letter, which its critics generally ignore. It is divided into two parts.

The first part is entitled "Biblical and Theological Foundations." It is in turn subdivided into two sections. First comes a rich refflection on biblical themes of creation, covenant, and community; on the primacy of justice and solidarity with the poor in the biblical vision. This is followed by an elaboration of "Ethical Norms for Economic Life," which do not rely explicitly on the language or authority of Scripture—a response to the realities of secularization and pluralism that Tawney explored in their origins.

The bishops know that their words must be understandable and persuasive, at least in part, to those outside their religious tradition as well as to those within it. The first subsection speaks in a distinctly Christian voice; the second tries to address all citizens in a rationally defensible manner as accessible to the nonbeliever as the believer.

There are three things to be noted about this first part of the letter. One was emphasized in the press coverage—the bishops' outspoken insistence on the needs of the poor. Not so widely understood was how this insistence was part of an intensely social and communitarian vision. The bishops' starting point for evaluating the economy is *human dignity*, and human dignity is "realized in community with others." The bishops' focus was not on material deprivation per se but on whatever—material deprivation included, of course—kept people from being active participants in their communities. Respect for human dignity, in this participatory, communitarian sense, requires three things: a minimum level of material security; an opportunity for self-realization and community contribution through work; institutions that enhance social solidarity.

This emphasis on social solidarity led the bishops not only to endorse affirmative action and comparable worth as concepts relevant to correcting the effects of racial and sexual discrimination; it led them to two other controversial judgments. One was the conclusion that while they saw numerous justifications for inequalities of reward, the degree of *gross inequality* in income and wealth in America—quite independent of the absolute amount of well-being afforded those at lower levels—was itself "morally unacceptable." Second, the bishops called for an "experiment in economic democracy": an acceptance of economic rights— rights to minimum economic provision, to a worthwhile job, to an active role in directing one's work—parallel to the founding fathers' innovations in political democracy.

While the letter is definite and perhaps even radical in setting forth the standards by which an economy such as America's should be evaluated, it is simultaneously modest and even reticent—far too reticent, some would say—in plumping for any particular diagnosis of the economy's problems: "There is no clear consensus about the nature of the problems facing the country or about the best ways to address these problems effectively."

Again and again the bishops note the complexity of these issues. They don't pretend the church has all the answers, but they do think it can "make an important contribution to finding the right path." Again and again the bishops acknowledge that people of good will, Catholics among them, will disagree about particular economic policies. The bishops "expect and welcome debate." "There is certainly room for pluralism within the Church on these matters. . . . We do not seek to foreclose discussion."

By and large, it was not this first part of the bishops' draft, on ethical norms, that attracted most attention; it was the second part, on specific applications. Pastoral letters, it seems, are unlike loans: it is never the principle that earns the interest—but the distinction between the two parts of the letter is essential for understanding the bishops' work. In an introduction to the second part, they are utterly clear about the difference between their policy applications and what went before:

> The movement from principle to practice is a complex and sometimes difficult task. . . . Ethical values in themselves do not dictate specific kinds of programs or provide the blueprints for action. Rather, our principles must interact with empirical data, with historical, social and political realities, and with competing demands for limited resources. The effectiveness of our prudential judgments in this area will depend not only on the moral force of our principles, but also on the empirical accuracy of our information. . . . In certain cases, the same principles interpreted differently or combined with other assumptions may lead to different conclusions.

The bishops then repeat something that they said in their pastoral letter on nuclear weaponry:

> We do not intend that our treatment of each of these [specific] issues carry the same moral authority as our statement of universal moral principles and formal Church teaching. . . .

And so the bishops conclude:

> We expect that on complex economic questions a diversity of opinions on specific policy applications will exist, even among those who hold the same moral principles. . . . We urge mutual respect among different groups as they carry on this dialogue. For this process of reflection and dialogue will be most constructive if it is characterized not only by conviction and commitment, but also by civility and charity.

This, presumably, is the arrogance and "tone of magisterial righteousness" that Mr. Krauthammer (no stranger to either) finds so insufferable in the letter. This, no doubt, is the basis for the peroration of the article in *Commentary* by Peter Berger who, after writing a rather fine-grained critique of what is by his own account no radical document, suddenly declaims:

> Human lives are at stake: by what right, then, do these men appear before us, wrapped in the mantle of authority of prophets and popes stretching back to ancient Israel, and dare to tell us that one set of highly precarious policy choices represents the will of God in our time?

It is, I admit, tedious to cite chapter and verse of the bishops' letter to refute the fatuousness of Krauthammer or the bluster of Berger. It might be more tedious yet to note all the further acknowledgments of complexity and uncertainty to be found throughout the second part of the draft. In discussing the difficulties of achieving a national commitment to full employment, for instance, the draft explicitly states that the problem derives not only from our shortage of good will but "is also a consequence of conflicting interpretations of what causes unemployment. . . . No single all-purpose cure is available." Government job programs have been marked by both "successes and failures," from which we can learn. Here, evidently, is what Mr. Will considers a "flight from complexity" or the refusal to admit intellectual difficulties or "entertain[ing] a doubt about government programs."

I don't want to pretend that there are no real problems with the bishops' letter or that nothing stands between them and their critics that is more substantial than the fog of condescension and polemic. Nonetheless, the disparity between the bishops' text and its critics' reports is dramatic enough to cry out for some explanation. Has functional illiteracy really made such inroads among my fellow journalists and editorial writers? Why do the bishops' critics so regularly up the ante in order to make their work of demolition that much easier? If the bishops condemn an aspect of the American economy as "morally unacceptable," then, supposedly, they have cursed it root and branch. If the bishops decry inequality, then, supposedly, they are calling, as Mr. Novak wrote, for the federal government to "have new and sweeping powers" to set limits on everyone's income and wealth.

Perhaps what we are seeing here is simply the territorial imperative. Neither Mr. Buckley nor Mr. Will nor Mr. Krauthammer nor Mr. Berger nor Mr. Novak are known for any contribution to the discipline of economics. They are not so much economists but, in their spheres, a species of aspiring bishops; one group of preachers defending turf against a rival group.

Less speculative, I believe, is the role a deep-seated stereotype may have played not only in the critics' characterization of the draft letter but in their very reading of it. It is the stereotype of the clergyman as an unworldly, moralistic, and at least pretentious, if not hypocritical, do-gooder. Like other stereotypes, this one is based on some bit of reality. But readers of the letter ought to consider another possibility. Consider that the committee drafting this letter was constituted of intelligent individuals, most of whom must even meet a large payroll and supervise a sizable network of activities and organizations. Assume that they actually listened to the approximately 125 individuals who appeared before them over several years of hearings and that these hearings, if nothing else, exposed them to multiple viewpoints and multiple complexities.

It may be consoling to some of the letter's critics to suppose that if the final product reached conclusions they don't favor this was so because of a "routine acceptance of liberal assumptions" or "childlike innocence." This supposition is somewhat arrogant. It excludes the possibility that the bishops knew very well what they were doing and, whether with ultimate wisdom or not, adopted a number of liberal positions on the basis of informed and considered judgments.

If one discards these mentioned stereotypes of the bishops, the lines of criticisms advanced against their letter by no means dissolve entirely, but they do appear in a new perspective. This is especially so when the bishops' draft is compared with the rival document form the Simon/Novak commission. It is true, for example, that there are lacunae in the bishops' considerations and references. There were undoubtedly alternative positions they did not sufficiently explore, as many on their left, it should be noted, as on their right.

But the same is true—with a vengeance—of the Simon/Novak letter. Its references to economic literature are far more ideologically "bunched" than those of the bishops. The point is not to argue the superiority of the bishops' letter to the Simon/Novak one—although I don't think that argument would be hard to make—but to note that as soon as moral teachers try at all to touch base with the real world, in our day they cannot avoid *some* alignment in the battles of social science, even as they strive to withhold canonization from Lord Keynes or Milton Friedman or Karl Marx.

The bishops are determined to avoid leaving their teaching at the high level of generality that invites every interpretation—and hence the charge of being platitudinous. They want to avoid the strategem of the 18th century divines whom Tawney wrote about and who, confronted with the vigor of an independent science of economics, began to "formulate the ethical principles of Christianity in terms of a comfortable ambiguity, and rarely indicate with any precision their application to commerce, finance, and the ownership of property."

When the bishops extend themselves to specific applications, they recognize the unavoidable danger of casting their lot with a particular school of economic thought—especially at a time when the disarray of contending schools is as great as it is today. Their strategy, therefore, is to cast this part of the letter in the form of a pedagogical stimulus. The topics they address "are illustrative topics intended to exemplify the interaction of moral values and economic issues in our day. . . . This document," they insist, "is not a technical blueprint for economic reform, but rather an attempt to foster a serious moral analysis of economic justice." In sum, this is their best attempt to show how the general norms drawn from Scripture and the social demands of human dignity apply to specific issues; others are welcome to reach different conclusions—provided they make the moral connections in a similarly serious and scrupulous fashion.

This defense of the bishops' procedure assumes, of course, that the general approach taken in their policy recommendations is at least a highly plausible one—and this many of their critics obviously deny. Once again it is interesting to turn to the Simon/Novak alternative. That document argues the case for an entrepreneurial capitalism relatively free of government regulation or efforts to redistribute income. In its support the Simon/Novak letter includes a lengthy "Table of Comparative Economic Measures" listing over 160 of the world's nations, and categorizing them as either *capitalist, mixed capitalist, capitalist-statist, mixed socialist, or socialist.* Each nation is rated according to its degree of political and economic freedom plus its per capita Gross National Product as of 1978 and a measure of material well-being called the Physical Quality of Life Index.

If one returns to the source from which this table came (a study published by Freedom House), one finds the following description of the "mixed capitalist" category: "Mixed capitalist systems . . . provide social services on a large scale through governmental or other nonprofit institutions, with the result that private control over property is sacrificed to egalitarian purposes. These nations still see capitalism as legitimate, but its legitimacy is accepted grudgingly by many in government."

Now I don't think that it would be unfair to say that the bishops' letter points more or less in the direction of such mixed capitalist regimes, while the Simon/Novak letter points in the direction of distinctly capitalist ones. That is why it is noteworthy that the very table reproduced in the Simon/Novak letter shows the mixed capitalist economies equaling the capitalist ones in freedom and excelling them in physical quality of life and in per capita Gross National Product.

And so, step by step, we are forced back from the second part of the bishops' draft, which has stirred all the controversy, to the first part. By and large, the letter's critics avoid confronting the bishops on this section. Everyone agrees on these principles, they suggest; it is only how we put them into operation that is at issue. *But does everyone really agree?* Do we really agree that an economy is to be evaluated not simply by the aggregate or average wealth it produces but by the way that wealth is distributed so that none experience exclusion? Or by the way the work that produces this wealth is organized, so that the everyday activity of all is imbued with meaning? Or by the way institutions foster participation and solidarity rather than passivity and isolation?

For all the genius and subtlety of the mind of Adam Smith—often as rashly caricatured by modern liberals as the bishops have been by their critics—it seems obvious to me that *he* did not accept the criteria the bishops set forth. Adam Smith was concerned about the well-being of the poor as well as that of the average person. But that well-being he defined largely in terms of material subsistence and consumption, and he saw it as precisely the product of the transformation whose description by Tawney began these observations: the division of life—

> into its elements—politics, business, and spiritual exercises; each assumes a separate and independent vitality and obeys the laws of its own being. . . . separate and parallel compartments, between which a due balance should be maintained, but which have no vital connection with each other.

It is noteworthy that what Tawney saw as a key problem of the modern world, this division, the Simon/Novak committee simply proposes as its solution. It presents this divison of the social system into a separate political system, economic system, and moral-cultural system as a uniquely American innovation, in effect linking capitalism to our pride in America's political freedoms and institutions. These different systems are to serve as checks and balances, supports and correctives for one another. This is surely an improvement over the monolithic social system of a theocratic or totalitarian society.

Unfortunately, the Simon/Novak schema provides little guidance for determining when, short of theocracy or totalitarianism, the "separate and parallel compartments," to use Tawney's words, are no longer in "due balance." This is particularly so since the Simon/Novak letter did not risk, as the bishops did, going into particulars in detail. The bishops, on the other hand, have tried to propose what Tawney would call a "vital connection" between these separate compartments by their uncompromising moral stand on human solidarity and on the rights of the vulnerable and the excluded, and by their somewhat more tentative proposal for "economic democracy."

That the bishops' letter has proved controversial is said to stem not from its premises, which are unexceptionable, but from its concrete suggestions, which are said to be impractical and radical. I would argue, on the contrary, that the bishops' specific applictions, though debatable, are relatively modest and open-ended. In the end, it is their very premises that sharply challenge the deeply rooted assumptions of the present moment.   ■

CHAPTER 13

Foreign Policy and National Security

Because the basic aim of any country's foreign policy is to preserve its existence and security as a nation, foreign policy involves both war and peace, as well as economic matters.

Isolationism—noninvolvement in foreign affairs, especially outside our own hemisphere—was long a key characteristic of American foreign policy. After becoming deeply involved in World War I, we returned again to an isolationist policy that lasted until we were plunged into World War II in 1941. With that devastating conflict, our isolationist policy was permanently abandoned, replaced by one of *internationalism*—principally built around East-West issues and our aim of containing the infuence of the Soviet Union.

In our own hemisphere, however, our policy has always been characterized by *interventionism*, based upon the assumption that the United States has special interests and rights in this part of the world. This policy has, many times over the years, caused us to intervene militarily in a number of countries, and, since World War II, this intervention has not been confined to our own hemisphere. Thus, for example, we have fought major wars in Vietnam and Korea, we have been involved in the overthrow of governments in Guatemala and Chile, we have supported governments against rebel forces in countries like El Salvador, and we have supported rebel forces against governments in such countries as Nicaragua and Angola.

As with the making of other kinds of policy, foreign policy issues get on the agenda as a result of the influence of events and actors. The president, backed up by the foreign policy bureaucracy (especially the State Department, the Defense Department, and the intelligence establishment) is the dominant actor in America's foreign policy. But Congress plays an important role, too, especially in limiting the actions of the president.

In this chapter, we will first consider the role of the president in U. S.

foreign policy. Then, we will turn to the critical relationship between the United States and the U. S. S. R. Following that, we will give our attention to a debate on two important policy issues: the "Star Wars" program and intervention in Nicaragua. Finally, we will examine the subject of the rise and fall of the importance of human rights in American foreign policy.

THE PRESIDENT AND FOREIGN POLICY

The U. S. Constitution makes the president the principal actor in the field of U. S. foreign policy—although, as with other presidential powers, there is some overlapping of the foreign policy powers of the president and the Congress. The president has the power to appoint ambassadors and Cabinet officials, such as the Secretary of State and the Secretary of Defense (all subject to Senate confirmation, of course). He or she is commander-in-chief of the armed forces (although Congress has the sole power to declare war). He or she can decide which foreign nations to recognize. The president also has the power to negotiate treaties (subject to Senate ratification).

In addition to these constitutional powers, the president is the dominant actor in the making of U. S. foreign policy because he or she controls essential information, because he or she is looked to for the management of crises, and because of his or her role in personal diplomacy.

In 1973, reacting particularly to U. S. involvement in an undeclared war in Vietnam, the Congress passed the War Powers Act—over President Nixon's veto. This measure was an attempt by the legislative branch to redress the balance of power between it and the executive branch in regard to foreign policy, a balance that the Congress felt had swung too far in favor of the president. In an article excerpted here, international relations professor Michael Rubner examines the present status of the War Powers Act in the light of President Reagan's ordered invasion of the Carribean island nation of Grenada and the Supreme Court's decision in the case of *Immigration and Naturalization Service* v. *Chadha* (excerpted in Chapter 9 on the presidency).

Following that is an article by former President Richard Nixon on "Superpower Summitry," written on the eve of President Reagan's 1985 meeting with Soviet Communist Party General Secretary Mikhail Gorbachev. Nixon, who, himself, held important summit meetings during his term in office, not only discusses U.S.-Soviet issues, but also touches on the importance of such personal diplomacy initiatives by U. S. presidents.

THE WAR POWERS ACT AND THE INVASION OF GRENADA
Michael Rubner

On the morning of 25 October 1983, President Ronald Reagan announced that 1,900 U.S. Marines and Army Rangers, joined by 300 troops from six Caribbean states, had launched a predawn assault on the island of Granada. The President explained that he had ordered the invasion for three reasons: to protect the nearly 1,000 American citizens—most of them medical students at St. George's University School of Medicine—whose lives had been allegedly jeopardized by actions of a military junta that had gained control of the island after a bloody coup a few days earlier; to "forestall further chaos"; and "to help in the restoration of democratic institutions in Grenada."

Because of the unexpectedly stiff resistance by Cuban and Grenadian forces, the invading contingent was eventually augmented by approximately 4,000 American troops. Following the successful evacuation of U.S. citizens, the Pentagon announced on 2 November that armed hostilities had ceased and that American troop withdrawal would begin shortly. In the meantime, the ruling military junta was dissolved and de facto authority devolved on the British-appointed Governor-General of Grenada, Sir Paul Scoon. By mid-November Scoon announced the appointment of a nine-person advisory council to help administer the island's affairs until a new government would be elected sometime in 1984. On 15 December, the last U.S. combat forces departed Grenada, leaving 300 noncombat American servicemen to insure internal security and to train the 300 troops from neighboring Caribbean islands in maintenance of law and order. Although relatively swift and ostensibly successful, the invasion led to substantial loss of life. According to the Pentagon, 18 American soldiers were killed and 116 were wounded. Cuban forces were estimated to have suffered 24 dead and 59 wounded, while Grenadian military casualties were put at 45 killed and 337 wounded.

While much has been written about the events that precipitated the invasion, the military and political repercussions of the war, and the disputed legality of the venture under international law, there has been no systematic analysis of the nexus between the decision to invade Grenada and the 1973 War Powers Resolution. Passed over President Richard Nixon's veto on 7 November 1973, the War Powers Resolution established various procedures to "insure that the collective judgment of both the Congress and the President will apply to the introduction of United States Armed Forces into hostilities." This article addresses three questions: To what extent did the Reagan administration comply with the requirements stipulated in the War Powers Resolution? How did Congress respond to the administration's interpretation of its obligations under the War Powers Resolution? What can be learned from the Grenada episode about the utility of the War Powers Resolution as a tool for securing legislative participation in future decisions involving deployment of American forces abroad?

It should be stressed at the outset that Congress and the White House could not reach agreement on the ground rules under which the post-invasion debate on the War Powers Resolution was to be waged. Like its predecessors, the Reagan administration never acknowledged the constitutionality of the legislation. Yet while they resorted to circumlocutory rhetoric during the Grenada imbroglio, administration officials made their opposition to the 1973 Resolution increasingly clear in a series of statements shortly before and after the invasion.

For example, in July 1983, after the U.S. Supreme Court declared unconstitutional a legislative veto provision of the Immigration and Nationality Act in *Immigration and Naturalization Service (INS)* v. *Chadha,* Deputy Secretary of State Kenneth W. Dam contended that the Chadha decision also invalidated the section of the War Powers Resolution, 5(c), requiring the immediate withdrawal of U.S. troops from hostilities if the Congress so directs by concurrent resolution. Similarly, when he reluctantly accepted a congressional resolution that invoked the War Powers Act and authorized the continued participation of U.S. Marines in the Multinational Force in Lebanon for eighteen months, Reagan stated on 12 October 1983 that his signature was "not to be viewed as any acknowledgement that the President's constitutional authority can be impermissibly infringed by statute."[1] Such assaults on the War Powers Resolution reached a climax in late March 1984, when Secretary of State George Shultz challenged the constitutionality of the entire act and told a Senate subcommittee that the administration's ability to conduct its foreign policy had been "constantly undermined" by congressional interference.

On the other hand, bipartisan majorities have demonstrated continous strong support in Congress for the 1973 resolution. The predominant congressional sentiment on the status of the legislation was most succinctly expressed by Senator Gary Hart (D-Col.) shortly after the start of the Grenadian invasion, when he noted that

> . . . the War Powers Act is still the law of the land and is still in full force and effect. It still binds all citizens of our country up to and including the President of the United States. And we expect the President, absent a change or repeal in that law, to obey it.[2]

In light of these diametrically opposed interpretations of the constitutionality of the 1973 law and because of various ambiguities within the statute, an acrimonious dispute between the executive and legislative branches following the invasion of Grenada was inevitable.

---

1. *New York Times,* 13 October 1983.
2. U.S. Congress, Senate, 98th Cong., 1st sess., 28 October 1983, *Congressional Record* 129:14869.

CONSULTATIONS

Section 3 of the 1973 War Powers Resolution stipulates that "The President *in every possible instance* shall consult with Congress *before* introducing United States Armed Forces into hostilities or into situations where imminent involvement in hostilities is clearly indicated by the circumstances." The President is also enjoined to consult regularly with Congress until the forces cease to engage in hostilities or are removed from such situations. There can be no doubt that the invasion of Grenada was one type of situation that the framers had in mind when they inserted the consultation requirement in the War Powers Resolution. After all, the invading forces were engaged in fierce combat as soon as they landed on the island, and twelve Cuban soldiers and two American Marines were killed during the first ten hours of the operation. Hence, the basic issue that needs to be ascertained is the extent to which the Reagan administration complied with the consultation clause.

From the very beginning, administration officials claimed that the White House had fully met its legal obligations to consult Congress about U.S. troop deployment in Grenada. For example, during hearings held by the Senate Foreign Relations Committee on 27 October 1983, Deputy Secretary of State Kenneth Dam asserted that "there was consultation with the leadership—bipartisan leadership of the House and Senate." Responding to persistent questioning by Senator Claiborne Pell (D-R.I.), Dam insisted that "we did consult to the maximum degree consistent with the safeguarding of American lives, both military and civilians."[3] However, a careful reconstruction of the sequence of events that took place immediately before and after the decision to invade had been reached clearly shows that the Reagan administration circumvented the requirement to consult with Congress before deploying troops in Grenada.

Several sources confirm that the final order permitting U.S. forces to proceed with the invasion was issued by President Reagan around 6 P.M. on Monday, 24 October 1983. About two to three hours later, a bipartisan group of five congressional leaders, including House Speaker Thomas P. O'Neill (D-Mass.), House Majority Leader Jim Wright (D-Tex.), House Minority Leader Robert H. Michel (R-Ill.), Senate Majority Leader Howard H. Baker (R-Tenn.), and Senate Minority Leader Robert C. Byrd (D-W.Va.), was quietly whisked into the White House. The congressmen were then briefed by the President about the imminent invasion. According to various accounts by those present at that meeting, congressional advice was not solicited nor did any meaningful consultations take place. Speaker O'Neill, for example, admitted that "we weren't asked for advice," adding that "we were informed what was taking place." Likewise, Senator Baker acknowledged on the Senate floor that

---

3. U.S. Congress, Senate Committee on Foreign Relations, *The Situation in Grenada*, Hearing. 98th Cong., 1st sess., 27 October 1983, 11.

I was with the minority leader at the White House on Monday night when the President called in the joint bipartisan leadership to advise us of this operation in advance. I use the term "advise" because it is true that we were not consulted in the sense that there was no solicitation of opinion, but we were told of it in advance, for which I am grateful.[4]

Senator Byrd concurred, expressing concern that

. . . the administration only tells the Senate after the administration makes its decision. It informs us then that it is going to do this and that. It does not ask for the advice of the Senate through the Senate leadership . . . . I think we are entitled to more than that.[5]

None of the legislators present at the Monday evening session raised any objections to the operation, and at the end of the meeting, Speaker O'Neill reportedly turned to Reagan and said: "God bless you, Mr. President. And good luck." On Tuesday, 25 October, at approximately 8:15 A.M., the President briefed the entire congressional leadership on the invasion that had begun about three hours earlier. There is no evidence that additional executive-legislative "consultations" ever took place on any aspect of the Grenada invasion while the operation was being carried out.

The record thus suggests that the Reagan administration violated both the letter and spirit of Section 3 of the War Powers Resolution. It should be emphasized that during deliberations on the 1973 Resolution, the House Foreign Affairs Committee devoted much attention to the meaning of "consultation" as used in Section 3 and unequivocally rejected the notion that consultation was equivalent to mere transmission of information. In its 1973 report, the committee stated that "consultation in this provision means that a decision is pending on a problem and that members of Congress are being asked by the President for their advice and opinions."[6] Furthermore, since the stated intent of the resolution is to secure the collective judgment of both Congress and the president in decisions involving the introduction of U.S. troops into hostilities, it cannot be reasonably argued that merely briefing a group of legislators about imminent action based on a decision that had already been finalized qualifies as applying the judgment of Congress to such decision. This argument was articulated most emphatically by Senator Pell during the Foreign Relations Committee hearings on the situation in Grenada, when he pointed out that "there is a world of difference between being consulted and being asked do we think this is wise or not, or being informed, saying we are doing this at 5 A.M. tommorow."[7]

In defense of the Reagan administration's behavior, it might be argued that the phrase requiring consultation "in every possible instance" was deliberately

---

4. U.S. Congress, Senate, 98th Cong., 1st sess., 29 October 1983, *Congressional Record* 129:14912
5. Ibid., 14913.
6. U.S. Congress, House, Committee on Foreign Affairs. House Rep. 287, 93rd Cong., 1st sess., 1973. Cited in Robert Zutz, "The Recapture of the S.S. *Mayaguez:* Failure of the Consultation Clause of the War Powers Resolution," *New York University Journal of International Law and Politics 8* (Winter 1976): 468.
7. Senate Committee on Foreign Relations, *Situation in Grenada,* 11.

inserted into Section 3 in order to provide the president discretion concerning the feasibility, form, and timing of consultation with Congress. Indeed, several scholars have suggested that the physical inability to ocommunicate with key legislators, the need for an immediate reaction to an emergency, and the fear that sensitive information would be leaked, might render prior consultation with Congress impossible or undesireable and that the ultimate decision in such cases rests with the president. It is apparent, however, that none of the circumstances that might have reasonably recused President Reagan from the obligation to consult Congress was present in the case at hand.

First, Congress was in session in October 1983 and legislative leaders were physically available in Washington for meetings with the President. Furthermore, the sequence of events leading to the ultimate decision to deploy U.S. troops leaves no doubt whatsoever that there had been ample opportunity and sufficient time for meaningful executive-legislative deliberations before acting. According to administration officials, discussions on the use of military force in Grenada were initiated with friendly Caribbean states as early as 15 October 1983. Two days later, President Reagan gave the go-ahead for the planning of a noncombatant evacuation operation in Grenada to an interagency group with representatives from the State Department, CIA, Joint Chiefs of Staff (JCS), and the Department of Defense. On 20 October, the National Security Council's Special Situation Group, chaired by Vice President George Bush, drew up a National Security Decision Directive (NSDD) instructing the Joint Chiefs to plan for both a non-combatant evacuation of Americans and a complete military seizure of the island. The NSDD was initialed by the President on Friday, 21 October. Perhaps the best proof for the contention that up to this point the situation in Grenada was not viewed as a crisis requiring immediate action is provided by the fact that Reagan, Secretary of State George Shultz, and National Security Adviser Robert C. McFarlane left Washington later that very evening for a weekend of rest at the Augusta National Golf Club in Georgia.

The decision to refine the NSDD by transforming it into an action plan to "land U.S. and allied Caribbean military forces in order to take control of Grenada no later than Tuesday" (25 October) was made at a meeting of the Special Situation Group, in which the President, Shultz, and McFarlane participated via a telephone hookup, on Saturday, 22 October. It was the disaster at Marine barracks in the outskirts of Beirut that brought the President and his entourage back to Washington early Sunday, 23 October, and after two lengthy meetings with his top advisers, Reagan gave his tentative approval to the modified NSDD later that evening. The invasion plans were refined in a meeting between the President, Secretary of Defense Caspar Weinberger, and the JCS on Monday afternoon, and it was only *after* the President had sent a cable to Prime Minister Margaret Thatcher advising her of his impending decision, and *after* he had signed the final directive ordering the invasion, that he met with the bipartisan congressional leadership. Since the planning for deployment of U.S. forces in Grenada stretched over several days rather than a few hours, any claim that the White House did not have the necessary time to seek congressional advice remains totally unpersuasive.

There is some evidence that the administration made an effort to maintain a facade of normalcy while planning for the operation proceeded apace. That might explain why the President deliberately decided to stay in Augusta on Saturday, 22 October, several hours after the request for American military intervention had been relayed from the Organization of Eastern Caribbean States (OECS) to Shultz. The concern for maximizing secrecy would also explain why the bipartisan congressional leadership group was brought into the White House basement through the Old Executive Office Building on the eve of 24 October. However, whether the fear of premature leaks was a legitimate excuse for avoiding prior consultation with Congress remains a highly debatable proposition for several reasons.

First, the secrecy of the plan may have been already compromised by reports in the Caribbean press and on Grenadian radio more than two days before the invasion that such an operation was being planned by Caribbean leaders. Second, on 28 October, Wesley L. McDonald, commander of U.S. forces in the Atlantic region, acknowledged that the Cubans had known that "U.S. intervention was likely" and that they had prepared for it. Third, after a meeting with President Reagan in Washington on 6 November, Jamaica's Prime Minister, Edward Seaga, revealed that General Hudson Austin, the leader of the Grenadian junta before the invasion, had been told of the invasion plan nearly thirty-six hours before it was carried out. The White House never challenged this claim. Finally, and most importantly, Reagan and his closest advisers may have fallen prey to the dubious assumption that consultation with a small group of legislative leaders is necessarily more dangerous to national security than are discussions between the President and members of his staff and cabinet. The prevalent belief that the executive branch enjoys an inherent monopoly over the ability to maintain secrecy was challenged on the Senate floor by Minority Leader Byrd, who noted that

> There are few people, there are at least a few who can keep a secret here, and I would say that the Senate can be trusted as much as the Defense Department can be or the State Department can be or the White House can be to keep a secret.[8]

The exclusion of Congress from prior consultation in violation of Section 3 of the War Powers Resolution had two major consequences. First, it invited both opponents and supporters of the invasion in Congress to criticize the decision on purely procedural grounds and to assert the institutional prerogatives of Congress. For example, Representative Robert G. Torricelly (D-N.J.) reminded the White House that

> . . . the law reads "in any case, the President shall consult with Congress. In any case." It does not say in some cases. It does not say in all cases except Grenada. It does not say in all cases except when the Cubans are involved. It says the President shall consult with the Congress in all cases.[9]

---

8. U.S. Congress, Senate, 98th Cong., 1st sess., 29 October 1983, *Congressional Record* 129:14913.

9. U.S. Congress, House Committee on Foreign Affairs, *Grenada War Powers: Full Compliance Reporting and Implementation.* Markup on H.J. Res. 402, 27 October 1983. 98th Cong., 1st sess., 1983, 12.

Similar sentiments were expressed by Representative Robert W. Edgar (D-Pa.), who lamented that "the President failed to adequately consult Congress in planning and executing the invasion," and by Representative Mervyn M. Dymally (D.Calif.), who complained that "once again the Congress of the United States was in on the landing, but not the takeoff."[10] Likewise, Representative Dante B. Fascell (D-Fla.), one of the authors of the War Powers Resolution and a supporter of the invasion, stated that he was "deeply distressed that the law was not complied with so that the Congress could have also shared in the responsibility of this commitment of U.S. troops and lives."[11]

Second, and more significantly, by leaving Congress completely out in the cold, the White House may have deprived itself of a potentially useful source of advice in the policy formation phase. Long after the last U.S. combat forces had left Grenada, some basic questions about the wisdom of the invasion decision remain unanswered: Were American lives in fact threatened by actions of the Revolutionary Military Council in Grenada before the invasion? Why did the administration ignore assurances from the military junta that Americans on the island were not in danger and that they would be permitted to leave if they so desired? If evacuation of civilians was indeed necessary, could it have been accomplished without the use of force through assistance of intermediaries or with the help of the Red Cross? Did concern for the safety of American lives justify the overthrow of the Grenadian government and takeover of the entire island in apparent violation of the United Nations and Organization of American States (OAS) charters? Could the security of the allegedly-threatened Caribbean states have been enhanced by interposing American naval forces in the area? Was is prudent to proceed without prior consultation with major U.S. allies?

Ordinarily, such pointed questions would have been raised in the predecision stage by State Department officials, who are led by traditional bureaucratic orientations to urge caution and to search for alternative diplomatic options in crisis situations. In this instance, however, a strange bureaucratic role reversal took place, as the main impetus for a large-scale military operation came from State Department diplomats, while the Defense Department and the JCS were urging delay, further study, and restraint. Specifically, as early as 17 October, officials from the Department of State's Bureau of Inter-American Affairs, backed by Undersecretary for Political Affairs Lawrence Eagleburger, began pressing for military contingency planning for an evacuation operation in Grenada, while representatives from the JCS refused to even acknowledge the need for such planning. At the following interagency meeting two days later, the military personnel reluctantly agreed to discuss a limited action to evacuate Americans from Grenada, while State Department officials argued strongly for military takeover of the entire island. The JCS and Weinberger continued to urge caution with respect to Grenada following the murderous onslaught against the U.S. Marines barrack in Beirut on 23 October. According to one senior official, the JCS "were dismayed by what happened in Beirut that morning, and were not in the mood

---

10. U.S. Congress, House, 98th Cong., 1st sess., 26 October 1983, *Congressional Record* 129:8639, 8644.
11. Ibid., 8691

to get into another situation where we would take additional casualties."[12] Secretary of State Shultz, on the other hand, reportedly convinced the President to "strike while the iron is hot."

Under these unusual and tense circumstances, it is likely that the President's team could have benefited from continuous consultation with congressional leaders. If nothing else, a select group of legislators, considerably less strongly attached to vested bureaucratic stakes, would have been in an ideal position to raise sharp questions about the reasonableness of competing objectives and the costs and benefits of various alternative options. Such additional input from an external source might have prevented the premature foreclosure of options, could have altered the terms of the debate, and might even have tipped the scales in favor of the Pentagon's more restrained and conservative posture. It is a tragic, yet telling fact, that in attempting to ascertain the likely impact that congressional participation might have had on the quality of the final decision in this case, one is necessarily compelled to rely on speculation.

REPORTING AND TRIGGERING THE SIXTY-DAY CLOCK

Section 4(a) of the 1973 War Powers Resolution stipulates that in the absence of a declaration of war, in any case in which American armed forces are introduced "into hostilities or into situations where imminent involvement in hostilities is clearly indicated by the circumstances," or "into the territory, airspace or waters of a foreign nation, while equipped for combat," or "in numbers which substantially enlarge United States Armed Forces equipped for combat already located in a foreign nation," the president must submit within forty-eight hours a written report to the Speaker of the House and the President pro tempore of the Senate. Such report must identify the circumstances compelling the deployment of armed forces, the constitutional and legislative authority under which such deployment is taking place, and the estimated scope and length of the hostilities or military involvement. The president is further required to submit periodic reports to the Congress on the status of hostilities and their anticipated duration so long as U.S. forces continue to be engaged. Section 5(b) stipulates that within sixty days after a report is submitted pursuant to Section 4(a) (1), the president must terminate deployment of U.S. forces, unless Congress has declared war or has specifically authorized such deployment, extended the sixty-day period by law, or is unable to meet as a result of an attack on the U.S. The sixty-day period may be extended up to thirty additional days if the president determines and certifies to Congress in writing that such extension is necessary for safe and prompt removal of troops. The president is compelled to terminate such deployment at any time if Congress so directs him by concurrent resolution.

On the afternoon of 25 October 1983, less than twelve hours after U.S. forces had landed in Grenada, President Reagan sent a written report to Senator Strom

---

12. *New York Times*, 7 November 1983.

Thurmond (R-S.C.), president pro tem of the Senate, and to House Speaker O'Neill. Claiming to be "consistent with the War Powers Resolution," the letter notified Congress that approximately 1,900 U.S. Army and Marine Corps personnel, supported by some 300 troops from Jamaica, Barbados, and various OECS members, had begun landing on Grenada at about 5:00 A.M. The objectives of the operation were identified as "assisting the restoration of conditions of law and order and of governmental institutions to the island of Grenada, and to facilitate the protection and evacuation of United States citizens." The President noted that the deployment was being undertaken "pursuant my constitutional authority with respect to the conduct of foreign relations, and as Commander-in-Chief of the United States Armed Forces." The report also stated that because "it is not possible at this time" to predict the duration of deployment, "our forces will remain only so long as their presence is required."[13]

Thus, President Reagan had seemingly complied with the reporting provisions of Section 4(a). His report was filed with the designated congressional leaders well within the specified deadline, described the conditions that prompted the invasion and identified its objectives, cited the constitutional authority on which the decision was based, and while being imprecise about the duration of the operation, at least contained a commitment to terminate it promptly. In fact, however, Reagan's report opened a Pandora's box.

First, the President notified Congress that he was filing the report "consistent with the War Powers Resolution" instead of acknowledging that he was "informing Congress on this matter *under* the War Powers Resolution." Critics of the President in both the House and Senate became necessarily alarmed by his deliberate choice of words because the "consistent with" formula had been used by Reagan himself in the case of Lebanon and by his predecessors to avoid conceding the validity of the War Powers Resolution.

Second, the President's letter did not state explicitly that U.S. troops landing in Grenada were being introduced "into hostilities or into situations where imminent involvement in hostilities is clearly indicated by the circumstances." This proved to be a crucial omission because pursuant to Section 5(b), it is only the submission of a "hostilities" report under Section 4(a)(1) that triggers the automatic sixty-day termination provision. Because none of the other reports required by Section 4 set the sixty-day clock ticking, and because Reagan failed to specify which type of report he was filing, considerable ambiguity emerged on the question of whether the sixty-day limit had been automatically invoked by his report.

Third, the resulting confusion was further compounded by the administration's reluctance to provide a clear and unequivocal indication that it intended to comply with the War Powers Resolution. Thus, when he was asked by Senator Pell, "Do you consider the time clock running now under the War Powers Resolution?" Deputy Secretary of State Dam kept running in circles, finally admitting

---

13. The complete text of the President's report may be found in U.S. Congress, Senate, 98th Cong., 1st sess., 26 October 1983, *Congressional Record* 129:14610.

that "the administration does not have a view to express on that position, and, therefore, I cannot give you an administration answer." Such nebulous responses, coupled with Reagan's failure to cite any specific provision of the 1973 Resolution or to indicate a termination date, eventually convinced substantial majorities in Congress that the central issue raised by the President's report was "whether the executive branch alone is going to be able to place forces of this country into hostilities indefinitely without coming to the Congress of the United States as the War Powers Act requires."[14]

That issue was addressed directly by Representative Clement J. Zablocki (D-Wis.) on 26 October 1983, when he introduced H.J. Res. 402, declaring that Congress "determines that the requirements of section 4(a)(1) of the War Powers Resolution became operative on October 25, 1983, when United States Forces were introduced into Grenada." The measure intended to eliminate confusion by declaring that the sixty-day time limit had been triggered by the President's report. After it refused to accept an amendment by Representative George W. Crockett (D-Mich.) that would have required the President to withdraw American forces from Grenada no later than 24 November 1983, the House Foreign Affairs Committee approved the Zablocki measure on 27 October by a lopsided vote of 33 to 2. On 1 November, following a brief and perfunctory floor debate, H.J. Res. 402 was adopted by the full House by vote of 403 to 23. The measure was supported by 256 Democrats and 147 Republicans.

Language identical to H.J. Res. 402 was also introduced by Senator Gary Hart (D-Col.) in the form of an amendment to a bill increasing the national debt ceiling. It was approved by the Republican-controlled Senate on 28 October in a bipartisan vote of 64 to 20. However, on 31 October, the version of the debt limit bill containing the Hart amendment was defeated, and the amendment itself was eventually omitted from the final debt limit bill that was approved by the House-Senate conference committee on 17 November. On the following day Congress adjourned without passing any joint legislation that would have invoked the War Powers Resolution in reference to the invasion of Grenada. Senate Minority Leader Byrd described the actions of both chambers on this issue "like two ships passing in the night," noting that "the Senate acted on one vehicle; the House of Representatives acted on another. But both houses have acted 'finding' that the War Powers Act sections 4(a) and 5(b) have been triggered."[15] Thus, in the strictly legal sense, Reagan was taken off the hook by a procedural impasse.

Perhaps the most instructive conclusion to be drawn from the debate over H.J. Res. 402 is that the extremely brief yet heated exchanges in the House and Senate focused almost exclusively on questions of institutional prerogatives rather than on the wisdom of the decision to invade Grenada. As the following excerpts show, one legislator after another sought to drive a wedge between procedural and substantive issues, insisting that it was imperative to concentrate on the former at the expense of the latter:

---

14. U.S. Congress, House, 98th Cong., 1st sess., 26 October 1983, *Congressional Record* 129:8697.

15. U.S. Congress, Senate, 98th Cong., 1st sess., 28 October 1983, *Congressional Record* 129:14876, and 17 November 1983, *Congressional Record* 129:16593.

Rep. Clement J. Zablocki (D-Wis.): the resolution is not, nor is it intended to be, critical of the President or his action in ordering the invasion of Grenada. House Joint Resolution 402 does not pass judgment on this action.[16]

Rep. Robert J. Lagomarsino (R-Calif.): It is important to emphasize that the purpose of this resolution is not to determine the merits of the President's actions. It is merely to establish that the timeclock is running . . . .[17]

Sen. Gary Hart (D-Col.): This amendment has nothing to do with whether we should be there at all. It does not raise the question of whether the U.S. citizens' lives or security or safety were in danger. It does not . . . question the authority of the President to have done what he did . . . . Whether we disagree or agree with the policy, whether or not we think it is wise, the issue is, will the President be bound by the laws of the United States or will he not? That is the only issue.[18]

The President's report thus provided additional impetus for the congressional penchant to transform substantive issues into controversies over procedures and institutional rights. As a result, the merit of Reagan's decision to invade Grenada never received the close legislative scrutiny that it surely deserved.

Questions may also be raised about the extent to which the White House complied with its obligation to keep Congress informed of developments in Grenada after the start of hostilities. The administration did send one additional report to Speaker O'Neill and Senate President pro tem Thurmond on 9 November 1983, informing Congress that U.S. military forces on the island had been reduced to 2,700. It also claimed that it was still not possible to predict the precise withdrawal date for the remaining troops and promised that American servicemen will continue to withdraw as their functions are gradually taken over by a peacekeeping force composed of units from neighboring Caribbean states. At other times, however, the administration was much less forthcoming with information. For example, even after being briefed by intelligence officials in a closed session on 31 October, several House members complained of being kept in the dark. Representative Gerry E. Studds (D-Mass.), a member of the House Foreign Affairs Committee who had attended the meeting, stated that "it reminded me of how little we know . . . . They didn't satisfy anyone. They didn't even satisfy friendly Republicans who support the policy and asked leading questions. Likewise, while admitting that the administration had responded to his earlier requests for details about White House deliberations before the invasion, Representative Ronald V. Dellums (D-Calif.) complained that the replies had still left "voids."

It must also be noted that the administration barred journalists from Grenada until the third day of the invasion, thereby depriving Congress and the American public of vital details at a crucial stage of the operation. And it was because "the media [had] been substantially restricted from obtaining and providing

---

16. House Committee on Foreign Affairs, *Granada War Powers*, 1.
17. U.S. Congress, House, 98th Cong., 1st sess., 31 October 1983, *Congressional Record* 129:8888.
18. U.S. Congress, Senate, 98th Cong., 1st sess., 28 October 1983, *Congressional Record* 129:14869.

detailed information concerning the situation in Grenada" that Minority Leader Byrd proposed appointing a Senate fact-finding mission to visit the island and to submit a factual report as soon as possible.[19] While Byrd argued that such first-hand information was essential to enable the Senate to meet its reponsibilities pursuant to provisions of the War Powers Resolution, the administration resisted this idea because of the "logistics" involved and because "we're trying to avoid the aura of any long-term commitment" to Grenada. The legislative branch eventually prevailed and between 4–8 November, three congressional delegations visited Grenada: a fourteen-member bipartisan House group headed by Majority Whip Thomas S. Foley (D–Wash.) and Minority Leader Robert H. Michel, a team of four Republican House members sponsored by the National Defense Council, and a one-person mission carried out by Senator John G. Tower (R-Tex.). An uninhibited flow of information between the White House and Capitol Hill would have obviated the need for such missions.

IMPLICATIONS AND CONCLUSIONS

In the aftermath of Grenada, Congress has four options with respect to the 1973 War Powers Resolution. It can repeal the resolution, accept the status quo, enforce the existing legislation more vigorously, or amend the resolution. Entirely different implications flow from each of these alternatives.

Repeal of the legislation has been favored by conservatives who claim that such legislative restrictions on the president's power as commander-in-chief are unconstitutional, impractical, and dangerous because they deny the chief executive maximum flexibility in times of crisis. It is for these reasons that a bill for repeal of the War Powers Resolution was introduced by Senator Barry Goldwater (R-Ariz.) on 31 October, shortly after the fighting in Grenada had subsided. However, in justifying this measure, Goldwater did not make a single reference to the Grenadian venture, perhaps because he could not find a shred of evidence that in this instance the legislation constituted "a dangerous impediment to taking necessary actions in defense of the freedoms of our citizens and the security of our Nation . . . ."[20]

While repeal might indeed avoid a serious constitutional confrontation in a future international crisis, the fact remains that the War Powers Resolution is the only potentially effective legal mechanism currently available to insure some legislative participation in decisions involving use of American forces in hostilities in the absence of a formal declaration of war. Ultimately, one wonders whether conservatives of Goldwater's persuasion would be content to rely on congressional appointment, appropriations, and impeachment powers as the sole

---

19. U.S. Congress, Senate, 98th Cong., 1st sess., 31 October 1983, *Congressional Record* 129:14970.
20. U.S. Congress, Senate, 98th Cong., 1st sess., 31 October 1983, *Congressional Record* 129:15082.

checks against a chief executive bent on using American forces against right-wing regimes in undeclared wars.

Acceptence of the status quo, on the other hand, carries the risk that White House occupants will continue to circumvent the law by excluding Congress from prior consultations in crisis situations, with the resulting loss of potentially useful legislative input before critical decisions are made final. Furthermore, as the Grenada episode clearly demonstrates, semantic ambiguities in the present law fail to insure the automatic triggering of time limits on American troop deployments in hostilities and shift the burden of invoking such limits from the White House, where it had been originally lodged, back to Congress. As a result, legislators are forced to waste precious time on procedural issues and institutional prerogatives, while the substantive merit of presidential policies remains largely unexamined.

Current executive practice and legal ambiguities notwithstanding, Congress could attempt to enforce compliance with the War Powers Resolution through various means that are theoretically available to it. For example, in the absence of a prior declaration of war, Congress could pass a concurrent resolution urging immediate withdrawal of armed forces from hostilities. Furthermore, as Robert Zutz has pointed out, Congress could also seek a court injunction to prevent the president from acting until he complies with existing legislation. Confronting a defiant chief executive, Congress could also vote to bar expenditure of funds needed to finance presidentially initiated military ventures. As a last resort, Congress could impeach a president for violating the law.

Indeed, attempts to exploit such Congressional prerogatives were initiated by various legislators in the case of Grenada. It is instructive, however, that all of these efforts ended in utter failure. For example, on 27 October 1983, Representative Dymally, who was joined by sixteen Democratic colleagues, introduced a concurrent resolution that "expressed the sense of the Congress that the United States should recognize the right of the people of Grenada to territorial integrity, calling upon the President immediately to remove United States Armed Forces from Grenada." The measure was forwarded to the House Committee on Foreign Affairs where it died. On the following day, Representative Don Edwards (D-Calif.) introduced a joint resolution, cosponsored by nine Democrats and nine Repbulicans, "declaring that the President violated the constitutional prerogatives of the Congress to declare war when he ordered United States Armed Forced to invade Grenada on 25 October 1983, and requiring the immediate withdrawal" of these forces from the island. This resolution was never reported out of the House Foreign Affairs Committee. On 10 November, Representative Theodore S. Weiss (D-N.Y.) introduced a resolution calling for the impeachment of Ronald Reagan for "the high crime or misdemeanor of ordering the invasion of Grenada in violation of the Constitution of the United States, and other high crimes and misdemeanors ancillary thereto." This measure, too, died in the House Judiciary Committee.

In addition, eleven members of Congress sought a court injunction ordering the President to remove American troops from Grenada and requesting judicial determination that the invasion was unconstitutional because it had violated the power of Congress to declare war. However, the court denied jurisdiction in this case because the injunction would have forced the judiciary to "unnecessarily and unwisely interfere with the legislative process and raise significant separation of power concerns." It should be noted that the Congress made no attempt to deny funds for the Grenada operation, and as will be argued and demonstrated below, such a move would not have received the necessary legislative support even if it had been initiated.

The Grenada episode makes perfectly clear that it is not the absence of consitutional or legal powers that prevents effective enforcement of the War Powers Resolution. Rather, in this as well as in previous cases in which the legislation had been violated, Congress was unwilling to secure strict compliance with the law because it was severely constrained by political circumstances over which it had very little control.

First, in the absence of full information, overwhelming bipartisan majorities in both the House and Senate readily accepted the President's description of the invasion as an essential rescue operation and were willing to support it on the sole condition that American forces would be pulled out as soon as the evacuation and the other stated objectives had been achieved. Indeed, from the very beginning and throughout the Grenadian venture, Congress was continually bombarded with a steady stream of assurances from the White House that U.S. troops would be deployed for an extremely short duration, falling well within the sixty-day limit stipulated in the War Powers Resolution. For example, on 25 October, Secretary of State Shultz announced that "our troops will leave as soon as they possibly can . . . . I think they will be leaving very very promptly."[21] On 28 October, President Reagan stated in his nationally televised address that "it's our intention to get our men out as soon as possible."[22] At his press conference on 3 November, the President insisted that the operation was "a successful rescue mission" and proclaimed that "our objectives have been achieved and as soon as the logistics permit, American personnel will be leaving."[23] And on 16 November, the administration announced that U.S. combat troops would be withdrawn by 23 December. Given this constant barrage of promises and concrete evidence of gradual troop removal, it should not come as a surprise that most members of Congress opted for a "wait and see" posture. Eventually, the last American combat forces were withdrawn on the forty-ninth day of the operation, thus rendering compliance with the sixty-day time limit a moot issue.

Second, any potentially massive legislative criticism of presidential conduct was simply suppressed as events in the Grenadian drama kept unfolding. First, the publication of pictures of returning medical students kissing American soil, together with the nearly unanimous praise for the invasion by the evacuees, convinced even the more ardent congressional skeptics that the President's swift deci-

21. *New York Times*, 26 October 1983.
22. Ibid., 29 October 1983.
23. Ibid., 4 November 1983.

sion had been fully justified, even if it did not strictly adhere to the requirements of the War Powers Resolution. Such sentiments were further reinforced by the administration's claim that U.S. forces in Grenada had discovered huge quantities of Cuban and Soviet arms stockpiles as well as secret military agreements between the island's former rulers and Cuba, the USSR, and North Korea. Thus, the invasion seemed to have been much more successful than had been initially anticipated.

Third, as a result of these fortuitous developments and because it also provided a timely outlet for pent-up frustration in the wake of the Beirut disaster, the invasion became such an extremely popular venture with the American public that Congress was left with the choice of putting up or shutting up. There is indeed substantial evidence that public opinion aligned itself solidly behind the President. For example, in a *New York Times*/CBS poll conducted 27 October 1983, 55 percent of the respondents approved the decision to invade Grenada, while only 31 percent registered disapproval. Likewise, an ABC News sample the night of the President's 27 October address on TV showed 64 percent favoring the invasion before the speech, and 86 percent endorsing the move after the speech. This poll also found that 74 percent agreed with the statement, "I feel good about Grenada because it showed that American can use its power to protect our own interests." Similarly, a Gallup poll conducted for *Newsweek* on 26–27 October showed that 53 percent approved and 34 percent disapproved U.S. participation in the invasion. The "rally around the flag" phenomenon is also evident in a post-invasion poll taken by the *Washington Post* and ABC News showing that 63 percent approved the way President Reagan was handling the presidency, the highest level in two years. Finally, in a *Time* poll taken during the first week in December, 58 percent agreed that the invasion was in the best interest of the nation, while only 32 percent disagreed. In view of such overwhelming outpouring of support for the President, his critics in Congress were in no position to prolong debate over Reagan's compliance with the War Powers Resolution and the wisdom of his policy. The mood of Congress was best described by Senator Daniel P. Moynihan (D-N.Y.), who noted that "the move is popular and therefore there's no disposition in the Senate to be opposed to it."[24]

The already slim hope that the Democratic-controlled House would take on the White House on the War Powers question evaporated completely when key Democratic leaders flip-flopped on the propriety of the invasion. Particularly noticeable here was the complete turnabout of Speaker O'Neill, who had initially insisted that "we can't go the way of gunboat dimplomacy" and that the policy was "wrong" and "frightening." However, on 8 November, O'Neill admitted that a House fact-finding mission had convinced him that "sending American forces into combat was justified under these particular circumstances." The fact-finding mission also had a sobering effect on one of its key members, Representative Michael D. Barnes (D-Md.), chairman of the House Foreign Affairs Subcommittee on Western Hemisphere Affairs and a leading critic of President Reagan's

24. *New York Times*, 4 November 1983.

policies toward Central America and the Caribbean. Following a four-day visit to Grenada and Barbados, Barnes was persuaded that the danger to American citizens was "adequate justification" for the invasion.

Thus, the invasion of Grenada drives home a lesson that should have been absorbed in 1975, when American forces were used to rescue the captured S.S. *Mayaguez*. Namely, that in low-intensity conflict situations, the political power of Congress to constrain the president through strict enforcement of the War Powers Resolution is severely limited if it is not dead altogether. There are no assurances, however, that future crises will necessarily follow the *Mayaguez* and Grenada model – the use of a relatively small force in a geographically confined area where the U.S. can quickly establish superiority in pursuit of limited objectives that can be secured with minimal casualties. These precedents do not vitiate the need for effective legal mechanisms that would enable Congress to have some impact on decisions involving use of American forces in future hostilities. While certain political realities will inevitably remain beyond its control, Congress can nevertheless take a step in the right direction by removing serious ambiguities and weaknesses from the existing war powers legislation.

The Grenada episode confirms that Congress paid little attention to the language of Section 3 when the War Powers Resolution was originally drafted. The terse wording in that section allows the president considerable discretion on such questions as when consultation must occur, who must be involved, and what actions constitute consultation. Congress can reduce executive discretion on these matters in several ways. First, instead of mandating consultation "in every possible instance," Section 3 could be amended to require consultation "at least twenty-four hours prior to any presidential decision to commit U.S. forces under any of the circumstances contemplated by Section 4(a)(1)." The president would be exempted from this requirement only in those situations in which he is unable to initiate consultation as a result of an armed attack upon the United States.

Another major problem with Section 3 is its failure to specify the identity of those members of Congress whom the president is required to consult. Hence, several legal scholars have argued that meaningful consultation could best be promoted by an amendment that would explicitly designate those congressional leaders from each party who must be involved in consultation. Here, several options could be considered. Former Senator Jacob Javits suggested that the designees come from the Senate Foreign Relations and House Foreign Affairs Committees. Alternatively, law professor Thomas Franck has proposed designating two members, a Republican and Democrat, from each of the committees in the Senate and House dealing with foreign affairs, armed services, and intelligence, two members from each of the foreign affairs appropriations subcommittees, as well as the two senior leaders of both parties in the two chambers. In any event, the bipartisan congressional group should remain sufficiently small to minimize the risk of leaks, and its members would have to agree to be permanently available for consultation, either in person or by electronic communication, much like the members of the Senate Select Committee on Intelligence.

To insure that executive-legislative dialogue is meaningful rather than perfunctory—as it surely was in the case of Grenada—Section 3 could be further amended by adopting Senator Thomas Eagleton's proposal that requires the president to "discuss fully and seek the advice and counsel" of the designated congressional group, instead of merely "to consult." It would also be prudent to require direct presidential involvement in such exchanges whenever time permits it.

Finally, to close the huge loopholes that shifted the burden of triggering the sixty-day time limit from the White House to Congress in the Grenada case, Michael Glennon has recommended sensible amendments for Section 4 of the War Powers Resolution. One would provide a clear definition of "hostilities"; no such definition is included in the present law. An additional change would require the president to specify which type of report he is filing under Section 4(a) and to designate a "hostilities" report as such. This would restore automaticity to the sixty-day triggering mechanism and hopefully help avoid the regrettable procedural impasse that occurred in the Grenada case.

Of course, there are at least two major unresolved issues that must be confronted promptly if the amended legislation is to fulfill its intended purposes. First, both branches must find mutually agreeable means for determining the constitutionality of the act. Second, since the Supreme Court's ruling in the *Chadha* case casts doubts about the validity of the legislative veto provision in the War Powers Resolution, the executive and legislative branches would have to reach consensus on the legality of legislative vetoes, especially in cases involving exercise of the constitutionally-mandated power of Congress to declare war.

The power to order armed forces into hostilities is among the most awesome that governments exercise. It is debatable whether the American founders, who ardently believed in the principle that authority over fundamental decisions should be shared, ever intended to lodge the war power exclusively in the hands of one individual or solely in one branch. Indeed, those wielding the power of the sword ought to heed the eloquent admonition by former Senator Jacob Javits, the principal author of the War Powers Resolution, that "the President is not the Commander-in-Chief of the American people; he is the Commander-in-Chief of the armed forces alone—a very different and much more limited function."[25] By amending the War Power Resolution along the lines suggested above, Congress could take a giant step forward in reconciling its power to declare war with the powers of the president as commander-in-chief. That the need for such reconciliation is paramount cannot be doubted. It remains to be seen whether executive and legislative leaders have the vision and the will to resolve the war powers controversy in the aftermath of Grenada.   ■

---

25. Jacob K. Javits, "The War Powers Resolution and the Constitution: A Special Introduction," in Demetrios Caraley, ed., *The President's War Powers: From the Federalist to Reagan* (New York: The Academy of Political Science, 1984), 3.

SUPERPOWER SUMMITRY
Richard Nixon

Forty years ago, U.S. nuclear power was indispensable in ending World War II. In the postwar era, American nuclear superiority was indispensable in deterring Soviet probes that might have led to World War III. But that era is over, and we live in the age of nuclear parity, when each superpower has the means to destroy the other and the rest of the world.

In these strategic circumstances, summit meetings between leaders of the United States and the Soviet Union have become essential if peace is to be preserved. Such meetings will contribute to the cause of peace, however, only if both leaders recognize that tensions between the two nations are due not to the fact that we do *not* understand each other but to the fact that we *do* understand that we have diametrically opposed ideological and geopolitical interests. Most of our differences will never be resolved. But the United States and the Soviet Union have one major goal in common: survival. Each has the key to the other's survival. The purpose of summit meetings is to develop rules of engagement that could prevent our profound differences from bringing us into armed conflict that could destroy us both.

With this limited but crucially important goal in mind, we must disabuse ourselves from the start of the much too prevalent view that if only the two leaders, as they get to know each other, could develop a new "tone" or a new "spirit" in their relationship, our problems would be solved and tensions reduced. If history is any guide, evaluating a summit meeting in terms of the "spirit" it produces is evidence of failure rather than success. The spirits of Geneva in 1955, of Camp David in 1959, of Vienna in 1961 and of Glassboro in 1967 each produced a brief improvement in the atmosphere, but no significant progress on resolving major issues. Spirit and tone matter only when two leaders of nations with similar interests have a misunderstanding that can be resolved by their getting to know each other. Such factors are irrelevant when nations have irreconcilable differences, which is the case as far as the United States and the Soviet Union are concerned.

The obsession with style over substance among some observers is ludicrous. The fact that General Secretary Mikhail Gorbachev has a firm handshake, excellent eye contact, a good sense of humor and dresses fashionably is no more relevant to his policies than the fact that Khrushchev wore ill-fitting clothes, drank too much and spoke a crude Russian. Anyone who reaches the top in the Soviet hierarchy is bound to be a dedicated communist and a strong, ruthless leader who supports the Soviet foreign policy of extending Soviet domination into the non-communist world. We can "do business" with Gorbachev, but only if we recognize that the business we have to deal with involves intractable differences between competitive states.

President Reagan will be urged to prove to Mr. Gorbachev that he is sincerely dedicated to peace and that, despite his tough rhetoric, he is really a very nice man. President Reagan does not have to prove that he is for peace. Mr. Gorbachev knows that. What is vitally important is that he also understand that President Reagan is a strong leader, one who is fair and reasonable, but who will, without question, take action to protect American interests when they are threatened.

Debates about ideology will serve no useful purpose. Mr. Gorbachev is as dedicated to his ideology as President Reagan is to his. Neither is going to convert the other.

In the postwar era, no two leaders come to a summit with more political support at home or more endowed with charm and charisma. But for one to try to charm the other would bring not affection but contempt; this would certainly be Mr. Gorbachev's reaction. An essential element of a new relationship is not sentimental expressions of friendship but hard-headed mutual respect. In 1959, before I met Khrushchev, British Prime Minister Harold Macmillan told me that he sensed in his meetings with the Soviet leaders that, above all, they "wanted to be admitted as members of the club." This is a small price to pay for laying the foundations for a new structure of peace in the world.

II

Can two powers with diametrically opposed geopolitical interests avoid war and develop a peaceful relationship? It is important to recognize clearly the major dangers which could lead to nuclear war. In descending order of likelihood they are:

1) War by accident, where one side launches a nuclear attack because a mechanical malfunction creates the mistaken impression that the other side has launched an attack;

2) Nuclear proliferation, which could put nuclear weapons in the hands of a leader of a minor revolutionary or terrorist power who would be less restrained from using nuclear weapons than the major powers have been;

3) Escalation of small wars in areas where the interests of the superpowers are both involved, such as the Middle East and the Persian Gulf;

4) War by miscalculation, where a leader of one superpower understimates the will of the leader of the other to take utlimate risks to defend his interests.

In all four of these scenarios, the United States and the Soviet Union have a mutual interest in reducing the danger and risks which could lead to a nuclear war. They are, therefore, areas where tough-minded diplomacy culminating in agreements at the summit level can play a constructive role.

The next most likely danger is a Soviet preemptive strike to liquidate the Chinese nuclear arsenal. This is not a danger at the present time because China lacks the industrial base and military capacity to be a serious threat to the Soviet Union. But as China begins to develop such a capacity in the future, a Soviet leader could decide that it is better to strike before China becomes a major nuclear power. A nuclear war between major powers, like the Soviet Union and China, could escalate into a world war. That is why it is in the interest of the United States and the West to welcome, not oppose, efforts on the part of the Soviet Union and the People's Republic of China to reduce tensions.

The least likely danger of nuclear war is a Soviet nuclear attack on Western Europe or the United States. The Soviet leaders are and will continue to be dedicated to extending communist domination over non-communist nations. But they are not madmen, and they are not fools. No matter how confident they are that they can win a nuclear war, it would be at the risk of great destruction to the Soviet homeland. Having Europe and the United States reduced to nuclear wastelands would be the bitter fruit of such a "victory." World war has become obsolete as an instrument of policy between the two superpowers. That is why the primary danger, as far as the United States and Western Europe are concerned, is not destruction in war but surrender to nuclear coercion.

Reducing the danger of nuclear war involves arms control, but it is a mistake to support arms control as desirable in itself and to believe that any agreement is better than none. The primary purpose of arms control is to reduce the danger of war. It is not the existence of arms, but political differences that lead to their use, which leads to war. A bad agreement that opens the way to Soviet superiority increases the danger of war. Even a good agreement will not prevent war if political differences lead to armed conflict. Thus, an agreement reducing arms but not linked to restraints on political conduct would not contribute to peace. If political differences escalate into war, it is no comfort to know that each side has the capacity to destroy the other only two times rather than twenty times.

President Reagan has been unfairly criticized for adhering to the SALT II (Strategic Arms Limitation Talks) treaty negotiated by President Jimmy Carter but not approved by the Senate. The critics contend that the reason the Soviet Union is ahead and that we are behind in land-based strategic missiles is because the Soviets are cheating on the arms control agreements and because those agreements restricted our strategic programs. There is no question that the Soviets will do all that is allowed under an arms control agreement and will stretch it to the outer limits and indeed will cheat if they can get away with it. But they gained their superiority in strategic land-based missiles not because of what *they* did in violation of arms control agreements but because of what *we* did *not* do within the limits allowed by the agreements. We must also face up to the hard reality that without a credible arms control initiative, it would be impossible to get congressional approval for adequate defense budgets to match the Soviet effort or to retain the support of our allies.

It is contended that because of the flaws in the agreements and the Soviet practice of violating them, the United States would be better off without any agreement. Yet, while there is strong evidence that the Soviet Union is probably violating provisions of SALT I and SALT II, it is complying with the limits on the fractionation of warheads agreed to in SALT II. If President Reagan had decided not to continue complying with SALT II, the Soviet Union would not consider itself to be bound by these provisions and limitations either; it could attach 30 warheads to each of its 300 giant SS-18 intercontinental ballistic missiles rather than the 10 allowed under the treaty. This would mean an increase of 6,000 warheads in the Soviet arsenal. The United States has no missiles of this size which would allow us to match such an action by the Soviets.

Looking to the future, without a new arms control agreement, even if the United States were to continue its own arms program at the levels requested by President Reagan rather than the far lower levels approved by Congress, and if the Soviets were to continue their program at current levels, the Soviet Union will be further ahead in nuclear missiles in 1990 than it is today.

If we are to prevent otherwise inevitable Soviet superiority, our only option is to negotiate a new, verifiable arms control agreement based on strict parity that denies a first-strike capability to the Soviet Union as well as to ourselves. What is most urgent is to remove the threat of the SS-18s and the new ICBMs, the SS-24 and SS-25, which are designed not to attack our cities in retaliation for an attack on the Soviet Union but for a decisive first strike against our missile sites. Many senators and congressmen have voted for the 40 MX missiles in the hope that they would be an effective bargaining chip in the Geneva negotiations. But the Soviets are not philanthropists. They will not cut back their 300 SS-18s to only 40 without getting something in return.

That is why, contrary to the critics' contention, the President's Strategic Defense Initiative (SDI) is indispensable to arms control. Without it, the Soviet Union would have no incentive to limit its offensive weapons. It is important, however, to distinguish among three different defensive systems.

A defensive system to protect our entire population would make nuclear weapons obsolete and thus replace deterrence as our defense against nuclear weapons. But for such a system to be effective against an all-out Soviet attack, it would have to be virtually leakproof. In view of the dramatic scientific breakthroughs made in my lifetime, I do not contend, as some do, that this is impossible. But we cannot base our *current* strategic planning on a system which, at best, will not be ready for full deployment until the next century.

A system that defends our missile sites, however, is possible in ten years or less. Even if it is only 30-percent effective, it would effectively deny the Soviet Union a first-strike capability against our missile sites. The purpose of such a defensive system would be not to replace deterrence but to strengthen it.

The third kind of system, a thin population defense, which would not be adequate against an all-out Soviet attack but *would* be effective against an accidental launch or an attack by a minor nuclear power, is also feasible within the next ten years. This is an area where the Soviet Union could agree with us that developing and deploying such a limited system is in their interest as well as ours.

President Reagan is correct in insisting that research on all aspects of the SDI is not negotiable, both because a ban on research is not verifiable and because if there is even a remote chance to develop a total population defense it should be a priority goal of our defense establishment. We also must have in mind that the Soviet Union is spending twice as much as we are on defense against nuclear weapons.

But deployment, as distinguished from research, for defense of our missile fields is the ultimate bargaining chip, just as was the case with SALT I. We should agree to limit our deployment of defensive weapons *only* if the Soviets significantly reduce and limit their offensive weapons. The choice is Gorbachev's. Either the Soviets cut back on their offensive forces or we will deploy defensive forces to match their buildup.

III

Arms control and political issues must go forward together. Progress on arms control can lead to stability and the reduction of political tensions. Reduction of political tensions can lead to a better climate for reaching an arms control agreement that is fair to both sides. Those who contend that we should seek arms control regardless of what happens on political issues should bear in mind that what destroyed any chance for Senate approval of the SALT II treaty was the Soviet invasion of Afghanistan. Today, there is no chance that the Senate would approve an arms control treaty at a time when the Soviet Union is supporting anti-U.S. forces in El Salvador and Nicaragua.

A summit agenda, therefore, should have as its first priority not arms control but the potential flash points for U.S.-Soviet conflicts. It is highly doubtful that we would have agreed to SALT I in 1972 had we not settled in the Berlin Agreement of 1971 those issues which had led to so many crises since the end of World War II. A similar opportunity is presented in the Middle East and Central America today.

The most difficult and potentially dangerous issue which brings the two nations into confrontation is the Soviet policy of supporting revolutionary movements against non-communist governments in the Third World. The Brezhnev Doctrine of 1968, announced after Soviet troops crushed a rebellion against the communist government of Czechoslovakia, proclaimed that Soviet conquests in Eastern Europe were irreversible. Putting it simply, Brezhnev said, "what's mine is mine." By Soviet probes in Latin America, Africa, the Persian Gulf and the Mideast against allies and friends of the United States, that doctrine has been extended to mean "what's yours is mine." The Soviet leaders must be made to understand that it would be both irrational and immoral for the United States and the West to accept the doctrine that the Soviet Union has a right to support wars of liberation in the non-communist world without insisting on our right to defend our allies and friends under assault and to support true liberation movements against pro-Soviet regimes in the Third World.

We cannot expect the Soviets to cease being communists, dedicated to expanding communist influence and domination in the world. But we must make it clear to the Soviets that military adventurism will destroy the chances for better relations between the United States and the Soviet Union. We must also make it clear that the revised Brezhnev Doctrine of not only defending but extending communism will be answered by a Reagan Doctrine of defending and extending freedom. Our only common interest is to conduct ourselves in such a way that such conflicts do not escalate into nuclear confrontation.

In view of the danger of proliferation of nuclear weapons, both nations have a mutual interest in working together to combat international terrorism, whether promoted by states or individuals. With the progress that is being made in the technology of miniaturazation, the time is not far off when the danger of breaking the nuclear threshold will come from individuals and not only nations. If the nuclear genie gets out of the bottle, the fallout could affect all nations and particularly those which have nuclear weapons. The Soviets should be asked to join us in a declaration that terrorists and those who give aid and comfort to terrorists are guilty of an international crime and should be dealt with accordingly.

While we should hold the Soviets accountable for the actions they take that are opposed to our interests, we should recognize that they are not responsible for all of the troubles in the world. The income gap between nations that produce raw materials and those that consume them, famine due to climatic causes, radical Muslim fundamentalist and terrorist movements emanating from Libya and Iran—all of these problems would exist even if the Soviet Union did not exist. But rather than exploiting such problems, the Soviet Union should join the United States and other Western nations in combating them. The Soviets should be especially concerned about the rise of Muslim fundamentalism not only because one-third of the population of the Soviet Union is Muslim, but also because the Muslim revolution competes with the Soviet revolution for the support of people in Third World nations.

There is one phase of our competition which should be brought under control—competing with each other in fueling the arms race in the Third World. U.S. and Soviet arms sales to Third World countries run to billions of dollars. Most of these countries are desperately poor, and they need economic assistance far more than they need additional arms. For the Soviet Union to arm India, while the United States arms Pakistan, can only end in tragedy for the people of both countries. Even though these are only non-nuclear arms, they are instruments of war, and small wars always have the potential of escalating into nuclear wars. There is no prospect for reducing arms sales soon, if at all, but both the United States and the U.S.S.R. have an interest in controlling them and not letting them drag us into conflict.

IV

Turning to collateral issues, while it is an illusion that trade by itself will lead to peace, an increase in unsubsidized trade in nonmilitary items can provide a strong incentive for the Soviet Union to avoid conduct that increases political tensions between our two countries. Trade and political issues are inexorably linked. For the United States to increase trade, which the Soviets need and want, at a time when they are engaging in political activities that are opposed to our interests, would be stupid and dangerous. No nation should subsidize its own destruction.

One of the most widely held misconceptions is that person-to-person programs and cultural exchange will significantly reduce tensions. As a longtime supporter of such programs, I must reluctantly point out that this is not the case. "Getting to know you" is not the issue between the Soviet Union and the United States. What are called the three Cs—consular, cultural and commercial issues—will and should receive appropriate attention at summit meetings. But since Soviet authorities decide who is to go to the United States and what and whom foreigners can see in the Soviet Union, no one should be under any illusion that agreements in such peripheral areas by themselves have any significant effect on the nature of the conflict between the two superpowers.

The most highly charged emotional issue is that of human rights abuses in the Soviet Union. The Soviets insist that under no circumstances will they allow their internal policies to be a subject for negotiation with another government. We should make human rights a top-priority *private* issue but not a *public* issue. We saw this principle in practice in 1972. In my summit conversations with Brezhnev, I privately urged that he lift limitations on Jewish emigration in order to gain support for détente in the United States. A record 37,000 exit visas were granted in that year. The following year, the Jackson-Vanik Amendment to the trade bill put public pressure on the Soviets to increase Jewish emigration. The Soviets reacted by sharply *reducing* the number of visas rather than *increasing* them.

V

For the past five years I have strongly urged holding annual summit meetings. Such meetings can serve useful purposes apart from reaching any major substantive agreements. Most important, they can substantially reduce the risk of war from miscalculation. This will be the case not because the two leaders will charm each other or find that they like each other, but because they will understand each other's interests, respect each other's strength, and know the limits beyond which they cannot go without running the risk of armed conflict. This was a factor after the 1973 summit which probably helped to convince Brezhnev that I was not bluffing later in the year (October 1973) when I ordered an alert of our forces to back up our demand that he not intervene unilaterally in the Middle East War.

Moreover, when a summit meeting is scheduled, it inhibits one side from engaging in actions that would be clearly against the interests of the other during the period before the meeting; thus each party will have an incentive to avoid conduct which might poison the atmosphere. This factor probably also played a role in cooling the 1973 crisis.

A summit meeting is also a very useful tool to get a bureaucracy moving. The Soviet bureaucracy is notoriously and maddeningly slow, rigid and inflexible. The U.S. bureaucracy is not free of such faults. There is nothing like the deadline of a summit to knock heads together and to shape up a bureaucracy. The danger which must be avoided is pressure, especially from the bureaucracy, for agreements for agreements' sake to ensure the success of the summit. It is far better to have no agreement at all than to negotiate a bad one.

IV

One hundred and fifty years ago, Alexis de Tocqueville observed with incredible foresight:

> There are at the present time two great nations in the world which seem to bend toward the same end although they start from different points: I allude

to the Russians and the Americans—the Anglo-American relies upon personal interest to accomplish his ends and gives free scope to the unguided exertions and common sense of the citizens; the Russian centers all the authority of society in a single arm: the principal instrument of the former is freedom, of the latter servitude. Their starting point is different and their courses are not the same; yet each of them seems to be marked out by the will of heaven to sway the destinies of half the globe.

This was written long before the communists came to power in Russia. We must recognize that while Russians and Americans can be friends, our governments are destined by history to be adversaries. Yet while we are destined to be adversaries, we have a mutual interest in avoiding becoming enemies in a suicidal war. This requires a candid and honest recognition of our irreconcilable and permanent differences, not a superficial glossing-over of them. A difference not recognized can be dangerous. A difference recognized can be controlled.

The one absolute certainty about the Soviet-American relationship is that the struggle in which we are engaged will last not just for years but for decades. In such a struggle, one advantage the Soviet Union has over the United States is that its foreign policy has consistency and continuity. The leaders change but the policies remain the same. Khrushchev wore short-sleeved shirts and Brezhnev wore French cuffs, but both set the same foreign policy goals: the extension of Soviet domination and influence in the world.

Every eight years and sometimes every four years, American policy, with bipartisanship virtually ended by the Vietnam War, oscillates between the extremes of underestimating and overestimating the Soviet threat. What is needed is a steady, consistent policy with bipartisan support that does not change from one administration to another. This is a long struggle with no end in sight. Whatever their faults, the Soviets will be firm, patient and consistent in pursuing their foreign policy goals. We must match them in this respect. Gorbachev, at 54, is a man who does not to be in a hurry. He may live long enought to deal with as many as five American presidents. We must not give him the opportunity to delay making a deal with one president in the hope that he might get a better one from the president who is to succeed him.   ∎

THE UNITED STATES AND THE U.S.S.R.

Since World War II, the foreign policy of the United States has been primarily one of the East-West focus—based upon our relations with, and the actions and policies of, the Soviet Union.

Beginning, particularly with the administration of President Richard Nixon, ours was a foreign policy aimed toward *détente*, or relaxation of tensions, with Russia. But relations became strained again following the inauguration of President Ronald Reagan. He referred to the Soviet Union as "an evil empire," hardened the U. S. position in regard to negotiated arms control, while presiding over a military buildup and inaugurating the new Strategic Defense Initiative, or "Star Wars," program, and viewed a number of trouble spots in the world, such as Nicaragua, essentially as representing East-West struggles.

Reprinted here is an article that attempts to put relations between the United States and the Soviet Union in historical perspective. The author of the article is Raymond L. Garthoff, former U.S. Ambassador to Yugoslavia and now senior fellow at Brookings Institute. He asserts that both countries have misunderstood and overreacted to the other. He argues that both countries should work together for crisis avoidance and crisis management and for mutually advantageous arms control.

UNITED STATES RELATIONS WITH THE SOVIET UNION
Raymond L. Garthoff

American-Soviet relations stand in need of a redefinition of goals and means. Anyone who in the heyday of détente a decade ago may have forgotten or misjudged the continuation of competition and of an adversarial relationship has been sharply reminded of it since Afghanistan. The fragility of the structure of cooperation erected early in the 1970s was evident in its collapse at the end of the decade. The absence of mutual trust is, in the mid-1980s, stark and clear. Dispelling illusions about détente can be useful. What is not useful—indeed is dangerous—is to resurrect in their place cold war myths and misperceptions. It is also not useful for each superpower to try to hold the other to a standard of international behavior that it does not itself always observe. A misreading by one side of the motivation and intentions of the other, and action on that basis, is akin to Don Quixote's charge against windmills of imagined threatening and evil strength. But the danger is much greater than misapplied chivalry and energy. It is the risk of giving substance to a sharper and deeper conflict than would have been justified by a sound understanding and sober evaluation of real conflicts of interest and the real requirements for competition—and, equally important, of the opportunities still available to realize areas of cooperation in serving mutual interests, including, above all, survival in a nuclear world.

The imperative of coexistence and the reality of competition remain. So do the problems of reconciling them. Thoughtful study of the experience of the 1970s is of the highest importance in order to learn as much as possible about the requirements and conditions for—and limitations on—cooperation, and about the nature and forms of competition. That knowledge can contribute to the design of policies and a policy process for the future that can help to work toward a world order that, while short of the ideal or preference of any one ideology or nation, will nevertheless preserve the essential peace. Without that peace, no idea or people in our day can survive.

FOCUSING ON THE PROBLEM

The essential requirements are political wisdom and courage on the part of the leaders of the two superpowers. While the sources of political understanding and bases for political action are many and complex, among them is a further need for analytical understanding of the situation. While that alone is not sufficient, consistent and coherent action is not likely without it. Evidently, there is need for improved understanding both in Moscow and Washington. The problems in reaching better understanding of realities, and in bringing such action to bear on policy and on the conduct of relations, differ in the two societies, but are great in both cases. In this article my principal focus will be on American policy. While clearer understanding is necessary in both countries, any improvement in either is to the good.

American studies of relations between the United States and the Soviet Union are usually, perhaps necessarily, undertaken by students of Soviet affairs. While expertise on the Soviet Union is essential, its emphasis has tended to lead to an overconcentration on Soviet motives, objectives, and actions in what is a complex reciprocal interacting relationship. For example, such studies customarily identify the subject as "Soviet-American relations," unconsciously attributing the focal role to the Soviet Union and usually overstating Soviet initiative. The United States is unconsciously and implicitly assigned a more reactive role. This approach can distort the analysis. Soviet policy in general, and in its relationship to the United States in particular, is often reactive. In addition, from the Soviet perspective, the American role is much more active and initiatory. Moreover, in describing a relationship between adversaries, attribution of the intiative often carries connotations of a more activist role and offensive design, so that even the wording may imply more than is realized. While there is no completely neutral solution, it is important to bear the point in mind.

In framing U.S. policy toward the Soviet Union, it is necessary not only to examine both American and Soviet objectives and courses of action, but also what may be termed courses of interaction. Reactions of the Soviet leaders to any U.S. action obviously should be considered, although in reality they are not always weighed. But far too little attention is paid to a further chain of interactions. Similarly, effects on other countries, including unintended effects, should be anticipated to the extent possible. The perceptions of an adversary and of others should be part of such evaluations. Finally, the extent of unity and consistency of one's own objectives and policy course, and of the course of interaction with the other side, should be calculated.

The interactions of U.S. and Soviet policy have overlapped with complex interactions in East-West European relations, in the triangle of relations involving China, and in many situations and some conflicts born of local developments around the world. In short, it is necessary to think in terms of developing a strategy of U.S. policy in terms of the interplay of U.S. and Soviet strategies in a broad context of world politics.

Regrettably, the record indicates a progressive decline in such strategic policy making in the United States from the early 1970s to the mid-1980s. While the Nixon-Kissinger leadership showed lamentable miscalculation in a number of cases, it did proceed from an understanding of the need for a policy strategy. It exaggerated its own ability to control and manage events, but at least it sought to do so in pursuit of a purposeful strategy. The Carter administration vacillated notoriously, and moved from a pursuit of détente to confrontation. While the Reagan administration certainly has had aims, it has had a much less coherent strategy. Moreover, by misconstruing many aspects of both Soviet policy and world politics, it has had much less success in meeting its own aims than it could have had. It has also failed to set and reach other aims that would have been in the interest of the United States.

One necessary condition is to discard illusory aims of either a comprehenseive settlement of differences and achievement of a complete accommodation of U.S. and Soviet interests—a goal sometimes misattributed to détente—or U.S. victory in a contest with the Soviet Union, as aspiration of some proponents of confrontation. The real question is how best to manage the relationship of mixed competition and cooperation between rivals.

It is not easy to deal with the dialectical relationship between competition and cooperation. This relationship is a reality, but it is difficult to articulate in terms that command the necessary public support. It is also, for that and other reasons, very difficult to manage without competition getting out of hand and leading to confrontation. Yet that undesirable outcome is not necessary.

THE FAILURE OF DÉTENTE

The détente of the 1970s did not succeed, in the view of most Americans, because of Soviet actions that contravened what the United States understood détente to mean. Either the Soviet leaders abused détente, or if they did act in accordance with it, détente itself was flawed. Americans have blamed both the Soviet Union and détente itself for a mounting series of disquieting developments.

In the Soviet view, the joint détente effort of the 1970s has been willfully abandoned by the United States. The leaders of the United States have, since the late 1970s, preferred to seek advantages from a policy of confrontation, renewed an American quest for military superiority, and been unwilling to accept strategic and political parity. And the Soviet leaders intend to do all they consider necessary not to permit the United States again to gain a strategic advantage over them. In the avowed Soviet view, however, détente remains an objective, continues to be Soviet policy, and can be a common policy again if and when the United States returns to it.

This difference in perspective—like so many differences in American and Soviet perspective and perception—makes it difficult for Americans and Soviets even to conduct parallel assessments of the détente effort of the 1970s in order to diagnose the causes of its failure. Indeed, such assessments are scarcely deemed necessary in either Washington or Moscow. On each side, the actions of the other are virtually taken for granted as having been responsible for the breakdown of détente. The present climate of mutual hostility and suspicion does not encourage detached and dispassionate consideration.

There is a misleading, even dangerous, tendency in the United States by both advocates and opponents of efforts to improve relations to consider détente an entity in its own right and to assume that there is a single policy of détente. This tendency leads to judgments that "détente was tried and failed," or that "détente was betrayed," or that "détente was never really tried." Such oversimplified approaches only mislead.

Americans have feared that the United States was providing more than its share of cooperation, while the Soviet Union was more vigorously devoting itself to competition. This view is one-sided. So, too, on the other hand, is the Soviet belief that American leaders have consciously chosed to abandon détente for confrontation and that American disenchantment with détente was not seriously influenced by Soviet actions. There is much that can be learned and applied to present problems, and future efforts to deal with them, from reflection of the causes of the failure of the American-Soviet détente of the 1970s.

DIFFERENCES IN BASIC CONCEPTIONS

Formeost among the causes of the ultimate failure of détente in the 1970s was a fatal difference in the conception of its basic role by the two sides. The American leaders saw it (in Henry Kissinger's words) as a way of "managing the emergence of Soviet power" into world politics in an age of nuclear parity. The Soviet leaders envisaged it as a way of managing the transition of the United States from its former superiority to a more modest role in world politics in an age of nuclear parity. Thus each saw itself as the manager of a transition of the other. Moreover, both had diverging images of the world order, and although that fact was well enough understood, its implications were not. Thus, underlying the attempts by each of the two powers to manage the adjustment of the other to a changing correlation of forces in the world there were even more basic parallel attempts by both to modify the fundamental world order—in different directions.

The Soviet leaders, conditioned by their Marxist-Leninist ideology, believe that a certain historical movement will ultimately lead to the replacement of capitalism (imperialism) in the world by socialism (communism). But this transition must now occur in a world made incalcuably more dangerous by massive arsenals of nuclear weapons. Peaceful coexistence and détente are seen as offering a path to neutralize this danger by ruling out war between states, permitting historical change to occur, as the Soviets believe it must, through fundamental indigenous social-economic-political processes. While Marxist-Leninists do not shun the use of military force or any other instrument of power if it is expedient, they do not see military power as the fundamental moving force of history. On the contrary, they see it as a possible ultimate recourse of the doomed capitalist class ruling the imperialist citadels of the West. There is, therefore, no ideological barrier to or reservation about pursuing a policy of détente aimed at preventing a nuclear war. Quite the contrary, détente represents a policy aimed at providing stability to a world order that allows progressive revolutionary historical change. This ideological propensity reinforces pragmatic recognition of the need to avoid nuclear war.

The American leadership and people, not holding a deterministic ideology, have been much less sure of themselves and of the trend of history. Insofar as they hold an ideology for a global order, it is one of pluralism, which does not assume the whole world will choose an American-style democratic and free enterprise system. The world order is seen as one that should provide stability and at least protect the democratic option for peoples. Occasionally there have been crusades to extirpate communism in the world; a fringe represented today by Norman Podhoretz, for example, who criticizes the Reagan administration for failing wholeheartedly to rally a new assault on communism and against the Soviet Union. But the dominant American aim has been to contain and deter Soviet or Soviet-controlled communist expansion and to promote a pluralistic and free world order. What has varied and what periodically has been at issue is the relative weight to be placed, on the one hand, on containment achieved by building positions of counterposing power, and on the other, on cooperation pursued by seeking common ground for mutual efforts to reduce tension and accommodate the differing interests of the two sides. There have been varied judgments in both countries about whether objective circumstances at any given time permit the latter approach or require the former, and, therefore, about whether détente is feasible or confrontation is necessary.

When Nixon and Kissinger developed a strategy of détente to replace confrontation, the underlying expectation was that as the Soviet Union became more and more extensively engaged in an organic network of relations with the existing world order it would gradually become reconciled to that order. Ideological expectations of global revolutionary change would become attenuated and philosophical, rather than actively political. Avoidance of the risks of nuclear war was essential; hence there was acceptance of peaceful coexistence and of efforts at strategic arms limitation and other negotiations.

The common American and Soviet recognition of the need to avert war was, and is, of fundamental significance. But there remained radically different visions of the course world history would follow and, therefore, of the pattern of world politics. This divergence in world views naturally affected the policies of the two powers. The difference was well known in a general way; its implications for the two superpowers' respective actions, and, therefore, for their mutual relations and for détente, were not, however, sufficiently understood. This gap led to unrealistic expectations that were not met and that undermined confidence in détente.

American perceptions of a Soviet drive for world domination are rooted in the U.S. image of the ideological expectations of the Soviets for the future. The

United States sees a relentless, inexorable Soviet drive for world communism under the leadership and control of Moscow, and military means as the most—some would say only—successful Soviet instrument. The Soviet leaders in turn see, since the late 1970s, a reborn American pursuit of military superiority as the basis for a policy of intimidation. (In U.S. terms, an aggressive use of "escalation dominance.") The ultimate aim is world domination in a Pax Americana. Rather than attribute to Americans an underlying ideological expectation for the future, they see a nostalgia for the past, an atavistic reaching back for a time when imperialism ruled the world and, more proximately, for a time when the United States had nuclear superiority. In the Soviet view, the United States did carry out a policy of intimidation (for example, compelling the withdrawal of Soviet missiles from the territory of an ally, Cuba, in 1962).

We have not even begun to analyze critically the underlying postulates of either the American or the Soviet conceptions. For example, consider the Soviet proposition that "the class struggle" and "national liberation struggle" are not and cannot be affected by détente. With the exception of a minuscule minority that accepts the Soviet line uncritically, most Americans see that proposition as communist mumbo-jumbo being used as a transparently self-serving argument to excuse pursuit of Soviet interest. In fact, a Soviet leader considers that proposition to be a self-evident truth: détente is a policy, while the class struggle is an objective phenomenon in the historical process that cannot be abolished by policy decision, even if the Soviet leaders wanted to do so. While there is a self-serving dimension to the Soviet proposition, it is not cynical artifice. To the contrary, it is sincerely believed. On a logical plane, to whatever extent the Soviet premise is true, it is crystal clear that any inevitable historical process cannot be stopped by some agreement between the two states.

It is, fortunately, not necessary to assume a prior meeting of the minds of the leaders of the two powers on ideological conceptions as a prerequisite to agreements based on calculated mutual advantage. While ideological conditioning and belief do influence policy, they do not determine it. Questions about the historical process can and should be left to history. The critical question is not whether there is a global class struggle or national liberation struggle, as defined by Marxist-Leninism, but what the Soviet leadership is going to do about it. While the Soviet leadership accepts a moral commitment to aid the world revolutionary process, it is also ideologically obliged to do so only in ways that do not weaken or risk the attainments of socialism in the USSR. Moreover, the ideology also holds that world revolutionary processes are indigenous. Revolution cannot be exported. Neither can counterrevolution. But both can be aided by external forces. Here the Soviet prescription naturally stresses the ultimate failure, but present danger, of an imperialist export of counterrevolution (for example, American support to the authorities in El Salvador, its destabilizing actions against Nicaragua, and the invasion of Grenada). While the Soviet Union expresses support of genuine revolutions and national liberation movements, it is careful and selective in what support is provides, as ideologically sanctioned prudence requires.

In approaching the question of what is a proper and consistent code of conduct with respect to Soviet—and American—behavior in the Third World, each side needs to understand the perspective of the other. Each, naturally, will retain its own view of the historical process, as well as of its own national interests. Differences of concrete interests will remain to be reconciled, but failure to understand each other's viewpoint seriously compounds the problem.

FAILURE TO USE COLLABORATIVE MEASURES

A second cause of the collapse of détente was the failure to make greater use of collaborative measures to meet the requirements of security. National military power is bound to remain a foundation of national security in the foreseeable future. But it need not be the first, or usual, or sole, recourse. The American-Soviet détente involved efforts to prevent and manage crises, and to regulate the military balance through arms control and arms limitation. In the final analysis, however, those efforts—while useful and potentially significant—were almost entirely dependent on the political relationship, and in large measure withered with it.

The effort to achieve strategic arms limitations treaties (SALT) marked the first, and the most daring, attempt to follow a collaborative approach in meeting military security requirements. It involved an unprecedented joint consideration of ways to control the most vital (or fatal) element of national power—the arsenals of strategic nuclear weaponry. Early successes held great promise, but also showed the limits of the readiness of both superpowers to take this path. SALT also generated problems of its own and provided a focal point for objection by those who did not wish to see either regulated military parity or political détente. The final lesson of the failure to ratify SALT II was that arms control cannot stand alone nor sustain a political détente that does not support itself. Even the early successes of SALT I, which contributed to an upsurge of détente and were worthwhile on their own merits, became a bone of contention as détente came under fire.

The widely held American view that SALT tried to do too much is, in my view, a misjudgment: the real flaw was the failure of SALT to do enough. There were remarkable initial successes in the agreement on parity as an objective, on stability of the strategic arms relationship as a necessary condition, and on the control imposed on strategic defensive competition in antiballistic missile (ABM) systems. But there was insufficient political will (and perhaps political authority) to bite the bullet and ban or sharply limit multiple independently-targeted reentry vehicles (MIRVs)—the key to controlling the strategic offensive arms race. Both sides share the blame for this failure, but especially the United States, which led a new round of the arms competition when it couuld safely have held back (in view of the ABM Treaty) long enough to make a real effort to ban MIRVs. The failure to control MIRVs was ultimately the key to the essential failure in the 1970s to stabilize the military dimension of parity, and it contributed indirectly to the overall fall of détente.

Too little attention has been paid to the efforts in the 1970s to devise a regime of crisis management and crisis avoidance. Paradoxically, the relatively more successful steps in this direction are rarely remembered because they do not seize attention as do political frictions. The agreements of 1971 on averting war by accident or miscalculation and on upgrading the hot line, the agreement of 1972 on avoiding incidents at sea between the U.S. and Soviet navies, and the agreement of 1973 on prevention of nuclear war have played a positive role. In addition, there were mutlilateral confidence-building measures in the European security framework. The one instance sometimes charged to have been a failure of collaberation was in fact, if anything, a success: the defusing of the pseudocrisis between the two superpowers in October 1973 at the climax of the fourth Arab-Israeli war.

FAILURE TO DEFINE A CODE OF CONDUCT

A third cause of the failure of American-Soviet détente in the 1970s was the inability of the superpowers to transform the recognition of strategic parity into a common political standard to govern their competitive actions in the world. The divergent conceptions of détente and of the world order underlay this failure, but these were compounded by other factors. One was the unreadiness of the United States, in conceding nominal strategic parity, also to concede political parity. Another was a reciprocated hubris in which each superpower applied a one-sided double standard in perceiving and judging the behavior of the other. The basic principles of mutual relations and a code of conduct were never thrashed out with the necessary frank discussion of differing views, a failure that gave rise to a facade of agreement that not only affected public, but to some extent even leadership, expectations. Expectations based on wishful thinking about the effects of the historical process, or based on overconfidence about a country's managerial abilities to discipline the behavior of the other side, were doomed to failure. Paradoxically, these inflated expectations coexisted on both sides with underlying excessive and projected fears and imputations of aggressive hostility, which resurfaced when the expectations were not met. That this process influenced wider political constituencies (a much wider body politic in the United States) only compounded a situation that affected the leadership as well.

DIVERGENT PERCEPTIONS AND DOUBLE STANDARDS

The United States applied a double standard to Soviet behavior in occupying Afghanistan in 1979 (and earlier to a series of Soviet moves in the Third World). President Jimmy Carter's pained confession of having learned more about Soviet intentions from Afghanistan than from anything else only illustrated the fact. The Soviet intervention in Afghanistan was not justified by the standards of a world order endorsed by the community of nations and in principle by the Soviet Union as well as by the United States. But this fact does not alter (although it effectively obscured) that in practice the United States and the Soviet Union each apply fundamentally different standards to their own behavior than they do to that of the rival superpower and others. There was also an important failure in the case of Afghanistan (as well as in many other cases) by both the United States and the Soviet Union to recognize the perceptions, and motivations, and security interests, of the other side, whether accepting them or not.

The dominant American perception of the motive behind the Soviet intervention in Afghanistan was that it was an egregious example of aggressive expansionism, unprovoked, unless perhaps by a temptation that arose from declining American military power. The Soviets were seen as unaffected by détente unless they were using that policy to cover expansionist moves. The occupation of Afghanistan was seen as dangerous to American interests because it represented a steppingstone for Soviet advancement toward a vital western interest—assured access to oil from the Persian Gulf.

The Soviet leaders, given their perception of events, saw the attribution to them of offensive purposes and threats to the Persian Gulf region, stressed in the prevailing American perception, not merely as incorrect, but as not representing a real assessment by the American leadership, and indeed as a hostile act. Their view seemed to be borne out by the official American response, which included not only a new containment strategy (the Carter Doctrine) and quasi alliance with China, but also the dismantling of virtually the entire set of American-Soviet relations developed over a decade of détente. The Soviet leaders concluded that this reaction represented the preferred American policy. The American administration was using Afghanistan as a pretext for doing what it desired; to mobilize American and, to some extent, world opinion in support of an intensified arms race and an anti-Soviet political line of confrontation. This interpretation fitted the Soviet evaluation of the trend in American policy. It also conveniently removed the Soviet action in Afghanistan as a cause of the collapse of détente.

In the Soviet perception, it was the United States that was acting in a manner inconsistent with the implicit code of conduct of détente. The United States was not recognizing vital Soviet interest in its security sphere, as the Soviets had done when, after the western-supported overthrow of leftist regimes in Chile and Portugal, their criticism of American action had not been permitted to interfere with state relations. On the contrary, the United States was directly challenging them and unnecessarily converting the Afghanistan affair into a broad global political challenge, while discarding the achievements of détente. In the Soviet perception, moreover, the United States was ignoring Soviet parity as a superpower and applying a double standard. In 1965 the United States had, for example, introduced its own military forces and changed the leadership in the Dominican Republic—a country on the American periphery and in the American political, economic, and security sphere. How, the Soviets might have asked, is the Monroe Doctrine essentially different from the Brezhnev Doctrine? While voicing criticism, the Soviet Union had not made that or other comparable American actions, including intervention in Vietnam, a touchstone of Soviet-American relations. Indeed, it had not done so even on the occasion of the American escalation in bombing Hanoi and mining Haiphong in May 1972. Those events had not been permitted to derail the first Brezhnev-Nixon summit meeting and the signing of SALT I. Now the United States was putting the signed SALT II Treaty on the shelf and cutting economic, consular, and even cultural and sports relations, and in addition was mounting a strident propaganda campaign and pressing its allies and others to join in a wide range of anti-Soviet actions.

Indeed, the United States was applying a double standard to Soviet actions not only as compared with U.S. actions, but as compared with China as well. After all, only months before the United States had, while nominally expressing disapproval, done nothing when China invaded neighboring communist Vietnam. The United States even proceeded with a planned visit to China by its secretary of treasury, who while there signed an agreement for broadened bilateral economic relations that provided most-favored-nation status, which continued to be denied to the Soviet Union.

The Soviet perception in this case is little understood in the United States. For their part, the Soviets have failed to recognize American perceptions in this whole episode. The example of Afghanistan also illustrates Soviet difficulty in recognizing that western actions are often reactions to things the Soviets have done, rather than part of a hostile design that would have led to those same actions under any circumstances. The reverse is also true: the West has difficulty recognizing Soviet perceptions of a threat (one that it does not see itself) as the cause of some Soviet actions. Further, the West does not recognize that the Soviets often do not perceive sufficiently the reactive motive for western countermeasures.

The consistent failure of each side to sense and recognize the different perspective and perceptions of the other has been strongly detrimental to the development of their relations, compounding their real differences. The dangers of the failure of each side to recognize the effects of its own misperceptions are also too little appreciated, as are the dangers of its failure to perceive the implications of differing perceptions. Frequently during the 1970s and 1980s it has been unconsciously assumed that the other side was bound to see something in a certain way. That belief has led to serious errors or distortions in assessing the intentions and motivations of the other side. Rather than recognize a differing perception, judging it to be a valid alternative perception or misperception, both sides typically ascribe a different and usually malevolent purpose to each other. This tendency has, for example, characterized the assessment each has made of the military programs of the other, as well as of many of the political moves. Even when an attempt is made to take account of different ways of thinking, each side usually applies stereotypes of "communist" or "imperialist" modes of calculation to the other side, but in a superficial way that stresses the expansionist or aggressive image of the adversary. The result is usually no more than to provide a self-satisfying illusion that the perceptual factor has been taken into account.

COMPETITION UNDER DÉTENTE

In the United States, many in the 1970s saw a cumulative series of Soviet interventions involving military means, often with proxies—Angola, Ethiopia, Kampuchea, Afghanistan—that they believed formed a pattern of Soviet expansion and aggrandizement inconsistent with détente or were at least induced by a weakness of U.S. will and military power. Hence the need to rebuild that power and reassert that will; and hence the heightened suspicion of détente.

In fact, the history of diplomatic, political, and interventionist activity during the last decade is much more extensive and complex—and much less one-sided. Certainly from the Soviet perspective, not only has the Soviet role been more limited and more justified than the United States would concede, but the American role has been more active and less benign. For example, in Soviet eyes, during the decade of the 1970s the U.S. policy toward China moved from triangular diplomacy to active alignment on an anti-Soviet platform. The United States came to offer military assistance to China and established intelligence collection facilities in China directed at the Soviet Union. The United States coordinated hostile activities, for example in Afghanistan, with China. And it encouraged China to invade Vietnam and to arm the Cambodian forces of Pol. Pot.

In the Middle East, the United States arranged the defection of Anwar Sadat's Egypt—and of the Sudan, Somalia, and to some degree Iraq. It effectively squeezed the Soviet Union out of a role in the Middle East peace process, despite repeated assurances that it would not do so. The United States used the Iranian hostage crisis to mobilize a major new military presence in Southwest Asia, which it subsequently maintained. In Africa, U.S. allies and proxies repeatedly and blatantly intervened with military force—Portugal before 1974; France in numerous cases; France, Belgium, Morocco, and Egypt in Zaire; Zaire, South Africa and others in Angola in 1975, albeit unsuccessfully. Using covert operations, the United States assisted in the overthrow of an elected Marxist, Salvador Allende in Chile and, with European assistance, of the Marxist-supported Vasco dos Santos Goncalves in Portugal. America was silent when Indonesia suppressed the revolt of formerly Portuguese Timor. A number of Southeast Asian mountain people were used as American proxies in that region. In South Vietnam, the United States used South Korean and Thai proxy troops, and Australian, Philippine, and other support contingents, along with its own armed forces. It encouraged anti-Soviet activity in Poland and Afghanistan, in the latter case with covert military assistance to the rebels and with Pakistani assistance and Egyptian arms paid for by Saudi Arabia. More recently, the United States has orchestrated covert operations against Sandinista Nicaragua from Honduras and Costa Rica. And the United States itself invaded Grenada and established a friendly nonsocialist regime there.

The deterioration of relations during the latter half of the 1970s not only reflected some of these developments but also contributed to them. For the most part the actions of the two powers stemmed not from Soviet or American initiatives, but as responses to local events.

There also were conscious policies of assertive competition by *both* powers throughout the period of nominal détente. Recall, for example, the U.S. policy initiatives in the immediate aftermath of the first summit meeting in Moscow in 1972, the summit that launched détente. President Richard Nixon flew directly from the Soviet Union to Iran. One purpose of his visit was to establish the Shah as, in effect, American proconsul in the region, in keeping with the Nixon Doctrine. The Shah was promised virtually any American arms he wanted. A contributory reason for the Shah's deputation that was not apparent was to follow through on some conversations with the Chinese and to signal to them U.S. intention to build regional positions of strength around the Soviet Union, détente notwithstanding. In addition, while in Teheran the President accepted the Shah's proposal to arm covertly the Iraqi Kurds. (Iraq had just signed a treaty of friendship with the Soviet Union.) Thus the Kurds became proxies of the United States, Iran, and Israel, which joined in providing support in order to tie the Iraqi army down. And there was a later chapter to this American initiative: the Shah persuaded and induced President Mohammad Daoud of Afghanistan in 1975–78 to move away from his previous close alignment with the Soviet Union, to improve relations with Pakistan, and to crack down on Afghan leftists. It was Daoud's arrest of Nur Mohammad Taraki, Babrak Karmal, Hafizullah Amin, and others in April 1978 — not some plot concocted in Moscow — that led the Khalq military faction to mount a coup and depose him, turning the government over to the People's Democratic Party and setting in train the developments within Afghanistan that culminated in the Soviet intervention.

From Iran, President Nixon flew to Poland, where he was greeted by stirring public acclaim, demonstratively showing not only that the United States would support more or less nonaligned communist regimes (Nixon had visited Romania in 1969 and Yugoslavia in 1970, as well as China in 1972), but also that no part of the Soviet alliance was offbounds to American interest under détente.

As a directed result of the U.S. handling of the Middle East question at the détente summit meeting, Sadat — who was already secretly in touch with the United States — six weeks later expelled the 20,000 Soviet military advisers (and Soviet reconnaissance aircraft) from Egypt.

Only a few months later, in September 1972, China and Japan — with American encouragement — renewed diplomatic relations. And in December new armed clashes occurred on the Sino-Soviet border.

Further, upon President Nixon's return to Washington from the summit he not only urged ratification of the SALT I agreements, but also an increase in strategic arms. Secretary of Defense Melvin Laird even conditioned his support for SALT on congressional approval of new military programs, which he justified as necessary so as to be able to negotiate "from a position of strength," wittingly or not invoking a key symbol of the cold war.

It is not the purpose of this brief recapitulation of some examples of vigorous American competitive activity to argue either that the Soviet perception of American responsibility for the decline and fall of détente is justified, or that the United States was wrong to compete with the Soviet Union. Individual actions have been wise or unwise on their merits, and good or bad in their consequences — as is true of various Soviet actions. But Americans need to recognize that not only the Soviet Union but also the United Staes was "waging détente" in the 1970s — and Americans are not justified in concluding that the Soviet

Union was violating some agreed, clear, and impartial standard to which the United States in practice adheres. With respect to a Soviet readership, this same point about the application of a double standard would equally need to be recognized.

Both sides have in fact sought advantages. Surely Nixon and Kissinger, and Brezhnev and Gromyko, never believed that the other side, or that *either* side, would fail to seek advantages at the expense of the other just because they had agreed, in a document on Basic Principles on Mutual Relations, that "efforts to obtain unilateral advantage at the expense of the other, directly or indirectly, are inconsistent with these objectives" (those objectives being "reciprocity, mutual accommodation and mutual benefit").

Moreover, on the whole, since 1972 the leaders of the United States have probably been at least as inclined as those of the Soviet Union to ignore the further elaboration of that same basic principle–"The recognition of the security interests of the Parties based on the principle of equality." Some Americans, including leaders, have spoken and acted as though the Soviet Union had *no* legitimate security interests. Under the confrontational approach of the Reagan administration, the very legitimacy of the Soviet system has been repeatedly challenged by the President himself, at least during the years 1981–1983.

While both sides throughout the decade recognized their continuing competitive and even adversarial relationship (although the image of that relationship was distorted), they publicly muted this fact–until serious differences emerged. Then both sanctimoniously accused the other of violating an agreed code of conduct. Especially in the United States, this disjunction between private appreciation by its leadership of the political competition, and failure to acknowledge in publicly, contributed to later disillusionment with the détente process itself. In the Soviet Union it has been easier to continue to advocate détente while blaming the other side for renewing tensions.

Both the United States and the Soviet Union have acted in ways contrary to the spirit and letter of a code of conduct for détente as set forth in the Basic Principle to which both committed themselves in 1972. Each has seen its own actions as compatible with pursuit of a *realistic* policy of détente. Each, however, has sought to hold the other side to its own *idealized* view of détente. As a result, each has been disappointed in and critical of the actions of the other. The Soviet leaders, however, adjusted their expectations more realistically, seeing no better alternative than to continue an imperfect détente. This was the Soviet judgment even though the United States was seen as taking advantage of détente in the continuing competition, and even though détente proved less of a restraint on the United States than the Soviets had hoped and expected. Hence the Soviets advocated détente even after the U.S. repudiated in in January 1980 and elected Ronald Reagan. In the United States, on the other hand, dissatisfaction with the failure of detente to restrain Soviet behavior as expected, and to provide as much leverage on Soviet internal affairs as some had hoped it would, eroded public support for détente. Moreover, it was believed that some other course, containment (under Carter from 1978 on, above all in 1980) or even a declared policy of confrontation (under the Reagan administration from 1981 through 1983), was a possible and preferable alternative. In practice, containment, alone or laced with confrontation, proved—as had an idealized détente—not to be "the answer," or even a viable policy.

THE INTERPLAY OF STRATEGIES

Both sides have showed themselves guilty of strategic myopia. For example, both have sought marginal military advantages that have had not only the predictable effects of prompting counterbalancing actions by the other side, but also had adverse and unintended negative impact on political relations.

One broad and significant example of a different kind also illustrates this point well. Too little attention has been paid, on both sides, to the important interrelationships that derive from the interplay of their political strategies. The Carter and Reagan adminstrations have seen rapprochement with China as contributing to the containment of the Soviet Union, and, therefore, as reinforcement in reinstraining Soviet policy. They have failed to consider whether the tightening noose of a grand encirclement (the United States, NATO, China, Japan), as seen in Moscow, may have impelled the Soviet Union towards more active measures to prevent that incirclement (as in Afghanistan and potentially in Iran) and to leapfrogging to accomplish a counter-encirclement (as in Vietnam against China, and in Syria, South Yemen, and Ethiopia in the Middle East). The Soviet Union in turn has underestimated the extent to which actions it may have regarded as defensive and counter-encircling (largely the same list) have in fact—and not just in propaganda—been perceived in the West and China as offensive moves and thus contributed to the development of the very coalition of encirclement that they were intended to counter.

One important change in the American strategy of global competition exacerbated this inattention to the interplay of strategies. The transition from Henry Kissinger and a strategy of détente in the period form 1969 to 1976 to that of Zbigniew Brzezinski in 1978–79 (continued in the post-détente strategies since 1980) was characterized by a shift from a contest of maneuver in a system with two predominant powers to a positional conflict of two sides. Relations with China can illustrate. Kissinger avoided aligning the United States with either the Soviet Union or China against the other and secured a balancing position in triangular diplomacy. Under this approach, the United States could improve relations with both powers and improve its overall position in the process. After 1978 the United States shifted to a relationship with China designed to place pressure on the Soviet Union by aligning China with the United States in a coalition the latter would dominate. Thereafter, if the United States improved relations with either power, it would make its relations with the other worse. Moreover, the Chinese, once freed of the fear of American-Soviet alignment, reasserted their own independence from alignment with the United States and to an extent gained the balancing position in a reordered triangle.

THE ARMS RACE AND THE MILITARY BALANCE

A fourth cause of the decline in confidence in détente in the 1970s was the view widely held on both sides that the other side was seeking and acquiring military capabilities in excess of what it needed for deterrence and defense, and, therefore, was not adhering to détente. This is a complex question. For example, the limits under SALT reduced some previously important areas of concern and uncertainties in projecting the military balance—notably with respect to ABMs. But another effect was that the rather complex real strategic balance was artificially simplified in the general understanding (and not just that of the general public) to certain highlighted indexes, thereby increasing sensitivity to a symbolic arithmetical "balance." And national means of intelligence, which are given high credibility when it comes to identifying a threat, are regarded with a more jaundiced eye when called upon to monitor and verify compliance with an arms limitation agreement.

In any event, during the latter half of the 1970s, concern mounted in the United States over why the Soviet Union was engaged in what has been termed a relentless continuing arms build-up. At the same time U.S. military programs were justified as meeting that build-up. In turn, the Soviet Union saw the American build-up as designed to restore the United States to a position of superiority.

Throughout the preceding two decades of cold war and cold peace, the United States had maintained a clear strategic nuclear superiority. As the Soviet Union continued to build its strategic forces, despite earlier agreed strategic arms limitaitons, new fears and suspicions arose in the United States. Unfortunately, the actual consolidation of parity in the latter 1970s was not in synchronization with the political acceptance and public impression of parity in the early 1970s. What the Soviets saw as finally closing the gap through programs of weapons deployment, which they saw as fully consonant both with the terms of the SALT agreement and with achievement of parity, many in the United States saw as a Soviet pursuit of advantages that violated at least the spirit, if not the letter, of SALT and that threatened to go beyond parity to superiority. The real inconsistency was between the continuing Soviet deployments and the American public's expectation derived from SALT. The interim freeze of 1972 had set a level with respect to the deployment of forces, including some construction under way that had not yet been completed by the Soviet Union. In addition, it had limited only the level of strategic missile launchers, not of warheads, and the Soviets, who were behind in terms of arming their strategic missile force with MIRVs, sought to catch up in the years following. If the Soviet strategic deployments had occurred more nearly at the time of American deployment, and both countries had agreed to accept parity and stop at the same time (and not merely at the same level), the public perception would have been quite different.

While a desire to influence public opinion played a part in inflating presentations of the military threat posed by the other side, there were real build-ups on both sides. In part, then, perceptions of both sides of a hostile arms build-up were genuine. But both sides were unduly alarmist in exaggerating the military capabilities – and in imputing aggressive intentions – of the other.

A U.S. misestimate of the pace of Soviet military outlays in the period from 1977 to 1983 also contributed to the exaggerated impression of a relentless Soviet build-up. The fact of a deliberate cut in Soviet military expenditure from an annual real increase of 4–5 percent in the first half of the 1970s to only 2 percent from 1976 until 1983, with a stagnation at zero percent annual increase in military procurement for those seven years, was not recognized until 1983. While the Soviet military program continued at a high level, the significance of this Soviet reduction in the growth of military outlays was missed. And from the Soviet standpoint, the U.S. public insistence that there was a continuous Soviet increase, and use of that allegation to justify a real American and NATO build-up in the late 1970s and early 1980s, was perceived as reflecting a malevolent design rather than a mistaken intelligence assessment.

The Soviet Union did not serve its own best interests or the interests of détente by continuing to be so secretive about its military forces and programs. The case of the U.S. misestimate of Soviet military spending is one clear illustration. To cite but one other significant example, the argument of the USSR that its SS-20 intermediate-range ballistic missile deployment represented only modernization of a long-standing theater missile force, and timely indication that it would replace a like number of older, larger-yield weapons, might have convinced some in the West who were uncertain and fearful as to the purpose behind the Soviet deployment. A strategic dialogue before NATO decided on a counterdeployment might have permitted some preventive arms control without the heightened tension and less promising ex facto attempt at arms limitations on intermediate-range nuclear forces (INF).

The INF deployments and the failed attempt at INF arms control in the late 1970s and early 1980s illustrate the close connection between arms control and political as well as military relationships. The INF situation became a major political issue between East and West, and also within the West. What the Soviet leaders had intended to be military modernization was perceived instead as a political-military challenge, and it spurred a western counteraction. The NATO counteraction, which in turn was intended to reassure western opinion and to insure deterrence, instead was perceived in Moscow as an American threat that tied West Europe more closely into U.S. designs to regain overall military superiority with which to intimidate the Soviet Union. This perception of the American purpose led the Soviet leaders to attempt to head off the NATO deployment altogether – and when that attempt failed, to mount demonstrative military countermeasures through new deployments. The NATO alliance maintained the consensus to proceed with deployment, defeating the Soviet attempts to head it off. But it was a pyrrhic victory, as the issue weakened the basic social-political support for the alliance, while the resulting renewed Soviet build-up did not allay the concerns that had led to the NATO deployment. Neither side added to its security, only to the strain on political relations.

CONCLUSIONS

The essence of détente, as a practical proposition, was an agreement on mutual accommodation to a political competition in which each side would limit its actions in important (but, unfortunately, not well-defined) ways in recognition of the common shared interest in avoiding the risks of uncontrolled confrontation. Détente called for political adjustments, both negotiated and unilateral. It did not involve a classical division of the world into spheres of hegemonic geopolitical interests. Rather, it was a compact calling for self-restraint on each side in recognition of the interests of the other to the extent necessary to prevent sharp confrontation. While this general concept and approach were accepted by both sides, regrettably each side had differing conceptions of the proper restraint it—and the other side—should assume. This discrepancy led to reciprocal feelings of having been let down by the other side. From the outset there was insufficient recognition of the need for more frank exchanges of views and collaboration in dealing with differences of interest. With time, these efforts collapsed. Both sides showed that they were not ready to accommodate the interests of the other. An additional complicating factor was the inability of the U.S. leadership to manage and control its own policy. But more important, on both sides there was a serious inability to perceive the viewpoint and interest of the other. This gap grew, rather than lessened, with time and experience. As a consequence, trust—which was never very great—declined.

Naiveté has been charged to advocates of détente. But while some may have had unrealistic aims and expectations, the American leaders and practitioners of détente (Nixon, Kissinger, Brzezinski, and Cyrus Vance) were not as naive as were the critics and challengers who preferred to remain blind both to the strength and vigor of U.S. global competition and to the limits on Soviet power and policy. The critics of détente have seen both American and Soviet power and the exercise of that power from opposite ends of a telescope—a greatly exaggerated image of relentless Soviet build-up and use of power in a single-minded offensive expansionist policy and a grossly distorted image of U.S. passivity and impotence in the world.

There has also been a strong tendency on both sides to attribute to the other side exaggerated strength, control over events, and consistency both in purpose and in implementation of policy. What makes this irony dangerous is that each side acts on its perceptions of the intentions and power of its adversary in ways that tend to make these perceptions self-fulfilling prophecies.

Both powers have also been reluctant to acknowledge, even to recognize, failures of their own political systems. Instead, they have been only too ready to project responsibility onto the other side. Thus, for example, Soviet claims of American responsibility for internal opposition in Afghanistan and Poland serve (among other purposes) as an alibi for failures of Soviet-style socialism. American charges of Cuban and Soviet responsibility for revolution in Central America are similarly more convenient than acknowledging failures of reactionary "capitalist" regimes to provide for needed peaceful change. In addition to reflecting genuine fears based on perceived vulnerabilities, it is simply easier to project hostile intervention than to admit failures to facilitate or permit peaceful change within respective areas of predominant influence.

Thus, apart from differing conceptions of détente, there have been very important differences in perceptions not only of the motivations of the other side, but of the very reality of world politics. Détente, if it is revived (probably without that name), must be recognized as one complex basis for a competitive relationship, not as an alternative to competition. That has been the reality, and the fact must be recognized.

As we look to the future, the problem of managing the continuing global geopolitical competition between the Soviet Union and the United States remains a central issue. Whether a code of conduct, or rules of the game, can be agreed upon is a question. But some increased reciprocal understanding and genuine reciprocity and restraint is required, whether agreed principles are formulated or not. So is the need to work together in crisis avoidance and crisis management. Another major need is to resume the process of arms control. Regrettably the prospect is very clouded. Both sides need to be more prepared to meet the legitimate security requirements of the other in mutually advantageous agreements involving mutual sacrifices of military forces and options. At the present juncture, the picture is especially grim because of a quixotic quest by President Reagan for a miracle cure through his Star Wars strategic defense initiative and his failure to recognize its prejudicial impact on arms control, not only on further agreements but on maintaining existing arms limitations, and to appreciate the possible value of arms control.

This review may seem to close on a pessimistic note. Indeed, at the present juncture it would be misleading to be optimistic. Yet the basic foundations are there for possible serious steps to mitigate the American-Soviet confrontation and rivalry. And we can learn from the history of the recent past if we study it. ■

IS THE "STAR WARS" PROGRAM SOUND NATIONAL POLICY?

In 1983, President Ronald Reagan proposed the "establishment of a comprehensive and intensive research program, the Strategic Defense Initiative, aimed at eventually eliminating the threat posed by nuclear armed ballistic missiles." This program was soon dubbed "Star Wars."

The proposal immediately touched off a controversy in Congress over issues of nuclear strategy and arms control. The Soviet Union raised serious objections to the program. Some scientists questioned its technological feasibility. Professors at some universities opposed participation in the research involved.

Here, we present a debate on the issue. First, Fred C. Ikle, U.S. Under Secretary of Defense for Policy, argues in favor of the program as being necessary to reduce the risk of nuclear destruction.

Next, U.S. Senator William Proxmire (D-Wisconsin) takes the opposing view. He says such a system is probably unworkable and would increase, not decrease, the risk of nuclear war.

The question which they are addressing, then, is: Is the "Star Wars" program sound national policy?

YES, IT WILL REDUCE THE RISK OF NUCLEAR DESTRUCTION
Fred C. Ikle

ALMOST A YEAR AGO, President Reagan offered a hopeful vision of the future, based on a program to "counter the awesome Soviet missile threat with measures that are defensive." Many Americans welcomed this initiative, sensing that it could provide a road to escape from the confrontation of ever-more destructive missiles forces. But there were others who had doubts about the initiative, and some who are still strongly opposed to it.

Several developments have come together at this time that have made the President's initiative timely:

First, the continuing growth of the ballistic missile threat from the Soviet Union that could force upon us ever more difficult improvements in our offensive forces for second-strike deterrence.

Second, advances in technologies relevant for ballistic missile defense that require us to reassess the feasibility of various defensive systems.

Third, the substantial, ongoing Soviet efforts for ballistic missile and air defense, in particular the Soviet research and development programs for ballistic missile defenses and the fact that the Soviet Union has now deployed a large radar in Central Siberia which almsot certainly violates the ABM Treaty.

Clearly, the role of ballistic missile defenses must be viewed in the context of the overall military and political requirements of the United States. A decision to deploy ballistic missile defenses would have major implications for nuclear strategy, the prevention of nuclear war, deterrence of aggression, and arms reduction. Our policy on missile defenses must be shaped with this broad context in mind. To permit informed and prudent decisions we have to conduct research on many aspects of the relevant technology and develop a range of specific choices.

It seems plausible that components of a multi-layered defense could become deployed earlier than a complete system. Such intermediate versions of a ballistic missile defense system, while unable to provide the protection available from a completed multi-tiered system, may nevertheless offer useful capabilities. A research and development program that provides options to deploy such intermediate capabilities would be an important hedge against an acceleration in the Soviet strategic buildup. And if such intermediate systems were actually deployed, they could play a useful role in defeating limited nuclear attacks and in enhancing deterrence against large attacks.

One of the criticisms that has been levelled against ballistic missile defense is the allegation that such defenses would overturn principles of deterrence that have worked throughout the nuclear age. This criticism is based on amnesia — forgetting the true history of the nuclear age.

We recognize full well that there are many important uncertainties that will not be resolved until more is known about the technical characteristics of defensive systems, the future arms policies of the Soviet Union, the prospects for arms reduction agreements, and the Soviet response to U.S. initiatives. Important questions to be addressed are: (1) the absolute and relative effectiveness of future U.S. and Soviet defensive systems and how this effectiveness is perceived by each side; (2) the vulnerabilities of the defensive systems (both real and perceived); (3) the size, composition, and vulnerabilities of each side's offensive forces; and (4) the overall U.S.-Soviet military balance. While these uncertainties cannot be fully resolved, we will learn more about them with the passage of time. Our assessment of these issues should, of course, affect our design and deployment decisions.

Despite these uncertainties, a vigorous R&D program is essential to assess and provide options for future ballistic missile defenses. At a minimum, such a program is necessary to ensure that the United States will not be faced in the future with a one-sided Soviet deployment of highly effective ballistic missile defenses to which the only U.S. answer would be a further expansion of our offensive forces, such as the addition of penetration aids and more launchers. Such a situation would be fraught with extremely grave consequences for our security and that of our allies.

There is no basis for assuming that decisions on the deployment of defensive systems rest solely with the United States. On the contrary, Soviet history, doctrine, and programs (including an active program to modernize the existing Moscow defense, the only operational ballistic missile defense in existence) all indicate that the Soviets are more likely and better prepared than we to deploy ballistic missile defenses whenever they deem it to their advantage.

Since long-term Soviet behavior cannot reliably be predicted, we must be prepared to respond flexibly. A U.S. research and development program on ballistic missile defense that provides a variety of deployment options will help resolve the many uncertainties we now confront, and over time offers us flexibility to respond to new opportunities. By contrast, without the research and development program, we condemn future U.S. Presidents—and future Congresses—to remain locked into the present exclusive emphasis on deterrence through offensive systems alone.

Over time, our reseach and development on ballistic missile defense might induce a shift in Soviet emphasis from ballistic missiles, with the problems they pose for stability, in favor of air-breathing forces with slower flight times. By constraining Soviet efforts to maintain offensive forces (and making them more costly), U.S. options to deploy ballistic missile defenses might increase our leverage in inducing the Soviets to agree to mutual reductions in offensive nuclear forces. In turn, such reductions could reinforce the potential of defensive systems to stabilize deterrence. Reductions of the magnitude proposed by the United States in the Strategic Arms Reduction Talks (START) would be effective in this regard.

In its initial stages, a U.S. ballistic missile defense research and development program would be consistent with existing U.S. treaty obligations. Were we later to decide on deployment of a widespread defense of the United States, the ABM Treaty would have to be revised. If the result of the research and development program warranted such a decision in the future, it would be appropriate to address it in the context of a joint consideration of offensive and defensive systems. This was the context contemplated at the outset of the SALT negotiations; but while we reached an agreement in limiting defenses, our anticipations of associated limitations on offensive forces have not been realized.

Both the Soviet national interest and traditional themes in Soviet strategic thought give reason to expect that the Soviets will respond with an increased shift toward defensive forces relative to offensive forces. The nature of a cooperative U.S.-Soviet transition to defensive forces would depend on many factors, including the technical aspects of each side's defensive systems, their degree of similarity or dissimilarity, and whether U.S. and Soviet systems would be ready for deployment in the same period. Because of the present uncertainties, no detailed blueprint for arms control in such a transition period can be drawn at this time. A list of arms control measures might include agreed schedules for introducing the defensive systems of both sides, and associated schedules for reduction in ballistic missiles and other nuclear forces. Confidence-building measures and controls on devices designed specifically to attack or degrade the other side's defensive systems are other potential arms control provisions.

If both the United States and the Soviet Union deployed defensive systems against a range of nuclear threats, it would not diminish the need to strengthen U.S. and allied conventional military capabilities. Moreover, if the United States in such a future period decided to realize the protection offered by a fully effective strategic defense, we would also require air defenses. The integration of defenses against air-breathing vehicles with defenses against ballistic missiles requires further study.

Defense against ballistic missiles offers new possibilities for enhanced deterence of deliberate attack, greater safety against accidental use of nuclear weapons of unintended nuclear escalation, and new opportunities and scope for arms control. The extent to which these possibilities can be realized will depend on how our present uncertainties about technical feasibility, costs, and Soviet response are resolved.

The essential purpose of the U.S. strategic defense initiative is to diminish the risk of nuclear destruction. In contrast with continued, sole reliance on the threat of nuclear retaliation, the purpose is to provide for a safer, less menacing way of preventing nuclear war in the decades to come.

Some of the most fervent opposition to ballistic missile defenses is ideological. That is to say, it is not based on facts, but on fixed beliefs. Any proposed revision of this belief is attacked as heresy, any internal inconsistencies of the belief are ignored. Thus, you may have one and the same person:

One, applaud the Biological Weapons Convention because it prohibits offensive use of biological weapons, while defenses are permitted;

Two, oppose binary chemical weapons for deterrence, but support defensive chemical warfare equipment; and

Three, turn these rules upside down for nuclear arms, by supporting offensive arms but opposing defensive ones. The ideological opponents to nuclear defense also seems to forget that the basic premise of banning missile defenses has been disproven. The premise was that the prohibition of such defenses would permit us to curb the growth in offensive arms. But after the ABM Treaty the Soviet offensive build-up continued as if there had been no change.

A curious aspect of the ideology against missile defenses is the notion that outer space must be reserved for offensive missiles, so that they can travel without obstruction to create holocaust on earth. The ideology demands a sanctuary in outer space that excludes any protection for the cities we live in, but offers a free ride for the missiles that could destroy our cities.

The American people, in reacting to the President's initiative, and in various opinion polls, have already shown that they do not agree with these ideologues. They are more pragmatic. They support an intiative that offers hope for the future. They do not wish to preserve for the next generation the present nightmare of huge and unimpeded missile forces, constantly poised for mass destruction.   ∎

NO, IT IS UNWORKABLE AND WILL INCREASE RISK OF WAR

William Proxmire

THE TWO HOTTEST CONCERNS of the American people at this moment are the threat of nuclear war and the colossal deficits that threaten to cripple our economy. We in the Congress will be called upon to decide a little later this year whether or not to spend $2 billion next year and $24 billion over the next 5 years for research on an antiballistic missile defense. Obviously, we should spend whatever it takes to protect this country against the ultimate tragedy of a nuclear attack. But there is every reason to believe that the following disastrous results will follow a decision to fund this part of the administration's military budget. First, we would increase, not decrease, the danger of nuclear war. Second, we would end up spending not $24 billion but hundreds of billions, perhaps more than $1 trillion, on such a system. Third, it would almost certainly fail to work. Fourth, to the extent that it did somehow succeed, it would greatly reduce our deterrent capability.

This "Star Wars" defense is dead wrong on two counts. First, it makes a profound military mistake. It assumes that a superpower today can prevent or even win a nuclear war by relying on defensive military measures. It ignores the obvious fact that ever since World War I, more than 65 years ago, technology has overwhelmed the most elaborate military defenses. In the 1930's the French built their "impregnable" Maginot Line with the firm assurance that the elaborate series of armed pill boxes, organized to maximize crossfire and defeat the most determined onslaught, would frustrate the most determined kind of German assault. But what happened? The Germans hit the defenses with blinding speed in a blitzkrieg attack and simply waltzed around the famed Maginot Line.

Again, 12 or 14 years ago, both the United States and the Soviet Union seemed well on their way to the construction of antiballistic missile systems very similar to the antimissile defenses the Reagan Administration now wants to fund. I vividly recall the Senate floor debate on funding that antiballistic missile system, Critics of the system at that time contended that any ABM system we could construct, no matter how brilliantly conceived, deployed, and operated, could be easily defeated at a fraction of the cost of the defensive ABM system. At that time the going estimate was the expenditure of $1 on offense could overwhelm $10 spent on any defensive weapon designed to stop nuclear missiles. The surprise, the mobility, the choice of timing for attack, the level of attack—whether from a high altitude or hugging the ground or even from ground transported weapons—all of these elements would favor the offense. Furthermore, the offense could pour in successive waves of missiles in an endless series until the defense was exhausted. In addition, in a military milieu in which technology changes swiftly and drastically, even the most elaborate kind of defense against nuclear attack could be overcome at any time with an equally elaborate offense and at a fraction of the cost.

Second, the "Star Wars" defense is wrong because it strives to achieve peace by extending an arms race that simply cannot be won. What is worse, it accelerates an arms race that not only fails to build national security but literally contributes to insecurity. We will end up spending hundreds of billions of dollars and find ourselves less safe.

At the beginning of this speech, I warned that any success this expenditure achieved would simply reduce and maybe destroy deterrence—the basis of our security in this nuclear world for the past 30 years. How could this happen? Here is how: Suppose we found that the Russians were on the verge of some kind of magical breakthrough that would render our massive nuclear deterrent capability useless. What would we do? Would we quietly accept world domination by the Soviet Union and an end to our freedom? What do you think? Put it the other way. Suppose the Soviet Union found that the United States was truly succeeding in building a truly effective antimissile system that made all their missiles useless. What would they do? Would they seriously consider a preemptive strike before we had put the final touches on our "Star Wars" defense? Of course, they would.

Above all, if this Nation mistakenly proceeds down this path, we would obviously violate the Anti-Ballistic Missile Treaty of 1972. We would greatly dim the prospect of effective arms control agreements any time in the foreseeable future. We would be taking a long and tragic step toward a nuclear holocaust.

The first reason this Congress should not accept the President's recommendation and appropriate $2 billion for 1985 and commit ourselves to $25 billion over the next five years is because it will not work.

The Congressional Office of Technology Assessment issued a report saying "that a comprehensive antiballistic missile system should not serve as the basis of public expectation or national policy."

If we can win an arms control agreement on which we can rely that will limit and reduce nuclear weapons on both sides, we will not need to spend billions of dollars on this dreamy Star Wars defense.

Offensive arms control is dead in the water. Frankly, it is hard to construct a scenario more likely to keep it dead than for the Congress to comply with the Presidential request to fund the President's Star Wars program.

Why would funding the Star Wars defensive ABM program gut any real prospect of limiting offensive nuclear arms? Just put yourself in the position of the Russians. The only way we can expect to frustrate a Soviet missile attack is for the Soviets to agree to limit their offensive nuclear force in an arms control agreement with us.

Would they do this? Are they crazy? Why in the world would the Soviet Union agree to limit their nuclear arsenals in a mutual agreement with the United States when such an accommodation with the Soviet Union is the only way we can stop their missiles and destroy their deterrent capability. It is what has made them a superpower. Are they going to enter into an arms control agreement that will kill their deterrence? Of course not.

What a ridiculous dilemma this whole Star Wars gambit has driven this country into. The Soviet Union has vigorously protested the U.S. intention of building an elaborate antiballistic missile system. They see it as a very serious threat to their painfully constructed nuclear deterrent. Now we are told that for the program to work, we need to secure an arms control agreement with the Soviet Union to limit and reduce offensive nuclear weapons. So we cannot make this fabulously expensive defensive system operate effectively unless the Soviets agree—that is right, the Soviets agree—to limit their offensive missiles so we can gain this super advantage over them.

In my 27 years in this body I have seen some ridiculous proposals for spending the public's money. Indeed, I have given well over 100 Golden fleeces to various agencies for throwing the public's money away over the past 9 years, but this baby takes the cake. We are asked to spend $2 billion in 1985 and $25 billion over the next 5 years just for the research on this program. The program itself will obviously cost hundreds of billions of dollars. There is no way it can work unless the Soviet Union decides to accommodate us by agreeing to limit their offensive missiles so that we can destroy whatever deterrent power their nuclear arsenal now possesses. Does anyone believe the Soviet Union will make President Reagan's Star Wars a big success by agreeing that it will not build the offensive missiles to overcome it?

As a program for defending this country, the Reagan proposal is so ridiculously bad that I cannot believe the President seriously expected to win with it. This program, if carried out, will not defend this country. But it will accomplish something else. It will kill nuclear arms control. It drives a spike right through the heart of any basis for United States-Soviet agreement on limiting offensive missiles. It leaves nuclear arms control dead. Far more is riding on whether or not the Congress agrees to fund this antiballistic missile system than a disagreement on nuclear weapons policy. If the Congress goes ahead, nuclear arms control will be dead for a very long time. There would be no way the Russians would agree to it—not ever.

The Star Wars proponents have two arguments designed to appeal to peace advocates. First, they claim that their antiballistic missile defense is exactly that: a defense. It would not attack. It would defend. It would not initiate war. It would reduce or prevent the casualties of war. Even if it should be used first it would be used to anticipate an enemy attack. And second, these nuclear weapons would never be used against people, always lethal nuclear weapons on the other side. These Star Wars proponents argue that nuclear war has previously been viewed as an offensive operation. A weapons program designed to wreak the total destruction of an enemy. Now, with the Star Wars, here come the boys with the white hats: the good guys—the A Team—Lifesavers not life destroyers. Guardians of peace because missile defense would stop missile attack.

And that's not all. The proponents of Star Wars contend that defensive antimissile activity can supplement arms control, not kill it. They argue that Star Wars can operate in the interest of both the Soviet Union and the United States. They argue it can provide either side or both sides the assurance that there is an option other than massive civilization-ending retaliation; that is, intercepting and destroying the incoming missiles of the other side. Presumably a President warned that the Russians had launched an ICBM attack would not be faced with a choice between doing nothing and pressing a button that would set the world on fire. He would have the option of putting out the fire by intercepting and destroying most, and perhaps all, of the incoming missiles.

What validity does this argument have? Is it conceivably possible that we could develop a defensive missile system that would work? Could we intercept and shoot down enough offensive enemy missiles to prevent total destruction? Is it possible that both sides could agree to a balance that would make nuclear war less instead of more likely? Is all this just a happy—maybe a slap-happy—dream? How about it? Is it possible? Well, anything is possible.

After all if we could put an American on the moon for $25 billion with the technology of the 1960's why could we not shoot down moving missiles with technology of the 1980's or 1990's for 10 or 20 times that much, say $250 billion or $500 billion. Maybe we can succeed with Star Wars, maybe we cannot. But why not try? Certainly there is no price we could pay, no burden we could bear that would be too great to prevent the total devastation of a nuclear attack on our country.

So what is wrong with "Star Wars"? What is wrong is that there is no real prospect that a defensive antimissile system would work. None. None. It will not work. Why not? Because whatever dynamic progress we can expect from a defense against missiles, we can surely anticipate an equally potent and opposite reaction from offensive missiles. At this moment where does the advantage lie? Clearly and obviously with the offensive. Even the staunchest proponents of Star Wars agree that offensive missiles have a massive advantage over any kind of a defensive antimissile system using presently researched and deployed weapons. But they say give us time; give us time; the Star Wars people plead, and we will construct a defense that will knock out all or almost all offensive incoming missiles.

At this point I have a confession. I believe that on this limited point, they are right. Yes, indeed, 20 years or maybe even 10 or 5 years from now with our lasers and other advanced technology, we will have the defensive technology to intercept and destroy incoming missiles that are deployed today. Then why not go ahead? There is an easy answer: If we do proceed, the other side will proceed too, but not with today's offensive missile technology and not with an antimissile technology that simply matched the defensive system missile for missile but with a highly intensified offensive missile program. The proponents of Star Wars have loaded the dice in this argument. They hand us a phony scenario. They make the patently ridiculous assumption that only the defense will be dynamic and progressive. They assume the offense will stand still, frozen, paralyzed. Armed with that utterly unrealistic assumption they predict victory for the defense. Of course, this is nonsense. Certainly without a negotiated mutual nuclear freeze both superpowers will continue to refine, modernize, and improve their offensive nuclear weapons. Whatever technological advantage might be temporarily with antiballistic missile defense, the offense will swiftly move to overcome. Will the offense succeed? Of course, they will. Why would they not? The offense can take its own initiative. After all the offense will always have the advantage of selecting the time of attack and the place. It can concentrate its resources on the targets it selects.

For example, Star Wars proponents do not even try to defend against such offensive nuclear weapons as groundhugging cruise missiles. So what is to prevent a superpower frustrated by antimissile defense from simply sliding under the defensive screen with cruise missiles? The answer—nothing. Nothing.

Several times I have asked the proponents of Star Wars when they have appeared before our Appropriations Committee what they would do about cruise missiles. They say they do not have an answer to that. They are not trying to defend against cruise missiles, only trying to defend against the missiles they can defend against which is the intercontinental ballistic missiles.

The Star Wars proponents contend that we have to move into a massive strategic defense because the Russians are already deeply into it. But the SDI advocates' demands are based on the usual Pentagon approach to selling expensive hardware to Congress—that the Russians are 10 feet tall. Russia, indeed, has a long record of stressing defense, but there is little or no significant evidence. If we proceed with Star Wars, it will become a trillion-dollar boondoggle.

So how do we defend against nuclear war? One way: Stop the arms race. Stop it cold. Stop it now with a negotiated, mutual, verifiable, and comprehensive nuclear freeze. ■

IS THE REAGAN POLICY TOWARD NICARAGUA CORRECT?

In 1979, a leftist revolution overthrew the Nicaraguan government of General Anastasio Somozo Debayle, whom the United States had long backed. President Jimmy Carter took a moderate approach to this development and adopted a policy of "friendly cooperation" with the new Sandinista government (named for a Nicaraguan hero who had been killed in 1934 fighting against the American-installed government). President Carter offered American aid, hoping to influence the Sandinista government toward democracy.

The Reagan administration inaugurated a much different policy, stopping aid and demanding that Nicaragua end its support for leftist guerillas in neighboring El Salvador. A U.S. military buildup in Honduras was undertaken. First covertly, and then openly, the U.S. supported "contra" military forces, which it had helped to organize and which sought to overthrow the Sandinista government.

The policies of the Reagan administration caused great debate in Congress. In 1984, Congress cut of military aid to the "contras," but voted "humanitarian" aid for them. In 1985, President Reagan renewed his request for military aid ($70 million), as well as continued humanitarian aid ($30 million). The following year, after first defeating it, the U.S. House of Representatives narrowly adopted the Reagan proposal.

U.S. Senator John East (R-North Carolina) supported President Reagan's Nicaraguan policy. In a statement before the U.S. Senate that is reprinted here, he says so, and he even opposes an amendment by U.S. Senator Edward M. Kennedy (D-Massachusetts) to prohibit use of American troops in Nicaragua.

The opposing view is taken by U.S. Senator Jeff Bingaman (D-New Mexico), who objects to the Reagan administration's pursuit of a military solution in Nicaragua and Central America.

The question these two senators address is: Is the Reagan policy toward Nicaragua correct?

YES, WE MUST STOP SOVIET AND CUBAN INTERVENTION IN CENTRAL AMERICA
John P. East

Former Secretary of State Henry Kissinger has indicated that in order to accomplish the very ends [to prohibit use of U.S. troops in Nicaragua] that the supporters of this amendment seek—namely, a more equitable social and economic system—that in order to build that infrastructure, there must be a shield, if you will, a military shield, in view of Soviet-Cuban military intervention in the area, behind which this process can take place. If you eliminate the military option completely, you certainly telegraph to the enemy the idea that they are free to pursue a military solution.

I recall that when President Duarte was here—at that time, President-elect—he said it is a very complex situation. It is military, it is social, and it is economic. But his point was that if you have one army on one side and one army on the other and one is armed and the other is not armed, the armed army will win and you, in fact, will have a military solution.

If, in fact, we say and we telegraph to the people in this area and to the world that the United States, under no circumstances, would give sufficient latitude to the President to utilize our conventional military capability, I think you bring about what President Duarte was talking about—namely, that there will be a military solution, and it will be imposed by the Soviet Union and Cuba and those military forces it is backing in that area.

I think it is simply impossible in our time to micromanage American foreign policy, let along defense decisions, from the floor of the U.S. Senate. To do so will greatly imperil the effectiveness of this country to meet the very serious challenge it meets today from the Soviet Union and her surrogates in every continent in the world.

Let me put it another way: If we do fail in Central America, if the Marxist take control of the military solution, who will be held accountable? Yes, the President will be. I say that if we are going to hold him, as Commander in Chief, and his principal spokesman and formulator for American foreign policy responsible, we had better give him enough elbow room to do that which is necessary in order for his policies to succeed.

But if we try to micromanage every move he makes, we cannot hold him responsible. I think our policy will fail, and you will see, yes, a military solution in central America, and it will be dictated by Moscow, Havana, and Managua. That is what is going on currently.

Invariably, in a debate of this kind, I often find it interesting that our most honorable and patriotic opponents say there must be a political solution, in citing Vietnam. Of course, as Duarte has pointed out, if you do not have the military shield, you will not have a political solution; you will have a military solution, and it will be imposed by the superior military forces, which in this case, again, would be those forces in the area backed by the Soviet Union and by Cuba.

The current struggle in the world today, going on right now in the underdeveloped world, is of a guerilla type. It does not candidly lend itself to formal declarations. It does not lend itself to micromanagement from the floor of the U.S. Senate. Guerilla warfare is the key to military success in our time.

Alexander Solzhenitsyn remarked one time, "You need not worry about nuclear war in your time." Why? "Because," he said, "they are taking you with their bare hands," and they are. They are doing it in every part of the world. Solzhenitsyn said he did not think the West had read the Communist Manifesto. He did not think they had read the works of Lenin.

The point was that you would take the soft underbelly of the world, the underdeveloped continents of Asia, Latin America, and Central America. You would do it militarily. Yes, you would do it through guerilla warfare. Those are the realities of warfare in our time. They cannot be denied. Solzhenitsyn is correct: We are losing. We lost in Southeast Asia. Cam Ranh Bay, which used to be a military base, is now a Soviet base. Yes, we were told we were looking for a political solution. What did we get? A military solution, Soviet and Vietnamese imposed. Then they moved into Cambodia, and so it continues.

The same scenario is being repeated in Central America. The same problem exists in Africa. It would exist in the Middle East, were it not for the strength of Israel. Syria and the PLO, backed by the Soviet Union, would impose a military solution in Lebanon—indeed, throughout the entire Middle East. Would it make sense to say to the Israelis, for example, "Disarm"? Or, should we say that we would never, ever, under any circumstances, intervene? That simply telegraphs to the Soviet Union and her surrogates that military solutions are possible. It rules out the potential for political solution. It rules out the shield to which Henry Kissinger has referred.

How are you going to build the infrastructure for social and economic justice and social and economic growth and development where the enemy, the opposition, is free to shoot its way to power, as President Duarte put it?

Recently we adopted overwhelmingly, as I recall, an amendment supporting the Monroe Doctrine concept of 1823, which stated that the United States would not accept foreign intervention and military presence in the New World from the Old. This is precisely what we are allowing to happen now in Central America. The Soviet Union and Cuba are intervening in Central America. They are supplying the armed support to Nicaragua, all out of proportion to the needs of Nicaragua to defend itself.

If you tie the hands of the President of the United States publicly in the Senate and the House and say that under no circumstances can he do this without formal declarations or authorizations, and so forth, it simply telegraphs to Managua, to Havana, and to Moscow: "Gentlemen, full steam ahead." And what will we get? A military solution—the very thing that the proponents, the very honorable proponents, of this amendment [to prohibit use of U.S. troops] hope to avoid.

Let me end on this thought in terms of the reality of international relations of our time. There is no question about it. It has been spelled out carefully that the Marxist-Leninist solution is through military guerrilla operation to take the soft underdeveloped parts of the world and ultimately, as Marx and Lenin stated it, "You surround the urban industrial continents of Europe, of North America, including ultimately now Japan, and they in time will fall like ripe fruit."

We have to develop the acumen, the astuteness, the alertness, the ability to respond to that military challenge and it is of a guerilla warfare nature, and hence we must allow the President the latitude, because we will hold him accountable now, will we not? We will not bear the burden, we will not accept responsibility if the military solution is imposed. We will point down Pennsylvania Avenue to the White House and say they failed, he failed.

I leave us with this thought: Has the United States no area in the world where we have self-interest to assert?

We were told during the Vietnam conflict that was distant, far away, and it was none of our concern. We were told in the Middle East that that perhaps is distant and far away and none of our concern. We are told that Africa is distant and far away and none of our concern.

And now, we are in our own hemisphere. We are in Central America. We see the Monroe Doctrine repudiated de facto, and once again it seems to me the thrust of what the proponents of this amendment are saying again is we have no self-interest.

I ask you this: Where do we, as one of the two great superpowers in the world, have a self-interest?

The Soviet Union moves with impunity into Afghanistan. It sends its surrogates, such as Syria, into Central America. It sends its surrogates into Africa in the form of Cuban troops and into Ethiopia, Angola, and Mozambique. It sends the PLO into Central America. It sends the Eastern European forces into Central America. It sends Cuban forces into Central America. In the Far East it takes over again Southeast Asia, uses Cam Ranh Bay, our former base, as its own base of operation. It gives the moral, logistic support to Vietnam to take over Cambodia, to threaten Thailand, and to broaden and expand its power in that whole part of the world.

Apparently, we have no self-interests in either we are told.

Now, here we are right in our own hemisphere and, again, it seems to me it is the old refrain: So we have no self-interest there. It makes no difference.

But is has been pointed out repeatedly if you allow Nicaragua to become the model in Central America, El Salvador will fall, Costa Rica will fall, Honduras will fall, Guatemala will fall, and Belize will fall. The pressure will be on Mexico and it ultimately will have no option except to itself to succumb to what? Yes, a military solution imposed by Moscow, Havana, and Managua.

Now, as has been pointed out repeatedly between the Rio Grande and the Panama Canal are 100 million people. We have heard this before, but let me say it. I think it is worth repeating. We have learned from past experience that at least 10 percent of the population invariably flees when the Communists take over. All the voting is one way. Where they can vote with their feet, they come here.

Look at the poor pathetic boat people who went out and drifted in the South China Sea, just waiting for any vessel to come along and pick them up. Is it not curious where people have a choice, they leave? They leave the Communist system. We have to build up walls to keep them out. They have to build up walls to keep them in.

Now, I ask this, and in this case they would not even have to get into boats, they would simply walk. If they take over that area between the Rio Grande and the Panama Canal, of 100 million people, 10 million will move northward across the Rio Grande. How will you stop it? Will you machinegun them down? Of course you will not.

It will create enormous economic and social disruption in our country and it poses an enormous geopolitical threat to the peace and the freedom and the security and the well-being of this country. It jeopardizes not only your freedom and mine in our time, but that of our children and our grandchildren.

This amendment is a part of that whole fabric of thinking that seems to operate on the assumption that nothing is going on in the world today of consequence. I put it this way: We fiddle while Rome burns. We are excused by two facts. We do not know, first, that we fiddle and, second, we do not know that Rome burns. But Rome is burning in Central America and if you do not allow the President of the United States, who has the responsibility as the Commander in Chief under the separation of power, who has the principal responsibility for the conduct of foreign policy and for the protection of this country, the latitude to do what must be done in this area, I think that what you are going to see is all Central America fall under Soviet and Cuban control and domination and the whole Caribbean basin will simply become a dominant sphere of Soviet influence, military influence.

That I find totally unacceptable. Totally unacceptable from whose standpoint? From not only those people in that part of the world who must fall under this tyranny, but from the standpoint of the security, the freedom, and the well-being of this country.

So, I urge my colleagues to reflect very seriously on this. The stakes are high in Central America. They are in our own hemisphere, and if we will not defend our friends, our democratic friends, such as Duarte, in our own hemisphere, I simply question, gentlemen, who will we help? Who will we defend?

It is an eminently fair question to ask where would you draw the line—anywhere? Apparently not.

And that would be the great tragedy of our time and World War II has been subtly lost and it has been lost to Moscow. It has been lost to the Marxist-Leninist world vision. And it is over with a whimper.

And I suspect in due course, as Marx and Lenin predicted, the industrial urban continents of North America, Europe, and Japan will eventually have to succumb to the realities of power in their time. Solzhenitsyn has said the world is finite in geography. At some point the balance tips against you.

I do not know if it has occurred or not. He said psychologically it occurred in Vietnam. Perhaps it has. But it will have occurred, as a matter of reality, if we tie the hands of the President of the United States and allow the Soviet Union and Cuba and her surrogates such as in Managua to take over that area.

It is a very heavy question we face; I think the most serious facing this Congress and this country at this point in our history. And I vigorously disassociate myself from this amendment. I vigorously oppose it. And I hope my colleagues would reflect long and hard and repudiate it, vote it down.   ■

NO, WE SHOULD NOT PURSUE A MILITARY SOLUTION
Jeff Bingaman

In my view, our overall policy in Central America is misguided for at least three major reasons. The basic problem with our policy in the region, as I see it and as it is evolving and becoming evident to us through events, is that we are putting a tremendous emphasis and reliance upon military measures and military means to achieve our objectives there.

Our policy in that area of the world has not historically allowed for the necessary change to occur, which is inevitably going to occur in many of these Third World countries. We have opted for stability instead of change in most cases, and we have used military measures of various kinds to insure and enforce that stability. I believe we are in real danger of doing that once again in Central America.

The first of the major problems I see with our policy in Central America is this country's support of what are referred to in the press so widely as the contras. These are Nicaraguans, primarily, who are engaged in a guerrilla action against the Sandinista government with the express purpose of overthrowing that government.

It is well known and no longer secret or covert in any way that this country is providing the financial support, the arms, the supplies necessary to carry on that activity. I understand that there were initially efforts to keep this subject covert, to keep it a secret war.

The guerrillas are engaged in raids in Nicaragua and are involved in trying through various means to destroy some of the infrastructure in that country—roads, bridges, power lines. They have mined harbors, they have done numerous other things which they believe will help to destabilize that government and eventually bring it down.

I believe very strongly that this policy is wrong, primarily because it is

...ounterproductive. It is a policy which is having the effect of strengthening the support that the Nicaraguans are giving to the Sandinista government. It is very naturally causing the Nicaraguan people to rally around their own government to resist what they see as largely a foreign invasion. I have heard predictions that there was an imminent uprising by the Nicaraguan people to rally around the contras and overthrow the Sandinista government; but I have seen no evidence to support that position.

On the contrary, I believe that the popularity or strength of the Sandinistas is being cemented into place by virtue of the action that we are supporting through this contra activity.

Another major concern which we need to worry about in connection with the support of the contras is what happens when we decide or someone decides that this secret war, this contra activity, is no longer a proper course to pursue. What happens to these 10,000 to 18,000 troops who are armed and who are engaged in these activities? Where do they go? Where do they go with those weapons that have been issued to them? This is not a recipe for reducing conflict in Central America. This is not a recipe for reducing violence in Central America. I think the claim that this is necessary in order to interdict arms shipments which go through Nicaragua to El Salvador is becoming a thin justification indeed at this point.

I do not doubt that there were arms going through Nicaragua to El Salvador guerrillas and there may still be a level of arms going through there: I have no information one way or another. But I think clearly the main purpose of that guerilla activity today is not the interdiction of arms, it is the overthrow of the Sandinista government.

I believe it is wrong for us to support that; it is wrong for us to try to over-throw a government with which we have diplomatic relations, and whether we do it through direct action by our own troops or whether we do it through aid and assistance to others to accomplish that end is, I think, beginning to cut things fairly thin.

That is a major concern with our policy in Central America, one that I believe this Congress should take a strong stand to stop.

A second and very serious concern that I also believe Congress needs to focus on and, hopefully, come to grips with is what I see as a very major buildup of our military presence in Honduras. We have seen, starting last year, a series of exercises, military exercises or maneuvers as they were described to us, and they were described to us initially as very routine in nature, the type of exercises that our troops engage in throughout the world; no major reason to consult with Congress prior to the beginning of those exercises.

As I have watched these exercises take place and have toured some of the facilities that have been constructed in connection with them, in December when I was in Honduras, and when I have heard the testimony given with regard to this, it has become clear to me that the exercises are really being used by the military, perhaps for some training but also to accomplish two other fairly nonex-plicit goals. Those goals that we are attempting to accomplish and are ac-complishing through these exercises, as I see it, are that we are arriving at a point where we permanently station a significant number of U.S. troops in Honduras.

The second byproduct of these exercises, which has not been adequately discussed in my view, is that as part of the exercises we are building a very substantial military infrastructure, not just for the use of the Hondurans but for the use of U.S. troops as well. And again this is being done in my view without adequate discussion, without adequate consideration by the Congress.

Clearly, the argument can be made either way, that we should have a military infrastructure, military facilities, military personnel in the thousands stationed in Honduras, or that we should not. I conclude and argue that we should not. But whether you argue we should or we should not, the process of establishing that should be one which allows a public debate and a debate in Congress over whether it is going to happen.

I believe that we are already very far down the road toward building a significantly military infrastructure in Honduras without this body or without the Congress ever having adequately debated whether that is the policy of this Government or should be the policy of this Government.

So that is the second major difficulty that I see with our policy in Central America today, the first being the contra activity which I do not believe we should continue to support, the second being the major buildup in our military presence in Honduras, both in personnel and in facilities. I believe that having that military presence cuts off diplomatic options for us. Having a constantly increasing military presence reduces the opportunity for us to reach any kind of agreement for the lessening of tensions in that region. And clearly if we are going to have a two-track policy, one where we talk about our support of the Contadora process, as this administration does at every opportunity, and on the other hand constantly escalating military presence in the region, which goes directly contrary to the goals and the objectives of the Contadora nations, then it needs to be recognized by the American people. I believe it is a major concern we need to be addressing in this debate.

The third concern is that we are going in my view to a very heightened reliance on military resources to deal with the problems of Central America. We had testimony before the Armed Services Committee which I found to be very startling. This was filed testimony in open hearing. General Gorman, who is the commander in chief of Southcom out of Panama, gave us statistics as to the level of our present military support and what that is moving to in the future. I think that is interesting to look at.

First, in the area of military training, in 1983, the United States participated and helped in the training of 3,300 Central American soldiers for the various governments that we are allied with in that region. But in 1984, that figure goes from 3,300 to an estimated figure of 25,000 to 29,000 troops we are going to be engaged in training in Central America. That is an eightfold increase in 1 year, and I think that is the kind of statistic this Senate needs to focus on; that is a major increase in our military involvement.

When you look at the military assistance dollars, in 1983 we provided $126 million, and in 1984, for Central America as a whole we would provide $373 million in military assistance, a threefold increase in the amount of our military aid in 1 year.

I gather that we would provide assistance to pretty much anybody else down there who opposed the Sandinistas, if they asked for it, and in whatever amounts they asked for it.

I am not one—and I want to make this clear—who believes that we should cut off military assistance to El Salvador. I have been there. I have met with many people in that country, in the government and not in the government, who are very concerned that the fragile situation there not be allowed to disintegrate entirely. With the election results pending and all the rest, I do not favor this Government cutting off military aid to El Salvador.

I think the argument we are engaged in now is a proper one as to the level of that aid. It is a proper exercise to debate what conditions should be attached to that aid. But unless we see a takeover of that government by elements who have views completely contrary to our views of what is appropriate activity for government, I think we need to continue with a program of trying to allow that country to salvage its situation and defend itself against guerrilla activity.

I do not think we should approve additional military assistance very lightly and in a pro forma manner.

Is the main ingredient of our plan that Congress is willing to go along with military assistance, or are we going to have a willingness to do some other things and to keep the military assistance at the lowest possible level?

The history of that region would indicate that the stronger the military becomes in those countries, the more problems there are with human rights violations and the more problems there are with necessary reforms being stalled.

I think that for us to continue with an unrelenting buildup of the military in Honduras and El Salvador, absent a strong case being made that that buildup is absolutely essential, is a major mistake. In Honduras, I see the buildup of the military as largely unjustified. The military there is in complete control. I know of no external threat presently facing Honduras. To argue that the Honduran military has to be large enough to defend itself against the Nicaraguan military in the case of an invasion from outside comes close to being absurd.

I hope that in the course of this discussion in the Senate we can come to some rational decisions about whether we should support contra activity indefinitely in Central America, about whether we should engage in a major military buildup in Honduras, and also come to rational decisons about the level of military aid we should be willing to support in countries like El Salvador and Honduras.

The American people do not want a war in Central America and the American people are not persuaded that there is a military solution to the problems of Central America. This Senator shares in that skepticism. ∎

HUMAN RIGHTS AND AMERICAN FOREIGN POLICY

President Jimmy Carter made support for human rights an important element in U.S. foreign policy. His administration attempted (though not always consistently) to press other nations—through the giving or withholding of aid, for example—toward recognition of the human rights of their citizens. President Reagan put the human rights emphasis on the back burner. Among other things, his administration differentiated between "totalitarian" and "authoritative" regimes.

In the article by Jerome J. Shestack excerpted here, the author maintains that a return to the kind of strong human rights foreign policy the Carter administration followed would be in the national security interests of the United States, increasing our influence abroad, promoting world stability, and enhancing popular domestic support for America's foreign policy.

THE RISE AND DECLINE OF HUMAN RIGHTS IN U.S. FOREIGN POLICY
Jerome J. Shestack

 . . . The real impetus for an international commitment to the protection of human rights came as a phoenix of world order rising from the ashes of the Nazi experience and the Holocaust. The Nazi purification laws, the establishment of concentration camps, and the barbaric executions of the Holocaust had all been carried out according to German law. As World War II drew to a close, the cry "Never Again" became translated by many who gathered to establish the United Nations into a determination to protect the rights of the individual through the medium of international law.

Hence, the Preamble to the Charter of the United Nations affirms the dignity and worth of each person and the equal rights of men and women. Article I states that the purpose of the Charter is to maintain peace and promote respect for human rights and fundamental freedoms. Articles 55 and 56 encourage respect for human rights and pledge the members' cooperation with the United Nations' efforts to promote human rights.

These provisions may seem sparse, perhaps, considering the length of the U.N. Charter. Still, even this much coverage must be regarded as a striking achievement considering the weak position of human rights under international law until that time. However, while the Charter guaranteed human rights, it did not define them. Their definition was the next step. . . .

An entire system of rights is precisely what was envisioned by the United Nations concept. Shortly after the creation of the U.N., the drafting of the Universal Declaration of Human Rights began. Among the human rights pioneers instrumental in that development were Rene Cassin and Eleanor Roosevelt, whose 100th anniversary we celebrate shortly. They and other drafters were clearly influenced by natural rights theory, as is evident in the opening statement of the Declaration: "Whereas recognition of the inherent dignity and of the equal and inalienable rights of all members of the human family is the foundation of freedom, justice and peace in the world . . . " Similarly, Article 1 provides: "All human beings are born free and equal in dignity. They are endowed with reason and conscience and should act toward one another with a spirit of brotherhood."

Concepts of "inherent dignity" and "inalienable rights" have natural rights roots. Whether or not all of the nations that accepted the Universal Declaration were of common philosophic heart, the important point is that the Universal Declaration delineated the basic rights that were to be part of the system of world order and that were to be embodied in international law through international covenants.

The member nations of the United Nations did accept the Universal Declaration of Human Rights on December 10, 1948, since then known as Human Rights Day. What does the Declaration provide?

The Declaration is a pledge of rights for the world. The first twenty-one articles specify certain civil and political rights – the right to life, liberty, and a fair trial; the right to freedom of conscience, expression and association; the right to leave one's country and return to it; freedom from arbitrary arrest, detention and exile; and similar rights. The next nine articles specify social and economic rights. They include the right to a decent standard of living, to social security, to work and leisure, to health care, and to education.

The notion was that the Universal Declaration of Human Rights would set a "standard of achievement" for all peoples, which would be followed by subsequent treaties with force in international law and influenced by conforming domestic legislation and, ultimately, with a system of implementation.

In 1946, the Economic and Social Council of the United Nations created the United Nations Commission on Human Rights, which was to have primary jurisdiction over human rights matters. The Commission drafted a Covenant on Civil and Political Rights and a Covenant on Economic, Social and Cultural Rights. In the 1970's, these Covenants were ratified by the requisite number of nations and came into force.

These two Covenants have their own respective provinces, with some overlap. The rights specified in the Covenant on Civil and Political Rights essentially represent the values of western-oriented humanism, of the kind we find in our own Bill of Rights. They are sometimes called "negative rights" in that they impose restraints upon government: thou shalt not torture, thou shalt not deny the right to a fair trial, thou shalt not abridge freedom of religion, or freedom of association, or freedom of conscience.

The Covenant of Economic, Social and Cultural Rights, in contrast delineates a series of rights which are grounded in a commitment to equality and distributive justice: the right to food, clothing, housing, and education; the right to work, leisure, fair wages, and decent working conditions; protection for the family; and the right to physical and mental health. These rights have been called "affirmative rights." Sometimes they are viewed as goals or aspirations. That is, a government may earnestly wish to provide these rights to its citizens, but may not be able to do so; the necessary resources simply may not be available. The Covenant itself recognizes that economic and social rights can only be realized "progressively." . . .

In addition to the two major Covenants, others were established in specialized fields such as genocide, slavery, refugees, racial discrimination, and the rights of women. The Covenants and the human rights treaties encompass a broad spectrum of human rights. The vision was beautiful—one of freedom and human dignity. Yet, nation after nation engaged in abuse by torture, mass executions, arbitrary detention, and other oppression. The litany of human rights abuses is despairing. For most people the real world was the one described by Hobbes: life was mean, poor, brutish and short.

Many roadblocks have prevented the realization of human rights aspirations. One formidable obstacle has been the continued virulence of nationalism, which has produced a crop of strong, often ruthless leaders who believe that they can only maintain power and reach their goals through repression of dissent and suppression of participatory democracy.

A second obstacle has been the jealous guarding of domestic jurisdiction. Article 2(7) of the United Nations Charter, prohibiting interference in domestic affairs, has been frequently invoked to prevent examination of a nation's human rights abuses. The developing nations, in particular, after years of colonialsim, have been understandably suspicious of any intrusion by the West, whether on behalf of human rights values or anything else. The Soviet bloc, moreover, sought to shield its own poor record.

Another obstacle has been that human rights issues are constantly politicized and manipulated in the log-rolling politics of the United Nations. One tactic employed is the attempt to create a division between civil and political rights on the one hand and social and economic rights on the other, using one set of values to denigrate the other. More often than not, those exploiting this tactic are faithful to neither set of rights.

Finally, human rights issues lacked a champion among the major powers. Like most causes without a powerful advocate, the quest for protection of human rights languished. The United States, during the 1960's and most of the 1970's, was certainly not a champion of interntional human rights. To use a State Department term, human rights in United States foreign policy was a "nonstarter." The United States almost never spoke out publicly against violations of human rights and rarely quietly. Its record on international human rights was a bleak one of nonfeasance.

It is a commonplace that nations act only according to their own national interests. But our own perceptions as well as history teach us that many nations often fail to pursue courses of action which ultimately prove not to be in their best interests. Of course, delineation of national interest is not easy. The contours remain amorphous and imprecise. Often it represents an after the fact label to rationalize the way in which a particular state policy was executed. For the United States, the concept of national interest inevitably embodies a network of conflicting interests and values, since three different voices—the President, the Congress, and the Public—all consider themselves legitimate articulators of the national interest.

Unless a convincing argument can be made to support the proposition that a strong human rights policy serves the United States' interest, such a policy will not be pursued. It is thus necessary to analyze and understand the elements of the national interest that are likely to be affected by a strong human rights policy. What are the compelling reasons why our national interest is served by an emphasis on international human rights?

One important benefit to the national interest in focusing on human rights is that such a focus enables us to be effective in addressing one of the major issues on the global agenda. Human rights demands have surfaced more dramatically in this generation than in others for a variety of reasons. One reason is the spread of literacy and education; another is that increased communications heightened expectations; another is that human rights aspirations are infectious. The end result is that human rights have become a central item on the global agenda, appealing to the aspirations and yearnings of people on every continent.

Championing human rights affords the United States a unique opportunity to be an important influence on that agenda and to address those aspirations. For the United States, it is a particularly appealing role. This country was one of the first to be founded on the idea of independence and freedom for all, and during the two centuries of our history we have gone through a constant struggle to make that idea a reality, a struggle still in progress. Despite our own imperfections—witness Vietnam—the United States has generally been regarded as possessing an immense potential to realize the aspirations of individual freedom and the benefits that stem from it. This image of America has always had a great deal of popular appeal around the world.

The advocacy of human rights also serves our security interests. Repression of human rights is a source of instability and uprisings within nations and can impair peaceful relations between nations. It is naive to think that repressive nations will prove to be reliable friends or staunch allies. Experience has too often shown the contrary. We and other democratic nations would be more secure if all countries had a common purpose based on respect for human rights.

Even under a traditional *realpolitik* analysis, there are good reasons for having a strong human rights foreign policy. There is an ideological competition for world leadership between Communist and Western ideologies for the hearts and minds of men, as the cliché goes. What can the West offer to counter the honeyed appeal of Communist promises? Strength in armaments? That is hardly appealing, as protestors and placards the world over teach us daily. Business enterprise? This has been seen all too often as exploitation, especially among developing nations. But human rights and individual development are something different. Here is a drum beat to which men and women everywhere will respond; here is a vision which can generate popular support among masses of people. The Soviets fear Western dedication to a strong human rights policy because of their own dismal record and because they sense the power that ideas of freedom can exert. Our advocacy of human rights not only advances the human condition, but also confounds and isolates our adversaries and helps in reinforcing our claim to world leadership.

Finally, I believe it is in our national interest to have a foreign policy which reflects the fundamental values of the American people and therefore commands popular support. An emphasis on human rights fills that prescription. Individual rights have long been a focus for shared purpose in the American tradition. Surely, fostering a sense of shared purpose among our people is in the national interest. Nor should we forget that there is a connection between the failure to support human rights abroad and the erosion of human rights at home. While the correlation is imprecise, we protect our own liberties by concern for the liberties of others.

Each of these factors standing alone has a certain fragility; yet, in the aggregate, I believe they make a compelling case for the proposition that pursuit of human rights protections in our foreign policy serves critical facets of our national interest.

I do not suggest that human rights is the *only* consideration in determining what is in our national interest. There are other competing interests, such as national security, trade, strategic alliances, and arms control. Deciding between competing claims which cannot be harmonized is always difficult and often agonizingly so. What is necessary, however, is to ensure that human rights are represented in that competition. For many years, human rights had not been even an element in the calculus of our foreign policy. The Carter administration, for the first time, brought human rights into the calculus.

If we appaise the human rights record of the Carter administration, with the benefit now of three years of hindsight, there is much to criticize. Mr. Carter's early formulations of human rights policy had an almost homiletic character. They resembled moral preachments rather than formulations of policy, and they created a climate of raised expectations which could not be fulfilled. As the Administration progressed, Cyrus Vance and Warren Christopher began to shape our human rights policy in a coherent fashion and made it a strong element of U.S. foreign policy. Undoubtedly, many mistakes were made, and the Carter administration never succeeded in justifying some of its inconsistencies.

Despite such deficiencies, Mr. Carter did successfully establish the United States as the champion of critical items on the world agenda—human rights and Third World development. For the first time, the United States conveyed to the world the message that it stood for the international protection of human rights.

Mr. Carter also succeeded in limiting the unfortunate identification of the United States with repugnant regimes by cutting off military and economic aid to the most flagrant violators of human rights. Through bilateral negotiations, a substantial number of political prisoners were released in several Latin American and Asian countries. The number of disappearances fell in Argentina, torture declined in Brazil, and imprisonment decreased in Chile. Emigration of Jews from the Soviet Union reached the highest level ever.

At the United Nations, the member nations came to realize that international protection of human rights was of genuine concern to the United States. The United States organized a human rights bloc at the United Nations. This bloc was successful, for the first time, in obtaining the passage of significant human rights resolutions at the U.N. Commission on Human Rights, in creating working groups on disappearances, in raising the Sakharov issue before the United Nations, and in pursuing other objectives.

Overall, the Carter administration made significant progress on human rights issues. There was the fall of dictators, such as Amin in Uganda, Somoza in Nicaragua, and Bokassa in the Central African Empire. There were movements in Peru, Ecuador, Nigeria, Bolivia, and Brazil away from militiary *de facto* regimes toward constitutional governments. There developed an open electoral process in Portugal and the Dominican Republic. The Carter administration, of course, cannot claim full credit for all of these developments, but it did, at least, contribute to them.

Certainly, due to efforts of the Carter administration, many lives were saved and that is no trifling benefit. Even for those who remained repressed, there was hope and encouragement. I served at the United Nations during the later years at the Carter administration, and there is no doubt that the nations of the world, and, perhaps just as importantly, our own ambassadors, understood that human rights were of genuine concern to the United States.

When the Reagan administration came into office, it immediately began to demonstrate hostility toward human rights considerations. Launching attacks on the human rights policy of the Carter administration became almost a cottage industry in the west wing of the White House. In his first press conference, Secretary of State Alexander Haig declared that "international terrorism will take the place of human rights" as a foreign policy priority. Reagan administration officials quickly cuddled up to, indeed embraced, the repressive regimes of Latin America, Asia and South Africa. Only in the context of a Cold War approach to the Soviet Union was a human rights stance maintained.

At the State Department, senior officials began to speak of eliminating the State Department's Human Rights Bureau. The *coup de grace* to human rights policy was struck when Ernest Lefever, an outspoken opponent of an active human rights policy, was nominated by the President to head the Bureau. . . . Although the Senate Foreign Relations Committee overwhelmingly rejected his nomination, the White House insisted that Lefever was "the man for the job" until Lefever himself asked to be withdrawn from consideration.

Since then, a bit battered by that fight, the Administration has eased its open hostility to human rights and has increasingly offered at least lip service to human rights concerns – indeed, sometimes in impeccable prose. But the underlying philosophy and approach has remained the same and it should be articulated and understood.

The basic approach of the current administration to foreign policy, which also affects human rights issues, is ideological. The ideology is based on two premises. The first premise is that the United States represents the forces of good in this world, and that the Soviet Union represents the forces of evil. The working second premise is that everything follows from the first premise. . . . Early on, the Administration adopted a foreign policy model based on the distinction between totalitarian and authoritarian states.

A totalitarian regime is one in which ideology requires the complete and systematic management of human life by the state. The term was delineated by

Hannah Arendt in her brilliant essay on totalitarianism. The Nazi and Stalin regimes were the archtypes of the totalitarian state.

An authoritarian regime is a dictatorship which controls virtually all of the areas of civil and political freedom. It does not, however, seek control over every element of life. Some matters, such as religious worship and form of economic enterprise, are left to private direction, provided that they are not exercised in a way that resists or is hostile to the regime in any way.

Utilizing this model, the Administration categorized human rights violations by Communist dictators as totalitarian and violations by anti-Communist dictators as authoritarian. Carrying the model forward, the doctrine holds that human rights abuses by totalitarian states should be decried and attacked. Those by the authoritarian states should *not* be. Indeed, because of their anti-Soviet posture, such governments should be supported and should receive military and economic assistance whenever it is possible to overcome Congressional restraints on such aid.

A rational reason given to justify this disparate treatment is that authoritarian states have a potential for democratization. In contrast, experience has shown that totalitarian regimes seldom drift towards democratic institutions, since any such drift is quickly suppressed, as was the case in Poland.

Models are useful when they establish general principles from which particular outcomes can be predicted. But they can be dangerous when artificial constructions are mistaken for descriptions of the real world. From a human rights viewpoint, the Administration's model is untenable because it ignores the essence of what is at stake. In the human rights universe, abuse is abuse and torture is torture, no matter who the perpetrators may be. It is certainly no solace to the mother whose son was abducted and tortured in Argentina, or the the black man banned in South Africa, that the outrage was committed by an authoritarian regime rather than a totalitarian one.

Even from the perspective of political science, the model does not lend itself simply to Communist and anti-Communist categorizations. Yugoslavia and Poland during the Solidarity period may be less abusive than Chile or Paraguay. What shall we do when an authoritarian regime, such as that of the Philippines' President Marcos, blatantly violates human rights while a totalitarian state, like Romania, does so more discretely? The authoritarian regime of South Africa is harsher in its treatment of blacks than the Soviet Union is in its treatment of Jews. Moreover, there may be totalitarian regimes, such as China, which are relatively friendly to the United States while there may also be authoritarian regimes, such as Syria, which are not.

The totalitarian-authoritarian dichotomy, as adopted by the Reagan administration, is not often articulated today because it has been so vigorously attacked by human rights proponents. Nevertheless, the theory it reflects continues as the *eminence grise* of the Reagan administration's human rights policy, and it is the rationale for the double standard that this Administration applies to human rights. Strikingly, the fact that authoritarian regimes do indeed have a potential for democratization which is generally lacking in totalitarian regimes should lead to an even stronger interest in *pressing* human rights concerns in authoritarian regimes in order to propel them toward democratic measures. Moreover, we often possess the leverage to impose such pressure on these regimes. Yet, the Reagan administration has put little or no pressure on a Pinochet, a Strassner, a Viola or a Marcos. Thus, anti-Communist blinders continue to serve as an excuse for the Administration to woo even the worst of the authoritarians.

Another factor underlying the Reagan administrtion's approach to human rights is its view of national security, which is related to its ideological approach to foreign policy. Concern over our national security is the reason most often advanced as the basis for deflecting a human rights initiative. Much evil has been done in the name of national security. National security was used to justify illegal wiretaps, break-ins, a private police force, and the Watergate cover-up. Protection of our national security was the rationale for sending 500,000 American soldiers to Vietnam in order to prevent a Communist take-over. Concern for our national security was used to justify the Cambodian invasion, carpet bombing, My Lai, chemical defoliation, free fire zones, and the destruction of villages in order to save them. National security is now used as a reason for not pressuring South Korea and as a reason for invading Grenada. Whenever the Administrtion determines that it wants to provide military assistance to a country whose record on human rights record is deficient, it does so in the name of national security.

Perhaps the truest measure of any administration's commitment to human rights is the extent to which it will invoke national security considerations to override human rights concerns. For example, the current administration's embrace of Marcos of the Philippines is rationalized by the need to maintain bases in Clark Field as a matter of national security. Many military experts concede, however, that given our other footholds in the Pacific, such bases are largely unnecessary.

If an administration is forthright in its approach to national security, there are relatively few situations in which concern for national security will provide sufficient reason for not pressing for the protection of human rights. In a given situation, it may be that national security interests should prevail over human rights concerns. In such situations, the administration should make clear what the security interest is that would justify overriding human rights initiatives. The current administration has been, and, indeed, the Carter administration was as well, too quick to find national security excuses for foregoing human rights concerns. More often than not, the respective interests are not mutually exclusive.

There are many ways in which the Administration's philosophy has been translated into practices which are counter-productive to progress in human rights. The write-off of economic and cultural rights from the human rights agenda, the certification for aid of human rights offenders, the comfort given to repressive rulers, and the downplay of human rights in the embassies and at the State Department, are striking examples. Another example is the failure of this administration to use its most effective tool—our ability to marshal world opinion—in combatting human rights abuses. The Reagan administration has failed completely to do so in the case of the so-called authoritarian states.

There is a strange mystique about world opinion. Even repressive rulers like to present faces of concern for humanitarian goals. Perhaps this is due to shame or embarrassment; perhaps it is due to fear of their populace. Perhaps the aim is to win favor with allies, trading partners, or the investment community. Or perhaps (as a media friend once cynically observed) it is simply because public relations secretly rules the world. Whatever the psychological, political, or sociological causes, focusing world attention on human rights abuses is a valuable tool to effect at least limited redress, often bringing about concessions designed to placate both external condemnation and domestic opposition.

World opinion is also important in that it signals and encourages the populace of a repressive nation. Repressive rulers invariably distrust the populace, which possesses dormant power to overthrow them. Repressors are particularly nervous about world opinion because of its potential for stimulating yearnings among the populace, encouraging the growth of opposition leaders, and stimulating demands for the observance of rights.

The Reagan administration does give public signals in the human rights area, but all too often gives off the wrong ones. Expressions of support and other indicia of encouragement are frequently offered to repressive rulers in Argentina, Chile, the Philippines, Korea, and South Africa. The people of those nations view such support as a signal that the United States supports repressive regimes. The practice is not merely careless or naive diplomacy. It is calculated to bolster regimes that the Administration wishes to support because of their anti-Communist postures.

Administration spokesmen claim that the Administration can be more effective in ameliorating human rights abuses by authoritarian nations through the use of quiet diplomacy. Quiet diplomacy is often desirable, and the Carter administration utilized it frequently. But quiet diplomacy loses its effectiveness if the violating state knows that the quiet diplomacy will not be accompanied by a readiness to publicly marshal world opinion against the abuser. The leaders of many authoritarian states know that this Administration will not use this effective weapon against them. Hence, the Administration's quiet diplomacy is handicapped and, too often, unproductive.

With respect to Soviet violations of human rights, the Administration has been outspoken, but the declarations lose much of their credibility since they are made in a Cold War context and are under the disability that results from employing a double standard.

This is a rather bleak picture of the current state of United States foreign policy with respect to human rights. Nonetheless, the outlook for the future is not entirely gloomy. Public opinion is bound to have an impact on United States foreign policy and a human rights emphasis remains popular with the American public. Continued Congressional support of human rights measures surely reflects the belief of the legislators that their constituents support such measures. Recognition of the strength of public opinion has made the current Administration more cautious in its recent public expressions on human rights issues. The ideology may not have changed but there appears to be an increased receptivity to human rights initiatives, if only in response to the proximity of election day. The polls are always a force to be reckoned with for those who fashion foreign policy. . . .   ■

THE UNITED STATES CONSTITUTION

We the People of the United States, in Order to form a more perfect Union, establish justice, insure domestic Tranquility, provide for the common defence, promote the general Welfare, and secure the Blessings of Liberty to ourselves and our Posterity, do ordain and establish this Constitution for the United States of America.

ARTICLE I

Section 1.

All legislative Powers herein granted shall be vested in a Congress of the United States, which shall consist of a Senate and a House of Representatives.

Section 2.

The House of Representatives shall be composed of Members chosen every second Year by the People of the several States, and the Electors in each State shall have the Qualifications requisite for Electors of the most numerous Branch of the State Legislature.

No Person shall be a Representative who shall not have attained to the Age of twenty five Years, and been seven Years a Citizen of the United States, and who shall not, when elected, be an Inhabitant of that State in which he shall be chosen.

Representatives and direct Taxes shall be apportioned among the several States which may be included within this Union, according to their respective Numbers, which shall be determined by adding to the whole Number of free Persons, including those bound to Service for a Term of Years, and excluding Indians not taxed, three fifths of all other Persons.[1] The actual Enumeration shall be made within three years after the first Meeting of the Congress of the United States, and within every subsequent Term of ten Years, in such Manner as they shall by Law direct. The Number of Representatives shall not exceed one for every thirty Thousand, but each State shall have at Least one Representative; and until such enumeration shall be made, the State of New Hampshire shall be entitled to chuse three, Massachusetts eight, Rhode-Island and Providence Plantations one, Connecticut five, New York six, New Jersey four, Pennsylvania eight, Delaware one, Maryland six, Virginia ten, North Carolina five, South Carolina five, and Georgia three.

When vacancies happen in the Representation from any State, the Executive Authority thereof shall issue Writs of Election to fill such Vacancies.

The House of Representatives shall chuse their Speaker and other Officers; and shall have the sole Power of Impeachment.

---

[1]"Other Persons" being black slaves. Modified by Amendment XIV, Section 2.

Section 3.

The Senate of the United States shall be composed of two Senators from each State, chosen by the Legislature thereof, for six Years; and each Senator shall have one Vote.

Immediately after they shall be assembled in Consequence of the first Election, they shall be divided as equally as may be into three Classes. The Seats of the Senators of the first Class shall be vacated at the Expiration of the second Year, of the second Class at the Expiration of the fourth Year, and of the third Class at the Expiration of the Sixth Year, so that one third may be chosen every second Year; and if Vacancies happen by Resignation, or otherwise, during the Recess of the Legislature of any State, the Executive thereof may make temporary Appointments until the next Meeting of the Legislature, which shall then fill such Vacancies.[2]

No Person shall be a Senator who shall not have attained to the Age of thirty Years, and been nine Years a Citizen of the United States, and who shall not, when elected, be an Inhabitant of the State for which he shall be chosen.

The Vice President of the United States shall be President of the Senate, but shall have no Vote, unless they be equally divided.

The Senate shall chuse their other Officers, and also a President pro tempore, in the Absence of the Vice President, or when he shall exercise the Office of President of the United States.

The Senate shall have the sole power to try all impeachments. When sitting for that Purpose, they shall be on Oath or Affirmation. When the President of the United States is tried the Chief Justice shall preside: And no Person shall be convicted without the Concurrence of two thirds of the Members present.

Judgment in Cases of Impeachment shall not extend further than to removal from Office, and disqualification to hold and enjoy any Office of honor, Trust or Profit under the United States: but the Party convicted shall nevertheless be liable and subject to Indictment, Trial, Judgment and Punishment, according to Law.

Section 4.

The Times, Places and Manner of holding Elections for Senators and Representatives, shall be prescribed in each State by the Legislature thereof; but the Congress may at any time by Law make or alter such Regulations, except as to the Places of chusing Senators.

The Congress shall assemble at least once in every Year, and such Meeting shall be on the first Monday in December, unless they shall by Law appoint a different Day.[3]

Section 5

Each House shall be the Judge of the Elections, Returns and Qualifications of its own Members, and a Majority of each shall constitute a Quorum to do Business; but a smaller Number may adjourn from day to day, and may be authorized to compel the Attendance of absent Members, in such Manner, and under such Penalties as each House may provide.

Each House may determine the Rules of its Proceedings, punish its

[2]Provisions changed by amendment XVII.
[3]Provisions changed by Amendment XX, Section 2.

Members for disorderly Behaviour, and, with the Concurrence of two thirds, expel a Member.

Each House shall keep a Journal of its Proceedings, and from time to time publish the same, excepting such Parts as may in their Judgment require Secrecy; and the Yeas and Nays of the Members of either House on any question shall, at the Desire of one fifth of those Present, be entered on the Journal.

Neither House, during the Session of Congress, shall, without the Consent of the other, adjourn for more than three days, nor to any other Place than that in which the two Houses shall be sitting.

Section 6.

The Senators and Representatives shall receive a Compensation for their Services, to be ascertained by Law, and paid out of the Treasury of the United States. They shall in all Cases, except Treason, Felony and Breach of the Peace, be privileged from Arrest during their Attendance at the Session of their respective Houses, and in going to and returning from the same; and for any Speech or Debate in either House, they shall not be questioned in any other Place.

No Senator or Representative shall, during the Time for which he was elected, be appointed to any civil Office under the Authority of the United States, which shall have been created, or the Emoluments whereof shall have been encreased during such time; and no Person holding any Office under the United States, shall be a Member of either House during his Continuance in Office.

Section 7.

All Bills for raising Revenue shall originate in the House of Representatives; but the Senate may propose or concur with Amendments as on other Bills.

Every Bill which shall have passed the House of Representatives and the Senate, shall, before it become a Law, be presented to the President of the United States; If he approve he shall sign it, but if not he shall return it, with his Objections to that House in which it shall have originated, who shall enter the Objections at large on their Journal, and proceed to reconsider it. If after such Reconsideration two thirds of that House shall agree to pass the Bill, it shall be sent, together with the Objections, to the other House, by which it shall likewise to be reconsidered, and if approved by two thirds of that House, it shall become a Law. But in all such Cases the Vote of both Houses shall be determined by yeas and Nays, and the Names of the Persons voting for and against the Bill shall be entered on the Journal of each House respectively. If any Bill shall not be returned by the President within ten Days (Sundays excepted) after it shall have been presented to him, the Same shall be a Law, in like Manner as if he had signed it, unless the Congress by their Adjournment prevent its Return, in which Case it shall not be a Law.

Every Order, Resolution, or Vote to which the Concurrence of the Senate and House of Representatives may be necessary (except on a question of Adjournment) shall be presented to the President of the United States; and before the Same shall take Effect, shall be approved by him, or being disapproved by him, shall be repassed by two thirds of the Senate and House of Representatives, according to the Rules and Limitations prescribed in the Case of a Bill.

Section 8.

The Congress shall have Power To lay and collect Taxes, Duties, Imposts and Excises, to pay the Debts and provide for the common Defence and general Welfare of the United States; but all Duties, Imposts and Excises shall be uniform throughout the United States;

To borrow Money on the credit of the United States;

To regulate Commerce with foreign Nations, and among the several States, and with the Indian Tribes;

To establish an uniform Rule of Naturalization, and uniform Laws on the subject of Bankruptcies throughout the United States;

To coin Money, regulate the Value thereof, and of foreign Coin, and fix the Standard of Weights and Measures;

To provide for the Punishment of counterfeiting the Securities and current Coin of the United States;

To establish Post Offices and post Roads;

To promote the Progress of Science and useful Arts, by securing for limited Times to Authors and Inventors the exclusive Right to their respective Writings and Discoveries;

To constitute Tribunals inferior to the supreme Court;

To define and punish Piracies and Felonies committed on the high Seas, and Offences against the Law of Nations;

To declare War, grant Letters of Marque and Reprisal, and make Rules concerning Captures on Land and Water;

To raise and support Armies, but no Appropriation of Money to that Use shall be for a longer Term than two Years;

To provide and maintain a Navy;

To make Rules for the Government and Regulation of the land and naval Forces;

To provide for calling forth the Militia to execute the Laws of the Union, suppress Insurrections and repel Invasions;

To provide for organizing, arming, and disciplining, the Militia, and for governing such Part of them as may be employed in the Service of the United States, reserving to the States respectively, the Appointment of the Officers, and the Authority of training the Militia according to the discipline prescribed by Congress;

To exercise exclusive Legislation in all Cases whatsoever, over such District (not exceeding ten Miles square) as may, by Cession of particular States, and the Acceptance of Congress, become the Seat of the Government of the United States, and to exercise like Authority over all Places purchased by the Consent of the Legislature of the State in which the Same shall be, for the Erection of Forts, Magazines, Arsenals, dock-Yards, and other needful Buildings;—And

To make all Laws which shall be necessary and proper for carrying into Execution the foregoing Powers, and all other Powers vested by this Constitution in the Government of the United States, or in any Department or Officer thereof.

Section 9.

The Migration or Importation of such Persons as any of the States now existing shall think proper to admit, shall not be prohibited by the Congress prior to the Year one thousand eight hundred and eight, but a Tax, or duty may be imposed on such Importation, not exceeding ten dollars for each Person.

The Privilege of the Writ of Habeas Corpus shall not be suspended, unless when in Cases of Rebellion or Invasion the public Safety may require it.

No Bill of Attainder or ex post facto Law shall be passed.

No Capitation, or other direct, Tax shall be laid, unless in Proportion to the Census or Enumeration herein before directed to be taken.

No Tax or Duty shall be laid on Articles exported from any State.

No Preference shall be given by any Regulation of Commerce or Revenue to the Ports of one State over those of another; nor shall Vessels bound to, or from, one State, be obliged to enter, clear, nor pay Duties in another.

No Money shall be drawn from the Treasury, but in Consequence of Appropriations made by Law; and a regular Statement and Account of the Receipts and Expenditures of all public Money shall be published from time to time.

No Title of Nobility shall be granted by the United States: And no Person holding any Office for Profit or Trust under them, shall, without the Consent of the Congress, accept of any present, Emolument, Office, or Title, of any kind whatever, from any King, Prince, or foreign State.

Section 10.

No State shall enter into any Treaty, Alliance, or Confederation; grant Letters of Marque and Reprisal; coin Money; emit Bills of Credit; make any Thing but gold and silver Coin a Tender in Payment of Debts; pass any Bill of Attainder, ex post facto Law, or Law impairing the Obligation of Contracts, or grant any Title of Nobility.

No State shall, without the Consent of the Congress, lay any Imposts of Duties on Imports or Exports, except what may be absolutely necessary for executing its inspection Laws: and the net Produce of all Duties and Imposts, laid by any State on Imports or Exports, shall be for the Use of the Treasury of the United States; and all such Laws shall be subject to the Revision and Controul of the Congress.

No State shall, without the Consent of Congress, lay any Duty of Tonnage, keep Troops, or Ships of War in time of Peace, enter into any Agreement or Compact with another State, or with a foreign Power, or engage in War, unless actually invaded, or in such imminent Danger as will not admit of delay.

ARTICLE II

Section 1.

The executive Power shall be vested in a President of the United States of America. He shall hold his Office during the Term of four years, and, together with the Vice President, chosen for the same Term, be elected, as follows:

Each State shall appoint, in such Manner as the Legislature thereof may direct, a Number of Electors, equal to the whole Number of Senators and Representatives to which the State may be entitled in Congress: but no Senator or Representative, or Person holding an Office of Trust or Profit under the United States, shall be appointed an Elector.

The Electors shall meet in their respective States, and vote by Ballot for two Persons, of whom one at least shall not be an Inhabitant of the same State with themselves. And they shall make a List of all the Persons voted for, and of the Number of Votes for each; which List they shall sign and certify, and transmit sealed to the Seat of the Government of the United States, directed to the President of the Senate. The President of the Senate shall, in the Presence of the Senate and House of Representatives, open all the Certificates, and the Votes shall then be counted. The Person having the greatest Number of Votes shall be the President, if such Number be a Majority of the whole Number of Electors appointed, and if there be more than one who have such Majority, and have an equal Number of Votes, then the House of Representatives shall immediately chuse by Ballot one of them for President; and if no Person have a Majority, then from the five highest on the List the said House shall in like Manner chuse the President. But in chusing the President, the Votes shall be taken by States, the Representation from each State having one Vote; A quorum for this Purpose shall consist of a Member or Members from two thirds of the States, and a Majority of all the States shall be necessary to a Choice. In every Case, after the Choice of the President, the Person having the greatest Number of Votes of the Electors shall be the Vice President. But if there should remain two or more who have equal Votes, the Senate shall chuse from them by Ballot the Vice President.[4]

The Congress may determine the Time of chusing the Electors, and the Day on which they shall give their Votes; which Day shall be the same throughout the United States.

No Person except a natural born Citizen, or a Citizen of the United States, at the time of the Adoption of this Constitution, shall be eligible to the Office of President; neither shall any Person be eligible to that Office who shall not have attained to the Age of thirty five Years, and been fourteen Years a Resident within the United States.

In Case of the Removal of the President from Office, or of his Death, Resignation, or Inability to discharge the Powers and Duties of the said Office, the Same shall devolve on the Vice President, and the Congress may by Law provide for the Case of Removal, Death, Resignation or Inability, both of the President and Vice President, declaring what Officer shall then act as President, and such Officer shall act accordingly, until the Disability be removed, or a President shall be elected.

The President shall, at stated Times, receive for his Services, a Compensation, which shall neither be encreased nor diminished during the Period for which he shall have been elected, and he shall not receive within that Period any other Emolument from the United States, or any of them.

Before he enter on the Execution of his Office, he shall take the following Oath of Affirmation: –"I do solemnly swear (or affirm) that I will faithfully execute the Office of President of the United States, and will to the best of my Ability, preserve, protect and defend the Constitution of the United States."

Section 2.

The President shall be Commander in Chief of the Army and Navy of the United States, and of the Militia of the several States, when called into the actual Service of the United States; he may require the Opinion, in writing, of the principal Officer in each of the executive Departments, upon any Subject relating to the Duties of their respective Offices, and he shall have Power to grant Reprieves and Pardons for Offences against the United States, except in Cases of Impeachment.

He shall have Power, by and with the Advice and Consent of the Senate, to make Treaties, provided two thirds of the Senators present concur; and he shall nominate, and by and with the Advice and Consent of the Senate, shall appoint Ambassadors, other public Ministers and Consuls, Judges of the supreme Court, and all other Officers of the United States, whose Appointments are not herein otherwise provided for, and which shall be established by Law: but the Congress may by Law vest the Appointment of such inferior Officers, as they think proper in the President alone, in the Courts of Law, or in the Heads of Departments.

The President shall have power to fill up all Vacancies that may happen during the Recess of the Senate, by granting Commissions which shall expire at the end of their next Session.

Section 3.

He shall from time to time give to the Congress Information of the State of the Union, and recommend to their Consideration such Measures as he shall judge necessary and expedient; he may, on extraordinary Occasions, con-

---

[4]Provisions superseded by Amendment XII.

vene both Houses, or either of them, and in Case of Disagreement between them, with Respect to the Time of Adjournment, he may adjourn them to such Time as he shall think proper; he shall receive Ambassadors and other public Ministers; he shall take Care that Laws be faithfully executed, and shall Commission all the Officers of the United States.

Section 4.

The President, Vice President and all civil Officers of the United States, shall be removed from Office on Impeachment for, and Conviction of Treason, Bribery, or other high Crimes and Misdemeanors.

ARTICLE III

Section 1.

The judicial Power of the United States, shall be vested in one supreme Court, and in such inferior Courts as the Congress may from time to time ordain and establish. The Judges, both of the supreme and inferior Courts, shall hold their Offices during good Behaviour, and shall, at stated Times, receive for their Services, a Compensation, which shall not be diminished during their Continuance in Office.

Section 2.

The judicial Power shall extend to all Cases in Law and Equity, arising under this Constitution, the Laws of the United States, and Treaties made, or which shall be made, under their Authority; — to all Cases affecting Ambassadors, other public Ministers and Consuls; — to all Cases of admiralty and maritime Jurisdiction; — to Controversies to which the United States shall be a Party; — to Controversies between two or more states; — between a State and Citizens of another State; — between Citizens of different States; — between Citizens of the same State claiming Lands under Grants of different States, and between a State, or the Citizens thereof, and foreign States, Citizens or Subjects.[5]

In all other Cases affecting Ambassadors, other public Ministers and Consuls, and those in which a State shall be Party, the supreme Court shall have original Jurisdiction. In all the other Cases before mentioned, the supreme Court shall have appellate Jurisdiction, both as to Law and Fact, with such Exceptions, and under such Regulations as the Congress shall make.

The Trial of all Crimes, except in Cases of Impeachment, shall be by Jury; and such Trial shall be held in the State where the said Crimes shall have been committed, but when not committed within any State, the Trial shall be at such Place or Places as the Congress may by Law have directed.

Section 3.

Treason against the United States, shall consist only in levying War against them, or in adhering to their Enemies, giving them Aid and Comfort. No person shall be convicted of Treason unless on the Testimony of two Witnesses to the same overt Act, or on Confession in open Court.

The Congress shall have Power to declare the Punishment of Treason,

---

[5]Clause changed by Amendment XI.

but no Attainder of Treason shall work Corruption of Blood, or Forfeiture except during the Life of the Person attainted.

ARTICLE IV

Section 1.
Full Faith and Credit shall be given in each State to the public Acts, Records, and judicial Proceedings of every other State. And the Congress may by general Laws prescribe the Manner in which such Acts, Records and Proceedings shall be proved, and the Effect thereof.

Section 2.
The Citizens of each State shall be entitled to all Privileges and Immunities of Citizens in the several States.

A Person charged in any State with Treason, Felony, or other Crime, who shall flee from Justice, and be found in another State, shall on Demand of the executive Authority of the State from which he fled, be delivered up, to be removed to the State having Jurisdiction of the Crime.

No Person held to Service or Labour in one State, under the Laws thereof, escaping into another, shall, in Consequence of any Law or Regulation therein, be discharged from such Service or Labour, but shall be delivered up on Claim of the Party to whom such Service or Labour may be due.

Section 3.
New States may be admitted by the Congress into this Union; but no new State shall be formed or erected within the jurisdiction of any other State; nor any State be formed by the Junction of two or more States, or Parts of States, without the Consent of the Legislatures of the States concerned as well as of the Congress.

The Congress shall have Power to dispose of and make all needful Rules and Regulations respecting the Territory or other Property belonging to the United States; and nothing in this Constitution shall be so construed as to Prejudice any Claims of the United States, or of any particular State.

Section 4.
The United States shall guarantee to every State in this Union a Republican Form of Government, and shall protect each of them against Invasion; and on Application of the Legislature, or of the Executive (when the Legislature cannot be convened) against domestic Violence.

ARTICLE V

The Congress, whenever two thirds of both Houses shall deem it necessary, shall propose Amendments to this Constitution, or, on the Application of the Legislatures of two thirds of the several States, shall call a Convention for proposing Amendments, which, in either Case, shall be valid to all Intents and Purposes, as Part of this Constitution, when ratified by the Legislatures of three fourths of the several States, or by Conventions in three fourths thereof, as the one or the other Mode of Ratification may be proposed by the Congress; Provided that no Amendment which may be made prior to the Year One thousand eight hundred and eight shall in any Manner affect the first and fourth Clauses in the Ninth Section of the first Article; and that no State, without its Consent, shall be deprived of its equal Suffrage in the Senate.

ARTICLE VI

All Debts contracted and Engagements entered into, before the Adoption of this Constitution, shall be as valid against the United States under this Constitution, as under the Confederation.

This Constitution, and the Laws of the United States which shall be made in Pursuance thereof; and all Treaties made, or which shall be made, under the Authority of the United States, shall be the supreme Law of the Land; and the Judges in every State shall be bound thereby, any Thing in the Constitution or Laws of any State to the Contrary notwithstanding.

The Senators and Representatives before mentioned, and the Members of the several State Legislatures, and all executive and judicial Officers, both of the United States and of the several States, shall be bound by Oath or Affirmation, to support this Constitution; but no religious Test shall ever be required as a Qualification to any Office or public Trust under the United States.

ARTICLE VII

The Ratification of the Conventions of nine States shall be sufficient for the Establishment of this Constitution between the States so ratifying the Same.

Done in Convention by the Unanimous Consent of the States present the Seventeenth Day of September in the Year of our Lord one thousand seven hundred and Eighty seven and of the Independence of the United States of America and the Twelfth[6] IN WITNESS whereof We have here unto subscribed our Names.

[AMENDMENT I]

Congress shall make no law respecting an establishment of religion, or prohibiting the free exercise thereof; or abridging the freedom of speech, or of the press, or the right of the people peacably to assemble, and to petition the Government for a redress of grievances.

[AMENDMENT II]

A well regulated Militia being necessary to the security of a free State, the right of the people to keep and bear Arms, shall not be infringed.

---

[6]The Constitution was submitted on September 17, 1787, by the Constitutional Convention, was ratified by the conventions of several states at various dates up to May 29, 1790, and became effective on March 4, 1789.

[AMENDMENT III]

No Soldier shall, in time of peace be quartered in any house, without the consent of the Owner, nor in time of war, but in a manner to be prescribed by law.

[AMENDMENT IV]

The right of the people to be secure in their persons, houses, papers, and effects, against unreasonable searches and seizures, shall not be violated, and no Warrants shall issue, but upon probable cause, supported by Oath or affirmation, and particularly describing the place to be searched, and the persons or things to be seized.

[AMENDMENT V]

No person shall be held to answer for a capital, or otherwise infamous crime, unless on a presentment or indictment of a Grand Jury, except in cases arising in the land or naval forces, or in the Militia, when in actual service in time of War or public danger; nor shall any person be subject for the same offence to be twice put in jeopardy of life or limb; nor shall be compelled in any criminal case to be a witness against himself, nor be deprived of life, liberty, or property, without due process of law; nor shall private property be taken for public use, without just compensation.

[AMENDMENT VI]

In all criminal prosecutions, the accused shall enjoy the right to a speedy and public trial, by an impartial jury of the State and district wherein the crime shall have been committed, which district shall have been previously ascertained by law, and to be informed of the nature and cause of the accusation; to be confronted with the witnesses against him; to have compulsory process for obtaining witnesses in his favor, and to have the Assistance of Counsel for his defence.

[AMENDMENT VII]

In Suits at common law, where the value in controversy shall exceed twenty dollars, the right of trial by jury shall be preserved, and no fact tried by a jury, shall be otherwise re-examined in any court of the United States, than according to the rules of the common law.

[AMENDMENT VIII]

Excessive bail shall not be required, nor excessive fines imposed, nor cruel and unusual punishments inflicted.

[AMENDMENT IX]]

The enumeration in the Constitution, of certain rights, shall not be construed to deny or disparage others retained by the people.

[AMENDMENT X]

The powers not delegated to the United States by the Constitution, nor prohibited by it to the States, are reserved to the States respectively, or to the people.[7]

[AMENDMENT XI]

The judicial power of the United States shall not be construed to extend to any suit in law or equity, commenced or prosecuted against one of the United States by Citizens of another State, or by Citizens or Subjects of any Foreign State.[8]

[AMENDMENT XII]

The Electors shall meet in their respective states, and vote by ballot for President and Vice-President, one of whom, at least, shall not be an inhabitant of the same state with themselves; they shall name in their ballots the person voted for as President, and in distinct ballots the person voted for as Vice-President, and they shall make distinct lists of all persons voted for as President, and of all persons voted for as Vice-President, and of the number of votes for each, which lists they shall sign and certify, and transmit sealed to the seat of the government of the United States, directed to the President of the Senate;—The President of the Senate shall, in the presence of the Senate and House of Representatives, open all the certificates and the votes shall then be counted;—The person having the greatest number of votes for President, shall be the President, if such number by a majority of the whole number of Electors appointed; and if no person have such majority, then from the persons having the highest numbers not exceeding three on the list of those voted for as President, the House of Representatives shall choose immediately, by ballot, the President. But in choosing the President, the votes shall be taken by states, the representation from each state having one vote; a quorum for this purpose shall consist of a member or members from two-thirds of the states, and a majority of all the states shall be necessary to a choice. And if the House of Representatives shall not choose a President whenever the right of choice shall devolve upon them, before the fourth day of March next following, then the Vice-President shall act as President, as in the case of the death or other constitutional disability of the President.—The person having the greatest number of votes as Vice-President, shall be the Vice-President, if such number be a majority of the whole number of Electors appointed, and if no person have a majority, then from the two highest numbers on the list, the Senate shall choose the Vice-President; a quorum for the purpose

---

[7]The first ten amendments were all proposed by Congress on September 25, 1789, and were ratified and adoption certified on December 15, 1791.
[8]Proposed by Congress on March 4, 1794, and declared ratified on January 8, 1798.

shall consist of two-thirds of the whole number of Senators, and a majority of the whole number shall be necessary to a choice. But no person constitutionally ineligible to the office of President shall be eligible to that of Vice-President of the United States.[9]

[AMENDMENT XIII]

Section 1.

Neither slavery nor involuntary servitude, except as a punishment for crime whereof the party shall have been duly convicted, shall exist within the United States, or any place subject to their jurisdiction.

Section 2.

Congress shall have power to enforce this article by appropriate legislation.[10]

[AMENDMENT XIV]

Section 1.

All persons born or naturalized in the United States and subject to the jurisdiction thereof, are citizens of the United States and the State wherein they reside. No State shall make or enforce any law which shall abridge the privileges or immunities of citizens of the United States; nor shall any State deprive any person of life, liberty, or property, without due process of law; nor deny to any person within its jurisdiction the equal protection of the laws.

Section 2.

Representatives shall be apportioned among the several States according to their respective numbers counting the whole number of persons in each State, excluding Indians not taxed. But when the right to vote at any election for the choice of electors for President and Vice-President of the United States, Representatives in Congress, the Executive and Judicial officers of a State, or the members of the Legislature thereof, is denied to any of the male inhabitants of such State being twenty-one years of age and citizens of the United States, or in any way abridged, except for participation in rebellion or other crime, the basis of representation therein shall be reduced in the proportion which the number of such male citizens shall bear to the whole number of male citizens twenty-one years of age in such State.

Section 3.

No person shall be a Senator or Representative in Congress, or elector of President and Vice President or hold any office, civil or military, under the United States or under any State, who, having previously taken an oath, as a member of Congress, or as an officer of the United States, or as a member of any State legislature or as an executive or judicial officer of any State to support the Constitution of the United States, shall have engaged in insurrection or rebellion against the same, or given aid or comfort to the enemies thereof. But Congress may by a vote of two-thirds of each House, remove such disability.

---

[9]Proposed by Congress on December 9, 1803; declared ratified on September 25, 1804; supplemented by Amendments XX and XXIII.
[10]Proposed by Congress on January 31, 1865; declared ratified on December 18, 1865.

Section 1.

...alidity of the public debt of the United States authorized by law,
...ng debts incurred for payment of pensions and bounties for services
... suppressing insurrection or rebellion, shall not be questioned. But neither
the United States nor any State shall assume or pay any debt or obligation
incurred in aid of insurrection or rebellion against the United States, or any
claim for the loss or emancipation of any slave; but all such debts, obligations and claims shall be held illegal and void.

Section 5.

The Congress shall have power to enforce, by appropriate legislation,
the provisions of this article.[11]

[AMENDMENT XV]

Section 1.

The right of citizens of the United States to vote shall not be denied or
abridged by the United States or by any State on account of race, color, or
previous condition of servitude.

Section 2.

The Congress shall have power to enforce this article by appropriate
legislation.[12]

[AMENDMENT XVI]

The Congress shall have power to lay and collect taxes on incomes, from
whatever source derived, without apportionment among the several States,
and without regard to any census or enumeration.[13]

[AMENDMENT XVII]

The Senate of the United States shall be composed of two Senators from
each State, elected by the people thereof, for six years; and each Senator shall
have one vote. The electors in each State shall have the qualifications requisite
for electors of the most numerous branch of the State legislatures.

When vacancies happen in the representation of any State in the Senate,
the executive authority of such State shall issue writs of election to fill such
vacancies: *Provided,* That the legislature of any State may empower the executive thereof to make temporary appointments until the people fill the vacancies by election as the legislature may direct.

This amendment shall not be so construed as to affect the election or
term of any Senator chosen before it becomes valid as part of the Constitution.[14]

---

[11]Proposed by Congress on June 13, 1866; declared ratified on July 28, 1868.
[12]Proposed by Congress on February 26, 1869; declared ratified on March 30, 1870.
[13]Proposed by Congress on July 12, 1909; declared ratified on February 25, 1913.
[14]Proposed by Congress on May 13, 1912; declared ratified on May 31, 1913.

[AMENDMENT XVIII]

Section 1.

After one year from the ratification of this article the manufacture, sale, or transportation of intoxicating liquors within, the importation thereof into, or the exportation thereof from the United States and all territory subject to the jurisdiction thereof for beverage purposes is hereby prohibited.

Section 2.

The Congress and the several States shall have concurrent power to enforce this article by appropriate legislation.

Section 3.

This article shall be inoperative unless it shall have been ratified as an amendment to the Constitution by the legislatures of the several States, as provided in the Constitution, within seven years from the date of the submission hereof to the States by the Congress.[15]

[AMENDMENT XIX]

The right of citizens of the United States to vote shall not be denied or abridged by the United States or by any State on account of sex.

Congress shall have power to enforce this article by appropriate legislation.[16]

[AMENDMENT XX]

Section 1.

The terms of the President and Vice President shall end at noon on the 20th day of January, and the terms of Senators and Representatives at noon on the 3d day of January, of the years in which such terms would have ended if this article had not been ratified; and the terms of their successors shall then begin.

Section 2.

The Congress shall assemble at least once in every year, and such meeting shall begin at noon on the 3d day of January, unless they shall by law appoint a different day.

Section 3.

If, at the time fixed for the beginning of the term of the President, the President elect shall have died, the Vice President elect shall become President. If a President shall not have been chosen before the time fixed for the beginning of his term, or if the President elect shall have failed to qualify, then the Vice President elect shall act as President until a President shall have

---

[15]Proposed by Congress on December 18, 1917; declared ratified on January 29, 1919; repealed by Amendment XXI.

[16]Proposed by Congress on June 4, 1919; declared ratified on August 26, 1920.

alified; and the Congress may by law provide for the case wherein neither a President elect nor a Vice President elect shall have qualified, declaring who shall then act as President, or the manner in which one who is to act shall be selected, and such person shall act accordingly until a President or Vice President shall have qualified.

Section 4.

The Congress may by law provide for the case of the death of any of the persons from whom the House of Representatives may choose a President whenever the right of choice shall have devolved upon them, and for the case of the death of any of the persons from whom the Senate may choose a Vice President whenever the right of choice shall have devolved upon them.

Section 5.

Sections 1 and 2 shall take effect on the 15th day of October following the ratification of this article.

Section 6.

This article shall be inoperative unless it shall have been ratified as an amendment to the Constitution by the legislatures of three-fourths of the several States within seven years from the date of its submission.[17]

[AMENDMENT XXI]

Section 1.

The eighteenth article of amendment to the Constitution of the United States is hereby repealed.

Section 2.

The transportation or importation into any States, Territory, or possession of the United States for delivery or use therein of intoxicating liquors, in violation of the laws thereof, is hereby prohibited.

Section 3.

This article shall be inoperative unless it shall have been ratified as an amendment to the Constitution by conventions in the several States, as provided in the Constitution, within seven years from the date of the submission hereof to the States by the Congress.[18]

[AMENDMENT XXII]

Section 1.

No person shall be elected to the office of the President more than twice, and no person who had held the office of President, or acted as President, for more than two years of a term to which some other person was elected President shall be elected to the office of the President more than once. But this Article shall not apply to any person holding the office of President when the Article was proposed by the Congress, and shall not prevent any person who may be holding the office of President, or acting as President, during

---

[17]Proposed by Congress on March 2, 1932; declared ratified on February 6, 1933.
[18]Proposed by Congress on February 20, 1933; declared ratified on December 5, 1933.

the term within which this Article becomes operative from holding the office of President or acting as President during the remainder of such term.

Section 2.

This article shall be inoperative unless it shall have been ratified as an amendment to the Constitution by the legislatures of three-fourths of the several States within seven years from the date of its submission to the States by the Congress.[19]

[AMENDMENT XXIII]

Section 1.

The District constituting the seat of Government of the United States shall appoint in such manner as the Congress shall direct:

A number of electors of President and Vice President equal to the whole number of Senators and Representatives in Congress to which the District would be entitled if it were a State, but in no event more than the least populous State; they shall be in addition to those appointed by the States, but they shall be considered, for the purposes of the election of President and Vice President, to be electors appointed by a State; and they shall meet in the District and perform such duties as provided by the twelfth article of amendment.

Section 2.

The Congress shall have power to enforce this article by appropriate legislation.[20]

[AMENDMENT XXIV]

Section 1.

The right of citizens of the United States to vote in any primary or other election for President or Vice President, for electors for President or Vice President, or for Senator or Representative in Congress, shall not be denied or abridged by the United States or any state by reason of failure to pay any poll tax or other tax.

Section 2.

The Congress shall have the power to enforce this article by appropriate legislation.[21]

[AMENDMENT XXV]

Section 1.

In case of the removal of the President from office or his death or resignation, the Vice President shall become President.

---

[19]Proposed by Congress on March 24, 1947; declared ratified on March 1, 1951.
[20]Proposed by Congress on June 16, 1960; declared ratified on April 3, 1961.
[21]Proposed by Congress on August 27, 1962; declared ratified on January 23, 1963.

Section 2.

Whenever there is a vacancy in the office of the Vice President, the President shall nominate a Vice President who shall take the office upon confirmation by a majority vote of both houses of Congress.

Section 3.

Whenever the President transmits to the President pro tempore of the Senate and the Speaker of the House of Representatives his written declaration that he is unable to discharge the powers and duties of his office, and until he transmits to them a written declaration to the contrary, such powers and duties shall be discharged by the Vice President as Acting President.

Section 4.

Whenever the Vice President and a majority of either the principal officers of the executive departments or of such other body as Congress may by law provide, transmit to the President pro tempore of the Senate and the Speaker of the House of Representatives their written declaration that the President is unable to discharge the powers and duties of his office, the Vice President shall immediately assume the powers and duties of the office as Acting President.

Thereafter, when the President transmits to the President pro tempore of the Senate and the Speaker of the House of Representatives his written declaration that no inability exists, he shall resume the powers and duties of his office unless the Vice President and a majority of either the principal officers of the executive department or of such other body as Congress may by law provide, transmit within four days to the President pro tempore of the Senate and the Speaker of the House of Representatives their written declaration that the President is unable to discharge the powers and duties of his office. Thereupon Congress shall decide the issue, assembling within 48 hours for that purpose if not in session. If the Congress, within 21 days after receipt of the latter written declaration, or, if Congress is not in session, within 21 days after Congress is required to assemble, determines by two-thirds vote of both houses that the President is unable to discharge the powers and duties of his office, the Vice President shall continue to discharge the same as Acting President; otherwise, the President shall resume the powers and duties of his office.[22]

[AMENDMENT XXVI]

Section 1.

The right of citizens of the United States, who are 18 yers of age or older, to vote shall not be denied or abridged by the United States or any state on account of age.

Section 2.

The Congress shall have the power to enforce this article by appropriate legislation.[23]

---

[22]Proposed by Congress on July 6, 1965; declared ratified on February 10, 1967.
[23]Proposed by Congress on March 23, 1971; declared ratified on June 30, 1971.

Acknowledgments

Acknowledgments

4 – From "The Intellectual Origins of the American Constitution" by Gordon S. Wood, NATIONAL FORUM, Fall 1984. Reprinted by permission of NATIONAL FORUM: THE PHI KAPPA PHI JOURNAL, vol. LXIV, No. 4, and the author.

10 – Reprinted with permission of Macmillan Publishing Company from AN ECONOMIC INTERPRETATION OF THE CONSTITUTION OF THE UNITED STATES by Charles A. Beard. Copyright 1913, 1935 by Macmillan Publishing Company, renewed 1941 by Charles A. Beard, renewed 1963 by William Beard and Miriam Beard Vagts.

14 – Robert E. Brown, CHARLES BEARD AND THE CONSTITUTION: A CRITICAL ANALYSIS OF "AN ECONOMIC INTERPRETATION OF THE CONSTITUTION." Copyright © 1956, 1984 renewed by Princeton University Press. Excerpt, pp. 194–200, reprinted with permission of Princeton University Press.

19 – From "The Founding Fathers: A Reform Caucus in Action" by John P. Roche, AMERICAN POLITICAL SCIENCE REVIEW, 1961, Vol. 55, pp. 799–816. Reprinted by permission of the American Political Science Association and John P. Roche.

57 – From MANAGING FEDERALISM: STUDIES IN INTERGOVERNMENTAL RELATIONS by Arnold M. Howitt. Copyright © 1984, Congressional Quarterly, Inc. Reprinted by permission.

77 – From "The Constitution and Free Expression" by A.E. Dick Howard. Reprinted by permission of NATIONAL FORUM: THE PHI KAPPA PHI JOURNAL, Vol. LXIV, No. 4, Fall 1984, and the author.

85 – From DEFENDING MY ENEMY: AMERICAN NAZIS, THE SKOKIE CASE, AND THE RISKS OF FREEDOM by Aryeh Neier. Copyright © 1979 by Aryeh Neier. Reprinted by permission of the publisher, E.P. Dutton, a division of New American Library.

106 – Reprinted from Judith A. Baer: EQUALITY UNDER THE CONSTITUTION: RECLAIMING THE FOURTEENTH AMENDMENT. Copyright © 1983 by Cornell University Press. Used by permission of the publisher.

108 – From "The Meaning of Equality in America" by Sidney Verba and Gary R. Orren, POLITICAL SCIENCE QUARTERLY, Fall 1985. Copyright © 1985 by The Academy of Political Science. Reprinted by permission.

119 – From "Civil Rights Since Brown: 1954–1984" by Tom Bradley. Reprinted by permission from THE CENTER MAGAZINE, September/October 1984, a publication of The Center for the Study of Democratic Institutions in Santa Barbara, California.

120 – From "Still Two Nations – One White, One Black?" by Barbara Jordan, HUMAN RIGHTS Magazine (Fall 1985), published by the Section of Individual Rights and Responsibilities of the American Bar Association. Copyright © 1985 by the American Bar Association. Reprinted by permission of the ABA Press and the author.

122, 126 – "Equality of Opportunity Is Enough" by Clarence M. Pendelton, Jr., and "Equality of Result Is Required" by Douglas B. Huron. From HUMAN RIGHTS Magazine (Fall 1985), published by the Section of Individual Rights and Responsibilities of the American Bar Association. Copyright © 1985 by the American Bar Association. Reprinted by permission of ABA Press and the authors.

351—From Thomas E. Cronin, THE STATE OF THE PRESIDENCY, 2nd ed., pp. 129–139. Copyright © 1980 by Thomas E. Cronin. Reprinted by permission of Little, Brown and Company.

364—"For a One-Term, Six-Year Presidency" by Griffin B. Bell, Herbert Brownell, William E. Simon and Cyrus R. Vance, THE NEW YORK TIMES, December 31, 1985. Copyright © 1985 by The New York Times Company. Reprinted by permission.

366—"Against One-Term, Six-Year President" by Arthur Schlesinger, Jr., THE NEW YORK TIMES, January 10, 1986. Copyright © 1986 by The New York Times Company. Reprinted by permission.

368—From the book THE PRESIDENTIAL CHARACTER: PREDICTING PERFORMANCE IN THE WHITE HOUSE by James David Barber. Copyright © 1977 by James David Barber. Reprinted by permission of the publisher Prentice-Hall, Inc., Englewood Cliffs, NJ 07632.

378—From Michael Nelson, "The Psychological Presidency" in Michael Nelson, ed., THE PRESIDENCY AND THE POLITICAL SYSTEM. Copyright © 1984 Congressional Quarterly, Inc. Reprinted by permission.

391—"The Press and the President: There They Go Again" by George E. Reedy, COLUMBIA JOURNALISM REVIEW, May/June 1983. Copyright © 1983 Graduate School of Journalism, Columbia University. Reprinted by permission.

394—"The TV News Conference at 25" by Wayne King, THE NEW YORK TIMES, January 25, 1985. Copyright © 1985 The New York Times Company. Reprinted by permission.

399—From "A Short, Ironic History of Bureaucracy" by Michael Nelson, JOURNAL OF POLITICS, Vol. 44, No. 3, 1982. Copyright © 1982 by the Southern Political Science Association. Reprinted by permission.

442—From "The Judiciary: The Origins of Judicial Review" by Warren E. Burger, NATIONAL FORUM, Fall 1984. Copyright © The Honor Society of Phi Kappa Phi, 1984. Reprinted by permission.

445—"Inside View of the High Court" by William J. Brennan, Jr., THE NEW YORK TIMES Magazine, October 6, 1963. Copyright © 1963 by The New York Times Company. Reprinted by permission.

451—Excerpts from THE MEMOIRS OF EARL WARREN. Copyright © 1977 by Nina E. Warren, as executrix of the estate of Earl Warren. Reprinted by permission of Doubleday & Company, Inc.

459—From "A Bench Happily Filled: Some Historical Reflections on the Supreme Court Appointment Process" by Henry Abraham, JUDICATURE, February 1983. Reprinted by permission of the author.

470—"The Court That Tilted and Veered" by Richard Lacayo, TIME, June 30, 1986. Copyright © 1986 Time Inc. All rights reserved. Reprinted by permission.

472—From "Reaganizing the Judiciary: The First Term Appointments" by Sheldon Goldman, JUDICATURE, May 1985. Reprinted by permission of the author.

485—"Federal Law Gets a Reagan-Meese Stamp" by Stewart Powell. Reprinted by permission from U.S. NEWS & WORLD REPORT issue of June 30, 1986. Copyright © 1986, U.S. News & World Report.

500—"The Leverage of Our Wealthiest 400" by Lester C. Thurow, THE NEW YORK TIMES, October 11, 1984. Copyright © 1984 by The New York Times Company. Reprinted by permission.

501—From "How to Get the Poor Off Our Conscience" by John Kenneth Galbraith, HARPER'S MAGAZINE. Copyright © 1985 by Harper's Magazine. All rights reserved. Reprinted from the November issue by special permission.

505—From "Hard Times: The Public On Poverty" by I.A. Lewis and William Schneider, PUBLIC OPINION, June/July 1985, pp. 2–5, 59–60. Reprinted with permission of the American Enterprise Institute.

512—From "Have the Poor Been Losing Ground?" by Charles Murray, POLITICAL SCIENCE QUARTERLY, Fall 1985. Copyright © 1985 by The Academy of Political Science. Reprinted by permission.

526—From "How the Welfare System Promotes Economic Security" by Sar. A. Levitan,

POLITICAL SCIENCE QUARTERLY, Fall 1985. Copyright © 1985 by The Academy of Political Science. Reprinted by permission.

539—From PASTORAL LETTER ON CATHOLIC SOCIAL TEACHING AND THE U.S. ECONOMY (Second Draft) by the National Conference of Catholic Bishops, October 7, 1985. Copyright © 1985 by the United States Catholic Conference, Washington, DC. A Third Draft was issued June 4, 1986. Anticipated release of Final text is November 1986. Copies of all drafts are available from: OPPS, U.S. Catholic Conference, 1312 Mass. Ave., N.W., Washington, DC 20005.

550—From "The Bishops and Their Critics" by Peter Steinfels, DISSENT, Spring 1985. Copyright © 1985 by the Foundation for the Study of Independent Social Ideas, Inc. Reprinted by permission.

561—From "The Reagan Administration, the 1983 War Powers Resolution, and the Invasion of Grenada" by Michael Rubner, POLITICAL SCIENCE QUARTERLY, Winter 1985–86. Copyright © 1985 by The Academy of Political Science. Reprinted by permission.

578—From "Superpower Summitry" by Richard Nixon. Reprinted by permission of FOREIGN AFFAIRS, Fall 1985. Copyright © 1985 by the Council on Foreign Relations, Inc.

586—From "American-Soviet Relations in Perspective" by Raymond L. Garthoff, POLITICAL SCIENCE QUARTERLY, Winter 1985–86. Copyright © 1985 by The Academy of Political Science. Reprinted by permission.

604, 607—From "Is the Administration's 'Star Wars' Strategic Defense Initiative Sound National Policy?" THE CONGRESSIONAL DIGEST, March 1985. Copyright © 1985 by the Congressional Digest Corp., Washington, DC. Reprinted by permission.

613, 617—From the debate over Soviet and Cuban intervention in Central America in THE CONGRESSIONAL DIGEST, November 1984. Copyright © 1984 by the Congressional Digest Corp., Washington, DC. Reprinted by permission.